# Mathematica™

## A System for Doing Mathematics by Computer

## Stephen Wolfram

*Mathematica* **was designed and implemented by:**
**Stephen Wolfram, Daniel Grayson, Roman Maeder,**
**Henry Cejtin, Theodore Gray, Stephen Omohundro,**
**David Ballman and Jerry Keiper**

**Addison-Wesley Publishing Company, Inc.**
*The Advanced Book Program*

Redwood City, California • Menlo Park, California
Reading, Massachusetts • New York • Amsterdam
Don Mills, Ontario • Sydney • Bonn • Madrid
Singapore • Tokyo • San Juan • Wokingham, United Kingdom

*Mathematica* is a trademark of Wolfram Research Inc.

IRIS is a trademark of Silicon Graphics, Inc.

Macintosh is a trademark of Apple Computer, Inc.

POSTSCRIPT is a trademark of Adobe Systems Incorporated.

Sun-3 is a trademark of Sun Microsystems, Inc.

TEX is a trademark of the American Mathematical Society.

UNIX is a trademark of AT&T.


**Library of Congress Cataloging-in-Publication Data**

Wolfram, Stephen
    *Mathematica*: A System for Doing Mathematics by Computer / Stephen Wolfram
    p.    cm.
    Includes index.
    ISBN 0-201-19334-5;  0-201-19330-2 (pbk).
    1. *Mathematica* (Computer program) 2. Mathematics–Data processing.
  I. Title.
  QA76.95.W65 1988
510'.28'553—dc19                                                                 87-24628
                                                                                      CIP

**BCDEFGHIJ-DO-898**
Second printing: August, 1988

# About the Developers of *Mathematica*

**Stephen Wolfram** was responsible for the overall design of *Mathematica*. He also wrote much of the basic code in the kernel of *Mathematica*, as well as the text of this book.

Wolfram was born in London in 1959. He was educated at Eton, Oxford and Caltech, and received his PhD in theoretical physics from Caltech in 1979.

After two years on the faculty at Caltech, Wolfram moved to the Institute for Advanced Study in Princeton. In 1986, he moved from there to the University of Illinois, to become Director of the Center for Complex Systems Research, and Professor of Physics, Mathematics and Computer Science.

Wolfram's research has covered many areas of physics, mathematics and computer science. His early work (1976–1980) was primarily in high-energy physics, quantum field theory and cosmology.

In recent years, Wolfram has been a leader in the development of the new field of complex systems research. Complex systems research is concerned with the study of systems whose component parts are simple, but whose overall behavior is complex. Beginning in 1982, Wolfram pioneered the application of a class of computational models known as cellular automata to complex systems that arise in mathematics and physics. Wolfram's work on cellular automata has been widely applied in many different fields. It has led to new models for biological and physical pattern formation, and to new approaches to studies of chaos and randomness. In 1984, Wolfram invented a fast encryption system based on cellular automata, and in 1985, he was co-inventor of a new approach to computational fluid dynamics. In 1986, he founded the journal *Complex Systems*.

Much of Wolfram's work has involved the use and development of new computer techniques. In 1980–1981, Wolfram led the development of the SMP computer algebra system. More recently, Wolfram has worked on the development of algorithms for massively parallel computers.

Wolfram has been a consultant for many organizations, including Los Alamos National Lab, Bell Labs and Thinking Machines Corporation. He received a MacArthur Prize Fellowship in 1981.

**Daniel R. Grayson** wrote many of the mathematical parts of *Mathematica*, including arbitrary-precision arithmetic, equation solving, matrix manipulations, power series and elliptic functions. He also wrote the precompiler for the extension of the C programming language used in developing *Mathematica*.

Grayson is currently Professor of Mathematics at the University of Illinois. After receiving his PhD in mathematics from MIT in 1976, Grayson worked at Columbia University and the Institute for Advanced Study, before moving to the University of Illinois in 1982. Grayson's main research interest is algebraic K-theory, a branch of mathematics which brings together ideas from algebraic geometry, linear algebra and number theory. Grayson has used computers extensively to study conjectures in number theory. Before working on *Mathematica*, Grayson developed an interactive computer system for number theory research.

**Roman E. Maeder** was responsible for symbolic integration, polynomial factorization, and other polynomial operations in *Mathematica*. Maeder received his PhD from ETH in Zurich in 1986, with a thesis on the mathematical theory of programming languages. Since 1983, Maeder has worked on computer algebra, and its applications to mathematics education. He has organized "mathematical laboratories" for graduate courses in computer mathematics, first at ETH and more recently in the Mathematics Department at the University of Illinois.

**Henry Cejtin** wrote the final versions of many central routines in *Mathematica*, and helped to rationalize many aspects of the overall design of the system. Cejtin's work has alternated between pure mathematics and software development. His main mathematical research has been in algebraic geometry. He received a PhD in mathematics from Northwestern University in 1985, and has taught at Northwestern and the University of Illinois in Chicago. Cejtin has also been involved in a number of major software development projects. In 1983, he was responsible for parts of the UNIX-like operating system developed by Mark Williams Company.

**Theodore Gray** created the front ends for *Mathematica* on the Macintosh and other computers. Before working on *Mathematica*, Gray did graduate work in theoretical chemistry at Berkeley. In 1985, he was the author of a Macintosh system for teaching linear algebra.

**Stephen M. Omohundro** wrote the three-dimensional graphics code for *Mathematica*. Omohundro received his PhD in mathematical physics from Berkeley in 1985. In 1985–86 he worked at Thinking Machines Corporation on algorithms for massively parallel computation. He was co-designer of the extension of LISP used on the Connection Machine computer. In 1986, Omohundro moved to the University of Illinois to become Assistant Professor in the Department of Computer Science, and a member of the Center for Complex Systems Research. His current research is primarily concerned with the development of general algorithms for machine learning. He is currently working on his second book, tentatively entitled "Geometric Learning in Vision, Graphics and Robotics".

**David Ballman** was responsible for many aspects of the external system interface for *Mathematica*. Ballman has been involved in a range of computer hardware and software projects, first at the University of Minnesota, and, more recently, at the University of Illinois.

**Jerry Keiper** wrote the code for evaluation of special functions (`Gamma`, `Zeta`, `BesselJ`, etc.) in *Mathematica*, as well as for various numerical operations (`NIntegrate`, `NSum`, `FindRoot`, etc.). Before working on *Mathematica*, Keiper earned two master's degrees in mathematics, did research on the Riemann zeta function, and built pipe organs.

## About the Cover Illustration

The front cover of this book shows a three-dimensional plot of the Riemann zeta function $\zeta(z)$ in the complex plane. The height of the surface is given by the absolute value of $\zeta(z)$; the color is related to the phase of $\zeta(z)$.

The Riemann zeta function arises particularly in number theory, where it gives an analytical representation of certain aspects of the distribution of prime numbers. One of the most commonly studied features of the zeta function is the Riemann hypothesis, which states that all complex zeroes of the zeta function must lie on the "critical line" $\mathrm{Re}(z) = \frac{1}{2}$.

The picture on the cover is obtained by looking up the critical line. The complex zeroes of the zeta function appear as dips nestled in the side of the "mountain" on the left.

The *Mathematica* input used to generate the plot was
`Plot3D[{Abs[Zeta[x + I y]]`, *shading*`}, {x, -5, 9}, {y, 0.75, 30}`, *options*`]`. *shading* was
`HSBColor[1/2 + ArcTan[5 Arg[z]/2]/Pi, 1, 1]`, where `HSBColor` is defined in `Colors.m`. The options used were: `PlotRange->{0,9}`, `ViewPoint->{0.15,-2,1.1}`, `PlotPoints->80`,
`Boxed->False`, `BoxRatios->{1,1,0.8}`.

The plot took a few minutes to produce on a Sun 3/260 computer. The POSTSCRIPT version of the plot was converted into a bit map, and then color separated for printing by Spectral Effects Ltd. using a Silicon Graphics Iris computer.

# ■ Contents

## 4. *Mathematica* as a Computer Language

## Appendix A. Some Examples of *Mathematica* Packages

## Appendix B. *Mathematica* Reference Guide

## Index

# ■ What Is *Mathematica*™?

*Mathematica* is a general system for doing mathematical computation.

You can use *Mathematica* in many different ways. This section gives a brief survey of some of them. For specific examples of what *Mathematica* can do, see Chapter 0.

One way to use *Mathematica* is as a "calculator". You type in a calculation, and *Mathematica* immediately tries to do it. *Mathematica* does far more than a traditional electronic calculator would: as well as numerical operations, *Mathematica* can do symbolic and algebraic operations, and can generate graphics.

When you use *Mathematica* like a calculator, you are drawing on its built-in mathematical capabilities. But *Mathematica* is also a language, in which you can make your own definitions. You can write programs in *Mathematica*, working not only with numbers, but also with symbolic expressions and graphical objects.

You can use *Mathematica* as a language for representing mathematical knowledge. You can take mathematical relations from handbooks and textbooks and enter them almost directly into *Mathematica*. The basic approach is to give a sequence of "transformation rules" which specify how *Mathematica* should treat expressions with different forms.

As well as being a language, versions of *Mathematica* on many computers also serve as complete environments for computation. You can, for example, create "notebooks", which consist of ordinary text, mixed with graphics and "live" *Mathematica* input.

*Mathematica* is set up to fit in with other standard programs. You can use *Mathematica* to prepare input for, or analyse output from, external programs. What makes this possible is that *Mathematica* supports many standards, such as UNIX pipes and POSTSCRIPT, which are common to many modern programs.

## ■ 1. *Mathematica* Is a System for Doing Calculations

This section gives examples of the three main types of calculations that *Mathematica* can do: numerical, symbolic, and graphical. Each example consists of a short "dialog" with *Mathematica*. The lines labelled `In[n]` are what you would type in; the ones labelled `Out[n]` are what *Mathematica* would type back.

## A. Numerical Calculations

> *Example: Find the numerical value of* $\log(4\pi)$.
>
> Log[ 4 Pi ] is the *Mathematica* version of $\log(4\pi)$. The N tells *Mathematica* that you want a numerical result.
>
> ```
> In[1]:= N[ Log[ 4 Pi ] ]
> Out[1]= 2.53102
> ```
>
> Unlike a standard electronic calculator, *Mathematica* can give you answers to any number of decimal places. Here is $\log(4\pi)$ to 40 decimal places.
>
> ```
> In[2]:= N[ Log[ 4 Pi ], 40 ]
> Out[2]= 2.531024246969290792977891594269411847798
> ```

At the simplest level, *Mathematica* will do numerical calculations, just like a standard electronic calculator. *Mathematica* can, however, go far beyond a standard calculator. It can, for example, calculate with numbers of arbitrary precision. It can evaluate a wide range of mathematical functions, including all standard special functions of mathematical physics.

*Mathematica* works not only with single numbers, but also with more complicated structures. You can use *Mathematica*, for example, to do operations on matrices. The standard operations of numerical linear algebra are built into *Mathematica*. You can also use *Mathematica* to find Fourier transforms, least-squares fits, and so on. *Mathematica* can do numerical operations on functions, such as numerical integration and numerical minimization.

## B. Symbolic Calculations

> *Example: Find a formula for the integral* $\int x^4/(x^2 - 1)\,dx$.
>
> Here is the expression $x^4/(x^2 - 1)$ in *Mathematica*.
>
> ```
> In[3]:= x^4 / (x^2 - 1)
> 
>              4
>             x
> Out[3]= ---------
>                 2
>           -1 + x
> ```
>
> This tells *Mathematica* to integrate the previous expression. *Mathematica* finds an explicit formula for the integral.
>
> ```
> In[4]:= Integrate[%, x]
> 
>              3
>             x     Log[-1 + x]     Log[1 + x]
> Out[4]= x + -- + ----------- - ----------
>             3          2             2
> ```

The ability to deal with symbolic formulae, as well as with numbers, is one of the most powerful features of *Mathematica*. This is what makes it possible to do algebra and calculus with *Mathematica*.

*Mathematica* does many kinds of algebraic computations. It can expand, factor and simplify polynomials and rational expressions. It can solve polynomial equations, or systems of such equations. It can get algebraic results for many kinds of matrix operations.

*Mathematica* can also do calculus. It can evaluate derivatives and integrals symbolically. It can derive power series approximations.

## C. Graphics

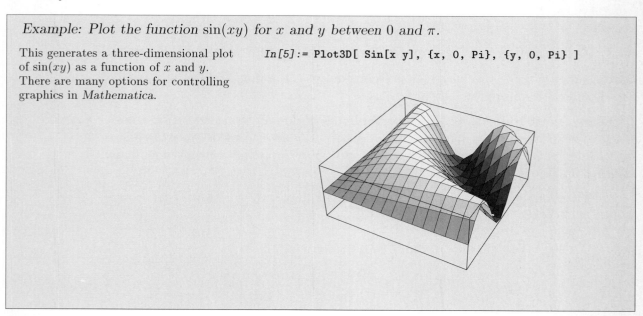

*Example: Plot the function* $\sin(xy)$ *for* $x$ *and* $y$ *between* $0$ *and* $\pi$.

This generates a three-dimensional plot of $\sin(xy)$ as a function of $x$ and $y$. There are many options for controlling graphics in *Mathematica*.

```
In[5]:= Plot3D[ Sin[x y], {x, 0, Pi}, {y, 0, Pi} ]
```

*Mathematica* does both two and three-dimensional graphics. You can plot functions or lists of data. The three-dimensional graphics that *Mathematica* produces can be quite realistic: they can, for example, include shading, color, and lighting effects.

You can use *Mathematica* to make two- and three-dimensional pictures. You supply a symbolic representation of the objects, say polygons, in the picture, and *Mathematica* will produce a graphical rendering of them.

## ■ 2. *Mathematica* Is a Programming Language

You can write programs in *Mathematica*, much as you would in a language like C. *Mathematica* is an interpreter: you can run your programs as soon as you have typed them in.

| | |
|---|---|
| This defines a function f which makes a table of the first *n* prime numbers. | `In[6]:= f[n_] := Table[Prime[i], {i, n}]` |
| You can use the definition of *f* immediately. Here is a table of the first 10 prime numbers. | `In[7]:= f[10]`<br>`Out[7]= {2, 3, 5, 7, 11, 13, 17, 19, 23, 29}` |

## ■ 3. *Mathematica* Is a System for Representing Mathematical Knowledge

*Mathematica* gives you a way to represent, and use, the kind of information that appears in tables of mathematical formulae.

Fundamental to much of *Mathematica* is the notion of "transformation rules", which specify how expressions of one form should be transformed into expressions of another form. Transformation rules are a very natural way to represent many kinds of mathematical relations.

Here are some relations that you could use to define your own logarithm function in *Mathematica*:

| Mathematical form | Mathematica form |
|---|---|
| $\log(1) = 0$ | `log[1] = 0` |
| $\log(e) = 1$ | `log[E] = 1` |
| $\log(xy) = \log(x) + \log(y)$ | `log[x_ y_] := log[x] + log[y]` |
| $\log(x^n) = n\log(x)$ | `log[x_^n_] := n log[x]` |

## ■ 4. *Mathematica* Is a Computing Environment

*Mathematica* gives you an environment in which to set up, run and document your calculations and programs.

There are two pieces to *Mathematica* on most computers: the "kernel", which does computations, and the "front end", which deals with user interaction. (These pieces do not necessarily have to be running on the same computer – you can use *Mathematica* over a network.)

The kernel works in the same way on all computers that run *Mathematica*. The front end, however, is set up to take advantage of the different capabilities of different kinds of computers.

On the Macintosh, for example, the *Mathematica* front end lets you use graphical tools to manipulate your input and output, and to insert extra text.

The *Mathematica* front end on the Macintosh takes advantage of the Macintosh's graphical capabilities.

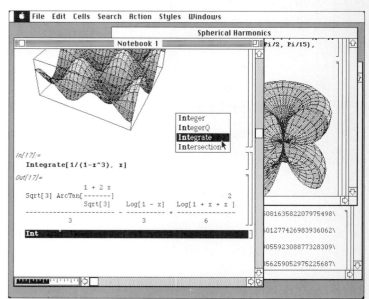

Many *Mathematica* front ends support "notebooks", which contain a mixture of text, graphics and *Mathematica* definitions.

There is a growing library of *Mathematica* notebooks which serve as "live textbooks" on a variety of different topics. You can read the text in a notebook to learn about a topic, and then use the *Mathematica* definitions in the notebook to do calculations.

Here is part of a *Mathematica* notebook about orthogonal polynomials. The material in the notebook is arranged in a hierarchical fashion, so you do not need to see details unless you want to.

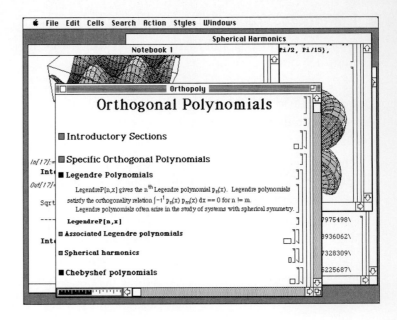

## ■ 5. *Mathematica* Is a Tool in the Standard Computing Environment

*Mathematica* interfaces to many elements of standard computing environments. Under UNIX, *Mathematica* can communicate with external programs through pipes.

You can format output from *Mathematica* as input to many kinds of programs. *Mathematica* can write out expressions in C or FORTRAN. It can also produce TEX, which you can typeset for papers and presentations.

*Mathematica* produces graphics using POSTSCRIPT. You can render the POST-SCRIPT on many different kinds of devices. You can also read it into other programs.

# ■ About This Book

## ■ What Is in this Book

This book has several parts, which are intended to be used in somewhat different ways.

- **This Introduction**: A superficial sketch of *Mathematica*, with some background discussion.

- **0. A Tour of *Mathematica***: Simple examples of the main features of *Mathematica*.

- **1. A Practical Introduction to *Mathematica***: A tutorial treatment of the features of *Mathematica* needed in most calculations.

- **2. The Structure of *Mathematica***: An exposition of the basic structure and principles of *Mathematica*.

- **3. Advanced Mathematics in *Mathematica***: A more complete discussion of the mathematical capabilities of *Mathematica*.

- **4. *Mathematica* as a Computer Language**: A discussion of *Mathematica* programming methodologies, and comparisons with other languages.

- **Appendix A: Some Examples of *Mathematica* Packages**: Parts of some application packages written in *Mathematica*.

- **Appendix B: *Mathematica* Reference Guide**: The definitive reference on *Mathematica*, including a list of all built-in *Mathematica* functions.

- **Summary of Functions**: A list of common built-in *Mathematica* functions, grouped according to type.

## ■ Who this Book Is Intended For

This book is intended for anyone who wants to use *Mathematica*: researchers, engineers, students, and others.

Most of Chapter 1 should be accessible to anyone with a high-school level knowledge of mathematics. It does not assume any prior experience with computers.

Chapter 2 assumes general familiarity with the concepts of computing, but requires almost no mathematical knowledge.

Chapter 3 is intended for those interested in using the more advanced mathematical features of *Mathematica*. Parts of it assume a knowledge of mathematics at an advanced college level.

Chapter 4 discusses programming language aspects of *Mathematica*, and assumes some knowledge of college-level computer science.

Appendix B is intended for those who are already familiar with *Mathematica*. Even if you have used many other computer systems, you should probably start by looking at Chapters 1 and 2, not at the Reference Guide.

## ■ What Is Not in this Book

This book describes the basic *Mathematica* system, as it exists on all computers that run *Mathematica*. The book does *not* discuss in any detail the aspects of *Mathematica* that vary from one computer to another. For information on these, you should look at the documentation that came with your computer, or with your copy of *Mathematica*.

This book is about the general principles of using *Mathematica*, not about its applications in specific areas. The examples in the book are intended to illustrate the principles of *Mathematica*, rather than to correspond to actual computations that arise in specific application areas. Other books will describe the use of *Mathematica* in particular application areas.

This book gives information on how to program in *Mathematica*, and how to create "packages" of *Mathematica* definitions. It does not, however, discuss how to write *Mathematica* "notebooks". The details of this vary from one computer system to another, and will be described elsewhere.

## ■ How to Read this Book

If at all possible, you should read this book in conjunction with using an actual *Mathematica* system. When you see examples in the book, you should try them out on your computer. (On some computer systems, you may be able to save some typing by getting the examples from the book on line, in the form of *Mathematica* notebooks.)

Whatever your background, you should make sure to look at the first three or four sections in Chapter 1. These sections describe the basics of how to use *Mathematica*.

The remainder of Chapter 1 shows you how to do many different kinds of computations with *Mathematica*. If you are trying to do a specific calculation, you will often find it sufficient just to look at the parts of Chapter 1 that discuss the features of *Mathematica* you need to use. A good approach is to try and find examples in the book which are close to what you want to do.

The emphasis in Chapter 1 is on using the basic functions that are built into

*Mathematica* to carry out various different kinds of computations.

Chapter 2, on the other hand, discusses the basic structure and principles that underlie all of *Mathematica*. Rather than describing a sequence of specific features, Chapter 2 takes a more global approach. If you want to learn how to create your own *Mathematica* functions, you should read Chapter 2.

Chapter 3 is intended for those with more sophisticated mathematical interests and knowledge. It covers the more advanced mathematical features of *Mathematica*, as well as describing some features already mentioned in Chapter 1 in greater mathematical detail.

Chapter 4 is primarily intended for experienced programmers. It discusses some of the common methodologies for programming, and describes how you can use them in *Mathematica*. The chapter also discusses analogies between *Mathematica* and some other computer languages. If you know one of these other languages well, looking at the section on that language may help you in learning *Mathematica*.

Each chapter is divided into a sequence of sections. There are two special kinds of sections, indicated by the following headings:

- **Advanced Topic**: Advanced material which can be omitted on a first reading.

- **Special Topic**: Material which applies only to certain computer systems.

Appendix A gives some examples of actual application packages written in *Mathematica*. If you have read Chapters 1 and 2 of the book, you should not have too much trouble seeing basically how these packages work. If you want to write your own *Mathematica* packages, you can use the ones in this appendix as models.

The main chapters in this book are intended to be pedagogical, and can meaningfully be read in a sequential fashion. Appendix B, however, is intended solely for reference purposes. Once you are familiar with *Mathematica*, you will probably find the list of functions in Appendix B the best place to look up details you need.

# ■ Background and Acknowledgements

## ■ Inside *Mathematica*

*Mathematica* is a C language program, about 150,000 lines long. (The front end of *Mathematica* for a computer like the Macintosh is an additional 50,000 lines.)

The original source code for *Mathematica* was actually written in our object-oriented extension of C, and then precompiled into standard C.

The internal code of *Mathematica* makes very few assumptions about the computer it is to be run on, beyond those implicit in the C language itself. As a result, the versions of *Mathematica* running on different computers come from essentially the same source code.

*Mathematica* does memory management with reference counts, so that pieces of memory are freed as soon as they stop being used. This means that *Mathematica* can make use of essentially all the memory that is available on a particular computer, without the need for operations such as garbage collection.

## ■ How this Book Was Produced

This book was produced by a highly automated process.

The original source for the book contains the main text, together with the *Mathematica* input for each of the examples. The first step in producing the book was to run *Mathematica* to generate the output for the examples. Generating the output in this automatic way guarantees that what is in this book agrees with what *Mathematica* actually does, at least as of the time the book was produced.

The text in this book was typeset using a combination of TeX and LaTeX. A number of new characters were constructed using METAFONT. The final typeset text was converted to POSTSCRIPT, where a number of elements were added.

The graphics in the body of the book were produced by *Mathematica* directly in POSTSCRIPT form.

The final POSTSCRIPT version of the book, which consisted of several hundred megabytes of data, was printed on a phototypesetter, and delivered as film to Addison-Wesley.

The picture on the front cover was produced by *Mathematica* in POSTSCRIPT form. (For more details, see the page following the copyright page at the beginning of the book.) The resulting POSTSCRIPT file was about 1.5 megabytes long. This was then converted into a 12 megabyte color bitmap. The color separation was done using a new computerized process developed by Spectral Effects Ltd. (Toronto).

## ■ The Background to *Mathematica*

*Mathematica* represents a synthesis of several different kinds of software:

- Interactive numerical languages such as BASIC.

- Interactive numerical systems, such as MathCAD, MATLAB and TK!Solver.

- Algebra systems, such as Macsyma, Maple. Reduce, Schoonschip, Scratchpad and SMP.

- Interpreted graphics languages, such as POSTSCRIPT.

- Numerical and symbolic list manipulation languages, such as APL and LISP.

- Structured programming languages, such as C and Pascal.

Aficionados of system design will find in *Mathematica* ideas from almost all the systems mentioned above.

The following are trademarks: MathCAD of MathSoft; TK Solver of Universal Technical Systems; Macsyma of Symbolics; SMP of Inference; POSTSCRIPT of Adobe.

## ■ Acknowledgements

My most important thanks go to my collaborators in the development of *Mathematica*. Without any one of them, *Mathematica* would not be what it is today. I thank all of them for taking the time away from their research that was needed to develop *Mathematica*.

We thank the following for making suggestions that led to algorithms and design features in *Mathematica*: Enrico Bombieri, Jonathan and Peter Borwein, David and Gregory Chudnovsky, Richard Crandall, John D'Angelo, Michael Filaseta, Bill Gosper. John Gray, Lyman Hurd, William Kahan, John Milnor, Peter Montgomery, Bruce Nemnich, Michael Stillman and Rico Tudor.

I thank David Ballman and Glen Herrmannsfeldt for the amazing feat of programming in C, *Mathematica*, LaTeX, TeX, METAFONT and POSTSCRIPT that was needed to format and typeset this book. I particularly thank Glen for taking so many months away from his semiconductor physics research to work on this project. I thank Johann George and John Herzig for doing the color separation for the cover picture. and John Herzig for doing the final phototypesetting of the book.

I thank Debra Lewis for her original encouragement to develop the "ultimate mathematics system". I thank her, and the many other test users of *Mathematica*, for their comments and suggestions.

I thank the faculty and administration of the University of Illinois for the support and encouragement they have given to the *Mathematica* project.

I thank Steven Jobs for suggesting the name *Mathematica*.

Finally, I am grateful to a number of people at Addison-Wesley: Allan Wylde, who organized everything, Karen Garrison, who dealt with production, and Marshall Henrichs, who made some suggestions on graphic design.

# Chapter 0:
# *A Tour of Mathematica*

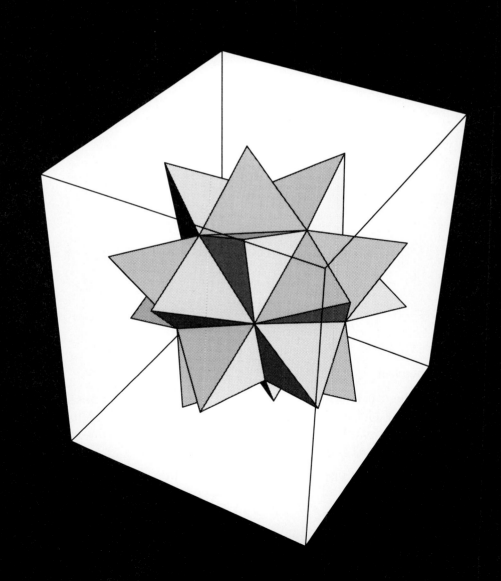

This chapter gives a quick look at various different aspects of *Mathematica*. The intention is not to show you how to use *Mathematica*, but rather to give you examples of what you can do once you know how to use *Mathematica*.

In some cases, you may be able to take what you see in this section, and adapt it for your own calculations. In most cases, however, you will have to read at least Chapter 1 before setting up your own calculations in *Mathematica*.

**About the illustration overleaf:**

This picture, like all the others which appear at the front of chapters in this book, was produced using *Mathematica*. This picture shows a stellated icosahedron. The definitions used come from the *Mathematica* package `Polyhedra.m`. The actual *Mathematica* command was
`Show[ Graphics3D[Stellate[Icosahedron[ ]]] ].`

For this and other chapter opener pictures, the default positions of light sources have been changed. The setting used is `LightSources -> {{{1,0,1}, GrayLevel[0.5]},}` `{{{1,1,1}, GrayLevel[0.6]}}`.

# ■ 0.1  Numerical Calculations

You can do arithmetic with *Mathematica* just as you would on a calculator. You type the input 5 + 7; *Mathematica* prints the result 12.

```
In[1]:= 5 + 7
Out[1]= 12
```

Unlike a calculator, however, *Mathematica* can give you *exact* results. Here is the exact result for $3^{100}$. The ∧ is the *Mathematica* notation for raising to a power.

```
In[2]:= 3 ^ 100
Out[2]= 515377520732011331036461129765621272702107522001
```

You can use the *Mathematica* function N to get approximate numerical results. The % stands for the last result. The answer is given in scientific notation.

```
In[3]:= N[%]
                       47
Out[3]= 5.15378 10
```

You can find numerical results to any degree of precision. This calculates $\sqrt{10}$ to 40 digits of precision.

```
In[4]:= N[ Sqrt[10], 40 ]
Out[4]= 3.162277660168379331998893544327185372
```

*Mathematica* can also handle complex numbers. Here is $(3+4i)^{10}$. In *Mathematica*, I stands for the imaginary number $\sqrt{-1}$.

```
In[5]:= (3 + 4 I) ^ 10
Out[5]= -9653287 + 1476984 I
```

*Mathematica* can evaluate all standard mathematical functions. Here is the value of the Bessel function $J_0(10.5)$.

```
In[6]:= BesselJ[0, 10.5]
Out[6]= -0.236648
```

Here is a root of $J_0(x)$ near $x = 10.5$.

```
In[7]:= FindRoot[BesselJ[0, x], {x, 10.5}]
Out[7]= {x -> 18.0711}
```

You can calculate mathematical functions to any precision. This gives the Riemann zeta function $\zeta(\frac{1}{2}+13i)$ to 40 digits of precision.

```
In[8]:= N[ Zeta[ 1/2 + 13 I ], 40 ]
Out[8]= 0.4430047825053681891978974413328491262 59 -
          0.6554830983211689430513696491913355062168 I
```

You can do numerical integrals. Here is the numerical value of $\int_0^\pi \sin(\sin(x))dx$.

```
In[9]:= NIntegrate[ Sin[Sin[x]], {x, 0, Pi} ]
Out[9]= 1.78649
```

*Mathematica* can do many kinds of exact computations with integers. FactorInteger gives the factors of an integer.

```
In[10]:= FactorInteger[ 20654065386 ]
Out[10]= {{2, 1}, {3, 2}, {43, 1}, {26684839, 1}}
```

# ■ 0.2  Graphics

Here is a plot of the function $\sin(x^3)$, with
$x$ ranging from $-2$ to $2$.

*In[1]:=* `Plot[ Sin[x^3], {x, -2, 2} ]`

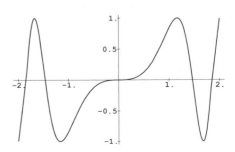

*Mathematica* chooses appropriate scales for
plots, even when there are singularities.

*In[2]:=* `Plot[ 1 / Sin[x], {x, 0, 10} ]`

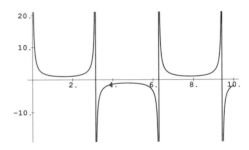

Here is a plot of the Riemann zeta function
along the critical line. *Mathematica*
automatically takes more samples of the
function where it needs to.

*In[3]:=* `Plot[ Abs[Zeta[1/2 + I y]], {y, 0, 40} ]`

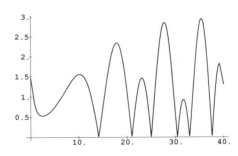

Here is one of the ways to get information
about the `Plot` function in *Mathematica*.

*In[4]:=* `?Plot`

```
Plot[f[x],{x,xmin,xmax}] plots a graph of f[x] as a
    function of x from xmin to xmax.
    Plot[{f1,f2,..},{x,xmin,xmax},(options)] plots functions
    f1,f2,..
```

# ■ 0.3  Three-Dimensional Plots

This makes a contour plot of the function $\sin(x)\sin(3y)$. The space between `Sin[x]` and `Sin[3y]` stands for multiplication.

*In[1]:=* `ContourPlot[ Sin[x] Sin[3y],`
`          {x, -2, 2}, {y, -2, 2} ]`

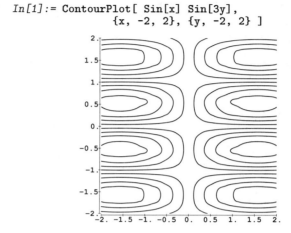

*Mathematica* can also make three-dimensional pictures.
*Mathematica* generates all its graphics in POSTSCRIPT, which can be interpreted for many displays and printers.

*In[2]:=* `Plot3D[ Sin[x] Sin[3y], {x, -2, 2}, {y, -2, 2} ]`

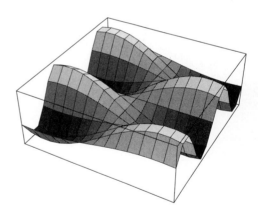

This redisplays the surface, as it would be
seen from a different view point.

*In[3]:= * `Show[ %, ViewPoint -> {1, 0, 1} ]`

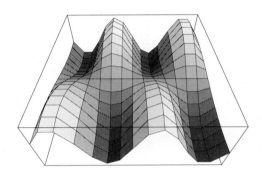

Here is the original picture, with a finer
grid of sample points, and with shading
determined by simulated illumination.

*In[4]:= * `Plot3D[ Sin[x] Sin[3y], {x, -2, 2}, {y, -2, 2},`
`PlotPoints -> 40, Lighting -> True ]`

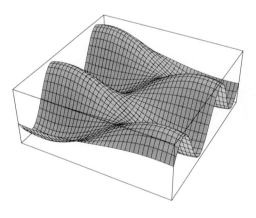

# ■ 0.4  Algebraic Formulae

*Mathematica* can work not only with numbers. but also with algebraic formulae. Here is the formula $(x + y)^2 - 9(2 + x)(x + y)$.

```
In[1]:= (x + y)^2 + 9 (2 + x) (x + y)
```

$$Out[1]= 9 \ (2 + x) \ (x + y) + (x + y)^2$$

This does the algebra to expand out products and powers.

```
In[2]:= Expand[ % ]
```

$$Out[2]= 18 \ x + 10 \ x^2 + 18 \ y + 11 \ x \ y + y^2$$

Here is the third power of the expression.

```
In[3]:= % ^ 3
```

$$Out[3]= (18 \ x + 10 \ x^2 + 18 \ y + 11 \ x \ y + y^2)^3$$

Expanding this gives a somewhat more complicated result.

```
In[4]:= Expand[ % ]
```

$$Out[4]= 5832 \ x^3 + 9720 \ x^4 + 5400 \ x^5 + 1000 \ x^6 +$$
$$17496 \ x^2 \ y + 30132 \ x^3 \ y + 17280 \ x^4 \ y + 3300 \ x^5 \ y +$$
$$17496 \ x \ y^2 + 32076 \ x^2 \ y^2 + 19494 \ x^3 \ y^2 +$$
$$3930 \ x^4 \ y^2 + 5832 \ y^3 + 12636 \ x \ y^3 + 8802 \ x^2 \ y^3 +$$
$$1991 \ x^3 \ y^3 + 972 \ y^4 + 1242 \ x \ y^4 + 393 \ x^2 \ y^4 +$$
$$54 \ y^5 + 33 \ x \ y^5 + y^6$$

Factoring the previous expression puts it in a much simpler form. This operation takes under a second on a Sun 3 computer.

```
In[5]:= Factor[ % ]
```

$$Out[5]= (x + y)^3 \ (18 + 10 \ x + y)^3$$

*Mathematica* can do many kinds of algebraic computations. This gives an exact formula for the integral $\int \frac{x}{1-x^3} \, dx$.

```
In[6]:= Integrate[ x / (1 - x^3), x ]
```

$$Out[6]= -(\frac{ArcTan[\frac{1 + 2 \ x}{Sqrt[3]}]}{Sqrt[3]}) - \frac{Log[-1 + x]}{3} + \frac{Log[1 + x + x^2]}{6}$$

You can also find approximate formulae. This computes the power series expansion of $\exp(-x)\sin(x)$ about the point $x = 0$ up to order $x^6$.

```
In[7]:= Series[ Exp[-x] Sin[2x], {x, 0, 6} ]
```

$$Out[7]= 2 \ x - 2 \ x^2 - \frac{x^3}{3} + x^4 - \frac{19 \ x^5}{60} - \frac{11 \ x^6}{180} + O[x]^7$$

# ■ 0.5 Solving Equations

You can use *Mathematica* to solve algebraic equations. Here is the equation $x^4 - 7x^3 + 3ax^2 = 0$.

```
In[1]:= x^4 - 7 x^3 + 3 a x^2 == 0
                2       3     4
Out[1]= 3 a x    - 7 x    + x    == 0
```

This solves the equation, giving formulae for the three solutions in terms of the parameter $a$.

```
In[2]:= Solve[ %, x ]
                    7 + Sqrt[49 - 12 a]
Out[2]= {{x ->  -------------------},
                          2

           7 - Sqrt[49 - 12 a]
{x ->  -------------------}, {x -> 0}, {x -> 0}}
                  2
```

You can solve sets of simultaneous equations.

```
In[3]:= Solve[ { a x + b y == 0, x - y == c } , {x, y} ]
                      b c          a c
Out[3]= {{x -> -(-------), y -> -------}}
                    -a - b        -a - b
```

*Mathematica* gives exact, closed-form, solutions to many kinds of equations.

```
In[4]:= Solve[ { x^3 + y^3 == 1, x + y == 2 } , {x, y} ]
                    6 - Sqrt[-6]         12 + 2 Sqrt[-6]
Out[4]= {{x -> -------------, y -> ---------------},
                        6                  12

           6 + Sqrt[-6]        12 - 2 Sqrt[-6]
{x -> -------------, y -> ---------------}}
                6                  12
```

There are some equations, however, where it is mathematically impossible to get closed forms for all the solutions. *Mathematica* gets the solutions it can, then leaves a symbolic representation of the ones that cannot be found.

```
In[5]:= Solve[ 1 + 8 x^3 + x^5 - 2 x^6 + 4 x^7 == 0, x ]
                    2 + 2 Sqrt[-3]          2 - 2 Sqrt[-3]
Out[5]= {{x -> -------------}, {x -> -------------},
                        8                      8
                                        5
          ToRules[Roots[1 + 2 x + x    == 0, x]]}
```

You can use *Mathematica* to get a numerical approximation to all the solutions.

```
In[6]:= N[ % ]
Out[6]= {{x -> 0.25 + 0.433013 I},
         {x -> 0.25 - 0.433013 I},
         {x -> -0.701874 - 0.879697 I},
         {x -> -0.701874 + 0.879697 I}, {x -> -0.486389},
         {x -> 0.945068 - 0.854518 I},
         {x -> 0.945068 + 0.854518 I}}
```

# ■ 0.6  Lists

This makes a list of the first twenty factorials.

```
In[1]:= Table[ n!, {n, 1, 20} ]
Out[1]= {1, 2, 6, 24, 120, 720, 5040, 40320, 362880,
          3628800, 39916800, 479001600, 6227020800,
          87178291200, 1307674368000, 20922789888000,
          355687428096000, 6402373705728000,
          121645100408832000, 2432902008176640000}
```

This takes the logarithm of each entry in the list, and evaluates the result numerically. Functions like Log have the property of being "listable", so that they apply separately to each element in a list.

```
In[2]:= N[ Log[ % ] ]
Out[2]= {0., 0.693147, 1.79176, 3.17805, 4.78749,
          6.57925, 8.52516, 10.6046, 12.8018, 15.1044,
          17.5023, 19.9872, 22.5522, 25.1912, 27.8993,
          30.6719, 33.5051, 36.3954, 39.3399, 42.3356}
```

Here is a plot of the entries in the list. The fact that the points lie close to a straight line is a consequence of the mathematical result that $\log n! \sim n \log n$ for large $n$.

```
In[3]:= ListPlot[ % ]
```

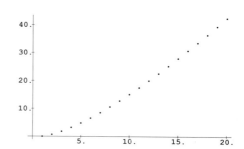

Fit finds least-squares fits to data. This finds the quadratic formula which gives the best fit to the list of numbers.

```
In[4]:= Fit[ %2, {1, x, x^2}, x ]
Out[4]= -2.02963 + 1.17902 x + 0.0531166 x
```

*Mathematica* uses lists to represent vectors. Here is the dot product of two three-dimensional vectors.

```
In[5]:= {x, y, z} . {a, b, c}
Out[5]= a x + b y + c z
```

You can also do purely symbolic operations with lists. Permutations gives all possible permutations of a list.

```
In[6]:= Permutations[{a, b, c}]
Out[6]= {{a, b, c}, {a, c, b}, {b, a, c}, {b, c, a},
          {c, a, b}, {c, b, a}}
```

Flatten "unravels" lists.

```
In[7]:= Flatten[%]
Out[7]= {a, b, c, a, c, b, b, a, c, b, c, a, c, a, b, c,
          b, a}
```

# ■ 0.7  Matrices

This generates a matrix whose $i, j^{\text{th}}$ element is $\frac{1}{i+j+1}$. *Mathematica* represents the matrix as a list of lists.

```
In[1]:= m = Table[ 1 / (i + j + 1), {i, 3}, {j, 3} ]

Out[1]= {{1/3, 1/4, 1/5}, {1/4, 1/5, 1/6}, {1/5, 1/6, 1/7}}
```

Here is the inverse of the matrix.

```
In[2]:= Inverse[ m ]
Out[2]= {{300, -900, 630}, {-900, 2880, -2100},
         {630, -2100, 1575}}
```

Multiplying the inverse by the original matrix gives an identity matrix.

```
In[3]:= % . m
Out[3]= {{1, 0, 0}, {0, 1, 0}, {0, 0, 1}}
```

This gives a new matrix, with a modified leading diagonal.

```
In[4]:= m - x IdentityMatrix[3]

Out[4]= {{1/3 - x, 1/4, 1/5}, {1/4, 1/5 - x, 1/6}, {1/5, 1/6, 1/7 - x}}
```

The determinant of the new matrix gives the characteristic polynomial for the original matrix.

```
In[5]:= Det[ % ]
```
$$Out[5]= \frac{1}{378000} - \frac{317\ x}{25200} + \frac{71\ x^2}{105} - x^3$$

This finds numerically the roots of the characteristic polynomial. These roots correspond to the eigenvalues of m.

```
In[6]:= N[ Solve[ % == 0, x ] ]
Out[6]= {{x -> 0.657051}, {x -> 0.000212737},
         {x -> 0.0189263}}
```

Using the function `Eigenvalues`, you can find the numerical eigenvalues of m directly.

```
In[7]:= Eigenvalues[ N[ m ] ]
Out[7]= {0.657051, 0.0189263, 0.000212737}
```

You can also find eigenvalues of symbolic matrices. Ending the line with `//ExpandAll` does expansions which lead to a slightly simpler result.

```
In[8]:= Eigenvalues[ {{a, b}, {-b, 2a}} ] // ExpandAll
```
$$Out[8]= \{\frac{3\ a}{2} + \frac{\text{Sqrt}[a^2 - 4\ b^2]}{2}, \frac{3\ a}{2} - \frac{\text{Sqrt}[a^2 - 4\ b^2]}{2}\}$$

## ■ 0.8  More Graphics

This reads in a file of *Mathematica* definitions for drawing polyhedra.

```
In[1]:= <<Polyhedra.m
```

This uses the definition for `Dodecahedron` in the file `Polyhedra.m` to produce a picture of a dodecahedron.

```
In[2]:= Show[ Graphics3D[ Dodecahedron[ ] ] ]
```

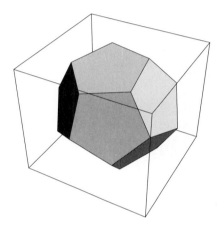

Here is a picture of a stellated icosahedron. The function `Stellate`, which is defined in the file `Polyhedra.m`, adds spikes to any polyhedron.

```
In[3]:= Show[ Graphics3D[ Stellate[ Icosahedron[] ] ] ]
```

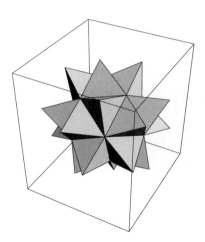

This reads in a file that gives functions for making three-dimensional parametric plots.

```
In[4]:= <<ParametricPlot3D.m
```

Here is a three-dimensional plot of the spherical harmonic $Y_3^1(\theta, \phi)$.

```
In[5]:= SphericalPlot3D[
            Abs[SphericalHarmonicY[3, 1, theta, phi]],
            {theta, 0, Pi, Pi/30}, {phi, 0, 2Pi, Pi/15} ]
```

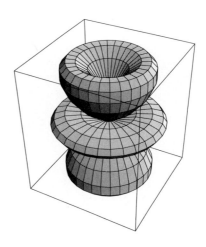

The file `CrystalStructure.m` contains specifications of some common crystal structures.

```
In[6]:= <<CrystalStructure.m
```

Here is a picture of the crystal structure of diamond.

```
In[7]:= Show[ DiamondPicture ]
```

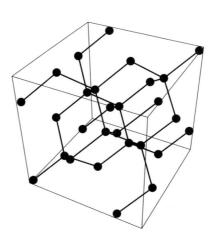

# ■ 0.9  Making Definitions in *Mathematica*

This defines a value for the variable v.

```
In[1]:= v = 1 + x
Out[1]= 1 + x
```

Now the value you have defined for v is used whenever v appears.

```
In[2]:= 5 + 2 v + 3 v^2
Out[2]= 5 + 2 (1 + x) + 3 (1 + x)²
```

You can actually define a value for any expression in *Mathematica*. This gives a value to w[2].

```
In[3]:= w[2] = 1 + 2 a
Out[3]= 1 + 2 a
```

Whenever w[2] appears, it is now replaced by its value. Since you have not yet specified any value for w[1], it stays unchanged.

```
In[4]:= w[1] + b w[2]
Out[4]= b (1 + 2 a) + w[1]
```

This defines a function f. The definition can be thought of as a rule for transforming expressions of the form f[*anything*].

```
In[5]:= f[x_] := x^2
```

The occurrences of f in an expression like this are transformed according to the rule you have just given.

```
In[6]:= f[3] + f[a+b]
Out[6]= 9 + (a + b)²
```

Here is the recursive rule for the factorial function.

```
In[7]:= fac[n_] := n fac[n-1]
```

This gives a rule for the end condition of the factorial function.

```
In[8]:= fac[1] = 1
Out[8]= 1
```

Here are the two rules you have defined for fac.

```
In[9]:= ?fac
fac
fac/: fac[1] = 1
fac/: fac[n_] := n fac[n - 1]
```

*Mathematica* can now apply these rules to find values for factorials.

```
In[9]:= fac[20]
Out[9]= 2432902008176640000
```

# ■ 0.10  Procedural Programming in *Mathematica*

Here is a simple *Mathematica* program that generates and expands products.

```
In[1]:= exprod[n_] :=
         Expand[ Product[ x + i, {i, 1, n} ] ]
```

This runs the program.

```
In[2]:= exprod[4]
                              2        3      4
Out[2]= 24 + 50 x + 35 x  + 10 x  + x
```

```
In[3]:= CF[x_Real, n_Integer?Positive] :=
         Block[ {
                  xi,
                  xp = x,
                  r = {}
                },
                Do[
                        xi = Floor[xp] ;
                        AppendTo[r, xi] ;
                        xp = 1 / (xp - xi) ,
                {n} ] ;
                Return [ r ]
         ]
```

Here is a more sophisticated *Mathematica* program, which finds continued fraction expansions for numbers. It uses standard structured programming constructs, just like C or Pascal.

The program builds up the list of partial quotients in the continued fraction by repeated division.

Having typed in the program, you can immediately use it to find the first 10 terms in the continued fraction expansion for $\pi$.

```
In[4]:= CF[ N[Pi], 10 ]
Out[4]= {3, 7, 15, 1, 292, 1, 1, 1, 2, 1}
```

# ■ 0.11  Defining Mathematical Relations in *Mathematica*

Here is an example of mathematical programming in *Mathematica*.

```
In[1]:= log[x_ y_] := log[x] + log[y]
```

This definition gives the mathematical rule $\log(xy) = \log(x) + \log(y)$.

*Mathematica* uses your definition to expand out this logarithm.

```
In[2]:= log[a b c^2 d]
```

$$Out[2]= \log[a] + \log[b] + \log[c^2] + \log[d]$$

You can add the rule $\log(x^n) = n \log(x)$.

```
In[3]:= log[x_ ^ n_] := n log[x]
```

Now logarithms of powers are also expanded out.

```
In[4]:= log[a b c^2 d]
Out[4]= log[a] + log[b] + 2 log[c] + log[d]
```

This shows all the definitions you have given for `log`.

```
In[5]:= ?log
log
log/: log[(x_) (y_)] := log[x] + log[y]

log/: log[(x_)^n_] := n log[x]
```

Here is a file of definitions for Laplace transforms in *Mathematica*. It follows closely what you would find in a standard book of mathematical tables.

After each /; is a condition for the applicability of each rule.

The text that appears between (* and *) is ignored by *Mathematica*.

```
In[5]:= !!Laplace.m

               (** Laplace transforms **)

BeginPackage["Laplace`"]

Laplace::usage =
  "Laplace[expr,t,s] gives the Laplace transform of expr."

(* constants *)
Laplace[c_,t_,s_] := c/s /; FreeQ[c,t]

(* linearity *)
Laplace[a_+b_,t_,s_] := Laplace[a,t,s] + Laplace[b,t,s]

(* pick off constants *)
Laplace[c_ a_,t_,s_] := c Laplace[a,t,s] /; FreeQ[c,t]

(* powers *)
Laplace[t_^n_.,t_,s_] := n!/s^(n+1) /;
                          (FreeQ[n,t] && n > 0)

(* products involving powers *)
Laplace[a_ t_^n_.,t_,s_] :=
      (-1)^n D[Laplace[a,t,s], {s, n}] /;
                          (FreeQ[n,t] && n > 0)

(* negative powers *)
Laplace[a_/t_,t_,s_] :=
          Block[ { v = Unique["s"] },
              Integrate[Laplace[a,t,v],{v,s,Infinity}]
          ]

(* exponentials *)
Laplace[a_. Exp[b_. + c_. t_],t_,s_] :=
              Laplace[a Exp[b],t,s-c] /;
 FreeQ[{b, c},t]

EndPackage[ ]
```

This reads in the file of Laplace transforms.

```
In[5]:= <<Laplace.m
```

Now you can do Laplace transforms in *Mathematica*. This finds the Laplace transform $\mathcal{L}[t^3 \exp(at)]$.

```
In[6]:= Laplace[ t^3 Exp[a t], t, s ]
```

$$Out[6]= \frac{6}{(-a + s)^4}$$

# ■ 0.12  Interfacing with *Mathematica*

*Mathematica* usually prints out expressions in an approximation to standard mathematical notation.

```
In[1]:= (a^2 + b^2)/(x + y)^3
```

$$Out[1]= \frac{a^2 + b^2}{(x + y)^3}$$

InputForm prints out expressions in a form that you can use as input to *Mathematica*. You can use a standard text editor to modify expressions in this form.

```
In[2]:= InputForm[ % ]
Out[2]//InputForm= (a^2 + b^2)/(x + y)^3
```

If you need to typeset the formulae you get from *Mathematica*, you can convert them into TEX input form using TeXForm.

```
In[3]:= TeXForm[ % ]
Out[3]//TeXForm=
    {{{a^2} + {b^2}}\over {{{\left( x + y \right) }^3}}}
```

FortranForm allows you to get your *Mathematica* results in a form that you can include in a FORTRAN program. *Mathematica* can also produce output for the C programming language.

```
In[4]:= FortranForm[ % ]
Out[4]//FortranForm= (a**2 + b**2)/(x + y)**3
```

You can use ReadList to read in data from files. This returns a list of the numbers in the file tour.dat.

```
In[5]:= ReadList["tour.dat", Number]
Out[5]= {15.6, 23.4, 1.77, 18.9, 20.7}
```

This executes the external command square5, then uses a pipe to read the list of numbers that it produces.

```
In[6]:= ReadList["!square5", Number]
Out[6]= {1, 4, 9, 16, 25}
```

# ■ 0.13 *Mathematica* Front Ends

Here is part of a *Mathematica* session on
a Macintosh.

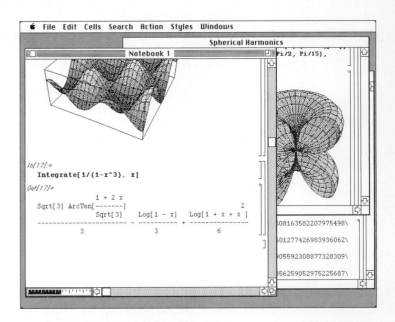

The Macintosh "front end" for
*Mathematica* makes use of the
Macintosh's graphical capabilities. It
lets you, for example, pick out
expressions graphically, and then paste
them in elsewhere. This example shows
a menu that lets you select *Mathematica*
commands to complete what you have
typed in.

You can still use the Macintosh front
end for *Mathematica* even if the main
part of your *Mathematica* calculation is
being run over a network on a larger
computer.

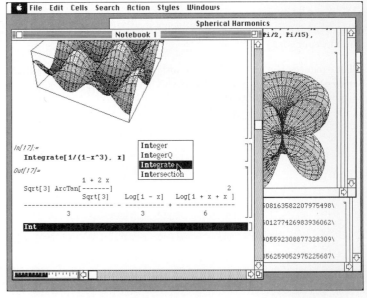

# ■ 0.14  Notebooks

*Mathematica* notebooks consist of a hierarchy of "cells". You can open up more cells when you need to see more detail.

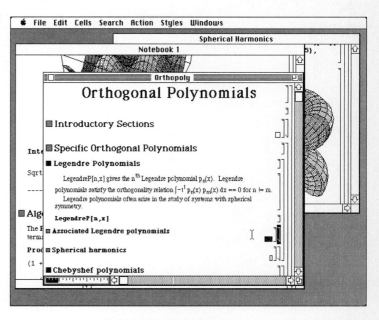

The cells can contain text, graphics or *Mathematica* commands. You can use *Mathematica* notebooks to build up "live" textbooks. You can write text that explains a topic, and then give *Mathematica* commands to implement it.

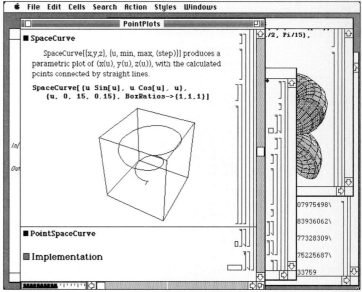

# Chapter One:
# *A Practical Introduction to Mathematica*

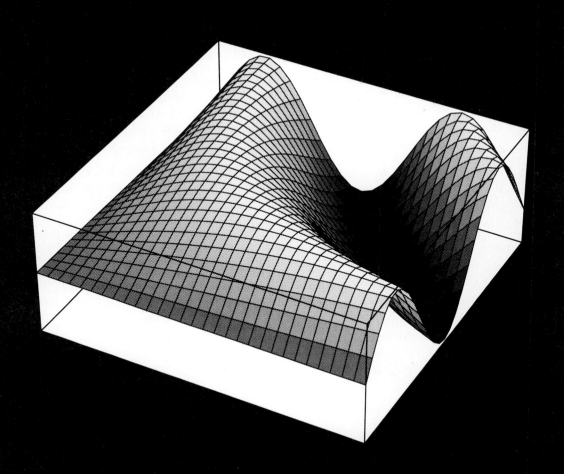

Starting to use *Mathematica* is about as easy as starting to use an electronic calculator. You type in your calculations, and *Mathematica* gives you back the results. The main thing you have to learn is how to describe your calculations in *Mathematica*'s language. Most of the time, you will find this language close to what you are used to from mathematics. However, not all the notations and conventions of mathematics can conveniently be used on a computer. As one simple example, many mathematical symbols do not appear on most computer keyboards. You will have to learn how to translate your calculations into *Mathematica*'s language.

This chapter starts by describing how to do numerical calculations with *Mathematica*. It shows you how to use *Mathematica* essentially like an electronic calculator. Once you have read the first few subsections of the chapter, you should be able to start making productive use of *Mathematica*. You will already have seen most of the basic elements that you need to do all kinds of calculations with *Mathematica*.

As you progress through the chapter, you will learn about many of the things that *Mathematica* can do. You will see how to do algebra with *Mathematica*, how to plot graphs, and how to create your own functions. By the time you have finished the chapter, you should have the working knowledge of *Mathematica* that you will need to do many kinds of practical problems.

What you see in this chapter is nevertheless in many respects just the surface of *Mathematica*. Underlying all the various features and capabilities described in this chapter, there is a powerful and general mechanism. Much of the time, you will never need to know about this mechanism. However, if you want to get the most out of *Mathematica*, you will have to understand it. Chapter 2 describes the structure of *Mathematica*, and gives you a more global picture of the system.

This chapter is a self-contained introduction to *Mathematica*. You should be able to read it even if you have never used a computer before. (You should look at the documentation that came with your copy of *Mathematica* to find out about the special features of your particular computer, and about using *Mathematica* on it.)

Most of the material in this chapter assumes no knowledge of mathematics beyond high-school level. The methods *Mathematica* uses to do calculations are often highly sophisticated, but that does not mean that you need to use any advanced mathematics in describing your calculation to *Mathematica*. Some parts of this chapter venture into slightly more complicated mathematics; if you do not understand it, skip that subsection – it will not be used elsewhere in the chapter. If you want to know the full mathematical details, try looking in Chapter 3.

**About the illustration overleaf:**

This picture was produced by the *Mathematica* command
`Plot3D[Sin[x y], {x, 0, Pi}, {y, 0, Pi}]` described in Section 1.8. The option setting
`PlotPoints->30` was used.

# ■ Running *Mathematica*

The details of installing and running *Mathematica* vary from one computer system to another.

If *Mathematica* came with your computer system, then it should be ready to use as soon as you have set up your computer.

If you bought *Mathematica* separately, then it should have come with installation instructions. The instructions are probably quite simple, but you should make sure to carry them out carefully and completely.

For details of how to run *Mathematica* on your particular computer system, you should look at the on-line documentation. On systems with standard terminal interfaces, the documentation is usually in a file called `README`. On systems with graphical interfaces, you should be able to get to on-line documentation by selecting the `About Mathematica` menu item.

Although the details of running *Mathematica* differ from one computer system to another, the structure of *Mathematica* calculations is the same in all cases. You enter input, *Mathematica* processes it, and then returns a result.

Throughout this book, "dialogs" with *Mathematica* are shown in the following way:

The computer prints `In[1]:=`. You just type in `2 + 2`. The line that starts with `Out[1]=` is the result from *Mathematica*.

```
In[1]:= 2 + 2
Out[1]= 4
```

Such dialogs may look slightly different on your computer. In particular, the `In[1]:=` may be inserted only *after* you type in your input.

When you read through this book, you should try out some of the examples on your own *Mathematica* system. Here are a few points to watch:

- Until you are familiar with *Mathematica*, make sure to type the input *exactly* as it appears in the book. Do not change any of the capital letters or brackets. Later, you will learn what things you can change. When you start out, however, it is important that you do not make any changes, otherwise you may not get the same results as in the book.

- You will see that the lines in each dialog are numbered in sequence. Most subsections in the book contain separate dialogs. To make sure you get exactly what the book says, you should start a new *Mathematica* session each time the book does.

▪ All the examples in this book assume that your computer or terminal uses a standard US ASCII character set. If you cannot find some of the characters you need on your keyboard, or if *Mathematica* prints out different characters than you see in the book, you will need to look at your computer documentation to find the correspondence with the character set you are using.

| | |
|---|---|
| Quit[ ] | end your *Mathematica* session |

A way to exit *Mathematica*.

# ■ 1.1  Numerical Calculations

## ■ 1.1.1  Arithmetic

You can do arithmetic with *Mathematica* just as you would on an electronic calculator.

| | |
|---|---|
| This is the sum of two numbers. | `In[1]:= 2.3 + 5.63`<br>`Out[1]= 7.93` |
| Here the / stands for division, and the ∧ stands for power. | `In[2]:= 2.4 / 8.9 ∧ 2`<br>`Out[2]= 0.0302992` |
| Spaces denote multiplication in *Mathematica*. You can use a * for multiplication if you want to. | `In[3]:= 2 3 4`<br>`Out[3]= 24` |
| You can type arithmetic expressions with parentheses. | `In[4]:= (3 + 4) ∧ 2 - 2 (3 + 1)`<br>`Out[4]= 41` |
| Spaces are not needed, though they often make your input easier to read. | `In[5]:= (3+4)∧2-2(3+1)`<br>`Out[5]= 41` |

| | |
|---|---|
| $x \wedge y$ | power |
| $-x$ | minus |
| $x/y$ | divide |
| $x\ y\ z$ or $x*y*z$ | multiply |
| $x+y+z$ | add |

Arithmetic operations in *Mathematica*.

Arithmetic operations in *Mathematica* are grouped according to the standard mathematical conventions. As usual, 2 ∧ 3 + 4, for example, means (2 ∧ 3) + 4, and not 2 ∧ (3 + 4). You can always control grouping by explicitly using parentheses.

| | |
|---|---|
| This result is given in scientific notation. Remember that spaces stand for multiplication. | `In[6]:= 2.4 ∧ 45`<br>`Out[6]= 1.28678 10`$^{17}$ |

You can enter numbers in scientific   *In[7]:=* **2.3 10^-70**
notation like this.
                                      *Out[7]=* 2.3 10$^{-70}$

## ■ 1.1.2 Exact and Approximate Results

A standard electronic calculator does all your calculations to a particular accuracy, say ten decimal digits. With *Mathematica*, however, you can often get *exact* results.

*Mathematica* gives an *exact* result for $2^{100}$,   *In[1]:=* **2 ^ 100**
even though it has 31 decimal digits.
                                                         *Out[1]=* 1267650600228229401496703205376

You can tell *Mathematica* to give you an approximate numerical result, just like a calculator, by ending your input with **//N**.

The **N** stands for "numerical". It must be a capital letter. Section 2.1 will explain what the **//** means.

This gives an approximate numerical result.   *In[2]:=* **2 ^ 100 //N**

                                               *Out[2]=* 1.26765 10$^{30}$

*Mathematica* can give results in terms of   *In[3]:=* **1/3 + 2/7**
rational numbers.
                                              *Out[3]=* $\dfrac{13}{21}$

**//N** always gives the approximate   *In[4]:=* **1/3 + 2/7 //N**
numerical result.
                                        *Out[4]=* 0.619048

| | |
|---|---|
| *expr* **//N** | give an approximate numerical value for *expr* |

Getting numerical approximations.

When you type in an integer like 7, *Mathematica* assumes that it is exact. If you type in a number like **4.5**, with an explicit decimal point, *Mathematica* assumes that it is accurate only to a fixed number of decimal places.

This is taken to be an exact rational number, and reduced to its lowest terms.

*In[5]:=* `452/62`

*Out[5]=* $\dfrac{226}{31}$

Whenever you give a number with an explicit decimal point, *Mathematica* produces an approximate numerical result.

*In[6]:=* `452.3/62`

*Out[6]=* `7.29516`

Here again, the presence of the decimal point makes *Mathematica* give you an approximate numerical result.

*In[7]:=* `452./62`

*Out[7]=* `7.29032`

When any number in an arithmetic expression is given with an explicit decimal point, you get an approximate numerical result for the whole expression.

*In[8]:=* `1. + 452/62`

*Out[8]=* `8.29032`

## ■ 1.1.3  Some Mathematical Functions

*Mathematica* includes a very large collection of mathematical functions. Section 3.2 gives the complete list. Here are a few of the common ones.

| | |
|---:|:---|
| Sqrt[$x$] | square root ($\sqrt{x}$) |
| Exp[$x$] | exponential ($e^x$) |
| Log[$x$] | natural logarithm ($\log_e x$) |
| Log[$b$, $x$] | logarithm to base $b$ ($\log_b x$) |
| Sin[$x$], Cos[$x$], Tan[$x$] | trigonometric functions (with arguments in radians) |
| ArcSin[$x$], ArcCos[$x$], ArcTan[$x$] | inverse trigonometric functions |
| $n$! | factorial (product of integers $1, 2, \ldots, n$) |
| Abs[$x$] | absolute value |
| Round[$x$] | closest integer to $x$ |
| Mod[$n$, $m$] | $n$ modulo $m$ (remainder on division of $n$ by $m$) |
| Random[ ] | pseudorandom number between 0 and 1 |
| Max[x, $y$, ...], Min[x, $y$, ...] | maximum, minimum of $x, y, \ldots$ |
| FactorInteger[$n$] | prime factors of $n$ (see page 346) |

Some common mathematical functions.

The arguments of all *Mathematica* functions are enclosed in *square brackets*.

The names of built-in *Mathematica* functions begin with *capital letters*.

Two important points about functions in *Mathematica*.

It is important to remember that all function arguments in *Mathematica* are enclosed in *square brackets*, not parentheses. Parentheses in *Mathematica* are used only to indicate the grouping of terms, and never to give function arguments.

This gives $e^{2.4}$. Notice the capital letter for Exp, and the *square brackets* for the argument.

```
In[1]:= Exp[2.4]
Out[1]= 11.0232
```

Just as with arithmetic operations, *Mathematica* tries to give exact values for mathematical functions when you give it exact input.

This gives $\sqrt{16}$ as an exact integer.

*In[2]:=* `Sqrt[16]`

*Out[2]=* 4

This gives an approximate numerical result for $\sqrt{2}$.

*In[3]:=* `Sqrt[2] //N`

*Out[3]=* 1.41421

The presence of an explicit decimal point tells *Mathematica* to give an approximate numerical result.

*In[4]:=* `Sqrt[2.]`

*Out[4]=* 1.41421

*Mathematica* cannot work out an exact result for $\sqrt{2}$, so it leaves the original form. This kind of "symbolic" result is discussed in Section 1.4.

*In[5]:=* `Sqrt[2]`

*Out[5]=* Sqrt[2]

Here is the exact integer result for $30 \times 29 \times ... \times 1$. Computing factorials like this can give you very large numbers. You should be able to calculate at least up to 1000! in a reasonable amount of time.

*In[6]:=* `30!`

*Out[6]=* 265252859812191058636308480000000

This gives the approximate numerical value of the factorial.

*In[7]:=* `30! //N`

*Out[7]=* $2.65253\ 10^{32}$

| | |
|---|---|
| Pi | $\pi \simeq 3.14159$ |
| E | $e \simeq 2.71828$ |
| Degree | $\pi/180$: degrees to radians conversion factor |
| I | $i = \sqrt{-1}$ |
| Infinity | $\infty$ |

Some common mathematical constants.

Notice that the names of these built-in constants all begin with capital letters.

This gives the numerical value of $\pi^2$.

*In[8]:=* `Pi ^ 2 //N`

*Out[8]=* 9.8696

This gives the exact result for $\sin(\pi/2)$. Notice that the arguments to trigonometric functions are always in radians.

*In[9]:=* `Sin[Pi/2]`

*Out[9]=* 1

This gives the numerical value of sin(20°). Multiplying by the constant **Degree** converts the argument to radians.

*In[10]:=* **Sin[20 Degree] //N**

*Out[10]=* 0.34202

**Log[x]** gives logarithms to base $e$.

*In[11]:=* **Log[E ∧ 5]**

*Out[11]=* 5

You can get logarithms in any base $b$ using **Log[b, x]**. As in standard mathematical notation, the $b$ is optional.

*In[12]:=* **Log[2, 256]**

*Out[12]=* 8

## ■ 1.1.4  Arbitrary Precision Calculations

When you use **//N** to get a numerical result, *Mathematica* does what a standard calculator would do: it gives you a result to a fixed number of significant figures. You can also tell *Mathematica* exactly how many significant figures to keep in a particular calculation. This allows you to get numerical results in *Mathematica* to any degree of precision.

| | |
|---|---|
| *expr*//N or  N[*expr*] | approximate numerical value of *expr* |
| N[*expr*, *n*] | numerical value of *expr* to *n* decimal digits |

Numerical evaluation functions.

This gives the numerical value of $\pi$ to a fixed number of significant digits. Typing **N[Pi]** is exactly equivalent to **Pi //N**.

*In[1]:=* **N[Pi]**

*Out[1]=* 3.14159

This gives $\pi$ to 40-digit accuracy.

*In[2]:=* **N[Pi, 40]**

*Out[2]=* 3.141592653589793238462643383279502884197

Here is $\sqrt{7}$ to 30-digit accuracy.

*In[3]:=* **N[Sqrt[7], 30]**

*Out[3]=* 2.64575131106459059050161575364

Doing any kind of numerical calculation can introduce small roundoff errors into your results. When you increase the numerical precision, these errors typically become correspondingly smaller. Making sure that you get the same answer when you increase numerical precision is often a good way to check your results.

The quantity $e^{\pi\sqrt{163}}$ turns out to be very close to an integer. To check that the result is not, in fact, an integer, you have to use sufficient numerical precision.

```
In[4]:= N[Exp[Pi Sqrt[163]], 50]
Out[4]= 262537412640768743.99999999999925007259719819
```

## ■ 1.1.5  Advanced Topic: Complex Numbers

You can enter complex numbers in *Mathematica* just by including the constant `I`, equal to $\sqrt{-1}$. Make sure you type a capital `I`.

This gives the imaginary number result $2i$.

```
In[1]:= Sqrt[-4]
Out[1]= 2 I
```

This gives the ratio of two complex numbers.

```
In[2]:= (4 + 3 I) / (2 - I)
Out[2]= 1 + 2 I
```

Here is the numerical value of a complex exponential.

```
In[3]:= Exp[2 + 9 I] //N
Out[3]= -6.73239 + 3.04517 I
```

| | |
|---|---|
| `x + I y` | the complex number $x + i\,y$ |
| `Re[z]` | real part |
| `Im[z]` | imaginary part |
| `Conjugate[z]` | complex conjugate $z^*$ or $\overline{z}$ |
| `Abs[z]` | absolute value $|z|$ |
| `Arg[z]` | the argument $\phi$ in $|z|e^{i\phi}$ |

Complex number operations.

## ■ 1.1.6  Getting Used to *Mathematica*

This section has given you a first glimpse of *Mathematica*. If you are used to other computer systems, you will be beginning to see some of the ways that *Mathematica* is different.

Arguments of functions are given in *square brackets*.

Names of built-in functions have their first letters capitalized.

Multiplication can be represented by a space.

Powers are denoted by ∧.

Numbers in scientific notation are entered for example as `2.5 10∧-4`.

Some superficial differences between *Mathematica* and other systems.

At first, you may find some of these differences confusing. You should realize, however, that there are good reasons for *Mathematica* to be set up the way it is.

Many systems use parentheses both for grouping, and for giving function arguments. In *Mathematica*, parentheses are used strictly for grouping, and square brackets are used for function arguments. The standard mathematical use of parentheses for functions is often confusing. For example, does $c(1 + x)$ mean `c[1+x]` or `c*(1+x)`? Many systems insist that multiplication be indicated by an explicit star. The use of square brackets for function arguments in *Mathematica* makes this unnecessary, and allows you to type expressions like `c(1+x)` in standard mathematical notation.

You may also wonder about the use of long names for built-in *Mathematica* functions. Would it not be easier if the function to generate a pseudorandom number were called `Rand`, rather than `Random`?

There is a convention in *Mathematica* that all function names are spelled out as full English words, unless there is a standard mathematical abbreviation for them. The great advantage of this scheme is that it is *predictable*. Once you know what a function does, you will usually be able to guess exactly what its name is. If the names were abbreviated, you would always have to remember exactly which shortening of the standard English words was used.

Most implementations of *Mathematica* are capable of *command completion* (see Section 1.3). Once you have typed the beginning of a function name, you can get the system to try and complete it. As a result, you very rarely end up having to type the whole function name.

Another feature of built-in *Mathematica* names is that they all start with capital letters. In later sections, you will see how to define variables and functions of your own. The capital letter convention makes it easy to distinguish built-in objects. If *Mathematica* used `i` to represent $\sqrt{-1}$, then you would never be able to use `i` as the name of one of your variables.

# ■ 1.2  Building Up Calculations

## ■ 1.2.1  Using Previous Results

When you build up a calculation, you will often need to use previous results that you have got. In *Mathematica*, % always stands for your last result.

You will have noticed that all the input and output lines in *Mathematica* are numbered. You can use these numbers to refer to your previous results.

| | |
|---|---|
| % | the last result generated |
| %% | the next-to-last result |
| %$n$ | the result on output line Out[$n$] |

Ways to refer to your previous results.

Here is the first result.

```
In[1]:= 77 ^ 2
Out[1]= 5929
```

This adds 1 to the last result.

```
In[2]:= % + 1
Out[2]= 5930
```

This uses both the last result, and the result on line 1.

```
In[3]:= 3 % + % ^ 2 + %1
Out[3]= 35188619
```

With many front ends for *Mathematica*, you can "scroll back" to see earlier parts of your session. More advanced front ends also often allow you to pick out previous results graphically, without referring to them explicitly by line numbers.

## ■ 1.2.2  Defining Variables

When you do long calculations, it is often convenient to give *names* to your intermediate results. Just as in standard mathematics, or in other computer programming languages, you can do this by introducing named *variables*.

This sets the value of the *variable* x to be 5.

```
In[1]:= x = 5
Out[1]= 5
```

Whenever x appears, *Mathematica* now replaces it with the value 5.

```
In[2]:= x ^ 2
Out[2]= 25
```

| | |
|---|---|
| This assigns a new value to x. | *In[3]:=* `x = 7 + 4`<br>*Out[3]=* 11 |
| pi is set to be the numerical value of $\pi$ to 40 digit accuracy. | *In[4]:=* `pi = N[Pi, 40]`<br>*Out[4]=* 3.141592653589793238462643383279502884197 |
| Here is the value you defined for pi. | *In[5]:=* `pi`<br>*Out[5]=* 3.141592653589793238462643383279502884197 |
| This gives the numerical value of $\pi^2$, to the same accuracy as pi. | *In[6]:=* `%^2`<br>*Out[6]=* 9.8696044010893586188344909998761511353137 |

| | |
|---|---|
| $x$ = *value* | assign a value to the variable $x$ |
| $x$ = $y$ = *value* | assign a value to both $x$ and $y$ |
| $x$ =. | remove any value assigned to $x$ |

Assigning values to variables.

It is very important to realize that values you assign to variables are *permanent*. Once you have assigned a value to a particular variable, the value will be kept until you explicitly remove it. The value will, of course, disappear if you start a whole new *Mathematica* session.

Forgetting about definitions you made earlier is one of the most common sources of confusion when using *Mathematica*. If you set x = 5, *Mathematica* assumes that you *always* want x to have the value 5, until or unless you explicitly tell it otherwise. Particularly when you are using variables to represent symbolic quantities (see Section 1.4), it is very important that you remove any values you have defined when you finish using them.

Values you assign to variables stay until you explicitly change or remove them.

An important point to remember when using *Mathematica*.

The variables you define can have almost any names. There is no limit on the length of their names. One constraint, however, is that variable names can never *start* with numbers. x2 could be a variable, but 2x means 2*x.

*Mathematica* uses both upper and lower-case letters. You should make sure, however, that the names of your variables at least begin with lower-case letters.

This will avoid confusion with built-in *Mathematica* objects, such as those in Section 1.1.3, whose names always start with upper-case letters.

| | |
|---|---|
| aaaaa | a variable name containing only lower-case letters |
| Aaaaa | a built-in object whose name begins with a capital letter |

Naming conventions.

You can type formulae involving variables in *Mathematica* almost exactly as you would in mathematics. There are a few important points to watch, however.

x y means x times y

xy with no space is the variable with name xy

5x means 5 times x

x∧2y means (x∧2) y, not x∧(2y)

Some points to watch when using variables in *Mathematica*.

## ■ 1.2.3  Making Lists of Objects

In doing calculations, it is often convenient to collect together several objects, and treat them as a single entity. *Lists* give you a way to make collections of objects in *Mathematica*.

A list like {3, 1, 6, 2} is a collection of four objects. You can treat it just like a single object. You can do arithmetic with it, assign it as the value of a variable, and so on.

Here is a list of three numbers.

```
In[1]:= {3, 5, 1}
Out[1]= {3, 5, 1}
```

This adds 2 to each of the numbers in the list.

```
In[2]:= % + 2
Out[2]= {5, 7, 3}
```

You can do any arithmetic operation on the list.

```
In[3]:= %∧2 + % + 1
Out[3]= {31, 57, 13}
```

You can name the list v.

*In[4]:=* **v = %**

*Out[4]=* {31, 57, 13}

When you ask for v, you get the list.

*In[5]:=* **v**

*Out[5]=* {31, 57, 13}

Now you can subtract one from each element of v.

*In[6]:=* **v - 1**

*Out[6]=* {30, 56, 12}

Like other arithmetic operations, division is done on each element of the lists in turn.

*In[7]:=* **v / (v - 1)**

*Out[7]=* {$\frac{31}{30}$, $\frac{57}{56}$, $\frac{13}{12}$}

All the mathematical functions in Section 1.1.3 can be applied to lists.

*In[8]:=* **Exp[-2 %] / 5  //N**

*Out[8]=* {0.0253214, 0.0261174, 0.0229118}

| | |
|---|---|
| Range[$n$] | create the list {1, 2, 3, ..., $n$} |
| Range[$n_1$, $n_2$] | create the list {$n_1$, $n_1$+1, ..., $n_2$} |
| Range[$n_1$, $n_2$, $dn$] | create the list {$n_1$, $n_1$+$dn$, ..., $n_2$} |

A function that creates lists.

This gives a list of the first five integers.

*In[9]:=* **Range[5]**

*Out[9]=* {1, 2, 3, 4, 5}

Here are the first five squares.

*In[10]:=* **Range[5]^2**

*Out[10]=* {1, 4, 9, 16, 25}

This gives a list of integers in the range -2 to 2.

*In[11]:=* **Range[-2, 2]**

*Out[11]=* {-2, -1, 0, 1, 2}

This gives a list of numbers from 0 to 1 in steps of 0.2.

*In[12]:=* **Range[0, 1, 0.2]**

*Out[12]=* {0, 0.2, 0.4, 0.6, 0.8, 1.}

Section 1.7 discusses many other ways to create lists in *Mathematica*.

## ■ 1.2.4 Manipulating Elements of Lists

When you are doing calculations, you most often want to treat a whole list as a single object. Sometimes, however, you need to pick out individual elements of the list.

The elements in *Mathematica* lists are numbered in order. The first element has "index" 1. In this respect, lists in *Mathematica* work very much like "arrays" in other computer languages.

| | |
|---:|:---|
| {a, b, c} | a list |
| *list*[[i]] | the $i^{th}$ element of *list* (the first element is *list*[[1]]) |
| *list*[[{i, j, ...}]] | a list of the $i^{th}$, $j^{th}$, ... elements of *list* |
| *list*[[i]] = *value* | reset the $i^{th}$ element of *list* |
| *list*[[i, j, ...]] | an element of a nested list |

Operations on list elements.

| | |
|:---|:---|
| Here is a list of four elements. | In[1]:= {5, 1, 6, 2}<br>Out[1]= {5, 1, 6, 2} |
| This extracts the third element of the list. | In[2]:= %[[3]]<br>Out[2]= 6 |
| Here is a list of numbers, assigned the name w. | In[3]:= w = Range[0, 2, 0.4]<br>Out[3]= {0, 0.4, 0.8, 1.2, 1.6, 2.} |
| This picks out the second element of w. | In[4]:= w[[2]]<br>Out[4]= 0.4 |
| This gives elements 2, 3 and 4. | In[5]:= w[[ {2,3,4} ]]<br>Out[5]= {0.4, 0.8, 1.2} |
| You can use Range to specify the indices for *ranges* of elements. | In[6]:= w[[ Range[2,5] ]]<br>Out[6]= {0.4, 0.8, 1.2, 1.6} |
| This resets the second element of w. | In[7]:= w[[2]] = 10<br>Out[7]= 10 |

If you ask for w, you will see that it has          *In[8]:= w*
now been modified.                                  *Out[8]= {0, 10, 0.8, 1.2, 1.6, 2.}*

## ■ 1.2.5  The Four Kinds of Bracketing in *Mathematica*

We have now introduced all the four kinds of bracketing used in *Mathematica*. Each
kind of bracketing has a very different meaning. It is important that you remember
all of them.

| | |
|---:|:---|
| (*term*) | parentheses for grouping |
| *f*[*x*] | square brackets for functions |
| {*a*, *b*, *c*} | curly brackets (braces) for lists |
| *v*[[*i*]] | double brackets for indexing |

The four kinds of bracketing in *Mathematica*.

When the expressions you type in are complicated, it is often a good idea to put
extra space inside each set of brackets. This makes it somewhat easier for you to
see matching pairs of brackets. *v*[[ {*a*, *b*} ]] is, for example, easier to recognize
than *v*[[{*a*, *b*}]].

# ■ 1.3 Using the *Mathematica* System

## ■ 1.3.1 *Mathematica* Front Ends

There are really two parts to the *Mathematica* system: a "kernel" that actually does computations, and a "front end" which manages interaction with the user.

When you type in 2 + 2, it is the kernel that computes the result 4. The front end is responsible for reading your input, and displaying the final result.

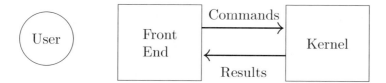

Most of this book is about what the kernel of *Mathematica* can do. This section, however, discusses some aspects of *Mathematica* front ends.

The kernel of *Mathematica* works in the same way on all computers that run *Mathematica*. This means for example that any of the dialogs with *Mathematica* which you have seen so far would run exactly the same on any kind of computer.

Although the kernel works the same, there can be very different front ends for *Mathematica* on different computers. The basic idea is for the front end to take advantage of whatever graphical or other capabilities each particular kind of computer has.

For information about the front end for *Mathematica* on your particular computer, you should look at the documentation that came with your system. This section discusses generalities, and does not give all the details you need to make use of a particular *Mathematica* front end.

---

Line-by-line (e.g. printing terminal).

Full screen text (e.g. standard display terminal).

Graphical (e.g. Macintosh).

---

Three types of *Mathematica* front ends.

The dialogs in this book essentially correspond to what you get by using *Mathematica* with a line-by-line front end. *Mathematica* prints a "prompt" of the form In[*n*]:=. You type your input, and *Mathematica* responds by printing out a result.

On many modern personal computers and workstations, however, there are *Mathematica* front ends which make more sophisticated interactions possible. Different front ends in general have different capabilities, but there are a number of typical features.

The first thing that more sophisticated front ends typically give you is the ability to browse through all the previous lines in your *Mathematica* session. When you are trying to work out what input to give next, you will often find it useful to "scroll backwards", and look through previous results that you got. If you have any kind of full-screen display, you should be able to get a *Mathematica* front end which allows you to do this kind of thing.

Browse through your *Mathematica* session.

Work with *Mathematica* from several different windows.

Have *Mathematica* find possible completions for parts of command names you type.

Search for text in your *Mathematica* session.

Copy and paste text and *Mathematica* expressions.

Animate graphical images, and digitize graphical input.

Some things you can do with more sophisticated front ends.

Here is a picture of the screen of a Macintosh computer that is running *Mathematica*.

There are two *Mathematica* windows on the screen. On the right-hand side of each window is a "scroll bar". You can move the scroll bar with the mouse, to look at different sections of your *Mathematica* session.

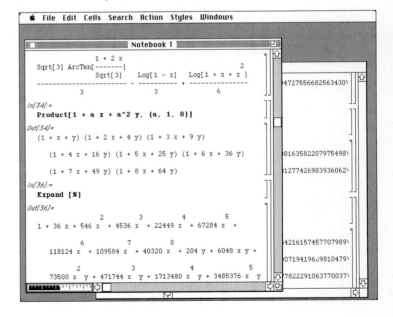

Although different front ends for *Mathematica* may look very different, it is important to remember that the actual commands you give to do calculations in *Mathematica* are the same in all cases. The only thing that changes is exactly how you construct and enter the commands, and how your results are displayed.

Advanced *Mathematica* front ends can save you a lot of typing. Instead of having to enter each line of input explicitly, you can often construct your input by pasting together pieces of text that you pick up from different places using graphical tools. The pieces of text may come from input that you gave earlier in your session, or from output that *Mathematica* generated.

Another important feature of advanced *Mathematica* front ends is that they typically give you a number of ways to organize the results you get from *Mathematica* calculations. Many front ends for example allow you to use multiple windows for *Mathematica* input and output. You can then use different windows for different parts of your calculation.

## ■ 1.3.2 Special Topic: Notebooks

More advanced front ends for *Mathematica* often support objects called "notebooks".

A notebook is a file that contains text and graphics, mixed with *Mathematica* input and output.

Here is a *Mathematica* notebook on a Macintosh in which text has been inserted to document lines in a *Mathematica* session. On a Macintosh, you can choose a variety of different fonts and styles for your text.

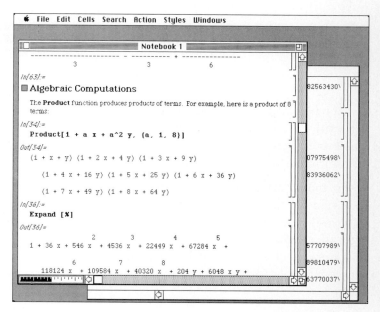

One application of notebooks is simply to use them as a way of organizing and documenting your *Mathematica* calculations.

Another important way to use notebooks is as computerized analogs of textbooks. You can put in a notebook the same kind of text and graphics that would appear in a standard textbook. In addition, however, you can include *Mathematica* input that sets up the calculations described in the text. In this way, you can use the notebook as something like a "live" textbook. You can read the text to learn about a topic, and then execute the associated *Mathematica* input, to actually perform a *Mathematica* calculation.

Here is a notebook about orthogonal polynomials. The notebook contains text about orthogonal polynomials, together with *Mathematica* definitions that allow you to do calculations with orthogonal polynomials.

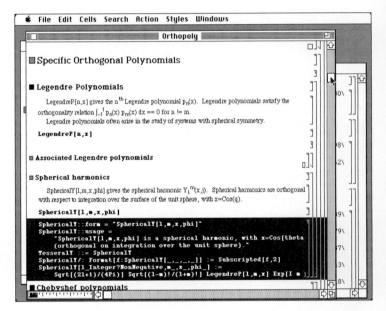

*Mathematica* notebooks are typically broken up into a sequence of "cells". Each cell can contain one piece of *Mathematica* input or output, or a paragraph of text, or a piece of graphics. When you edit a notebook, you typically operate on complete cells in much the same way as you operate on individual characters of text.

In many *Mathematica* notebooks, it is convenient to organize the cells into a hierarchy of "hypercells". Each section of a notebook, for example, may be a single hypercell, containing a sequence of many individual cells. *Mathematica* front ends typically allow you to "close" hypercells, so that only their headings are visible. If you see a closed hypercell whose heading seems relevant, you can typically use graphical tools to "open" the hypercell, and see the details of the cells inside it.

The notebook on orthogonal polynomials is organized into a hierarchy of "hypercells". This shows the hypercells corresponding to sections in the notebook. One hypercell is "open", showing the next set of cells and hypercells inside it.

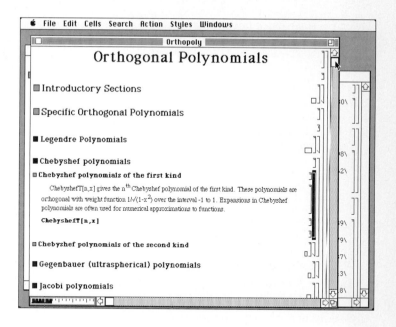

### ■ 1.3.3 Getting Information from *Mathematica*

You will often need to look up information on *Mathematica* functions that you want to use. In more sophisticated *Mathematica* front ends, there are usually graphical ways to request information on a particular object. In all cases, however, you can use what is discussed in this section to get information directly from the *Mathematica* kernel.

| | |
|---|---|
| ?*Name* | show information on *Name* |
| ??*Name* | show extra information on *Name* |
| ?*Aaaa*\* | show information on all objects whose names begin with *Aaaa* |
| ?++ etc. | get information on special input forms |

Ways to get information on *Mathematica* objects.

This gives information on the built-in function Log.

```
In[1]:= ?Log

Log[z] gives the natural logarithm of z (logarithm to
    base E). Log[b, z] gives the logarithm to base b.
```

This gives some extra information on Log. Attributes will be discussed in Section 2.2.18.

```
In[1]:= ??Log

Log[(base:E), x] gives the logarithm of x (default is
    natural log).
Attributes[Log] = {Listable, Protected}
```

This gives information on all *Mathematica* objects whose names begin with L. When there is more than one object, *Mathematica* just gives you the name of each of them.

```
In[1]:= ?L*

LCM             LerchPhi        ListContourPlot
Label           Less            ListDensityPlot
LaguerreL       LessEqual       ListPlot
Last            Level           ListPlot3D
LatticeReduce   LightSources    Listable
LeafCount       Lighting        Literal
Left            Limit           Locked
LegendreP       Line            Log
LegendreQ       LineBreak       LogIntegral
LegendreType    LinearSolve     LogicalExpand
Length          List
```

*?Aaaa* will give you information on the particular object whose name you specify. Using the "metacharacter" *, however, you can get information on collections of objects with similar names. The rule is that * is a "wild card" which can stand for any sequence of ordinary characters. So, for example, ?L* gets information on all objects whose names consist of the letter L, followed by any sequence of characters.

You can put a * anywhere in the string you ask ? about. For example, ?*Expand would give you all objects whose names *end* with Expand. ?x*0 would give you objects whose names start with x, and end with 0, and have any sequence of characters in between. (You may notice that the way you use * to specify names in *Mathematica* is similar to the way you use * in UNIX and other operating systems to specify file names.)

You can ask for information on most of the special input forms that *Mathematica* uses. This asks for information about the := operator.

```
In[1]:= ?:=

a:=b or SetDelayed[a,b] defines that the value of a is
    always the current value of b (delayed assignment).
```

## ■ 1.3.4  Special Topic: Terminating Input Lines

When you type input to *Mathematica*, you have to give some indication of when your input is finished. Exactly what "termination character" you should type depends on the front end you are using.

| | |
|---|---|
| line-by-line | RETURN |
| full screen text | CONTROL-X |
| graphical | SHIFT-RETURN |

Typical termination characters used in *Mathematica* front ends.

The *Mathematica* kernel can only process complete *Mathematica* input expressions. Much of the time, your whole input will only be one line long, so that you type the termination character as soon as you get to the end of the line.

If you have a long piece of input, however, you may have to let it continue for several lines. With most *Mathematica* front ends, you can just type RETURN at the end of each line, and then give the termination character when you reach the end of your whole input expression.

When you use *Mathematica* with a line-by-line front end, *Mathematica* will go on reading each successive line you type until it has got a complete expression. This means, for example, that *Mathematica* will go on reading lines of input that you type, until all open parentheses are closed, however many lines this takes. (Note that if you enter a completely blank line, *Mathematica* will throw away your input up to that point, so that you can start over again.)

| | |
|---|---|
| *Mathematica* knows that the first line cannot be your whole expression, so it waits for you to give more input on the next line. | `In[1]:= 3 + 4 +`<br>`        5`<br><br>`Out[1]= 12` |
| *Mathematica* will wait for as long as is needed to get a complete expression. | `In[2]:= ( 3`<br>`        + 4`<br>`        + 5`<br>`        )`<br><br>`Out[2]= 12` |

If you know that your input will go on for several lines, it is often a useful trick to open parentheses on the first line, then close them only when you get to the very end of your input.

## ■ 1.3.5 Sequences of Operations

You can type in a sequence of *Mathematica* operations just by separating them with semicolons. (You can think of the semicolons as like the statement delimiters in languages like C.)

| | |
|---|---|
| This does three operations on the same line. The semicolons separate different operations. | *In[1]:=* **x = 4; y = 6; z = 7**<br>*Out[1]=* 7 |
| If you put a semicolon at the end of your input, *Mathematica* will print no output. | *In[2]:=* **x = 8;** |
| However, you can always use % to refer to the expression that *Mathematica would* have given as output. | *In[3]:=* **%**<br>*Out[3]=* 8 |

You can think of putting a semicolon at the end of your input as like adding an extra "empty operation", which yields no output to be printed.

| | |
|---|---|
| $expr_1$; $expr_2$; $expr_3$ | do several operations, giving the result of the last one |
| $expr_1$; $expr_2$; | do the operations, but print no output |

Ways to do sequences of operations in *Mathematica*.

## ■ 1.3.6 Interrupting Calculations

There will probably be times when you want to stop *Mathematica* in the middle of a calculation. Perhaps you realize that you asked *Mathematica* to do the wrong thing. Or perhaps the calculation is just taking a long time, and you want to find out what is going on.

The way that you interrupt a *Mathematica* calculation depends on what front end you are using.

| | |
|---|---|
| textual front ends | type CONTROL-C |
| graphical front ends | type CONTROL-. or CONTROL-C, or click the **stop** button |

Some typical ways to interrupt calculations in *Mathematica*.

On some computer systems, it may take *Mathematica* a perceptible time to respond to your interrupt. When *Mathematica* does respond, it will typically give you a menu of possible things to do. Exactly what is on this menu will depend on what computer system you are using.

| | |
|---|---|
| `continue` | continue the calculation |
| `show` | show what *Mathematica* is doing |
| `abort` | abort this particular calculation |
| `exit` | exit *Mathematica* completely |

Some typical options when you interrupt a calculation in *Mathematica*.

## ■ 1.3.7  Messages from *Mathematica*

*Mathematica* usually goes about its work silently, giving output only when it has finished doing the calculations you asked for.

However, if it looks as if *Mathematica* is doing something you definitely did not intend, *Mathematica* will usually print a message to warn you.

The square root function should have only one argument. *Mathematica* prints a message to warn you that you have given two arguments here.

```
In[1]:= Sqrt[4, 5]
Sqrt::argct: Sqrt called with 2 arguments.
Out[1]= Sqrt[4, 5]
```

Each message has a name. You can switch off messages using `Off`.

```
In[2]:= Off[Sqrt::argct]
```

The message `Sqrt::argct` has now been switched off, and will no longer appear.

```
In[3]:= Sqrt[4, 5]
Out[3]= Sqrt[4, 5]
```

This switches `Sqrt::argct` back on again.

```
In[4]:= On[Sqrt::argct]
```

| | |
|---|---|
| `Off[`*Function*`::`*tag*`]` | switch off (suppress) a message |
| `On[`*Function*`::`*tag*`]` | switch on a message |

Functions for controlling message output.

## ■ 1.3.8  *Mathematica* Packages

There are a large number of functions built into the kernel of *Mathematica*. These functions provide the core of fundamental mathematical knowledge and capabilities that make *Mathematica* work. They do not, however, deal with the specific needs of every possible application area.

For many kinds of calculations, the functions that are built into *Mathematica* will be quite sufficient. However, if you are doing specialized calculations in a particular area, such as electrical engineering or particle physics, you may want to use more specialized functions. You may perhaps want a function for node voltage analysis or for Dirac gamma matrix algebra. There are no functions for these things built into *Mathematica*. However, you can always *construct* such functions from the more general ones that are built into *Mathematica*.

You will often be able to get a "package", which contains the *Mathematica* definitions for the functions you need. Each package is a file of *Mathematica* input, which you can read into *Mathematica* to "teach" it about a particular set of functions. Appendix A gives a few examples of *Mathematica* packages.

| |
|---|
| `<<`*name*        read in a *Mathematica* package |

Reading in a *Mathematica* package.

This reads in a *Mathematica* package called CombinatorialFunctions.m.

`In[1]:= <<CombinatorialFunctions.m`

The function `Subfactorial` was defined in the file you just read in.

`In[2]:= Subfactorial[10]`

`Out[2]= 1334961`

Many *Mathematica* front ends provide ways for you to search through all the *Mathematica* packages on your system to try and find references to a particular topic. *Mathematica* packages are also often available in the form of notebooks, which include explanatory text, as well as *Mathematica* function definitions.

## ■ 1.3.9 Special Topic: Using Files

If you use *Mathematica* with a graphical front end, you will probably never need to know about the file manipulation capabilities of *Mathematica* discussed in this section.

You can store *Mathematica* input and output in standard (plain text) files, which you can, for example, read and edit with a text editor.

When you are building up large calculations, you will often find it convenient to store some of your intermediate results in files. You can also store *Mathematica* definitions in files, and read them in when you need them. In fact, when you are making complicated definitions, you may find it best to work on them in a file, using an external text editor, and only later read them into *Mathematica*. If you subsequently want to change the definitions, you can just edit the file, and read it in again. (If you want to work like this, you should make sure it does not cause any trouble to execute the commands in your files more than once.)

It is a convention that all files containing *Mathematica* input have names that end with a `.m` suffix. When you look through all the files you have, you can then quickly recognize which of them are *Mathematica* input.

| | |
|---|---|
| `<<`*name* | read in a file of *Mathematica* input |
| `!!`*name* | display the contents of a file |
| `Save["`*name*`", ` $x_1$`, ` $x_2$`, ...]` | save definitions for variables |
| *x* `>>` *name* | put the value of *x* into the file *name* |
| *x* `>>>` *name* | append the value of *x* to *name* |
| `!`*command* | execute an external (operating system) command (available only on some computer systems) |

Functions for manipulating files without using a graphical front end.

| | |
|---|---|
| This sets the variable x to 6. | `In[1]:= x = 6`<br>`Out[1]= 6` |
| This saves the definition you have made for x in the file `tmp.m`. Do not forget to put quotes around the file name. | `In[2]:= Save["tmp.m", x]` |
| This displays the contents of the file `tmp.m`. You do not need quotes around the file name here. | `In[3]:= !!tmp.m`<br>`x = 6` |
| This sets y to 7. | `In[3]:= y = 7`<br>`Out[3]= 7` |
| This adds the definition of y to the file `tmp.m`. | `In[4]:= Save["tmp.m", y]` |
| The file `tmp.m` now contains definitions for both x and y. | `In[5]:= !!tmp.m`<br>`x = 6`<br>`y = 7` |

This reads in the file `tmp.m`, executing the assignments for the variables `x` and `y` just as if you had typed them directly into *Mathematica*.

```
In[5]:= <<tmp.m
Out[5]= 7
```

This executes the external operating system command `rm tmp.m`. What external commands, if any, you can execute, will depend on what particular computer system you are using. This example is for a standard UNIX operating system. The command removes the file `tmp.m`.

```
In[6]:= !rm tmp.m
```

This calculates the value of `10!`, and puts the result in the file `tmp`.

```
In[6]:= 10! >> tmp
```

Now the file `tmp` contains the value of `10!`.

```
In[7]:= !!tmp
3628800
```

Reading in `tmp` gives the result you stored.

```
In[7]:= <<tmp
Out[7]= 3628800
```

This *appends* `20!` to the file `tmp`. If you use `>>` instead of `>>>`, you overwrite what was previously in the file.

```
In[8]:= 20! >>> tmp
```

If you are familiar with the UNIX shell, you will recognize the *Mathematica* operators `>>` and `<<` as being analogous to the UNIX redirection operators `>` and `<`. The *Mathematica* operator `>>>` is analogous to the UNIX operator `>>`. (*Mathematica* uses the single characters `>` and `<` to represent the standard relational operators "greater than" and "less than".)

When you ask for a file using `<<`, *Mathematica* will search a sequence of directories to try and find it. The directories it searches are specified by the value of `$Path`, as discussed in Section 2.6.17.

# ■ 1.4  Formulae

## ■ 1.4.1  Symbolic Computation

One of the most important things about *Mathematica* is that it can do *symbolic*, as well as *numerical* calculations. This means that *Mathematica* can work with algebraic formulae as well as with numbers.

| | |
|---|---|
| This assigns p to have the numerical value 2. | `In[1]:= p = 2`<br>`Out[1]= 2` |
| Using the numerical value for p, *Mathematica* can work out the numerical value of this expression. | `In[2]:= 3p - p + 2`<br>`Out[2]= 6` |
| q has no numerical value in this case. *Mathematica* can nevertheless simplify this expression *symbolically*. | `In[3]:= 3q - q + 2`<br>`Out[3]= 2 + 2 q` |

| | |
|---|---|
| numerical computation | 3 + 62 - 1 $\longrightarrow$ 64 |
| symbolic computation | 3x - x + 2 $\longrightarrow$ 2 + 2 x |

Numerical and symbolic computations.

| | |
|---|---|
| You can type any algebraic expression into *Mathematica*. The expression is printed out in an approximation to standard mathematical notation. | `In[6]:= -1 + 2x + x^3`<br>`Out[6]= -1 + 2 x + x`$^3$ |
| *Mathematica* automatically carries out standard algebraic simplifications. Here it combines $x^2$ and $-4x^2$ to get $-3x^2$. | `In[7]:= x^2 + x - 4 x^2`<br>`Out[7]= x - 3 x`$^2$ |

You can type in any algebraic expression, using the operators listed on page 25. You can use spaces to denote multiplication. Be careful not to forget the space in x y. If you type in xy with no space, *Mathematica* will interpret this as a single symbol, with the name xy, not as a product of the two symbols x and y.

| | |
|---|---|
| *Mathematica* rearranges and combines terms using the standard rules of algebra. | `In[8]:= x y + 2 x^2 y + y^2 x^2 - 2 y x`<br>`Out[8]= -(x y) + 2 x`$^2$` y + x`$^2$` y`$^2$ |

Here is another algebraic expression.

*In[9]:=* **(x + 2y + 1)(x - 2)∧2**

$Out[9]= (-2 + x)^2 (1 + x + 2 y)$

The function **Expand** multiplies out products and powers.

*In[10]:=* **Expand[%]**

$Out[10]= 4 - 3 x^2 + x^3 + 8 y - 8 x y + 2 x^2 y$

**Factor** does essentially the inverse of **Expand**.

*In[11]:=* **Factor[%]**

$Out[11]= (-2 + x)^2 (1 + x + 2 y)$

## ■ 1.4.2  Representing Formulae

You should be able to type most kinds of mathematical formulae into *Mathematica* in a form that closely resembles the standard mathematical notation. You can use any of the functions in *Mathematica* in a symbolic fashion.

Here is a more complicated formula. (This occurs in an approximation to $\pi$ due to Ramanujan.) Make sure that you put parentheses in the right places when you type in a formula like this.

*In[1]:=* **Sqrt[8]/9801 (4n)! (1103 + 26390 n) /**
　　　　　**(n!∧4 396∧(4n))**

$$Out[1]= \frac{2 \text{ Sqrt}[2] \ (4 \ n)! \ (1103 + 26390 \ n)}{9801 \ 396^{4 \ n} \ n!^4}$$

Mathematica has a large repertoire of rules for transforming expressions that you type in. These include the standard rules of algebra, such as $x - x = 0$, together with much more sophisticated rules involving higher mathematical functions.

*Mathematica* uses standard rules of algebra to replace $(\sqrt{1+x})^4$ by $(1+x)^2$.

*In[2]:=* **Sqrt[1 + x]∧4**

$Out[2]= (1 + x)^2$

*Mathematica* knows no rules for this expression, so it leaves the expression in the original form you gave.

*In[3]:=* **Sqrt[1 + Cos[x]]**

$Out[3]= Sqrt[1 + Cos[x]]$

The notion of transformation rules is a very general one. In fact, you can think of the whole of *Mathematica* as simply a system for applying a collection of transformation rules to many different kinds of expressions.

The general principle that *Mathematica* follows is simple to state. It takes any expression you input, and gets results by applying a succession of transformation rules, stopping when it knows no more transformation rules that can be applied.

> Take any expression, and apply transformation rules until the result no longer changes

The fundamental principle of *Mathematica*.

*Mathematica* knows two rules which it can apply to this expression. The first one makes the transformation `Cos[x]-2Cos[x]` $\longrightarrow$ `-Cos[x]`. The second rule puts the `Cos` and `Sin` terms into a "standard order", in this case alphabetical.

```
In[4]:= Sin[x] + Cos[x] - 2 Cos[x]
Out[4]= -Cos[x] + Sin[x]
```

### ■ 1.4.3 Assigning Symbolic Values

Just as you can assign numerical values to variables in *Mathematica*, as discussed in Section 1.2.2, so also you can assign symbolic values.

This assigns `y` to have the symbolic value `1 + x`.

```
In[1]:= y = 1 + x
Out[1]= 1 + x
```

Whenever you ask for `y`, you now get the expression `1 + x`.

```
In[2]:= y
Out[2]= 1 + x
```

When you type in an expression involving `y`, *Mathematica* replaces `y` everywhere by the value you assigned to it.

```
In[3]:= 1 - y^2
Out[3]= 1 - (1 + x)^2
```

This clears the value you assigned to `y`.

```
In[4]:= y =.
```

Now `y` simply "stands for itself", and is no longer replaced by `1 + x`.

```
In[5]:= 1 - y^2
Out[5]= 1 - y^2
```

In most computer languages, variables are essentially used just as names to refer to objects like numbers that are generated at intermediate stages in computations. In *Mathematica*, as in standard mathematics, you can also use variables like `y` in a purely symbolic fashion.

If you assign no value to `y`, then any time `y` appears in an expression, *Mathematica* will leave it unchanged. But even though *Mathematica* does not change `y` itself, it can still apply transformation rules to expressions that *involve* `y`. So, for example, it will replace `y-y` by `0` even though you have given no specific value to `y`.

The point is that rules like this are correct whatever the value of y may be, so they can be used even when *Mathematica* knows no specific value for y.

When you use *Mathematica*, you will usually have some variables with specific values, and some which "stand for themselves" and have no value defined. It is important not to confuse which variables you are using in which way at a particular point in your *Mathematica* session.

One of the most common mistakes in using *Mathematica* is to assign a value to a variable at one point, and then to forget this, and try to use the variable in a purely symbolic fashion much later. To avoid this problem, it is important that you remove values for variables when you have finished using them. You can always check whether a particular variable has a value at a particular time just by typing the variable, and seeing what result you get.

---

Always remove values for symbols using x = . when you have finished with them

---

A very important point to remember when using symbols in *Mathematica*.

### ■ 1.4.4  Making Replacements

Making an *assignment* like x = 3 tells *Mathematica* to replace x by 3 *whenever* x appears. Often, you will need to make replacements in a more controlled fashion. For example, you may just need to replace x by 3 in a *particular* expression.

You can do this in *Mathematica* by typing *expr*/.x->3. This takes the expression *expr* and replaces all the occurrences of x in *expr* by 3. You must type -> as a pair of characters with no space in between. You can think of x->3 as representing a "replacement" in which "x goes to 3". The operator /. is also typed as a pair of characters with no space in between. You can think of it as representing evaluation of the expression "at the point" specified by the replacement.

| | |
|---|---|
| This replaces x by 1+a in the expression 1+x∧2. | `In[1]:= 1 + x∧2 /. x -> 1+a`<br><br>$Out[1]= 1 + (1 + a)^2$ |
| Making a replacement for x using /. has no effect on the value of x. | `In[2]:= x`<br>`Out[2]= x` |
| You can do several replacements at once by putting them in a list. | `In[3]:= (x + y) (x - y)∧2 /. {x -> 3, y -> 1 - a}`<br><br>$Out[3]= (3 - (1 - a))^2 (4 - a)$ |

| | |
|---|---|
| $x$ = *value* | define a value for $x$ which will always be used |
| $x$ =. | remove any value defined for $x$ |
| *expr* /. $x$ -> *value* | replace $x$ by *value* in the expression *expr* |
| *expr* /. {$x$ -> *xval*, $y$ -> *yval*} | perform several replacements |

Assignments and replacements.

You can mix assignments and replacements.

This assigns a value to the symbol t.

```
In[4]:= t = 1 + x^2
         
Out[4]= 1 + x
```
$$Out[4]= 1 + x^2$$

This finds the value of t, and then replaces x by 2 in it.

```
In[5]:= t /. x -> 2
Out[5]= 5
```

This finds the value of t for a different value of x.

```
In[6]:= t /. x -> 5a
              2
Out[6]= 1 + 25 a
```
$$Out[6]= 1 + 25\ a^2$$

This finds the value of t when x is replaced by Pi, and then evaluates the result numerically.

```
In[7]:= t /. x -> Pi //N
Out[7]= 10.8696
```

## ■ 1.4.5  Transforming Algebraic Expressions

There are often many different ways to write the same algebraic expression. As one example, the expression $(1 + x)^2$ can be written as $1 + 2x + x^2$. *Mathematica* provides a large collection of functions for converting between different forms of algebraic expressions.

| | |
|---|---|
| Expand[*expr*] | multiply out products and powers, writing the result as a sum of terms |
| Factor[*expr*] | write *expr* as a minimal product of terms |

Two common functions for transforming algebraic expressions.

Expand gives the "expanded form", with products and powers multiplied out.

```
In[1]:= Expand[ (1 + x)^2 ]
                        2
Out[1]= 1 + 2 x + x
```
$$Out[1]= 1 + 2\ x + x^2$$

Factor recovers the original form.

*In[2]:=* **Factor[ % ]**

*Out[2]=* $(1 + x)^2$

It is easy to generate complicated expressions with **Expand**.

*In[3]:=* **Expand[ (1 + x + 3 y)^4 ]**

*Out[3]=* $1 + 4 x + 6 x^2 + 4 x^3 + x^4 + 12 y + 36 x y +$
$36 x^2 y + 12 x^3 y + 54 y^2 + 108 x y^2 + 54 x^2 y^2 +$
$108 y^3 + 108 x y^3 + 81 y^4$

**Factor** often gives you simpler expressions.

*In[4]:=* **Factor[ % ]**

*Out[4]=* $(1 + x + 3 y)^4$

There are some cases, though, where **Factor** can give you more complicated expressions.

*In[5]:=* **Factor[ x^10 - 1 ]**

*Out[5]=* $(-1 + x) (1 + x) (1 - x + x^2 - x^3 + x^4)$
$(1 + x + x^2 + x^3 + x^4)$

In this case, **Expand** gives the "simpler" form.

*In[6]:=* **Expand[ % ]**

*Out[6]=* $-1 + x^{10}$

## ■ 1.4.6 Simplifying Algebraic Expressions

There are many situations where you want to write a particular algebraic expression in the "simplest possible form". Although it is difficult to know exactly what one means in all cases by the "simplest form", a worthwhile practical procedure is to look at many different forms of an expression, and pick out the one that involves the smallest number of parts.

| | |
|---|---|
| Simplify[*expr*] | try to find the form of *expr* with the smallest number of parts, by applying a sequence of different algebraic transformations |

Simplifying algbraic expressions.

**Simplify** writes $x^2 + 2x + 1$ in factored form.

*In[1]:=* **Simplify[x^2 + 2x + 1]**

*Out[1]=* $(1 + x)^2$

Simplify leaves $x^{10} - 1$ in expanded form, since for this expression, the factored form is larger.

```
In[2]:= Simplify[x^10 - 1]
                  10
Out[2]= -1 + x
```

You can often use **Simplify** to "clean up" complicated expressions that you get as the results of computations.

Here is the integral of $\frac{1}{x^4-1}$. Integrals are discussed in more detail in Section 1.5.

```
In[3]:= Integrate[1/(x^4-1), x]
         -ArcTan[x]     Log[-1 + x]     Log[1 + x]
Out[3]= ───────────  +  ───────────  -  ───────────
             2               4               4
```

Differentiating the result from **Integrate** should give back your original expression. In this case, as is common, you get a more complicated version of the expression.

```
In[4]:= D[%, x]
             1               1                1
Out[4]= ─────────────  -  ─────────────  -  ─────────────
        4 (-1 + x)        4 (1 + x)                    2
                                             2 (1 + x )
```

Simplify succeeds in getting back the original, more simple, form of the expression.

```
In[5]:= Simplify[%]
               1
Out[5]= ─────────────
                 4
         -1 + x
```

For many simple algebraic calculations, you may find it convenient to use **Simplify** quite routinely on your results.

In more complicated calculations, however, you often need to exercise more control over the exact form of answer that you get. In addition, when your expressions are complicated, **Simplify** may spend a long time testing a large number of possible forms, in its attempt to find the simplest one.

## ■ 1.4.7  Advanced Topic: Putting Expressions into Different Forms

Complicated algebraic expressions can usually be written in many different ways. *Mathematica* provides a variety of functions for converting expressions from one form to another.

In most applications, the commonest of these functions are **Expand**, **Factor** and **Simplify**. However, particularly when you have "rational" expressions that contain quotients, there are other functions that you may need to use.

| | |
|---|---|
| Expand[*expr*] | multiply out products and powers |
| ExpandAll[*expr*] | apply **Expand** everywhere |
| Factor[*expr*] | reduce to a product of factors |
| FactorTerms[*expr*] | pull out common factors from each term |
| Together[*expr*] | put all terms over a common denominator |
| Apart[*expr*] | separate into terms with simple denominators |
| Cancel[*expr*] | cancel common factors between numerators and denominators |
| Collect[*expr*, *x*] | group together powers of *x* |
| Simplify[*expr*] | try a sequence of algebraic transformations and give the smallest form of *expr* found |

Functions for transforming algebraic expressions.

Here is a rational expression that can be written in many different forms.

$In[1]:=$ e = (x - 1)^2 (2 + x) / ((1 + x) (x - 3)^2)

$$Out[1]= \frac{(-1 + x)^2 (2 + x)}{(-3 + x)^2 (1 + x)}$$

Expand expands out the numerator, but leaves the denominator in factored form.

$In[2]:=$ **Expand[e]**

$$Out[2]= \frac{2}{(-3 + x)^2 (1 + x)} - \frac{3 x}{(-3 + x)^2 (1 + x)} + \frac{x^3}{(-3 + x)^2 (1 + x)}$$

ExpandAll expands out everything, including the denominator.

$In[3]:=$ **ExpandAll[e]**

$$Out[3]= \frac{2}{9 + 3 x - 5 x^2 + x^3} - \frac{3 x}{9 + 3 x - 5 x^2 + x^3} + \frac{x^3}{9 + 3 x - 5 x^2 + x^3}$$

**Together** collects all the terms together over a common denominator.

$In[4]:=$ **Together[%]**

$$Out[4]= \frac{2 - 3 x + x^3}{9 + 3 x - 5 x^2 + x^3}$$

**Apart** breaks the expression apart, into terms with simple denominators.

$In[5]:=$ **Apart[%]**

$$Out[5]= 1 + \frac{5}{(-3 + x)^2} + \frac{19}{4 (-3 + x)} + \frac{1}{4 (1 + x)}$$

**Factor** factors everything, in this case reproducing the original form.

$In[6]:=$ **Factor[%]**

$$Out[6]= \frac{(-1 + x)^2 (2 + x)}{(-3 + x)^2 (1 + x)}$$

According to **Simplify**, the original form is the simplest way to write the expression.

$In[7]:=$ **Simplify[e]**

$$Out[7]= \frac{(-1 + x)^2 (2 + x)}{(-3 + x)^2 (1 + x)}$$

Getting algebraic expressions into the form you want is something of an art. In most cases, the best thing to do is to "experiment", trying different transformations until you get what you want.

When you have an expression in a single variable, you can choose to write it as a sum of terms, a product, and so on. If you have an expression with several variables, there is an even wider selection of possible forms. You can, for example, choose to group terms in the expression so that one or another of the variables is "dominant".

Here is an algebraic expression in two variables.

$In[8]:=$ **v = Expand[(3 + 2x + y)^3]**

$$Out[8]= 27 + 54 x + 36 x^2 + 8 x^3 + 27 y + 36 x y +$$
$$12 x^2 y + 9 y^2 + 6 x y^2 + y^3$$

This groups together terms in **v** that involve the same power of **x**.

$In[9]:=$ **Collect[v, x]**

$$Out[9]= 27 + 8 x^3 + 27 y + 9 y^2 + y^3 + x^2 (36 + 12 y) +$$
$$x (54 + 36 y + 6 y^2)$$

This groups together powers of y.        *In[10]:=* `Collect[v, y]`

*Out[10]=* 27 + 54 x + 36 x$^2$ + 8 x$^3$ + y$^3$ + y$^2$ (9 + 6 x) +

y (27 + 36 x + 12 x$^2$)

Even when one restricts oneself to algebraic expressions, there are many different ways to write any particular expression. If one goes beyond purely algebraic expressions, and includes, for example, higher mathematical functions, the variety of possible forms becomes still greater. As a result, it is totally infeasible to have a specific function in *Mathematica* to produce each possible form. Instead, as described in Chapter 2, *Mathematica* allows you to set up arbitrary transformation rules to convert between different forms.

### ■ 1.4.8 Picking Out Pieces of Algebraic Expressions

| | |
|---|---|
| `Coefficient[`*expr, form*`]` | the coefficient of *form* in *expr* |
| `Exponent[`*expr, form*`]` | the maximum power of *form* in *expr* |
| `Numerator[`*expr*`]` | the numerator of *expr* |
| `Denominator[`*expr*`]` | the denominator of *expr* |

Functions to pick out pieces of algebraic expressions.

Here is an algebraic expression.        *In[1]:=* `e = Expand[(1 + 3x + 4y^2)^2]`

*Out[1]=* 1 + 6 x + 9 x$^2$ + 8 y$^2$ + 24 x y$^2$ + 16 y$^4$

This gives the coefficient of x in e.        *In[2]:=* `Coefficient[e, x]`

*Out[2]=* 6 + 24 y$^2$

`Exponent[`*expr, y*`]` gives the highest power        *In[3]:=* `Exponent[e, y]`
of *y* that appears in *expr*.        *Out[3]=* 4

**Coefficient** and **Exponent** are effectively functions for working with *polynomials*. They work only on expressions that are explicitly written out as sums of terms, in the form you get from **Expand**.

**Numerator** and **Denominator** work on rational expressions.

Here is a rational expression.

$In[4]:= \texttt{r = (1 + x)/(2 (2 - y))}$

$Out[4]= \dfrac{1 + x}{2 (2 - y)}$

Denominator picks out the denominator.

$In[5]:= \texttt{Denominator[\%]}$

$Out[5]= \texttt{2 (2 - y)}$

Denominator gives 1 for expressions that are not quotients.

$In[6]:= \texttt{Denominator[x\^{}2]}$

$Out[6]= \texttt{1}$

### ■ 1.4.9  Working with Large Symbolic Expressions

When you do symbolic calculations, it is very easy to end up with extremely complicated expressions. Often, you will not even want to *see* the complete result of a computation.

If you end your input with a semicolon, *Mathematica* will do the computation you asked for, but will not display the result. You can nevertheless use % or Out[*n*] to refer to the result.

Even though you may not want to see the *whole* result from a computation, you often do need to see its basic form. You can use **Short** to display the *outline* of an expression, omitting some of the terms.

Ending your input with ; stops *Mathematica* from displaying the complicated result of the computation.

$In[1]:= \texttt{Expand[(x + 5 y + 10)\^{}4] ;}$

You can still refer to the result as %. //Short displays a one-line outline of the result. The <<*n*>> stands for *n* terms that have been left out.

$In[2]:= \texttt{\% //Short}$

$Out[2]//Short= \texttt{10000 + 4000 x + <<12>> + 625 } y^4$

This shows a three-line version of the expression. More parts are now visible.

$In[3]:= \texttt{Short[\%, 3]}$

$Out[3]//Short=$

$$10000 + 4000\ x + 600\ x^2 + 40\ x^3 + x^4 + 20000\ y +$$
$$6000\ x\ y + <<5>> + 5000\ y^3 + 500\ x\ y^3 + 625\ y^4$$

This gives the total number of terms in the sum.

$In[4]:= \texttt{Length[\%]}$

$Out[4]= \texttt{15}$

| | |
|---|---|
| *command* ; | execute *command*, but do not print the result |
| *expr* // Short | show a one-line outline form of *expr* |
| Short[*expr*, *n*] | show an *n*-line outline of *expr* |

Some ways to shorten your output.

### ■ 1.4.10  The Limits of *Mathematica*

In just one *Mathematica* command, you can easily specify a calculation that is far too complicated for any computer to do. For example, you could ask for Expand[(1+x)^(10^100)]. The result of this calculation would have $10^{100}+1$ terms – more than the total number of particles in the universe.

You should have no trouble working out Expand[(1+x)^100] on any computer that can run *Mathematica*. But as you increase the exponent of (1+x), the results you get will eventually become too big for your computer's memory to hold. Exactly at what point this happens depends not only on the total amount of memory your computer has, but often also on such details as what other processes happen to be running when you try to do your calculation.

If you do run out of memory in the middle of a calculation, most versions of *Mathematica* have no choice but to stop immediately. As a result, it is important to plan your calculations so that they never need more memory than your computer has.

Even if the result of an algebraic calculation is quite simple, the intermediate expressions that you generate in the course of the calculation can be very complicated. This means that even if the final result is small, the intermediate parts of a calculation can be too big for your computer to handle. If this happens, you can usually break your calculation into pieces, and succeed in doing all the pieces on their own. You should know that the internal scheme which *Mathematica* uses for memory management is such that once part of a calculation is finished, the memory used to store intermediate expressions that arose is immediately made available for new expressions.

Memory space is the most common limiting factor in *Mathematica* calculations. Time can also, however, be a limiting factor. You will usually be prepared to wait a second, or even a minute, for the result of a calculation. But you will less often be prepared to wait an hour or a day, and you will almost never be able to wait a year.

One class of calculations where time is often the limiting factor are those that effectively involve searching or testing a large number of possibilities. Integer factorization is a classic example. At some level, the problem of factoring an integer always seems to boil down to something related to testing a large number of candidate factors. As far as we know now, the number of cases to test can increase almost as fast as the exponential of the number of digits in the integer we are trying to factor. As a result, the time needed to factor integers can increase very rapidly with the size of the integers you try to factor. In practice, you will find that `FactorInteger[k]` will give a result almost immediately when $k$ has, say, less than 15 digits. But when $k$ has 40 digits, `FactorInteger[k]` will often take an unmanageably long time.

In the field of computational complexity theory, an important distinction is drawn between algorithms which are "polynomial time", and those which are not. A polynomial time algorithm can always be executed in a time that increases only like a polynomial in the length of the input. Non-polynomial time algorithms may take times that increase exponentially with the length of their input.

The internal code of *Mathematica* uses polynomial time algorithms whenever they are known. There are some problems, however, for which no polynomial time algorithms are known. In such cases, *Mathematica* has no choice but to use non-polynomial time algorithms, which may take times that increase exponentially with the length of their input. Integer factorization is one such case. Other cases include factoring polynomials and solving equations when the number of variables involved becomes large.

Even when the time needed to do a computation does not increase exponentially, there will always come a point where the computation is too large or time-consuming to do on your particular computer system. As you work with *Mathematica*, you should develop some feeling for the limits on the kinds of calculations you can do in your particular application area.

---

Doing arithmetic with numbers containing a few thousand digits.

Expanding out a polynomial that gives a few hundred terms.

Factoring a polynomial in two variables with a hundred terms.

Applying a recursive rule a few thousand times.

Finding the numerical inverse of a $50 \times 50$ matrix.

Formatting a few pages of output.

---

Some operations that typically take a few seconds on a 1987 workstation.

## ■ 1.4.11  Tagging Objects with the Names of Symbols

There are many ways to use symbols in *Mathematica*. So far we have concentrated on using symbols to store values, and to represent mathematical variables. This section describes another way to use symbols in *Mathematica*.

The basic idea is to use symbols as "tags" for different types of objects.

Working with physical units gives one simple example. When you specify the length of an object, you want to give not only a number, but also the units in which the length is measured. In standard notation, you might write a length as 12 meters.

You can imitate this notation almost directly in *Mathematica*. You simply use a symbol `meters` to indicates the units of our measurement.

| | |
|---|---|
| The symbol `meters` here acts as a "tag", which indicates the units used. | `In[1]:= 12 meters`<br>`Out[1]= 12 meters` |
| You can add lengths like this. | `In[2]:= % + 5.3 meters`<br>`Out[2]= 17.3 meters` |
| This gives a speed. | `In[3]:= % / (25 seconds)`<br><br>$Out[3]= \dfrac{0.692 \text{ meters}}{\text{seconds}}$ |
| This converts to a speed in feet per second. | `In[4]:= % /. meters -> 3.28084 feet`<br><br>$Out[4]= \dfrac{2.27034 \text{ feet}}{\text{seconds}}$ |

# ■ 1.5 Mathematical Operations in *Mathematica*

## ■ 1.5.1 Symbolic Mathematics

*Mathematica*'s ability to deal with symbolic expressions, as well as numbers, allows you to use it for many kinds of mathematics.

Calculus is one example. With *Mathematica*, you can differentiate an expression *symbolically*, and get a formula for the result.

This finds the derivative of $x^n$.

```
In[1]:= D[ x^n , x ]
                -1 + n
Out[1]= n x
```

Here is a slightly more complicated example.

```
In[2]:= D[x^2 Log[x + a], x]

                                2
                               x
Out[2]= 2 x Log[a + x]  +  -----
                           a + x
```

| | |
|---|---|
| $D[f, x]$ | the (partial) derivative $\frac{\partial f}{\partial x}$ |
| $Integrate[f, x]$ | the indefinite integral $\int f \, dx$ |
| $Integrate[f, \{x, xmin, xmax\}]$ | the definite integral $\int_{xmin}^{xmax} f \, dx$ |
| $Sum[f, \{i, imin, imax\}]$ | the sum $\sum_{i=imin}^{imax} f$ |
| $Product[f, \{i, imin, imax\}]$ | the product $\prod_{i=imin}^{imax} f$ |
| $Solve[lhs==rhs, x]$ | solution to an equation for $x$ |
| $Solve[\{lhs_1==rhs_1, lhs_2==rhs_2\}, \{x_1, x_2\}]$ | |
| | solution to a set of simultaneous equations for the $x_i$ |
| $Series[f, \{x, x_0, order\}]$ | a power series expansion of $f$ about the point $x = x_0$ |
| $Limit[f, x->x_0]$ | the limit $\lim_{x \to x_0} f$ |

Some mathematical operations.

# ■ 1.5.2  Differentiation

| | |
|---|---|
| Here is the derivative of $x^n$ with respect to $x$. | `In[1]:= D[ x^n , x ]`<br><br>`Out[1]= n x`$^{-1 + n}$ |
| *Mathematica* knows the derivatives of all the standard mathematical functions. | `In[2]:= D[ ArcTan[x] , x ]`<br><br>`Out[2]=` $\dfrac{1}{1 + x^2}$ |
| This differentiates three times with respect to x. | `In[3]:= D[ x^n, {x, 3} ]`<br><br>`Out[3]= n x`$^{-3 + n}$ `(-2 + n) (-1 + n)` |

The function `D[x^n, x]` really gives a *partial* derivative, in which n is assumed not to depend on x. *Mathematica* has an another function, called `Dt`, which finds *total* derivatives, in which all variables are assumed to be related. In mathematical notation, `D[f, x]` is like $\frac{\partial f}{\partial x}$, while `Dt[f, x]` is like $\frac{df}{dx}$. You can think of `Dt` as standing for "derivative total".

| | |
|---|---|
| `Dt` gives a *total derivative*, which assumes that n can depend on x. `Dt[n, x]` stands for $\frac{dn}{dx}$. | `In[4]:= Dt[ x^n , x ]`<br><br>`Out[4]= n x`$^{-1 + n}$ `+ x`$^{n}$ `Dt[n, x] Log[x]` |
| This gives the total differential $d(x^n)$. `Dt[x]` is the differential $dx$. | `In[5]:= Dt[ x^n ]`<br><br>`Out[5]= n x`$^{-1 + n}$ `Dt[x] + x`$^{n}$ `Dt[n] Log[x]` |

|  |  |
|---|---|
| `D[f, x]` | partial derivative $\frac{\partial}{\partial x} f$ |
| `D[f, x`$_1$`, x`$_2$`, ...]` | multiple derivative $\frac{\partial}{\partial x_1} \frac{\partial}{\partial x_2} ...f$ |
| `D[f, {x, n}]` | repeated derivative $\frac{\partial^n f}{\partial x^n}$ |
| `Dt[f]` | total derivative $df$ |
| `Dt[f, x]` | total derivative $\frac{d}{dx} f$ |

Some differentiation functions.

As well as treating variables like $x$ symbolically, you can also treat functions in

*Mathematica* symbolically. Thus, for example, you can find formulae for derivatives of `f[x]`, without specifying any explicit form for the function `f`.

| | |
|---|---|
| *Mathematica* does not know how to differentiate `f`, so it gives you back a symbolic result in terms of `f'`. | *In[6]:=* `D[ f[x], x ]`<br><br>*Out[6]=* `f'[x]` |

| | |
|---|---|
| *Mathematica* uses the chain rule to simplify derivatives. | *In[7]:=* `D[ 2 x f[x^2], x ]`<br><br>*Out[7]=* $2\ f[x^2]\ +\ 4\ x^2\ f'[x^2]$ |

## ■ 1.5.3  Integration

| | |
|---|---|
| Here is the integral $\int x^n\ dx$ in *Mathematica*. | *In[1]:=* `Integrate[x^n, x]`<br><br>*Out[1]=* $\dfrac{x^{1+n}}{1+n}$ |

| | |
|---|---|
| Here is a slightly more complicated example. | *In[2]:=* `Integrate[1/(x^4 - a^4), x]`<br><br>*Out[2]=* $\dfrac{-\text{ArcTan}[\frac{x}{a}]}{2\ a^3}\ +\ \dfrac{\text{Log}[1-\frac{x}{a}]}{4\ a^3}\ -\ \dfrac{\text{Log}[1+\frac{x}{a}]}{4\ a^3}$ |

*Mathematica* knows how to do many kinds of integrals. It can integrate any rational expression (ratio of polynomials), at least so long as the denominator does not involve too high a power of $x$. *Mathematica* can also integrate expressions that include exponential, logarithmic and trigonometric functions, so long as the resulting integrals can be given in terms of this same set of functions.

There are however many integrals for which no explicit formulae can be given, at least in terms of standard mathematical functions. Even a seemingly innocuous integral like $\int \frac{\log(1+2x)}{x}\ dx$ can, for example, only be done in terms of the dilogarithm function `PolyLog[2, x]`. And an integral like $\int \sin(\sin(x))\ dx$ simply cannot be done in terms of any of the functions that are defined in standard mathematical handbooks. Section 3.5.7 discusses how *Mathematica* treats different kinds of integrals.

| | |
|---|---|
| *Mathematica* can do integrals like this. | *In[3]:=* `Integrate[ Log[x]^2 (1 + x^2)/x , x ]`<br><br>*Out[3]=* $\dfrac{x^2}{4}\ -\ \dfrac{x^2\ \text{Log}[x]}{2}\ +\ \dfrac{x^2\ \text{Log}[x]^2}{2}\ +\ \dfrac{\text{Log}[x]^3}{3}$ |

This integral simply cannot be done in terms of standard mathematical functions. As a result, *Mathematica* just leaves it undone.

```
In[4]:= Integrate[ Sin[Sin[x]], x ]
Out[4]= Integrate[Sin[Sin[x]], x]
```

Here is the definite integral $\int_a^b \log(x)\,dx$.

```
In[5]:= Integrate[ Log[x], {x, a, b} ]
Out[5]= a - b - a Log[a] + b Log[b]
```

*Mathematica* cannot give you a formula for this definite integral.

```
In[6]:= Integrate[ Sin[Sin[x]], {x, 0, 1} ]
Out[6]= Integrate[Sin[Sin[x]], {x, 0, 1}]
```

You can still get a numerical result, though.

```
In[7]:= N[ % ]
Out[7]= 0.430606
```

| | |
|---|---|
| Integrate[*f*, *x*] | the indefinite integral $\int f\,dx$ |
| Integrate[*f*, {*x*, *xmin*, *xmax*}] | the definite integral $\int_{xmin}^{xmax} f\,dx$ |
| Integrate[*f*, {*x*, *xmin*, *xmax*}, {*y*, *ymin*, *ymax*}] | the multiple integral $\int_{xmin}^{xmax} dx \int_{ymin}^{ymax} dy\, f$ |

Integration.

This evaluates the multiple integral $\int_0^1 dx \int_0^x dy\,(x^2 + y^2)$. The variables appear in Integrate in the same order as in the standard mathematical notation: with the outermost one *first*.

```
In[8]:= Integrate[ x^2 + y^2, {x, 0, 1}, {y, 0, x} ]
Out[8]= 1
        -
        3
```

## ■ 1.5.4  Sums and Products

This constructs the sum $\sum_{i=1}^{7} \frac{x^i}{i}$.

```
In[1]:= Sum[x^i/i, {i, 1, 7}]
              2   3   4   5   6   7
             x   x   x   x   x   x
Out[1]= x +  -- + -- + -- + -- + -- + --
             2   3   4   5   6   7
```

You can leave out the lower limit if it is equal to 1.

```
In[2]:= Sum[x^i/i, {i, 7}]
              2   3   4   5   6   7
             x   x   x   x   x   x
Out[2]= x +  -- + -- + -- + -- + -- + --
             2   3   4   5   6   7
```

This makes $i$ increase in steps of 2, so that only odd-numbered values are included.

$In[3]:=$ **Sum[x^i/i, {i, 1, 5, 2}]**

$Out[3]= x + \dfrac{x^3}{3} + \dfrac{x^5}{5}$

Products work just like sums.

$In[4]:=$ **Product[x + i, {i, 1, 4}]**

$Out[4]= (1 + x) (2 + x) (3 + x) (4 + x)$

---

| | |
|---|---|
| **Sum**[$f$, {$i$, $imin$, $imax$}] | the sum $\sum_{i=imin}^{imax} f$ |
| **Sum**[$f$, {$i$, $imin$, $imax$, $di$}] | the sum with $i$ increasing in steps of $di$ |
| **Sum**[$f$, {$i$, $imin$, $imax$}, {$j$, $jmin$, $jmax$}] | |
| | the nested sum $\sum_{i=imin}^{imax} \sum_{j=jmin}^{jmax} f$ |
| **Product**[$f$, {$i$, $imin$, $imax$}] | the product $\prod_{i=imin}^{imax} f$ |

Sums and products.

*Mathematica* gives an exact result for this sum.

$In[5]:=$ **Sum[1/i^3, {i, 1, 20}]**

$Out[5]= \dfrac{33665881463886437 6538323}{2803462653224387 20204800}$

Here is the numerical value.

$In[6]:=$ **N[ % ]**

$Out[6]= 1.20087$

*Mathematica* cannot give you an exact result for this infinite sum.

$In[7]:=$ **Sum[1/i^3, {i, 1, Infinity}]**

$Out[7]= Sum[i^{-3}, \{i, 1, Infinity\}]$

You can still get a numerical result.

$In[8]:=$ **N[ % ]**

$Out[8]= 1.20206$

*Mathematica* also has a notation for multiple sums and products. **Sum**[$f$, {$i$, $imin$, $imax$}, {$j$, $jmin$, $jmax$}] represents a sum over $i$ and $j$, which would be written in standard mathematical notation as $\sum_{i=imin}^{imax} \sum_{j=jmin}^{jmax} f$. Notice that in *Mathematica* notation, as in standard mathematical notation, the range of the *outermost* variable is given *first*.

This is the multiple sum $\sum_{i=1}^{3}\sum_{j=1}^{i} x^i y^j$. Notice that the outermost sum over i is given first, just as in the mathematical notation.

```
In[9]:= Sum[x^i y^j, {i, 1, 3}, {j, 1, i}]

           2       3     2  2     3  2     3  3
Out[9]= x y + x  y + x   y + x   y  + x   y  + x   y
```

The way you specify the ranges of variables in **Sum** and **Product** is an example of the rather general *iterator notation* that *Mathematica* uses. You will see this notation again when we discuss generating tables and lists using **Table** (Section 1.7.2), and when we describe **Do** loops (Section 2.5.2). The function **Range** also uses essentially the same notation.

| | |
|---|---|
| *{imax}* | iterate *imax* times, without incrementing any variables |
| *{i, imax}* | *i* goes from 1 to *imax* in steps of 1 |
| *{i, imin, imax}* | *i* goes from *imin* to *imax* in steps of 1 |
| *{i, imin, imax, di}* | *i* goes from *imin* to *imax* in steps of *di* |
| *{i, imin, imax}, {j, jmin, jmax},* ... | *i* goes from *imin* to *imax*, and for each value of *i*, *j* goes from *jmin* to *jmax*, etc. |

*Mathematica* iterator notation.

## ■ 1.5.5 Equations

Section 1.2.2 discussed *assignments* such as *x* = *y* which *set* *x* equal to *y*. This section discusses *equations*, which *test* equality. *x* == *y* *tests* whether *x* is equal to *y*.

This *tests* whether 2 + 2 and 4 are equal. The result is the symbol **True**.

```
In[1]:= 2 + 2 == 4

Out[1]= True
```

It is very important that you do not confuse *x* = *y* with *x* == *y*. *x* = *y* is an *imperative* statement that actually causes an assignment to be done. *x* == *y* merely *tests* whether *x* and *y* are equal, and causes no explicit action. If you have used the C programming language, you will recognize that the notation for assignment and testing in *Mathematica* is just the same as in C.

| | |
|---|---|
| $x$ = $y$ | assigns $x$ to have value $y$ |
| $x$ == $y$ | tests whether $x$ and $y$ are equal |

Assignments and tests.

This *assigns* x to have value 4.

```
In[2]:= x = 4
Out[2]= 4
```

If you ask for x, you now get 4.

```
In[3]:= x
Out[3]= 4
```

This *tests* whether x is equal to 4. In this case, it is.

```
In[4]:= x == 4
Out[4]= True
```

x is equal to 4, not 6.

```
In[5]:= x == 6
Out[5]= False
```

This removes the value assigned to x.

```
In[6]:= x = .
```

The tests we have used so far just involve numbers, and always give a definite answer, either **True** or **False**.  You can also do tests on symbolic expressions.

*Mathematica* cannot get a definite result for this test unless you give x a specific numerical value.

```
In[7]:= x == 5
Out[7]= x == 5
```

If you replace x by the specific numerical value 4, the test gives **False**.

```
In[8]:= % /. x -> 4
Out[8]= False
```

Even when you do tests on symbolic expressions, there are some cases where you can get definite results. An important one is when you test the equality of two expressions that are *identical*. Whatever the numerical values of the variables in these expressions may be, *Mathematica* knows that the expressions must always be equal.

The two expressions are *identical*, so the result is **True**, whatever the value of x may be.

```
In[9]:= 2 x + x^2 == 2 x + x^2
Out[9]= True
```

Mathematica does not try to tell whether these expressions are equal. In this case, using `Expand` would make them have the same form.

```
In[10]:= 2 x + x^2 == x (2 + x)
                  2
Out[10]= 2 x + x  == x (2 + x)
```

Expressions like `x == 4` represent *equations* in *Mathematica*. There are many functions in *Mathematica* for manipulating and solving equations.

This is an *equation* in *Mathematica*. Subsection 1.5.7 will discuss how to solve it for `x`.

```
In[11]:= x^2 + 2 x - 7 == 0
                      2
Out[11]= -7 + 2 x + x  == 0
```

You can assign a name to the equation.

```
In[12]:= eqn = %
                      2
Out[12]= -7 + 2 x + x  == 0
```

If you ask for `eqn`, you now get the equation.

```
In[13]:= eqn
                      2
Out[13]= -7 + 2 x + x  == 0
```

## ■ 1.5.6 Advanced Topic: Logical Operations

| | |
|---|---|
| $x == y$ | equal |
| $x\ !=\ y$ | unequal |
| $x > y$ | greater than |
| $x >= y$ | greater than or equal |
| $x < y$ | less than |
| $x <= y$ | less than or equal |
| $x == y == z$ | all equal |
| $x\ !=\ y\ !=\ z$ | all unequal (distinct) |
| $x > y > z$, etc. | strictly decreasing, etc. |

Relational operators.

This tests whether 10 is less than 7. The result is `False`.

```
In[1]:= 10 < 7
Out[1]= False
```

| | |
|---|---|
| Not all the numbers are unequal, so this gives `False`. | `In[2]:= 3 != 2 != 3`<br>`Out[2]= False` |
| You can mix `<` and `<=`. | `In[3]:= 3 < 5 <= 6`<br>`Out[3]= True` |
| *Mathematica* does not know whether this is true or false. | `In[4]:= x > y`<br>`Out[4]= x > y` |

| | |
|---|---|
| `!`$p$ | not |
| $p$ `&&` $q$ `&&` ... | and |
| $p$ `||` $q$ `||` ... | or |
| `Xor[`$p$`, ` $q$`, ...]` | exclusive or |
| `Implies[`$p$`, ` $q$`]` | implication $p \Rightarrow q$ |
| `If[`$p$`, ` $t$`, ` $f$`]` | give $t$ if $p$ is `True`, and $f$ if $p$ is `False` |
| `LogicalExpand[`$expr$`]` | expand out logical expressions |

Logical operations.

| | |
|---|---|
| Both tests give `True`, so the result is `True`. | `In[5]:= 7 > 4 && 2 != 3`<br>`Out[5]= True` |

You should remember that the logical operations `==`, `&&` and `||` are all *double characters* in *Mathematica*. (If you have used the C programming language, you will recognize this notation as being the same as in C.)

| | |
|---|---|
| *Mathematica* does not know whether this is true or false. | `In[6]:= p && q`<br>`Out[6]= p && q` |
| *Mathematica* leaves this expression unchanged. | `In[7]:= (p || q) && !(r || s)`<br>`Out[7]= (p || q) && !(r || s)` |
| You can use `LogicalExpand` to expand out the terms. | `In[8]:= LogicalExpand[ % ]`<br>`Out[8]= p && !r && !s || q && !r && !s` |

## ■ 1.5.7  Solving Equations

An expression like `x∧2 + 2 x - 7 == 0` represents an *equation* in *Mathematica*. You will often need to *solve* equations like this, to find out for what values of x they are true.

This gives the two solutions to the quadratic equation $x^2 + 2x - 7 = 0$. The solutions are given as replacements for x.

```
In[1]:= Solve[x∧2 + 2x - 7 == 0, x]

                 -2 + 4 Sqrt[2]              -2 - 4 Sqrt[2]
Out[1]= {{x ->  ---------------}, {x ->  ---------------}}
                       2                         2
```

Here are the numerical values of the solutions.

```
In[2]:= N[ % ]
Out[2]= {{x -> 1.82843}, {x -> -3.82843}}
```

You can take the list of replacements produced by `Solve`, and use `/.` to substitute them into an expression involving x.

```
In[3]:= x∧2 + 3 x /. %
Out[3]= {8.82843, 3.17157}
```

`Solve` always tries to give you explicit *formulae* for the solutions to equations. However, it is a basic mathematical result that, for sufficiently complicated equations, explicit algebraic formulae cannot be given. If you have an algebraic equation in one variable, and the highest power of the variable is at most four, then *Mathematica* can always give you formulae for the solutions. However, if the highest power is five or more, it may be mathematically impossible to give explicit algebraic formulae for all the solutions.

*Mathematica* can always solve algebraic equations in one variable when the highest power is less than five.

```
In[4]:= Solve[x∧4 - 5 x∧2 - 3 == 0, x]

                 Sqrt[5 + Sqrt[37]]
Out[4]= {{x ->  ------------------},
                     Sqrt[2]

                    Sqrt[5 + Sqrt[37]]
        {x ->  -(------------------)},
                        Sqrt[2]

                 Sqrt[5 - Sqrt[37]]
        {x ->  ------------------},
                     Sqrt[2]

                    Sqrt[5 - Sqrt[37]]
        {x ->  -(------------------)}}
                        Sqrt[2]
```

It can solve some equations that involve higher powers.

```
In[5]:= Solve[x^6 == 1, x]
```

$$Out[5]= \{\{x \to 1\},\ \{x \to E^{\frac{I}{3}Pi}\},\ \{x \to E^{\frac{2\,I}{3}Pi}\},$$
$$\{x \to -1\},\ \{x \to E^{\frac{4\,I}{3}Pi}\},\ \{x \to E^{\frac{5\,I}{3}Pi}\}\}$$

There are some equations, however, for which it is mathematically impossible to find explicit formulae for the solutions. *Mathematica* uses the function `Roots` to represent the solutions in this case.

```
In[6]:= Solve[2 - 4 x + x^5 == 0, x]
```

$$Out[6]= \{\text{ToRules}[\text{Roots}[-4\ x + x^5 == -2, x]]\}$$

Even though you cannot get explicit formulae, you can still find the solutions numerically.

```
In[7]:= N[ % ]
```

$$Out[7]= \{\{x \to -1.51851\},\ \{x \to -0.116792 - 1.43845\ I\},$$
$$\{x \to -0.116792 + 1.43845\ I\},\ \{x \to 0.508499\},$$
$$\{x \to 1.2436\}\}$$

You can also use *Mathematica* to solve sets of simultaneous equations. You simply give the list of equations, and specify the list of variables to solve for.

Here is a list of two simultaneous equations, to be solved for the variables $x$ and $y$.

```
In[8]:= Solve[{a x + y == 0, 2 x + (1-a) y == 1}, {x, y}]
```

$$Out[8]= \{\{x \to -(\frac{1}{-2 + a - a^2}),\ y \to \frac{a}{-2 + a - a^2}\}\}$$

Here are some more complicated simultaneous equations. The two solutions are given as two lists of replacements for x and y.

```
In[9]:= Solve[{x^2 + y^2 == 1, x + 3 y == 0}, {x,y}]
```

$$Out[9]= \{\{x \to \frac{-3}{\text{Sqrt}[10]},\ y \to \frac{1}{\text{Sqrt}[10]}\},$$
$$\{x \to \frac{3}{\text{Sqrt}[10]},\ y \to -(\frac{1}{\text{Sqrt}[10]})\}\}$$

*Mathematica* can solve any set of simultaneous *linear* equations. It can also solve a large class of simultaneous polynomial equations. Even when it does not manage to solve the equations explicitly, *Mathematica* will still usually reduce them to a much simpler form.

You can use sets of simultaneous equations in *Mathematica* to represent collections of relations or constraints between different quantities. You can then use `Solve` to find the values of some of the quantities in terms of others.

Here is an equation that relates x and a. You do not need to put the equation in a list, but it makes things slightly easier to read.

```
In[10]:= eqn = { x == 2 a + 1 }
Out[10]= {x == 1 + 2 a}
```

This solves the equation, giving a formula for x in terms of a.

```
In[11]:= Solve[eqn, x]
Out[11]= {{x -> 1 + 2 a}}
```

You can also solve the equation for a in terms of x.

```
In[12]:= Solve[eqn, a]
```
$$Out[12]= \{\{a \to \frac{-1 + x}{2}\}\}$$

Here is a pair of equations that give relations between x and y.

```
In[13]:= eqns = { x == 3 a + y, y == 9 x - 4 }
Out[13]= {x == 3 a + y, y == -4 + 9 x}
```

You can solve these equations to find x and y in terms of a.

```
In[14]:= Solve[eqns, {x, y}]
```
$$Out[14]= \{\{x \to \frac{1}{2} - \frac{3\,a}{8}, \; y \to \frac{1}{2} - \frac{27\,a}{8}\}\}$$

You can also use the equations to get formulae for a and x in terms of y.

```
In[15]:= Solve[eqns, {a, x}]
```
$$Out[15]= \{\{a \to \frac{-y}{3} + \frac{4 + y}{27}, \; x \to \frac{4 + y}{9}\}\}$$

There are some kinds of calculations that are particularly suited to a style of computation in which one sets up a collection of equations, and then uses `Solve` to get the results one wants.

The standard *Mathematica* style is to give a sequence of assignments, which specify the value of one variable in terms of others. So, for example, you might make the assignment x = 2 a + 1, followed by y = 2 x + 9. If you then ask for y, *Mathematica* will find its value by applying the assignments you have just made.

You can also set up this calculation in terms of *equations*. Instead of making definite assignments that give the value of one variable in terms of others, you can simply write down *equations* that relate the values of different variables. Then, to find, say, the value of y, you explicitly *solve* these equations for y.

Here are some equations for x and y.

```
In[16]:= eqn = {x == 2 a + 1, y == 2 x + 9}
Out[16]= {x == 1 + 2 a, y == 9 + 2 x}
```

You can find the value of y by explicitly solving the equations for y.

```
In[17]:= Solve[eqn, y]
Out[17]= {{y -> 9 + 2 x}}
```

You can also "work backwards", and find the value of a in terms of y.

$In[18]:=$ `Solve[eqn, a]`

$Out[18]=$ `{{a ->` $\frac{-1 + x}{2}$ `}}`

This finds the values of both x and a.

$In[19]:=$ `Solve[eqn, {x, a}]`

$Out[19]=$ `{{x ->` $\frac{-9 + y}{2}$ `, a -> ` $-(\frac{1}{2}) + \frac{-9 + y}{4}$ `}}`

When you set up a calculation using assignments, you are essentially defining a specific set of "inputs", from which you compute a specific set of "outputs". When you use equations, you are giving relations with no definite "direction". It is only when you call `Solve` to find the value of a particular variable that you are imposing a definite direction.

Setting up calculations using equations, rather than assignments, is particularly convenient if you need to "work backwards" from your "output" to find appropriate "inputs". You can equally well use `Solve` to solve for the "output" in terms of the "input", or for the "input" in terms of the "output".

When you use a large set of equations in *Mathematica*, it is a bit like setting up a "spreadsheet", whose cells correspond to your variables. Whenever you need to find the value for a particular cell, you simply call `Solve` for the variable that corresponds to that cell. Of course, *Mathematica* can handle much more complicated mathematical relations between cells than a traditional spreadsheet program could.

When you are working with sets of equations in several variables, it is often convenient to reorganize the equations by eliminating some variables between them.

This eliminates y between the two equations, giving a single equation for x.

$In[20]:=$ `Eliminate[{a x + y == 0, 2 x + (1-a) y == 1}, y]`

$Out[20]=$ `-(a x) +` $a^2$ `x == 1 - 2 x`

If you have several equations, there is no guarantee that there exists *any* consistent solution for a particular variable.

There is no consistent solution to these equations, so *Mathematica* returns {}, indicating that the set of solutions is empty.

$In[21]:=$ `Solve[{x==1, x==2}, x]`

$Out[21]=$ `{}`

There is also no consistent solution to these equations for almost all values of a.

$In[22]:=$ `Solve[{x==1, x==a}, x]`

$Out[22]=$ `{}`

The general question of whether a set of equations has any consistent solution is quite a subtle one. For example, for most values of a, the equations {x==1, x==a} are inconsistent, so there is no possible solution for x. However, if a is equal to 1, then the equations *do* have a solution. Solve is set up to give you *generic* solutions to equations. It discards any solutions that exist only when special constraints between parameters are satisfied.

If you use Reduce instead of Solve, *Mathematica* will however keep *all* the possible solutions to a set of equations, including those that require special conditions on parameters.

This shows that the equations have a solution only when a == 1. The notation x==1 && x==a represents the requirement that *both* x==1 *and* x==a should be True.

```
In[23]:= Reduce[{x==1, x==a}, x]
Out[23]= a == 1 && x == 1
```

This gives the complete set of possible solutions to the equation. The answer is stated in terms of a combination of simpler equations. && indicates equations that must simultaneously be true; || indicates alternatives.

```
In[24]:= Reduce[a x + b == 0, x]
```
$$Out[24]= a \,!\!= 0 \;\&\&\; x == -\left(\frac{b}{a}\right) \;||\; a == 0 \;\&\&\; b == 0$$

This gives a more complicated combination of equations.

```
In[25]:= Reduce[a x^2 + b == 0, x]
```
$$Out[25]= a \,!\!= 0 \;\&\&\; \left(x == \frac{I\ \mathrm{Sqrt}[b]}{\mathrm{Sqrt}[a]} \;||\; x == \frac{-I\ \mathrm{Sqrt}[b]}{\mathrm{Sqrt}[a]}\right) \;||$$
$$a == 0 \;\&\&\; b == 0$$

You can use LogicalExpand to manipulate the set of equations.

```
In[26]:= LogicalExpand[%]
```
$$Out[26]= a \,!\!= 0 \;\&\&\; x == \frac{I\ \mathrm{Sqrt}[b]}{\mathrm{Sqrt}[a]} \;||$$
$$a \,!\!= 0 \;\&\&\; x == \frac{-I\ \mathrm{Sqrt}[b]}{\mathrm{Sqrt}[a]} \;||\; a == 0 \;\&\&\; b == 0$$

| `Solve[`*lhs*`==`*rhs*`, x]` | solve an equation for $x$ |

`Solve[{`*lhs₁*`==`*rhs₁*`, `*lhs₂*`==`*rhs₂*`, ...}, {x, y, ...}]`

$\qquad$ solve a set of simultaneous equations for $x, y, \ldots$

`Eliminate[{`*lhs₁*`==`*rhs₁*`, `*lhs₂*`==`*rhs₂*`, ...}, {x, ...}]`

$\qquad$ eliminate $x, \ldots$ in a set of simultaneous equations

`Reduce[{`*lhs₁*`==`*rhs₁*`, `*lhs₂*`==`*rhs₂*`, ...}, {x, y, ...}]`

$\qquad$ give a set of simplified equations, including all possible solutions

Functions for solving and manipulating equations.

## ■ 1.5.8  Power Series

The mathematical operations we have discussed so far are *exact*. Given precise input, their results are exact formulae.

In many situations, however, you do not need an exact result. It may be quite sufficient, for example, to find an *approximate* formula that is valid, say, when the quantity x is small.

This gives a power series approximation to $(1 + x)^n$ for $x$ close to 0, up to terms of order $x^3$.

```
In[1]:= Series[(1 + x)^n, {x, 0, 3}]
```

$$Out[1]= 1 + n\ x + \left(\frac{-n}{2} + \frac{n^2}{2}\right) x^2 + \left(\frac{n}{3} - \frac{n^2}{2} + \frac{n^3}{6}\right) x^3 + O[x]^4$$

Here is an approximation for $x$ close to 1.

```
In[2]:= Series[(1 + x)^n, {x, 1, 2}]
```

$$Out[2]= 2^n + \frac{2^n\ n\ (-1 + x)}{2} + 2^n \left(\frac{-n}{8} + \frac{n^2}{8}\right) (-1 + x)^2 +$$

$$O[-1 + x]^3$$

*Mathematica* knows the power series expansions for many mathematical functions.

```
In[3]:= Series[Exp[-a t] (1 + Sin[2 t]), {t, 0, 4}]
```

$$Out[3]= 1 + (2 - a)\ t + \left(-2\ a + \frac{a^2}{2}\right) t^2 +$$

$$\left(-\left(\frac{4}{3}\right) + a^2 - \frac{a^3}{6}\right) t^3 + \left(\frac{4\ a}{3} - \frac{a^3}{3} + \frac{a^4}{24}\right) t^4 + O[t]^5$$

If you give it a function that it does not know, **Series** writes out the power series in terms of derivatives.

$In[4]:=$ **Series[1 + f[t], {t, 0, 3}]**

$Out[4]= (1 + f[0]) + f'[0] \ t + \dfrac{f''[0] \ t^2}{2} + \dfrac{f^{(3)}[0] \ t^3}{6} + $

$O[t]^4$

Here is a simple power series, accurate to order $x^5$.

$In[5]:=$ **Series[Exp[x], {x, 0, 5}]**

$Out[5]= 1 + x + \dfrac{x^2}{2} + \dfrac{x^3}{6} + \dfrac{x^4}{24} + \dfrac{x^5}{120} + O[x]^6$

When you do operations on a power series, the result is computed only to the appropriate order in **x**.

$In[6]:=$ **%^2 (1 + %)**

$Out[6]= 2 + 5 \ x + \dfrac{13 \ x^2}{2} + \dfrac{35 \ x^3}{6} + \dfrac{97 \ x^4}{24} + \dfrac{55 \ x^5}{24} + O[x]^6$

This turns the power series back into an ordinary expression.

$In[7]:=$ **Normal[%]**

$Out[7]= 2 + 5 \ x + \dfrac{13 \ x^2}{2} + \dfrac{35 \ x^3}{6} + \dfrac{97 \ x^4}{24} + \dfrac{55 \ x^5}{24}$

Now the square is computed *exactly*.

$In[8]:=$ **%^2**

$Out[8]= (2 + 5 \ x + \dfrac{13 \ x^2}{2} + \dfrac{35 \ x^3}{6} + \dfrac{97 \ x^4}{24} + \dfrac{55 \ x^5}{24})^2$

Applying **Expand** gives a result with ten terms.

$In[9]:=$ **Expand[%]**

$Out[9]= 4 + 20 \ x + 51 \ x^2 + \dfrac{265 \ x^3}{3} + \dfrac{467 \ x^4}{4} + \dfrac{1505 \ x^5}{12} + $

$\dfrac{7883 \ x^6}{72} + \dfrac{1385 \ x^7}{18} + \dfrac{24809 \ x^8}{576} + \dfrac{5335 \ x^9}{288} + \dfrac{3025 \ x^{10}}{576}$

| | |
|---|---|
| **Series[***expr*, {*x*, $x_0$, *n*}**]** | find the power series expansion of *expr* about the point $x = x_0$ to at most *n* terms |
| **Normal[***series***]** | truncate a power series to give an ordinary expression |

Power series operations.

## ■ 1.5.9  Limits

Here is the expression $\frac{\sin(x)}{x}$.

```
In[1]:= t = Sin[x]/x
```

$$Out[1]= \frac{Sin[x]}{x}$$

If you replace x by 0, the expression becomes 0/0, and you get an indeterminate result.

```
In[2]:= t /. x->0
```

```
                                      1
Power::infy: Infinite expression  -  encountered.
                                      0
```

```
Infinity::indt:
        Indeterminate expression 0 ComplexInfinity
            encountered.
```

```
Out[2]= Indeterminate
```

If you find the numerical value of $\frac{\sin(x)}{x}$ for $x$ close to 0, however, you get a result that is close to 1.

```
In[3]:= t /. x->0.01
```

```
Out[3]= 0.999983
```

This finds the *limit* of $\frac{\sin(x)}{x}$ as $x$ approaches 0. The result is indeed 1.

```
In[4]:= Limit[t, x->0]
```

```
Out[4]= 1
```

| Limit[expr, x->x_0] | the limit of expr as x approaches $x_0$ |
|---|---|

Limits.

## ■ 1.5.10  Numerical Mathematics

Exact symbolic results are usually very desirable when they can be found. In many calculations, however, it is not possible to get symbolic results. In such cases, you must resort to numerical methods.

| | |
|---|---|
| `N[`*expr*`]` | numerical value of an expression (see Section 1.1) |
| `NIntegrate[`*f*`, {`*x*`, `*xmin*`, `*xmax*`}]` | numerical approximation to $\int_{xmin}^{xmax} f \, dx$ |
| `NSum[`*f*`, {`*i*`, `*imin*`, Infinity}]` | numerical approximation to $\sum_{imin}^{\infty} f$ |
| `NRoots[`*poly*`==0, `*x*`]` | numerical approximations to the roots of a polynomial |
| `FindRoot[`*lhs*`==`*rhs*`, {`*x*`, `*x₀*`}]` | search for a numerical solution to the equation, starting with $x=x_0$ |
| `FindMinimum[`*f*`, {`*x*`, `*x₀*`}]` | search for a minimum of $f$, starting with $x=x_0$ |

Some numerical operations.

*Mathematica* cannot get an exact formula for this integral.

```
In[1]:= Integrate[Sin[Sin[x]], {x, 1, 2}]
Out[1]= Integrate[Sin[Sin[x]], {x, 1, 2}]
```

You can, however, ask for an approximate numerical result.

```
In[2]:= N[ % ]
Out[2]= 0.81645
```

Sometimes you just want to do an integral numerically from the start, without having *Mathematica* first try to do it analytically.

```
In[3]:= NIntegrate[Sin[Sin[x]], {x, 1, 2}]
Out[3]= 0.81645
```

`NIntegrate` uses an adaptive scheme, which can cope with weak singularities at the end points.

```
In[4]:= NIntegrate[1/Sqrt[x], {x, 0, 1}]
Out[4]= 2.
```

This finds a numerical approximation to a root of the equation $\cos(x) = x$ near the point $x = 1$.

```
In[5]:= FindRoot[Cos[x] == x, {x, 1}]
Out[5]= {x -> 0.739085}
```

This finds a numerical approximation to the minimum of $x \sin(x)$ close to $x = 2\pi$. The result is a list: the first entry is the minimum value of the function; the second entry is the point at which the minimum occurs.

```
In[6]:= FindMinimum[x Sin[x], {x, 2Pi}]
Out[6]= {-4.81447, {x -> 4.913187501303}}
```

## ■ 1.5.11  Mathematics in *Mathematica* Packages

This section has described some of the many mathematical operations that are built into *Mathematica*. Many further mathematical operations are defined in external *Mathematica* packages, as discussed in Section 1.3.8.

*Mathematica* does not intrinsically know how to do Laplace transforms. This reads in a *Mathematica* package for doing Laplace transforms.

```
In[1]:= <<Laplace.m
```

Now *Mathematica* can do Laplace transforms.

```
In[2]:= Laplace[(1 + 2 t) Exp[-2 t], t, s]
```

$$Out[2]= \frac{2}{(2 + s)^2} + \frac{1}{2 + s}$$

You will have to look on your particular computer system to see what *Mathematica* packages are available. One point to be careful about is that if you ever use a name like **Laplace** *before* you read in the package that defines **Laplace**, then *Mathematica* may get confused about whether it should use your version of **Laplace**, or the one that was defined in the package. Page 316 discusses this issue in more detail.

| | |
|---|---|
| `Fourier.m` | symbolic Fourier transforms and their inverses |
| `Laplace.m` | Laplace transforms and their inverses |
| `ODE.m` | functions for manipulating and solving ordinary differential equations |
| `RungeKutta.m` | numerical integration of differential equations |
| `Trigonometry.m` | trigonometric identities and simplification rules |
| `VectorAnalysis.m` | vector analysis |

A few common *Mathematica* packages.

## ■ 1.5.12  Manipulating Numerical Data

| | |
|---|---|
| `Mean[data]` | mean (average value) |
| `Median[data]` | median (central value) |
| `Variance[data]` | variance |
| `StandardDeviation[data]` | standard deviation |

Basic statistics functions from the package `Statistics.m`.

Unless it was automatically loaded when you started *Mathematica*, you first need to read in the *Mathematica* statistics package.

```
In[1]:= <<Statistics.m
```

Here is some "data".

```
In[2]:= data = {4.3, 7.2, 8.4, 5.8, 9.2, 3.9}
Out[2]= {4.3, 7.2, 8.4, 5.8, 9.2, 3.9}
```

This gives the mean of your data.

```
In[3]:= Mean[data]
Out[3]= 6.46667
```

Here is the variance.

```
In[4]:= Variance[data]
Out[4]= 3.91222
```

When you have numerical data, it is often convenient to find a simple formula that approximates it. If you plotted the data as a curve, you could think of trying to "fit" a line or a simple curve through your data. The function Fit is built in to *Mathematica*; you do not need to read in any packages to get it.

Fit[$\{y_1, y_2, ...\}$, $\{f_1, f_2, ...\}$, x]
fit the values $y_n$ to a linear combination of functions $f_i$

Fit[$\{\{x_1, y_1\}, \{x_2, y_2\}, ...\}$, $\{f_1, f_2, ...\}$,x]
fit the points $(x_n, y_n)$ to a linear combination of the $f_i$

Functions for fitting curves, built in to *Mathematica*.

This generates a table of the numerical values of the exponential function. Table will be discussed in Section 1.7.2.

```
In[5]:= data = Table[ Exp[x/5.] , {x, 7}]
Out[5]= {1.2214, 1.49182, 1.82212, 2.22554, 2.71828,
         3.32012, 4.0552}
```

This finds a least-squares fit to data of the form $c_1 + c_2 x + c_3 x^2$. The elements of data are assumed to correspond to values 1, 2, ... of $x$.

```
In[6]:= Fit[data, {1, x, x^2}, x]
Out[6]= 1.09428 + 0.0986337 x + 0.0459482 x^2
```

This finds a fit of the form $c_1 + c_2 x + c_3 x^3 + c_4 x^5$.

```
In[7]:= Fit[data, {1, x, x^3, x^5}, x]
Out[7]= 0.96806 + 0.246829 x + 0.00428281 x^3 -
        0.00000657948 x^5
```

| This gives a table of $x$, $y$ pairs. | `In[8]:= data = Table[ {x, Exp[Sin[x]]} , {x, 0., 1., 0.2}]` |
|---|---|
| | `Out[8]= {{0., 1.}, {0.2, 1.21978}, {0.4, 1.47612},` |
| | `       {0.6, 1.75882}, {0.8, 2.04901}, {1., 2.31978}}` |

| This finds a fit to the new data, of the form $c_1 + c_2 \sin(x) + c_3 \sin(2x)$. | `In[9]:= Fit[%, {1, Sin[x], Sin[2x]}, x]` |
|---|---|
| | `Out[9]= 0.989559 + 2.04199 Sin[x] - 0.418176 Sin[2 x]` |

One common way of picking out "signals" in numerical data is to find the Fourier transform or "frequency spectrum" of the data.

| `Fourier[`*data*`]` | numerical Fourier transform |
|---|---|
| `InverseFourier[`*data*`]` | inverse Fourier transform |

Fourier transforms.

| Here is a simple square pulse. | `In[10]:= data = {1, 1, 1, 1, -1, -1, -1, -1}` |
|---|---|
| | `Out[10]= {1, 1, 1, 1, -1, -1, -1, -1}` |

| This takes the Fourier transform of the pulse. | `In[11]:= Fourier[data]` |
|---|---|
| | `Out[11]= {0., 0.707107 + 1.70711 I, 0.,` |
| | `          0.707107 + 0.292893 I, 0., 0.707107 - 0.292893 I,` |
| | `          0., 0.707107 - 1.70711 I}` |

# ■ 1.6  Adding Your Own Functions

## ■ 1.6.1  Defining Functions

In this chapter, we have seen many examples of functions that are built into *Mathematica*. In this section, we discuss how you can add your own simple functions to *Mathematica*. Chapter 2 will describe in much greater detail the mechanisms for adding functions to *Mathematica*.

As a first example, consider adding a function called f which squares its argument. The *Mathematica* command to define this function is f[x_] := x^2. The _ (referred to as "blank") on the left-hand side is very important; exactly what it means will be explained in Section 2. For now, just remember to put a _ on the left-hand side, but not the right-hand side, of your definition.

| | |
|---|---|
| This defines the function f. Notice the _ on the left-hand side. | *In[1]:=* **f[x_] := x^2** |
| f squares its argument. | *In[2]:=* **f[a+1]** |
| | *Out[2]=* $(1 + a)^2$ |
| The argument can be a number. | *In[3]:=* **f[4]** |
| | *Out[3]=* 16 |
| Or it can be a more complicated expression. | *In[4]:=* **f[3x + x^2]** |
| | *Out[4]=* $(3 \ x + x^2)^2$ |
| You can use f in a calculation. | *In[5]:=* **Expand[f[(x+1+y)]]** |
| | *Out[5]=* $1 + 2 \ x + x^2 + 2 \ y + 2 \ x \ y + y^2$ |
| This shows the definition you made for f. What /: means will be discussed in Chapter 2. | *In[6]:=* **?f** |
| | f |
| | f/: f[x_] := $x^2$ |

| | |
|---|---|
| `f[x_] := x^2` | define the function `f` |
| `?f` | show the definition of *f* |
| `Clear[f]` | clear all definitions for *f* |

Defining a function in *Mathematica*.

The names like **f** that you use for functions in *Mathematica* are just symbols. As a result, you should make sure to avoid using names that begin with capital letters, to prevent confusion with built-in *Mathematica* functions. You should also make sure that you have not used the names for something else earlier in your session.

*Mathematica* functions can have any number of arguments.

$$In[6]:= \text{hump}[x_-, xmax_-] := (x - xmax)^2 / xmax$$

You can use the **hump** function just as you would any of the built-in functions.

$$In[7]:= 2 + \text{hump}[x, 7/(3+5)]$$

$$Out[7]= 2 + \frac{8 \left(-\left(\frac{7}{8}\right) + x\right)^2}{7}$$

This gives a new definition for **hump**, which overwrites the previous one.

$$In[8]:= \text{hump}[x_-, xmax_-] := (x - xmax)^4$$

The new definition is displayed.

$$In[9]:= \text{?hump}$$

hump

$$\text{hump}/: \ \text{hump}[x_-, xmax_-] := (x - xmax)^4$$

This clears all definitions for **hump**.

$$In[9]:= \text{Clear}[\text{hump}]$$

## ■ 1.6.2 Functions as Procedures

In many kinds of calculations, you may find yourself typing the same input to *Mathematica* over and over again. You can save yourself a lot of typing by defining a *function* that contains your input commands.

This constructs a product of three terms, and expands out the result.

$$In[1]:= \text{Expand}[ \ \text{Product}[x + i, \{i, 3\}] \ ]$$

$$Out[1]= 6 + 11 x + 6 x^2 + x^3$$

| | |
|---|---|
| This does the same thing, but with four terms. | `In[2]:= Expand[ Product[x + i, {i, 4}] ]`<br><br>`Out[2]= 24 + 50 x + 35 x$^2$ + 10 x$^3$ + x$^4$` |

This defines a function `exprod` which constructs a product of *n* terms, then expands it out.

```
In[3]:= exprod[n_] :=
            Expand[ Product[ x + i, {i, 1, n} ] ]
```

Every time you use the function, it will execute the **Product** and **Expand** operations.

```
In[4]:= exprod[5]

Out[4]= 120 + 274 x + 225 x$^2$ + 85 x$^3$ + 15 x$^4$ + x$^5$
```

The functions you define in *Mathematica* are essentially "procedures" that execute the commands you give. You can have several steps in your procedures, separated by semicolons. Section 2.5 describes the full procedural programming capabilities of *Mathematica*.

The result you get from the whole function is simply the last expression in the procedure. Notice that you have to put parentheses around the procedure when you define it.

```
In[5]:= cex[n_, i_] := ( t = exprod[n];
            Coefficient[t, x^i] )
```

This "runs" the procedure.

```
In[6]:= cex[5, 3]
Out[6]= 85
```

## ■ 1.6.3 Special Topic: Saving Your Definitions

Any function you define in *Mathematica* will last for the whole of your session, unless you explicitly **Clear** it. However, if you want to use the same function again in future sessions, then you explicitly have to save it.

You can save the definitions of functions in exactly the same way as you save definitions of variables.

| | |
|---|---|
| `Save["filename", f$_1$, f$_2$, ...]` | save definitions of functions in a file |
| `<<filename` | read in a file of definitions |

Saving and restoring function definitions.

This defines a function `f`.

```
In[1]:= f[x_] := x^2
```

g is defined in terms of f.

*In[2]:=* **g[x_] := 3 f[x] + f[x∧2]**

This saves in the file **gdef.m** the definition of **g**, together with any subsidiary definitions that are needed.

*In[3]:=* **Save["gdef.m", g]**

The file contains the definition of **f** as well as **g**, since **g** depends on **f**.

*In[4]:=* **!!gdef.m**

**g/: g[x_] := 3*f[x] + f[x∧2]**

**f/: f[x_] := x∧2**

# ■ 1.7 Lists

## ■ 1.7.1 Collecting Objects Together

We first encountered lists in Section 1.2.3 as a way of collecting numbers together.
You can use lists to collect together any kind of expression.

Here is a list of numbers.

```
In[1]:= {2, 3, 4}
Out[1]= {2, 3, 4}
```

This gives a list of symbolic expressions.

```
In[2]:= x^% - 1
Out[2]= {-1 + x , -1 + x , -1 + x }
                  2        3        4
```

You can differentiate these expressions.

```
In[3]:= D[%, x]
Out[3]= {2 x, 3 x , 4 x }
               2     3
```

Or you can find their values when x is replaced with 3.

```
In[4]:= % /. x -> 3
Out[4]= {6, 27, 108}
```

The mathematical functions that are built in to *Mathematica* are mostly set up so that they act separately on each element of a list.    This is, however, not true of all functions in *Mathematica*. Unless you set it up specially, a new function f that you introduce will treat lists just as single objects. Sections 2.1.5 and 2.4.6 will describe how you can use **Map** and **Thread** to apply a function like this separately to each element in a list.

## ■ 1.7.2 Making Tables of Values

You can use lists as tables of values. You can generate the tables, for example, by evaluating an expression for a sequence of different parameter values.

This gives a table of the values of $i^2$, with $i$ running from 1 to 6.

```
In[1]:= Table[i^2, {i, 6}]
Out[1]= {1, 4, 9, 16, 25, 36}
```

Here is a table of $\sin(n\pi/5)$ for $n$ from 0 to 4.

```
In[2]:= Table[Sin[n Pi/5], {n, 0, 4}]
Out[2]= {0, Sin[Pi/5], Sin[2 Pi/5], Sin[3 Pi/5], Sin[4 Pi/5]}
```

| | |
|---|---|
| This gives the numerical values. | *In[3]:=* **N[%]** |
| | *Out[3]=* {0., 0.587785, 0.951057, 0.951057, 0.587785} |

You can also make tables of formulae.

*In[4]:=* **Table[x^i + 2i, {i, 5}]**

*Out[4]=* $\{2 + x, 4 + x^2, 6 + x^3, 8 + x^4, 10 + x^5\}$

**Table** uses exactly the same "iterator" notation as the functions **Sum** and **Product**, which were discussed in Section 1.5.4.

*In[5]:=* **Product[x^i + 2i, {i, 5}]**

*Out[5]=* $(2 + x) (4 + x^2) (6 + x^3) (8 + x^4) (10 + x^5)$

This makes a table with values of x running from 0 to 1 in steps of 0.25.

*In[6]:=* **Table[Sqrt[x], {x, 0, 1, 0.25}]**

*Out[6]=* {0, 0.5, 0.707107, 0.866025, 1.}

You can perform other operations on the lists you get from **Table**.

*In[7]:=* **%^2 + 3**

*Out[7]=* {3, 3.25, 3.5, 3.75, 4.}

**TableForm** displays lists in a "tabular" format. Notice that both the words in the name **TableForm** begin with capital letters.

*In[8]:=* **% // TableForm**

```
3
3.25
3.5
3.75
```

*Out[8]//TableForm=* 4.

All the examples so far have been of tables obtained by varying a single parameter. You can also make tables that involve several parameters. These "multidimensional" tables are specified using the standard *Mathematica* iterator notation, discussed in Section 1.5.4.

This makes a table of $x^i + y^j$ with $i$ running from 1 to 3 and $j$ running from 1 to 2.

*In[9]:=* **Table[x^i + y^j, {i, 3}, {j, 2}]**

*Out[9]=* $\{\{x + y, x + y^2\}, \{x^2 + y, x^2 + y^2\},$
$\{x^3 + y, x^3 + y^2\}\}$

The table in this example is a *list of lists*. The elements of the outer list correspond to successive values of $i$. The elements of each inner list correspond to successive values of $j$, with $i$ fixed.

Sometimes you may want to generate a table by evaluating a particular expression many times, without incrementing any variables.

This creates a list containing four copies of the symbol x.

```
In[10]:= Table[x, {4}]
Out[10]= {x, x, x, x}
```

This gives a list of four pseudorandom numbers. `Table` re-evaluates `Random[ ]` for each element in the list, so that you get a different pseudorandom number.

```
In[11]:= Table[Random[ ], {4}]
Out[11]= {0.626136, 0.593602, 0.740102, 0.928052}
```

| | |
|---|---|
| Table[*f*, {*imax*}] | give a list of *imax* values of *f* |
| Table[*f*, {*i*, *imax*}] | give a list of the values of *f* as *i* runs from 1 to *imax* |
| Table[*f*, {*i*, *imin*, *imax*}] | give a list of values with *i* running from *imin* to *imax* |
| Table[*f*, {*i*, *imin*, *imax*, *istep*}] | use steps of *istep* |
| Table[*f*, {*i*, *imin*, *imax*}, {*j*, *jmin*, *jmax*}, ...] | generate a multidimensional table |
| TableForm[*list*] | display a list in tabular form |

Functions for generating tables.

You can use the operations discussed in Section 1.2.3 to extract elements of the table.

This creates a 2 × 2 table, and gives it the name m.

```
In[12]:= m = Table[i - j, {i, 2}, {j, 2}]
Out[12]= {{0, -1}, {1, 0}}
```

This extracts the first sublist from the list of lists that makes up the table.

```
In[13]:= m[[1]]
Out[13]= {0, -1}
```

This extracts the second element of that sublist.

```
In[14]:= %[[2]]
Out[14]= -1
```

This does the two operations together.

```
In[15]:= m[[1,2]]
Out[15]= -1
```

This displays m in a "tabular" form.

```
In[16]:= TableForm[m]
                        0    -1
Out[16]//TableForm= 1    0
```

|                      |                                                            |
|----------------------|------------------------------------------------------------|
| $t[[i]]$             | give the $i^{\text{th}}$ sublist in $t$                    |
| $t[[\{i_1,\ i_2,\ ...\}]]$ | give a list of the $i_1{}^{\text{th}}$, $i_2{}^{\text{th}}$, ... parts of $t$ |
| $t[[i,\ j,\ ...]]$   | give the part of $t$ corresponding to $t[[i]][[j]]...$      |

Ways to extract parts of tables.

As we mentioned in Section 1.2.3, you can think of lists in *Mathematica* as being analogous to "arrays". Lists of lists are then like two-dimensional arrays. When you lay them out in a tabular form, the two indices of each element are like its $x$ and $y$ coordinates.

You can use **Table** to generate arrays with any number of dimensions.

This generates a three-dimensional $2 \times 2 \times 2$ array. It is a list of lists of lists.

```
In[17]:= Table[i j^2 k^3, {i, 2}, {j, 2}, {k, 2}]
Out[17]= {{{1, 8}, {4, 32}}, {{2, 16}, {8, 64}}}
```

## ■ 1.7.3  Vectors and Matrices

Vectors and matrices in *Mathematica* are simply represented by lists and lists of lists, respectively.

|                      |                                                            |
|----------------------|------------------------------------------------------------|
| $\{a,\ b,\ c\}$      | vector $(a, b, c)$                                         |
| $\{\{a,\ b\},\ \{c,\ d\}\}$ | matrix $\begin{pmatrix} a & b \\ c & d \end{pmatrix}$ |

The representation of vectors and matrices by lists.

This is a $2 \times 2$ matrix.

```
In[1]:= m = {{a, b}, {c, d}}
Out[1]= {{a, b}, {c, d}}
```

Here is the first row.

```
In[2]:= m[[1]]
Out[2]= {a, b}
```

Here is the element $m_{12}$.

```
In[3]:= m[[1,2]]
Out[3]= b
```

This is a two-component vector.

```
In[4]:= v = {x, y}
Out[4]= {x, y}
```

p and q are treated as scalars.

*In[5]:=* **p v + q**

*Out[5]=* {q + p x, q + p y}

Vectors are added component by component.

*In[6]:=* **v + {xp, yp} + {xpp, ypp}**

*Out[6]=* {x + xp + xpp, y + yp + ypp}

This takes the dot ("scalar") product of two vectors.

*In[7]:=* **{x, y} . {xp, yp}**

*Out[7]=* x xp + y yp

You can also multiply a matrix by a vector.

*In[8]:=* **m . v**

*Out[8]=* {a x + b y, c x + d y}

Or a matrix by a matrix.

*In[9]:=* **m . m**

*Out[9]=* {{$a^2$ + b c, a b + b d}, {a c + c d, b c + $d^2$}}

Or a vector by a matrix.

*In[10]:=* **v . m**

*Out[10]=* {a x + c y, b x + d y}

This combination makes a scalar.

*In[11]:=* **v . m . v**

*Out[11]=* x (a x + c y) + y (b x + d y)

The way *Mathematica* uses lists to represent vectors and matrices, you never have to distinguish between "row" and "column" vectors.

| | |
|---|---|
| Table[*f*, {*i*, *n*}] | build a length-*n* vector by evaluating *f* with *i*=1, *i*=2, ..., *i*=*n* |
| Array[*a*, *n*] | build a length-*n* vector of the form {a[1], a[2], ...} |
| *list*[[*i*]] | give the *i*<sup>th</sup> element in the vector *list* |
| ColumnForm[*list*] | display the elements of *list* in a column |
| Table[*f*, {*i*, *m*}, {*j*, *n*}] | build an *m* × *n* matrix by evaluating *f* with *i* ranging from 1 to *m* and *j* ranging from 1 to *n* |
| Array[*a*, {*m*, *n*}] | build an *m* × *n* matrix with *i*, *j*<sup>th</sup> element a[*i*, *j*] |
| IdentityMatrix[*n*] | generate an *n* × *n* identity matrix |
| DiagonalMatrix[*list*] | generate a square matrix with the elements in *list* on the diagonal |
| *list*[[*i*]] | give the *i*<sup>th</sup> row in the matrix *list* |
| *list*[[*i*, *j*]] | give the *i*, *j*<sup>th</sup> element in matrix *list* |
| MatrixForm[*list*] | display *list* in matrix form |

Functions for vectors and matrices.

This builds a $3 \times 3$ matrix s with elements $s_{ij} = i + j$.

```
In[12]:= s = Table[i+j, {i, 3}, {j, 3}]
Out[12]= {{2, 3, 4}, {3, 4, 5}, {4, 5, 6}}
```

This displays s in standard two-dimensional matrix format.

```
In[13]:= MatrixForm[s]
                    2   3   4
                    3   4   5
Out[13]//MatrixForm= 4   5   6
```

This gives a vector with "symbolic elements". You can use this in deriving general formulae that are valid with any choice of vector components.

```
In[14]:= Array[a, 4]
Out[14]= {a[1], a[2], a[3], a[4]}
```

This gives a $3 \times 2$ matrix with symbolic elements. Chapter 2.1.14 will discuss how you can produce other kinds of elements with **Array**.

```
In[15]:= Array[p, {3, 2}]
Out[15]= {{p[1, 1], p[1, 2]}, {p[2, 1], p[2, 2]},
           {p[3, 1], p[3, 2]}}
```

This generates a 3 × 3 diagonal matrix.

*In[16]:=* `DiagonalMatrix[{a, b, c}]`

*Out[16]=* `{{a, 0, 0}, {0, b, 0}, {0, 0, c}}`

| | |
|---:|:---|
| *c m* | multiply by a scalar |
| *a* . *b* | matrix product |
| `Inverse[`*m*`]` | matrix inverse |
| `Det[`*m*`]` | determinant |
| `Transpose[`*m*`]` | transpose |
| `Eigenvalues[`*m*`]` | eigenvalues |
| `Eigenvectors[`*m*`]` | eigenvectors |
| `Eigenvalues[N[`*m*`]], Eigenvectors[N[`*m*`]]` | |
| | numerical eigenvalues and eigenvectors |

Some mathematical operations on matrices.

Here is a 2 × 2 matrix of symbolic variables, that was defined above.

*In[17]:=* `m`

*Out[17]=* `{{a, b}, {c, d}}`

This gives its determinant.

*In[18]:=* `Det[m]`

*Out[18]=* `-(b c) + a d`

Here is the transpose of `m`.

*In[19]:=* `Transpose[m]`

*Out[19]=* `{{a, c}, {b, d}}`

This gives the inverse of `m` in symbolic form.

*In[20]:=* `Inverse[m]`

$$Out[20]= \{\{\frac{d}{-(b\ c)\ +\ a\ d},\ -(\frac{b}{-(b\ c)\ +\ a\ d})\},$$
$$\{-(\frac{c}{-(b\ c)\ +\ a\ d}),\ \frac{a}{-(b\ c)\ +\ a\ d}\}\}$$

Here is a particular 3 × 3 rational matrix known as a "Hilbert matrix".

*In[21]:=* `h = Table[1/(i+j+1), {i, 3}, {j, 3}]`

$$Out[21]= \{\{\frac{1}{3},\ \frac{1}{4},\ \frac{1}{5}\},\ \{\frac{1}{4},\ \frac{1}{5},\ \frac{1}{6}\},\ \{\frac{1}{5},\ \frac{1}{6},\ \frac{1}{7}\}\}$$

This gives its inverse.

*In[22]:=* **Inverse[h]**

*Out[22]=* {{300, -900, 630}, {-900, 2880, -2100},

{630, -2100, 1575}}

Taking the dot product of the inverse with the original matrix gives the identity matrix.

*In[23]:=* **% . h**

*Out[23]=* {{1, 0, 0}, {0, 1, 0}, {0, 0, 1}}

Here is a $3 \times 3$ matrix.

*In[24]:=* **r = Table[i+j+1, {i, 3}, {j, 3}]**

*Out[24]=* {{3, 4, 5}, {4, 5, 6}, {5, 6, 7}}

**Eigenvalues** gives the eigenvalues of the matrix.

*In[25]:=* **Eigenvalues[r]**

*Out[25]=* $\{0, \dfrac{15 + \text{Sqrt}[249]}{2}, \dfrac{15 - \text{Sqrt}[249]}{2}\}$

This gives a numerical approximation to the matrix.

*In[26]:=* **rn = N[r]**

*Out[26]=* {{3., 4., 5.}, {4., 5., 6.}, {5., 6., 7.}}

Here are numerical approximations to the eigenvalues.

*In[27]:=* **Eigenvalues[rn]**

*Out[27]=* $\{15.3899, -0.389867, 4.6843 \ 10^{-18}\}$

Section 3.7 discusses a number of other matrix operations that are built in to *Mathematica*.

## ■ 1.7.4  Finding the Structure of a List

| | |
|---|---|
| Length[*list*] | the number of elements in *list* |
| Dimensions[*list*] | the dimensions of a list that forms an array |
| VectorQ[*list*] | test whether *list* has the structure of a vector |
| MatrixQ[*list*] | test whether *list* has the structure of a matrix |
| TensorRank[*list*] | find the rank of *list*, when viewed as a tensor |
| MemberQ[*list, form*] | test whether *form* is an element of *list* |
| Count[*list, form*] | the number of times *form* appears as an element of *list* |
| FreeQ[*list, form*] | test whether *form* occurs nowhere in *list* |
| Position[*list, form*] | the positions at which *form* occurs in *list* |

Functions for finding the structure of lists.

Length gives the number of elements in a list.

```
In[1]:= Length[{a,b,c,d}]
Out[1]= 4
```

The list {} has zero elements.

```
In[2]:= Length[{}]
Out[2]= 0
```

This shows that a is an element of {a, b, c}.

```
In[3]:= MemberQ[{a, b, c}, a]
Out[3]= True
```

On the other hand, d is not.

```
In[4]:= MemberQ[{a, b, c}, d]
Out[4]= False
```

This counts the number of times that a appears as an element of the list.

```
In[5]:= Count[{a, a, a+1, b, a}, a]
Out[5]= 3
```

This assigns m to be the $3 \times 3$ identity matrix.

```
In[6]:= m = IdentityMatrix[3]
Out[6]= {{1, 0, 0}, {0, 1, 0}, {0, 0, 1}}
```

Here are the dimensions of m.

```
In[7]:= Dimensions[m]
Out[7]= {3, 3}
```

This shows that 0 does occur *somewhere* in m.

```
In[8]:= FreeQ[m, 0]
Out[8]= False
```

This gives a list of the positions at which 0 occurs in m.

```
In[9]:= Position[m, 0]
Out[9]= {{1, 2}, {1, 3}, {2, 1}, {2, 3}, {3, 1}, {3, 2}}
```

The functions Count and Position, as well as MemberQ and FreeQ, can in fact be used not only to search for particular list elements, but also for classes of elements which match particular "patterns". (Cases gives the actual elements that occur.) Section 2.3.5 will discuss how this works.

## ■ 1.7.5  Getting Pieces of Lists

| | |
|---|---|
| First[*list*] | the first element in *list* |
| Last[*list*] | the last element |
| *list*[[*n*]] | the $n^{\text{th}}$ element |
| *list*[[-*n*]] | the $n^{\text{th}}$ element from the end |
| *list*[[{$n_1$, $n_2$, ...}]] | the list of elements $n_1$, $n_2$, ... |
| {$x_1$, $x_2$, ...} = {$y_1$, $y_2$, ...} | assign each $x_i$ to the corresponding $y_i$ |
| Take[*list*, *n*] | the first *n* elements in *list* |
| Take[*list*, -*n*] | the last *n* elements |
| Take[*list*, {*m*, *n*}] | elements *m* through *n* (inclusive) |
| Rest[*list*] | *list* with its first element dropped |
| Drop[*list*, *n*] | *list* with its first *n* elements dropped |
| Drop[*list*, -*n*] | *list* with its last *n* elements dropped |
| Drop[*list*, {*m*, *n*}] | *list* with elements *m* through *n* dropped |

Functions for picking out pieces of lists.

We will use this list for the examples.

```
In[1]:= t = {a,b,c,d,e,f,g}
Out[1]= {a, b, c, d, e, f, g}
```

Here is the last element of t.

```
In[2]:= Last[t]
Out[2]= g
```

This gives the third element.

```
In[3]:= t[[3]]
Out[3]= c
```

This gives a list of the first and fourth elements.

```
In[4]:= t[[ {1, 4} ]]
Out[4]= {a, d}
```

This sets x to the first element of the list, and y to the second one.

```
In[5]:= {x, y} = %
Out[5]= {a, d}
```

The symbol x, for example, now has value a.

```
In[6]:= x
Out[6]= a
```

This gives the first three elements.

```
In[7]:= Take[t, 3]
Out[7]= {a, b, c}
```

This gives the last three elements.

```
In[8]:= Take[t, -3]
Out[8]= {e, f, g}
```

This gives elements 2 through 5 inclusive.

```
In[9]:= Take[t, {2, 5}]
Out[9]= {b, c, d, e}
```

This gives t with the first element dropped.

```
In[10]:= Rest[t]
Out[10]= {b, c, d, e, f, g}
```

This gives t with its first three elements dropped.

```
In[11]:= Drop[t, 3]
Out[11]= {d, e, f, g}
```

This gives t with just its third element dropped.

```
In[12]:= Drop[t, {3, 3}]
Out[12]= {a, b, d, e, f, g}
```

| | |
|---|---|
| *list*[[*i*, *j*, ...]] | the element *list*[[*i*]][[*j*]]... |
| *list*[[{*i₁*, *i₂*, ...}, {*j₁*, *j₂*, ...}, ...]] | |
| | the list of elements obtained by picking out parts $i_1$, $i_2$, ... at the first level, etc. |

Extracting parts of nested lists.

Here is a list of lists.

```
In[13]:= t = {{a, b, c}, {d, e, f}}
Out[13]= {{a, b, c}, {d, e, f}}
```

This picks out the first sublist.

```
In[14]:= t[[1]]
Out[14]= {a, b, c}
```

This picks out the second element in the first sublist.

```
In[15]:= t[[1, 2]]
Out[15]= b
```

This is equivalent to t[[1, 2]], but is clumsier to write.

```
In[16]:= t[[1]][[2]]
Out[16]= b
```

This gives a list containing two copies of the second part of t, followed by one copy of the first part.

```
In[17]:= t[[{2, 2, 1}]]
Out[17]= {{d, e, f}, {d, e, f}, {a, b, c}}
```

For each of the parts picked out on the previous line, this gives a list of their second and third parts.

```
In[18]:= t[[{2, 2, 1}, {2, 3}]]
Out[18]= {{e, f}, {e, f}, {b, c}}
```

Section 2.1 will show how all the functions in this section can be generalized to work not only on lists, but on any *Mathematica* expressions.

The functions in this section allow you to pick out pieces that occur at particular positions in lists. Section 2.3.5 will show how you can use functions like **Select** and **Cases** to pick out elements of lists based not on their positions, but instead on their properties.

## ■ 1.7.6  Adding Elements to Lists

| | |
|---|---|
| `Prepend[`*list*, *element*`]` | add *element* at the beginning of *list* |
| `Append[`*list*, *element*`]` | add *element* at the end of *list* |
| `Insert[`*list*, *element*, *n*`]` | insert *element* at position *n* in *list* |
| `Insert[`*list*, *element*, -*n*`]` | insert at position *n* counting from the end of *list* |

Functions for adding elements to lists.

This gives a list with x prepended.

```
In[1]:= Prepend[{a, b, c}, x]
Out[1]= {x, a, b, c}
```

This adds x at the end.

```
In[2]:= Append[{a, b, c}, x]
Out[2]= {a, b, c, x}
```

This inserts x so that it becomes element number 2.

```
In[3]:= Insert[{a, b, c}, x, 2]
Out[3]= {a, x, b, c}
```

Negative numbers count from the end of the list.

```
In[4]:= Insert[{a, b, c}, x, -2]
Out[4]= {a, b, x, c}
```

## ■ 1.7.7  Combining Lists

| | |
|---|---|
| `Join[`*list1*, *list2*, ...`]` | concatenate lists together |
| `Union[`*list1*, *list2*, ...`]` | combine lists, removing repeated elements, and sorting the result |

Functions for combining lists.

`Join` concatenates any number of lists together.

```
In[1]:= Join[{a, b, c}, {x, y}, {c, {d, e}, a}]
Out[1]= {a, b, c, x, y, c, {d, e}, a}
```

`Union` combines lists, keeping only distinct elements.

```
In[2]:= Union[{a, b, c}, {c, a, d}, {a, d}]
Out[2]= {a, b, c, d}
```

### ■ 1.7.8  Advanced Topic: Lists as Sets

*Mathematica* usually keeps the elements of a list in exactly the order you originally entered them. If you want to treat a *Mathematica* list like a mathematical *set*, however, you may want to ignore the order of elements in the list.

| | |
|---|---|
| Union[*list1*, *list2*, ...] | give a list of the distinct elements in the *list*$_i$ |
| Intersection[*list1*, *list2*, ...] | give a list of the elements that are common to all the *list*$_i$ |
| Complement[*universal*, *list1*, ...] | give a list of the elements that are in *universal*, but not in any of the *list*$_i$ |

Set theoretical functions.

Union gives the elements that occur in *any* of the lists.

```
In[1]:= Union[{c, a, b}, {d, a, c}, {a, e}]
Out[1]= {a, b, c, d, e}
```

Intersection gives only elements that occur in *all* the lists.

```
In[2]:= Intersection[{a, c, b}, {b, a, d, a}]
Out[2]= {a, b}
```

Complement gives elements that occur in the first list, but not in any of the others.

```
In[3]:= Complement[{a, b, c, d}, {a, d}]
Out[3]= {b, c}
```

### ■ 1.7.9  Rearranging Lists

| | |
|---|---|
| Sort[*list*] | sort the elements of *list* into a standard order |
| Union[*list*] | sort elements, removing any duplicates |
| Reverse[*list*] | reverse the order of elements in *list* |
| RotateLeft[*list*, *n*] | rotate the elements of *list* *n* places to the left |
| RotateRight[*list*, *n*] | rotate *n* places to the right |
| RotateLeft[*list*], RotateRight[*list*] | |
| | rotate by one position |

Functions for rearranging lists.

This sorts the elements of a list into a standard order. In simple cases like this, the order is alphabetical or numerical.

```
In[1]:= Sort[{b, a, c, a, b}]
Out[1]= {a, a, b, b, c}
```

This sorts the elements, removing any duplicates.

```
In[2]:= Union[{b, a, c, a, b}]
Out[2]= {a, b, c}
```

This reverses the list.

```
In[3]:= Reverse[{a, b, c, d}]
Out[3]= {d, c, b, a}
```

This rotates ("shifts") the elements in the list two places to the left.

```
In[4]:= RotateLeft[{a, b, c, d, e}, 2]
Out[4]= {c, d, e, a, b}
```

You can rotate to the right by giving a negative displacement, or by using `RotateRight`.

```
In[5]:= RotateLeft[{a, b, c, d, e}, -2]
Out[5]= {d, e, a, b, c}
```

## ■ 1.7.10  Advanced Topic: Rearranging Nested Lists

You will encounter nested lists if you use matrices, or generate multidimensional arrays and tables. Rearranging nested lists can be a complicated affair, and you will often have to experiment to get the right combination of commands.

| | |
|---|---|
| `Transpose[`*list*`]` | interchange the top two levels of lists |
| `Transpose[`*list*`, `*n*`]` | interchange the top level with the $n^{\text{th}}$ level |
| `Flatten[`*list*`]` | flatten out all levels in *list* |
| `Flatten[`*list*`, `*n*`]` | flatten out the top *n* levels in *list* |

Functions for rearranging nested lists.

Here is a 3 × 2 array.

```
In[1]:= t = {{a, b}, {c, d}, {e, f}}
Out[1]= {{a, b}, {c, d}, {e, f}}
```

You can rearrange it to get a 2 × 3 array.

```
In[2]:= Transpose[t]
Out[2]= {{a, c, e}, {b, d, f}}
```

This "flattens out" sublists. You can think of it as effectively just removing the inner sets of braces.

```
In[3]:= Flatten[t]
Out[3]= {a, b, c, d, e, f}
```

Here is a $2 \times 2 \times 2$ array.                  *In[4]:=* `t = Table[i^2 +j^2 +k^2, {i, 2}, {j, 2}, {k, 2}]`

                                                         *Out[4]=* `{{{3, 6}, {6, 9}}, {{6, 9}, {9, 12}}}`

This flattens out all the levels.                        *In[5]:=* `Flatten[t]`

                                                         *Out[5]=* `{3, 6, 6, 9, 6, 9, 9, 12}`

This flattens only the first level of sublists.          *In[6]:=* `Flatten[t, 1]`

                                                         *Out[6]=* `{{3, 6}, {6, 9}, {6, 9}, {9, 12}}`

There are many other operations you can perform on nested lists. We will discuss some more of them when we look at `Map`, `Apply`, `Scan` and `Level` in Section 2.1.

## ■ 1.7.11  Grouping Together Elements of Lists

| | |
|---|---|
| `Partition[`*list*`, ` *n*`]` | partition *list* into *n* element pieces |
| `Partition[`*list*`, ` *n*`, ` *d*`]` | use offset *d* for successive pieces |

Functions for grouping together elements of lists.

Here is a list.                                          *In[1]:=* `t = {a, b, c, d, e, f, g}`

                                                         *Out[1]=* `{a, b, c, d, e, f, g}`

This groups the elements of the list in pairs.            *In[2]:=* `Partition[t, 2]`

                                                         *Out[2]=* `{{a, b}, {c, d}, {e, f}}`

This groups elements in triples. There is no overlap between the triples.            *In[3]:=* `Partition[t, 3]`

                                                         *Out[3]=* `{{a, b, c}, {d, e, f}}`

This makes triples of elements, with each successive triple offset by just one element.            *In[4]:=* `Partition[t, 3, 1]`

                                                         *Out[4]=* `{{a, b, c}, {b, c, d}, {c, d, e}, {d, e, f},`
                                                              `{e, f, g}}`

You can think of `Partition` as a kind of inverse to `Flatten`.

## ■ 1.7.12  Mathematical Operations on Lists

Section 2.1 will discuss in detail how to do mathematical operations on lists. Here are a couple of cases that often occur in practice; Section 2.1 will give many generalizations.

| | |
|---|---|
| Apply[Plus, *list*] | add up all the elements in *list* |
| Apply[Times, *list*] | multiply together all the elements in *list* |

Simple mathematical operations on lists.

This adds all the elements in a list.

```
In[1]:= Apply[Plus, {a, b, c, d}]
Out[1]= a + b + c + d
```

## ■ 1.7.13  Advanced Topic: Combinatorial Operations

You can use lists to set up many kinds of combinatorial calculations. Here are a
few examples.

| | |
|---|---|
| Permutations[*list*] | give all possible orderings of *list* |
| Outer[List, *list₁*, *list₂*, ...] | give lists of elements in the *listᵢ* combined in all possible ways |
| OrderedQ[*list*] | give True if the elements of *list* are in order |
| Signature[*list*] | give the signature of the permutation needed to put *list* into standard order |

Some combinatorial operations on lists.

This gives the 3! = 6 possible
permutations of three elements.

```
In[1]:= Permutations[{a,b,c}]
Out[1]= {{a, b, c}, {a, c, b}, {b, a, c}, {b, c, a},
         {c, a, b}, {c, b, a}}
```

This combines the list elements in all
possible ways. This operation is analogous
to a mathematical "outer product" (see
Section 3.7.12).

```
In[2]:= Outer[List, {a, b}, {c, d}]
Out[2]= {{{a, c}, {a, d}}, {{b, c}, {b, d}}}
```

# ■ 1.8  Graphics

## ■ 1.8.1  Basic Plotting

| | |
|---|---|
| Plot[*f*, {*x*, *xmin*, *xmax*}] | plot *f* as a function of *x* from *xmin* to *xmax* |
| Plot[{*f₁*, *f₂*, ...}, {*x*, *xmin*, *xmax*}] | |
| | plot several functions together |

Basic plotting functions.

This plots a graph of $\sin(x)$ as a function of *x* from 0 to $2\pi$.

*In[1]:=* Plot[Sin[x], {x, 0, 2Pi}]

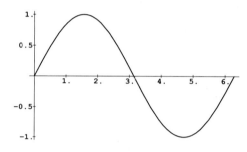

You can plot functions that have singularities. *Mathematica* will try to choose appropriate scales.

*In[2]:=* Plot[Tan[x], {x, -3, 3}]

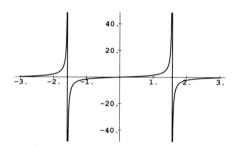

You can give a list of functions to plot.

*In[3]:=* Plot[{Sin[x], Sin[2x], Sin[3x]}, {x, 0, 2Pi}]

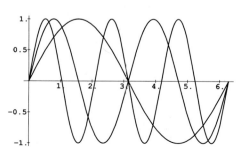

On many systems, you have to "initialize" graphics in *Mathematica*, specifying for example, what kind of graphics device you are using. The information which came with your copy of *Mathematica* should tell you how to do what is needed. Section B.7.8 discusses some general features of graphics initialization in *Mathematica*.

■ **1.8.2  Specifying Options**

When *Mathematica* plots a graph, it has to make many choices. It has to work out what the scales should be, where the function should be sampled, and so on. Most of the time, *Mathematica* will probably make pretty good choices. However, if you want to get the very best possible pictures for your particular purposes, you may have to help *Mathematica* in making some of its choices.

There is a general mechanism for specifying "options" in *Mathematica* functions. Each option has a definite name. As the last argument to a function like `Plot`, you can include a sequence of rules of the form *name->value*, which give the values of various options. Any option for which you do not give an explicit replacement is taken to have its "default" value.

| option name | default value | |
|---|---|---|
| PlotRange | Automatic | the range of coordinates to include in the plot: you can give {*ymin*, *ymax*} or {{*xmin*, *xmax*}, {*ymin*, *ymax*}}; **All** tells *Mathematica* to include all points |
| PlotLabel | None | an expression to be printed as a label for the plot |
| Framed | False | whether to draw a frame around the plot |
| AspectRatio | 1/GoldenRatio | the height-to-width ratio for the plot; **Automatic** sets it from the absolute $x$ and $y$ coordinates |
| Axes | Automatic | what axes to include: **None** gives no axes; {*x*, *y*} specifies an axis origin |
| AxesLabel | None | labels to be put on the axes: *ylabel* specifies a label for the $y$ axis, {*xlabel*, *ylabel*} for both axes |
| Ticks | Automatic | {*xtick*, *ytick*} gives positions of $x$ and $y$ tick marks: each can be **None** for no tick marks, {$t_1$, $t_2$, ...} for explicit positions |
| PlotColor | True | whether to generate color graphics |
| DisplayFunction | $DisplayFunction | how to display graphics; **Identity** causes no display |
| PlotStyle | Automatic | a list of lists of graphics primitives to use for each curve (see Section 1.8.13) |
| PlotPoints | 25 | the minimum number of points at which to sample the function |
| MaxBend | 10. | the maximum kink angle between successive segments of a curve |
| PlotDivision | 20. | the maximum factor by which to subdivide in sampling the function |

Some of the options for Plot. The first set of options can also be used in Show.

A function like **Plot** has many options that you can set. Usually you will have to use at most a few of these at a time. If you want to optimize a particular plot, you will probably do best to "experiment", trying a sequence of different settings for various options.

Each time you produce a plot, you can specify options for it. The next section will also discuss how you can change the options, even once you have produced a plot.

| | |
|---|---|
| `Automatic` | use internal algorithms |
| `None` | do not include this |
| `All` | include everything |
| `True` | do this |
| `False` | do not do this |

Some common settings for various options.

A plot with all options having their default values.

`In[1]:= Plot[Sin[x^2], {x, 0, 3}]`

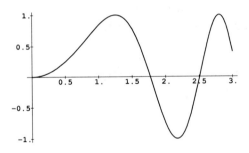

The replacement for the option `PlotRange` gives explicit $y$ limits for the graph. With the $y$ limits specified, the bottom of the curve is cut off. Remember to use capital letters for *each word* when you give options like `PlotRange` that have multi-word names.

`In[2]:= Plot[Sin[x^2], {x, 0, 3}, PlotRange -> {0, 1.2}]`

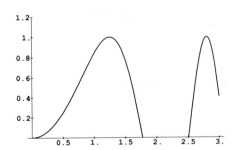

This specifies labels for the $x$ and $y$ axes. The expressions you give as labels are printed just as they would be if they appeared as *Mathematica* output. You can give any piece of text by putting it inside a pair of double quotes.

```
In[3]:= Plot[Sin[x^2], {x, 0, 3},
            AxesLabel -> {"x value", "Sin[x^2]"} ]
```

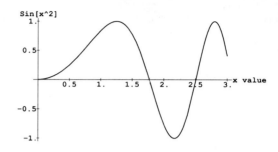

You can give several options at the same time, in any order. `Axes -> None` suppresses the drawing of axes; setting `PlotLabel` sets up a label for the graph.

```
In[4]:= Plot[Sin[x^2], {x, 0, 3}, Axes -> None,
            PlotLabel -> "Sin[x^2]"]
```

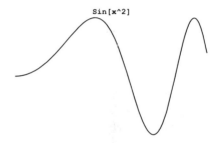

This puts tick marks at intervals of 0.4 on the $x$ axis, and leaves the positioning of tick marks on the $y$ axis up to *Mathematica*. Remember that `Range[0, 3, .4]` produces a list of numbers running from 0 to 3 in steps of 0.4.

```
In[5]:= Plot[Sin[x^2], {x, 0, 3},
            Ticks -> {Range[0, 3, .4], Automatic}]
```

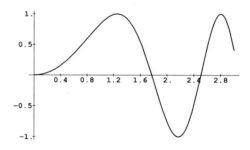

Setting the `AspectRatio` option changes the whole shape of your plot. `AspectRatio` gives the ratio of width to height. Its default value is the inverse of the Golden Ratio – supposedly the most pleasing shape for a rectangle.

`In[6]:= Plot[Sin[x^2], {x, 0, 3}, AspectRatio -> 1]`

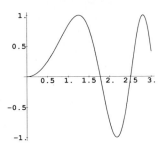

When *Mathematica* makes a plot, it tries to set the $x$ and $y$ scales to include only the "interesting" parts of the plot. If your function increases very rapidly, or has singularities, the parts where it gets too large will be cut off. By specifying the option `PlotRange`, you can control exactly what ranges of $x$ and $y$ coordinates are included in your plot.

| | |
|---|---|
| `Automatic` | show at least a large fraction of the points, including the "interesting" region (the default setting) |
| `All` | show all points |
| `{ymin, ymax}` | show a specific range of $y$ values |
| `{xrange, yrange}` | show the specified ranges of $x$ and $y$ values |

Settings for the option `PlotRange`.

*Mathematica* always tries to plot functions as smooth curves. As a result, in places where your function wiggles a lot, *Mathematica* will use more points. In general, *Mathematica* tries to *adapt* its sampling of your function to the form of the function. There is, however, a limit, which you can set, to how finely *Mathematica* will ever sample a function.

The function $\sin(\frac{1}{x})$ wiggles infinitely often when $x \simeq 0$. *Mathematica* tries to sample more points in the region where the function wiggles a lot, but it can never sample the infinite number that you would need to reproduce the function exactly. As a result, there are slight glitches in the plot.

`In[7]:= Plot[Sin[1/x], {x, -1, 1}]`

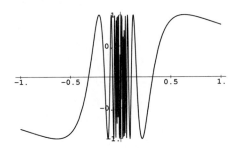

It is important to realize that since *Mathematica* can only sample your function at a limited number of points, it can always miss features of the function. By increasing `PlotPoints`, you can make *Mathematica* sample your function at a larger number of points. Of course, the larger you set `PlotPoints` to be, the longer it will take *Mathematica* to plot *any* function, even a smooth one.

### ■ 1.8.3 Advanced Topic: Setting Options Globally

If you do not specify a particular value for an option to a function like `Plot`, *Mathematica* will automatically use a default value for the option. If you want to use the *same* value many times for a particular `Plot` option, you may find it convenient to change the default value for that option.

| | |
|---|---|
| `function[arguments, ..., name->value, ...]` | |
| | specify options in a function |
| `Options[function]` | show the current list of defaults |
| `SetOptions[function, name->value, ...]` | |
| | reset defaults |

Commands for changing default values of options.

### ■ 1.8.4 Redrawing and Combining Plots

*Mathematica* saves information about every plot you produce, so that you can later redraw it. When you redraw plots, you can change some of the options you use.

| | |
|---|---|
| `Show[plot]` | redraw a plot |
| `Show[plot, option->value]` | redraw with options changed |
| `Show[plot_1, plot_2, ...]` | draw several plots together |
| `Options[plot]` | show the options used for a particular plot |
| `InputForm[plot]` | show the information that is saved about a plot |

Functions for manipulating plots.

Here is a simple plot. -Graphics- is usually printed on the output line to stand for the information that *Mathematica* saves about the plot.

*In[1]:=* `Plot[ChebyshevT[7, x], {x, -1, 1}]`

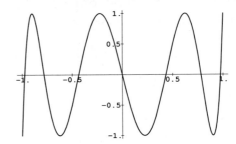

This redraws the plot from the previous line.

*In[2]:=* `Show[%]`

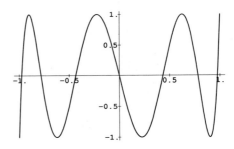

When you redraw the plot, you can change some of the options. This changes the choice of *y* scale.

*In[3]:=* `Show[%, PlotRange -> {-1, 2}]`

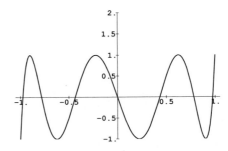

This takes the plot from the previous line, and changes another option in it.

*In[4]:=* `Show[%, PlotLabel -> "A Chebyshev Polynomial"]`

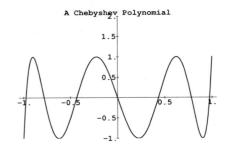

By using **Show** with a sequence of different options, you can look at the same plot in many different ways. You may want to do this, for example, if you are trying to find the best possible setting of options.

You can also use **Show** to combine plots. It does not matter whether the plots have the same scales: *Mathematica* will always choose new scales to include the points you want.

This sets gj0 to be a plot of $J_0(x)$ from $x = 0$ to 10.

*In[5]:=* **gj0 = Plot[BesselJ[0, x], {x, 0, 10}]**

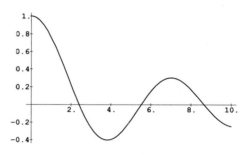

Here is a plot of $Y_1(x)$ from $x = 1$ to 10.

*In[6]:=* **gy1 = Plot[BesselY[1, x], {x, 1, 10}]**

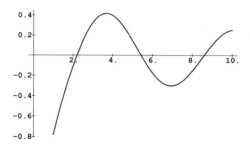

This shows the previous two plots combined into one. Notice that the scale is adjusted appropriately.

*In[7]:=* **Show[gj0, gy1]**

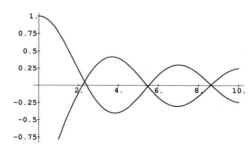

When you make a plot, *Mathematica* saves the list of points it used, together with some other information. Using what is saved, you can redraw plots in many different ways with `Show`. However, you should realize that whatever options you specify, `Show` still has the same basic set of points to work with. So, for example, if you set the options so that *Mathematica* displays a small portion of your original plot magnified, you will probably be able to see the individual sample points that `Plot` used. Options like `PlotPoints` can only be set in the original `Plot` command itself. (*Mathematica* always plots the actual points it has; it avoids using smoothed or splined curves, which can give misleading results in mathematical graphics.)

Here is a simple plot.                     *In[8]:=* `Plot[Cos[x], {x, -Pi, Pi}]`

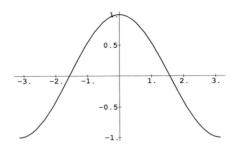

This shows a small region of the plot in a       *In[9]:=* `Show[%, PlotRange -> {{0, .3}, {.92, 1}}]`
magnified form. At this resolution, you can
see the individual line segments that were
produced by the original `Plot` command.

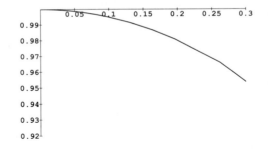

## ■ 1.8.5  Special Topic: Graphics on Different Devices

Sophisticated *Mathematica* front ends have capabilities built in for controlling the display, saving and printing of *Mathematica* graphics. If you use *Mathematica* with a sophisticated front end, you will probably never need to know the details of how *Mathematica* sends graphics to different kinds of devices.

This section describes in general terms how *Mathematica* produces and renders graphics. For details on how to use *Mathematica* graphics on your particular computer system, you should look at the documentation which came with your copy of *Mathematica*.

*Mathematica* produces all graphics in two stages. First, *Mathematica* generates a representation of your graphics in the standard PostScript page description language. This representation does not depend on resolution, or other details, of your output device.

The second stage in generating graphics is to render the PostScript description on a particular output device. This is usually done by the *Mathematica* front end, or by a program completely external to *Mathematica*. Particularly when you make elaborate three-dimensional plots, the final rendering step may take a substantial amount of time.

The fact that *Mathematica* generates graphics in two stages makes it potentially possible to get the best of every different kind of output device. This is particularly important for three-dimensional plots, where shading and hidden surface elimination ultimately have to be carried out at the resolution appropriate for every different kind of output device.

When you start up *Mathematica*, you may have to tell it what graphics output devices you want to use. The documentation that came with your copy of *Mathematica* should tell you how to do this; typically you have to read in a file of definitions.

| | |
|---|---|
| `Display["`*file*`", `*plot*`]` | save the PostScript form of a plot in a file |

Saving the PostScript for a plot.

## ■ 1.8.6 Advanced Topic: Parametric Plots

Section 1.8.1 described how to plot curves in *Mathematica* in which you give the $y$ coordinate of each point as a function of the $x$ coordinate. You can also use *Mathematica* to make *parametric* plots. In a parametric plot, you give both the $x$ and $y$ coordinates of each point as a function of a third parameter, say $t$.

| | |
|---|---|
| `ParametricPlot[{`$f_x$`, `$f_y$`}, {`*t*`, `*tmin*`, `*tmax*`}]` | |
| | make a parametric plot |
| `ParametricPlot[{{`$f_x$`, `$f_y$`}, {`$g_x$`, `$g_y$`}, ...}, {`*t*`, `*tmin*`, `*tmax*`}]` | |
| | plot several parametric curves together |
| `ParametricPlot[{`$f_x$`, `$f_y$`}, {`*t*`, `*tmin*`, `*tmax*`}, AspectRatio -> Automatic]` | |
| | attempt to preserve the shapes of curves |

Functions for generating parametric plots.

Here is the curve made by taking the $x$ coordinate of each point to be `Sin[t]` and the $y$ coordinate to be `Sin[2t]`.

*In[1]:=* **ParametricPlot[{Sin[t], Sin[2t]}, {t, 0, 2Pi}]**

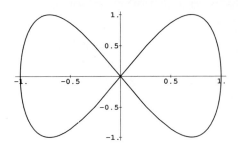

The "shape" of the curve produced depends on the ratio of height to width for the whole plot.

*In[2]:=* **ParametricPlot[{Sin[t], Cos[t]}, {t, 0, 2Pi}]**

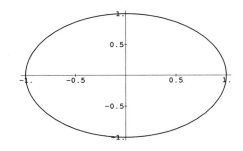

Setting the option `AspectRatio` to `Automatic` makes *Mathematica* preserve the "true shape" of the curve, as defined by the actual coordinate values it involves.

*In[3]:=* **Show[%, AspectRatio -> Automatic]**

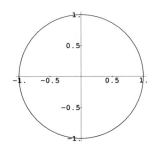

| | |
|---|---|
| `{r[t] Cos[t], r[t] Sin[t]}` | polar plot with radius $r[t]$ at angle $t$ |
| `{Re[f], Im[f]}` | phase or Argand diagram of a complex function |
| `{Log[f], Log[x]}` | log-log plot |

Some types of parametric plots.

This defines a function `r`.

*In[4]:=* **r[t_] := (3 Cos[t]^2 - 1)/2**

This gives a plot in polar coordinates, with r[t] as the radius function at angle t.

*In[5]:=* `ParametricPlot[{r[t] Cos[t], r[t] Sin[t]}, {t, 0, 2Pi}]`

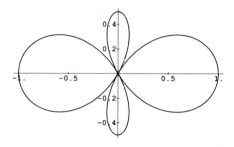

This makes a log-log plot of $x^2 + x^6$ as a function of $x$.

*In[6]:=* `ParametricPlot[{Log[x], Log[x^2 + x^6]}, {x, 1, 4}]`

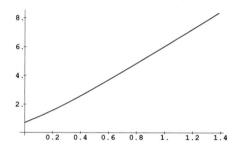

## ■ 1.8.7  Advanced Topic: Plotting Tables of Functions

When you ask *Mathematica* to plot an object, say $f$, as a function of $x$, there are two possible approaches it can take. One approach is first to try and evaluate $f$, presumably getting a symbolic expression in terms of $x$, and then subsequently evaluate this expression numerically for the specific values of $x$ needed in the plot. The second approach is first to work out what values of $x$ are needed, and only subsequently to evaluate $f$ with those values of $x$.

If you type `Plot[f, {x, xmin, xmax}]` it is the second of these approaches that is used. This has the advantage that *Mathematica* only tries to evaluate $f$ for specific numerical values of $x$; it does not matter whether sensible values are defined for $f$ when $x$ is symbolic.

There are, however, some cases in which you need *Mathematica* to evaluate $f$ before it starts to make a plot. One common case is when $f$ is a command that generates a table of functions. You want to have *Mathematica* first produce the table, and then evaluate the functions, rather than trying to produce the table afresh for each value of $x$. You can do this by typing `Plot[Release[f], {x, xmin, xmax}]`.

The `Release` tells *Mathematica* not to "hold" *f* unevaluated.

This makes a plot of the Bessel functions $J_n(x)$ with $n$ running from 1 to 4. The `Release` tells *Mathematica* first to make the table of functions, and only *then* to evaluate them for particular values of x.

*In[1]:=* `Plot[Release[Table[BesselJ[n, x], {n, 4}]],`
                   `{x, 0, 10}]`

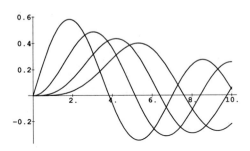

---

| | |
|---|---|
| `Plot[`*f*`, {`*x*`, `*xmin*`, `*xmax*`}]` | *first* choose specific numerical values for *x*, then evaluate *f* for each value of *x* |
| `Plot[Release[`*f*`], {`*x*`, `*xmin*`, `*xmax*`}]` | *first* evaluate *f*, then choose specific numerical values of *x* |
| `Plot[Release[Table[`*f*`, ...]], {`*x*`, `*xmin*`, `*xmax*`}]` | generate a list of functions, and then plot them |

Methods for setting up objects to plot.

The issue of what order to use in choosing *x*, and in evaluating *f*, arises not only in `Plot`, but also in other iteration functions, such as `Sum` and `Table`. Section 2.2.19 discusses the general principles of evaluation for such functions.

## ■ 1.8.8  Three-Dimensional Plotting

| | |
|---|---|
| `Plot3D[`*f*`, {`*x*`, `*xmin*`, `*xmax*`}, {`*y*`, `*ymin*`, `*ymax*`}]` | make a three-dimensional plot of *f* as a function of the variables *x* and *y* |

Basic 3D plotting function.

This makes a three-dimensional plot of the
function $\sin(xy)$.

`In[1]:= Plot3D[Sin[x y], {x, 0, 3}, {y, 0, 3}]`

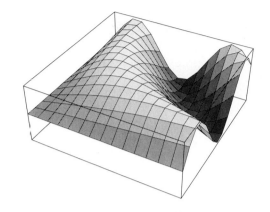

There are many options for three-dimensional plots in *Mathematica*.

The first set of options are similar to those you use for standard two-dimensional
plots.

| option name | initial default value | |
|---|---|---|
| PlotRange | Automatic | the range of coordinates to include in the plot: you can specify All, {$zmin$, $zmax$} or {{$xmin$, $xmax$}, {$ymin$, $ymax$}, {$zmin$, $zmax$}} |
| PlotLabel | None | a label for the plot |
| Framed | False | whether to draw a frame around the plot |
| AspectRatio | 1 | the height-to-width ratio for the whole plot |
| PlotColor | True | whether to generate color graphics |
| PlotPoints | 15 | the number of points in each direction at which to sample the function; {$n_x$, $n_y$} specifies different numbers in the $x$ and $y$ directions |

Some basic options for `Plot3D`. The first set of options can also be used in `Show`.

This redraws the plot on the previous line, with options changed. With this setting for `PlotRange`, only the part of the surface in the range $-0.5 \le z \le 0.5$ is shown.

*In[2]:=* **Show[%, PlotRange -> {-0.5, 0.5}]**

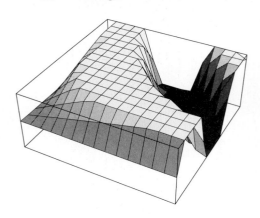

When you make the original plot, you can choose to sample more points. You will need to do this to get good pictures of functions that wiggle a lot.

*In[3]:=* **Plot3D[Sin[x] Sin[y], {x, -10, 10}, {y, -10, 10}, PlotPoints -> 40]**

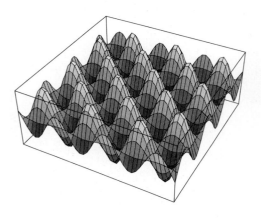

You can think of the pictures you get from `Plot3D` as being like simulated photographs. There are several options for `Plot3D` and `Show` that parallel choices you would make in taking a real photograph.

| option name | initial default value | |
|---|---|---|
| VoewPoint | {1.3, -2.4, 2} | the point from which to look at the surface |
| Boxed | True | whether to draw a box around the surface |
| BoxRatios | {1, 1, 0.4} | side length ratios for the box that encloses the surface |

Options to Plot3D and Show for viewing surfaces.

The most important option is where you put the camera relative to the surface. You can see very different features of the surface by putting the camera in different places.

When *Mathematica* draws a three-dimensional object, it effectively encloses the object in a transparent cuboidal box. With the default setting Boxed->True, it draws the edges of this box explicitly. You can also squash or extend the box in different directions by setting the option BoxRatios.

The ViewPoint option allows you to specify the coordinates {x, y, z} of the camera relative to the center of the box. The coordinates are scaled so that the longest side of the box has length 1. If you use a cubical box, coordinates between $-\frac{1}{2}$ and $\frac{1}{2}$ will therefore be inside the box. The default setting for ViewPoint corresponds to a "generic position", for which coincidental alignments between different parts of your object are unlikely.

Here is a surface, viewed from the default "camera position" {1.3, -2.4, 2}.

*In[4]:=* **g = Plot3D[Sin[x y], {x, 0, 3}, {y, 0, 3}]**

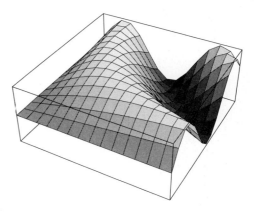

This redraws the picture, with the camera directly in front. Notice the perspective effect that makes the back of the box look much smaller than the front.

*In[5]:=* `Show[%, ViewPoint -> {0, -2, 0}]`

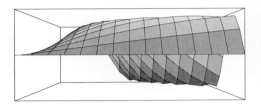

Moving the camera position further away reduces the perspective effect.

*In[6]:=* `Show[%, ViewPoint -> {0, -4, 0}]`

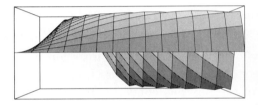

Here the camera points towards one of the sides of the box.

*In[7]:=* `Show[%, ViewPoint -> {0, -1, 1}]`

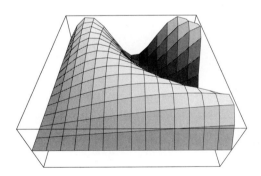

This moves the camera further away, reducing the perspective. The picture is automatically scaled so that the longest side of the box has the same apparent length.

*In[8]:=* **Show[%, ViewPoint -> {0, -4, 4}]**

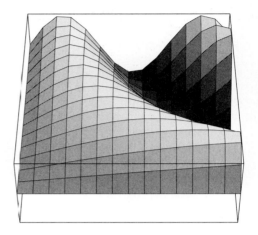

This shows the surface drawn in a cubical box.

*In[9]:=* **Show[%, BoxRatios -> {1, 1, 1}]**

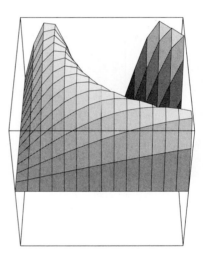

Setting `Boxed->False` stops the box from being drawn.

`In[10]:= Show[%, Boxed -> False]`

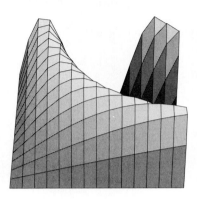

| {0, -2, 0} | directly in front |
| {0, -2, 2} | in front and up |
| {0, -2, -2} | in front and down |
| {-2, -2, 0} | left-hand corner |
| {2, -2, 0} | right-hand corner |
| {0, 0, 2} | directly above |

Typical choices of the `ViewPoint` option.

The human visual system is not particularly good at understanding complicated mathematical surfaces. As a result, you need to generate pictures that contain as many clues as possible about the form of the surface.

Camera positions slightly above the surface are usually best. It is typically a good idea to keep the camera close enough to the surface that there is some perspective effect. Having a box explicitly drawn around the surface is helpful in recognizing the orientation of the surface.

There are several options for how the actual surface should be shown in `Plot3D`.

| option name | default value | |
|---|---|---|
| HiddenSurface | True | whether parts of the surface that are obscured should be hidden |
| Shading | True | whether the surface should be shaded, or left white |
| Mesh | True | whether an $xy$ mesh should be drawn on the surface |

Options for rendering surfaces in Plot3D and Show.

Here is a plot with the default settings for surface rendering options.

*In[11]:=* g = Plot3D[Exp[-(x∧2+y∧2)], {x, -2, 2}, {y, -2, 2}]

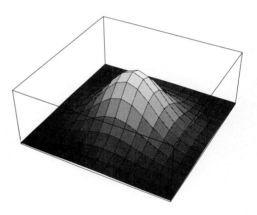

This shows the surface without the mesh drawn. It is usually much harder to see the form of the surface if the mesh is not there.

*In[12]:=* Show[g, Mesh -> False]

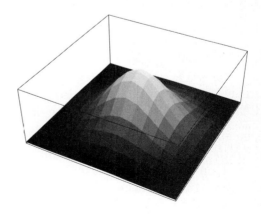

This shows the surface with no shading. Some display devices may not be able to show shading.

*In[13]:=* **Show[g, Shading -> False]**

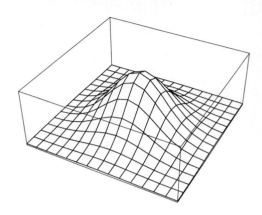

Here is the picture without hidden surface removal. The surface is now like a "wire frame" that you can see through.

*In[14]:=* **Show[%, HiddenSurface -> False]**

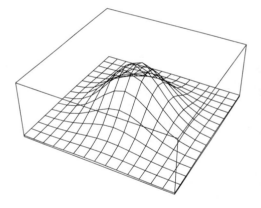

The inclusion of shading and a mesh are usually great assets in understanding the form of a surface. On some vector graphics output devices, however, you may not be able to get shading. You should also realize that when shading is included, it may take a long time to render the surface on your output device.

A final element of realism that you can include in the three-dimensional pictures produced by *Mathematica* is simulated *illumination*. The darkness of shading at a particular point on the surface is usually determined just by its height. However, if you set **Lighting -> True**, *Mathematica* will shade the surface to simulate illumination. (There are nevertheless no shadows produced.)

| option name | default value | |
|---|---|---|
| Lighting | False | whether to include simulated illumination |
| AmbientLight | GrayLevel[0.] | isotropic ambient light |
| LightSources | (see below) | directions and colors of point light sources, specified by $\{\{\{x_1,y_1,z_1\}, i_1\}, \{\{x_2,y_2,z_2\}, i_2\}, ...\}$ |

Options for simulated illumination.

You can specify two components to the illumination of an object. First, you can set **AmbientLight** to specify diffuse isotropic lighting, which gives a uniform shading over the whole surface. Second, you can specify point light sources with particular positions and colors. The effect of all these light sources is added together to determine the shading of each point on the surface. The surface is always assumed to reflect all the light that reaches it.

If you have a color output device, *Mathematica* should be able to give you graphics in color. Simulated lighting is often a good way to introduce color into a picture. If you specify a color picture, the colors will simply be averaged to give a gray level when you use a black-and-white display device.

If you set **Lighting->True**, but do not explicitly set **AmbientLight** or **LightSources**, *Mathematica* will use its default arrangement of simulated lighting. This consists of three point light sources, respectively red, green and blue, with no ambient light. The point light sources are placed at 45° angles on the right-hand side of the object.

| | |
|---|---|
| GrayLevel[*gray*] | gray level between 0 (black) and 1 (white) |
| RGBColor[*r*, *g*, *b*] | red, green, blue color intensities, each between 0 and 1 |

*Mathematica* gray level and color specifications.

Unless you specify otherwise, `Plot3D` shades surfaces with gray levels determined by the height of each point on the surface.

*In[15]:=* **Plot3D[Sin[x y], {x, 0, 3}, {y, 0, 3}]**

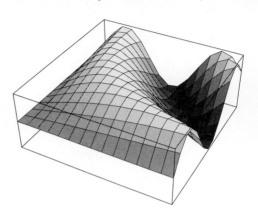

This shows the same surface, with shading determined by simulated illumination. The default illumination, used here, has three light sources of different colors on the upper right. A particular square on the surface is brightest if its orientation is normal to the direction of the light sources.

*In[16]:=* **Show[%, Lighting -> True]**

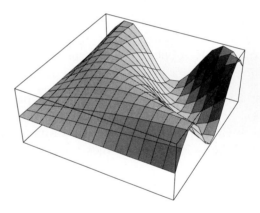

If you have no light sources, the surface is uniformly shaded with gray from the ambient light.

```
In[17]:= Show[%, AmbientLight -> GrayLevel[0.7],
                 LightSources -> {}]
```

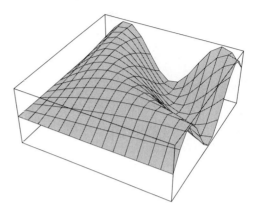

With no ambient light, parts of the surface away from the point light source are black.

```
In[18]:= Show[%, AmbientLight -> GrayLevel[0.],
                 LightSources -> {{{-1, -1, 1}, GrayLevel[0.8]}}]
```

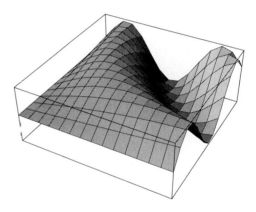

Another option that you can set in **Plot3D** concerns the way that "clipped" surfaces are shown. Clipping is simple in two-dimensional graphics: lines that extend outside the plot are just truncated. In three-dimensional graphics, clipping is more complicated. *Mathematica* always cuts off surfaces when they cross the rectangular box that it uses for three-dimensional pictures. The option **ClipFill** specifies what is shown in the places where the surface is clipped.

| | |
|---|---|
| None | leave out clipped parts of the surface, so that you can see through |
| Automatic | show the clipped part of the surface with the same shading as an actual surface in the same position would have (default setting) |
| GrayLevel[*i*] or RGBColor[*r*, *g*, *b*] | |
| | show the clipped part of the surface with a particular gray level or color |
| {*bottom*, *top*} | give different specifications for parts that are clipped at the bottom and top |

Settings for the ClipFill option.

Here is a three-dimensional plot in which the top and bottom of the surface are clipped. With the default setting for ClipFill, the clipped parts are shown as they would be if they were part of the actual surface.

*In[19]:=* **Plot3D[Sin[x y], {x, 0, 3}, {y, 0, 3},**
            **PlotRange -> {-.5, .5}]**

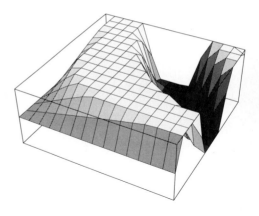

With `ClipFill->None`, parts of the surface which are clipped are left out, so that you can "see through" the surface there. *Mathematica* always leaves out parts of the surface that correspond to places where the value of the function you are plotting is not a real number.

*In[20]:=* **Show[%, ClipFill -> None]**

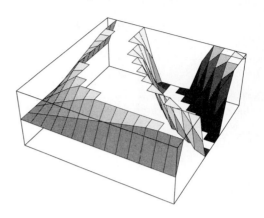

This makes the bottom clipped face white (gray level 1), and the top one black.

*In[21]:=* **Show[%, ClipFill -> {GrayLevel[1], GrayLevel[0]}]**

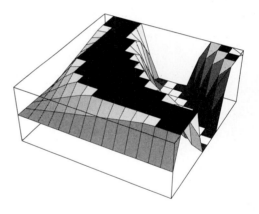

## ■ 1.8.9  Advanced Topic: Shading Surfaces with Functions

The last section discussed how you can shade surfaces either according to their height, or according to the effects of simulated illumination.

With *Mathematica*, you can also specify explicitly how each part of a surface is to be shaded.

---

`Plot3D[{f, s}, {x, xmin, xmax}, {y, ymin, ymax}]`

> plot a surface corresponding to $f$, shaded according to the function $s$

Specifying shading functions for surfaces.

This shows a surface whose height is determined by the function `Sin[x y]`, but whose shading is determined by `GrayLevel[x/3]`.

*In[1]:=* `Plot3D[{Sin[x y], GrayLevel[x/3]},`
`{x, 0, 3}, {y, 0, 3}]`

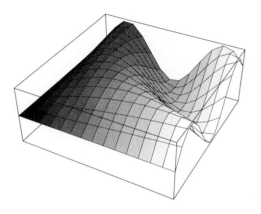

You can use either `GrayLevel` or `RGBColor` to specify a shading function for a surface. You can get many different effects by choosing different shading functions. If you effectively want to display an extra coordinate, you can often do this using a color shading function.

### ■ 1.8.10  Contour Plots

When you are trying to understand the form of a particular surface, it is often useful to look at the surface in several different ways. `Plot3D` gives you a realistic three-dimensional picture of the surface. You can use `ContourPlot` to get a "topographic map" of the surface.

---

`ContourPlot[f, {x, xmin, xmax}, {y, ymin, ymax}]`

> make a contour plot of $f$

Contour plots.

This gives a contour plot of the function $\sin(x)\sin(y)$.

*In[1]:=* `ContourPlot[Sin[x] Sin[y], {x, -2, 2}, {y, -2, 2}]`

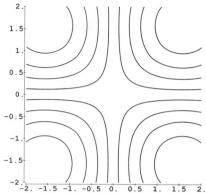

The "contour lines" are just like those in a standard topographical map. They join points on the surface that have the same height. The contour lines correspond to an evenly-spaced sequence of $z$ values.

| *option name* | *default value* | |
| --- | --- | --- |
| PlotPoints | 15 | number of evaluation points in each direction |
| PlotRange | Automatic | the range of values to be included; you can specify {*zmin*, *zmax*}, All, etc. |
| ContourLevels | 10 | number of contour lines between *zmin* and *zmax* |
| ContourSpacing | Automatic | spacing in $z$ between successive contour lines |

Some options for `ContourPlot`.

This increases the density of contour lines shown.

*In[2]:=* `Show[%, ContourLevels -> 40]`

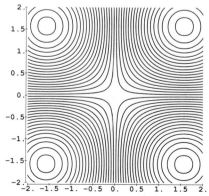

If you do not evaluate your function on a fine enough grid, there may be inaccuracies in your contour plot. One point to realize is that irregularities become obvious in `Plot3D` and `ContourPlot` in somewhat complementary circumstances. `Plot3D` gives an irregular surface if your function varies too rapidly. `ContourPlot`, on the other hand, gives a regular pattern of contour lines when your function varies rapidly, but can give irregular contour lines when the function is almost flat.

## ■ 1.8.11 Density Plots

If you have a display device that shows gray scales or color well, then a good alternative to contour plots are *density plots*. In a density plot, the height of the function at each point is shown by shading.

| |
| --- |
| `DensityPlot[f, {x, xmin, xmax}, {y, ymin, ymax}]`<br>make a density plot |

Density plots.

This is a density plot. Lighter regions are higher.

`In[1]:= DensityPlot[Sin[x] Sin[y], {x, -2, 2}, {y, -2, 2}]`

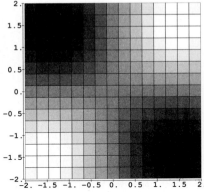

You can get rid of the mesh like this. The
results do not usually look as nice as they
do when you include the mesh.

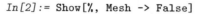

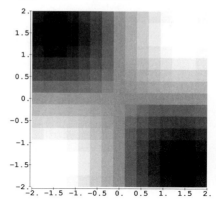

## ■ 1.8.12  Plotting Lists of Data

So far, we have discussed how you can use *Mathematica* to make plots of *functions*.
You give *Mathematica* a function, and it builds up a curve or surface by evaluating
the function at many different points.

This section describes how you can make plots from lists of data, instead of
functions. (Section 1.9 discusses how to read data from external files and programs.)
The *Mathematica* commands for plotting lists of data are direct analogs of the ones
discussed above for plotting functions.

| | |
|---|---|
| `ListPlot[{`$y_1$`, `$y_2$`, ...}]` | plot $y_1$, $y_2$, ... at $x$ values 1, 2, ... |
| `ListPlot[{{`$x_1$`, `$y_1$`}, {`$x_2$`, `$y_2$`}, ...}]` | |
| | plot points $(x_1, y_1)$, ... |
| `ListPlot[`*list*`, PlotJoined -> True]` | |
| | plot a line through the points |
| `ListPlot3D[{{`$z_{11}$`, `$z_{12}$`, ...}, {`$z_{21}$`, `$z_{22}$`, ...}, ...}]` | |
| | make a three-dimensional plot of the array of heights $z_{xy}$ |
| `ListContourPlot[`*array*`]` | make a contour plot from an array of heights |
| `ListDensityPlot[`*array*`]` | make a density plot |

Functions for plotting lists of data.

Here is a list of values.

*In[1]:=* **t = Table[i∧2, {i, 10}]**

*Out[1]=* {1, 4, 9, 16, 25, 36, 49, 64, 81, 100}

This plots the values.

*In[2]:=* **ListPlot[t]**

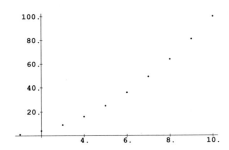

This puts a line through the points.

*In[3]:=* **ListPlot[t, PlotJoined -> True]**

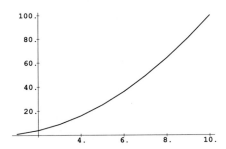

This gives a list of *x*, *y* pairs.

*In[4]:=* **Table[{i∧2, 4 i∧2 + i∧3}, {i, 10}]**

*Out[4]=* {{1, 5}, {4, 24}, {9, 63}, {16, 128}, {25, 225},
           {36, 360}, {49, 539}, {64, 768}, {81, 1053},
           {100, 1400}}

This plots the points.

*In[5]:=* **ListPlot[%]**

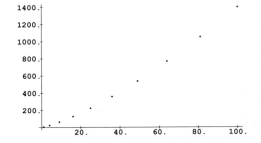

This gives a rectangular array of values. The array is quite large, so we end the input with a semicolon to stop the result from being printed out.

*In[6]:=* **t3 = Table[Mod[y, x], {x, 20}, {y, 20}] ;**

This makes a three-dimensional plot of the array of values.

*In[7]:=* **ListPlot3D[t3]**

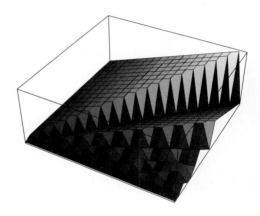

You can redraw the plot using Show, as usual.

*In[8]:=* **Show[%, ViewPoint -> {1.5, -0.5, 0}]**

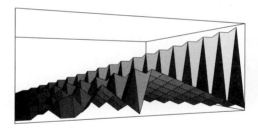

This gives a density plot of the array of values.                    $In[9]:=$ `ListDensityPlot[t3]`

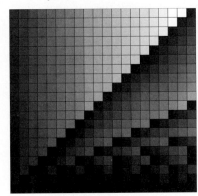

## ■ 1.8.13 Advanced Topic: Building Up Two-dimensional Graphics

All plots in *Mathematica* are built up from lists of *graphics primitives*.    Functions like `Plot` work by producing appropriate lists of graphics primitives, and then displaying them. This section discusses how you can work directly with *Mathematica* graphics primitives. If you only need to make plots of functions or data, then commands like `Plot` and `ListPlot` should be quite sufficient, and you will not need to read this section. If, on the other hand, you want to make more complicated diagrams and pictures in *Mathematica*, then you will need to use the graphics primitives discussed in this section.

| | |
|---|---|
| `Graphics[`*list*`]` | representation of two-dimensional graphics |
| `Show[`*graphics*`]` | display graphics |

Representation and display of graphics.

`Plot` creates an appropriate graphics object, and then displays it.                    $In[1]:=$ `Plot[Sin[x], {x, 0, 3}]`

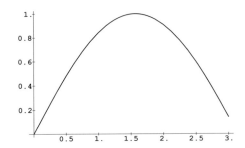

This shows the internal form of the
graphics object. It contains a list of
graphics primitives.

```
In[2]:= InputForm[%]

Out[2]//InputForm=
    Graphics[{GrayLevel[0],
        {Line[{{0., 0.}, {0.125, 0.124675},
            {0.25, 0.247404}, {0.375, 0.366273},
            {0.5, 0.479426}, {0.625, 0.585097},
            {0.75, 0.681639}, {0.875, 0.767544},
            {1., 0.841471}, {1.125, 0.902268},
            {1.1875, 0.927437}, {1.25, 0.948985},
            {1.3125, 0.966827}, {1.375, 0.980893},
            {1.40625, 0.986493},
            {1.4375, 0.991129},
            {1.46875, 0.994798},
            {1.48437, 0.996268}, {1.5, 0.997495},
            {1.51562, 0.998478},
            {1.52344, 0.998879},
            {1.53125, 0.999218},
            {1.53906, 0.999497},
            {1.54687, 0.999714}, {1.55078, 0.9998},
            {1.55469, 0.99987},
            {1.55859, 0.999926},
            {1.5625, 0.999966}, {1.56641, 0.99999},
            {1.57031, 1.}, {1.57422, 0.999994},
            {1.57812, 0.999973},
            {1.58203, 0.999937},
            {1.58594, 0.999885},
            {1.59375, 0.999737},
            {1.60156, 0.999527},
            {1.60937, 0.999256}, {1.625, 0.998531},
            {1.64062, 0.997563},
            {1.65625, 0.996351},
            {1.6875, 0.993198},
            {1.71875, 0.989075}, {1.75, 0.983986},
            {1.8125, 0.970932}, {1.875, 0.954086},
            {2., 0.909297}, {2.125, 0.85032},
            {2.25, 0.778073}, {2.375, 0.693685},
            {2.5, 0.598472}, {2.625, 0.49392},
            {2.75, 0.381661}, {2.875, 0.263446},
            {3., 0.14112}}]}},
        {PlotRange -> Automatic,
         AspectRatio -> GoldenRatio^(-1),
         DisplayFunction -> Display["stdout", #1] & ,
         PlotColor -> Automatic, Axes -> Automatic,
         PlotLabel -> None, AxesLabel -> None,
         Ticks -> Automatic, Framed -> False}]
```

Show displays graphics.

```
In[3]:= Show[%]
```

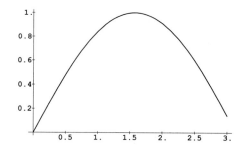

| | |
|---|---|
| Point[{$x$, $y$}] | point at position $x, y$ |
| Line[{{$x_1$, $y_1$}, {$x_2$, $y_2$}, ...}] | line through the points $(x_1, y_1)$, $(x_2, y_2)$, ... |
| Rectangle[{$xmin$, $ymin$}, {$xmax$, $ymax$}] | |
| | filled rectangle |
| Polygon[{{$x_1$, $y_1$}, {$x_2$, $y_2$}, ...}] | |
| | filled polygon with the specified list of corners |
| CellArray[{{$a_{11}$, $a_{12}$, ...}, {$a_{21}$, ...}, ...}] | |
| | rectangular array of gray levels between 0 and 1 |
| CellArray[$array$, {{$xmin$, $ymin$}, {$xmax$, $ymax$}}, {$zmin$, $zmax$}] | |
| | array of gray levels between $zmin$ and $zmax$ drawn in the rectangle defined by $xmin$, $ymin$, $xmax$, $ymax$ |
| Text[$expr$, {$x$, $y$}] | the text of $expr$, centered at the point $(x, y)$ (see below) |
| GrayLevel[$i$] | display objects that follow at an intensity (gray level) $i$ between 0 (*black*) and 1 (*white*) |
| RGBColor[$r$, $g$, $b$] | display (if possible) with the specified red, green and blue color intensities (each between 0 and 1) (see below) |
| PointSize[$s$] | give points a size $s$ *measured as a fraction of the width of whole plot* |
| Thickness[$t$] | display lines with a thickness $t$ *measured as a fraction of the width of whole plot* |
| Dashing[{$d_1$, $d_2$, ...}] | display lines as a sequence of dashed segments, with lengths $d_1$, $d_2$, ... *measured as a fraction of the width of whole plot* |

Two-dimensional graphics primitives.

Here are graphics primitives representing two lines.

```
In[4]:= g = Graphics[ {Line[{{-1,-1},{1,1}}],
                       Line[{{-1,1},{1,-1}}]} ]

Out[4]= -Graphics-
```

Show displays the graphics.                     *In[5]:=* **Show[%]**

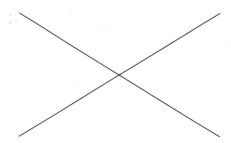

You can use any of the standard options for     *In[6]:=* **Show[%, Axes -> Automatic]**
Show. When you create your own graphics,
the default setting for **Axes** is **None**.

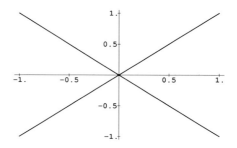

Here is an ordinary *Mathematica* plot.         *In[7]:=* **Plot[Sin[x], {x, -1, 1}]**

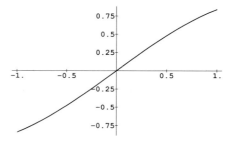

You can combine this with your graphics          *In[8]:=* **Show[%, g]**
primitives.

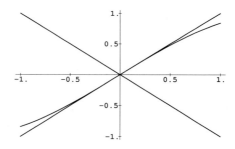

Here are the coordinates of the corners of a pentagon.

```
In[9]:= pentagon =
    Table[ N[{Sin[2 Pi n/5], Cos[2 Pi n/5]}], {n, 5} ]
Out[9]= {{0.951057, 0.309017}, {0.587785, -0.809017},
    {-0.587785, -0.809017}, {-0.951057, 0.309017},
    {0., 1.}}
```

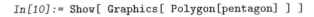

This displays the pentagon. With the default choice of aspect ratio, it comes out somewhat squashed.

```
In[10]:= Show[ Graphics[ Polygon[pentagon] ] ]
```

This chooses the aspect ratio so that the shape of the pentagon is preserved.

```
In[11]:= Show[ %, AspectRatio -> Automatic ]
```

This gives a pentagon with intensity 0.4. Remember that intensity 0 is black, and 1 is white.

```
In[12]:= Show[ Graphics[ { GrayLevel[0.4],
        Polygon[pentagon] } ],
        AspectRatio -> Automatic ]
```

This draws two pentagons superimposed.
Later graphics primitives always overwrite
earlier ones.

```
In[13]:= Show[ Graphics[
           { GrayLevel[0.4], Polygon[pentagon],
             GrayLevel[0.8],
             Polygon[pentagon + Table[{0.5, 0.5}, {5}]]
           } ], AspectRatio -> Automatic ]
```

Remember that the scales given in the
graphics primitives `PointSize`, `Thickness`
and `Dashing` are always measured relative
to the width of the whole plot.

```
In[14]:= Show[ Graphics[ { Line[{{-2, -2}, {2, 2}}],
           PointSize[0.1], Point[{0,1}], Point[{1,0}] } ] ]
```

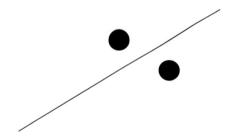

| option name | default value | |
|---|---|---|
| PlotRange | Automatic | range of coordinates to include in the plot (**All** includes everything) |
| AspectRatio | 1/GoldenRatio | the height-to-width ratio for the whole plot; **Automatic** preserves the shapes of objects |
| Axes | None | whether axes are drawn |
| PlotColor | True | whether color is used |

Some options for `Graphics` and `Show`.

There are two ways to specify the positions of objects in a plot: absolute coordinates and scaled coordinates.

| | |
|---|---|
| $\{x,\ y\}$ | absolute coordinate values |
| Scaled[$\{x,\ y\}$] | scaled coordinates, running from 0 to 1 in each direction |

Two ways to specify position in a plot.

You can use the graphics primitive **Text** to include text in your plots.

| | |
|---|---|
| Text[*expr*, $\{x,\ y\}$] | text centered at $(x, y)$ |
| Text[*expr*, $\{x,\ y\}$, $\{-1,\ 0\}$] | left-hand end at $(x, y)$ |
| Text[*expr*, $\{x,\ y\}$, $\{1,\ 0\}$] | right-hand end at $(x, y)$ |
| Text[*expr*, $\{x,\ y\}$, $\{0,\ 1\}$] | centered above $(x, y)$ |
| Text[*expr*, $\{x,\ y\}$, $\{0,\ -1\}$] | centered below $(x, y)$ |
| Text[*expr*,$\{x,y\}$,$\{dx,dy\}$] | positioned so that $(x, y)$ is at relative coordinates $(dx, dy)$ within the box that bounds the text |

Ways to specify the position of text in a plot.

Here is text at various positions in a plot.

```
In[15]:= Show[ Graphics[ { Text[aaa, {0.75, 0.5}],
              Text[bbb, {0.75, 0.6}, {-1, 0}],
              Text[ccc, {0.75, 0.7}, {0, 1}] } ],
              Axes -> Automatic ]
```

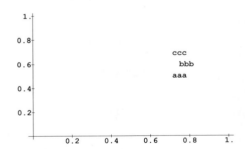

Exactly what font and style are used for the text in your plots will depend on the particular device and particular POSTSCRIPT interpreter you have. Section 2.6.10 discusses how you can get some control over the form of text in graphics.

If you have a color display device, you can use the **RGBColor** graphics primitive to generate color output. The external file **Colors.m** contains many specifications for colors.

| | |
|---|---|
| Black | `GrayLevel[0]` |
| White | `GrayLevel[1]` |
| Gray | `GrayLevel[0.5]` |
| Red | `RGBColor[1,0,0]` |
| Green | `RGBColor[0,1,0]` |
| Blue | `RGBColor[0,0,1]` |
| Yellow | `RGBColor[1,1,0]` |
| Cyan | `RGBColor[0,1,1]` |
| Magenta | `RGBColor[1,0,1]` |
| `HSBColor[`$h$`, `$s$`, `$b$`]` | color specified using hue, saturation and brightness |

Some color specifications from the file `Colors.m`.

You can use graphics primitives to specify different *styles* for curves drawn by `Plot` and `ListPlot`.

| | |
|---|---|
| `PlotStyle -> `*style* | specify a style for all curves |
| `PlotStyle -> {{`*style₁*`}, {`*style₂*`}, ...}` | specify styles to be used (cyclically) for a sequence of curves |
| `GrayLevel[0.5]` | gray |
| `RGBColor[1,0,0]`, etc. | red, etc. |
| `Thickness[0.05]` | thick |
| `Dashing[{0.05, 0.05}]` | dashed |
| `Dashing[{0.01, 0.05, 0.05, 0.05}]` | dot-dashed |

Styles for curves.

This makes a plot with the first curve having intensity 0.2, and the second one having intensity 0.7. Remember that intensity 0 is black. Notice that the graphics primitives for each curve have to be enclosed in a separate list.

```
In[16]:= Plot[{BesselJ[0, x], BesselJ[1, x]}, {x, 0, 10},
             PlotStyle -> {{GrayLevel[0.2]}, {GrayLevel[0.7]}}]
```

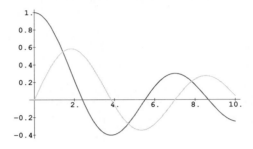

This makes a dashed curve.

```
In[17]:= Plot[ArcTan[x], {x, 0, 10},
             PlotStyle -> Dashing[{0.05, 0.05}]]
```

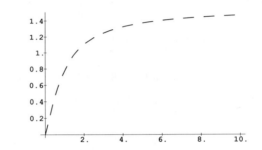

## ■ 1.8.14 Advanced Topic: Building Up Three-Dimensional Graphics

The functions `Plot3D` and `ListPlot3D` draw three-dimensional pictures of single *surfaces*. This section discusses how you can use *Mathematica*'s three-dimensional graphics primitives to build up more complicated three-dimensional pictures.

If you only use three-dimensional graphics to produce surfaces representing functions or lists of data, then you do not need to read this section. On the other hand, if you want to draw pictures of objects like polyhedra, this section will show you how to do it using three-dimensional graphics primitives.

| | |
|---|---|
| `Graphics3D[list]` | representation of three-dimensional graphics |
| `Show[graphics]` | display graphics |

Representation and display of three-dimensional graphics.

| | |
|---|---|
| `Point[{`$x$`, `$y$`, `$z$`}]` | point with coordinates $x$, $y$, $z$ |
| `Line[{{`$x_1$`, `$y_1$`, `$z_1$`}, {`$x_2$`, `$y_2$`, `$z_2$`}, ...}]` | |
| | line joining the points $(x_1, y_1)$, $(x_2, y_2)$, ... |
| `Polygon[{{`$x_1$`, `$y_1$`, `$z_1$`}, {`$x_2$`, `$y_2$`, `$z_2$`}, ...}]` | |
| | filled polygon with the specified list of corners |
| `GrayLevel[`$i$`]` | display objects that follow with an intensity $i$ |
| `RGBColor[`$r$`, `$g$`, `$b$`]` | display (if possible) with the specified red, green and blue color intensities |
| `PointSize[`$s$`]` | make points of size $s$ |
| `Thickness[`$t$`]` | use thickness $t$ for lines |
| `FaceForm[`*gfront*`, `*gback*`]` | show the fronts and backs of polygons in the specified `GrayLevel` or `RGBColor` |
| `EdgeForm[ ]` | do not draw lines at the edges of polygons |
| `EdgeForm[`*primitive*`]` | make polygon edges a particular `GrayLevel` or `RGBColor` |

Three-dimensional graphics primitives.

| | |
|---|---|
| This produces a list of 20 random points in three-dimensional space. | `In[1]:= pts =`<br>`    Table[Point[{Random[ ], Random[ ], Random[ ]}], {20}] ;` |

Here is a three-dimensional plot of the points.

*In[2]:=* **Show[ Graphics3D [ pts ] ]**

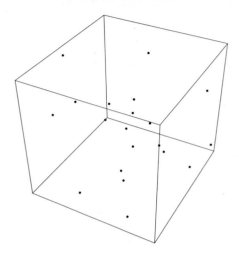

You can use Show to redraw the plot with different options.

*In[3]:=* **Show[ %, ViewPoint -> {8, 1, 1} ]**

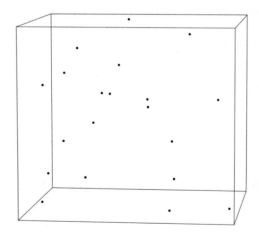

This draws the plot with much larger points.

`In[4]:= Show[ Graphics3D [ { PointSize[0.05], pts } ] ]`

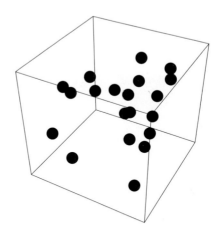

This defines a function that creates a random *n*-sided polygon.

```
In[5]:= ranpoly[n_] :=
          Polygon[ Table[ Random[ ], {n}, {3} ] ]
```

Here is a picture of a randomly-generated triangle.

`In[6]:= Show[ Graphics3D[ ranpoly[3] ] ]`

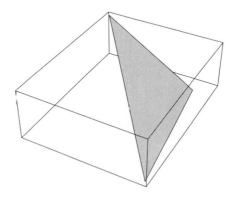

Here is a picture of 5 randomly-generated triangles. *Mathematica* hides the parts that are obscured.

*In[7]:=* **Show[ Graphics3D[ Table[ranpoly[3], {5}] ] ]**

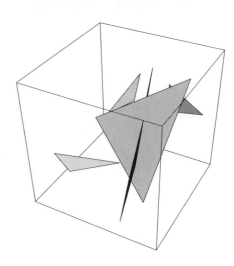

*Mathematica* assumes that all the polygons you give it are supposed to be planar. If you give a non-planar polygon, *Mathematica* will break the polygon into triangles, but not show any "seams" between the triangles.

*In[8]:=* **Show[ Graphics3D[**
          **Polygon[**
          **{{3, 0, 2}, {0, 2, 3}, {3, 3, 1}, {3, 3, 3}}**
          **] ]]**

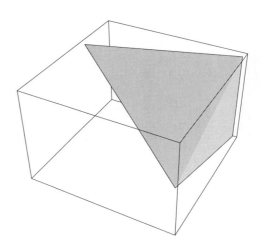

Putting in EdgeForm[ ] gets rid of the lines     *In[9]:=* Show[ Graphics3D[ {EdgeForm[ ], ranpoly[3],
at edges of polygons.                                                 ranpoly[3]} ] ]

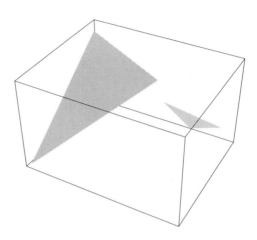

The way that shading and color are done in three-dimensional *Mathematica* graphics is flexible, but somewhat complicated.

There are two basic approaches. First, you can set Lighting -> False, and then the primitives GrayLevel and RGBColor to specify explicitly the shading of all the objects. Alternatively, you can set Lighting -> True, and generate polygon shadings from simulated illumination. You can then use GrayLevel and RGBColor to specify the *reflectance* of different polygons. The final shading of a polygon is determined by the *product* of its illumination and reflectivity. Lighting does not affect the shading of points and lines.

A final complication is that each polygon has two sides: a front and a back. By using the two arguments to the graphics primitive FaceForm you can specify different colors or reflectivities for the front and back. When you look at the *front* of the polygon, the corners, taken in the order that you specify them, appear in counter-clockwise order. Reversing the order of the corners interchanges the roles of front and back.

When you construct two-dimensional graphics, *Mathematica* always draws the objects you specify in the order you give them. Later objects are taken to obscure earlier ones. On the other hand, when you construct three-dimensional graphics, the order in which you specify different objects is essentially irrelevant. *Mathematica* will always order the objects so that objects "in front" obscure those "behind".

The file `Polyhedra.m` contains lists of graphics primitives representing regular polyhedra.

```
In[10]:= <<Polyhedra.m
```

Here are the graphics primitives for a tetrahedron centered at the origin. Note that each pair of faces shares a common edge.

```
In[11]:= Tetrahedron[ ]
Out[11]= {Polygon[{{0., 0., 1.},
            {-0.942809, 0., -0.333333},
            {0.471405, -0.834546, -0.333333}}],
         Polygon[{{0., 0., 1.},
            {0.471405, 0.834546, -0.333333},
            {-0.942809, 0., -0.333333}}],
         Polygon[{{0., 0., 1.},
            {0.471405, -0.834546, -0.333333},
            {0.471405, 0.834546, -0.333333}}],
         Polygon[{{-0.942809, 0., -0.333333},
            {0.471405, 0.834546, -0.333333},
            {0.471405, -0.834546, -0.333333}}]}
```

This displays the graphics primitives corresponding to a tetrahedron. Only two of the faces of the tetrahedron are visible from this angle.

```
In[12]:= Show[ Graphics3D[ % ] ]
```

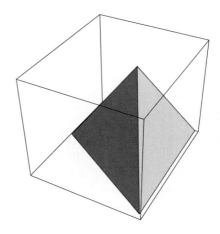

A further detail concerns how three-dimensional pictures are built up on interactive display devices. You can choose whether *Mathematica* draws every polygon, but covers up ones that are not visible in the final picture, or whether it only draws polygons or parts of polygons that are going to be visible.

| | |
|---|---|
| RenderAll->True | draw all polygons, starting from the back (default) |
| RenderAll->False | draw only those polygons or parts of polygons which are visible in the finished picture |

An option for rendering three-dimensional pictures.

If you set RenderAll->True, then your pictures will always be drawn from back to front. All polygons will be rendered, but the ones at the back will be covered up by ones in front. If you display a closed surface with RenderAll->True, you will see the insides of the surface while it is being drawn; the surface will typically be closed up only when the last polygons are added at the front of the picture.

With RenderAll->False, on the other hand, *Mathematica* renders only the polygons, or parts of polygons, that are visible in the final picture. As a result, you can never see the insides of closed surface, even while it is being drawn.

For reasonably simple pictures, without a large number of intersecting polygons, RenderAll->False will typically give you smaller POSTSCRIPT output. Particularly when there are a large number of intersecting polygons, however, RenderAll->False may take a very long time to run, and may give you larger POSTSCRIPT output. The final pictures you get are always independent of the setting you use for RenderAll; all that is affected is how your pictures are built up in time.

### ■ 1.8.15  Special Topic: Real-Time Graphics

There are some sophisticated front ends for *Mathematica* that allow you to do various kinds of real-time graphics.

You can often, for example, take sequences of pictures produced by *Mathematica*, and display them in rapid succession to make something like a "movie loop". In this way, you can "animate" two- and three-dimensional graphics.

On some computers, you can also feed representations of three-dimensional graphics produced by *Mathematica* into external programs which allow you to change viewing angles and other parameters interactively.

# ■ 1.9  Advanced Topic: Interfacing to Other Systems

## ■ 1.9.1  Reading Data Files

| | |
|---|---|
| `ReadList["`*file*`", Number]` | read numbers from a file, and return a *Mathematica* list of them |
| `ReadList["`*file*`", {Number, Number}]` | |
| | read pairs of numbers from a file |

Reading numerical data files.

If you have a table of numbers in a file, generated for example by an external program, you can read them into *Mathematica* using `ReadList`. The numbers in your file can be given in C or FORTRAN-like form, as `2.3E5` and so on. `ReadList` converts all numbers to the appropriate *Mathematica* form.

This shows the contents of the file
`rand.dat`.

```
In[1]:= !!rand.dat

22   4.5
108  2.2e3
204  4.77e6
```

This reads the file `rand.dat`, and returns a
list of the numbers in the file.

```
In[1]:= ReadList["rand.dat", Number]
```

$Out[1]= \{22, 4.5, 108, 2200., 204, 4.77\ 10^6\}$

This reads numbers from the file in pairs.

```
In[2]:= ReadList["rand.dat", {Number, Number}]
```

$Out[2]= \{\{22, 4.5\}, \{108, 2200.\}, \{204, 4.77\ 10^6\}\}$

## ■ 1.9.2  C and FORTRAN Programming Languages

*Mathematica* is a system for doing general mathematical computations. You may sometimes want to take results you have got from *Mathematica*, and plug them into various special-purpose programs you may have written in other programming languages.

The standard version of *Mathematica* supports both C and FORTRAN programming languages. You can have *Mathematica* write out expressions in the form you need for input to C and FORTRAN.

| | |
|---|---|
| CForm[*expr*] | write out *expr* so it can be used in a C program |
| FortranForm[*expr*] | write out *expr* for FORTRAN |

*Mathematica* output for programming languages.

Here is an expression, written out in standard mathematical form.

```
In[1]:= Expand[(1 + x + y)^2]
```

$$Out[1]= 1 + 2\ x + x^2 + 2\ y + 2\ x\ y + y^2$$

Here is the expression in FORTRAN form.

```
In[2]:= FortranForm[%]

Out[2]//FortranForm= 1 + 2*x + x**2 + 2*y + 2*x*y + y**2
```

Here is the same expression in C form. Macros for objects like Power are defined in the C header file mdefs.h that comes with most versions of *Mathematica*.

```
In[3]:= CForm[%]

Out[3]//CForm=
        1 + 2*x + Power(x,2) + 2*y + 2*x*y + Power(y,2)
```

## ■ 1.9.3 TeX Formatting System

When you are preparing documents for publication, you may need to use a full-function formatting system, such as TeX. You can use **TeXForm** to write out results from *Mathematica* in a form suitable for input to TeX.

| | |
|---|---|
| TeXForm[*expr*] | write out *expr* in TeX input form |

*Mathematica* output for formatting systems.

Here is an expression, written out in standard mathematical form.

```
In[1]:= (x + y)^2 / (x y)
```

$$Out[1]= \frac{(x + y)^2}{x\ y}$$

Here is the expression in TeX input form.

```
In[2]:= TeXForm[%]

Out[2]//TeXForm=
        {{{{\left( x + y \right) }^2}}\over {x y}}
```

Here is a more complicated example.

This is the standard *Mathematica* form of an expression.

```
In[3]:= Sum[ Sqrt[8]/9801 (4n)! (1103 + 26390 n) /
              (n!^4 396^(4n)), {n, 1, Infinity} ]
```

$$Out[3]= \text{Sum}\left[\frac{2\ \text{Sqrt}[2]\ (4\ n)!\ (1103 + 26390\ n)}{9801\ 396^{4\ n}\ n!^4},\right.$$

$$\{n,\ 1,\ \text{Infinity}\}]$$

Here is the expression in TEX input form.

```
In[4]:= TeXForm[%]
```

```
Out[4]//TeXForm=
        \sum_{n = 1}^{\infty}
            {{2 {\sqrt{2}} \left( 4 n \right) !
                \left( 1103 + 26390 n \right) }\over
            {9801 {{396}^{4 n}} {{n!}^4}}}
```

Here is the result of running the TEX input through TEX:

$$\sum_{n=1}^{\infty} \frac{2\sqrt{2}}{9801}\,(4n)!\frac{1103+26390n}{n!^4 396^{4n}}$$

**TeXForm** automatically converts a number of *Mathematica* symbol names to TEX forms.

| *Mathematica* form | TEX form |
|---|---|
| alpha, beta, gamma, etc. | $\alpha$, $\beta$, $\gamma$, etc. |
| ALPHA, BETA, GAMMA, etc. | $A$, $B$, $\Gamma$, etc. |
| I, E, Pi, Infinity | $i$, $e$, $\pi$, $\infty$ |

Some transformations made by TeXForm.

### ■ 1.9.4  Splicing *Mathematica* Output into External Files

If you have a C or FORTRAN program, or a TEX document, you may want to insert formulae or other data by "splicing in" output from *Mathematica*.

| | |
|---|---|
| Splice["*file*.mx"] | splice *Mathematica* output into an external file named *file*.mx, putting the results in the file *file*.x |
| Splice["*infile*", "*outfile*"] | splice *Mathematica* output into *infile*, sending the output to *outfile* |

Splicing *Mathematica* output into files.

The basic idea is to set up the definitions you need in a particular *Mathematica* session, then run `Splice` to use the definitions you have made to produce the appropriate output to insert into the external files.

```
#include "mdefs.h"

double f(x)
double x;
{
double y;

y = <* Integrate[Sin[x]^5, x] *> ;

return(2*y - 1) ;
}
```

A simple C program containing a *Mathematica* formula.

```
#include "mdefs.h"

double f(x)
double x;
{
double y;

y = -5*Cos(x)/8 + 5*Cos(3*x)/48 - Cos(5*x)/80 ;

return(2*y - 1) ;
}
```

The C program after processing with `Splice`.

## ■ 1.9.5  PostScript Page Description Language

As discussed in Section 1.8.5, *Mathematica* generates all its graphics in PostScript form. You will usually not need to look at the PostScript form: it will simply be rendered by your *Mathematica* front end.

However, if you want to send graphics from *Mathematica* to other output devices, or if you want to include the graphics in documents, you may need to get at the PostScript form directly.

| | |
|---|---|
| `Display["`*file*`", `*graphics*`]` | write the PostScript form of graphics into a file |

PostScript output.

For some purposes, you may need to edit the PostScript that *Mathematica* produces. You will find that most of the PostScript is quite simple. There are some complications, however, associated with text that is embedded in graphics: to allow for the different fonts available with different PostScript renderers, *Mathematica* leaves the final calculations about positioning of text to the PostScript interpreter.

## ■ 1.9.6 Special Topic: External Programs

*Mathematica* does many things well. There are, however, some things that are still best done outside of *Mathematica*. In such cases, you can call external programs from within *Mathematica*, and then, for example, get the results back into *Mathematica* for further processing.

One situation in which it is often convenient to use external programs is in working with special input or output devices. You can use an external program to control the device, and then transfer arrays of *Mathematica* data to or from the device.

If you already have an external program that does a particular calculation, it may be easier for you to do that calculation with your existing program, rather than to recode the algorithm in *Mathematica*. Even if the main part of your calculation is done by an external program, you can still use *Mathematica* to prepare the input, and to process the output.

On most computer systems (such as those with the UNIX operating system), the basic scheme that *Mathematica* uses to handle external programs is to run the programs and separate processes, and to communicate with them through pipes.

*Mathematica* is set up so that any commands which do input and output with files can also work with pipes.

| | |
|---|---|
| `<<`*file* | read in a file |
| `<<"!`*command*`"` | run an external command, and read in the output it produces |
| *expr* `>> "!`*command*`"` | feed the textual form of *expr* to an external command |
| `ReadList["!`*command*`", Number]` | run an external command, and read in a list of the numbers it produces |

Some ways to communicate with external programs.

| | |
|---|---|
| This feeds the expression x^2 + y^2 as input to the external command lpr, which, on a typical UNIX system, sends output to a printer. | *In[1]:=* x^2 + y^2 >> "!lpr" |

| | |
|---|---|
| Putting a ! at the beginning of a line causes the remainder of the line to be executed as an external command. squares is an external program which prints numbers and their squares. | *In[2]:=* !squares 4<br><br>1  1<br>2  4<br>3  9<br>4  16 |

| | |
|---|---|
| This runs the external command squares 4, then reads pairs of numbers from the output it produces. | *In[2]:=* ReadList["!squares 4", {Number, Number}]<br>*Out[2]=* {{1, 1}, {2, 4}, {3, 9}, {4, 16}} |

## ■ 1.9.7 Special Topic: External Functions

On many computer systems, *Mathematica* can not only execute complete external programs, but can also call individual functions inside appropriately-prepared external programs. In this way, you can set up an external program which contains a "library" of functions that can be accessed from *Mathematica*.

This kind of communication with external programs is again done through pipes. Packets of data, specifying the function to call, and the arguments to give, are sent from *Mathematica* through the pipe to the external program. Routines inside the external program then decode the packet, call the appropriate function, and then return the result to *Mathematica*. Versions of the routines that are needed for this decoding are usually distributed with *Mathematica* in source code form.

| | |
|---|---|
| StartProcess["*command*"] | execute an external program, and set up *Mathematica* definitions for the functions it contains |
| CallProcess["*command*", *f*, {arg$_1$, arg$_2$, ...}] | call the function *f* in an external process |
| EndProcess["*command*"] | stop an external process |

Calling functions in external processes.

The same basic mechanism that allows *Mathematica* to call functions inside an external program can also be used to allow an external program to call *Mathematica*. In this way, you can effectively treat *Mathematica* as a "library" that your external programs can call on.

# Chapter Two:
# *The Structure of*
# *Mathematica*

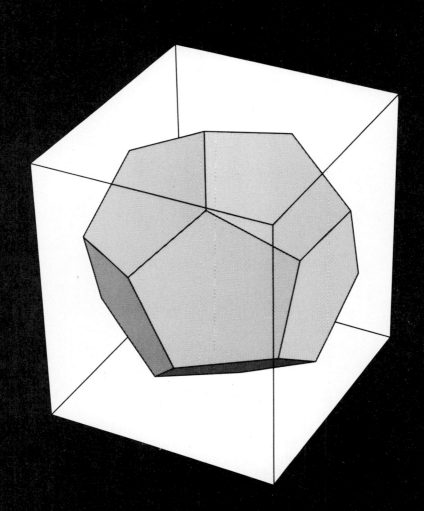

Chapter 1 introduced *Mathematica* by showing you how to use some of its more common features. This chapter looks at *Mathematica* in a different way.

Instead of discussing individual features, it describes the overall framework of *Mathematica*. You will be able to do many calculations in *Mathematica* without understanding the framework. However, if you want to use *Mathematica* to its fullest, you will need to know the framework. In addition, knowing the framework will help you remember how all the individual features of *Mathematica* work. In fact, you will probably often be able to "predict" how features work, without even reading the description.

This chapter assumes no advanced knowledge of computing. If you are an expert on computer languages, you may find it useful to look first at the Reference Guide. You should still read this chapter, though, to understand *why Mathematica* is constructed the way it is.

**About the illustration overleaf:**

This is a picture of a regular dodecahedron. The package `Polyhedra.m` includes the function `Dodecahedron`, which gives a list of graphics primitives representing the faces of a dodecahedron. The complete *Mathematica* command used to produce the picture was
`Show[ Graphics3D[Dodecahedron[ ]] ].`

# ■ 2.1 Expressions

## ■ 2.1.1 Everything Is an Expression

*Mathematica* handles many different kinds of things: mathematical formulae, lists, graphs, to name a few. Although they often look very different, *Mathematica* represents all of these things in one uniform way. They are all *expressions*.

A prototypical example of a *Mathematica* expression is `f[x, y]`. You might use `f[x, y]` to represent a mathematical function $f(x, y)$. The function is named `f`, and has two arguments, `x` and `y`.

You do not always have to write expressions in the form $f[x,y,...]$. For example, `x + y` is also an expression. When you type in `x + y`, *Mathematica* converts it to the standard form `Plus[x, y]`. Then, when it prints it out again, it gives it as `x + y`.

The same is true of other "operators", such as ∧ (`Power`) and / (`Divide`).

In fact, everything you type into *Mathematica* is treated as an expression.

| | |
|---:|:---|
| x + y + z | Plus[x, y, z] |
| x y z | Times[x, y, z] |
| x∧n | Power[x, n] |
| {a, b, c} | List[a, b, c] |
| a -> b | Rule[a, b] |
| a = b | Set[a, b] |

Some examples of *Mathematica* expressions.

You can see the full form of any expression by using `FullForm[`*expr*`]`.

Here is an expression.

```
In[1]:= x + y + z
Out[1]= x + y + z
```

This is the full form of the expression.

```
In[2]:= FullForm[%]
Out[2]//FullForm= Plus[x, y, z]
```

Here is another expression.

```
In[3]:= 1 + x∧2 + (y + z)∧2
```

$$Out[3]= 1 + x^2 + (y + z)^2$$

Its full form has several nested pieces.

```
In[4]:= FullForm[%]
Out[4]//FullForm=
     Plus[1, Power[x, 2], Power[Plus[y, z], 2]]
```

The object *f* in an expression *f*[x, y, ...] is known as the *head* of the expression. You can extract it using Head[*expr*]. Particularly when you write programs in *Mathematica*, you will often want to test the head of an expression to find out what kind of thing the expression is.

Head gives the "function name" f.

```
In[5]:= Head[f[x, y]]
Out[5]= f
```

Here Head gives the name of the "operator".

```
In[6]:= Head[a + b + c]
Out[6]= Plus
```

Everything has a head.

```
In[7]:= Head[{a, b, c}]
Out[7]= List
```

Numbers also have heads.

```
In[8]:= Head[23432]
Out[8]= Integer
```

You can distinguish different kinds of numbers by their heads.

```
In[9]:= Head[345.6]
Out[9]= Real
```

| | |
|---|---|
| Head[*expr*] | give the head of an expression: the *f* in *f*[x, y] |
| FullForm[*expr*] | display an expression in the full form used by *Mathematica* |

Functions for manipulating expressions.

## ■ 2.1.2  The Meaning of Expressions

The notion of expressions is a crucial unifying principle in *Mathematica*. It is the fact that every object in *Mathematica* has the same underlying structure that makes it possible for *Mathematica* to cover so many areas with a comparatively small number of basic operations.

Although all expressions have the same basic structure, there are many different ways that expressions can be used. Here are a few of the interpretations you can give to the parts of an expression.

| Meaning of f | Meaning of x,  y,  ... | Examples |
|---|---|---|
| Function | arguments or parameters | `Sin[x]`, `f[x, y]` |
| Command | arguments or parameters | `Expand[(x + 1)∧2]` |
| Operator | operands | `x + y`, `a = b` |
| Head | elements | `{a, b, c}` |
| Object type | contents | `RGBColor[r, g, b]` |

Some interpretations of parts of expressions.

Expressions in *Mathematica* are often used to specify operations. So, for example, typing in 2 + 3 causes 2 and 3 to be added together, while `Factor[x∧6 - 1]` performs factorization.

Perhaps an even more important use of expressions in *Mathematica*, however, is to maintain a structure, which can then be acted on by other functions. An expression like `{a, b, c}` does not specify an operation. It merely maintains a list structure, which contains a collection of three elements. Other functions, such as `Reverse` or `Dot`, can act on this structure.

The full form of the expression `{a, b, c}` is `List[a, b, c]`. The head `List` performs no operations. Instead, its purpose is to serve as a "tag" to specify the "type" of the structure.

You can use expressions in *Mathematica* to create your own structures. For example, you might want to represent points in three-dimensional space, specified by three coordinates. You could give each point as `point[x, y, z]`. The "function" `point` again performs no operation. It serves merely to collect the three coordinates together, and to label the resulting object as a `point`.

You can think of expressions like `point[x, y, z]` as being "packets of data", tagged with a particular head. Even though all expressions have the same basic structure, you can distinguish different "types" of expressions by giving them different heads. You can then set up transformation rules and programs which treat different types of expressions in different ways.

## ■ 2.1.3  Four Ways to Write Expressions

Internally, *Mathematica* represents a sum of two objects as `Plus[x, y]`. You can, however, enter this expression in the much more convenient form `x + y`. *Mathematica* also accepts alternative forms for standard expressions like *f* `[x, y, ...]`.

| | |
|---|---|
| $f[x, y]$ | standard form for $f[x, y]$ |
| $f @ x$ | prefix form for $f[x]$ |
| $x // f$ | postfix form for $f[x]$ |
| $x \sim f \sim y$ | infix form for $f[x, y]$ |

Four ways to write expressions in *Mathematica*.

This "postfix form" is exactly equivalent to $f[x + y]$.

```
In[1]:= x + y //f
Out[1]= f[x + y]
```

You will often want to add functions like N as "afterthoughts", and give them in postfix form.

```
In[2]:= 3^(1/4) + 1   //N
Out[2]= 2.31607
```

It is sometimes easier to understand what a function is doing when you write it in infix form.

```
In[3]:= {a, b, c} ~Join~ {d, e}
Out[3]= {a, b, c, d, e}
```

You should notice that // has very low "precedence". If you put //*f* at the end of any expression containing arithmetic or logical operators, the *f* is applied to the *whole expression*. So, for example, x+y //f means f[x+y], not x+f[y].

The prefix form @ works differently. f @ x + y is equivalent to f[x] + y, not f[x + y]. You can write f[x + y] in prefix form as f @ (x + y).

## ■ 2.1.4 Applying Functions by Name

The "name" *f* of a function, like everything else in *Mathematica*, is just an expression. As a result, you can have functions that take as arguments the *names* of other functions.

Nest[*f*, *x*, *n*] takes the "name" *f* of a function, and applies the function *n* times to *x*.

```
In[1]:= Nest[f, x, 5]
Out[1]= f[f[f[f[f[x]]]]]
```

Apply lets you apply a function to a list of arguments.

```
In[2]:= Apply[f, {a, b, c}]
Out[2]= f[a, b, c]
```

This gives the sum of the elements in a list.

```
In[3]:= Apply[Plus, {a, b, c}]
Out[3]= a + b + c
```

| Apply[*f*, *list*] | apply the function *f* to the elements in a list |
| Nest[*f*, *x*, *n*] | apply the function *f* nested *n* times to *x* |

Applying named functions to expressions.

## ■ 2.1.5  Applying Functions to Parts of Expressions

In an expression like f[{a, b, c}], the function f is applied to the *whole* of the list {a, b, c}. Often you will instead want to apply the function separately to *each* element in a list. You can do this using Map.

| | |
|---|---|
| This applies f separately to each element in the list. | *In[1]:=* Map[f, {a, b, c}] |
| | *Out[1]=* {f[a], f[b], f[c]} |
| | |
| This applies f to the whole list {a, b, c}. | *In[2]:=* f[{a, b, c}] |
| | *Out[2]=* f[{a, b, c}] |
| | |
| There are, however, some mathematical functions in *Mathematica* that automatically apply themselves to each element in a list. | *In[3]:=* Log[{a, b, c}] |
| | *Out[3]=* {Log[a], Log[b], Log[c]} |

You can use Map to apply a function to parts of any expression, not just lists.

| | |
|---|---|
| This applies f to each element of the sum. | *In[4]:=* Map[f, a + b + c] |
| | *Out[4]=* f[a] + f[b] + f[c] |
| | |
| Factor does not work its way inside the g. | *In[5]:=* Factor[ g[-1 + x^2, -1 + x^3] ] |
| | *Out[5]=* g[-1 + x$^2$, -1 + x$^3$] |
| | |
| You can use Map to apply Factor separately to each argument of g. | *In[6]:=* Map[Factor, %] |
| | *Out[6]=* g[(-1 + x) (1 + x), (-1 + x) (1 + x + x$^2$)] |

Map[*f*, *expr*] applies *f* to the "first level" of parts in *expr*. You can use MapAll[*f*, *expr*] to apply *f* to *all* the parts of *expr*.

| | |
|---|---|
| This defines a 2 × 2 matrix m. | *In[7]:=* m = {{a, b}, {c, d}} |
| | *Out[7]=* {{a, b}, {c, d}} |

Map applies f to the first level of m, in this case the rows of the matrix.

```
In[8]:= Map[f, m]
Out[8]= {f[{a, b}], f[{c, d}]}
```

MapAll applies f at *all* levels in m. If you look carefully at this expression, you will see an f wrapped around every part.

```
In[9]:= MapAll[f, m]
Out[9]= f[{f[{f[a], f[b]}], f[{f[c], f[d]}]}]
```

You can use **Map** and **MapAll** to apply either standard built-in *Mathematica* functions, or functions that you have defined yourself.

This defines a function of one argument which takes the first two elements of a list.

```
In[10]:= take2[list_] := Take[list, 2]
```

This applies take2 to each sublist.

```
In[11]:= Map[take2, {{a, b, c}, {c, a, b}, {c, c, a}}]
Out[11]= {{a, b}, {c, a}, {c, c}}
```

Sometimes you may find yourself defining a new function just in order to be able to use its name in **Map** or **MapAll**. Section 2.1.12 will show how to avoid this by using "pure functions" which do not have explicit names.

| | |
|---|---|
| Map[*f*, *expr*] | apply *f* to each part of the first level in *expr* |
| MapAll[*f*, *expr*] | apply *f* to all parts in *expr* |

Applying functions to parts of expressions.

## ■ 2.1.6  Advanced Topic: Shorter Forms for Function Application

| | |
|---|---|
| *f* @ *expr* | *f* [*expr*] |
| *f* @@ *expr* | Apply[*f*, *expr*] |
| *f* /@ *expr* | Map[*f*, *expr*] |
| *f* //@ *expr* | MapAll[*f*, *expr*] |

Shorter forms for function application.

This uses the whole object {x, y} as an argument to f, as discussed in Section 2.1.3.

```
In[1]:= f @ {x, y}
Out[1]= f[{x, y}]
```

This *applies* f to {x, y}, giving a result in which f has two arguments.

```
In[2]:= f @@ {x, y}
Out[2]= f[x, y]
```

This *maps* f over the elements of the list {x, y}.

```
In[3]:= f /@ {x, y}
Out[3]= {f[x], f[y]}
```

## ■ 2.1.7 Manipulating Expressions Like Lists

Since lists are just a particular kind of expression, it will come as no surprise that you can use most of the list manipulation functions from Section 1.7 on any expression.

Here is an expression that corresponds to a sum of terms.

```
In[1]:= t = 1 + x + x^2 + y^2
Out[1]= 1 + x + x^2 + y^2
```

Take[t, 2] takes the first two elements from t, just as if t were a list.

```
In[2]:= Take[t, 2]
Out[2]= 1 + x
```

Length gives the number of elements in t.

```
In[3]:= Length[t]
Out[3]= 4
```

This extracts the third part of t.

```
In[4]:= t[[3]]
Out[4]= x^2
```

You can use FreeQ[*expr*, *form*] to test whether *form* appears nowhere in *expr*.

```
In[5]:= FreeQ[t, x]
Out[5]= False
```

Here is a function with four arguments.

```
In[6]:= f[a, b, c, d]
Out[6]= f[a, b, c, d]
```

You can add an argument using Append.

```
In[7]:= Append[%, e]
Out[7]= f[a, b, c, d, e]
```

This reverses the arguments.

```
In[8]:= Reverse[%]
Out[8]= f[e, d, c, b, a]
```

There are a few extra functions that can be used with expressions, as discussed in Sections 2.4.5 and 2.4.6.

## ■ 2.1.8  Selecting Parts of Expressions Based on Criteria

Section 1.2.4 showed how you can pick out elements of lists based on their *positions*. Often, however, you will need to select elements based not on *where* they are, but rather on *what* they are.

Select[*list*, *f*] selects elements of *list* using the function *f* as a criterion. Select applies *f* to each element of *list* in turn, and keeps only those for which the result is True.

| | |
|---|---|
| This defines gt4 to test whether an expression is greater than 4. | *In[1]:=* gt4[e_] := e > 4 |
| This selects the elements of the list for which gt4 yields True, *i.e.* those which are numerically greater than 4. | *In[2]:=* Select[{2, 15, 1, a, 16, 17}, gt4]<br>*Out[2]=* {15, 16, 17} |

You can use Select to pick out pieces of any expression, not just elements of a list.

| | |
|---|---|
| This defines the function xfree[e] to give True if the symbol x does not appear anywhere in *e*. | *In[3]:=* xfree[e_] := FreeQ[e, x] |
| This gives a sum of terms involving x, y and z. | *In[4]:=* t = Expand[(x + y + z)^2]<br>*Out[4]=* $x^2 + 2 x y + y^2 + 2 x z + 2 y z + z^2$ |
| You can use Select to pick out only those terms in the sum that do involve the symbol x. | *In[5]:=* Select[t, xfree]<br>*Out[5]=* $y^2 + 2 y z + z^2$ |

| | |
|---|---|
| Select[*expr*, *f*] | select the elements in *expr* for which the function *f* gives True |

Selecting pieces of expressions.

Section 2.3.2 discusses some "predicates" that are often used as criteria in Select.

## ■ 2.1.9  Advanced Topic: Expressions as Trees

The expression x^3 + (1 + x)^2 consists of several nested pieces. Written out in full form, the expression is Plus[Power[x, 3], Power[Plus[1, x], 2]]. You can think of nested expressions like this as having a "tree" structure. (If you are familiar with "parse trees", you will notice the analogy with the structure of expressions.)

TreeForm prints out expressions to show their "tree" structure.

```
In[1]:= TreeForm[x^3 + (1 + x)^2]

Out[1]//TreeForm= Plus[|                    , |                         ]
                          Power[x, 3]    Power[|          , 2]
                                                Plus[1, x]
```

The top node in the tree consists of a `Plus`. From this node come two "branches", `x^3` and `(1 + x)^2`. From the `x^3`, there are then two other branches, `x` and `3`, which can be viewed as "leaves" of the tree.

All *Mathematica* expressions can be viewed as trees, although the trees are often quite complicated.

This matrix is a simple tree with just two levels.

```
In[2]:= TreeForm[{{a, b}, {c, d}}]

Out[2]//TreeForm= List[|              , |             ]
                         List[a, b]   List[c, d]
```

Here is a more complicated expression.

```
In[3]:= {{a b, c d^2}, {x^3 y^4}}

Out[3]= {{a b, c d }, {x  y }}
                   2      3  4
```

The tree for this expression has several levels. The representation of the tree here was too long to fit on a single line, so it had to be broken in two.

```
In[4]:= TreeForm[%]

Out[4]//TreeForm=
        List[|                                                       ,
              List[|                , |                             ]
                    Times[a, b]    Times[c, |              ]
                                              Power[d, 2]

              |                                 ]
        List[|                                ]
              Times[|              , |             ]
                     Power[x, 3]    Power[y, 4]
```

## ■ 2.1.10  Advanced Topic: Levels in Expressions

`Map` applies functions at the first level in expressions; `MapAll` applies functions at all levels. Sometimes you may need finer control over where functions are applied.

Looking at the trees that correspond to expressions, one can define a general notion of "levels" in expressions. The level of a particular part of an expression is simply the distance down the tree at which that expression occurs. (The top of the tree is considered to be level 0.)

| | |
|---|---|
| Map[*f*, *expr*, *n*] | apply *f* at all levels down to *n* in *expr* |
| Map[*f*, *expr*, {*n*}] | apply *f* just at level *n* in *expr* |

Applying functions to various levels in expressions.

Here is a sample expression.

$In[1] := t = \{\{a \ b, \ c \ d \wedge 2\}, \ \{x \wedge 3 \ y \wedge 4\}\}$

$Out[1] = \{\{a \ b, \ c \ d^2\}, \ \{x^3 \ y^4\}\}$

You can see the different levels in t from the tree form.

$In[2] := \text{TreeForm}[t]$

$Out[2]//TreeForm=$

```
    List[|
        List[|               , |                         ]
            Times[a, b]  Times[c, |                   ]
                                  Power[d, 2]

        |                                              ]
        List[|
            Times[|           , |                 ]
                  Power[x, 3]  Power[y, 4]
```

This applies f at level 1, just as Map[f, t] would.

$In[3] := \text{Map}[f, t, 1]$

$Out[3] = \{f[\{a \ b, \ c \ d^2\}], \ f[\{x^3 \ y^4\}]\}$

This applies f to level 2. Notice that f is nested exactly two deep.

$In[4] := \text{Map}[f, t, 2]$

$Out[4] = \{f[\{f[a \ b], \ f[c \ d^2]\}], \ f[\{f[x^3 \ y^4]\}]\}$

This applies f *only* at level 2.

$In[5] := \text{Map}[f, t, \{2\}]$

$Out[5] = \{\{f[a \ b], \ f[c \ d^2]\}, \ \{f[x^3 \ y^4]\}\}$

When you have got the hang of ordinary levels, you can try thinking about *negative levels*. Negative levels label parts of expressions starting at the bottom of the tree. Level –1 contains all the "leaves" of the tree: objects like symbols and numbers.

This applies f to parts at the bottom level of the t tree.

$In[6] := \text{Map}[f, t, \{-1\}]$

$Out[6] = \{\{f[a] \ f[b], \ f[c] \ f[d]^{f[2]}\}, \ \{f[x]^{f[3]} \ f[y]^{f[4]}\}\}$

You can think of expressions as having a "depth", equal to the maximum number of levels shown by TreeForm. In general, level –*n* in an expression is defined to consist of all subexpressions whose depth is *n*.

| | |
|---|---|
| Depth[*expr*] gives the "depth" of an expression. | *In[7]:=* **Depth[x^2]** |
| | *Out[7]=* 2 |

This applies f to all parts of t that have "depth" 3. You may have to look quite carefully at this result to see exactly how it works.

*In[8]:=* **Map[f, t, {-3}]**

*Out[8]=* {{a b, f[c d$^2$]}, {f[x$^3$ y$^4$]}}

| | |
|---|---|
| **Depth[*expr*]** | the total number of levels in *expr* |
| **Level[*expr*, *lev*]** | a list of the parts of *expr* at the levels specified by *lev* |

Testing and extracting levels.

Level gives a list of all parts of an expression at particular levels. The parts of t at level -1 are all symbols or numbers.

*In[9]:=* **Level[t, {-1}]**

*Out[9]=* {a, b, c, d, 2, x, 3, y, 4}

This gives a list of the parts of t strictly at level -2.

*In[10]:=* **Level[t, {-2}]**

*Out[10]=* {a b, d$^2$, x$^3$, y$^4$}

Here are the parts of t on levels 2 and below.

*In[11]:=* **Level[t, {2, Infinity}]**

*Out[11]=* {a, b, a b, c, d, 2, d$^2$, c d$^2$, x, 3, x$^3$, y, 4, y$^4$, x$^3$ y$^4$}

Here are the parts whose level specifications are between 2 and -2, inclusive.

*In[12]:=* **Level[t, {2, -2}]**

*Out[12]=* {a b, d$^2$, c d$^2$, x$^3$, y$^4$, x$^3$ y$^4$}

| | |
|---|---|
| *n* | levels 1 through *n* |
| **Infinity** | all levels |
| **{*n*}** | level *n* only |
| **{*n$_1$*, *n$_2$*}** | levels *n$_1$* through *n$_2$* |

Level specifications.

## ■ 2.1.11  Advanced Topic: Parts of Expressions

There are many times when you need to pick out or modify particular parts of an expression. The easiest way to do this, if your computer system allows it, is to select the parts graphically, using a pointing device such as a mouse.

If, however, your computer does not support this kind of interaction, or if you need to do these operations as part of a program, then you will need to read the rest of this section.

Section 1.2.4 described how you can pick out parts of lists by giving their integer "indices". The same approach can be used for arbitrary expressions, where now the indices label branches on the expression tree.

Picking out parts of arbitrary expressions is often much more complicated than picking out parts of lists. The problem is that the standard printed form of an expression may not correspond very closely to its tree representation. In setting up the printed form to mimic mathematical notation, the parts often get rearranged.

For small expressions, you can use `TreeForm[`*expr*`]` to see the explicit tree structure. For larger expressions, `FullForm[`*expr*`]` shows the arrangement of parts.

| | |
|---|---|
| Here is an expression. | *In[1]:=* t = 1 + (3 + x)^2 / y |
| | *Out[1]=* $1 + \dfrac{(3 + x)^2}{y}$ |
| This picks out the second term of t. | *In[2]:=* t[[2]] |
| | *Out[2]=* $\dfrac{(3 + x)^2}{y}$ |
| `FullForm` shows that the actual arrangement of parts in t is slightly different from what the usual printed form suggests. | *In[3]:=* FullForm[t] |
| | *Out[3]//FullForm=* |
| | Plus[1, Times[Power[y, -1], Power[Plus[3, x], 2]]] |
| Knowing the actual arrangement of parts, it is straightforward to pick out a particular piece. This finds the first subpart of t[[2]]. | *In[4]:=* t[[2,1]] |
| | *Out[4]=* $\dfrac{1}{y}$ |
| This finds the part labeled by indices 2, 1, 1. | *In[5]:=* t[[2,1,1]] |
| | *Out[5]=* y |

This is what happens if you ask for a part that does not exist.

$In[6]:=$ `t[[7]]`

$$\text{Part::width: Part 7 of } 1 + \frac{(3 + x)^2}{y} \text{ does not exist.}$$

$$Out[6]= (1 + \frac{(3 + x)^2}{y})[[7]]$$

You can think of the indices for a particular part in an expression as specifying the branches you need to take in order to get to that part by descending from the node of the tree.

You can reset parts of expressions in the same way as you reset parts of lists.

This resets a part of t.

$In[7]:=$ `t[[2,1,1]] = x`

$Out[7]=$ `x`

Now the form of t has been changed.

$In[8]:=$ `t`

$$Out[8]= 1 + \frac{(3 + x)^2}{x}$$

You can find out the indices for parts with a particular form using the function **Position**.

This gives a list of the indices for the positions of the two x's that appear in t.

$In[9]:=$ `Position[t, x]`

$Out[9]=$ `{{2, 1, 1}, {2, 2, 1, 2}}`

One way to apply a function to a particular part of an expression is to pick out that part, and then reset it to the result obtained by applying the function. An alternative is to use `MapAt`, which allows you to give the indices for a list of parts to which to apply a function.

This applies f to two parts of t.

$In[10]:=$ `MapAt[f, t, {{2, 1, 1}, {2, 2}}]`

$$Out[10]= 1 + \frac{f[(3 + x)^2]}{f[x]}$$

You have to use a nested list even if you only want to apply f to a single part. (A single list {2, 1, 1} would be ambiguous.)

$In[11]:=$ `MapAt[f, t, {{2, 1, 1}}]`

$$Out[11]= 1 + \frac{(3 + x)^2}{f[x]}$$

Section 1.2.4 discussed how you can use lists of indices to pick out several elements of a list at a time. You can use the same procedure to pick several parts in an expression at a time.

| | |
|---|---|
| This picks out elements 2 and 4 in the list, and gives a list of these elements. | `In[12]:= {a, b, c, d, e}[[{2, 4}]]`<br>`Out[12]= {b, d}` |
| This picks out parts 2 and 4 of the sum, and gives a *sum* of these elements. | `In[13]:= (a + b + c + d + e)[[{2, 4}]]`<br>`Out[13]= b + d` |

Any part in an expression can be viewed as being an argument of some function. When you pick out several parts by giving a list of indices, the parts are combined using the same function as in the expression.

| | |
|---|---|
| `expr[[n]]` | the $n^{\text{th}}$ part of *expr* |
| `expr[[-n]]` | the $n^{\text{th}}$ part, counting from the end |
| `expr[[n_1, n_2, ...]]` | the part of *expr* labeled by indices from the tree |
| `expr[[n]] = value` | reset part of an expression |
| `MapAt[f, expr, {{n_1, n_2, ...}, {m_1, m_2, ...}, ...}]` | apply *f* to a list of parts of *expr* |
| `Position[expr, form]` | find the positions of parts matching *form* in *expr* |
| `expr[[{n_1, n_2, ...}]]` | give a combination of several parts of an expression |

Functions for manipulating parts of expressions.

## ■ 2.1.12  Pure Functions

When you do an operation like `Map[f, expr]`, you have to specify a function *f* to apply. If there is already a function that does exactly what you want, then you can just give its name. Often, however, you may end up defining functions simply in order to use their names in `Map`.

| | |
|---|---|
| This defines a function h. | `In[1]:= h[x_] := f[x] + g[x]` |
| Now you can use h in Map. | `In[2]:= Map[h, {a, b, c}]`<br>`Out[2]= {f[a] + g[a], f[b] + g[b], f[c] + g[c]}` |

This section discusses a way to avoid defining functions like h simply in order to use their names in Map.

The function h in the example takes an argument $x$ and returns the result f[$x$] + g[$x$]. If we are only going to use h in Map, its actual name is quite irrelevant. We could avoid explicitly defining h at all if we had some object that would simply compute f[$x$] + g[$x$] when applied to any expression. We could then give this object, rather than h, to Map.

The object Function[x, f[x] + g[x]] plays the role of a "pure function" in *Mathematica*. This object can be applied to any argument $a$, to give the result f[$a$] + g[$a$].

This computes f[$x$] + g[$x$] for each element in the list.

```
In[3]:= Map[ Function[x, f[x] + g[x]], {a, b, c} ]
Out[3]= {f[a] + g[a], f[b] + g[b], f[c] + g[c]}
```

You can use Function to specify any kind of operation. For example, Function[z, z^2] corresponds to the operation of squaring an expression.

This applies the pure function Function[z, z^2] to the argument 1 + a.

```
In[4]:= Function[z, z^2] [1 + a]
Out[4]= (1 + a)²
```

You can treat a Function just like any other kind of expression.

```
In[5]:= t = Function[z, z^2]
Out[5]= Function[z, z²]
```

Now t stands for the pure function Function[z, z^2], so this gives the square of the argument 1 + a.

```
In[6]:= t[1 + a]
Out[6]= (1 + a)²
```

You can specify any operation as a "pure function" in the form Function[*variable*, *operation*]. Whenever you provide an argument for the pure function, it substitutes the argument for *variable*, and performs the *operation*. (If you know LISP or formal logic, you will recognize Function as being analogous to a $\lambda$ expression. It is also close to the mathematical notion of an "operator".)

You can specify any operation as a pure function.

```
In[7]:= Function[e, Expand[e^2]] [ 1 + x ]
Out[7]= 1 + 2 x + x²
```

You can use Function whenever you need to give a function.

```
In[8]:= Select[ {1, 7, 8, 2, 9}, Function[n, n > 4] ]
Out[8]= {7, 8, 9}
```

| | |
|---|---|
| `Function[`*variable, operation*`]` | a pure function that performs the operation on any argument you provide |
| `Function[{`$x_1$`,` $x_2$`, ...},` *operation*`]` | |
| | a pure function that can take several arguments |

A way to represent functions without giving them names.

The pure functions we have discussed so far take just one argument. You can also set up pure functions that can take several arguments.

This pure function expects two arguments.

```
In[9]:= t = Function[{x, y}, x + 2 y]
Out[9]= Function[{x, y}, x + 2 y]
```

a is substituted for x, and b for y, in the pure function.

```
In[10]:= t[a, b]
Out[10]= a + 2 b
```

If you give too many arguments, the remaining ones are ignored.

```
In[11]:= t[a, b, c]
Out[11]= a + 2 b
```

If you give too few arguments, you get a message.

```
In[12]:= t[a]
Function::count:
      Too many parameters {x, y} to be filled from
        Function[{x, y}, x + 2 y][a].
Out[12]= a + 2 y
```

## ■ 2.1.13  Advanced Topic: Shorter Forms for Pure Functions

By using pure functions, you can avoid giving explicit names to functions. You can also avoid giving names to the variables or "formal parameters" that appear in these functions.

It is clear that the actual name x of the variable in the pure function `Function[x, x∧2]` is entirely irrelevant. You can get a shorter form for the pure function by using the special object `#` as the variable, instead of the named symbol x. When `#` appears in a pure function, *Mathematica* assumes that it is the variable, without you explicitly saying so. As a result, `Function[#∧2]` is equivalent to `Function[x, x∧2]`.

The special object `#` is assumed to be the variable in the pure function `Function[#∧2]`.

```
In[1]:= Function[#∧2] [1 + a]
                    2
Out[1]= (1 + a)
```

You can save even more typing by using a & instead of spelling out `Function`. The form *operation*& is equivalent to `Function[operation]`.

| | |
|---|---|
| #∧2& is equivalent to `Function[x, x∧2]`. | *In[2]:=* **#∧2& [1 + a]** |
| | *Out[2]=* $(1 + a)^2$ |
| Using # and & allows for some very compact notation. | *In[3]:=* **Map[#∧2&, {a, b, c}]** |
| | *Out[3]=* $\{a^2, b^2, c^2\}$ |

| | | |
|---|---:|---|
| | **#** | the first variable in a pure function |
| | **#***n* | the $n^{\text{th}}$ variable |
| | **##** | the sequence of all variables in a pure function |
| | **##***n* | the sequence of variables, starting with the $n^{\text{th}}$ one |
| | *operation*& | short form for `Function[operation]`; never forget the & when using this form |

Short forms for pure functions.

| | |
|---|---|
| Here is a pure function with two arguments. | *In[4]:=* **(#1∧2 + #2∧2)& [x, y]** |
| | *Out[4]=* $x^2 + y^2$ |
| ## stands for *all* the arguments you give. | *In[5]:=* **f[##, ##]& [x, y]** |
| | *Out[5]=* **f[x, y, x, y]** |

## ■ 2.1.14  Advanced Topic: Making Lists out of Functions

| | |
|---|---|
| Array[f, n] | generate a length n list of the form {f[1], f[2], ...} |
| Array[f, {n₁, n₂, ...}] | generate a $n_1 \times n_2 \times$ ... nested list, each of whose entries consists of f applied to its indices |
| NestList[f, x, n] | generate a list of the form {x, f[x], f[f[x]], ...}, where f is nested up to n deep |
| Accumulate[f, list] | cumulatively applies f to pairs of elements in *list* |

Making lists from functions.

This makes a list of 5 elements, each of the form p[i].

```
In[1]:= Array[p, 5]
Out[1]= {p[1], p[2], p[3], p[4], p[5]}
```

Here is another way to produce the same list.

```
In[2]:= Table[p[i], {i, 5}]
Out[2]= {p[1], p[2], p[3], p[4], p[5]}
```

This produces a list whose elements are $i + i^2$.

```
In[3]:= Array[Function[i, i + i^2], 5]
Out[3]= {2, 6, 12, 20, 30}
```

This generates a 2 × 3 matrix whose entries are m[i, j].

```
In[4]:= Array[m, {2, 3}]
Out[4]= {{m[1, 1], m[1, 2], m[1, 3]},
        {m[2, 1], m[2, 2], m[2, 3]}}
```

This produces a list of the first four "iterates" of f. The list includes the argument x itself, and so has length 5.

```
In[5]:= NestList[f, x, 4]
Out[5]= {x, f[x], f[f[x]], f[f[f[x]]], f[f[f[f[x]]]]}
```

This gives a list of the first three iterated derivatives of $x^n$.

```
In[6]:= NestList[Function[y, D[y, x]], x^n, 3]
```
$$Out[6]= \{x^n, n\, x^{-1 + n}, n\, x^{-2 + n}\,(-1 + n),$$
$$n\, x^{-3 + n}\,(-2 + n)\,(-1 + n)\}$$

Functions like `NestList` and `Map` allow you to apply functions to single expressions. `Array` and `Apply` can deal with sequences of any number of expressions. `Accumulate` is intended specifically for dealing with functions that take exactly two arguments.

Here is a list of four elements.

```
In[7]:= Range[4]
Out[7]= {1, 2, 3, 4}
```

This shows the result of "accumulating" f over the list.

```
In[8]:= Accumulate[f, %]
Out[8]= {1, f[1, 2], f[f[1, 2], 3], f[f[f[1, 2], 3], 4]}
```

If you accumulate Plus over a list, you get a list of cumulative sums.

```
In[9]:= Accumulate[Plus, Range[5]]
Out[9]= {1, 3, 6, 10, 15}
```

## ■ 2.1.15 Advanced Topic: Applying Functions with Side Effects

| | |
|---|---|
| Scan[*f, expr*] | evaluates *f* applied to each element of *expr* in turn |
| Scan[*f, expr, lev*] | evaluates *f* applied to parts of *expr* on levels specified by *lev* |

Evaluating functions on parts of expressions.

Here is a list of three elements.

```
In[1]:= t = {a, b, c}
Out[1]= {a, b, c}
```

Map constructs a new list in which f has been applied to each element of t.

```
In[2]:= Map[f, t]
Out[2]= {f[a], f[b], f[c]}
```

Scan evaluates the result of applying a function to each element, but does not construct a new expression.

```
In[3]:= Scan[Print, t]

a
b
c
```

Functions like Map allow you to create expressions with parts modified. Sometimes you simply want to go through an expression, applying a particular function to some parts of it, but not building a new expression. A typical case is when the function you apply has certain "side effects", such as making assignments, or generating output.

Scan visits the parts of an expression in a depth-first walk, with the leaves visited first.

```
In[4]:= Scan[Print, 1 + x^2, Infinity]

1
x
2
 2
x
```

You can use Return to stop scanning the expression tree.

```
In[5]:= Scan[(Print[#]; If[# > 2, Return[found]])&,
            {1, 2, 3, 4}]
1
2
3

Out[5]= found
```

# ■ 2.2 Transformation Rules and Definitions

## ■ 2.2.1 Evaluating Expressions

The operation of *Mathematica* can be summarized by saying that when you type in an expression, *Mathematica evaluates* it to give you a result. The process of evaluation can involve many different kinds of operations. If you typed in the expression 6 + 7, evaluation would consist in applying a procedure for adding integers, to give you the result 13. If you typed in x - 3x + 1, rules for simplification would be applied to give you the result 1 - 2x. If you had set x = 5, then x would be replaced by 5, and 1 - 2x would be reduced to -9.

Section 2.1 discussed how all the different kinds of objects that *Mathematica* deals with are represented in one uniform way: as expressions. The operations that *Mathematica* performs to evaluate expressions can also be viewed in a uniform way. All the operations consist of applying *transformation rules* to change expressions from one form to another.

There are many different kinds of transformation rules. Section 1.4.1 mentioned some rules that *Mathematica* uses to carry out algebraic simplifications on sums of terms. Definitions of functions can also be thought of as rules. So, for example, f[x_] := x^2 can be thought of as defining a rule for transforming all expressions of the form f[*anything*]. Later, we will discuss how you can add many different kinds of transformation rules to *Mathematica*.

When *Mathematica* evaluates an expression, it goes on applying transformation rules until it can find no more rules to apply. The *result* of the evaluation is the expression produced at this point.

The result of a particular evaluation depends on the transformation rules that *Mathematica* "knows" when it does the evaluation. If you add new rules, *Mathematica* may be able to take the evaluation of a particular expression further.

When *Mathematica* evaluates an expression like 2 + x, its first step is to try and find any value that you may have defined for x. Assuming there is no value for x, *Mathematica* then tries to find transformation rules for the expression 2 + x. None of the rules for sums of terms discussed in Section 1.4.1 apply, so the expression 2 + x will be the final result. If you subsequently assigned a value to x, this expression could be evaluated further. Without a value specified for x, *Mathematica* will, however, give the "symbolic" result 2 + x, which involves the "undetermined parameter" x. As we have discussed at some length, one of the most crucial features of *Mathematica* is its ability to produce this kind of symbolic result.

If you type in the expression f[3], *Mathematica* will again try to find rules to evaluate it. If you had given a definition for f[x_], then *Mathematica* would use this definition. But if it can find no such definition, *Mathematica* leaves the expression f[3] unchanged, just as it leaves the symbol x unchanged in 2 + x.

| | |
|---|---|
| *Mathematica* evaluates 3 + 5 to give 8, but can then find no rules for f[8], so leaves it unchanged. | `In[1]:= f[3 + 5]`<br>`Out[1]= f[8]` |

| | |
|---|---|
| *Mathematica* finds no rules for f[*anything*], but still applies algebraic simplification rules to collect together the f[4] terms. | `In[2]:= f[4] + 3 f[4] + 2 f[5]`<br>`Out[2]= 4 f[4] + 2 f[5]` |

| | |
|---|---|
| Once again f is treated as an "unknown function". | `In[3]:= t = f[2] + f[x]`<br>`Out[3]= f[2] + f[x]` |

| | |
|---|---|
| This specifies a transformation rule for f[*anything*]. | `In[4]:= f[x_] = x^2`<br>`Out[4]= x`$^2$ |

| | |
|---|---|
| Now the expression t defined above can be evaluated further, using the transformation rule you have defined for f[x_]. | `In[5]:= t`<br>`Out[5]= 4 + x`$^2$ |

## ■ 2.2.2 Specifying Transformation Rules

There are many kinds of transformation rules built into *Mathematica*. These include rules for doing arithmetic, rules for simplifying algebraic expressions, rules for differentiation, and so on.

Perhaps *Mathematica*'s most powerful feature is that you can add your own rules to supplement, or even override, the ones that are built in. You can "teach" *Mathematica* about new kinds of functions and objects by giving it the rules it needs to manipulate them.

As Section 1.3 discussed, there is a growing library of packages which contain the rules needed for many different kinds of *Mathematica* applications.

We have already discussed two simple kinds of transformation rules that you can set up in *Mathematica*. When you define the value of a "variable", say x = 1 - b, you are specifying the transformation rule that whenever x appears, it is to be replaced by 1 - b. When you define a "function", say f[x_] = x^2, you are specifying the transformation rule that any expression of the form f[*anything*] should be replaced by *anything*^2.

*Mathematica* allows you to specify very general kinds of transformation rules for expressions. You can essentially define any expression to have any value.

| | |
|---|---|
| This sets the expression `f[6]` to have value 14. It specifies the rule that whenever `f[6]` appears, it is to be replaced by 14. | *In[1]:=* `f[6] = 14`<br><br>*Out[1]=* `14` |
| `f[6]` is replaced according to the rule you have just defined. No rule is known for `f[7]`, so it is left unchanged. | *In[2]:=* `a f[6] + b f[7]`<br><br>*Out[2]=* `14 a + b f[7]` |
| You can also specify a rule for `f[a]`. | *In[3]:=* `f[a] = 8a`<br><br>*Out[3]=* `8 a` |
| If you ask about `f`, *Mathematica* shows you all the rules that have been defined for it. | *In[4]:=* `?f`<br>`f`<br>`f/: f[6] = 14`<br><br>`f/: f[a] = 8 a` |
| Now `f[a]` is replaced using the rule that has been defined. There is no rule known for `f[b]`. | *In[4]:=* `f[a] + f[b]`<br><br>*Out[4]=* `8 a + f[b]` |

In the sections that follow, we will discuss how to define and use transformation rules for various kinds of expressions.

### ■ 2.2.3 Indexed Variables

One simple way to set up an "array" in *Mathematica* is to create an explicit list of elements. You can define a list, say `a = {x, y, z}`, then access the elements using `a[[i]]`. One problem with this approach is that you have to fill in all the elements of the list when you first create it. You cannot just fill in the elements you need at a particular time.

You can use transformation rules to set up objects like arrays in a somewhat more flexible fashion.

The idea is simply to define values for expressions like `a[i]`. You can fill in these values when you want to, in any order.

| | |
|---|---|
| This defines a value for `a[1]`. | *In[1]:=* `a[1] = 9`<br><br>*Out[1]=* `9` |

| | |
|---|---|
| This defines a value for a[2]. | *In[2]:=* **a[2] = 7** |
| | *Out[2]=* 7 |

This shows all the values you have defined
for expressions associated with a so far.

*In[3]:=* **?a**

a
a/: a[1] = 9
a/: a[2] = 7

You can define a value for a[5], even
though you have not yet given values to
a[3] and a[4].

*In[3]:=* **a[5] = 0**

*Out[3]=* 0

Defining values for a[i] does not affect the
value of a itself.

*In[4]:=* **a**

*Out[4]=* a

This generates an explicit list of the values
of the a[i].

*In[5]:=* **Table[a[i], {i, 5}]**

*Out[5]=* {9, 7, a[3], a[4], 0}

Here is another way to make the same list.

*In[6]:=* **Array[a, 5]**

*Out[6]=* {9, 7, a[3], a[4], 0}

You can think of a[i] as being like an "indexed" or "subscripted" variable.
(Section 2.6.7 describes how to make $i$ actually print as a subscript.)

| | |
|---|---|
| a[*i*] = *value* | add or overwrite a value |
| a[*i*] | access a value |
| a[*i*] =. | remove a value |
| ?a | show all defined values |
| Clear[a] | clear all defined values |
| Table[a[i], {i, 1, *n*}] or Array[a, *n*] | |
| | convert to an explicit List |

Manipulating indexed variables.

## ■ 2.2.4  Symbolic Indices

You can think of an expression such as a[k] as being like an "indexed variable",
where instead of being a number, the index is now the symbol k.

| | |
|---|---|
| This defines a value for a[k]. | *In[1]:=* **a[k] = 4** |
| | *Out[1]=* 4 |

| | |
|---|---|
| You can define values for a[*i*] with other "indices", symbolic or numerical. | *In[2]:=* **a[0] = a[kp] = 0** |
| | *Out[2]=* 0 |

| | |
|---|---|
| This shows all the values associated with a so far. | *In[3]:=* **?a** |
| | a |
| | a/: a[k] = 4 |
| | a/: a[kp] = 0 |
| | a/: a[0] = 0 |

You can use definitions for objects with symbolic indices to build up simple "databases".

| | |
|---|---|
| This defines the "object" **area** with "index" **square** to have value 1. | *In[3]:=* **area[square] = 1** |
| | *Out[3]=* 1 |

| | |
|---|---|
| This adds another result to the **area** "database". | *In[4]:=* **area[triangle] = 1/2** |
| | *Out[4]=* $\dfrac{1}{2}$ |

| | |
|---|---|
| Here are the entries in the **area** database so far. | *In[5]:=* **?area** |
| | area |
| | area/: area[square] = 1 |
| | area/: area[triangle] = $\dfrac{1}{2}$ |

| | |
|---|---|
| You can use these definitions wherever you want. You have not yet assigned a value for area[pentagon]. | *In[5]:=* **4 area[square] + area[pentagon]** |
| | *Out[5]=* 4 + area[pentagon] |

## ■ 2.2.5  Using Rules to Define Functions

Section 1.6.1 discussed how you can define *functions* in *Mathematica*. In a typical case, you would type in f[x_] = x^2 to define a function f. (Actually, the definitions in Section 1.6 used the := operator, rather than the = one. Section 2.2.10 will explain exactly when to use := and =.)

A definition like f[x_] = x^2 can be thought of as a transformation rule. The definition specifies that whenever an expression of the form f[*anything*] occurs, it is to be replaced by *anything*∧2.

This kind of "function definition" can be compared with the definitions like f[a] = b for "indexed variables" discussed in the last section. A definition like f[a] = b specifies that whenever the *particular* expression f[a] occurs, it is to be replaced by b. But the definition says nothing about expressions like f[y], where f appears with another "index".

To define a "function", you need to specify values for expressions of the form f[x], where the "argument" x can be *any* expression. This is what the _ (pronounced "blank") in f[x_] means. The _ stands for *any expression*. You can think of it as a "blank space", where any expression could be inserted.

The pattern x_ also stands for any expression, but gives the expression the *name* x. Now you can understand how f[x_] = x∧2 specifies a transformation rule for all expressions of the form f[*anything*]. The *anything* is referred to as x, so the result *anything*∧2 is written as x∧2.

| | |
|---|---|
| f[x] = *value* | definition for a *specific expression* x |
| f[x_] = *value* | definition for *any expression*, referred to as x |

The difference between defining an indexed variable and a function.

Making definitions for f[2] or f[a] can be thought of as being like giving values to various elements of an "array" named f. Making a definition for f[x_] is like giving a value for a set of "array elements" with arbitrary "indices". In fact, you can actually think of any function as being like an array with an arbitrarily-variable index.

In mathematical terms, you can think of f as a *mapping*. When you define values for, say, f[1] and f[2], you specify the image of this mapping for various discrete points in its domain. Defining a value for f[x_] specifies the image of f on a continuum of points.

Since definitions for objects f[1], f[a] and f[x_] are all just treated as transformation rules, you can mix these definitions in any way.

This defines a transformation rule for the *specific expression* f[x].

```
In[1]:= f[x] = u
Out[1]= u
```

When the specific expression f[x] appears, it is replaced by u. Other expressions of the form f[*argument*] are, however, not modified.

```
In[2]:= f[x] + f[y]
Out[2]= u + f[y]
```

This defines a value for f with *any* *expression* as an "argument".

In[3]:= f[x_] = x^2

$$Out[3]= x^2$$

The old definition for the *specific* *expression* f[x] is still used, but the new general definition for f[x_] is now used to find a value for f[y].

In[4]:= f[x] + f[y]

$$Out[4]= u + y^2$$

This removes all definitions for f.

In[5]:= Clear[f]

It is very convenient to define mathematical functions using transformation rules. An example is the factorial function. This function is in fact built in to *Mathematica* (it is written n!). However, as an illustration, we will show how you could define the function for yourself.

The mathematical definition of the factorial function is: $f(1) = 1$; $f(n) = n\,f(n-1)$. This mathematical definition can immediately be thought of in terms of transformation rules. For any $n$, $f(n)$ should be replaced by $n\,f(n-1)$, except that $f(1)$ should simply be replaced by 1.

You can enter the mathematical definition of factorial almost directly into *Mathematica*, in the form: f[1] = 1;   f[n_]  := n f[n-1].

The exact distinction between = and := will be discussed in Section 2.2.10. For now, a good procedure is to use := whenever there is a _, and = when there is not.

Here is the value of the factorial function with argument 1.

In[6]:= f[1] = 1

Out[6]= 1

Here is the general recursion relation for the factorial function.

In[7]:= f[n_]  := n f[n-1]

Now you can use these definitions to find values for the factorial function.

In[8]:= f[10]

Out[8]= 3628800

The results are the same as you get from the built-in version of factorial.

In[9]:= 10!

Out[9]= 3628800

This shows the definitions made for your factorial function f. Notice that the definition for the specific expression f[1] comes before the general definition for f[n_].

In[10]:= ?f

```
f
f/: f[1] = 1

f/: f[n_] := n f[n - 1]
```

The example of the factorial function illustrates several important points.

When you enter the expression `f[10]`, *Mathematica* follows its general principle of applying transformation rules until no more rules apply. Its first step is to apply the rule `f[n_] := n f[n-1]` to get the result `10 f[9]`. Then it applies this rule eight more times to the succession of expressions `f[9]`, `f[8]`, etc. Finally, the expression `f[1]` is generated. Now *Mathematica* applies the rule `f[1] = 1`. Collecting all the intermediate terms together, it gets the final result `3628800`.

An important point is that *Mathematica* tries to apply the specific rule for `f[1]` *before* it applies the general rule for `f[n_]`.

This is an example of a principle that *Mathematica* follows. When you give a sequence of transformation rules, *Mathematica* arranges them so that the *most specific rules come first*. Then, when it tries to apply the rules, it tests them in order. If a specific rule does apply, then it is used; only if none of the specific rules apply will the later, more general, rules be used. If *Mathematica* cannot decide whether a new rule is more or less specific than the ones it already knows, it puts the new rule at the end of the list.

For the factorial function, the "end condition" `f[1] = 1` is a specific rule, which is placed before the general rule `f[n_] := n f[n-1]`. The order in which *Mathematica* puts the rules does not depend on the order in which you typed the definitions for `f[1]` and `f[n_]`.

Many mathematical functions can conveniently be defined by giving a few special cases, and then a general formula. Often, as for the factorial function, the general formula will be *recursive*, in the sense that it defines one instance of the function in terms of other instances of the same function.

Whenever you have a recursive formula, you must be careful to make sure that you specify all the necessary "end conditions". If you forgot to give the value of `f[1]` for the factorial function, then evaluating `f[10]` would lead to an infinite sequence of `f`'s, with successively more negative arguments. If *Mathematica* gets into this kind of infinite loop, you can always stop it by making an interrupt as discussed in Section 1.3.6. You can then type in the end conditions, and try the computation again.

## ■ 2.2.6  A First Encounter with Patterns

The `x_` that appears in `f[x_]` is an example of an important kind of object in *Mathematica* known as a *pattern*. Patterns are a way of representing *classes of expressions* in *Mathematica*. A single pattern can stand for a whole class of possible expressions. By giving transformation rules for patterns, you can define rules for classes of expressions.

The basic object that appears in *Mathematica* patterns is _ (pronounced "blank"). The fundamental rule is that _ *stands for any expression*. As an example, the pattern f[_] can thus stand for any expression of the form f[*anything*]. The pattern x^_ could stand for any power of x. The pattern _^_ represents any power of any expression.

In general, a pattern can stand for a particular expression if there is a way of "filling in the blanks" (_ objects) in the pattern so as to get the expression. _^_ stands for (1 + x)^3 because the first _ can be filled in with 1 + x and the second one with 3.

Each time a particular pattern is used, say in a transformation rule, _ can stand for a different expression. In one case, _ might stand for a + b; in another 2 - a. It is often convenient to name the expression that _ stands for in a particular case.

The pattern x_ can again stand for any expression, but now the expression is given the *name x*. You can use the symbol x to represent the expression, say on the right-hand side of a definition.

| | |
|---|---|
| f[n_] | f with any "argument", named n |
| f[n_, m_] | f with two arguments, named n and m |
| x^n_ | x to any power, with the power named n |
| x_^n_ | any expression to any power |
| a_ + b_ | a sum of two expressions |
| {a1_, a2_} | a list of two expressions |
| f[n_, n_] | f with two *identical* arguments |

Some examples of patterns.

| | |
|---|---|
| This defines a rule for g when its argument is a power. | *In[1]:=* g[x_^y_] := y h[x] |
| This uses the rule for g. | *In[2]:=* g[(1 + x)^2] |
| | *Out[2]=* 2 h[1 + x] |
| Here is a more complicated transformation rule. | *In[3]:=* g[(x_ + y_)^n_ + c_] := n hp[x, y] + c |

| | |
|---|---|
| This uses the more complicated transformation rule. | *In[4]:=* `g[(a + b)∧3 + x∧2]`<br><br>*Out[4]=* $x^2$ + 3 hp[a, b] |

When you have a pattern in which a named blank such as `n_` occurs several times, the blank must stand for the *same expression* each time. As a result, a pattern like `f[n_,n_]` can stand for `f[a+b, a+b]`, but not for `f[a, b]`.

| | |
|---|---|
| This defines a value for `f` with two identical arguments. | *In[5]:=* `f[n_, n_] := 2n` |
| This defines a value for the general case of two arbitrary arguments. | *In[6]:=* `f[n_, m_] := g[n+m]` |
| This shows the values defined for `f`. Notice that the more specific case with two identical arguments is given first. | *In[7]:=* `?f`<br><br>`f`<br>`f/: f[n_, n_]  :=  2 n`<br><br>`f/: f[n_, m_]  :=  g[n + m]` |
| With two identical arguments, the first rule for `f` is used. | *In[7]:=* `f[1 + x, 1 + x]`<br><br>*Out[7]=* `2 (1 + x)` |
| With different arguments, the second rule is used. | *In[8]:=* `f[1 - x, 1 + x]`<br><br>*Out[8]=* `g[2]` |

## ■ 2.2.7  Specifying Mathematical Relations

One of the most important ways you can use transformation rules for patterns is to specify *mathematical relations*. If you look through a handbook of mathematics, you will find many formulae that give relations between mathematical functions.

One such mathematical relation might be $\log(\exp(x)) = x$.

You can interpret this relation as being a transformation rule for a pattern. It states that whenever you have an expression of the form `log[exp[`*anything*`]]`, it can be "simplified" to *anything*.

You can enter this transformation rule almost directly into *Mathematica*, just by giving the definition `log[exp[x_]]  := x`.

| | |
|---|---|
| This specifies a relation for the logarithm function. | *In[1]:=* `log[exp[x_]]  := x` |

Now the relation is used to "simplify" expressions involving `log`.

```
In[2]:= log[exp[y^2+1]]

Out[2]= 1 + y
          2
```

You can now go on and add other transformation rules for the `log` function.

Two standard mathematical relations for logarithm functions are: $\log(xy) = \log(x) + \log(y)$; $\log(x^n) = n \log(x)$.

Once again, these relations can be entered almost directly into *Mathematica* as transformation rules for patterns: `log[x_ y_] := log[x] + log[y]`; `log[x_^n_] := n log[x]`.

This gives the rule for expanding logarithms of products.

```
In[3]:= log[x_ y_] := log[x] + log[y]
```

Here is the rule for logarithms of powers.

```
In[4]:= log[x_^n_] := n log[x]
```

This shows all the rules defined for `log`.

```
In[5]:= ?log

log
log/: log[exp[x_]]  := x
log/: log[(x_) (y_)] := log[x] + log[y]

                n_
log/: log[(x_)  ]  := n log[x]
```

This is "simplified" using the rule for logarithms of powers.

```
In[5]:= log[(1+x)^5]
Out[5]= 5 log[1 + x]
```

This is simplified using the rule for logarithms of products. The rule gives the expansion for a product of just two expressions, so it had to be applied three times in this case.

```
In[6]:= log[a b c d]

Out[6]= log[a] + log[b] + log[c] + log[d]
```

Here is a more complicated example. The various transformation rules you have defined for `log` are each used several times to get the final result.

```
In[7]:= log[(1+x)^2 y^2] + log[x^3 (1-y)^4] +
            log[exp[a b] x^2]

Out[7]= a b + 5 log[x] + 2 log[y] + 2 log[1 + x] +
         4 log[1 - y]
```

These examples begin to show the power of "mathematical programming" in *Mathematica*. Section 2.3 gives some more details of how to use patterns in specifying mathematical relations. Section 4.1 discusses the general methodology of "mathematical programming".

## ■ 2.2.8 Giving Rules for Built-in Functions

The last few sections have discussed how you can specify rules for functions that you introduce into *Mathematica*.

You can use exactly the same methods to add new transformation rules for functions that are already built in to *Mathematica*. This capability is powerful, but potentially dangerous. *Mathematica* will always follow the rules you give it. This means that if the rules you give are incorrect, then *Mathematica* will give you incorrect answers.

To avoid the possibility of changing built-in functions by mistake, *Mathematica* "protects" all built-in functions from redefinition. If you want to give a definition for a built-in function, you have to remove the protection first. After you give the definition, you should usually restore the protection, to prevent future mistakes.

| | |
|---|---|
| `Unprotect[`*f*`]` | remove protection |
| `Protect[`*f*`]` | add protection |

Protection for functions.

Built-in functions are usually "protected", so you cannot redefine them.

```
In[1]:= Log[7] = 2
Set::write: Symbol Log is write protected.
Out[1]= 2
```

This removes protection for Log.

```
In[2]:= Unprotect[Log]
Out[2]= {Log}
```

Now you can give your own definitions for Log. This particular definition is not mathematically correct, but *Mathematica* will still allow you to give it.

```
In[3]:= Log[7] = 2
Out[3]= 2
```

*Mathematica* will use your definitions whenever it can, whether they are mathematically correct or not.

```
In[4]:= Log[7] + Log[3]
Out[4]= 2 + Log[3]
```

This removes the incorrect definition for Log.

```
In[5]:= Log[7] =.
```

This restores the protection for Log.

```
In[6]:= Protect[Log]
Out[6]= {Log}
```

You can define your own rules to add new features and capabilities to existing built-in functions.

There is no transformation rule for logarithms of products built in to *Mathematica*.

```
In[7]:= Log[a b c]

Out[7]= Log[a b c]
```

You can add the rule yourself. You need to unprotect Log before making the assignment.

```
In[8]:= (
   Unprotect[Log] ;
   Log[x_ y_] := Log[x] + Log[y] ;
   Protect[Log]
   )

Out[8]= {Log}
```

Now *Mathematica* knows how to expand out logarithms of products.

```
In[9]:= Log[a b c]

Out[9]= Log[a] + Log[b] + Log[c]
```

?Log just gives you a message about the built-in Log function.

```
In[10]:= ?Log

Log[z] gives the natural logarithm of z (logarithm to
   base E). Log[b, z] gives the logarithm to base b.
```

??Log shows you all the information *Mathematica* has about Log, including the transformation rule you just added.

```
In[10]:= ??Log

Log[z] gives the natural logarithm of z (logarithm to
   base E). Log[b, z] gives the logarithm to base b.
Attributes[Log] = {Listable, Protected}
Log/: Log[(x_) (y_)] := Log[x] + Log[y]
```

You can also set up your own transformation rules that override some of the rules built into *Mathematica*. *Mathematica* always tries to use your rules *before* it uses built-in ones.

There is a built-in rule for simplifying Log[Exp[*expr*]].

```
In[10]:= Log[Exp[y]]

Out[10]= y
```

You can give your own rule for Log[Exp[*expr*]].

```
In[11]:= (
   Unprotect[Log] ;
   Log[Exp[expr_]] := logexp[expr] ;
   Protect[Log] ;
   )
```

Your rule overrides the built-in one.

```
In[12]:= Log[Exp[y]]

Out[12]= logexp[y]
```

The transformation rules that are built in to *Mathematica* are intended to be appropriate for the broadest possible range of calculations. You may find cases, however, where you do not like what the built-in rules do. In such cases, you can always give your own rules to override the ones that are built in.

### ■ 2.2.9  Making Replacements for Patterns

You can think of a mathematical relation as being a statement that two mathematical expressions are equal. So, for example, the trigonometric formula $\sin(2x) = 2\sin(x)\cos(x)$ states that the sine of a double angle is equal to a product of trigonometric functions.

From a formula like this, you can derive several different transformation rules for trigonometric functions. Two of the possible rules are:
`Sin[2 x_] -> 2 Sin[x] Cos[x]` and `Sin[x_] Cos[x_] -> Sin[2 x] / 2`.

These rules effectively use the trigonometric formula "in opposite directions". Depending on exactly what calculation you are doing, you may want to use either one of these rules.

Making a *Mathematica definition* such as `Sin[2 x_] := 2 Sin[x] Cos[x]`, specifies that *whenever* an expression of the form `Sin[2 x_]` is encountered, it should be replaced by `2 Sin[x] Cos[x]`. Often, however, you do not want a transformation like this to be made in such an automatic way. Instead, you may simply want to set up the rule, and then apply it only "on request".

You can use *replacements* to specify transformation rules that are to be made in this kind of controlled way. Section 1.4.4 discussed making replacements for symbols. Like definitions, replacements in *Mathematica* can be made for any kinds of expression, including a pattern.

| | |
|---|---|
| Here is an expression involving trigonometric functions. | `In[1]:= t = Sin[2 x] + Sin[2 y z] + Sin[z]`<br>`Out[1]= Sin[2 x] + Sin[z] + Sin[2 y z]` |
| This makes a replacement for expressions that match the pattern `Sin[2 x_]`. | `In[2]:= t /. Sin[2 x_] -> 2 Sin[x] Cos[x]`<br>`Out[2]= 2 Cos[x] Sin[x] + Sin[z] + 2 Cos[y z] Sin[y z]` |
| This makes a replacement for all expressions of the form `Sin[x_]`. | `In[3]:= t /. Sin[x_] -> 2 Sin[x/2] Cos[x/2]`<br>`Out[3]= 2 Cos[x] Sin[x] + 2 Cos[`$\frac{z}{2}$`] Sin[`$\frac{z}{2}$`] +`<br>     `2 Cos[y z] Sin[y z]` |

You will often find it convenient to give "names" to transformation rules that you are going to use in replacements.

| This assigns the "name" `sinexp` to the transformation rule. | `In[4]:= sinexp = Sin[2 x_] -> 2 Sin[x] Cos[x]`<br><br>`Out[4]= Sin[2 (x_)] -> 2 Cos[x] Sin[x]` |
|---|---|
| The value of `sinexp` is the transformation rule. | `In[5]:= sinexp`<br><br>`Out[5]= Sin[2 (x_)] -> 2 Cos[x] Sin[x]` |
| Now the rule can be requested "by name". | `In[6]:= Sin[2 (1 + x)^2] /. sinexp`<br><br>`Out[6]= 2 Cos[(1 + x)^2] Sin[(1 + x)^2]` |

| *pattern* := *value* | define a transformation rule to be used automatically |
|---|---|
| *rule* = *pattern* -> *value* | give a name to a transformation rule |
| *expression* /. *rule* | apply a named rule |

Functions for setting up replacements.

You can also use replacements for patterns to do some simple kinds of "mathematical editing" on expressions. For example, you can drop all terms of the form x^_ in a sum, just by applying a rule that replaces them with 0.

| This expression involves various powers of x. | `In[7]:= Expand[(1 + x + y)^3]`<br><br>`Out[7]= 1 + 3 x + 3 x^2 + x^3 + 3 y + 6 x y + 3 x^2 y +`<br><br>`       3 y^2 + 3 x y^2 + y^3` |
|---|---|
| Making this replacement drops all terms involving powers of x in the expression. | `In[8]:= % /. x^_ -> 0`<br><br>`Out[8]= 1 + 3 x + 3 y + 6 x y + 3 y^2 + 3 x y^2 + y^3` |

You should realize that the rules discussed here make transformations based on the *structure* of expressions. Section 3.4.10 discusses the function `AlgebraicRules`, which allows you to set up rules based directly on the *algebraic form* of expressions.

## ■ 2.2.10  Defining Functions with = and :=

You will have noticed that there are two different assignment operations in *Mathematica*, represented by the = and := operators.

The basic difference between = and := has to do with *when* the expression on the right-hand side of the assignment is evaluated.

| | |
|---|---|
| *lhs* = *rhs* (immediate assignment) | *rhs* is evaluated when the assignment is made |
| *lhs* := *rhs* (delayed assignment) | *rhs* is evaluated each time the value of *lhs* is requested |

The two types of assignments in *Mathematica*.

This makes a *delayed* assignment. Whenever f[x_] is evaluated, the current value of % at that time will be used.

```
In[1]:= f[x_] := % + 2x
```

Here is an expression.

```
In[2]:= 1 + y^2
```
$$Out[2]= 1 + y^2$$

This makes an *immediate* assignment. The current value 1 + y^2 is immediately used, so that the actual assignment done is effectively g[x_] = 1 + y^2 + 2x.

```
In[3]:= g[x_] = % + 2x
```
$$Out[3]= 1 + 2\ x + y^2$$

Here is an expression.

```
In[4]:= 2 + z
```
$$Out[4]= 2 + z$$

f uses the *current* value of %, here 2 + z. g uses the value of % from the time when the assignment was made.

```
In[5]:= {f[a], g[a]}
```
$$Out[5]= \{2 + 2\ a + z,\ 1 + 2\ a + y^2\}$$

You can see from this example that both = and := can be useful, but they mean different things, and you must be careful about which one you use in a particular case.

One rule of thumb is the following. If you think of an assignment as giving the "value" of an expression, use the = operator. If instead you think of the assignment as giving a "command" for finding the value, use the := operator.

This defines the function ex to execute the "command" Expand. Every time ex is evaluated, the "command" will be re-executed.

```
In[6]:= ex[x_] := Expand[(1 + x)^2]
```

The definition of ex maintains the Expand "command", ready for execution.

```
In[7]:= ?ex
```
```
ex
ex/: ex[x_] := Expand[(1 + x)^2]
```

Expand is called when the function ex is evaluated.

*In[7]:=* ex[y + 2]

*Out[7]=* 9 + 6 y + y$^2$

If you make the original assignment with =, then the expansion is carried out immediately.

*In[8]:=* iex[x_] = Expand[(1 + x)^2]

*Out[8]=* 1 + 2 x + x$^2$

The definition for iex now contains the expanded form. The Expand "command" is not maintained.

*In[9]:=* ?iex

iex

iex/: iex[x_] = 1 + 2 x + x$^2$

Now the expression 2 + y is simply substituted into the already expanded form 1 + 2 x + x^2. The Expand command is not re-executed.

*In[9]:=* iex[y + 2]

*Out[9]=* 1 + 2 (2 + y) + (2 + y)$^2$

| | |
|---|---|
| *lhs* = *rhs* | *rhs* is intended to be the "final value" of *lhs* (e.g. f[x_] = 1 - x^2) |
| *lhs* := *rhs* | *rhs* gives a "command" or "program" to be executed whenever you ask for the value of *lhs* (e.g. f[x_] := Expand[1 - x^2]) |

Interpretations of assignments with the = and := operators.

You will probably find that you use := more often than = in defining functions. If you are in doubt about which to use, it is probably better to try the := operator.

There is nevertheless one common situation where you need to use = to define a function. If you do a calculation, and get an answer in terms of a symbolic parameter, say x, you will often want to go on and find results for various specific values of x. One way to do this is to take your answer, and make a sequence of replacements for x in it. It is usually more convenient, however, to define a *function*, whose argument gives the value you want to use for x.

Here is an expression involving x.

*In[10]:=* D[Log[Sin[x]]^2, x]

$$Out[10]= \frac{2 \ Cos[x] \ Log[Sin[x]]}{Sin[x]}$$

This defines a *function* whose argument is the value to be taken for x.

```
In[11]:= dlog[x_] = %
          2 Cos[x] Log[Sin[x]]
Out[11]= ---------------------
                Sin[x]
```

This evaluates the expression taking x to be 2.5.

```
In[12]:= dlog[2.5]
Out[12]= 1.37446
```

Here x is taken to be 1 + a.

```
In[13]:= dlog[1 + a]
          2 Cos[1 + a] Log[Sin[1 + a]]
Out[13]= ----------------------------
                  Sin[1 + a]
```

An important point to notice in this example is that there is nothing "magical" about the name x that appears in the x_ pattern. It is just a symbol, and can be part of a result that you got in a completely different computation.

### ■ 2.2.11 Defining Functions that Remember Values They Have Found

When you make a function definition using :=, the value of the function is recomputed every time you ask for it. In some kinds of calculations, you may end up asking for the same function value many times. You can save time in these cases by having *Mathematica* remember all the function values it finds. Here is an "idiom" for defining a function that does this.

f[x_] := f[x] = *rhs*      define a function which remembers values that it finds

Defining a function that remembers values it finds.

This defines a function f which stores all values that it finds.

```
In[1]:= f[x_] := f[x] = f[x - 1] + f[x - 2]
```

Here are the end conditions for the recursive function f.

```
In[2]:= f[0] = f[1] = 1
Out[2]= 1
```

Here is the original definition of f.

```
In[3]:= ?f
f
f/: f[1] = 1
f/: f[0] = 1
f/: f[x_] := f[x] = f[x - 1] + f[x - 2]
```

This computes `f[5]`. The computation involves finding the sequence of values `f[5]`, `f[4]`, ... `f[2]`.

```
In[3]:= f[5]
Out[3]= 8
```

All the values of `f` found so far are explicitly stored.

```
In[4]:= ?f
f
f/: f[1] = 1
f/: f[0] = 1
f/: f[2] = 2
f/: f[3] = 3
f/: f[4] = 5
f/: f[5] = 8
f/: f[x_] := f[x] = f[x - 1] + f[x - 2]
```

If you ask for `f[5]` again, *Mathematica* can just look up the value immediately; it does not have to recompute it.

```
In[4]:= f[5]
Out[4]= 8
```

You can see how a definition like `f[x_] := f[x] = f[x-1] + f[x-2]` works. The function `f[x_]` is defined to be the "program" `f[x] = f[x-1] + f[x-2]`. When you ask for a value of the function `f`, the "program" is executed. The program first calculates the value of `f[x-1] + f[x-2]`, then saves the result as `f[x]`.

It is often a good idea to use functions that remember values when you implement mathematical *recursion relations* in *Mathematica*. In a typical case, a recursion relation gives the value of a function $f$ with an integer argument $x$ in terms of values of the same function with arguments $x - 1$, $x - 2$, etc. The Fibonacci function definition $f(x) = f(x-1) + f(x-2)$ used above is an example of this kind of recursion relation. The point is that if you calculate say $f(10)$ by just applying the recursion relation over and over again, you end up having to recalculate quantities like $f(5)$ many times. In a case like this, it is therefore better just to *remember* the value of $f(5)$, and look it up when you need it, rather than having to recalculate it.

There is of course a trade-off involved in remembering values. It is faster to find a particular value, but it takes more memory space to store all of them. You should usually define functions to remember values only if the total number of different values that will be produced is comparatively small.

Defining functions that remember values they have found is sometimes called "dynamic programming".

# ■ 2.2.12  Assigning Variables with = and :=

You will have noticed that the input and output lines in *Mathematica* are labeled respectively with `In[n]:=` and `Out[n]=`. We can now explain what these labels mean.

The basic point is that there are two "arrays", `In` and `Out`. Each input or output line is assigned as the value for an element in these arrays. As a result, you can manipulate `In[n]` and `Out[n]` just like any other subscripted variables. You can for example see all your output lines so far by typing `??Out`. (With most *Mathematica* front ends, you will be able to do this particular thing much more conveniently just by scrolling backwards.)

As their label indicates, output lines are given as immediate assignments for `Out[n]`. Input lines, on the other hand, are given as delayed assignments, using `:=`. This means that the "command" you give on each input line is maintained in an unevaluated form. If you ask for a particular line `In[n]` again, *Mathematica* will automatically re-execute the command that appeared on that line.

| | |
|---|---|
| Here is an expression. | `In[1]:= (x+1)^2` |
| | `Out[1]= (1 + x)`$^2$ |
| This input line gives the command to expand the latest expression generated. | `In[2]:= Expand[%]` |
| | `Out[2]= 1 + 2 x + x`$^2$ |
| Here is another expression. | `In[3]:= (1 + x + y)^2` |
| | `Out[3]= (1 + x + y)`$^2$ |
| This "re-executes" the command you typed in on line 2. Now % refers to the expression (1 + x + y)^2. | `In[4]:= In[2]` |
| | `Out[4]= 1 + 2 x + x`$^2$ ` + 2 y + 2 x y + y`$^2$ |

The difference between = and := assignments is just the same for single variables as for functions. If you type *x* = *value*, then *value* is immediately evaluated, and the result is assigned to the variable *x*. On the other hand, if you type *x* := *value*, then *value* is not immediately evaluated. Instead, it is evaluated afresh each time *x* is used.

The difference between = and := is particularly important when you set up chains of assignments that define values for a sequence of variables.

| | |
|---|---|
| This assigns a value to a. | *In[5]:=* **a = 1** |
| | *Out[5]=* 1 |

| | |
|---|---|
| This defines a *delayed value* for r. | *In[6]:=* **r := a + 2** |

| | |
|---|---|
| Every time you ask for r, the expression a + 2 is evaluated afresh, using whatever the current value of a is. | *In[7]:=* **r** |
| | *Out[7]=* 3 |

| | |
|---|---|
| This resets the value of a. | *In[8]:=* **a = 2** |
| | *Out[8]=* 2 |

| | |
|---|---|
| The new value of a is now used in finding the current value of r. | *In[9]:=* **r** |
| | *Out[9]=* 4 |

| | |
|---|---|
| This defines an *immediate value* for s. The expression a + 3 is immediately evaluated using the current value of a. The result is that s is simply assigned the value 5. | *In[10]:=* **s = a + 3** |
| | *Out[10]=* 5 |

| | |
|---|---|
| This changes the value of a again. | *In[11]:=* **a = 7** |
| | *Out[11]=* 7 |

| | |
|---|---|
| Once again, the value of r is found using the new value of a. | *In[12]:=* **r** |
| | *Out[12]=* 9 |

| | |
|---|---|
| s, on the other hand, was defined with an *immediate assignment*, so it still has its original value, and is unaffected by the change in the value of a. | *In[13]:=* **s** |
| | *Out[13]=* 5 |

When you use variables just to give names to intermediate results in your calculations, you will usually want to make immediate assignments, using the = operator.

You can use := to set up variables whose values you want to find in a variety of different "environments". You can make a delayed assignment for an object *t* using *t := value*. Then you can try out various different assignments for the objects on which *t* depends. Every time you ask for *t*, a new value for it is found, based on the current values of the objects on which it depends.

| | |
|---|---|
| This defines a delayed value for t. | *In[14]:=* **t := {a, Factor[x^a - d], Factor[x^a + d], d}** |

| | |
|---|---|
| This sets a to 2. | `In[15]:= a = 2`<br>`Out[15]= 2` |
| Now d is set to 1. | `In[16]:= d = 1`<br>`Out[16]= 1` |
| If you ask for t, you get the result with the current values of a and d. | `In[17]:= t`<br>`Out[17]= {2, (-1 + x) (1 + x), 1 + x`$^2$`, 1}` |
| This resets a. | `In[18]:= a = 4`<br>`Out[18]= 4` |
| This gives the result for t, based on the new value of a. | `In[19]:= t`<br>`Out[19]= {4, (-1 + x) (1 + x) (1 + x`$^2$`), 1 + x`$^4$`, 1}` |

The "variable" t in the example above is used much like a "function". In fact, you could have given all definitions in terms of a function t[ ], with no arguments, instead of in terms of a plain variable t. It is probably slightly clearer to use a variable rather than a function with no arguments.

There are some calculations where setting up a sequence of variables with delayed values that depend on other variables can be quite convenient. As a general matter, however, it is usually best to avoid setting things up so that one object has a "hidden", implicit, dependence on other objects. It is all too easy in cases like this just to forget about some dependence that exists.

It is usually much better to avoid dependence on "global variables", and instead to specify all dependences explicitly by having them appear as the arguments to functions.

## ■ 2.2.13  Setting up Rules with `->` and `:>`

Just as you can make both immediate and delayed definitions in *Mathematica*, you can also set up both immediate and delayed transformation rules.

| | |
|---|---|
| *lhs* `->` *rhs* | *rhs* is evaluated when the rule is given |
| *lhs* `:>` *rhs* | *rhs* is evaluated when the rule is used |

Two types of transformation rules in *Mathematica*.

You should use :> whenever you need to "execute a program" to evaluate the right-hand side of the transformation rule.

$$In[1]:= \texttt{t = f[(1+x)^2] + f[(1-x)^2] + g[(1+x)^2]}$$

$$Out[1]= \texttt{f[(1 - x)}^2\texttt{] + f[(1 + x)}^2\texttt{] + g[(1 + x)}^2\texttt{]}$$

This replacement executes the "program" f[Expand[x]] on each object of the form f[x_].

$$In[2]:= \texttt{t /. f[x_] :> f[Expand[x]]}$$

$$Out[2]= \texttt{f[1 - 2 x + x}^2\texttt{] + f[1 + 2 x + x}^2\texttt{] + g[(1 + x)}^2\texttt{]}$$

An immediate replacement would have performed the Expand when the replacement was first given, and in this case would not have done what you wanted.

$$In[3]:= \texttt{f[x_] -> f[Expand[x]]}$$

$$Out[3]= \texttt{f[x_] -> f[x]}$$

## ■ 2.2.14  Advanced Topic: Controlling the Action of Rules

When you make a replacement with *expr /. rules*, each of the rules is tried *only once*.

Sometimes you will need to go on trying rules over and over again, until the expression you are working on no longer changes. You can do this using *expr //. rules*. You can think of the notation //. as representing an extension of the standard /. notation for replacements.

The /. operator applies the rule only once.

$$In[1]:= \texttt{f[5] /. f[x_] -> x f[x-1]}$$

$$Out[1]= \texttt{5 f[4]}$$

//. goes on trying to apply the rules in order, until none of them apply any more.

$$In[2]:= \texttt{f[5] //. \{f[1] -> 1, f[x_] -> x f[x-1]\}}$$

$$Out[2]= \texttt{120}$$

Both *expr /. rules* and *expr //. rules* try to apply each rule to *every part* of the expression *expr*.

Sometimes, you may need to apply rules only to a specific part of an expression. Replace[*expr, rules*] tries to apply *rules* to the whole of *expr*; it does not apply the rules to any of the subparts of *expr*.

You can use Replace, together with Map and MapAt, to control exactly which parts of an expression a replacement is applied to.

| | |
|---|---|
| The operator /. tries to apply rules to all the parts of an expression. | *In[3]:=* **f[x]^2 /. f[x] -> a**<br><br>*Out[3]=* a$^2$ |
| Replace applies rules only to the whole expression. | *In[4]:=* **Replace[f[x]^2, f[x]^2 -> b]**<br>*Out[4]=* b |
| No replacement is done here. | *In[5]:=* **Replace[f[x]^2, f[x] -> a]**<br><br>*Out[5]=* f[x]$^2$ |

| | |
|---|---|
| *expr /. rules* | apply *rules* to all parts of *expr* just once |
| *expr //. rules* | apply *rules* to all parts of *expr* repeatedly, until the result no longer changes |
| Replace[*expr, rules*] | apply *rules* just once, to the whole of *expr* only |

Types of replacement.

### ■ 2.2.15  Advanced Topic: Associating Rules with Different Objects

When you make a definition like f[x_] = x^2, it is pretty clear that this should be associated with the "object" f, and, for example, displayed when you type ?f.

But what should a definition like g[x_] + g[y_] := g[x y] be associated with? The full form of the left-hand side is Plus[g[x_], g[y_]]. Looking at this form, one might think of associating the definition with Plus. The way *Mathematica* is set up, this would certainly work. However, it is not the best thing to do, either from the point of organization, or efficiency.

When you see a mathematical formula like $g(x) + g(y) = g(xy)$, you usually think of it as a relation concerning the object $g$, not a relation about addition. In this case, it would be more natural to associate a *Mathematica* definition such as g[x_] + g[y_] := g[x y] with g than with Plus.

| | |
|---|---|
| *g/: lhs := rhs* | define a transformation rule to be associated with the "object" *g* |

Defining a rule to be associated with a particular object.

| | |
|---|---|
| This rule is associated with f. | *In[1]:=* **f[g[x_], g[y_]] := rhs[x ,y]** |

| | |
|---|---|
| This shows the rules associated with f. | *In[2]:=* ?f |
| | f<br>f/: f[g[x_], g[y_]] := rhs[x, y] |
| The g/: tells *Mathematica* to associate this rule with g, rather than with Plus. | *In[2]:=* **g/: g[x_] + g[y_] := rhs[x, y]** |
| Here are the rules associated with g. | *In[3]:=* ?g |
| | g<br>g/: g[x_] + g[y_] := rhs[x, y] |
| The rule you gave is used. | *In[3]:=* g[a] + g[b] |
| | *Out[3]=* rhs[a, b] |
| You can also associate this rule with g. | *In[4]:=* **g/: f[g[x_], g[y_]] := rhs[x, y]** |
| Now both rules appear. | *In[5]:=* ?g |
| | g<br>g/: g[x_] + g[y_] := rhs[x, y]<br>g/: f[g[x_], g[y_]] := rhs[x, y] |

The ability to associate rules with different objects is very important when you use *Mathematica* expressions to represent "packets of data".

You might want to introduce a mathematical object called quat that has special addition and multiplication properties. One way to do this would be to set up special addition and multiplication functions for quat objects. A much more convenient way to do it, however, is to use the standard addition and multiplication functions, but to add special rules associated with quat objects.

Some rules you could add for quat objects would be quat/: quat[x_] + quat[y_] := *value* and quat/: quat[x_] quat[y_] := *value*. You can think of these rules as "extending the domain" of addition and multiplication to include quat objects.

(If you are familiar with other computer languages, you may think of quat as specifying a "type". Assignments associated with quat can then be used to "extend" or "overload" operators to allow for arguments of type quat. From the point of view of object-oriented systems, you could think of quat as corresponding to a type of "object". The definitions you give for quat then specify "methods" associated with different operations or "messages".)

Another case where you should use `/:` is in building up "databases" that give a variety of properties for a particular object. A sequence of definitions like `area[pentagon]` = *value*, `perimeter[pentagon]` = *value*, ..., could be associated with each of the quantities `area`, `perimeter`, and so on. It is much more natural, however, to use `/:` to associate all these definitions with the object `pentagon`.

| | |
|---|---|
| This associates the definition with the object `square`. | `In[5]:= square/: area[square] = 1`<br>`Out[5]= 1` |
| Here is another definition, again associated with `square`. | `In[6]:= square/: perimeter[square] = 4`<br>`Out[6]= 4` |
| Here are the definitions for `square` that you have given. | `In[7]:= ?square`<br>`square`<br>`square/: area[square] = 1`<br>`square/: perimeter[square] = 4` |

You can use `/:` to associate a particular assignment with any symbol that appears in the left-hand side. A very common case is one where the assignment should be associated with the argument $g$ in an expression like $f[g]$ or $f[g[arguments]]$. You can save typing $g/:$ by using the special assignment operators `^=` and `^:=`.

| | |
|---|---|
| $f[g]$ `^=`*value*   or   $f[g[args]]$ `^=`*value* | make assignments to be associated with $g$, rather than $f$ |
| $f[g]$ `^:=`*value*   or   $f[g[args]]$ `^:=`*value* | make delayed assignments associated with $g$ |
| $f[arg_1, arg_2, ...]$ `^=`*value* | make assignments associated with the heads of *all* the $arg_i$ |

Shorter ways to make assignments associated with function arguments.

| | |
|---|---|
| Using `^=` makes *Mathematica* associate the assignment with the argument `triangle`, rather than the function `area`. | `In[7]:= area[triangle] ^= 1/2`<br>$Out[7]= \dfrac{1}{2}$ |

If you have a function with several arguments, `^=` makes assignments associated with *each* of the arguments. This is particularly useful when all the arguments have the same head, as in the case of `quat[x_] + quat[y_] ^:=` *value*. You should be careful not to add extra definitions by mistake when different arguments have different heads.

## ■ 2.2.16  Defining Numerical Values

When you define a mathematical function, you will often want to give approximate numerical rules for it, as well as exact symbolic ones.

| | |
|---|---|
| N[*expr*] = *value* | define a numerical value |

Defining a numerical value.

This specifies an exact value for f[1].

```
In[1]:= f[1] = ax
Out[1]= ax
```

This defines an approximate numerical value for f[x_].

```
In[2]:= N[f[x_]] := N[Sum[x^-i/i^2, {i, 20}]]
```

Only the exact definition is automatically used.

```
In[3]:= f[1] + f[6]
Out[3]= ax + f[6]
```

This uses the numerical definition.

```
In[4]:= N[%]
Out[4]= 0.17418 + ax
```

The numerical definition is automatically associated with f, rather than N.

```
In[5]:= ?f
f
f/: f[1] = ax
                                 -i
                                x
f/: N[f[x_]] := N[Sum[---, {i, 20}]]
                                 2
                                i
```

## ■ 2.2.17  Advanced Topic: Reducing Expressions to Standard Form

The fact that addition is *associative* means that you can insert parentheses anywhere in a sum of terms, without changing the value of the sum. As a result, expressions like (a + b) + c, a + (b + c) and a + b + c, that have different parenthesization, are all mathematically equal. In many senses, however, the most "natural" form for all these expressions is the unparenthesized one a + b + c. You can think of this unparenthesized form as being the "standard" or "canonical" form for the sum of terms.

If you enter a sum of terms into *Mathematica*, it will always try to remove parentheses so as to reduce the sum to the standard form.

*Mathematica* removes the parentheses to give this sum in the standard, unparenthesized, form.

```
In[1]:= (a + b) + c
Out[1]= a + b + c
```

Whenever *Mathematica* knows that a function is associative, it tries to remove parentheses (or nested invocations of the function) to get the function into a standard "flattened" form.

A function like addition also has the property of being commutative, which means that expressions like a + c + b and a + b + c with terms in different orders must be equal. Once again, *Mathematica* tries to put all such expressions into a "standard" form. The standard form it chooses is the one in which all the terms are in a definite order, corresponding roughly to alphabetical order.

*Mathematica* sorts the terms in this sum into a standard order.

```
In[2]:= c + a + b
Out[2]= a + b + c
```

| | |
|---|---|
| flat (associative) | $f(f(a), b)$, etc. are equivalent to $f(a, b)$ |
| orderless (commutative) | $f(b, c, a)$, etc. are equivalent to $f(a, b, c)$ |

Two important properties that *Mathematica* uses in reducing functions to standard form.

There are several reasons to try and put expressions into standard forms. The most important is that if two expressions are really in standard form, it is obvious whether they are equal or not.

When the two sums are put into standard order, they are immediately seen to be equal, so that two **f**'s cancel, leaving the result 0.

```
In[3]:= f[a + c + b] - f[c + a + b]
Out[3]= 0
```

You could imagine finding out whether a + c + b was equal to c + a + b by testing all possible orderings of each sum. It is clear that simply reducing both sums to standard form is a much more efficient procedure.

One might think that *Mathematica* should somehow automatically reduce *all* mathematical expressions to a single standard canonical form. With all but the simplest kinds of expressions, however, it is quite easy to see that you do not want the *same* standard form for all purposes.

For polynomials, for example, there are two obvious standard forms, which are good for different purposes. The first standard form for a polynomial is a simple sum of terms, as would be generated in *Mathematica* by applying the function Expand. This standard form is most appropriate if you need to add and subtract polynomials.

There is, however, another possible standard form that you can use for polynomials. By applying Factor, you can write any polynomial as a product of irreducible factors. This canonical form is useful if you want to do operations like division.

Expanded and factored form are in a sense both equally good standard forms for polynomials. Which one you decide to use simply depends on what you want to use them for. As a result, *Mathematica* does not automatically put polynomials into one of these two forms. Instead, it gives you functions like Expand and Factor that allow you explicitly to put polynomials in whatever form you want.

| | |
|---|---|
| Here is a list of two polynomials that are mathematically equal. | $In[4]:=$ t = {x^2 - 1, (x + 1)(x - 1)} <br><br> $Out[4]=$ {-1 + x$^2$, (-1 + x) (1 + x)} |
| You can write both of them in expanded form just by applying Expand. In this form, the equality of the polynomials is obvious. | $In[5]:=$ Expand[t] <br><br> $Out[5]=$ {-1 + x$^2$, -1 + x$^2$} |
| You can also see that the polynomials are equal by writing them both in factored form. | $In[6]:=$ Factor[t] <br><br> $Out[6]=$ {(-1 + x) (1 + x), (-1 + x) (1 + x)} |

Although it is clear that you do not always want expressions reduced to the *same* standard form, you may wonder whether it is at least *possible* to reduce all expressions to *some* standard form.

There is a basic result in the mathematical theory of computation which shows that it is, in fact, not always possible. You cannot guarantee that any finite sequence of transformations will take any two arbitrarily chosen expressions to a standard form.

In a sense, this is not particularly surprising. If you could in fact reduce all mathematical expressions to a standard form, then it would be quite easy to tell whether any two expressions were equal. The fact that so many of the difficult problems of mathematics can be stated as questions about the equality of expressions suggests that this is not always easy.

# ■ 2.2.18  Advanced Topic: Specifying Attributes

In addition to defining explicit transformation rules, *Mathematica* allows you to specify certain *attributes*, which describe "general properties" of functions. You should be careful to set up any attributes you need for a particular function *before* you try to give transformation rules for it. *Mathematica* needs to know the attributes that a function has in order to set the transformation rules correctly.

| | |
|---|---|
| `Attributes[f]` | give the attributes of $f$ |
| `Attributes[f] = {`$attr_1$`, `$attr_2$`, ...}` | set the attributes of $f$ |
| `Attributes[f] = {}` | set $f$ to have no attributes |
| `SetAttributes[f, attr]` | add *attr* to the attributes of $f$ |
| `ClearAttributes[f, attr]` | remove *attr* from the attributes of $f$ |
| `Orderless` | commutative function (arguments are sorted into standard order, and $f[a, b]$ is equivalent to $f[b, a]$ etc. in pattern matching) |
| `Flat` | associative function (arguments are "flattened out", and $f[f[a, b], c]$ is equivalent to $f[a, b, c]$ etc.) |
| `OneIdentity` | $f[f[a]]$ etc. are equivalent to $a$ for pattern matching |
| `Listable` | $f$ is automatically "threaded" over lists that appear as arguments (e.g. $f[\{a,b\}]$ becomes $\{f[a], f[b]\}$) |
| `Constant` | all derivatives of $f$ are zero |
| `Protected` | values of $f$ cannot be changed |
| `Locked` | attributes of $f$ cannot be changed |
| `ReadProtected` | values of $f$ cannot be read |
| `HoldFirst` | the first argument of $f$ is not evaluated |
| `HoldRest` | all but the first argument of $f$ is not evaluated |
| `HoldAll` | all the arguments of $f$ are not evaluated |

The complete list of attributes for symbols in *Mathematica*.

Many built-in functions have attributes; you should not try to modify them.

*In[1]:=* **Attributes[Plus]**

*Out[1]=* {Flat, Listable, OneIdentity, Orderless, Protected}

This defines a new function f to be "orderless" or commutative.

*In[2]:=* **SetAttributes[f, Orderless]**

Now the arguments of f are automatically sorted into standard order.

*In[3]:=* **f[b, a, c, a]**

*Out[3]=* f[a, a, b, c]

This defines g to be an associative and commutative function.

*In[4]:=* **SetAttributes[g, {Flat, Orderless}]**

The nested g's are flattened out, and the arguments are sorted.

*In[5]:=* **g[g[b, a], c, g[a]]**

*Out[5]=* g[a, a, b, c]

This defines a transformation rule for g.

*In[6]:=* **g[x_, x_] := dg[x]**

The attributes of g are used in applying the transformation rule.

*In[7]:=* **g[a,b,a,c,d]**

*Out[7]=* g[b, c, d, dg[g[a]]]

You can get rid of the g nested inside the dg by setting g to have the attribute OneIdentity.

*In[8]:=* **SetAttributes[g, OneIdentity]**

After you change its attributes, you should clear any values you defined for g.

*In[9]:=* **Clear[g]**

Now you must redo the definitions.

*In[10]:=* **g[x_, x_] := dg[x]**

With the attribute OneIdentity set, the nested g is gone.

*In[11]:=* **g[a,b,a,c,d]**

*Out[11]=* g[b, c, d, dg[a]]

This shows the definitions for g, including Attributes.

*In[12]:=* **?g**

```
g
Attributes[g] = {Flat, OneIdentity, Orderless}
g/: g[x_, x_] := dg[x]
```

This defines h to be Listable.

*In[12]:=* **SetAttributes[h, Listable]**

Now h is automatically "threaded" over lists.

```
In[13]:= h[{a, b}, {c, d}, e]
Out[13]= {h[a, c, e], h[b, d, e]}
```

This defines c to be a constant in differentiation.

```
In[14]:= SetAttributes[c, Constant]
```

c is now treated as a constant.

```
In[15]:= Dt[c x^2 + b + c, x]
Out[15]= 2 c x + Dt[b, x]
```

This stops values of i from being set or changed. You can also set the Protected attribute for a symbol simply by calling Protect[s].

```
In[16]:= SetAttributes[i, Protected]
```

Now you cannot set values of i. Unless you set the Locked attribute, you can always go back and remove the Protected attribute.

```
In[17]:= i = 7
Set::write: Symbol i is write protected.
Out[17]= 7
```

This makes the first argument of j not be evaluated.

```
In[18]:= SetAttributes[j, HoldFirst]
```

The first argument of j is not evaluated.

```
In[19]:= j[1 + 1, 1 + 1]
Out[19]= j[1 + 1, 2]
```

This function resets the value of its argument to special. You need to set the HoldFirst attribute of j to make sure its argument is not evaluated before being used in the assignment.

```
In[20]:= j[v_] := v = special
```

## ■ 2.2.19  Advanced Topic: How Evaluation Works

Evaluate the head of the expression.

Evaluate each element in turn.

Reorder, thread over lists, or flatten, if the function requires it.

Apply any rules you have specified.

Apply any built-in rules.

Evaluate the result.

The standard evaluation procedure for *Mathematica* expressions.

*Mathematica* goes through essentially the same evaluation procedure for any expression. Here is a simple example, where we assume that `a = 7`.

| | |
|---|---|
| `2 a x + a^2 + 1` | here is the original expression |
| `Plus[Times[2, a, x], Power[a, 2], 1]` | this is the internal form |
| `Times[2, a, x]` | this is evaluated first |
| `Times[2, 7, x]` | a is evaluated to give 7 |
| `Times[14, x]` | rules for `Times` give this result |
| `Power[a, 2]` | this is evaluated next |
| `Power[7, 2]` | here is the result after evaluating `a` |
| `49` | rules for `Power` give this result |
| `Plus[Times[14, x], 49, 1]` | here is the result after the arguments of `Plus` have been evaluated |
| `Plus[50, Times[14, x]]` | rules for `Plus` give this result |
| `50 + 14 x` | the result is printed like this |

A simple example of evaluation in *Mathematica*.

You can watch some of the evaluation process in *Mathematica* by switching on "tracing" using the command `On[ ]`.

First set a to 7.

```
In[1]:= a = 7
Out[1]= 7
```

Now switch on tracing.

```
In[2]:= On[ ]
```

This shows the stages in the evaluation procedure.

```
In[3]:= 2 a x + a^2 + 1
a::trace: a —> 7.
Times::trace: 2 7 x —> 14 x.
a::trace: a —> 7.
                 2
Power::trace: 7  —> 49.
Plus::trace: 14 x + 49 + 1 —> 1 + 49 + 14 x.
Plus::trace: 1 + 49 + 14 x —> 50 + 14 x.
Out[3]= 50 + 14 x
```

This switches off trace messages.

```
In[4]:= Off[ ]
```

## The Order of Rule Application

*Mathematica* stores rules associated with a particular object in a definite order. What order the rules are in will depend on the order in which you entered them, and on what reorderings were made by Set. You can find out what order the rules for a particular object are in by typing ?*f*. (If *f* has a usage message, you will have to type ??*f* to see the actual rules defined for *f*.)

When *Mathematica* evaluates an expression, it tries each of the rules associated with the expression in turn, and returns the result from the first rule that applies.

With an expression like *f*[*g*[x]], however, there are two possible sets of rules that can apply: those associated with *f*, and those associated with *g*. In a case like this, *Mathematica* follows the principle of *first* trying rules associated with *g*, and then, only if none of these apply, trying rules associated with *f*.

The general goal is to apply specific transformation rules before general ones. By applying rules associated with the arguments of a function before rules associated with the function itself, *Mathematica* allows you to give rules for special arguments that override the general rules for evaluation of the function with any arguments.

This defines a rule for f[g[x_]], to be associated with f.

```
In[1]:= f/: f[g[x_]] := frule[x]
```

| | |
|---|---|
| This defines a rule for `f[g[x_]]`, associated with g. | *In[2]:=* `g/: f[g[x_]] := grule[x]` |

| | |
|---|---|
| The rule associated with g is tried before the rule associated with f. | *In[3]:=* `f[g[2]]`<br>*Out[3]=* `grule[2]` |

| | |
|---|---|
| If you remove rules associated with g, the rule associated with f is used. | *In[4]:=* `Clear[g] ;   f[g[1]]`<br>*Out[4]=* `frule[1]` |

> Rules associated with *g* are applied before rules associated with *f* in the expression *f*[*g*[*x*]].

The order in which rules are applied.

*Mathematica* usually applies any built-in transformation rules for a particular object *after* it applies rules that you have explicitly given. *Mathematica* therefore evaluates an expression like *f*[*g*[*x*]] in four stages:

- Apply rules you have given associated with *g*;

- Apply built-in rules associated with *g*;

- Apply rules you have given associated with *f*;

- Apply built-in rules associated with *f*.

The fact that *Mathematica* applies rules associated with *g* before those associated with *f* in an expression like *f*[*g*[*x*]] is important for a number of purposes.

Given a rather generic operation such as composition, you may want to define special cases for particular kinds of objects. You will, however, usually also want to give general rules, in this example for the composition operation, to be used if none of the special cases apply.

| | |
|---|---|
| Here is a definition associated with q for composition of "q objects". | *In[5]:=* `q/: comp[q[x_], q[y_]] := qcomp[x, y]` |

| | |
|---|---|
| Here is a general rule for composition, associated with `comp`. | *In[6]:=* `comp[f_[x_], f_[y_]] := gencomp[f, x, y]` |

| | |
|---|---|
| If you compose two q objects, the rule associated with q is used. | *In[7]:=* `comp[q[1], q[2]]`<br>*Out[7]=* `qcomp[1, 2]` |

If you compose r objects, the general rule associated with comp is used.

```
In[8]:= comp[r[1], r[2]]
Out[8]= gencomp[r, 1, 2]
```

## Non-Standard Argument Evaluation

The standard *Mathematica* scheme for evaluating a function is first to evaluate the arguments to the function, and then to evaluate the function itself. There are some functions, however, that do not use this standard scheme. Instead, they either do not evaluate their arguments at all, or evaluate them in a special way that they themselves control.

Assignment functions are one example. If you type a = 1, the a on the left-hand side is not evaluated before the assignment is performed. You can see that there would be trouble if the a were to be evaluated. For example, you might previously have made the assignment a = 7. Then, if the a in a = 1 was evaluated, you would get the nonsensical expression 7 = 1.

Control structures are another important example of functions that evaluate their arguments in non-standard ways. For example, Do[*expr*, {*n*}] maintains *expr* in an unevaluated form, so that it can explicitly evaluate *expr* *n* separate times.

Hold is the prototypical example of a function that does not evaluate its arguments.

```
In[1]:= Hold[1 + 1]
Out[1]= Hold[1 + 1]
```

You can use hold to maintain an expression in unevaluated form, then evaluate it using Release.

```
In[2]:= Release[%]
Out[2]= 2
```

Functions that use non-standard argument evaluation carry attributes like HoldAll, which effectively specify that certain arguments are to be treated as if they were enclosed in Hold functions, and therefore to be left unevaluated. You can override the implicit Hold by giving function arguments of the form Release[*arg*].

| | |
|---|---|
| *f*[Release[*arg*]] | evaluate *arg* immediately, even though the attributes of *f* specify that it should be held |

Overriding non-standard argument evaluation.

The presence of the Release overrides the non-standard argument evaluation usually used by Hold.

```
In[3]:= Hold[Release[1 + 1]]
Out[3]= Hold[2]
```

This assigns a to have value b. The
left-hand side of an assignment like this is
not usually evaluated.

*In[4]:=* **a = b**

*Out[4]=* **b**

The assignment a = 7 would simply reset a
to 7. Release[a] evaluates to b, however,
before the assignment is done.

*In[5]:=* **Release[a] = 7**

*Out[5]=* **7**

As a result, it is b, rather than a, that is
set to 7.

*In[6]:=* **b**

*Out[6]=* **7**

## Evaluation in Assignments

| | |
|---|---|
| *symbol* = *value* | *symbol* is not evaluated; *value* is evaluated |
| *symbol* := *value* | neither *symbol* nor *value* are evaluated |
| *f* [*args*] = *value* | *args* are evaluated; left-hand side as a whole is not |
| *f* [Literal[*arg*]] = *value* | *f* [*arg*] is assigned, without evaluating *arg* |
| Release[*lhs*] = *value* | left-hand side is evaluated completely |

Evaluation in assignments.

When you type in something like f[1 + 1] = 2, *Mathematica* first evaluates the
arguments of f to get f[2] = 2, and only then performs the assignment. As a result,
*Mathematica* stores a transformation rule for f[2], rather than for f[1+1]. A
transformation rule for f[1+1] would not be particularly useful, since the expression
f[1+1] could never actually arise in the process of evaluation. Assuming that f does
not have any attributes such as HoldAll, f[1+1] will always be evaluated to f[2]
before any transformation rules are tried.

There are some cases, however, where it is necessary to make assignments with
the argument of the left-hand side, or some part of it, not evaluated. You can
do this by wrapping the function Literal around the parts that are not to be
evaluated. Literal is a HoldFirst function, which maintains its argument in an
unevaluated form. However, *Mathematica* replaces Literal[*expr*] by *expr* in the
actual expression that is assigned, but without evaluating *expr*.

Integrate assumes here that y_ is a
constant, and so gives the peculiar result
x_ y_ for the integral.

*In[1]:=* **Integrate[y_, x_]**

*Out[1]=* **(x_) (y_)**

*Mathematica* leaves integrals like this in a form that matches the pattern `Integrate[y_, x_]`.

```
In[2]:= Integrate[q[x], x]
Out[2]= Integrate[q[x], x]
```

This defines a value for `f` when its argument is any object of the form `Integrate[y_, x_]`. The `Literal` prevents `Integrate[y_, x_]` from being evaluated at the time of assignment.

```
In[3]:= f[Literal[Integrate[y_, x_]]] := fint[y, x]
```

The `Literal` has been stripped out of the expression, but `Integrate[y_, x_]` has been left unevaluated.

```
In[4]:= ?f
f
f/: f[Integrate[y_, x_]] := fint[y, x]
```

The pattern now matches in this case.

```
In[4]:= f[Integrate[q[x], x]]
Out[4]= fint[q[x], x]
```

## Iteration Functions

Iteration functions such as `Table` and `Sum`, as well as `Plot` and `Plot3D`, evaluate their arguments in a slightly complicated way.

First, the "iterator specification" that appears as the second argument of an expression like `Table[`*f*`, {`*i*`, `*imax*`}]` is evaluated. The object *i* cannot have a value at this point. If it does have a value, `Table` prints a message, and stops.

The expression *f* to be tabulated is maintained in an unevaluated form. The evaluation of `Table` involves assigning a succession of values to the iteration variable *i*, and in each case evaluating *f*. Finally, the value assigned to *i* is removed.

The fact that `Random[ ]` is evaluated four separate times means that you get four different pseudorandom numbers.

```
In[1]:= Table[Random[ ], {4}]
Out[1]= {0.626136, 0.593602, 0.740102, 0.928052}
```

The `Sum` in this case is evaluated separately for each value of *x*.

```
In[2]:= Table[Sum[x^i, {i, 8}], {x, 4}]
Out[2]= {8, 510, 9840, 87380}
```

Using `Release`, you can make the `Sum` be evaluated first.

```
In[3]:= Table[Release[Sum[x^i, {i, 8}]], {x, 4}]
Out[3]= {8, 510, 9840, 87380}
```

This defines `fac` to give the factorial when it has an integer argument, and to give `NaN` (standing for "Not a Number") otherwise.

```
In[4]:= fac[n_Integer] := n! ;  fac[x_] := NaN
```

In this form, `fac[i]` is not evaluated until an explicit integer value has been assigned to `i`.

```
In[5]:= Table[fac[i], {i, 5}]
Out[5]= {1, 2, 6, 24, 120}
```

Using `Release` forces `fac[i]` to be evaluated with `i` left as a symbolic object.

```
In[6]:= Table[Release[fac[i]], {i, 5}]
Out[6]= {NaN, NaN, NaN, NaN, NaN}
```

## Infinite Recursion

The general principle that *Mathematica* follows in evaluating expressions is to go on applying transformation rules until the expressions no longer change. This means, for example, that if you make an assignment like `x = x + 1`, *Mathematica* should go into an infinite loop. In fact, *Mathematica* stops after a definite number of steps, determined by the value of the global variable `$RecursionLimit`. You can always stop *Mathematica* earlier by explicitly interrupting it.

This assignment could cause an infinite loop. *Mathematica* stops after a number of steps determined by `$RecursionLimit`.

```
In[1]:= x = x + 1
General::recursion: Recursion depth of 256 exceeded.
Out[1]= 254 + Hold[1 + x]
```

When *Mathematica* stops without finishing evaluation, it returns a held result. You can continue the evaluation by explicitly calling `Release`.

```
In[2]:= Release[%]
General::recursion: Recursion depth of 256 exceeded.
Out[2]= 507 + Hold[1 + x]
```

An assignment like `x = x + 1` is obviously circular. When you set up more complicated recursive definitions, however, it can be much more difficult to be sure that the recursion terminates, and that you will not end up in an infinite loop. The main thing to check is that the right-hand sides of your transformation rules will always be different from the left-hand sides. This ensures that evaluation will always "make progress", and *Mathematica* will not simply end up applying the same transformation rule to the same expression over and over again.

Some of the trickiest cases occur when you have rules that depend on complicated `/;` conditions (see page 229). One particularly awkward case is when the condition involves a "global variable". *Mathematica* may think that the evaluation is finished because the expression did not change. However, a side effect of some other operation could change the value of the global variable, and so should lead to a new result in the evaluation. The best way to avoid this kind of difficulty is not to use global variables in `/;` conditions. If all else fails, you can type `Update[s]` to tell *Mathematica* to update all expressions involving *s*. `Update[ ]` tells *Mathematica* to update absolutely all expressions.

# ■ 2.3 Patterns

## ■ 2.3.1 When Patterns Match

Section 2.2.6 introduced patterns as a way of representing *classes* of expressions in *Mathematica*.

The basic way that you construct a pattern in *Mathematica* is to take an expression, and replace pieces of it by "blanks" (written _). Each blank can stand for *any* expression.

As a result, a pattern like f[_^_, _] stands for a class of expressions of the form f[*anything^anything, anything*].

You can think of this as giving the "outline" of an expression, but leaving "blanks" or "holes" in which arbitrary pieces can be inserted.

When you use patterns, particularly in transformation rules, it is often convenient to give "names" to the blanks. An object like x_ stands for a blank with the name *x*. The important rule is that different occurrences in a particular pattern of blanks with the *same name* must stand for the *same expression*. The pattern f[_,_] can stand for any expression of the form f[*x, y*], where *x* and *y* need not be the same. On the other hand, f[x_,x_] can *only* stand for expressions in which the two arguments of f are exactly the same.

| | |
|---|---|
| This gives a rule for the value of the function f with two identical arguments. | *In[1]:=* f[x_, x_] := p[x] |
| The rule applies to f[a, a], but not to f[a, b]. | *In[2]:=* f[a, a] + f[a, b]<br>*Out[2]=* f[a, b] + p[a] |

It is important to realize that patterns in *Mathematica* stand for classes of expressions with the same *structure*. Even though two expressions may be *mathematically equal*, they cannot be represented by the same *Mathematica* pattern unless they have the same structure.

Thus, for example, the pattern (1 + x_)^2 can stand for expressions like (1 + a)^2 or (1 + b^3)^2 that have the same *structure*. However, it cannot stand for the expression 1 + 2 a + a^2. Although this expression is *mathematically equal* to (1 + a)^2, it does not have the same *structure* as the pattern (1 + x_)^2.

The fact that patterns in *Mathematica* specify the *structure* of expressions is important in making it possible for you to set up transformation rules which change the *structure* of expressions, while leaving them mathematically equal.

It is worth realizing that in general it would be quite impossible for *Mathematica* to match patterns by mathematical, rather than structural, equivalence. In the case of expressions like (1 + a)∧2 and 1 + 2 a + a∧2, you can determine equivalence just by using functions like **Expand** and **Factor**. But, as we discussed on page 213 there is in general no way to find out whether an arbitrary pair of mathematical expressions are equal.

| | |
|---|---|
| With two identical arguments, the rule defined above applies. | *In[3]*:= **f[a∧2 - 1, a∧2 - 1]** <br><br> *Out[3]*= p[-1 + a$^2$] |

| | |
|---|---|
| Even though these arguments are mathematically equal, they are not structurally equivalent, so the pattern does not match. | *In[4]*:= **f[a∧2 - 1, (1 + a)(1 - a)]** <br><br> *Out[4]*= f[-1 + a$^2$, (1 - a) (1 + a)] |

Although *Mathematica* matches in a purely structural fashion, its notion of structural equivalence is quite sophisticated.

It considers, for example, two expressions like *x* + *y* and *y* + *x* to be equivalent. As a result, a pattern like g[x_ + y_, x_] in *Mathematica* can match both g[a + b, a] and g[a + b, b].

In fact, whenever *Mathematica* encounters an *orderless* or *commutative* function such as **Plus** or **Times** in a pattern, it effectively tests all the possible orders of arguments to try and find a match. Sometimes, there may be several orderings that lead to matches. In such cases, *Mathematica* just uses the first ordering it finds. For example, h[x_ + y_, x_ + z_] could match h[a + b, a + b] with x→a, y→b, z→b or with x→b, y→a, z→a. *Mathematica* tries the case x→a, y→b, z→b first, and so uses this match.

| | |
|---|---|
| This defines a transformation rule for the pattern g[x_ + y_, x_]. | *In[5]*:= **g[x_ + y_, x_] := p[x, y]** |

| | |
|---|---|
| This expression has exactly the same form as the pattern. | *In[6]*:= **g[a + b, a]** <br> *Out[6]*= p[a, b] |

| | |
|---|---|
| *Mathematica* matches the pattern by rearranging this expression as g[b + a, b]. | *In[7]*:= **g[a + b, b]** <br> *Out[7]*= p[b, a] |

| | |
|---|---|
| Here is a more complicated definition. | *In[8]*:= **h[x_ + y_, x_ + z_] := p[x, y, z]** |

This can match h[x_ + y_, x_ + z_] either with x → a or with x → b. *Mathematica* tries x → a first, and so uses this match.

```
In[9]:= h[a + b, a + b]
Out[9]= p[a, b, b]
```

In addition to being orderless, functions like **Plus** and **Times** also have the property of being *flat* or *associative*. This means that you can effectively "parenthesize" their arguments in any way, so that, for example, x + (y + z) is equivalent to x + y + z, and so on.

*Mathematica* takes account of flatness in matching patterns. As a result, a pattern like g[x_ + y_] can match g[a + b + c], with x → a and y → (b + c).

*Mathematica* uses the associativity of addition to write this expression as g[a + (b + c), a], so that it has the same form as the pattern g[x_ + y_, x_].

```
In[10]:= g[a + b + c, a]
Out[10]= p[a, b + c]
```

*Mathematica* uses the commutativity and associativity of addition to try several different arrangements of this expression. It finds a match when the expression is put in the form g[(b + d) + (a + c), b + d].

```
In[11]:= g[a + b + c + d, b + d]
Out[11]= p[b + d, a + c]
```

This does not match the pattern.

```
In[12]:= g[a, a]
Out[12]= g[a, a]
```

This matches the pattern, since a − b is treated as a + (−1 b).

```
In[13]:= g[a - b, a]
Out[13]= p[a, -b]
```

The associativity of **Plus** allows a pattern like x_ + y_ to match expressions like a + b or a + b + c. The pattern cannot, however, match the object a on its own.

Nevertheless, in certain situations, it is useful to think of a as the "sum" a + 0, and to allow it to match a sum of terms. The special notation x_ + y_. stands for a sum in which y_ is *optionally included*. The pattern x_ + y_. can match either an explicit sum of terms in which both x_ and y_ appear, or a single term x_, with y taken to be 0.

This pattern allows both sums of terms, and single terms.

```
In[14]:= k[x_ + y_.] := q[x, y]
```

This matches the pattern, with y taken to have its "default value" of 0.

```
In[15]:= k[a]
Out[15]= q[a, 0]
```

*Mathematica* can treat "optional arguments" like y_. in several standard functions. (Sections 2.3.6 and 2.3.7 discuss how you can set up your own defaults.)

|  |  |
|---|---|
| x_ + y_. | default for y is 0 |
| x_ y_. | default for y is 1 |
| x_^y_. | default for y is 1 |

Patterns with optional pieces.

| | |
|---|---|
| This definition applies to expressions *structurally* of the form g[*anything*∧*anything*]. | `In[16]:= g[x_^n_] := gp[x, n]` |
| The pattern matches this expression. | `In[17]:= g[a^b]`<br>`Out[17]= gp[a, b]` |
| The pattern does not match this expression, even though a+b could mathematically be considered as (a+b)∧1. | `In[18]:= g[a+b]`<br>`Out[18]= g[a + b]` |
| Now the exponent is specified as being *optional*. | `In[19]:= h[x_^n_.] := hp[x, n]` |
| The new pattern matches this expression. | `In[20]:= h[a^b]`<br>`Out[20]= hp[a, b]` |
| It also matches this pattern, with n → 1. | `In[21]:= h[a + b]`<br>`Out[21]= hp[a + b, 1]` |
| This is a common form of pattern. a_. + b_. x_ matches any linear function of x_. | `In[22]:= u[a_. + b_. x_, x_] := up[a, b]` |
| In this case, b → 1. | `In[23]:= u[1 + x, x]`<br>`Out[23]= up[1, 1]` |
| Here b → 1 and a → 0. | `In[24]:= u[y, y]`<br>`Out[24]= up[0, 1]` |

### ■ 2.3.2  Making Restrictions on Patterns and Transformation Rules

When you use a "blank" _ in a pattern, it can stand for absolutely any expression. Often you will want to restrict the class of expressions that a particular blank can represent. There are several ways to do this.

The first way is to use objects like _h or x_h which stand for expressions which must have head h.

| | |
|---|---|
| _ | any expression |
| x_ | any expression, to be named x |
| x_Integer | any integer, to be named x |
| x_Real | any approximate real number |
| x_Complex | any complex number |
| x_h | any object with head h |

Some basic pattern objects.

| | |
|---|---|
| This gives a transformation rule for the gamma function with an integer argument. | `In[1]:= gamma[n_Integer] := (n-1)!` |
| The rule applies to gamma with the integer argument 4, but not with the symbolic argument x. | `In[2]:= gamma[4] + gamma[x]`<br>`Out[2]= 6 + gamma[x]` |
| The rule does not apply to this expression because the object 4. has head Real, rather than Integer. | `In[3]:= gamma[4.]`<br>`Out[3]= gamma[4.]` |
| This defines a value for the function r when its first argument is a list, and its second argument is an integer. | `In[4]:= r[list_List, n_Integer] := list^n` |
| This matches the pattern in the rule defined for r. | `In[5]:= r[{a, b}, 3]`<br>`Out[5]= {a^3, b^3}` |
| This gives a rule for expressions with integer exponents. | `In[6]:= d[x_^n_Integer] := n x^(n-1)` |
| The rule is applied only in the cases with integer exponents. | `In[7]:= d[x^4] + d[(a+b)^3] + d[x^(1/2)]`<br>`Out[7]= 4 x^3 + 3 (a + b)^2 + d[Sqrt[x]]` |

You can think of making an assignment for f[x_Integer] as like defining a function f that must take an argument of "type" Integer. In many cases, you will need to have more complicated restrictions on the arguments that can be given to a particular function. Often these restrictions correspond to the mathematical conditions for the validity of a particular formula.

*Mathematica* provides a general mechanism for making restrictions on the applicability of transformation rules. At the end of any definition that you give, you can add /; *condition*, where the /; can be read as "such that".

| | |
|---|---|
| *lhs* := *rhs* /; *condition* | define a transformation rule to be applied only if the condition is satisfied |

Making a definition with a condition attached.

| | |
|---|---|
| This gives a rule for f that applies only when its argument n is positive. | *In[8]:=* **f[n_] := n! /; n > 0** |
| The rule for f is used only with positive arguments. | *In[9]:=* **f[6] + f[-4]**<br>*Out[9]=* 720 + f[-4] |
| This gives another rule for f with a different condition. | *In[10]:=* **f[n_] := fp[1-n] /; n < -1** |
| This shows all the rules you have defined for f. The rules are inserted and tested in the order you give them. (If a new rule has *exactly* the same condition attached as an older one, the older one is overwritten.) | *In[11]:=* **?f**<br>f<br>f/: f[n_] := n! /; n > 0<br>f/: f[n_] := fp[1 - n] /; n < -1 |
| Here is a rule with a more complicated condition attached. | *In[11]:=* **g[x_, y_] := pg[x, y] /; x > y+1 && x > 0** |
| *Mathematica* cannot find out whether a > 0 without knowing more about a. Unless a condition given with /; is explicitly **True**, *Mathematica* will not perform the transformation. | *In[12]:=* **g[a, b]**<br>*Out[12]=* g[a, b] |
| This is a common construction, implementing a feature of the "linearity" of a function h. | *In[13]:=* **h[a_ b_, x_] := a h[b, x] /; FreeQ[a, x]** |
| The terms independent of x are pulled out of each h. | *In[14]:=* **h[2 (1+x) x^2, x] + h[a b x, x]**<br>*Out[14]=* a b h[x, x] + 2 h[$x^2$ (1 + x), x] |

There are many functions in *Mathematica* for testing properties of expressions. It is a convention that functions of this kind whose names end with the letter **Q** are set up to give `False` if their tests are not explicitly satisfied.

| | |
|---|---|
| `NumberQ[`*expr*`]` | number |
| `IntegerQ[`*expr*`]` | integer |
| `EvenQ[`*expr*`]` | even number |
| `OddQ[`*expr*`]` | odd number |
| `PrimeQ[`*expr*`]` | prime number |
| `PolynomialQ[`*expr*`, {`$x_1$`, `$x_2$`, ...}]` | polynomial in $x_1$, $x_2$, ... |
| `VectorQ[`*expr*`]` | a list representing a vector |
| `MatrixQ[`*expr*`]` | a list of lists representing a matrix |
| `OrderedQ[{`*a*`, `*b*`, ...}]` | *a*, *b*, ... are in standard order |
| `MemberQ[`*expr*`, `*x*`]` | *x* is an element of *expr* |
| `FreeQ[`*expr*`, `*x*`]` | *x* appears nowhere in *expr* |
| `MatchQ[`*expr*`, `*form*`]` | *expr* matches the pattern *form* |
| `ValueQ[`*expr*`]` | a value has been defined for *expr* |
| `AtomQ[`*expr*`]` | *expr* has no subexpressions |

Functions that test properties of expressions.

561 is an integer, so the test returns True.

```
In[15]:= IntegerQ[561]
Out[15]= True
```

This gives `False`, since x is not *known* to be an integer.

```
In[16]:= IntegerQ[x]
Out[16]= False
```

You can explicitly specify that x is an integer. Section 2.2.15 explains the meaning of the /: operator.

```
In[17]:= x/: IntegerQ[x] = True
Out[17]= True
```

This overrides the default assumption that x is not an integer.

```
In[18]:= IntegerQ[x]
Out[18]= True
```

| | |
|---|---|
| This tests whether the elements of the list are in standard order. | `In[19]:= OrderedQ[{a,b,d}]`<br>`Out[19]= True` |

| | |
|---|---|
| The expression n is not a *member* of the list {x, x∧n}. | `In[20]:= MemberQ[{x, x∧n}, n]`<br>`Out[20]= False` |

| | |
|---|---|
| n does however appear *somewhere* in {x, x∧n}. | `In[21]:= FreeQ[{x, x∧n}, n]`<br>`Out[21]= False` |

You can use /; conditions to set up patterns that match complicated classes of expressions. The essential idea is to have a basic pattern which matches a wide range of expressions, and then to use /; conditions to give complicated restrictions on the expressions.

| | |
|---|---|
| This pattern matches only expressions that have the *structure* v[x_, 1 - x_]. | `In[22]:= v[x_, 1 - x_] := p[x]` |

| | |
|---|---|
| This expression has the appropriate structure, and is matched. | `In[23]:= v[a∧2, 1 - a∧2]`<br>`Out[23]= p[a`$^2$`]` |

| | |
|---|---|
| This expression does not have the appropriate structure, and so does not match. *Mathematica* does not, for example, try to "solve equations" to work out possible matches. | `In[24]:= v[4, -3]`<br>`Out[24]= v[4, -3]` |

| | |
|---|---|
| This pattern matches any expression w[x_, y_], with the added restriction that y == 1 - x. | `In[25]:= w[x_, y_] := p[x] /; y == 1 - x` |

| | |
|---|---|
| This expression matches the pattern. w[4, -3] is structurally of the form w[x_, y_]. In addition, the arguments 4 and -3 satisfy the condition y == 1 - x. | `In[26]:= w[4, -3]`<br>`Out[26]= p[4]` |

## ■ 2.3.3  An Example: Defining Your Own Integration Function

Now that we have introduced most of the basic features of patterns in *Mathematica*, we can use them to give a more or less complete example. We will show how you could define your own simple integration function in *Mathematica*.

From a mathematical point of view, the integration function is defined by a sequence of mathematical relations. By setting up transformation rules for patterns, you can implement these mathematical relations quite directly in *Mathematica*.

| mathematical form | Mathematica definition |
|---|---|
| $\int (y+z)\,dx = \int y\,dx + \int z\,dx$ | ```integrate[y_ + z_, x_] := ``` <br> ```    integrate[y, x] + integrate[z, x]``` |
| $\int cy\,dx = c \int y\,dx$ ($c$ independent of $x$) | ```integrate[c_ y_, x_] := ``` <br> ```    c integrate[y, x] /; FreeQ[c, x]``` |
| $\int c\,dx = cx$ | ```integrate[c_, x_] := c x /; FreeQ[c, x]``` |
| $\int x^n\,dx = \frac{x^{(n+1)}}{n+1}, \; n \neq -1$ | ```integrate[x_^n_., x_] := x^(n+1)/(n+1) /;``` <br> ```    FreeQ[n, x] && n != -1``` |
| $\int \frac{1}{ax+b}\,dx = \frac{\log(ax+b)}{a}$ | ```integrate[1/(a_. x_ + b_.), x_] := ``` <br> ```    Log[a x + b]/a /; FreeQ[{a,b}, x]``` |
| $\int e^{ax+b}\,dx = \frac{1}{a}\,e^{ax+b}$ | ```integrate[Exp[a_. x_ + b_.], x_] := ``` <br> ```    Exp[a x + b]/a /; FreeQ[{a,b}, x]``` |

Definitions for an integration function.

This implements the linearity relation for integrals: $\int (y+z)\,dx = \int y\,dx + \int z\,dx$.

```
In[1]:= integrate[y_ + z_, x_] :=
            integrate[y, x] + integrate[z, x]
```

The associativity of `Plus` makes the linearity relation work with any number of terms in the sum.

```
In[2]:= integrate[a x + b x^2 + 3, x]

Out[2]= integrate[3, x] + integrate[a x, x] +
                     2
           integrate[b x , x]
```

This makes `integrate` pull out factors that are independent of the integration variable x.

```
In[3]:= integrate[c_ y_, x_] :=
            c integrate[y, x] /; FreeQ[c, x]
```

*Mathematica* tests each term in each product to see whether it satisfies the `FreeQ` condition, and so can be pulled out.

```
In[4]:= integrate[a x + b x^2 + 3, x]

Out[4]= integrate[3, x] + a integrate[x, x] +
                   2
         b integrate[x , x]
```

This gives the integral $\int c\,dx = cx$ of a constant.

```
In[5]:= integrate[c_, x_] := c x /; FreeQ[c, x]
```

Now the constant term in the sum can be integrated.

```
In[6]:= integrate[a x + b x^2 + 3, x]
```

$$Out[6]= 3 \text{ x} + \text{a integrate}[\text{x, x}] + \text{b integrate}[\text{x}^2, \text{x}]$$

This gives the standard formula for the integral of $x^n$. By using the pattern x_^n_., rather than x_^n_, we include the case of $x^1 = x$.

```
In[7]:= integrate[x_^n_., x_] :=
          x^(n+1)/(n+1) /; FreeQ[n, x] && n != -1
```

Now this integral can be done completely.

```
In[8]:= integrate[a x + b x^2 + 3, x]
```

$$Out[8]= 3 \text{ x} + \frac{\text{a x}^2}{2} + \frac{\text{b x}^3}{3}$$

Of course, the built-in integration function **Integrate** (with a capital I) could have done the integral anyway.

```
In[9]:= Integrate[a x + b x^2 + 3, x]
```

$$Out[9]= 3 \text{ x} + \frac{\text{a x}^2}{2} + \frac{\text{b x}^3}{3}$$

Here are all the rules you have given for your **integrate** function so far.

```
In[10]:= ?integrate
integrate

integrate/:
      integrate[(y_) + (z_), x_] :=
        integrate[y, x] + integrate[z, x]
integrate/:
      integrate[(c_) (y_), x_] :=
        c integrate[y, x] /; FreeQ[c, x]
integrate/: integrate[c_, x_] := c x /; FreeQ[c, x]
integrate/:
```

$$\text{integrate}[(\text{x\_})^{\text{n\_.}}, \text{x\_}] :=$$

$$\frac{\text{x}^{\text{n + 1}}}{\text{n + 1}} \text{ /; FreeQ}[\text{n, x}] \text{ \&\& n != -1}$$

Here is the rule for integrating the reciprocal of a linear function. The pattern a_. x_ + b_. stands for any linear function of x; the optional argument b has default value 0; a has default 1. The condition FreeQ[{a,b}, x] checks that both a and b are independent of x.

```
In[10]:= integrate[1/(a_. x_ + b_.), x_] :=
            Log[a x + b]/a /; FreeQ[{a,b}, x]
```

Here both a and b take on their default values.

```
In[11]:= integrate[1/x, x]
Out[11]= Log[x]
```

Here is a more complicated case. The symbol a now matches 2 p.

```
In[12]:= integrate[1/(2 p x - 1), x]
         Log[-1 + 2 p x]
Out[12]= ---------------
              2 p
```

You can go on and add many more rules for integration. Here is a rule for integrating exponentials.

```
In[13]:= integrate[Exp[a_. x_ + b_.], x_] :=
           Exp[a x + b]/a /; FreeQ[{a,b}, x]
```

## ■ 2.3.4  Advanced Topic: Patterns for Algebraic Expressions

In trying to set up patterns for algebraic expressions, it is important to understand the standard form that *Mathematica* uses for algebraic expressions.

Here is a typical algebraic expression.

```
In[1]:= -1 / z^2 + 2 (x z)^2 y - z / y
         -2   z        2  2
Out[1]= -z   - - + 2 x  y z
              y
```

You can use FullForm to see the standard form that *Mathematica* uses for this kind of expression.

```
In[2]:= FullForm[%]
Out[2]//FullForm=
        Plus[Times[-1, Power[z, -2]],
          Times[-1, Power[y, -1], z],
          Times[2, Power[x, 2], y, Power[z, 2]]]
```

The standard internal form that *Mathematica* uses for algebraic expressions is essentially a sum of products of powers.

Any ratio of terms is converted into a product, with denominator terms having negative exponents. When the expression is printed out, however, the terms with negative exponents are again shown in the denominator. In the internal form, however, there are no ratios, as FullForm shows.

Patterns that you set up for algebraic expressions must follow the standard form that *Mathematica* uses. There is no point, for example, in having a pattern for a ratio that cannot actually appear in an algebraic expression.

| | |
|---|---|
| `x_ + y_` | a sum of two or more terms |
| `n_Integer x_` | $x$ multiplied by an integer other than 1 |
| `a_. + b_. x_` | a linear expression $a + bx$ |
| `x_ ^ n_` | $x^n$ with $n \neq 0, 1$ |
| `x_ ^ n_.` | $x^n$ with $n \neq 0$ |
| `a_. + b_. x_ + c_. x_^2` | a quadratic expression |

Some common patterns for algebraic expressions.

## ■ 2.3.5  Finding Expressions that Match a Pattern

When you have generated an expression, especially a large one, you often want to pick out just those pieces that have a particular form. You can describe the kind of pieces you want by setting up a pattern. Then you can use the following functions to find the pieces that match the pattern.

| | |
|---|---|
| `Cases[`*expr, form*`]` | give the elements in *expr* that match *form* |
| `Count[`*expr, form*`]` | give the number of elements in *expr* that match *form* |
| `Select[`*expr, test*`]` | give the elements of *expr* on which *test* gives `True` |
| `Position[`*expr, form*`]` | give a list of the positions of parts anywhere in *expr* that match *form* |

Functions for finding parts of expressions.

Here is a list.

```
In[1]:= t = {3, x, 4, x^2, x^3, 5}

Out[1]= {3, x, 4, x , x , 5}
                   2    3
```

This picks out the elements of the list `t` that have the form of `x` to a power.

```
In[2]:= Cases[t, x^_]

Out[2]= {x , x }
          2    3
```

This counts the number of elements in `t` that match `x^_`, without explicitly returning a list of them.

```
In[3]:= Count[t, x^_]

Out[3]= 2
```

| | |
|---|---|
| This picks out the integers in t. | *In[4]:=* `Cases[t, _Integer]` |
| | *Out[4]=* `{3, 4, 5}` |
| | |
| You can also use `Select` to pick out the integers. | *In[5]:=* `Select[t, IntegerQ]` |
| | *Out[5]=* `{3, 4, 5}` |
| | |
| This gives two positions at which 3 occurs in t. The second 3 is in the exponent of x^3. | *In[6]:=* `Position[t, 3]` |
| | *Out[6]=* `{{1}, {5, 2}}` |
| | |
| This gives all terms involving x^2 in the polynomial. | *In[7]:=* `Cases[Expand[(1 + x + y)^3], n_. x^2]` |
| | *Out[7]=* `{3 x , 3 x  y}` |

## ■ 2.3.6  Advanced Topic: Functions with Variable Numbers of Arguments

When you make an assignment like `f[x_, y_] := ` *value*, you are defining the value of the function `f` with two arguments. If you ask for values of `f` with different numbers of arguments, say `f[a]` or `f[a, b, c]`, *Mathematica* will not know their values.

You will sometimes need to define a function that can take a variable number of arguments. While a "single blank" _ stands for a single *Mathematica* expression, you can use a "double blank" __ to stand for any *sequence* of expressions.

| | |
|---|---|
| This defines a value for the function f with exactly two arguments. | *In[1]:=* `f[x_, y_] := x + y` |
| | |
| No values are defined for f with one or three arguments. | *In[2]:=* `f[a] + f[a, b, c]` |
| | *Out[2]=* `f[a] + f[a, b, c]` |
| | |
| This defines the function g with any sequence of (one or more) arguments. | *In[3]:=* `g[x__] := p[x] + q[x, x]` |
| | |
| The definition given for g applies, with x taken as the sequence (a, b, c). | *In[4]:=* `g[a, b, c]` |
| | *Out[4]=* `p[a, b, c] + q[a, b, c, a, b, c]` |
| | |
| Here is a more complicated definition, which picks out pairs of duplicated elements in h. | *In[5]:=* `h[a___, x_, b___, x_, c___] := hh[x] h[a, b, c]` |
| | |
| The rule is applied twice, picking out the two paired elements. | *In[6]:=* `h[2, 3, 2, 4, 5, 3]` |
| | *Out[6]=* `h[4, 5] hh[2] hh[3]` |

"Double blanks" __ stand for sequences of one or more expressions. "Triple blanks" ___ stand for sequences of zero or more expressions. You should be very careful whenever you use triple blank patterns. It is easy to make a mistake that can lead to an infinite loop. For example, if you define p[x_, y___] := p[x] q[y], then typing in p[a] will lead to an infinite loop, with y repeatedly matching a sequence with zero elements. Unless you are sure you want to include the case of zero elements, you should always use double blanks rather than triple blanks.

| | |
|---|---|
| _ | any single expression |
| $x$_ | any single expression, to be named $x$ |
| __ | any sequence of one or more expressions |
| $x$__ | sequence named $x$ |
| $x$__$h$ | sequence of expressions, all of whose heads are $h$ |
| $x$___ | sequence of zero or more expressions |

More kinds of pattern objects.

Notice that when you work with "flat" functions such as Plus and Times, variable numbers of arguments are automatically handled, without you explicitly needing to use double or triple blanks. Section 2.2.18 discusses how you can set up your own "flat" functions.

Sometimes you will want to define a function where certain arguments, if omitted, should be given "default values". The pattern $x$_:$v$ stands for an object that can be omitted, and replaced by the default value $v$.

This defines a function j with a required argument x, and optional arguments y and z, with default values 1 and 2, respectively.

*In[7]:=* j[x_, y_:1, z_:2] := jp[x, y, z]

The default value of z is used here.

*In[8]:=* j[a, b]

*Out[8]=* jp[a, b, 2]

Now the default values of both y and z are used.

*In[9]:=* j[a]

*Out[9]=* jp[a, 1, 2]

Some common functions, such as Plus, have built-in default values for their arguments. In these cases, you can use the special notation $x$_. to stand for an argument that can be omitted. In the case of arguments to Plus, $x$_. is in fact equivalent to $x$_:0. The notation $x$_. has the obvious advantage, however, that you do not need to specify the default value explicitly every time you set up a pattern. Section B.5.1 will discuss how you can set up your own "default defaults" for arguments in functions.

| | |
|---|---|
| $x\_ : v$ | an expression which, if omitted, is taken to have default value $v$ |
| $x\_.$ | an expression with a built-in default value |

Pattern objects with default values.

## ■ 2.3.7  Advanced Topic: Functions with Optional Arguments

When you define a complicated function, you will often want to have some of the arguments of the function be "optional". If you do not give those arguments explicitly, you want them to take on certain "default" values.

Built-in *Mathematica* functions use two basic methods for dealing with optional arguments. You can choose between the same two methods when you define your own functions in *Mathematica*.

The first method is to have the meaning of each argument determined by its position, and then to allow one to drop arguments, replacing them by default values. Almost all built-in *Mathematica* functions that use this method drop arguments from the end. For example, the built-in function `Flatten[`*list, n*`]` allows you to drop the second argument, which is taken to have a default value of `Infinity`.

You can implement this kind of "positional" argument using `_:` patterns.

| | |
|---|---|
| $f[x\_, \ k\_ : kdef] \ := \ value$ | a typical definition for a function whose second argument is optional |

Defining a function with positional arguments.

This defines a function with an optional second argument. When the second argument is omitted, it is taken to have the default value `Infinity`.

```
In[1]:= f[list_, n_:Infinity] := f0[list, n]
```

Here is a function with two optional arguments.

```
In[2]:= fx[list_, n1_:1, n2_:2] := fx0[list, n1, n2]
```

*Mathematica* assumes that arguments are dropped from the end. As a result m here gives the value of n1, while n2 has its default value of 2.

```
In[3]:= fx[k, m]

Out[3]= fx0[k, m, 2]
```

The second method that built-in *Mathematica* functions use for dealing with optional arguments is to give explicit names to the optional arguments, and then to allow their values to be given using transformation rules. This method is particularly convenient for functions like `Plot` which have a very large number of optional parameters, only a few of which usually need to be set in any particular instance.

The typical arrangement is that values for "named" optional arguments can be specified by including the appropriate transformation rules at the end of the arguments to a particular function. Thus, for example, the rule `PlotJoined->True`, which specifies the setting for the named optional argument `PlotJoined`, could appear as `ListPlot[`*list*`, PlotJoined->True]`.

When you set up named optional arguments for a function $f$, it is conventional to store the default values of these arguments as a list of transformation rules assigned to `Options[`*f*`]`.

| | |
|---|---|
| $f[x\_,\ opts\_\_\_]\ :=\ value$ | a typical definition for a function with named optional arguments |
| *name* `/.` {*opts*} `/.` `Options[`*f*`]` | replacements used to get the value of a named optional argument in the body of the function |

Named arguments.

This sets up default values for two named optional arguments opt1 and opt2 in the function fn.

```
In[4]:= Options[fn] := { opt1 -> 1, opt2 -> 2 }
```

This gives the default value for opt1.

```
In[5]:= opt1 /. Options[fn]

Out[5]= 1
```

The rule opt1->3 is applied first, so the default rule for opt1 in Options[fn] is not used.

```
In[6]:= opt1 /. opt1->3 /. Options[fn]

Out[6]= 3
```

Here is the definition for a function fn which allows zero or more named optional arguments to be specified.

```
In[7]:= fn[x_, opts___] := k[x, opt2/.{opts}/.Options[fn]]
```

With no optional arguments specified, the default rule for opt2 is used.

```
In[8]:= fn[4]

Out[8]= k[4, 2]
```

If you explicitly give a rule for opt2, it will     *In[9]:=* **fn[4, opt2->7]**
be used before the default rules stored in
Options[fn] are tried.                               *Out[9]=* k[4, 7]


■ **2.3.8  Advanced Topic: The Complete Structure of Patterns**

For most purposes, you should find it quite sufficient to use just the pattern objects
we have discussed so far.  In some advanced applications, however, you may also
have to use other *Mathematica* pattern objects.

| | |
|---:|:---|
| _ | any expression |
| x_ | any expression, given the name x |
| x:*pattern* | a pattern, given the name x |
| *pattern* ? *test* | a pattern that satisfies a test |
| _h | any expression with head h |
| __ | any sequence of one or more expressions |
| ___ | any sequence of zero or more expressions |
| x_:v | an expression with default value v |
| x_h:v | an expression with head h and default value v |
| x_. | an expression with a globally-defined default value |
| Optional[x_h] | an expression that must have head h, and has a globally-defined default value |
| *pattern*.. | a pattern repeated one or more times |
| *pattern*... | a pattern repeated zero or more times |

Pattern objects in *Mathematica*.


**Pattern Names**

You will find the construction x:*pattern* useful when you give a pattern to define
the structure of a part, but then want to give a single name to the whole part, so
that, for example, you can use it on the right-hand side of a transformation rule.

| | |
|---|---|
| This defines a function f whose argument can be *anything^anything*, with whole argument named x. | `In[1]:= f[x:_^_] := p[x]` |

x is the complete object a^b.

`In[2]:= f[a^b]`

$$Out[2]= p[a^b]$$

Here is a more complicated case. The exponent is called n, and the complete object is called x.

`In[3]:= g[x:_^n_] := p[x, n]`

Here x is a^b and n is b.

`In[4]:= g[a^b]`

$$Out[4]= p[a^b, b]$$

## Restricted Patterns

We have discussed two ways to restrict the expressions that a particular pattern can match. One is to use objects like `_Integer` that match only expressions with particular heads. Another, more general, approach that you can use in setting up transformation rules is to include a `/;` condition.

There is a third approach that *Mathematica* allows. You can restrict any pattern by using the construction *pattern* `?` *test*. The pattern will be considered to match a particular expression only if the result of applying *test* to the expression is `True`.

When you set up transformation rules, it is usually best to make restrictions using `/;` conditions. However, when you have to give individual patterns, as in functions like `Cases` and `Position`, you cannot use `/;`, so `?` is the only possibility.

In some sophisticated uses of transformation rules, it may also be important to make sure that *Mathematica* detects failure of pattern match before it has finished the whole pattern. In these cases, again, restrictions based on `?` may be appropriate.

This defines a value for h when its argument satisfies the `NumberQ` test. You could have made a definition for *integer* x using `x_Integer`, but there are several different heads that an arbitrary *number* can have.

`In[5]:= h[x_?NumberQ] := x^2`

The definition applies to h with any numerical argument.

`In[6]:= h[4.5] + h[3/2] + h[x]`

`Out[6]= 22.5 + h[x]`

This defines a value for i with positive integer arguments.

`In[7]:= i[x_Integer?Positive] := x^2`

This gives a definition for j when its argument is an integer x for which `Function[v, v > 2][x]` is True. In this case, a definition like `j[x_Integer] := x^2 /; x > 2` would probably be better.

`In[8]:= j[x_Integer?Function[v, v > 2]] := x^2`

| | |
|---|---|
| Positive[x] | strictly greater than zero |
| NonNegative[x] | greater than or equal to zero |
| Negative[x] | less than zero |
| NumberQ[x] | a number of any kind |

Functions for testing properties of expressions.

You can always explicitly give a pure function as the test to use in a ? construction. For some common tests, however, there are built-in *Mathematica* functions. Thus, for example, you can use `x_?NumberQ` to stand for any number, and `x_Integer?NonNegative` to stand for any non-negative integer. Note that a ? test is assumed to have failed if it does not explicitly come back True.

## Repetitive Patterns

The final element of patterns that we need to discuss is the "repetition operator". The object __ represents *any* sequence of expressions. You can use *pattern*.. to represent sequences of expressions, in which each expression matches a particular pattern.

This gives a definition for j when it has a sequence of arguments, all of the form k[*anything*]. The whole sequence of arguments is named x. (Using the pattern x__k would not guarantee that each k had exactly one argument.)

`In[9]:= j[x:k[_]..] := jp[x, x]`

The pattern matches in this case.

`In[10]:= j[k[1], k[2], k[3]]`

`Out[10]= jp[k[1], k[2], k[3], k[1], k[2], k[3]]`

It does not match in this case.

`In[11]:= j[k[1], 2, k[3]]`

`Out[11]= j[k[1], 2, k[3]]`

The arguments of s can be any sequence of cbjects of the form m[*anything*, *n*], where *n* must be the same for all the arguments.

```
In[12]:= s[x:m[_,n_]..] := sp[x, x]
```

This matches.

```
In[13]:= s[m[1,1], m[2,1], m[4,1]]
Out[13]= sp[m[1, 1], m[2, 1], m[4, 1], m[1, 1], m[2, 1],
         m[4, 1]]
```

This does not.

```
In[14]:= s[m[1,1], m[2,2]]
Out[14]= s[m[1, 1], m[2, 2]]
```

# ■ 2.4  Advanced Topic: Operators

## ■ 2.4.1  Manipulating the Heads of Expressions

The head $f$ of an expression like $f[x]$ is itself an expression, and you can manipulate it in a number of ways.

| | |
|---|---|
| You can use `Head` to extract the head of any expression. | `In[1]:= Head[a + b]`<br>`Out[1]= Plus` |
| You can test whether an expression has a particular head. | `In[2]:= Head[a + b] == Plus`<br>`Out[2]= True` |
| You can use `/.` to make replacements for the heads of expressions. | `In[3]:= f[1 - x]   /. f -> g`<br>`Out[3]= g[1 - x]` |
| If you set `p1` to `p2`, then `p1` will automatically be replaced by `p2`. The replacement is done even if `p1` appears as a head. | `In[4]:= p1 = p2;   p1[x, y]`<br>`Out[4]= p2[x, y]` |

You can set up patterns in which the head of an expression can be arbitrary.

| | |
|---|---|
| This defines a value for `ffun[`*anyhead*`[`*anyelem*`]]`. | `In[5]:= ffun[f_[x_]] := r[x, x]` |
| The pattern matches this expression. | `In[6]:= ffun[ h[5] ]`<br>`Out[6]= r[5, 5]` |
| It also matches this expression, which involves a built-in function. | `In[7]:= ffun[ Log[w] ]`<br>`Out[7]= r[w, w]` |

You can also give as an argument to a function an object which is to be used as the head of another expression.

| | |
|---|---|
| This definition takes `f` as an argument, then uses it as the head of an expression. | `In[8]:= pf[f_, x_] := f[x] + f[1-x]` |
| Here `f` is the "function" `hp`. | `In[9]:= pf[hp, 3]`<br>`Out[9]= hp[-2] + hp[3]` |

| | |
|---|---|
| f can just as well be a built-in function. | *In[10]:=* **pf[Log, q]** |
| | *Out[10]=* Log[q] + Log[1 - q] |

You can use transformation rules to pull out heads of expressions, and then potentially to use them elsewhere.

| | |
|---|---|
| This pulls out the head of an expression with a single element, and puts it in a list. | *In[11]:=* **pull[f_[x_]] := {f, x}** |
| This pulls out the head Log. | *In[12]:=* **pull[Log[1 + w]]** |
| | *Out[12]=* {Log, 1 + w} |
| This takes any function *f*[x] as an argument. | *In[13]:=* **sym[f_[x_]] := f[x] + f[1 - x]** |
| Here f matches Log. | *In[14]:=* **sym[Log[w]]** |
| | *Out[14]=* Log[w] + Log[1 - w] |

## ■ 2.4.2 Any Expression Can Be a Head

In most cases, you want the head *f* of an expression like *f*[x] to be a single symbol. There are, however, some situations where it is convenient to use more complicated expressions as heads.

*Mathematica* allows you to use any expression as a head.

| | |
|---|---|
| Here a+b is the head of the expression. | *In[1]:=* **(a + b)[x]** |
| | *Out[1]=* (a + b)[x] |
| This has f[p] as a head. | *In[2]:=* **f[p][x]** |
| | *Out[2]=* f[p][x] |
| You can use this kind of expression to give "indexed functions" as heads. | *In[3]:=* **f[3][x, y]** |
| | *Out[3]=* f[3][x, y] |
| When you give complicated expressions as heads, you must make sure to put in the appropriate parentheses. | *In[4]:=* **((1 + a)(1 + b))[x]** |
| | *Out[4]=* ((1 + a) (1 + b))[x] |

One situation in which we have already encountered the use of complicated expressions as heads is in working with pure functions (see Section 2.1.12). If you give **Function[***args*, *body***]** as the head of an expression, then the function is applied to any arguments you supply.

With the head `Function[x, x^2]`, the value of the expression is the square of the argument.

```
In[5]:= Function[x, x^2] [a + b]

Out[5]= (a + b)
               2
```

Another important use of more complicated expressions as heads is in implementing *functionals* and *functional operators* in mathematics.

As one example, consider the operation of differentiation. As will be discussed in Section 3.5.4, an expression like `f'` represents a *derivative function*, obtained from `f` by applying a functional operator to it. In *Mathematica*, `f'` is represented as `Derivative[1][f]`: the "functional operator" `Derivative[1]` is applied to `f` to give another function, represented as `f'`.

This expression has a head which represents the application of the "functional operator" `Derivative[1]` to the "function" `f`.

```
In[6]:= f'[x] // FullForm

Out[6]//FullForm= Derivative[1][f][x]
```

You can replace the head `f'` by another head, say `fp`. This effectively takes `fp` to be a "derivative function" obtained from `f`.

```
In[7]:= % /. f' -> fp

Out[7]= fp[x]
```

## ■ 2.4.3  Working with Operators

You can think of an expression like $f[x]$ as being formed by applying an *operator* $f$ to the expression $x$. You can get the sum of two expressions $x$ and $y$ just by writing $x + y$. If you have two operators $f$ and $g$, it is sometimes also useful to think about finding their sum.

Here is a sum of two expressions, that you can think of as the results of applying the "operators" f and g to x.

```
In[1]:= f[x] + g[x]

Out[1]= f[x] + g[x]
```

This expression represents the application of the sum of the operators f and g to x.

```
In[2]:= (f + g)[x]

Out[2]= (f + g)[x]
```

You can use `Through` to convert the expression to this form.

```
In[3]:= Through[%, Plus]

Out[3]= f[x] + g[x]
```

`Identity` is a very simple function that just returns its argument. It is useful when you try to build up operators.

```
In[4]:= Identity[x]

Out[4]= x
```

This corresponds to the mathematical operator $1 + \frac{\partial}{\partial x}$.

```
In[5]:= Identity + (D[#, x]&)

Out[5]= Identity + (D[#1, x] & )
```

*Mathematica* does not automatically apply the separate pieces of the operator to an expression.

```
In[6]:= % [x^2]
                                    2
Out[6]= (Identity + (D[#1, x] & ))[x ]
```

You can use `Through` to apply the operator.

```
In[7]:= Through[%, Plus]
                    2
Out[7]= 2 x + x
```

`Through` does nothing if the operation that appears in the head of the expression does not match the one you specify.

```
In[8]:= Through[(c f)[x], Plus]

Out[8]= (c f)[x]
```

| | |
|---|---|
| `Identity[`*expr*`]` | the identity function |
| `Through[`*p*`[`*f₁*`, `*f₂*`][x], `*q*`]` | give $p[f_1[x]\,,\ f_2[x]]$ if $p$ is the same as $q$ |
| `Operate[`*p*`, `*f*`[x]]` | give $p[f][x]$ |

Operations for working with operators.

This has a complicated expression as a head.

```
In[9]:= t = ((1 + a)(1 + b))[x]

Out[9]= ((1 + a) (1 + b))[x]
```

Functions like `Expand` do not automatically go inside heads of expressions.

```
In[10]:= Expand[%]

Out[10]= ((1 + a) (1 + b))[x]
```

`MapAll` also does not go inside heads of expressions.

```
In[11]:= MapAll[Expand, t]

Out[11]= ((1 + a) (1 + b))[x]
```

Rules applied with `/.` do work inside the heads of expressions.

```
In[12]:= t /. a->1

Out[12]= (2 (1 + b))[x]
```

You can use `Operate` to apply functions to the heads of expressions.

```
In[13]:= Operate[p, t]

Out[13]= p[(1 + a) (1 + b)][x]
```

This performs the expansion inside the head of `t`.

```
In[14]:= Operate[Expand, t]

Out[14]= (1 + a + b + a b)[x]
```

When you work with operators, it is important to remember that *Mathematica* always evaluates the head of an expression before it evaluates the rest of the expression. You can thus for example give rules to change the head of an expression, so that the operations that are done on its arguments are different.

| | |
|---|---|
| This sets `hh[1]` to be the symbol `Plus`. | *In[15]:=* `hh[1] = Plus` |
| | *Out[15]=* `Plus` |

| | |
|---|---|
| If you use `hh[1]` as the head of an expression, the elements get added together. | *In[16]:=* `hh[1][b, a, c]` |
| | *Out[16]=* `a + b + c` |

### ■ 2.4.4  Functional Composition

When you manipulate functions as objects in their own right, an operation you often need to perform is functional composition.

| | |
|---|---|
| `Compose[`$f_1$`, `$f_2$`, ..., `$f_k$`, x]` | compose expressions to give $f_1[f_2[...[f_k[x]]...]]$ |
| `Nest[f, x, n]` | apply $f$ composed $n$ times to $x$ |
| `HeadCompose[`$f_1$`, `$f_2$`, ..., `$f_k$`, x]` | compose expressions to give $f_1[f_2]...[f_k][x]$ |
| `Operate[p, f[x]]` | give $p[f][x]$ |
| `Operate[p, f[x], n]` | apply $p$ at level $n$ in $f$ |

Functional composition operations.

| | |
|---|---|
| This forms the composition of a, b and c, and applies the result to x. | *In[1]:=* `Compose[a, b, c, x]` |
| | *Out[1]=* `a[b[c[x]]]` |

| | |
|---|---|
| You can use `Compose` with `Outer` to do this. | *In[2]:=* `Outer[Compose, {a, b}, {x, y, z}]` |
| | *Out[2]=* `{{a[x], a[y], a[z]}, {b[x], b[y], b[z]}}` |

| | |
|---|---|
| `Nest[f, x, n]` composes the function $f$ with itself $n$ times, and applies the result to $x$. | *In[3]:=* `Nest[f, x, 4]` |
| | *Out[3]=* `f[f[f[f[x]]]]` |

| | |
|---|---|
| `Operate` performs an operation on the head of an expression. | *In[4]:=* `Operate[p, a[b][x]]` |
| | *Out[4]=* `p[a[b]][x]` |

HeadCompose constructs this slightly
peculiar expression. Remember that
function application groups to the left, so
the expression should be read
`((a[b])[c])[x]`.

*In[5]:=* `HeadCompose[a, b, c, x]`

*Out[5]=* `a[b][c][x]`

## ■ 2.4.5  Applying Distributive Laws

There are a number of properties that you often need to define when you treat
an object like $f$ as an "operator". Section 2.2.18 discussed how to define $f$ to be
associative and commutative. This section discusses making $f$ *distributive*.

If $f$ is distributive over **Plus**, then an expression like $f[a + b]$ can be "expanded" to give $f[a] + f[b]$. The function **Expand** performs this kind of expansion
using the distributivity of operators like **Times**.

You can use the function **Distribute** to expand expressions involving any operator $f$, and to implement the distributive law for this operator over operators like
**Plus**.

This "distributes" f over a + b.

*In[1]:=* `Distribute[ f[a + b] ]`

*Out[1]=* `f[a] + f[b]`

Here is a more complicated example.

*In[2]:=* `Distribute[ f[a + b, c + d] ]`

*Out[2]=* `f[a, c] + f[a, d] + f[b, c] + f[b, d]`

The result is the analogue of the expansion
of this product.

*In[3]:=* `Expand[ (a + b) (c + d) ]`

*Out[3]=* `a c + b c + a d + b d`

You can tell **Distribute** to distribute over
operators other than **Plus**. The result
contains all possible pairs of arguments.

*In[4]:=* `Distribute[ f[{a, b}, {c, d}], List ]`

*Out[4]=* `{f[a, c], f[a, d], f[b, c], f[b, d]}`

In this case you can get a similar result
using **Outer**.

*In[5]:=* `Flatten[ Outer[f, {a, b}, {c, d}] ]`

*Out[5]=* `{f[a, c], f[a, d], f[b, c], f[b, d]}`

When you apply the distributive law to two
operators $f$ and $g$, the results you get do
not necessarily have to contain the same
operators. You can tell **Distribute** exactly
which operators you want to distribute
over, and exactly what operators to insert
in the results.

*In[6]:=* `Distribute[ f[g[a, b], g[c, d]], g, f, gp, fp ]`

*Out[6]=* `gp[fp[a, c], fp[a, d], fp[b, c], fp[b, d]]`

| | |
|---|---|
| This is the kind of distribution that you need to do for an operator `exp` that is analogous to exponentiation. | *In[7]:=* `Distribute[ exp[a + b + c],`<br>`            Plus, exp, Times, exp ]`<br><br>*Out[7]=* `exp[a] exp[b] exp[c]` |

| | |
|---|---|
| `Distribute[`*f*`[a + b + ...], ...]]` | distribute *f* over sums to give<br>*f*[*a, ...*] + *f*[*b, ...*] + ... |
| `Distribute[`*f*`[args]`, *g*`]` | distribute *f* over any arguments which have head *g* |
| `Distribute[`*expr*, *g*, *f*`]` | distribute only when the head is *f* |
| `Distribute[`*expr*, *g*, *f*, *gp*, *fp*`]` | distribute *f* over *g* to give *fp* and *gp*, respectively |

Applying distributive laws.

## ■ 2.4.6 Threading Expressions

When you have a structure like a list, it is often convenient to apply a particular function "in parallel" to all the elements of the list. Functions that have the attribute `Listable` automatically get applied in this way. You can use `Thread` to do this with any function.

| | |
|---|---|
| `Thread[`*f*`[{`$a_1$, $a_2$`}, {`$b_1$, $b_2$`}]]` | thread *f* over lists to give {*f*[$a_1$, $b_1$], *f*[$a_2$, $b_2$]} |
| `Thread[`*f*`[args]`, *g*`]` | thread *f* over objects with head *g* in *args* |

Functions for threading expressions.

| | |
|---|---|
| Here is a function whose arguments are lists. | *In[1]:=* `f[{a1, a2}, {b1, b2}]`<br><br>*Out[1]=* `f[{a1, a2}, {b1, b2}]` |
| `Thread` applies the function "in parallel" to each element of the lists. | *In[2]:=* `Thread[%]`<br><br>*Out[2]=* `{f[a1, b1], f[a2, b2]}` |
| Arguments that are not lists get copied. | *In[3]:=* `Thread[ f[{a1, a2}, {b1, b2}, c, d] ]`<br><br>*Out[3]=* `{f[a1, b1, c, d], f[a2, b2, c, d]}` |
| Most built-in mathematical functions have the attribute `Listable`, and so automatically get threaded over lists. | *In[4]:=* `Log[{a, b, c}]`<br><br>*Out[4]=* `{Log[a], Log[b], Log[c]}` |

Log does not automatically get applied to both sides of structures other than lists, such as equations.

```
In[5]:= Log[x == y]

Out[5]= Log[x == y]
```

You can use Thread to apply functions to both sides of an equation.

```
In[6]:= Thread[%, Equal]

Out[6]= Log[x] == Log[y]
```

# ■ 2.5  Procedural Programming

## ■ 2.5.1  Procedures

When you build up calculations in *Mathematica*, you often need to string together sequences of "commands". You can do this using *procedures*. A procedure is simply a sequence of *Mathematica* expressions, separated by semicolons. The expressions in a procedure are evaluated in order, with the final result being the value of the last expression.

| | |
|---|---|
| Each element of the procedure is "executed" in turn. The final result is the value of the last expression. | `In[1]:= r = (1+x)^2; r = Expand[r]; r - 1`<br><br>$Out[1]= 2\ x\ +\ x^2$ |
| This defines the function f to be a procedure. You need to include the parentheses to make it clear that the whole procedure is to be the value of f. | `In[2]:= f[x_] := ( t = (1 + x)^2; t = Expand[t] )` |
| Evaluating the function executes the procedure. | `In[3]:= f[a + b]`<br><br>$Out[3]= 1 + 2\ a + a^2 + 2\ b + 2\ a\ b + b^2$ |
| A side effect of executing the procedure is to assign a value to the variable t. | `In[4]:= t`<br><br>$Out[4]= 1 + 2\ a + a^2 + 2\ b + 2\ a\ b + b^2$ |

When you set up procedures in *Mathematica*, you often need to use "temporary" variables to store values of intermediate results. You will usually want to arrange for each of these variables to be "local" to a particular procedure. You want to make sure that variables in two different procedures are independent, even if they happen to have the same name. For example, if two procedures both have a variable named t, you need to make sure that the value of t in each procedure is independent, otherwise you cannot, for example, expect to be able to call one of the procedures from within the other one.

You can use the construction `Block[{x, y, ...}, procedure]` to specify that a list of variables is to be treated as "local" to a particular procedure. Each time the procedure is executed, the original value of each local variable is saved, and is restored when the execution of the procedure is over. This means that you can define whatever value you want within the procedure without affecting the value outside. As a result, you can safely "nest" one procedure inside another, and thereby use *Mathematica* as a "block-structured" programming language.

| | |
|---|---|
| In this definition, u is declared as a "local" variable. | `In[5]:= g[x_] :=`<br>`    Block[ {u}, u = (1 + x)∧2; u = Expand[u] ]` |

g gives the same results as f did above.

`In[6]:= g[a + b]`

$$Out[6]= 1 + 2 a + a^2 + 2 b + 2 a b + b^2$$

However, since u is declared to be "local", the temporary value it gets during the computation of g is removed when the computation is finished.

`In[7]:= u`

`Out[7]= u`

| | |
|---|---|
| *command*;  *command*;  ... | a procedure consisting of a sequence of commands |
| `Block[{x, y, ...}, ` *procedure*`]` | declare the variables $x$, $y$, ... to be local to the procedure |
| `Block[{x = ` $x_0$`, y = ` $y_0$`, ...}, ` *procedure*`]` | |
| | specify initial values for local variables |

The basic structure of procedures.

For most purposes, the simple description of local variables given in this section will be quite adequate. The complete interaction between local variables, function arguments and so on in a symbolic language like *Mathematica* is necessarily, however, quite complicated. Section 2.5.10 discusses more of the details.

## ■ 2.5.2  Loops

Procedures let you give sequences of *Mathematica* operations to execute. You also often need to give operations that are to be executed repetitively, in some kind of "loop".

| | |
|---|---|
| `Do[`*expr*`, {`*i*`, `*imax*`}]` | evaluate *expr* repetitively, with *i* varying from 1 to *imax* in steps of 1 |
| `Do[`*expr*`, {`*i*`, `*imin*`, `*imax*`, `*istep*`}]` | evaluate *expr* with *i* varying from *imin* to *imax* in steps of *istep* |
| `Do[`*expr*`, {`*n*`}]` | evaluate *expr* *n* times |
| `Nest[`*f*`, `*expr*`, `*n*`]` | apply *f* to *expr* *n* times |
| `FixedPoint[`*f*`, `*expr*`]` | start with *expr*, and apply *f* repeatedly until the result no longer changes |
| `While[`*test*`, `*expr*`]` | evaluate *expr* repetitively, so long as *test* is `True` |
| `For[`*start*`, `*test*`, `*step*`, `*expr*`]` | evaluate *start*, then repetitively evaluate *step* and *expr*, until *test* fails |

Loop constructs.

This makes a loop with i running from 1 to 4. It prints the first four squares.

```
In[1]:= Do[Print[i^2], {i, 4}]
1
4
9
16
```

This makes a loop with k running from 2 to 4.

```
In[2]:= t = x; Do[t = 1/(1 + k t), {k, 2, 4}]; t
```

$$Out[2]= \cfrac{1}{1 + \cfrac{4}{1 + \cfrac{3}{1 + 2 x}}}$$

Here k runs from 0 to 5 in steps of 2.

```
In[3]:= r = 1; Do[r = (r + k)/(1 + k), {k, 0, 5, 2}]; r
Out[3]= 1
```

The way iteration is specified in **Do** is exactly the same as in functions like **Table** and **Sum**. Just as in those functions, you can set up several nested loops by giving a sequence of iteration specifications to **Do**.

| | |
|---|---|
| This loops over values of i from 1 to 4, and for each value of i, loops over j from 1 to i-1. | *In[4]:=* `Do[Print[{i,j}], {i, 4}, {j, i-1}]`<br><br>`{2, 1}`<br>`{3, 1}`<br>`{3, 2}`<br>`{4, 1}`<br>`{4, 2}`<br>`{4, 3}` |

One important point to remember is that, as in other iteration functions, the iteration variable in `Do` cannot have a value before the iteration starts. You can use `Block` to make sure that the iteration variable in `Do` is kept local.

| | |
|---|---|
| The iteration variable cannot already have a value before the iteration starts. | *In[5]:=* `m = 3; Do[Print[m^2], {m, 3}]`<br><br>`General::itervar:`<br>    `In iterator {m, 3}, variable m already has a value.`<br><br>*Out[5]=* `Do[Print[m ], {m, 3}]` $^2$ |
| The `Block` makes m local, so that it can be used in the Do. | *In[6]:=* `Block[{m}, Do[Print[m^2], {m, 3}]]`<br><br>`1`<br>`4`<br>`9` |

Sometimes you may want to repeat a particular operation a certain number of times, without changing the value of an iteration variable. You can specify this kind of repetition in `Do` just as you can in `Table` and other iteration functions.

| | |
|---|---|
| This repeats the assignment t = 1/(1+t) three times. | *In[7]:=* `t = x; Do[t = 1/(1+t), {3}]; t`<br><br>*Out[7]=* $\dfrac{1}{1 + \dfrac{1}{1 + \dfrac{1}{1 + x}}}$ |
| You can put a procedure inside Do. | *In[8]:=* `t = 67; Do[Print[t]; t = Floor[t/2], {3}]`<br><br>`67`<br>`33`<br>`16` |

`Do` allows you to repeat an operation many times. Often what you actually want to do is just to take an expression, and repeatedly apply the same function to it.

| | |
|---|---|
| `Nest` applies a function repeatedly. | *In[9]:=* `Nest[f, x, 3]`<br><br>*Out[9]=* `f[f[f[x]]]` |

This applies a pure function three times, giving the same result as the Do in the example above.

$In[10]:=$ `Nest[ Function[t, 1/(1+t)], x, 3 ]`

$$Out[10]= \cfrac{1}{1 + \cfrac{1}{1 + \cfrac{1}{1 + x}}}$$

Nest allows you to apply a function a specified number of times. In some cases, you may simply want to go on applying a function until the results you get no longer change. You will need to do this if you want to imitate evaluation in *Mathematica*, or the operation of the //. operator. FixedPoint goes on applying a function until it gets the same result on two successive occasions.

FixedPoint goes on applying a function until the result no longer changes.

$In[11]:=$ `FixedPoint[Function[t, Print[t];Floor[t/2]], 67]`

```
67
33
16
8
4
2
1
0
```

$Out[11]=$ 0

The function Do allows you to set up a loop in which iteration variables take on a fixed sequence of values. *Mathematica* also provides the somewhat more flexible iteration functions For and While, which allow you to perform a sequence of operations repeatedly, stopping when some arbitrary condition fails to be true.

The While loop continues until the condition fails.

$In[12]:=$ `n = 17; While[(n = Floor[n/2]) != 0, Print[n]]`

```
8
4
2
1
```

This is a very common form for a For loop. i++ increments the value of i.

$In[13]:=$ `For[i=1, i < 4, i++, Print[i]]`

```
1
2
3
```

Here is a more complicated For loop. Notice that the loop terminates as soon as the test i^2 < 10 fails. The body of the loop is not executed the last time through.

$In[14]:=$ `For[i=1; t=x, i^2 < 10, i++, t = t^2 + i;`
                   `Print[t]]`

$$1 + x^2$$
$$2 + (1 + x^2)^2$$
$$3 + (2 + (1 + x^2)^2)^2$$

The way `For` and `While` work in *Mathematica* is similar to the way they work in the C programming language. If you are familiar with C, however, you should be sure to notice that the roles of comma and semicolon are reversed in *Mathematica* `For` loops relative to C ones.

When you set up loops in *Mathematica*, particularly with `For` and `While`, you often want to update repeatedly the values of variables you are using. There are short ways to specify some of the more common operations of this kind.

| | |
|---:|:---|
| $i$++ | increment the value of $i$ by 1 |
| $i$-- | decrement $i$ |
| ++$i$ | pre-increment $i$ |
| --$i$ | pre-decrement $i$ |
| $i$ += $di$ | add $di$ to the value of $i$ |
| $i$ -= $di$ | subtract $di$ from $i$ |
| $x$ *= $c$ | multiply $x$ by $c$ |
| $x$ /= $c$ | divide $x$ by $c$ |
| {$x$, $y$} = {$y$, $x$} | interchange the values of $x$ and $y$ |
| `PrependTo`[*list*, *elem*] | prepend *elem* to the value of *list* |
| `AppendTo`[*list*, *elem*] | append *elem* |

Some operations that are often used in loops.

| | |
|:---|:---|
| This sets `t` to `x`, then increments `t` by the symbolic quantity `5y`, then returns the result for `t`. | `In[15]:= t = x; t += 5y; t`<br>`Out[15]= x + 5 y` |
| The value of `i++` is the value of `i` *before* the increment is done. | `In[16]:= i=5; Print[i++]; Print[i]`<br>`5`<br>`6` |
| The value of `++i` is the value of `i` *after* the increment. | `In[17]:= i=5; Print[++i]; Print[i]`<br>`6`<br>`6` |

The assignment {a, b} = {b, a} interchanges the values of the variables a and b.

```
In[18]:= (a=1; b=2; Print[{a,b}]; {a, b} = {b, a};
            Print[{a,b}])

{1, 2}
{2, 1}
```

You can make assignments of lists to permute values of variables in any way.

```
In[19]:= (a=1; b=2; c=3; Print[{a,b,c}];
            {a, b, c} = {c, a, b}; Print[{a,b,c}])

{1, 2, 3}
{3, 1, 2}
```

When you set up loops in *Mathematica*, you will often need to take a list, and successively add elements to it. The functions PrependTo and AppendTo allow you to manipulate lists "by name".

PrependTo[v, x] is equivalent to v = Prepend[v, x].

```
In[20]:= v = {a, b, c}; PrependTo[v, x]; v
Out[20]= {x, 3, 1, 2}
```

## ■ 2.5.3  Conditionals

In building procedures in *Mathematica*, you often need to specify that a set of operations is to be performed only if certain conditions are satisfied. *Mathematica* provides a number of "conditional structures" that allow you to do this.

| | |
|---|---|
| If[*test*, *then*, *else*] | execute *then* if *test* is True, and *else* if it is False |
| Which[$test_1$, $value_1$, $test_2$, ...] | evaluate $test_1$, ... in turn, giving the value associated with the first test that is True |
| Switch[*expr*, $form_1$, $value_1$, ...] | compare *expr* with $form_1$, $form_2$, ..., giving the value associated with the first form that it matches |

Basic conditional constructs.

The test gives False, and so the "*else*" expression y is returned.

```
In[1]:= If[7 > 8, x, y]
Out[1]= y
```

This defines a step function, with value 1 for x > 0, and −1 otherwise.

```
In[2]:= f[x_] := If[x > 0, 1, -1]
```

Here is another definition of the step function, using transformation rules with conditions attached. This kind of approach is often much better in *Mathematica* than using an explicit If statement.

```
In[3]:= g[x_] := 1 /; x > 0 ; g[x_] := -1 /; x <= 0
```

| | |
|---|---|
| This defines a function with three regions. Using `True` as the third test makes this the default case. | `In[4]:= h[x_] := Which[x < 0, x^2, x > 5, x^3, True, 0]` |
| This uses the first case in the `Which`. | `In[5]:= h[-5]` <br> `Out[5]= 25` |
| This uses the third case. | `In[6]:= h[x^2]` <br> `Out[6]= 0` |
| This defines a function that depends on the value of its argument modulo 3. | `In[7]:= r[x_] := Switch[Mod[x, 3], 0, a, 1, b, 2, c]` |
| `Mod[7, 3]` is 1, so this uses the second case in the `Switch`. | `In[8]:= r[7]` <br> `Out[8]= b` |
| The forms you use in `Switch` can be any patterns. The pattern _ matches any expression, so that in this case the last choice in the `Switch` is used if none of the others apply. | `In[9]:= Switch[Mod[x, 3], 0, a, 1, b, _, q]` <br> `Out[9]= q` |

One subtlety of conditionals in a symbolic system like *Mathematica* is that the conditions you specify may give neither `True` nor `False`. For example, `x == y` does not yield a definite truth value unless `x` and `y` have been given special values (such as numerical ones). As a result, the *Mathematica* `If` structure has a fourth element, which you can use to specify the result when the truth value of the condition is unknown.

| | |
|---|---|
| `If[test, then, else, unknown]` | the full form of `If`, including the result to give if *test* gives neither `True` nor `False` |
| `TrueQ[expr]` | give `True` if *expr* is `True`, and `False` otherwise |
| `SameQ[expr_1, expr_2]` | give `True` if two expressions are identical, and `False` otherwise |

Functions for dealing with symbolic conditions.

### ■ 2.5.4 Program Flow

When you use a procedure in *Mathematica*, its elements are usually executed one after another. In some cases, you may want to modify the order of execution. You may for example want to stop executing the elements, and just return the result you have. There are several functions that you can use to make these kinds of changes in the "flow" of your program.

| | |
|---|---|
| Return[*expr*] | return the value *expr*, exiting all procedures in a function |
| Break[ ] | exit the nearest enclosing While or For |
| Continue[ ] | go to the next step in While or For |
| Goto[*name*] | go to the element Label[*name*] in the current procedure |
| Throw[*expr*] | return *expr* as the value of nearest enclosing Catch (non-local return) |

Basic control flow constructs.

This defines a function which returns 0 if it finds that t == 0. You could just write t instead of Return[t] at the end of the procedure.

```
In[1]:= f[y_, x_] :=
          Block[ {t}, t = D[y, x]; If[t==0, Return[zero]];
              t = t^2 + 1; Return[t] ]
```

t is found to be 0, so zero is returned.

```
In[2]:= f[4, x]
Out[2]= zero
```

Now t is nonzero, so the rest of the procedure is executed.

```
In[3]:= f[x^2, x]
```
$$Out[3]= 1 + 4 x^2$$

This function "throws" overflow if its argument is greater than 10.

```
In[4]:= g[x_] := If[x > 10, Throw[overflow], x!]
```

overflow is not generated.

```
In[5]:= 2 + g[5]
Out[5]= 122
```

g[20] throws overflow, which is returned as the value of the enclosing Catch.

```
In[6]:= Catch[ 2 + g[20] ]
Out[6]= overflow
```

Now the Catch has no effect.

```
In[7]:= Catch[ 2 + g[5] ]
Out[7]= 122
```

If you are familiar with the C programming language, you will notice that Return, Break and Continue work essentially the same in *Mathematica* as in C.

### ■ 2.5.5  Handling Error Conditions

Most *Mathematica* functions produce warning messages if you try to use them in inappropriate ways. In writing programs, it is often important to check automatically whether any messages were generated during a particular calculation. If messages were generated, say as a consequence of producing indeterminate numerical results, then the result of the calculation may be meaningless.

| | |
|---|---|
| Check[*expr*, *failexpr*] | if no messages are generated during the evaluation of *expr*, then return *expr*, otherwise return *failexpr* |
| Check[*expr*, *failexpr*, $s_1$::$t_1$, $s_2$::$t_2$, ...] | |
| | check only for the messages $s_i$ |

Checking for warning messages.

Typing in 0/0 produces a warning message.

```
In[1]:= 0/0

General::dby0: Division by zero.

Infinity::indt:
      Indeterminate expression 0 ComplexInfinity
        encountered.

Out[1]= Indeterminate
```

This defines a function which computes 0/x. If a message is generated, the function returns the symbol meaningless.

```
In[2]:= f[x_] := Check[0/x, meaningless]
```

No message is generated, so the function returns 0/1.

```
In[3]:= f[1]

Out[3]= 0
```

This produces an error message, and so returns the second argument of Check.

```
In[4]:= f[0]

General::dby0: Division by zero.

Infinity::indt:
      Indeterminate expression 0 ComplexInfinity
        encountered.

Out[4]= meaningless
```

Check usually tests for all messages, including ones whose output has been suppressed using Off.

In some cases, however, you may want to test only for a specific set of messages, say ones associated with numerical overflow. You can do this by explicitly telling Check the names of the messages you want to look for.

## ■ 2.5.6  Functions that Return Multiple Values

It is sometimes convenient to write a function that returns several values at the same time. You can do this in *Mathematica* simply by making the function return a list of expressions. A convenient way to pick out each of the expressions in this returned list is just to assign the list as the value of a list of variables.

| | |
|---|---|
| This assigns a the value 1 and b the value 4. | *In[1]:=* `{a, b} = {1, 4}`<br>*Out[1]=* `{1, 4}` |
| Here is a function that returns a list of three values. | *In[2]:=* `f[x_] := {x, 1-x, 1+x}` |
| This assigns the variables a, b and c to be the three values returned by f. | *In[3]:=* `{a, b, c} = f[5]`<br>*Out[3]=* `{5, -4, 6}` |

## ■ 2.5.7  Formatting *Mathematica* Programs

When you write programs using procedures and loops, it is very important that you format them in a way that makes their structure clear. It is usually a good idea to put each element of a procedure on a separate line. You should indent the lines to indicate what loop or procedure they are in.

```
ToCycles[perm_?PermutationQ] :=
      Block[{a, t, n, l, i, len},
            len = Length[perm];
            a = {} ;
            t = Table[True, {len}];
            For[i=1, i<=len, i++,
                  If[t[[i]],
                        For[n = perm[[i]]; l = {}, t[[n]], n = perm[[n]],
                              t[[n]] = False; AppendTo[l, n]
                        ];
                        AppendTo[a, l]
                  ]
            ] ;
            Return[a]
      ]
```

A *Mathematica* program, illustrating formatting conventions.

Even if you just have a sequence of nested functions, it is often a good idea to put successive nesting levels on different lines, with progressively larger indents. If the sequence of nested functions is short enough, you can put them all on one line, but add spaces to emphasize the nesting.

```
FromCycles0[list_, c_] :=
        Block[{c1},
                c1 = RotateRight[c,1];
                Table[ list[ c1[[i]] ] = c[[i]], {i, 1, Length[c]} ]
        ]
```

A *Mathematica* definition, illustrating the use of spaces in nested functions.

## ■ 2.5.8  Documenting *Mathematica* Programs

| | |
|---|---|
| $f$::usage = "*text*" | text about a function |
| (* *text* *) | comment within a function |

Ways to document functions in *Mathematica*.

When you write a function in *Mathematica* that you intend to use in the future, it is a very good idea to put in some kind of documentation that tells you about the function. If you define a value for $f$::usage, this will be retrieved when you type ?$f$.

| | |
|---|---|
| Here is the definition of a function f. | *In[1]:=* **f[x_] := x^2** |
| Here is a "usage message" for f. | *In[2]:=* **f::usage = "f[x] gives the square of x."**<br>*Out[2]=* f[x] gives the square of x. |
| This gives the usage message for f. | *In[3]:=* **?f**<br>f[x] gives the square of x. |
| ??f gives all the information *Mathematica* has about f, including the actual definition. | *In[3]:=* **??f**<br>f[x] gives the square of x.<br>f/: f[x_] := x$^2$ |

When you define a function $f$, you can usually display its value using ?$f$. However, if you give a usage message for $f$, then ?$f$ just gives the usage message. Only when you type ??$f$ do you get all the details about $f$, including its actual definition.

If you ask for information using ? about just one function, *Mathematica* will print out the complete usage messages for the function. If you ask for information on several functions at the same time, however, *Mathematica* will just give you the name of each function.

If you use *Mathematica* notebooks, you can give complete documentation for your functions in text cells that surround the cells where you give the definitions.

Whether you are using notebooks or not, you can include text in the form of "comments" in your *Mathematica* input. Any text that you put between (* and *) will be ignored when a *Mathematica* expression is evaluated. (You can nest (* and *).)

| | |
|---|---|
| You can use comments anywhere in your input. | `In[3]:= If[a > b, (* then *) p, (* else *) q]`<br>`            (* This is a conditional *)`<br><br>`Out[3]= If[a > b, p, q]` |

## ■ 2.5.9 Debugging

Whenever you write long programs in *Mathematica*, or for that matter any other language, it is inevitable that you will make mistakes in them from time to time. You will often want to execute your program in steps, so that you can see exactly what it is doing.

Debug[*expr*] allows you to step through the evaluation of *expr*. Exactly how Debug works will depend on the computer system you are using.

| | |
|---|---|
| Debug[*expr*] | step through the evaluation of *expr* |
| Debug[*expr*, {*f*, *g*, ...}] | step through the evaluation of all calls to the functions *f*, *g*, ... |
| On[*f*] | display a trace of all calls to the function *f* |
| Off[*f*] | stop tracing *f* |
| On[ ] | trace of all function evaluations |
| Off[ ] | stop all tracing |

Functions for tracing and debugging.

When you stop the execution of a program in Debug, you can "inspect" the state you are in. You can do any operation, so long as it does not change the state. You cannot use any *Mathematica* function that resets the value of any variable.

| | |
|---|---|
| i | inspect current state |
| s | step through execution |
| n | continue to next expression |
| c | continue to the end of the current block |
| f | finish computation |
| a | abort computation |

Typical options when you stop the execution of a program in Debug.

## ■ 2.5.10  Advanced Topic: Function Arguments and Local Variables

In a symbolic language like *Mathematica*, the exact treatment of function arguments and local variables can be quite complicated.

The first issue to understand is how the argument x is treated in a function definition like f[x_]  := x^2.

*Mathematica* uses an approach known as *substitution semantics*. When it evaluates f[5], *Mathematica* simply takes the expression x^2 that forms the "body" of the function and substitutes 5 for x everywhere in it. The procedure is effectively to evaluate f[5] using the replacement x^2 /. x -> 5.

An alternative approach that *Mathematica* does not use would be temporarily to *assign* the function argument x to have value 5, and then to evaluate the body of the function with this assignment made.

The substitution semantics approach that *Mathematica* uses has several advantages. One of them is that it allows you to use the values of function arguments even in places where they would not usually be evaluated. This means, for example, that you can give as a function argument an object that appears in the body of the function on the left-hand side of an assignment, or inside the body of a pure function. The appropriate value is substituted for every occurrence of the function argument in the body of the function, whether or not it would be evaluated in that position.

One of the key issues in the treatment of function arguments is how significant the actual *names* of function arguments are. An advantage of substitution semantics is that it makes these actual names largely irrelevant. If *Mathematica* instead used temporary assignment, the names could be significant, and many problems would arise. For example, with a definition like f[x_]  := x^2, an expression such as `f[1+x]` would be difficult to evaluate. The first step in the evaluation would effectively be the assignment `x = 1+x`. If `x` had no explicit value defined, then this assignment would immediately lead to an infinite loop. Substitution semantics avoids these difficulties, by making just one pass through the body of the function, inserting the values given for the function arguments.

Another issue about the treatment of function arguments is the form in which their values are "passed" to the body of the function. In a standard *Mathematica* function that evaluates its arguments, it is just the values of the arguments that are passed to the body of the function. However, if you set a *Mathematica* function which does *not* evaluate certain arguments, then these arguments will be passed in exactly the form that you specify them.

| | |
|---|---|
| g is defined to assign a to have value b. | `In[1]:= g[a_, b_] := (a = b)` |

| | |
|---|---|
| This does the assignment x = y. | `In[2]:= g[x, y]`<br>`Out[2]= y` |

| | |
|---|---|
| The first step here is to evaluate x to give y. Then y is substituted for each occurrence of a in the body of g. The final assignment done is y = z. | `In[3]:= g[x, z]`<br>`Out[3]= z` |

| | |
|---|---|
| The value of x is unchanged, but y now evaluates to z. | `In[4]:= {x, y}`<br>`Out[4]= {z, z}` |

| | |
|---|---|
| This specifies that none of the arguments to h are to be evaluated. | `In[5]:= Attributes[h] = HoldAll` |

| | |
|---|---|
| Here is the same definition as we used for g. | `In[6]:= h[a_, b_] := (a = b)` |

| | |
|---|---|
| Now x is not evaluated before being passed to the function body. The final assignment that is done is therefore x = 2. | `In[7]:= h[x, 2]`<br>`Out[7]= 2` |

One point to remember when you set up functions in *Mathematica* is that the values of arguments are substituted *wherever* objects with the same name as those arguments appear in the body of the function. Thus, for example, you have to be careful that the names of local variables you use inside a `Block`, or in an iteration function like `Do`, `Table` or `Sum`, do not conflict with the names of the function arguments. (You must also avoid conflicts with arguments to functions that you define inside your main function.)

In general, the way that local variables are handled in *Mathematica* is as follows. Whenever a block is entered, the previous values of the variables which you declare to be local are effectively pushed on a stack. When the block is finished, the original values of the variables are restored.

When you are inside a `Block` with a local variable named *x*, there is no way for you to access a value that *x* has outside the block.

One complication occurs if you *return* the local variable *x* from a block, without having assigned it a value inside the block. In this case, *Mathematica* treats the returned expression as containing an object with name *x*. When the previous value of *x* is restored, evaluation of the object named *x* will give this previous value.

A final issue concerns a complicated interaction between the symbolic nature of *Mathematica*, and the treatment of function arguments and local variables.

| | |
|---|---|
| This function sums the value of the object *x* when i runs from 1 to 3. | `In[8]:= s[x_] := Sum[x, {i, 3}]` |

| | |
|---|---|
| The expression j∧2 is independent of i, and so the result is just 3 j∧2. | `In[9]:= s[j∧2]`<br><br>$Out[9]= 3\ j^2$ |

| | |
|---|---|
| The variable i that appears in the argument is now "captured" by Sum. The result is the value of Sum[i∧2, {i, 3}]. | `In[10]:= s[i∧2]`<br>`Out[10]= 14` |

The "capture" of symbolic function arguments by local variables in the body of a function can have both good and bad consequences. Sometimes it can be very confusing to have the name of a local variable conflict with a value you give for a function argument.

The best way to solve this problem is somehow to have the names of the local variables that appear in your functions be such that they will never appear in the values of function arguments. You can conveniently achieve the kind of "static scoping" that is needed by setting up "contexts" for symbol names, as discussed in Section 2.7.

# ■ 2.6  Input and Output

## ■ 2.6.1  Output Formats

| | |
|---|---|
| OutputForm[*expr*] | standard two-dimensional mathematical form |
| InputForm[*expr*] | one-dimensional form suitable for input to *Mathematica* |

Two basic output formats.

*Mathematica* usually prints expressions in an approximation to standard mathematical notation. It lays out the parts of the expression in two dimensions, using superscripts, built-up fractions, and so on.

This two-dimensional form is convenient for output, but is not suitable for input to *Mathematica*. The standard input that you type to *Mathematica* consists of lines of text with an effectively one-dimensional structure. Basic *Mathematica* input cannot contain superscripts and so on.

The function InputForm allows you to print *Mathematica* expressions in a form that *is* suitable for subsequent input to *Mathematica*.

Here is an expression printed in standard *Mathematica* output form. It involves superscripts and built-up fractions.

```
In[1]:= x^4/4 + 1/y^2
```
$$Out[1]= \frac{x^4}{4} + y^{-2}$$

Here is the same expression in a one-dimensional form suitable for input to *Mathematica*.

```
In[2]:= InputForm[%]

Out[2]//InputForm= x^4/4 + y^(-2)
```

Although the output from a *Mathematica* computation is usually printed in *Mathematica*'s standard output form, many *Mathematica* front ends in fact also store the input form of the *Mathematica* output. (Often they call the input and output forms "unformatted" and "formatted", respectively.) By storing the input forms of all expressions, *Mathematica* front ends allow you to give any expression you see as input to *Mathematica*. A common thing is to look at an expression in output form, then edit the input form of the expression, and use a piece of the text that you get as subsequent input to *Mathematica*.

Section 1.9 discussed some of the ways you can generate output from *Mathematica* that is suitable for input to other computer languages and programs.

| | |
|---|---|
| TeXForm[*expr*] | TEX input form |
| CForm[*expr*] | C language input form |
| FortranForm[*expr*] | FORTRAN input form |

*Mathematica* output suitable for input to other systems.

Here is an expression in standard *Mathematica* output form.

```
In[3]:= x^5/7 + y^3 - Log[y]
```

$$Out[3]= \frac{x^5}{7} + y^3 - Log[y]$$

Here is the same expression in a form suitable for input to the TEX typesetting system.

```
In[4]:= TeXForm[%]
Out[4]//TeXForm= {{{x^5}}\over 7} + {y^3} - \log (y)
```

Here is the expression in C language form. C macros for objects like `Power` are defined in the header file `mdefs.h`.

```
In[5]:= CForm[%]
Out[5]//CForm= Power(x,5)/7 + Power(y,3) - Log(y)
```

Here is the FORTRAN form.

```
In[6]:= FortranForm[%]
Out[6]//FortranForm= x**5/7 + y**3 - Log(y)
```

Section 1.9 discussed some of the details of TEX, C and FORTRAN output in *Mathematica*, and outlined how you can take this output, and "splice it" into external files.

## ■ 2.6.2  Short Output Form

When you generate a very large output expression in *Mathematica*, you often do not want to see the whole expression at once. Rather, you would first like to get an idea of the general structure of the expression, and then, perhaps, go in and look at particular parts in more detail.

The function `Short` gives you a way to have *Mathematica* print shortened forms of expressions.

| | |
|---|---|
| Short[*expr*] | print a one-line outline of *expr* |
| Short[*expr*, *n*] | print an *n*-line outline of *expr* |

Showing expressions in short form.

This generates a long expression. If the whole expression were printed out here, it would go on for 23 lines.

$In[1]:=$ `t = Expand[(1 + x + y)^12] ;`

This gives a one-line "outline" of t. The `<<87>>` indicates that 87 terms are omitted.

$In[2]:=$ `Short[t]`

$Out[2]//Short=$ $1 + 12 x + 66 x^2 + <<87>> + y^{12}$

Here is a four-line version of t. More terms are shown in this case.

$In[3]:=$ `Short[t, 4]`

$Out[3]//Short=$

$$1 + 12 x + 66 x^2 + 220 x^3 + 495 x^4 + 792 x^5 +$$

$$924 x^6 + 792 x^7 + 495 x^8 + <<77>> + 132 x y^{10} +$$

$$66 x^2 y^{10} + 12 y^{11} + 12 x y^{11} + y^{12}$$

You can use `Short` with other output forms, such as `InputForm`.

$In[4]:=$ `Short[InputForm[t]]`

$Out[4]//Short=$ `1 + 12*x + 66*x^2 + <<87>> + y^12`

When *Mathematica* generates output, it first effectively writes the output in one long row. Then it looks at the width of text you have asked for, and it chops the row of output into a sequence of separate "lines". Each of the "lines" may of course contain superscripts and built-up fractions, and so may take up more than one actual line on your output device. When you specify a particular number of lines in `Short`, *Mathematica* takes this to be the number of "logical lines" that you want, not the number of actual physical lines on your particular output device.

### ■ 2.6.3  Advanced Topic: Outputting Internal Representations

The form in which *Mathematica* prints an expression often bears little relation to the form in which the expression is actually stored. For most purposes, you will never need to know exactly how expressions are stored. However, if you want to manipulate the *structure* of an expression, particularly as part of a program, you may need to look at its internal form.

| | |
|---|---|
| `FullForm[`*expr*`]` | the explicit form of *expr* in functional notation |
| `TreeForm[`*expr*`]` | a representation of the expression tree for *expr* |
| `PrintForm[`*expr*`]` | the internal representation of the print form for *expr* |

Output forms that reveal internal representation.

| | |
|---|---|
| Here is an expression in standard *Mathematica* output form. | `In[1]:= x^2/3 + 1/y^2`<br><br>`Out[1]=` $\dfrac{x^2}{3} + y^{-2}$ |

| | |
|---|---|
| Here is the same expression in an explicit functional notation that mirrors the internal representation of the expression. | `In[2]:= FullForm[%]`<br>`Out[2]//FullForm=`<br>`   Plus[Times[Rational[1, 3], Power[x, 2]], Power[y, -2]]` |

| | |
|---|---|
| Here is a representation of the expression as a tree structure. | `In[3]:= TreeForm[%]`<br>`Out[3]//TreeForm=` |

```
Plus[|                                        , |          ]
       Times[|              , |           ]   Power[y, -2]
              Rational[1, 3]   Power[x, 2]
```

## ◼ 2.6.4  The Operation of Output Forms

There are two steps in every *Mathematica* calculation. First, *Mathematica* takes your input, and *evaluates* it, performing whatever mathematical operations you have specified. After that, it takes the result, and formats it for output.

Functions like `TeXForm` affect only the output formatting step. If you type in something like `TeXForm[expr]`, the expression *expr* will be evaluated, but the function `TeXForm` will stay wrapped around it, and will not evaluate in any way. However, when it reaches the output formatting step, the presence of the `TeXForm` function serves as a signal to the *Mathematica* output formatter to show the expression in TeX form.

| | |
|---|---|
| This sets the value of t to be an expression enclosed in the function `TeXForm`. When t prints out, the presence of `TeXForm` signals the output formatter to generate TeX form. | `In[1]:= t = TeXForm[a/b]`<br>`Out[1]//TeXForm= {a\over b}` |

| | |
|---|---|
| In full form, you can see the function `TeXForm` as part of the value of t. | `In[2]:= FullForm[t]`<br>`Out[2]//FullForm= TeXForm[Times[a, Power[b, -1]]]` |

It is very common to want to see an expression you are working with in various different output forms. Usually, when you apply a function like `TeXForm` to an expression, the function remains "wrapped" around your expression, and to recover your expression, you have to "dig" inside the function. In the particular case when your expression is the current output line `%`, *Mathematica* has a special mechanism which allows you to avoid "digging" inside functions like `TeXForm` to get your expression.

*Mathematica* recognizes when the outermost function in an output expression is the name of an output form (`InputForm`, `TeXForm`, etc.). In this case, *Mathematica* sets the value of `Out[n]` to be not the whole output expression, but instead the expression inside the output form function. This behavior is reflected in the special output label that *Mathematica* uses in this case. Instead of writing just `Out[n]=` at the beginning of your output, *Mathematica* writes something like `Out[n]//TeXForm=`. This label represents the fact that `TeXForm[Out[n]]` is the expression you have generated. As a result, `Out[n]` is the part *inside* the `TeXForm` function. This means that when you ask for %, or when you refer to the output line later on, you get your expression *without* `TeXForm` wrapped around it.

| | |
|---|---|
| The current output line is set to be the expression `a^2/b^2`, without `FortranForm` wrapped around it. | `In[3]:= FortranForm[(a/b)^2]`<br><br>`Out[3]//FortranForm= a**2/b**2` |
| % refers to the expression, without the `FortranForm` wrapped around it. | `In[4]:= %^2`<br><br>`Out[4]=` $\dfrac{a^4}{b^4}$ |

## ■ 2.6.5  Generating Tabular Output

| | |
|---|---|
| `TableForm[`*expr*`]` | print in tabular form |
| `MatrixForm[`*expr*`]` | print as a matrix |

Functions for tabular output.

| | |
|---|---|
| `TableForm` displays lists of expressions in columns. | `In[1]:= TableForm[{10!, 15!, 20!}]`<br><br>    3628800<br><br>    1307674368000<br><br>`Out[1]//TableForm= 2432902008176640000` |
| Here is a matrix, printed out as a list of lists in standard *Mathematica* output form. | `In[2]:= m = Table[i^j, {i, 3}, {j, 3}]`<br><br>`Out[2]= {{1, 1, 1}, {2, 4, 8}, {3, 9, 27}}` |

| | |
|---|---|
| TableForm displays the entries in the matrix in a two-dimensional array. | `In[3]:= TableForm[m]` |

```
                              1    1    1
                              2    4    8
Out[3]//TableForm= 3    9    27
```

| | |
|---|---|
| MatrixForm displays the entries in an array where every element is placed in an area of the same width and height. | `In[4]:= MatrixForm[m]` |

```
                               1    1    1
                               2    4    8
Out[4]//MatrixForm= 3    9    27
```

You can use `TableForm` and `MatrixForm` to display lists that are nested more than two levels deep. Successive dimensions are laid out alternately in horizontal and vertical directions.

## ■ 2.6.6  Advanced Topic: Defining Your Own Output Forms

When you introduce a new function into *Mathematica*, one of the things that you can specify is how the function should be printed out.

| | |
|---|---|
| `Format[`*expr*`]  :=` *form* | define the output form for *expr* |
| `Format[`*expr*`, ` *type*`]  :=` *form* | define the output form in a particular format |
| `FullForm[`*expr*`]` | display the full form of *expr*, ignoring any special output forms |

Defining output forms.

| | |
|---|---|
| This defines `pair` with two arguments to print like a list. | `In[1]:= Format[pair[x_, y_]] := {x, y}` |

| | |
|---|---|
| Now `pair` prints as a list. | `In[2]:= pair[a+b, c]` |
| | `Out[2]= {a + b, c}` |

| | |
|---|---|
| The list form was used only for output. Internally, this is still a `pair` function. | `In[3]:= FullForm[%]` |
| | `Out[3]//FullForm= pair[Plus[a, b], c]` |

It is important to understand that defining the output form of a function is quite independent of defining the *value* of the function. If you define the value of a function, say by making an assignment like `f[x_]:=`*value*, then every time the function appears in a calculation, *Mathematica* will replace it with the value you defined. On the other hand, defining the output form of a function, say with the assignment `Format[f[x_]]:=`*form*, does not affect the *value* of the function. With this assignment alone, `f[x]` will remain unevaluated when it appears in a calculation. However, when the calculation is finished and *Mathematica* is formatting the output, then any time that `f[x]` appears, it will be formatted in the way you specified.

When you make a definition like `Format[f[x_]]:=`*form*, the value *form* can be any *Mathematica* expression. When `f` is formatted, *form* is evaluated. As a result, you can have *Mathematica* do computations to work out the output form for `f`.

| | |
|---|---|
| This defines the output form of `rep` to be the result of replicating `x` `n` times. | `In[4]:= Format[rep[n_]] := Table[x, {n}]` |
| The list of four elements is created when `rep[4]` is formatted. | `In[5]:= rep[4]`<br>`Out[5]= {x, x, x, x}` |
| `rep[4]` only *prints* as a list. Internally, it is still just `rep[4]`. | `In[6]:= 1 + %`<br>`Out[6]= 1 + {x, x, x, x}` |

| | |
|---|---|
| `"text"` | a string containing arbitrary text |
| `HoldForm[`*expr*`]` | the output form of *expr*, with *expr* maintained unevaluated |

Functions that give literal output.

In general, the expression you assign as output forms for functions get evaluated when they are used. Often, however, you want to specify the output form of a function to be some literal object, which should not be evaluated.

One way to do this is to define the output form simply to be a specific string of text. The string can contain special characters, including newlines and so on, as discussed in Section 2.6.9.

Often, however, the arguments of your function have to appear in some way in the output form for the function. You can arrange for this by constructing the expression that represents the output form you want, and then enclosing this expression in a `HoldForm` function. The `HoldForm` function prevents the expression inside from being evaluated, but allows its output form to be used.

| | |
|---|---|
| This defines the function `pow` to have the printed form of a power, but with the power remaining unevaluated. | `In[7]:= Format[pow[x_,y_]] := HoldForm[x^y]` |

| | |
|---|---|
| This prints just like 2∧3, but without evaluating 2∧3. | $In[8]:=$ `pow[2, 3]` |
| | $Out[8]=$ $2^3$ |

You can use assignments like `Format[expr]:=`*form* to specify the output form for any expression or class of expressions. You can, for example, specify output forms for symbols in this way.

| | |
|---|---|
| This specifies that the output form of the symbol `catalan` should be the string "G". | $In[9]:=$ `Format[catalan] := "G"` |

| | |
|---|---|
| Whenever `catalan` appears, it is now printed out as G. Notice that in standard *Mathematica* output form, the double quotes around strings are not included. | $In[10]:=$ `catalan∧2/4` |
| | $Out[10]=$ $\dfrac{G^2}{4}$ |

When you make an assignment for `Format[`*expr*`]`, you are defining the output form for *expr* in the standard *Mathematica* output format (`OutputForm`). By making definitions for `Format[`*expr*, *type*`]`, you can specify output forms in other types of output format.

| | |
|---|---|
| This specifies the `TeXForm` for the symbol x. | $In[11]:=$ `Format[x, TeXForm] := "{\\bf x}"` |

| | |
|---|---|
| The output form for x that you specified is now used whenever the TEX form is needed. | $In[12]:=$ `TeXForm[1 + x∧2]` |
| | $Out[12]//TeXForm=$ `1 + {{{\bf x}}∧2}` |

## ■ 2.6.7 Advanced Topic: Mimicking Mathematical Notation

In creating your own output forms, the goal is often to mimic standard mathematical notation. One of the most common elements of standard notation is the use of subscripts and superscripts. Output forms for these are built in to *Mathematica*.

| | |
|---|---|
| `Subscripted[`$f[x_1, x_2, ...]$`]` | a function with arguments given as subscripts |
| `Subscripted[`$f$`[args], `$n$`]` | a function with the first $n$ arguments as subscripts |
| `Subscripted[`$f$`[args], `$\{d_0, d_1\}, \{u_0, u_1\}$`]` | arguments $d_0$ through $d_1$ as subscripts; $u_0$ through $u_1$ as superscripts |

Output forms that give subscripts and superscripts.

This gives an output form with both
arguments of a as subscripts.

$In[1]:=$ Subscripted[a[1, 2]]

$Out[1]=$ $a_{1,2}$

This defines a with any number of
arguments to be output with the
arguments as subscripts.

$In[2]:=$ Format[a[x__]]  := Subscripted[a[x]]

The subscripts can themselves contain
superscripts.

$In[3]:=$ a[x^2, y^2]

$Out[3]=$ $a_{x^2,y^2}$

You can specify what sequences of arguments to a function should be subscripts
or superscripts. The notation for each sequence is the same as in Take and Drop.
Any arguments that you do not explicitly specify as subscripts or superscripts are
output in standard functional notation.

This outputs the first two arguments as
subscripts, and the remainder in standard
functional notation.

$In[4]:=$ Subscripted[f[a, b, c, d], 2]

$Out[4]=$ $f_{a,b}[c,d]$

This gives the last argument as a subscript.

$In[5]:=$ Subscripted[f[a, b, c, d], -1]

$Out[5]=$ $f_d[a,b,c]$

Here the first two arguments of f are
printed as subscripts, and the last one is a
superscript. The remaining argument is
given in standard functional notation.

$In[6]:=$ Subscripted[f[a, b, c, d], 2, -1]

$Out[6]=$ $f_{a,b}^{d}[c]$

*Mathematica* allows you to go beyond just having subscripts and superscripts,
and to define any kind of two-dimensional output form. In a typical case, you
can build up a complicated two-dimensional form from a combination of horizontal
(SequenceForm) and vertical (ColumnForm) "boxes".

| | |
|---|---|
| SequenceForm[$f_1$, $f_2$, ...] | a sequence of objects, arranged horizontally |
| ColumnForm[{$f_1$, $f_2$, ...}] | a column of objects |
| ColumnForm[*list*, *h*, *v*] | a column with horizontal alignment *h* (Left, Center or Right), and vertical alignment *v* (Below, Center or Above) |
| Subscript[*x*] | a subscript |
| Superscript[*x*] | a superscript |

Objects for building up two-dimensional output forms.

SequenceForm concatenates the output forms of expressions, with no spaces in between.

```
In[7]:= SequenceForm["-+-", 1/x, "-+-"]
```
$$Out[7]= -+\frac{1}{x}+-$$

ColumnForm arranges lists of expressions in vertical columns.

```
In[8]:= ColumnForm[{"-+-", x + y, "-+-"}]
Out[8]= -+-
        x + y
        -+-
```

You can build up more complicated two-dimensional structures by nesting SequenceForm and ColumnForm.

```
In[9]:= SequenceForm[%, "***", %]
Out[9]= -+-   ***-+-
        x + y    x + y
        -+-      -+-
```

Subscript and Superscript are output as subscripts and superscripts.

```
In[10]:= f[Subscript[x], y, Superscript[z^2]]
```
$$Out[10]= f[\ , y, \ z^2\ ]$$
$$\qquad\qquad x$$

## ■ 2.6.8  Advanced Topic: Formatting Functions as Operators

| | |
|---|---|
| Prefix[$f$[$x$], $h$] | prefix form $h$  $x$ |
| Postfix[$f$[$x$], $h$] | postfix form $x$  $h$ |
| Infix[$f$[$x$, $y$, ...], $h$] | infix form $x$  $h$  $y$  $h$ ... |
| Prefix[$f$[$x$]] | standard prefix form $f$@$x$ |
| Postfix[$f$[$x$]] | standard postfix form $x$//$f$ |
| Infix[$f$[$x$, $y$, ...]] | standard infix form $x$~$f$~$y$~$f$~... |
| PrecedenceForm[$expr$, $n$] | an object to be parenthesized with a precedence level $n$ |

Output forms for operators.

This prints with f represented by the "prefix operator" <>.

```
In[1]:= Prefix[f[x], "<>"]
Out[1]= <>x
```

Here is output with the "infix operator" =*=.

```
In[2]:= s = Infix[{a, b, a/b, b/a}, " =*= "]
                         a          b
Out[2]= a =*= b =*= (-) =*= (-)
                         b          a
```

By default, the "infix operator" =*= is assumed to have "higher precedence" than Power, so no parentheses are inserted.

```
In[3]:= s^2
                         a          b 2
Out[3]= a =*= b =*= (-) =*= (-)
                         b          a
```

Here =*= is treated as an operator with precedence 100. This precedence turns out to be low enough that parentheses are inserted.

```
In[4]:= PrecedenceForm[s, 100]^2
                          a          b 2
Out[4]= (a =*= b =*= (-) =*= (-))
                          b          a
```

## ■ 2.6.9  Character Strings

All input and output in *Mathematica* ultimately consists of strings of characters. There are some situations in which you may find it convenient to work directly with strings of characters. You can give any string of text in *Mathematica* in the form "*text*".

You can put any text into a *Mathematica* string. The " are not displayed in standard *Mathematica* output format.

```
In[1]:= "This is a text string."
Out[1]= This is a text string.
```

| | |
|---|---|
| The " are given in input form. | *In[2]:=* **InputForm[%]** |
| | *Out[2]//InputForm=* "This is a text string." |
| The string "x" is not the same as the symbol x. In the standard output format, you do not see the " in the string "x". | *In[3]:=* **"x" != x** |
| | *Out[3]=* x != x |
| You can tell whether something is a string by looking at its head. | *In[4]:=* **Head["x"]** |
| | *Out[4]=* String |
| You can define transformation rules that involve strings. | *In[5]:=* **z["gold"] = 79** |
| | *Out[5]=* 79 |

Any standard printable character can appear in a *Mathematica* string. There are also ways to include special characters. You can use special characters to build up formats for special output devices.

| | |
|---|---|
| $a$ | an ordinary character |
| \" | a " to be included in a string |
| \n | a newline (line feed) |
| \t | a tab |
| \\*nnn* | a character with octal code *nnn* |

Special codes in *Mathematica* strings.

In *Mathematica*, a single character is represented as a string of length one. Most computer systems have a way of numbering characters, most often using ASCII codes. *Mathematica* can convert between strings, lists of characters, and ASCII codes.

| | |
|---|---|
| **Characters["*string*"]** | give a list of the characters in a string |
| **ToASCII["*c*"]** | give the ASCII code for a character |
| **FromASCII[*n*]** | construct a character from an ASCII code |

Conversions between strings, characters and ASCII codes.

| | |
|---|---|
| Here is a string. | *In[6]:=* **str = "The string."** |
| | *Out[6]=* The string. |

This gives a list of the characters in `str`. Each character is a string of length one.

*In[7]:=* `Characters[str]`

*Out[7]=* {T, h, e,  , s, t, r, i, n, g, .}

Here is the fifth character in `str`.

*In[8]:=* `%[[5]]`

*Out[8]=* s

`ToASCII` gives the numerical ASCII code for the character.

*In[9]:=* `ToASCII[%]`

*Out[9]=* 115

`FromASCII` converts from the code to the character.

*In[10]:=* `FromASCII[%]`

*Out[10]=* s

| | |
|---|---|
| `StringJoin[`*str₁*`, `*str₂*`, ...]` | join several strings together |
| `StringLength[`*string*`]` | give the number of characters in a string |
| *str₁* `==` *str₂* | test whether two strings are identical |

Some functions for manipulating character strings.

`StringJoin` joins strings together.

*In[11]:=* `StringJoin["The cat", " ", "in the hat"]`

*Out[11]=* The cat in the hat

You can apply `StringJoin` to a list of characters.

*In[12]:=* `Apply[StringJoin, {"a", "b", "c"}]`

*Out[12]=* abc

This finds the total number of characters in `str`.

*In[13]:=* `StringLength[str]`

*Out[13]=* 11

You can use the standard `==` operator to find out if two strings are identical.

*In[14]:=* `"x y" == "x y"`

*Out[14]=* True

When you work with expressions in *Mathematica*, you are usually concerned with their *structure*, whether mathematical or otherwise. Sometimes, however, you may want to manipulate or use an expression in a purely textual way. You can do this by converting the expression to a string.

| | |
|---|---|
| ToString[*expr*] | give the textual form of an expression as a string |
| ToExpression[*string*] | convert (if possible) a string to an expression |

Converting between expressions and strings.

This gives a string of the InputForm text of the expression.

```
In[15]:= ToString[x^2 + a/b]
Out[15]= a     2
         - + x
         b
```

This converts the string back to an expression.

```
In[16]:= ToExpression[%]
Out[16]= 2 a
```

You can use **ToString** and **ToExpression** to convert between names of symbols and strings. Sometimes, you may find it convenient to generate a sequence of symbols with different names. The *Mathematica* function **Unique** discussed in Section 2.7.2 allows you to do this.

## ■ 2.6.10  Advanced Topic: Font Specifications

When you give text to be included in graphics output, it is often possible to choose between a variety of fonts and sizes. With some *Mathematica* systems, you may also be able to make such choices for standard output from *Mathematica*.

| | |
|---|---|
| FontForm[*expr*, "*fontname*", *size*] | request a particular font and size for the printed form of *expr* |

Specifying fonts and sizes of output.

This shows text in different fonts and sizes in graphics output.

```
In[1]:= Show[Graphics[{
    Text[FontForm["Some text", "Plain", 14], {0.5, 0.2}] ,
    Text[FontForm["Some text", "Bold", 16], {0.5, 0.4}] ,
    Text[FontForm["Some text", "Italic", 18], {0.5, 0.6}]
},
    Framed->True ]]
```

One of the great complications in specifying styles for text output is that not all output devices have the same set of fonts and sizes available. As a result, the external program that actually produces output has to map the font name and size you give into ones that are available.

The "size" you specify in `FontForm` gives the basic height of characters in units of "points". One point is $\frac{1}{72}$ inches. The main text in this book, for example, is set in 11 point type.

## ■ 2.6.11 Producing Output

The most common way to use *Mathematica* is to type in an expression, then let *Mathematica* evaluate the expression, and print the final result. Sometimes, however, you may want to get *Mathematica* to print out expressions at intermediate stages in its operation.

| | |
|---|---|
| `Print[expr₁, expr₂, ...]` | print the $expr_i$, with no spaces in between, but with a newline (line feed) at the end |

Printing expressions.

Print prints its arguments, with no spaces in between, but with a newline (line feed) at the end.

```
In[1]:= Print[a, b]; Print[c]
ab
c
```

This prints a table of the first five integers     *In[2]:=* `Do[Print[i, "    ", i^2], {i, 5}]`
and their squares.

```
1    1
2    4
3    9
4    16
5    25
```

**Print** simply takes the arguments you give, and prints them out one after the other, with no spaces in between. In many cases, you will need to print output in a more complicated format. You can do this by giving an output form as an argument to **Print**.

This prints the matrix in the form of a         *In[3]:=* `Print[TableForm[{{1, 2}, {3, 4}}]]`
table.

```
1    2

3    4
```

| TextForm[*expr*] | output *expr* in a form suitable for inclusion inside ordinary text |
|---|---|
| StringForm["*cccc``cccc*", $x_1$, $x_2$, ...] | |
| | output a string in which successive `` are replaced by successive $x_i$ |
| StringForm["*cccc`i`cccc*", $x_1$, ...] | |
| | output a string in which each `i` is replaced by the corresponding $x_i$ |

Some output forms for generating formatted output.

**StringForm** allows you to format *Mathematica* output in a way that is somewhat analogous to the format directives used in languages like C and FORTRAN.

This generates output according to the        *In[4]:=* `StringForm["x=``, y=``", 3, (1 + u)^2]`
"format string" you have given.

*Out[4]=* x=3, y=(1 + u)$^2$

### ■ 2.6.12  Messages

Many built-in *Mathematica* functions print messages to warn you of possible errors. Each message that *Mathematica* prints has a unique name, of the form *symbol*::*tag*.

Section 1.3.7 discussed how you can use `On[s::t]` and `Off[s::t]` to switch on and off the printing of particular messages.

The text of a message with name $s::t$ is stored as the value of the object $s::t$, associated with the symbol $s$. You can change the text for a message simply by redefining the value of $s::t$. Messages are usually stored as strings containing `i` markers, in the form used by **StringForm**.

| | |
|---|---|
| If you give **Inverse** a singular matrix, it prints a warning message. | *In[1]:=* **Inverse[{{1,1},{2,2}}]** <br><br> Inverse::sing: Matrix {{1, 1}, {2, 2}} is singular. <br><br> *Out[1]=* Inverse[{{1, 1}, {2, 2}}] |
| The message is stored as a string to be used with **StringForm**. | *In[2]:=* **Inverse::sing** <br><br> *Out[2]=* Matrix `1` is singular. |

Most messages are associated directly with the functions that generate them. There are, however, some "general" messages, which can be produced by a variety of functions.

If you give the wrong number of arguments to a function $F$, *Mathematica* will warn you by printing the message $F::$**argct**. If *Mathematica* cannot find a message named $F::$**argct**, it will use the text of the "general" message **General::argct** instead. You can use **Off[$F::$argct]** to switch off the argument count message specifically for the function $F$. You can also use **Off[General::argct]** to switch off all messages that use the text of the general message.

| | |
|---|---|
| *Mathematica* prints a message if you give the wrong number of arguments to a built-in function. | *In[3]:=* **Sqrt[a, b]** <br><br> Sqrt::argct: Sqrt called with 2 arguments. <br><br> *Out[3]=* Sqrt[a, b] |
| The argument count message is a general one, used by many different functions. | *In[4]:=* **General::argct** <br><br> *Out[4]=* `1` called with `3` arguments. |

If something goes very wrong with a calculation you are doing, it is common to find that the same warning message is generated over and over again. This is usually more confusing than useful. As a result, *Mathematica* keeps track of all messages that are produced during a particular calculation, and stops printing a particular message if it comes up more than three times. Whenever this happens, *Mathematica* prints the message **General::stop** to let you know. If you really want to see all the messages that *Mathematica* tries to print, you can do this by switching off **General::stop**.

When you write programs in *Mathematica* you will often want to use the same mechanism for messages as built-in *Mathematica* functions do. One reason for this is that functions like **Check** which test for error conditions look for what messages have been produced.

| | |
|---|---|
| $s$::*tag* = *string* | define a message |
| Message[$s$::*tag*] | print a message |
| Message[$s$::*tag*, *expr₁*, ...] | print a message, replacing successive ` ` in it with successive *exprᵢ* |
| Messages[$s$] | show the messages associated with $s$ |
| Off[$s$::*tag*] | switch off a message, so that it is not printed |
| On[$s$::*tag*] | switch on a message |

Functions for manipulating messages.

| | |
|---|---|
| This defines a message, associated with f. | *In[5]:=* f::overflow = "Factorial too large." |
| | *Out[5]=* Factorial too large. |
| If x > 10, f gives the overflow message, then returns Infinity. | *In[6]:=* f[x_Integer] := If[x > 10, Message[f::overflow]; Infinity, x!] |
| The overflow message is displayed. | *In[7]:=* f[20] |
| | f::overflow: Factorial too large. |
| | *Out[7]=* Infinity |
| This switches off the overflow message. | *In[8]:=* Off[f::overflow] |
| The message is no longer given. | *In[9]:=* f[20] |
| | *Out[9]=* Infinity |
| This switches on the message again. | *In[10]:=* On[f::overflow] |
| Now the message is given. | *In[11]:=* f[20] |
| | f::overflow: Factorial too large. |
| | *Out[11]=* Infinity |
| This shows the messages associated with f. | *In[12]:=* Messages[f] |
| | *Out[12]=* f::overflow -> Factorial too large. |

| | |
|---|---|
| Here is a new message. | *In[13]:=* `f::new = "Overflow with x=``, Log[x]=``."` |
| | *Out[13]=* `Overflow with x=``, Log[x]=``.` |
| | |
| This prints the message, with each `` | *In[14]:=* `Message[f::new, 30, N[Log[30]]]` |
| replaced by an expression. | `f::new: Overflow with x=30, Log[x]=3.4012.` |

## ■ 2.6.13  Special Topic: Files

*Mathematica* provides various ways to use files that are stored on your computer.

The most common use of files in *Mathematica* is as a way of saving definitions that are needed in several different *Mathematica* sessions. The *Mathematica* library contains, for example, files of definitions that can be read into any *Mathematica* session when they are needed.

This section discusses some of the commands in *Mathematica* for reading and writing files. If you use *Mathematica* with a front end, then you may be able to save definitions and input directly using features of the front end, without ever needing to make use of the intrinsic file manipulation capabilities of *Mathematica*.

| | |
|---|---|
| `<<`*file* | read in a file |
| *expr* `>>` *file* | write an expression to a file |
| *expr* `>>>` *file* | append an expression to a file |
| `!!`*file* | display the contents of a file |

Basic input and output operations.

You can use `<<` to read in any file of *Mathematica* input. The result from `<<` is the last expression that was read from the file. (If the last line of the file is blank, then the last expression is taken to be `Null`.) If *Mathematica* finds a syntax error in the file, it reports the error, then stops reading the file.

| | |
|---|---|
| This reads in the file `Polyhedra.m`, which | *In[1]:=* `<<Polyhedra.m` |
| contains a sequence of *Mathematica* | |
| definitions. | |

The `>>` operator is essentially the inverse of the `<<` operator: it allows you to write out *Mathematica* expressions to a file, in a form that you can subsequently read in using the `<<` operator.

| | |
|---|---|
| This writes the expression x^2 + y^2 out to the file `tmp.m`. | `In[2]:= x^2 + y^2 >> tmp.m` |

| | |
|---|---|
| Here are the contents of `tmp.m`. The expression was written in **InputForm**. Note that `>>` overwrites any previous data in the file. | `In[3]:= !!tmp.m`<br>`x^2 + y^2` |

| | |
|---|---|
| Reading in `tmp.m` gives back the original expression. | `In[3]:= <<tmp.m`<br><br>$Out[3]= x^2 + y^2$ |

You can put any sequence of *Mathematica* commands into a file, and then read in the file, and execute the commands, using the `<<` operator. It is often convenient to prepare a file of commands outside of *Mathematica*, say using a standard text editor, and then read the file into *Mathematica* when it is ready.

Sometimes you may want to create a complete "script" for all the input to be given in a particular *Mathematica* session. The procedure for running *Mathematica* in this kind of "batch" mode differs from one computer system to another. Section B.7.2 gives some discussion of it.

## ■ 2.6.14  Special Topic: External Programs

*Mathematica* does many things well. However, there are some things that of convenience or necessity are best done by external programs.

On most computer systems (e.g. those running UNIX), you can run external programs from within *Mathematica*.

*Mathematica* provides a number of methods for "communicating" with external programs. All the methods that are currently supported ultimately involve the exchange of plain text between *Mathematica* and the external program.

---

Use files which can be read and written both by *Mathematica* and by an external program.

Use `<<"!`*command*`"` and `>>"!`*command*`"` to read or write expressions directly to an external program.

Use `RunThrough` to pass expressions through an external program.

Use `Read` with `"!`*command*`"` to read objects produced by an external program.

Use `StartProcess` and `CallProcess` to access individual functions in a suitably-prepared external program.

---

Ways to communicate with external programs in *Mathematica*.

*Mathematica* allows you to treat communication with external programs in much the same way as you treat input and output to files. Thus a command like *expr*`>>`*string* can be used either to write output to a file, or to send output to an external program.

If *string* is a standard file name, then *expr*`>>`*string* simply writes the text of *expr* to the file. If, on the other hand, *string* starts with a !, then it is interpreted as a command for running an external program. In this case, the textual form of *expr* is fed through a "pipe" as the input to the external program. Thus, for example, *expr*`>>lpr` writes *expr* to a file named *lpr*. *expr*`>>!lpr`, on the other hand, executes the external program `lpr`, giving the textual form of *expr* as its input. (On a typical UNIX system, `lpr` sends its input to a printer; as a result, *expr*`>>!lpr` causes a *Mathematica* expression to be printed.)

---

| | |
|---|---|
| *expr*`>>`*filename* | write an expression to a file |
| *expr*`>>"!`*command*`"` | send an expression through a pipe as input to an external program |

---

Writing expressions to files and external programs.

On most computer systems, the text that you give after ! is used directly as an operating system command. Since this text often contains spaces or other special characters, you will usually have to enclose !*command* in " when you give it in *Mathematica*.

You can use !*command* wherever you would usually use a standard file name. As well as sending *Mathematica* output to external programs using `>>!`*command*, you can also get *Mathematica* input from an external program using `<<!`*command*.

echo $TERM is a UNIX operating system command that prints the type of terminal you are using. The text output from this command is read as input to *Mathematica*.

```
In[4]:= <<"!echo $TERM"
Out[4]= vt100
```

## ■ 2.6.15  Special Topic: Writing Output to Files and Pipes

The operators >> and >>> are the standard *Mathematica* functions for writing output to files and pipes. There are some extensions to these functions which are often used.

| | |
|---|---|
| *expr* >> *file* | write an expression to a file, in input format |
| *expr* >>> *file* | append an expression to a file, in input format |
| OutputForm[*expr*] >> *file* | write an expression to a file, in output format |
| Display["*file*", *graphics*] | write graphics to a file, in POSTSCRIPT form |
| Save["*file*", $s_1$, $s_2$, ...] | save the complete definitions of the symbols $s_i$ in a file |
| Definition[*s*] >> *file* | write the definition of *s* to a file |
| FullDefinition[*s*] >> *file* | write the complete definition of *s* to a file, including definitions of any objects that *s* depends on |

Writing output to files.

All functions for writing output to files can also be used to send output through pipes to external commands. You can specify a pipe simply by giving an external command, prefaced by !, in place of a file name.

This writes the expression a/b to the file tmp.m.

```
In[1]:= a/b >> tmp.m
```

The operator >>> appends to a file.

```
In[2]:= c/d >>> tmp.m
```

The file tmp.m now contains both expressions, given in input form.

```
In[3]:= !!tmp.m
a/b
c/d
```

When you use >> and >>> to write expressions to files, the expressions are usually given in input format, so that they can be read back into *Mathematica*. Sometimes you may want to save expressions in other formats.

By specifying an explicit output form, you can override the default choice of input format.

```
In[3]:= OutputForm[x^2 + y^2] >> tmp.m
```

The expression was written to the file in output format.

```
In[4]:= !!tmp.m
         2    2
        x  + y
```

This writes out the expression in FORTRAN form.

```
In[4]:= FortranForm[x^2 + y^2] >> tmp.m
```

One of the most common reasons for using files is to save definitions of *Mathematica* objects, to be able to read them in again in a subsequent *Mathematica* session. The operators `>>` and `>>>` allow you to save *Mathematica* expressions in files. You can use the function `Save` to save complete definitions of *Mathematica* objects, in a form suitable for execution in subsequent *Mathematica* sessions.

This assigns a value to the symbol a.

```
In[5]:= a = 2 - x^2
                  2
Out[5]= 2 - x
```

You can use `Save` to write the definition of a to a file.

```
In[6]:= Save["afile.m", a]
```

Here is the definition of a that was saved in the file.

```
In[7]:= !!afile.m
a = 2 - x^2
```

When you define a new object in *Mathematica*, your definition will often depend on other objects that you defined before. If you are going to be able to reconstruct the definition of your new object in a subsequent *Mathematica* session, it is important that you store not only its own definition, but also the definitions of other objects on which it depends. The function `Save` looks through the definitions of the objects you ask it to save, and automatically also saves all definitions of other objects on which these depend. As a result, reading the output generated by `Save` back into a new *Mathematica* session should set up the definitions of your objects exactly as you had them before.

This defines a function f which depends on the symbol a defined above.

```
In[7]:= f[z_] := a^2 - 2
```

This saves the complete definition of f in a file.

```
In[8]:= Save["ffile.m", f]
```

The file contains not only the definition of f itself, but also the definition of the symbol a on which f depends.

```
In[9]:= !!ffile.m
f/: f[z_] := a^2 - 2
a = 2 - x^2
```

The function **Save** makes use of the output forms **Definition** and **FullDefinition**, which print as definitions of *Mathematica* symbols. In some cases, you may find it convenient to use these output forms directly.

The output form **Definition[f]** prints as the sequence of definitions that have been made for *f*.

```
In[9]:= Definition[f]
                              2
Out[9]=   f/: f[z_] := a  - 2
```

**FullDefinition[f]** includes definitions of the objects on which *f* depends.

```
In[10]:= FullDefinition[f]
                                 2
Out[10]=   f/: f[z_] := a  - 2
                       2
           a = 2 - x
```

## ■ 2.6.16  Advanced Topic: Low-Level Output Functions

You can think of **>>** and **>>>** as "high-level" *Mathematica* output functions. They are based on a set of lower-level output primitives. By using the output primitives directly, you can have more control over exactly how *Mathematica* produces output. You will often need to do this, for example, if you write programs that store intermediate data in files.

The basic low-level scheme for writing output in *Mathematica* is as follows. First, you call **OpenWrite** or **OpenAppend** to tell *Mathematica* that you want to write output to a particular file, and to specify in what form that output should be written. Then you call **Write** or **WriteString** to write your sequence of expressions or strings to the file. Finally, you call **Close** to tell *Mathematica* that you are finished with the file.

| | |
|---|---|
| OpenWrite["*file*"] | prepare to write output to a file, overwriting the previous contents of the file |
| OpenAppend["*file*"] | prepare to append output to a file |
| OpenWrite["*file*", *options*] | open a file, specifying options for how output is to be written to it |
| Write["*file*", *expr₁*, *expr₂*, ...] | write a sequence of expressions to a file, ending the output with a newline (line feed) |
| Write[{"*file₁*", "*file₂*", ...}, *expr₁*, ...] | |
| | write expressions to a list of files |
| WriteString["*file*", *str₁*, *str₂*, ...] | |
| | write a sequence of character strings to a file, with no extra newlines |
| Display["*file*", *graphics*] | write graphics output to a file, in POSTSCRIPT form |
| Close["*file*"] | tell *Mathematica* that you are finished with a file |
| ResetMedium["*file*", *options*] | reset the options for a file that is already open |
| ResetMedium[*options*] | reset options for your standard output |

Low-level output functions.

This gets ready to write to the file test.

```
In[1]:= OpenWrite["test"]
Out[1]= test
```

This writes a sequence of expressions to test, ending the output with a newline (line feed).

```
In[2]:= Write["test", a, b, c]
```

This writes another expression to test.

```
In[3]:= Write["test", x]
```

This tells *Mathematica* you have finished writing to the file test.

```
In[4]:= Close["test"]
Out[4]= test
```

This is what the file test now contains.

```
In[5]:= !!test
abc
x
```

By making a sequence of calls to Write, you can output a sequence of expressions to a file. There is some subtlety in the question of exactly how the expressions you give are placed in the file. The main issue is that in standard *Mathematica* output format, expressions have a two-dimensional structure. This means that if you write out a sequence of separate expressions, it is not clear how they should line up. What `Write` does is to output the expressions you give it, ending them with a newline (line feed). The next time you call `Write`, its output goes underneath what it produced before.

`Write` is appropriate for writing out complete *Mathematica* expressions. Sometimes, however, you may want to write out simple character strings, with complete control over where newlines are placed. The function `WriteString` allows you to write out character strings without inserting any extra newlines or other characters. Section 2.6.9 discusses various functions you can use to construct character strings, including the function `ToString`, which converts any *Mathematica* output form to a string.

| | |
|---|---|
| Open the file `test` for writing. | `In[5]:= OpenWrite["test"]`<br><br>`Out[5]= test` |
| This writes out the expressions `a^2` and `b^2`, with a string of spaces in between. | `In[6]:= Write["test", a^2, "     ", b^2]` |
| This closes the file. | `In[7]:= Close["test"]`<br><br>`Out[7]= test` |
| The expressions were all written in input form. As a result, `a^2` and `b^2` appear in a linear format. The string of spaces is displayed with explicit double quotes. | `In[8]:= !!test`<br>`a^2"     "b^2` |
| This writes out the same expressions, with the first two now explicitly given in output form. | `In[8]:= ( OpenWrite["test"];`<br>`        Write["test", OutputForm[a^2], OutputForm["     "],`<br>`b^2];`<br>`        Close["test"]`<br>`)`<br><br>`Out[8]= test` |
| The first expression is now given in two-dimensional form, and the spaces have no double quotes around them. | `In[9]:= !!test`<br>`  2`<br>`a       b^2` |

If you are familiar with the C programming language and the UNIX operating system, you will notice that the *Mathematica* functions `OpenWrite`, `OpenAppend`, `Close` and `WriteString` work in much the same way as the UNIX system calls `open`, `close` and `write`. One important difference, however, is that in *Mathematica* you always refer to files by their textual names, rather than through "file descriptors" or "file pointers".

Another point is that in *Mathematica* all the low-level output primitives can take lists of files, as well as single files. This allows you to write the same output to several files at once. It is often convenient to define an "output channel" that consists of a list of files to which you want to send a particular kind of output. There are several global variables that represent common output channels in *Mathematica*. Functions like `Print` and `Message` use these output channels to determine where to write their output.

| | |
|---|---|
| `$Output` | standard output (used by `Print`) |
| `$Echo` | files to which to echo each input line |
| `$Urgent` | files for urgent output (syntax error messages, etc.) |
| `$Messages` | files for messages (used by `Message`) |
| `$Display` | files for graphics output (used by `$DisplayFunction`) |

Output channels.

If you want to send a particular kind of output to a certain file, you can just add the file to the list for the corresponding output channel. (You can conveniently do this using the function `PrependTo`.) Thus, for example, if you want to keep a record of your complete *Mathematica* session in a file, you can simply add this file to the lists for the output channels `$Echo` and `$Output`. If you want to keep only the input you type, you can just add the file to the list for `$Echo`.

*Mathematica* supports a few "special files". On most computer systems, the *Mathematica* files `"stdout"` and `"stderr"` correspond to the standard output and error media, respectively.

*Mathematica* maintains a list of all the output (and input) files that are open at a particular time. The list is called `$$Media`. You can add and remove entries from this list using `OpenWrite`, `OpenAppend` and `Close`. You cannot, however, modify the list directly.

When you open a file, there are a number of options that you can give to specify how you want output to that file to be formatted. Even once a file is open, you can change the options for it using `ResetMedium`. If you want to know what options are set for a particular file, you can pick out the entry for the file in `$$Media`, and use the function `Options` on it.

You can change the options for your standard output medium by calling `ResetMedium` without giving an explicit file name.

| option | default | |
|--------|---------|---|
| FormatType | InputForm | the default output format to use |
| PageWidth | 78 | the width of the page |
| PageHeight | 22 | the height of the page |
| TextRendering | Plain | the default outputs text as plain characters; PostScript gives POSTSCRIPT |

Some options for output to files.

This opens the file `test`, specifying that the default output format for all output written to it should be `FortranForm`.

```
In[9]:= OpenWrite["test.m", FormatType -> FortranForm]
Out[9]= test.m
```

This writes output to `test`, using the default format type `FortranForm`.

```
In[10]:= Write["test.m", (a + b)^2]
```

This resets the options for `test`, so that future output to it will be done with default format type `InputForm`.

```
In[11]:= ResetMedium["test.m", FormatType -> InputForm]
```

This tells *Mathematica* you have finished using the file `test`.

```
In[12]:= Close["test.m"]
Out[12]= test.m
```

This tells *Mathematica* to write textual output to `test` in POSTSCRIPT form.

```
In[13]:= OpenWrite["test.m", TextRendering -> PostScript]
Out[13]= test.m
```

This writes an expression to `test`.

```
In[14]:= Write["test.m", (a + b)^2]
```

The expression was written in a form suitable for input to POSTSCRIPT.

```
In[15]:= !!test.m
0 0 moveto
/Plain findfont setfont
(\(a + b\)^2) show
```

You can use the function `Write` to output any standard *Mathematica* expression. If you want to output graphics, however, you must use `Display` instead.

The option `PageWidth` gives the width of the page available for textual output from *Mathematica*. All lines of output are broken so that they fit in this width. If you do not want any lines to be broken, you can set `PageWidth -> Infinity`. Usually, however, you will want to set `PageWidth` to the value appropriate for your particular output device. On many systems, you will have to run an external program to find out what this value is. Using `SetOptions`, you can make the default rule for `PageWidth` be, for example, `PageWidth :> <<"!devicewidth"`, so that an external program is run automatically to find the value of the option.

## ■ 2.6.17 Advanced Topic: Referring to Files

Many operating systems, such as UNIX, provide a number of mechanisms for referring to files without necessarily specifying their names or locations in full. *Mathematica* allows you to make use of such mechanisms in your operating system or "shell", and also adds some mechanisms of its own.

When you refer to a file in *Mathematica*, the first thing that *Mathematica* does is to scan the name you have given to see if it contains any special "metacharacters".

On most computer systems, *Mathematica* looks for the characters *, $, ~, ?, [, ", \, ` and '. If it finds any of these characters, then *Mathematica* passes the name you have given to your operating system or shell for interpretation. If you are using the UNIX operating system, then *name** and *$VARIABLE* constructions will be expanded at this point. Assuming that the result is a unique file, *Mathematica* will then use this file.

If you are using a file for *output*, then *Mathematica* makes no further transformations on its name: if the file does not exist, *Mathematica* will typically try to create it.

If, on the other hand, you are trying to access a file for input, say with the `<<` operator, then *Mathematica* uses a further mechanism to find the file you want.

On most computer systems, files are organized into "directories" or "folders". *Mathematica* can search for input files in a list of directories, not necessarily just your current directory. The full specification of a file is typically *directory/name*. When you ask for a file with a particular name, *Mathematica* can search for a file with that name in a sequence of directories. The sequence of directories that *Mathematica* searches is specified by strings in the list `$Path`. (This mechanism is similar to the path mechanism used in UNIX to search for programs.)

| | |
|---|---|
| . | current directory |
| .. | directory one level up in the hierarchy |
| ~ | home directory |

Special codes for specifying directories.

When you use <<*filename*, the file name you specify can contain not only alphanumeric characters, but also the metacharacters mentioned above, together with dot, slash and tilde. If it contains any other characters, however, you have to enclose it in double quotes.

## ■ 2.6.18  Special Topic: Running External Programs

| | |
|---|---|
| !*command* | "shell escape": take a complete line of *Mathematica* input, and run it as an external command |
| Run["*command*", $arg_1$, ...] | run an external command from within *Mathematica* |

Running external commands.

By starting a line with !, you can effectively direct the input you type not to *Mathematica*, but rather to your operating system. Anything after ! that you type on the line is taken as an external command to execute. Any output that the command generates is immediately displayed.

You should know that some *Mathematica* front ends cannot support this kind of interaction. They will usually give you other ways to execute external commands.

When you put an ! at the beginning of a line, the rest of the line is interpreted as an operating system command. The UNIX command date used in this example returns the current date and time.

```
In[1]:= !date

Sat Aug  6 15:02:22 CDT 1988
```

The way *Mathematica* uses !*command* is typical of the way "shell escapes" work in programs running under the UNIX operating system. You will usually be able to start an interactive shell just by typing ! on its own.

! allows you to execute external programs when you type input to *Mathematica*. You can also execute external programs from within a *Mathematica* program, using Run.

With Run, however, you can neither give input to the external program, nor receive output from it. (Under the UNIX operating system, both standard input and output for the external program are taken to be /dev/null.)

This executes the command date, but shows no output from it. The returned value is an "exit code" from the operating system.

```
In[1]:= Run["date"]

Sat Aug  6 15:02:22 CDT 1988

Out[1]= 0
```

You can use `Run` to execute a command that has some external effect. For example, you might use `Run` to print graphics data that you are building up in a particular file.

You can generate the commands that you want to use in `Run` from within *Mathematica*. All that `Run` does is to take the textual forms of any arguments you specify, and then join them together, with spaces in between, and using the resulting text as the command to execute.

Under most operating systems, you can specify a command, then give some "arguments" for it, separated by spaces. In this case, the first argument to `Run` gives the name of the "command"; subsequent arguments give the "arguments" of the command.

One way to execute an external program on data from *Mathematica* is first to put the data in a file, and then call the external program using `Run`, with the name of the file given as an appropriate argument. A much easier way to do this, however, is to make use of pipes.

| | |
|---|---|
| *expr* `>> "!`*command*`"` | run *command*, with the textual form of *expr* as input |
| `<<"!`*command*`"` | run *command*, and take its output as *Mathematica* input |
| `RunThrough["`*command*`", `*expr*`]` | run *command*, using *expr* as input, and reading the output back into *Mathematica* |
| `OpenTemporary[ ]` | open a temporary file, with a unique name |
| `OpenWrite["!`*command*`"]` | start executing *command*, and open a pipe to give input to it |
| `Write["!`*command*`", `*expr*`]` | send an expression to an external command through a pipe |
| `Display["!`*command*`", `*graphics*`]` | send POSTSCRIPT graphics to an external command |
| `Close["!`*command*`"]` | stop executing *command*, and close the pipe to it |

Running external commands with pipes.

When you use `<<"!`*command*`"`, the external command you specify is automatically started. *Mathematica* goes on taking input from the command until the command terminates.

When you use *expr*`>>"!`*command*`"`, the external command is again automatically started. *Mathematica* sends the textual form of *expr* as input to the command,

and then terminates the input.

You can use `>>` and `<<` to get data to and from external programs. Both of these operators can transmit data only in one direction. Sometimes you may need to send data from *Mathematica* to an external program, and then get results back to *Mathematica* from the same program.

The most general way to set up communication of this kind is to put data you generate into temporary files, and then to read and write these files from *Mathematica*. You can use the function `OpenTemporary[ ]` to open a temporary file with a unique name.

A more convenient way to set up two-way communication is to use the function `RunThrough`. This function starts an external command, sends the textual form of a *Mathematica* expression to it, and then takes its output and reads it back into *Mathematica*. Notice that in `RunThrough`, as in `Run`, the text of your external command is not prefaced by `!`.

This feeds the expression 78 to the external program `cat`, which in this case simply echoes the text of the expression. The output from `cat` is then read back into *Mathematica*.

```
In[2]:= RunThrough["cat", 78]

Out[2]= 78
```

Functions like `>>` and `RunThrough` first start an external program, then send a single piece of *Mathematica* output to the program. Sometimes you may want to start an external program, and then send a sequence of expressions to it. You can do this in essentially the same way as you write sequences of expressions to files.

The first step is to call `OpenWrite["!`*command*`"]`. This starts up the external program you specify. Then you can send a sequence of expressions to the program by calling `Write["!`*command*`", `*expr*`]` on each one. You can tell the external program that you have finished sending input to it by calling `Close["!`*command*`"]`.

Once you have started an external program using `OpenWrite`, it is important that every time you refer to the program you do so by giving exactly the same string. `OpenWrite` always returns the name of the object it opens. It is usually convenient to assign this name as the value of a variable, and then use the variable when you need to specify the program in `Write` and `Close`.

## ■ 2.6.19  Interactive Input

When you write programs in *Mathematica*, you will sometimes want a program to stop, and ask for input from the user.

| | |
|---|---|
| Input[ ] | read one input expression |
| Input["*prompt*"] | issue a prompt, then read one input expression |
| InputString[ ] | read a string of input |
| InputString["*prompt*"] | issue a prompt, then read a string |

Interactive input.

Input is intended for reading in complete *Mathematica* expressions. InputString, on the other hand, reads in arbitrary character strings. You should realize then when you evaluate Input or InputString, *Mathematica* waits until it has received the appropriate *Mathematica* expression, or character string. If you do not enter any input, *Mathematica* will just keep on waiting.

Particularly when you use *Mathematica* with a graphical front end, the mechanism by which Input and InputString actually get their input may be quite sophisticated. A typical thing is for Input and InputString to tell the front end to put up a "dialog box" into which the input can be entered.

## ■ 2.6.20  Special Topic: Reading Data from Files and Pipes

With << you can read the contents of a file as *Mathematica* input. However, if you have data that has been generated by an external program, it may not be in exactly the right form to be used as standard *Mathematica* input. For example, it may consist of a sequence of numbers, one to a line. You can use ReadList to read in such a sequence of numbers, and convert it to a *Mathematica* list.

| | |
|---|---|
| ReadList["*file*", *type*] | read a sequence of objects of a particular type from a file, and put them in a *Mathematica* list |
| ReadList["!*command*", *type*] | execute an external program, and read the objects it produces |

Reading lists of data.

| Byte | single byte of data, returned as an integer |
|---|---|
| Character | single character, returned as a one-character string |
| String | character string, terminated by a newline (line feed or return) |
| Real | approximate number in FORTRAN-like "E" notation |
| Number | exact or approximation number in FORTRAN-like notation |
| Expression | *Mathematica* expression |
| {$type_1$, $type_2$, ...} | a sequence of objects of various types |

Types of objects to read.

The file `cubes.dat` contains a table of numbers. The numbers in scientific notation are given in the form they would be generated by C or FORTRAN.

```
In[1]:= !!cubes.dat
128        2.09715E+6
256        1.67772E+7
512        1.34218E+8
```

This reads in the numbers in `cubes.dat`, and puts them all in a list.

```
In[1]:= ReadList["cubes.dat", Number]
```
$$Out[1]= \{128, 2.09715\ 10^6, 256, 1.67772\ 10^7, 512,$$
$$1.34218\ 10^8\}$$

This reads in each line of `cubes.dat` as a string. Using `InputForm` makes the form of the strings clear.

```
In[2]:= ReadList["cubes.dat", String] // InputForm
Out[2]//InputForm=
     {"128        2.09715E+6", "256        1.67772E+7",
      "512        1.34218E+8"}
```

This reads the numbers in `cubes.dat` in pairs, giving as a result a list of the pairs.

```
In[3]:= ReadList["cubes.dat", {Number, Number}]
```
$$Out[3]= \{\{128, 2.09715\ 10^6\}, \{256, 1.67772\ 10^7\},$$
$$\{512, 1.34218\ 10^8\}\}$$

You can specify any list structure in which to insert the numbers that you read.

```
In[4]:= ReadList["cubes.dat", {{Number}, {Number}}]
```
$$Out[4]= \{\{\{128\}, \{2.09715\ 10^6\}\}, \{\{256\}, \{1.67772\ 10^7\}\},$$
$$\{\{512\}, \{1.34218\ 10^8\}\}\}$$

If you use the type **Number**, *Mathematica* will give any number that does not contain an explicit decimal point as an integer. If you use `Real` instead, `ReadList` will give all the numbers it reads in approximate form. Notice that just as `ReadList` converts numbers from C or FORTRAN form to *Mathematica* form, so you can also use `CForm` and `FortranForm` to convert numbers in *Mathematica* to C and FORTRAN form.

---

`ReadList["`*file*`", Number]`      read a sequence of numbers from a file

`ReadList["`*file*`", {Number, Number}]`

read pairs of numbers from a file

`ReadList["`*file*`", Table[Number, {`*n*`}]]`

read numbers in blocks of *n* from a file

---

Typical ways to read numerical data.

The function `ReadList` works not only for reading data from a file, but also for reading data generated by an external program.

The external program `squares` *n* prints out numbers and their squares.

*In[5]:=* `!squares 3`

```
1  1
2  4
3  9
```

This runs the external program `squares 4`, then reads in pairs of numbers from the output, and puts the result in a list.

*In[5]:=* `ReadList["!squares 4", {Number, Number}]`

*Out[5]=* `{{1, 1}, {2, 4}, {3, 9}, {4, 16}}`

`ReadList` allows you to read in *all* the data from a file or pipe. Sometimes you may want to read data from a file one piece at time, perhaps doing tests each time to tell what kind of data to expect next.

---

`OpenRead["`*file*`"]`         open a file for reading

`Read["`*file*`"]`            read an expression from a file

`Read["`*file*`", `*type*`]`      read an object of the specified type from a file

`Close["`*file*`"]`           close a file

---

Functions for reading objects from files.

When you read individual pieces of data from files, *Mathematica* always remembers the "current point" in the file that you are at. When you call `OpenRead`, the current point is at the beginning of the file. Every time you call `Read` to read an object from the file, the current point moves on. If you try to read past the end of the file, `Read` returns the symbol `EndOfFile`.   You can get back to the beginning of the file by calling `Close`, and then calling `OpenRead` again.

This opens the file `cubes.dat` for reading.

> *In[6]:=* `f = OpenRead["cubes.dat"]`
>
> *Out[6]=* `cubes.dat`

This reads one number from `cubes.dat`.

> *In[7]:=* `Read[f, Number]`
>
> *Out[7]=* `128`

This reads a string from the file. `InputForm` makes the form of the string clear.

> *In[8]:=* `Read[f, String] // InputForm`
>
> *Out[8]//InputForm=* `"        2.09715E+6"`

This reads in the remaining numbers in the file, and puts them in a list.

> *In[9]:=* `ReadList[f, Number]`
>
> *Out[9]=* $\{256, 1.67772 \; 10^7, 512, 1.34218 \; 10^8\}$

This closes the file.

> *In[10]:=* `Close[f]`
>
> *Out[10]=* `cubes.dat`

If you call `Read` a few times, and then call `ReadList`, *Mathematica* will read from where you are to the end of the file, giving a list of the objects read.

Like `ReadList`, `Read` can also be used to read through pipes objects generated as output from external programs.

## ■ 2.6.21  Special Topic: Calling External Functions

Functions like `RunThrough` allow you to send input to an external program, and get back the results it generates. In many cases, you may not want to send input to the *whole* external program, but rather, you may want to call just one of the functions in the program.

On most computer systems, *Mathematica* provides a mechanism for doing this. The basic idea is for the external program to accept "packets" of input, that specify which function is to be called, and with what arguments.

There is a collection of utility functions, distributed in C, FORTRAN and other source code forms, which allow you to set up routines in the external program which "decode" packets received from *Mathematica*, and call the necessary functions.

There are also utility functions which allow the external program to send packets back to *Mathematica*, to request results from *Mathematica*.

These functions are discussed in slightly more detail in Section B.7.6.

| | |
|---|---|
| StartProcess["*command*"] | start an external program, and set up *Mathematica* functions to call the functions inside it |
| CallProcess["*command*", *f*, arg$_1$, arg$_2$, ...] | call the function *f* in the external program |
| EndProcess["*command*"] | terminate the external program |

Calling functions in external programs.

When you call the function StartProcess, it typically sets up a sequence of definitions for *Mathematica* functions which call functions in the external program, using CallProcess.

# ■ 2.7 Advanced Topic: The Naming of Things

## ■ 2.7.1 Aliases

It is conventional in *Mathematica* to name objects as explicitly as possible, typically using full English words. This means that names in *Mathematica* can sometimes get quite long.

If you use a particular long name very often, you may want to define a shorter "alias" for it. Especially in writing programs, however, the extra clarity you get by using an explicit, long, name much more than offsets any reduction in time or space that you might get from using a shorter alias.

| | |
|---|---|
| *input* ::= *translation* | specify a translation for an input symbol name |
| Alias["*input*"] | show any translation that has been defined for *input* |
| Alias[ ] | show all translations that have been defined |
| "*input*" ::=. | remove a translation for *input* |
| UnAlias[ ] | remove all translations |

Functions for defining aliases.

This defines int to be an alias for Integrate.

$In[1]:=$ **int ::= Integrate**

$Out[1]=$ Integrate

You can now type int instead of Integrate. What you gain in typing speed by doing this is usually not worth what you lose in clarity.

$In[2]:=$ **int[Sin[x]^3, x]**

$Out[2]=$ $\dfrac{-3\ \text{Cos}[x]}{4} + \dfrac{\text{Cos}[3\ x]}{12}$

Setting up an alias with int::=Integrate is in some respects like setting up a transformation rule with int:=Integrate. There is an important difference, however. An alias set up with int::=Integrate is used *wherever* int appears, whether it is evaluated or not. A transformation rule set up with int:=Integrate is only used, however, when int is *evaluated*.

This gives the translation for int that you have defined.

$In[3]:=$ **Alias["int"]**

$Out[3]=$ Integrate

This removes the translation for int.

$In[4]:=$ **"int" ::=.**

$Out[4]=$ int

| | |
|---|---|
| This sets up aa as an alias for Aardvark. | `In[5]:= aa ::= Aardvark`<br><br>`Out[5]= Aardvark` |

| | |
|---|---|
| Whenever you type aa, it is immediately replaced by Aardvark. You can thus use aa = *value* to define a value for Aardvark. | `In[6]:= aa = 6`<br><br>`Out[6]= 6` |

## ■ 2.7.2 Working with Names

In doing mathematical operations, the actual names that you give to particular symbols are essentially irrelevant. There are circumstances, however, when the form of names for symbols can be important. For example, you may want to find all symbols whose *names* start with the letter x.

If you type a particular symbol name, *Mathematica* will give you that symbol. Certain *Mathematica* functions, however, allow you to use character strings to refer to several different symbols at the same time. The character strings can contain special "metacharacters" which can stand for classes of other characters.

| | |
|---|---|
| `?`*nameform* | give information on all objects whose names have a particular form |
| `Names["`*nameform*`"]` | give a list of symbol names that have a particular form |
| `Clear["`*nameform*`"]` | clear the values of all symbols whose names have a particular form |

Functions that work with names.

| | |
|---|---|
| This prints a list of all objects whose names begin with B. | `In[1]:= ?B*` |

```
BaseForm         BesselY           Block
Begin            Beta              Bottom
BeginPackage     Binomial          BoxRatios
Below            Blank             Boxed
BernoulliB       BlankForm         Break
BesselI          BlankNullSequence Byte
BesselJ          BlankSequence     ByteCount
BesselK
```

| | |
|---|---|
| Here is a *Mathematica* list of symbols whose names begin with V. The entries in this list are all character strings. | `In[1]:= Names["V*"]`<br><br>`Out[1]= {ValueForm, ValueList, ValueQ, Variables,`<br>`        VectorQ, VerticalForm, ViewPoint}` |

This clears the values of all symbols whose names begin with **x**. Since there are no symbols with such names in the current *Mathematica* session, this does nothing here.

*In[2]:=* **Clear["x*"]**

|   |   |
|---|---|
| * | zero or more alphanumeric characters |
| ** | zero or more alphanumeric characters, or $ |
| @ | one or more lower-case letters |
| \* etc. | literal * etc. |

Metacharacters used in specifying names.

You can use metacharacters to give "patterns" for strings. You should realize, however, that these patterns have nothing to do with the kind of patterns for expressions that we discussed in Sections 2.2 and 2.3. They relate only to the textual form of strings.

| | |
|---|---|
| **StringMatchQ["*string*", "*pattern*"]** | yield **True** if *string* matches the textual pattern given, and **False** otherwise |

A function for textual pattern matching.

You can use metacharacters to build up "regular expressions" that stand for classes of strings. The regular expression **a*b**, for example, stands for any string that begins with **a**, ends with **b**, and has any number of other characters in between. **a*b*** stands for strings that start with **a**, then have any number of other characters, including at least one **b**.

The metacharacters provided in *Mathematica* include **@**, which stands for any sequence of lower-case letters. This metacharacter is useful when you want to work on user-defined symbols, whose names contain no upper-case letters.

In this case, the string matches the pattern you have given.

*In[3]:=* **StringMatchQ["aaaabbccbbb", "a*b*"]**

*Out[3]=* True

As well as recognizing symbols whose names have a particular form, you may sometimes want to *generate* automatically symbols with various different names. Given a character string such as "aaa", you can generate a symbol with that name using **ToExpression["aaa"]**.

Sometimes you may need to produce a symbol whose name is guaranteed not to have been used before. You can do this using the function `Unique`.

| | |
|---|---|
| `Unique["sss"]` | generate a symbol with a name of the form *sssnnn*, that has not been used before |

A function for generating symbols with unique names.

`Unique` generates a unique new symbol
every time it is called.

```
In[4]:= {Unique["a"], Unique["a"], Unique["b"]}
Out[4]= {a1, a2, b1}
```

You may sometimes need to use `Unique` to get names for "dummy variables" that you can be sure will not conflict with other variables. You should use `Unique` sparingly, however; if at all possible, call your variables `a[1]`, `a[2]`, etc., rather than `a1`, `a2`, etc.

### ■ 2.7.3  Using the Same Name for Different Things

In standard mathematical notation, one often ends up using the same symbol to mean several different things. In one context, for example, the symbol *p* might stand for a prime number; in another context, it might correspond to something very different, say momentum.

When you use *Mathematica*, you should always try to avoid choosing the same name for several different things. However, particularly when you use several packages at the same time, it is sometimes inevitable that the same name will be used in different places for different purposes.

*Mathematica* supports the notion of "contexts", which allow it to distinguish different uses of a particular name. Instead of just referring to a symbol by a name like `p`, you can specify the context for the symbol explicitly. Thus for example, you can type `NumberTheory`p` or `Physics`p` to distinguish symbols with the name `p` from two different contexts. Of course, if a particular name appears only in one context, you do not have to give the name of the context explicitly.

Every symbol that you use in *Mathematica* is in fact associated with one context or another. The full specification of any symbol is therefore *context`name*. The ` that appears here is called a *Mathematica* "context mark".

As one example, all built-in *Mathematica* objects are in the context `System``. The full specification of the function `Integrate`, for example, is therefore `System`Integrate`.

Many external packages that you read in to *Mathematica* set up their own

contexts.  Usually the names of the contexts are based on the names of the packages.
By having different contexts for different packages, one makes sure that objects from
one package cannot get confused with objects from another package.

| | |
|---|---|
| This is a symbol with name x in context a. | *In[1]:=* **a`x** |
| | *Out[1]=* **a`x** |

| | |
|---|---|
| a`x and b`x are different symbols.  They both have *name* x, but they have different contexts. | *In[2]:=* **a`x - b`x** |
| | *Out[2]=* **a`x - b`x** |

| | |
|---|---|
| This gives the context of a`x. | *In[3]:=* **Context[a`x]** |
| | *Out[3]=* **a`** |

| | |
|---|---|
| The context for built-in functions is System`. | *In[4]:=* **Context[Integrate]** |
| | *Out[4]=* **System`** |

| | |
|---|---|
| *context*`*name* | the full name of a symbol, with the context given explicitly |
| **Context[***symbol***]** | the context for a particular symbol |

Contexts for symbols.

### ■ 2.7.4  Setting Up Contexts for Packages

When you write a package in *Mathematica*, you usually want it to operate in a
way that is as independent of its "environment" as possible.  You do not want your
package to stop working just because the user, or some other package that has been
read in, happens to define a particular symbol to have some peculiar value.

The best way to make packages independent is to set up separate contexts for
each of them.  The standard *Mathematica* convention is to base the names of the
contexts on the name used for the file, with the .m suffix removed.

| | |
|---|---|
| `System`` | built-in *Mathematica* objects |
| *Package*`` | objects for export |
| *Package*``private`` | objects local to the package |
| *Needed$_1$*``, *Needed$_2$*``, ... | other contexts needed for definitions in the package |

Types of context used in a typical package.

Two kinds of objects are typically introduced in a package. The first kind are names of functions that are intended to be used outside the package. The second are names of functions and variables that are used only within the package. You can distinguish these two kinds of objects by putting the first ones in a context with a name of the form *Package*``, and the second ones in a context with a name of the form *Package*``private``. Once you are in the context *Package*``, you can refer to the context *Package*``private`` using the "relative context" notation `` `private` ``.

There is a standard sequence of context specifications that you can use when you set up a package. The later parts of this section will explain what these context specifications mean. For most purposes, however, you will simply be able to use the template given here.

| | |
|---|---|
| `BeginPackage["`*Package*`` `"]` | make *Package*`` and `System`` the only active contexts |
| `f::usage = "`*text*`", ...` | introduce the objects intended for export (and no others) |
| `Begin["`` `private` ``"]` | begin private context for package |
| `f[`*args*`] = `*value*`, ...` | give the main body of definitions in the package |
| `End[ ]` | end the private context |
| `EndPackage[ ]` | end the package, prepending the context *Package*`` to the global context path |

The standard sequence of context control commands in a package.

```
BeginPackage["Collatz`"]

Collatz::usage =
        "Collatz[n] gives a list of the iterates in the 3n+1 problem,
        starting from n. The conjecture is that this sequence always
        terminates."
```

```
Begin["`private`"]

Collatz[1] := {1}

Collatz[n_Integer]  := Prepend[Collatz[3 n + 1], n] /; OddQ[n] && n > 0

Collatz[n_Integer] := Prepend[Collatz[n/2], n] /; EvenQ[n] && n > 0

End[ ]

EndPackage[ ]
```

The package `Collatz.m`.

Giving `usage` messages at the beginning of a package can be thought of as essentially a trick for introducing in the appropriate context the objects you want to "export" from the package. The point is that when you define these messages, the only symbols you need to mention are exactly the ones you want to export.

When you actually come to give the definitions of the functions in a package, you need to make sure that the local variables and so on are introduced in a "private context" that is not readily accessible from outside the package. By doing this, you can avoid any possibility of confusion between local and global variables, as discussed in Section 2.5.10.

Sometimes you may need to set up a package which uses objects that are defined in other packages. You can tell *Mathematica* to read in the other packages when they are needed.

| | |
|---|---|
| `Needs["`*context*`\`"]` | reads in *context*.m if *context*` is not in the current list of active contexts |
| `BeginPackage["`*Package*`\`", "`*Needed$_1$*`\`", ...]` | begins a package, reading in other packages that are needed |

Functions for specifying interdependence of packages.

### ■ 2.7.5  Accessing Objects in Different Contexts

Particularly when you use many different packages at the same time, it is not uncommon to end up having a variety of different objects with the same name. In such cases, you will need to use contexts to distinguish the different objects.

There will always be one object with a particular name that you can refer to just by giving its name, without explicitly specifying its context. However, if you want to use other objects with the same name, then you will have to specify their contexts explicitly. In a typical case, the object that you can refer to without giving a context is the one that was defined most recently.

| | |
|---|---|
| *name* | the most recently defined object with a particular name |
| *context`name* | an object with a particular name in a specific context |
| ?*name* | give information on all objects with a particular name |
| ?*context`name* | give information on an object in a specific context |
| ?*context`** | give information on all objects in a context |

Typical ways to access objects in different contexts.

Many packages use objects internally that they do not intend "for export". Such objects will not be listed when you type ?*name*. If you want to see a list of these objects, you can get it by typing ?*`name*.

### ■ 2.7.6 Advanced Topic: Manipulating Whole Contexts

| | |
|---|---|
| ?*context`** | give information on all objects in a context |
| Names["*context`*"] | give a list of the names of all objects in a context |
| NameQ["*context`*"] | give **True** if there are any objects in a context |
| Remove["*context`*"] | remove all objects in a context |

Functions for manipulating whole contexts.

Like other packages, CombinatorialFunctions.m defines objects in its own context.

```
In[1]:= <<CombinatorialFunctions.m
```

This gives a list of strings corresponding to all the objects defined in the package.

```
In[2]:= Names["CombinatorialFunctions`*"]
Out[2]= {CatalanNumber, Fibonacci, Hofstadter,
    Subfactorial}
```

This removes all the objects in the context, both clearing their values, and removing their names from the list of known objects.

```
In[3]:= Remove["CombinatorialFunctions`*"]
```

## ■ 2.7.7  Advanced Topic: How Contexts Work

The most common use for contexts is in setting up packages. Section 2.7.4 gave the basic scheme that is usually used for contexts in packages. This section discusses the lower level "primitive" context mechanism in *Mathematica*.

At any point in a *Mathematica* session, there is always a "current context". When you type a name like p, *Mathematica* first looks in the current context to see if there is an object by that name. If it does not find any such object in your current context, *Mathematica* then searches a list of contexts in an attempt to find the object. If it fails to find the object in any of these contexts, then it creates a new object with the name you gave in your current context.

| | |
|---:|---|
| `$Context` | the current context |
| `$ContextPath` | the current context search path |
| `Begin["`*context*`` `` `"]` | switch to a new current context |
| `End[ ]` | revert to the previous context |
| `EndAdd[ ]` | revert to the previous context, adding the current context to the search path |

Basic context manipulation.

The way *Mathematica* searches for symbols in contexts specified by `$ContextPath` is somewhat analogous to the way it searches for files in directories specified by `$Path`. You can think of `Begin` as doing something like changing your working directory.

| | |
|---|---|
| When you start a *Mathematica* session, the current context is set to Global`. | `In[1]:= $Context`<br>`Out[1]= Global`` |
| When you type the name z, *Mathematica* creates a symbol by that name in the current context. | `In[2]:= z^2`<br>`Out[2]= z`$^2$ |
| This defines a value for z. | `In[3]:= z = 6`<br>`Out[3]= 6` |
| This resets the current context. | `In[4]:= Begin["New`"]`<br>`Out[4]= New`` |

Global\` is still in the context search path.

```
In[5]:= $ContextPath
Out[5]= {Global`, System`}
```

If you type z, you still get the symbol z in the Global\` context.

```
In[6]:= z
Out[6]= 6
```

This resets $ContextPath so as to exclude Global\`.

```
In[7]:= $ContextPath = {"System`"}
Out[7]= {System`}
```

If you now type z, *Mathematica* will now not be able to find any symbol with that name, so it creates a new symbol in the New\` context.

```
In[8]:= z
Out[8]= z
```

Typing the name y causes a symbol with that name to be created in the current context.

```
In[9]:= y = 9
Out[9]= 9
```

This reverts to the previous context, adding the current context to the context search path.

```
In[10]:= EndAdd[ ]
Out[10]= New`
```

If you now type z, you get the symbol named z in the Global\` context.

```
In[11]:= z
Out[11]= 6
```

This shows you all the objects named z.

```
In[12]:= ?*`z
z      New`z
```

There is no object in the Global\` context named y. *Mathematica* searches for an object named y in the contexts on the search path, and finds one in the New\` context.

```
In[12]:= y
Out[12]= 9
```

| | |
|---|---|
| *name* | a symbol in the current context, or found first on the search path |
| *context*\`*name* | a symbol in a specific context |
| \`*name* | a symbol in the current context |
| \`*context*\`*name* | a symbol in the "relative context" Context[]\`*context*\` |

Ways to refer to symbols in different contexts.

If you type z, *Mathematica* finds the symbol named z in your current context. This, on the other hand, finds the z in the New` context.

```
In[13]:= New`z
Out[13]= New`z
```

This defines a value for the z in the New` context.

```
In[14]:= New`z = 45
Out[14]= 45
```

Although any symbol you define must be in a particular context, aliases that you set up are global, and are not tied to a particular context. With an alias like mechp::=Mechanics`p, you can use mechp to refer to Mechanics`p, whatever your current context may be.

When you are working with a large number of different contexts, you may want to organize a hierarchy of contexts, a bit like a hierarchical file system. A context name can have any number of ` marks in. Thus for example, you could have a context called Physics`Mechanics` that you can view as subsidiary to the context Physics`. Once you are in the context Physics`, you can refer to Physics`Mechanics` relative to your current context as `Mechanics`.

An important point to realize is that a symbol "exists" as soon as its name has been mentioned, whether or not any value has been assigned to it. As a result, just typing x in a particular context can cause the x to be created in that context. Having an x in the current context will then hide any x's that appear in other contexts.

The x you have in the current context will interfere with other x's until you explicitly *remove* it. Clearing the value of x is not good enough. You have to actually take it entirely out of the system, so its name is no longer recognized.

| | |
|---|---|
| Clear[s] | clear the values of a symbol |
| Remove[s] | remove a symbol from the system |
| Remove["*context*`*"] | remove all symbols in a context |

Functions for getting rid of symbols.

This clears the value of z, and removes it entirely from the current context.

```
In[15]:= Remove[z]
```

Now when you type z, you get the object named z in the New` context.

```
In[16]:= z
Out[16]= 45
```

One case in which you may have to use Remove is when names that you have introduced conflict with names used in packages that you subsequently read in. When you enter a new name, a symbol with that name is created in your current context, typically the `Global`` context. When you read in a package, the objects it introduces are always put in the context for that package. Since in normal use, your current context will be `Global``, the symbols you created will hide symbols with the same name that were created by the package. In order to "see" the symbols from the package, you have to remove the symbols you created.

If you try to do a Laplace transform without reading in `Laplace.m`, *Mathematica* will just return an unevaluated result. By entering this input, however, you are creating the symbol `Laplace`, in the `Global`` context.

```
In[17]:= Laplace[t^2 Exp[t], t, s]
                t  2
Out[17]= Laplace[E  t , t, s]
```

When you read in `Laplace.m`, it creates a symbol `Laplace`, in the context `Laplace``.

```
In[18]:= <<Laplace.m
```

This shows all the symbols with name `Laplace`. The one that was created by `Laplace.m` is hidden by the one in the `Global`` context that you already created.

```
In[19]:= ?*`Laplace
Laplace          Laplace`Laplace
```

If you now try to do a Laplace transform, *Mathematica* will use *your* `Laplace` symbol, rather than the one from `Laplace.m`.

```
In[19]:= Laplace[t^2 Exp[t], t, s]
                t  2
Out[19]= Laplace[E  t , t, s]
```

This removes the `Laplace` symbol that you created.

```
In[20]:= Remove[Laplace]
```

Now *Mathematica* uses the `Laplace` symbol from `Laplace.m`, and computes the Laplace transform.

```
In[21]:= Laplace[t^2 Exp[t], t, s]
                2
Out[21]= -----------
                    3
          (-1 + s)
```

# ■ 2.8  Advanced Topic: Resource Management

## ■ 2.8.1  Time

| | |
|---|---|
| Timing[*expr*] | evaluate *expr*, and return a list of the result, and the CPU time it took |

Measuring computer time.

The actual time you wait to get the result of a calculation in *Mathematica* is a combination of several components.

First, there is the actual CPU time that is spent doing the computation. This is the time that is measured by Timing.

Second, there is time that your operating system spends in swapping *Mathematica* code and data on and off your mass storage device. On many computer systems, you will notice an extra delay the *first* time you use a particular *Mathematica* function. The extra time is spent in reading the code for the function off the mass storage device.

If your computer has a multi-tasking operating system (such as UNIX), the total time that elapses during a *Mathematica* computation also depends on the other things that your computer is doing.

One thing you should realize is that even the CPU time spent on a particular computation may be different the second time you do a computation. Many built-in *Mathematica* functions, for example, build internal tables only when you first use them in a particular way. Once these tables have been built, the functions will work much more quickly.

There are also a number of crucial optimizations that *Mathematica* uses internally to avoid re-evaluating expressions when it is not necessary. If you do the same calculation several times, it is possible that certain re-evaluations will be done on some, but not all, occasions. The result is that the CPU time spent doing the computation may vary.

This gives the CPU time used in computing 1000! on a particular kind of computer. The ; stops the value of the factorial from being printed, and returns Null instead.

```
In[1]:= Timing[1000!;]
Out[1]= {1.73333 Second, Null}
```

When you first ask for the factorial, *Mathematica* builds some internal tables. The second time you ask for it, it is much faster.

```
In[2]:= Timing[1000!;]
Out[2]= {0. Second, Null}
```

## ■ 2.8.2  Memory

Time is usually not a critical limitation in the computations that you do. At worst, you can always just wait longer to get your results. Memory space, on the other hand, can represent an insuperable barrier in a calculation.

If the intermediate expressions that you would generate in a particular calculation are larger than the memory you have available, then you will simply never be able to do that calculation on the computer system you are using.

*Mathematica* is quite careful about the way that it uses memory. Every time an intermediate expression that you generate is no longer needed, *Mathematica* immediately frees the memory that was allocated for it. (In technical terms, *Mathematica* uses a version of reference count memory management; as a result, it does not, for example, have to do "garbage collection".)

| | |
|---|---|
| MemoryInUse[ ] | the number of bytes of memory space currently being used by *Mathematica* |
| MaxMemoryUsed[ ] | the maximum number of bytes of memory used in this *Mathematica* session |
| ByteCount[*expr*] | the number of bytes of memory used to store *expr* |
| LeafCount[*expr*] | the number of terminal nodes in the expression tree for *expr* |
| Share[*expr*] | optimize the storage of *expr* |
| Share[ ] | optimize the storage of all expressions |

Memory management functions.

One issue that often comes up is exactly how much memory *Mathematica* can actually use on a particular computer system. Usually there is a certain amount of memory available for *all* processes running on the computer at a particular time. Sometimes this amount of memory is equal to the physical number of bytes of RAM in the computer. Often, it includes a certain amount of "virtual memory", obtained by swapping data on and off a mass storage device.

When *Mathematica* runs, it needs space both for data and for code. The complete code of *Mathematica* is typically at least one megabyte in size. For any particular calculation, only a small fraction of this code is usually used. However, in trying to work out the total amount of space available for *Mathematica* data, you should not forget what is needed for *Mathematica* code. In addition, you must include the space that is taken up by other processes running in the computer.

If there are fewer jobs running, you will usually find that your job can use more memory.

It is also worth realizing that the time needed to do a calculation can depend very greatly on how much physical memory you have. Although virtual memory allows you in principle to use large amounts of memory space, it is usually hundreds or even thousands of times slower to access than physical memory. As a result, if your calculation becomes so large that it needs to make use of virtual memory, it may run *much* more slowly.

Another point to realize is that under most operating systems, *Mathematica* can never really free memory that has once been allocated to it. The result from `MaxMemoryUsed[ ]` therefore usually gives not only the maximum amount of memory that your current *Mathematica* session has used, but also the total amount that the operating system has allocated to it.

There are various ways that you can save memory in a *Mathematica* session. The first is to remove values that you are no longer using. As soon you remove all references to a particular expression, *Mathematica* will free the memory associated with that expression.

You should remember, however, that any expression you got as output is stored as the value of the corresponding `Out[n]`. You can use `Clear[Out]` to get rid of these references to expressions.

The second way to save memory in storing expressions is to use the function `Share`. To see what `Share` does, you must understand some things about how *Mathematica* actually stores expressions.

Consider an expression like `f[1 + x, 1 + x]`. The two arguments `1 + x` are identical expressions. The question is whether internally, they are both actually stored in the same piece of computer memory, or whether there are two copies of `1 + x` at different places in computer memory. What `Share` does is to make sure that all expressions that are identical are actually stored in the same piece of computer memory. It effectively "shares" the memory that is used to store expressions.

The results that you get from `ByteCount` give the number of bytes that a particular expression takes *assuming that none of its subexpressions are shared*. As a result, `ByteCount` often gives you a substantial overestimate of the actual number of bytes of computer memory that a particular expression really uses.

## ■ 2.8.3  Advanced Topic: Stack Space

On most computer systems, the memory used by a running program is divided into two parts: memory explicitly allocated by the program, and "stack space". Every time an internal routine is called in the program, a certain amount of stack space is used to store parameters associated with the call. On many computer systems, the maximum amount of stack space that can be used by a program must be specified in advance. If the specified stack space limit is exceeded, the program usually just exits.

Results and intermediate expressions are all stored in memory that is explicitly allocated by *Mathematica*. However, calls of internal *Mathematica* routines use up stack space. The amount of stack space they use can become large if the routines are called recursively many times.

On most computer systems, it is difficult to control or even monitor directly the stack space used in a *Mathematica* session. Nevertheless, there is one important way that you can exercise somewhat indirect control over the amount of stack space used.

| | |
|---|---|
| `$RecursionLimit` | the number of levels of recursion now allowed |
| `$RecursionLimit=n` | set the number of levels of recursion allowed to $n$ |

Controlling the number of levels of recursion allowed during evaluation.

One of the primary sources of recursion in *Mathematica* is the evaluation of functions which are defined in terms of each other. The global variable `$RecursionLimit` specifies the number of levels of recursion that are allowed in the evaluation process. You should try to make sure that the limits you set are low enough that *Mathematica* should not run out of stack space simply as a result of doing recursive evaluations.

## ■ 2.8.4  Resource-Constrained Calculations

When you run *Mathematica* interactively, it is quite common to try a calculation, and to stop if it seems to be taking too long. If you use *Mathematica* in a batch-processing mode, you may not be able to monitor its progress, and to stop it if it is taking too long. The functions `TimeConstrained` and `MemoryConstrained`, however, allow you to try a calculation, and automatically stop it if it takes too much time or memory.

| | |
|---|---|
| TimeConstrained[*expr*, *t*] | tries to evaluate *expr*, stopping after *t* seconds |
| MemoryConstrained[*expr*, *b*] | tries to evaluate *expr*, stopping if more than *b* bytes of additional memory are requested |

Resource-constrained calculations.

The way that TimeConstrained and MemoryConstrained work is effectively to generate an interrupt if the constraints you specify are overrun. In many cases, *Mathematica* will not be able to stop immediately when the interrupt occurs, and so may well use up more time or memory than the constraint you gave. Whenever a calculation is interrupted, the result *Mathematica* returns is the symbol $Interrupted.

If you use TimeConstrained in programs you write, you should be sure to remember that different kinds of computers can run at very different speeds, so that TimeConstrained may give you different results.

# Chapter Three:
## *Advanced Mathematics in Mathematica*

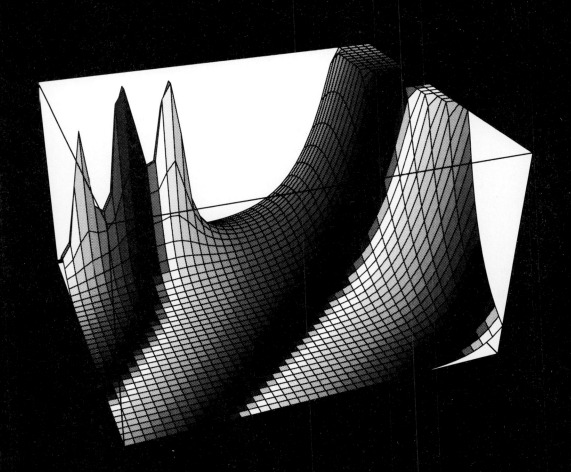

Chapter 1 described how to do basic mathematics with *Mathematica*. For many kinds of calculations, you will need to know nothing more. But if you do want to use more advanced mathematics, this chapter discusses how to do it in *Mathematica*.

This chapter goes through the various mathematical functions and methods that are built in to *Mathematica*. Some calculations can be done just by using these built-in mathematical capabilities. For many specific calculations, however, you will need to use application packages that have been written in *Mathematica*. These packages build on the mathematical capabilities discussed in this chapter, but add new functions for doing special kinds of calculations. Appendix A gives some examples of such packages.

Much of what is said in this chapter assumes a knowledge of mathematics at an advanced undergraduate level. If you do not understand a particular part of it, then you can probably assume that you will not need to use that part.

The emphasis in this chapter is on *what Mathematica* does, not *how* it does it. Except for a few cases in numerical mathematics, you should never need to know how *Mathematica* actually works inside.

**About the illustration overleaf:**

This is a picture of the Euler gamma function $\Gamma(z)$ in the complex plane. The height of the surface gives the absolute value of $\Gamma(z)$; the shading represents the phase of $\Gamma(z)$. You can see spikes at integer positions along the negative real axis, corresponding to poles in $\Gamma(z)$.

The actual *Mathematica* command used to produce this picture was
`Plot3D[{Abs[Gamma[x + I y]], `*shading*`}, {x, -2.5, 5}, {y, -6, 1}]`, where *shading* was
`GrayLevel[(Pi+Arg[Gamma[x+I y]])/(2Pi)]`. The following option settings were used:
`PlotRange->{0, 6}, ViewPoint->{-0.8, -2, 1.2}, BoxRatios->{1.2, 1, 0.7},`
`PlotPoints->40.`

# ■ 3.1  Numbers

## ■ 3.1.1  Types of Numbers

Four types of numbers are built into *Mathematica*.

| | |
|---|---|
| Integer | arbitrary-length exact integer |
| Rational | *integer*/*integer* in lowest terms |
| Real | approximate real number, with any specified precision |
| Complex | complex number of the form *number* + *number* I |

Intrinsic types of numbers in *Mathematica*.

Rational numbers always consist of a ratio of two integers, reduced to lowest terms.

*In[1]:=* **12344/2222**

*Out[1]=* $\dfrac{6172}{1111}$

Approximate real numbers are distinguished by the presence of an explicit decimal point.

*In[2]:=* **5456.**

*Out[2]=* 5456.

An approximate real number can have any number of digits.

*In[3]:=* **4.54543523454543523453452345234543**

*Out[3]=* 4.54543523454543523453452345234543

Complex numbers can have integer or rational components.

*In[4]:=* **4 + 7/8 I**

*Out[4]=* $4 + \dfrac{7\ I}{8}$

They can also have approximate real number components.

*In[5]:=* **4 + 5.6 I**

*Out[5]=* 4. + 5.6 I

| | |
|---|---|
| 123 | an exact integer |
| 123. | an approximate real number |
| 123.0000000000000 | an approximate real number with a certain precision |
| 123. + 0. I | a complex number with approximate real number components |

Several versions of the number 123.

You can distinguish different types of numbers in *Mathematica* by looking at their heads. (Although numbers in *Mathematica* have heads like other expressions, they do not have explicit elements which you can extract.)

| | |
|---|---|
| The object 123 is taken to be an exact integer, with head `Integer`. | *In[6]:=* **Head[123]** <br> *Out[6]=* Integer |

| | |
|---|---|
| The presence of an explicit decimal point makes *Mathematica* treat 123. as an approximate real number, with head `Real`. | *In[7]:=* **Head[123.]** <br> *Out[7]=* Real |

| | |
|---|---|
| `NumberQ[`*x*`]` | test whether *x* is any kind of number |
| `IntegerQ[`*x*`]` | test whether *x* is an integer |
| `EvenQ[`*x*`]` | test whether *x* is even |
| `OddQ[`*x*`]` | test whether *x* is odd |
| `PrimeQ[`*x*`]` | test whether *x* is a prime integer |
| `TrueQ[Head[`*x*`]==`*type*`]` | test the type of a number |

Tests for different types of numbers.

| | |
|---|---|
| `NumberQ[`*x*`]` tests for any kind of number. | *In[8]:=* **NumberQ[5.6]** <br> *Out[8]=* True |

| | |
|---|---|
| 5. is treated as a `Real`, so `IntegerQ` gives `False`. | *In[9]:=* **IntegerQ[5.]** <br> *Out[9]=* False |

If you use complex numbers extensively, there is one subtlety you should be aware of. When you enter a number like 123., *Mathematica* treats it as an approximate real number, but assumes that its imaginary part is exactly zero. Sometimes you may want to enter approximate complex numbers with imaginary parts that are zero, but only to a certain precision.

| | |
|---|---|
| When the imaginary part is the exact integer 0, *Mathematica* simplifies complex numbers to real ones. | `In[10]:= Head[ 123 + 0 I ]`<br>`Out[10]= Integer` |
| Here the imaginary part is only zero to a certain precision, so *Mathematica* retains the complex number form. | `In[11]:= Head[ 123. + 0. I ]`<br>`Out[11]= Complex` |
| When the imaginary part of a complex number would print as `0.`, *Mathematica* just prints the real part. | `In[12]:= 123. + 0. I`<br>`Out[12]= 123.` |

The distinction between complex numbers whose imaginary parts are exactly zero, or only zero to a certain precision, may seem like a pedantic one. However, when we discuss for example the interpretation of powers and roots of complex numbers in Section 3.2.7, the distinction will become significant.

One way to find out the type of a number in *Mathematica* is just to pick out its head using `Head[`*expr*`]`. For many purposes, however, it is better to use functions like `IntegerQ` which explicitly test for particular types. Functions like this are set up to return `True` if their argument is manifestly of the required type, and to return `False` otherwise. As a result, `IntegerQ[x]` will give `False`, unless you have assigned `x` an explicit integer value.

In doing symbolic computations, however, you may sometimes want to treat `x` as an integer, even though you have not assigned an explicit integer value to it. You can override the assumption that the symbol `x` is not an integer by explicitly making an assignment of the form `x/: IntegerQ[x] = True`. This assignment specifies that whenever you specifically test `x` with `IntegerQ`, it will give the result `True`. You should realize, however, that the assignment does not actually change the head of `x`, so that, for example, `x` will still not match `n_Integer`.

| | |
|---|---|
| `x` does not explicitly have head `Integer`, so `IntegerQ` returns `False`. | `In[13]:= IntegerQ[x]`<br>`Out[13]= False` |
| This specifies that `x` is in fact an integer. The `x/:` specifies that the rule is associated with `x`, not `IntegerQ`. | `In[14]:= x/: IntegerQ[x] = True`<br>`Out[14]= True` |
| The definition overrides the default assumption that `x` is not an integer. | `In[15]:= IntegerQ[x]`<br>`Out[15]= True` |

## ■ 3.1.2 Converting Between Types of Numbers

| | |
|---|---|
| N[$x$, $n$] | convert $x$ to an approximate real number with at most $n$ digits of precision |
| Rationalize[$x$] | give a rational number approximation to $x$ |
| Rationalize[$x$, $dx$] | give a rational number approximation to within tolerance $dx$ |

Functions that convert between different types of numbers.

| | |
|---|---|
| This gives a 30-digit real number approximation to 3/7. | *In[1]:=* **N[3/7, 30]**<br>*Out[1]=* 0.428571428571428571428571428571 |
| This takes the 30-digit number you have just generated, and reduces it to 20-digit precision. | *In[2]:=* **N[%, 20]**<br>*Out[2]=* 0.42857142857142857143 |
| This converts the result back to a rational number. | *In[3]:=* **Rationalize[%]**<br>*Out[3]=* $\dfrac{3}{7}$ |
| The numerical value of $\pi$ is not "sufficiently close" to a rational number to be converted. | *In[4]:=* **Rationalize[ N[Pi] ]**<br>*Out[4]=* 3.14159 |
| If you give a specific tolerance, **Rationalize** will give you a rational number approximation accurate to within that tolerance. | *In[5]:=* **Rationalize[ N[Pi], 10^-5 ]**<br>*Out[5]=* $\dfrac{355}{113}$ |

## ■ 3.1.3 Output Forms for Numbers

| | |
|---|---|
| NumberForm[$expr$, $n$] | print real numbers in $expr$ to $n$ digit precision |
| ScientificForm[$expr$] | print all real numbers in scientific notation |
| EngineeringForm[$expr$] | print all real numbers in engineering notation (exponents divisible by 3) |

Output forms for numbers in *Mathematica*.

| | |
|---|---|
| Here is $\pi^{60}$ to 35 decimal places. | `In[1]:= x = N[Pi^60, 35]` |
| | `Out[1]= 6745161642333967682001126958915.55914` |

This prints the number to 10 places.

`In[2]:= NumberForm[x, 10]`

`Out[2]//NumberForm= 6.745161642 10`$^{29}$

EngineeringForm writes real numbers so that their exponents are divisible by three.

`In[3]:= EngineeringForm[x]`

`Out[3]//EngineeringForm=`

`674.5161642333967682001269589155914 10`$^{27}$

You can give options to `NumberForm` to specify in more detail how you want both real numbers and integers to be printed.

| option | default value | |
|---|---|---|
| DigitBlock | Infinity | number of digits between breaks |
| NumberSeparator | "," | string to insert at breaks between blocks of digits |
| NumberPoint | "." | decimal point string |
| ExponentStep | 1 | size of steps in exponent |

Options for `NumberForm`.

Setting `DigitBlock->n` makes `NumberForm` insert a separator every *n* digits.

`In[4]:= NumberForm[30!, DigitBlock->3]`

`Out[4]//NumberForm=`

`265,252,859,812,191,058,636,308,480,000,000`

This writes the number in blocks of five digits, with spaces in between.

`In[5]:= NumberForm[30!, DigitBlock->5,`
`                    NumberSeparator->" "]`

`Out[5]//NumberForm=`

`265 25285 98121 91058 63630 84800 00000`

## ■ 3.1.4 Numbers in Other Bases

| | |
|---|---|
| $b$^^$nnnn$ | a number in base $b$ |
| BaseForm[x, $b$] | print with $x$ in base $b$ |

Numbers in other bases.

When the base is larger than 10, extra digits are represented by letters a–z.

The number $100101_2$ in base 2 is 37 in base 10.

```
In[1]:= 2^^100101
Out[1]= 37
```

This prints 37 in base 2.

```
In[2]:= BaseForm[37, 2]
Out[2]//BaseForm= 100101_2
```

Here is a number in base 16.

```
In[3]:= 16^^ffffaa00
Out[3]= 4294945280
```

You can do computations with numbers in base 16. Here the results are given in base 10.

```
In[4]:= 16^^fffaa2 + 16^^ff - 1
Out[4]= 16776096
```

This gives the results in base 16.

```
In[5]:= BaseForm[%, 16]
Out[5]//BaseForm= fffba0_{16}
```

You can give approximate real numbers, as well as integers, in other bases.

```
In[6]:= 2^^101.100101
Out[6]= 5.578125
```

Here are the first few digits of $\sqrt{2}$ in octal.

```
In[7]:= BaseForm[N[Sqrt[2], 30], 8]
Out[7]//BaseForm= 1.32404746317716746220426276612_8
```

## ■ 3.1.5 Numerical Precision

Integers and rational numbers in *Mathematica* are treated exactly. Real numbers, however, can usually only be treated approximately. The reason is that even to specify an arbitrary real number exactly can take an infinite number of digits. On a finite computer, therefore, one has to work with approximations to real numbers that involve only a finite number of digits.

In a symbolic system like *Mathematica*, however, you can nevertheless often represent real numbers exactly. For example, the symbol `Pi` is an exact representation of the mathematical constant $\pi$. However, when you ask for the numerical value of $\pi$ using `N`, *Mathematica* can give you only a finite precision result.

| | |
|---|---|
| `Precision[x]` | the number of decimal digits of precision in $x$ |
| `Accuracy[x]` | the number of significant digits to the right of the decimal point in $x$ |

Precision and accuracy of real numbers.

The precision of an exact integer is infinite.

```
In[1]:= Precision[3]
Out[1]= Infinity
```

This gives the numerical value of $\pi^{20}$ to 20 significant figures.

```
In[2]:= pi20 = N[Pi^20, 20]
Out[2]= 8769956796.0826994748
```

The precision is equal to the total number of decimal digits. *Mathematica* sometimes does computations to slightly more digits than you explicitly ask for.

```
In[3]:= Precision[pi20]
Out[3]= 20
```

The accuracy is the number of digits that appear to the right of the decimal point.

```
In[4]:= Accuracy[pi20]
Out[4]= 10
```

Whenever you enter a real number, *Mathematica* has to assign a definite precision to it. However, in the standard way of entering real numbers, you cannot explicitly specify the precision.

*Mathematica* always assumes that the digits you explicitly type in are accurate. The question is then whether you intend these digits to be followed by some number of zeroes, or not.

*Mathematica* distinguishes two kinds of approximate real numbers, and makes different assumptions about them. The first kind are "low precision numbers", that *Mathematica* assumes are always accurate to some definite "machine precision". (As discussed in Section 3.1.7, the machine precision is usually 16 decimal digits, but may vary from one computer system to another.)

The second kind of real numbers are "high precision" ones, which *Mathematica* assumes are accurate only to the number of digits you explicitly give.

> Low precision numbers (e.g 3.): assumed accurate to a definite machine precision.
>
> High precision numbers (e.g. 3.0000000000000000): assumed accurate only to the number of digits you explicitly give.

Two types of approximate real numbers in *Mathematica*.

| | |
|---|---|
| Here is a "high precision number". | `In[5]:= 3.000000000000000000000000000` |
| | `Out[5]= 3.` |
| | |
| The precision is equal to the number of digits you explicitly gave. | `In[6]:= Precision[ % ]` |
| | `Out[6]= 30` |
| | |
| 3. is a "low precision number". Its precision is equal to the fixed "machine precision". *Mathematica* effectively adds zeroes to the right of the decimal point until this precision is reached. | `In[7]:= Precision[ 3. ]` |
| | `Out[7]= 16` |
| | |
| Whenever you give just a few digits, *Mathematica* treats your numbers as "low precision", and assigns a definite machine precision to them. | `In[8]:= Precision[ 3.00 ]` |
| | `Out[8]= 16` |

In doing numerical computations, it is inevitable that you will sometimes end up with results that are less precise than you want. Particularly when you get numerical results that are very close to zero, you may well want to *assume* that the results should be exactly zero.

| | |
|---|---|
| `Chop[`*expr*`]` | replace all approximate real numbers in *expr* with magnitude less than $10^{-10}$ by 0 |
| `Chop[`*expr*`,` *dx*`]` | replace numbers with magnitude less than *dx* by 0 |

Removing numbers close to zero.

| | |
|---|---|
| Here is a $2 \times 2$ numerical matrix. | `In[9]:= m = {{2., -3.}, {4., -7.}}` |
| | `Out[9]= {{2., -3.}, {4., -7.}}` |
| | |
| Multiplying the matrix by its inverse should give an identity matrix. Instead, there are some small off-diagonal terms. | `In[10]:= Inverse[m] . m` |
| | `Out[10]= {{1., -7.10543 10^{-15}}, {2.66454 10^{-15}, 1.}}` |

You can use Chop to remove the off-diagonal terms.

```
In[11]:= Chop[%]
Out[11]= {{1., 0}, {0, 1.}}
```

## ■ 3.1.6  High Precision Calculations

When you do calculations with high precision numbers, *Mathematica* always keeps track of the precision of your results. *Mathematica* tries to give you results that are as accurate as possible, given the precision of the input you provided.

Here is the numerical value of $\pi^2$ to 30 significant figures.

```
In[1]:= N[ Pi^2, 30 ]
Out[1]= 9.86960440108935861883449099988
```

Operations like these give you results that have the same precision as your input.

```
In[2]:= 2 Sqrt[ % ] + 1
Out[2]= 7.28318530717958647692528676655901
```

If you multiply by a number with 20-digit precision, *Mathematica* gives you a 20-digit result.

```
In[3]:= % N[Sqrt[2], 20]
Out[3]= 10.299979438689827542833
```

When you multiply several numbers together, the general rule is that the result you get has the same precision as the least precise one of the numbers. When you add numbers, it is the *accuracy* of each number that enters, rather than its precision.

You will often find that you get results that are less precise than the input you gave. One common reason for this is "roundoff error": if you subtract two nearby numbers, the result is necessarily less precise than the numbers themselves. *Mathematica* always keeps track of the precision of the results you get.

Even though each number is given to high precision, their difference has much lower precision.

```
In[4]:= 1.11111111111111111 -
        1.111111111111111000
Out[4]= 1.11 10
```
$$Out[4]= 1.11 \cdot 10^{-16}$$

Here is the numerical value of log(3) to 30 significant figures.

```
In[5]:= N[ Log[3], 30 ]
Out[5]= 1.09861228866810969139524523692
```

The exponential of the finite precision approximation to log(3) differs from 3 in the last decimal place.

```
In[6]:= Exp[ % ]
Out[6]= 3.
```

The difference from the exact result is given to only one significant figure.

```
In[7]:= % - 3
```
$$Out[7]= -1. \cdot 10^{-33}$$

The precision of the output from a function can depend in a complicated way on the precision of the input. Functions that vary rapidly typically give less precise output, since the variation of the output associated with uncertainties in the input is larger. Functions that are close to constants can actually give output that is more precise than their input.

| | |
|---|---|
| Functions like `Sin` that vary rapidly typically give output that is less precise than their input. | `In[8]:= Sin[111111111.0000000000000000]`<br><br>`Out[8]= -0.29753510333494323` |

Here is $e^{-40}$ to 20 digit precision.

`In[9]:= N[Exp[-40], 20]`

$$Out[9]= 4.2483542552915889953 \ 10^{-18}$$

The result you get by adding 1 has a higher precision.

`In[10]:= 1 + %`

`Out[10]= 1.0000000000000000004248354255291588995 3293`

It is worth realizing that different ways of doing the same calculation can end up giving you results with very different precisions. Typically, if you once lose precision in a calculation, it is essentially impossible to regain it: in losing precision, you are effectively losing information about your result.

Here is a 40-digit number that is close to 1.

`In[11]:= x = N[1 - 10^-30, 40]`

`Out[11]= 0.9999999999999999999999999999999`

Adding 1 to it gives another 40-digit number.

`In[12]:= 1 + x`

`Out[12]= 1.9999999999999999999999999999999`

Most of the original precision has been maintained.

`In[13]:= Precision[%]`

`Out[13]= 44`

This way of computing `1 + x` loses precision.

`In[14]:= (x^2 - 1) / (x - 1)`

`Out[14]= 2.`

The result obtained in this way has quite low precision.

`In[15]:= Precision[%]`

`Out[15]= 15`

The internal algorithms that *Mathematica* uses to evaluate mathematical functions are set up to maintain as much precision as possible. In most cases, built-in *Mathematica* functions will give you results that have as much precision as can be justified on the basis of your input. In some cases, however, it is simply impractical to do this, and *Mathematica* will give you results that have lower precision. If you give higher precision input, *Mathematica* will use higher precision in its internal calculations, and you will usually be able to get a higher precision result.

The fact that different ways of doing the same calculation can give you different numerical answers, means, among other things, that comparisons between approximate real numbers must be treated with care. In testing whether two real numbers are "equal", *Mathematica* effectively finds their difference, and tests whether the result is "consistent with zero" to the precision given.

These numbers are equal to the precision given.

```
In[16]:= 3 == 3.000000000000000000
Out[16]= True
```

## ■ 3.1.7  Low Precision Calculations

When you type in a high precision number, such as 3.000000000000000000, *Mathematica* assumes that the number is accurate only to the precision you explicitly give. If you type in a number like 3., however, *Mathematica* effectively adds trailing zeroes to give the number some definite "machine precision".

*Mathematica* effectively adds trailing zeroes, to make a number accurate to the machine precision of 16 digits.

```
In[1]:= Precision[3.]
Out[1]= 16
```

When you work with low precision numbers, *Mathematica* carries out all calculations to the fixed machine precision.

The result is computed to the machine precision, then printed to a default of 6 decimal places.

```
In[2]:= Log[3.]
Out[2]= 1.09861
```

This calculation is again done to the machine precision. *Mathematica* does not print explicit zeroes after the decimal point in this case.

```
In[3]:= Exp[%]
Out[3]= 3.
```

Subtracting 3 gives the difference from the exact result. This difference is again computed to the machine precision.

```
In[4]:= % - 3
Out[4]= 4.44089 10
```
$$4.44089 \times 10^{-16}$$

The difference has the same precision as your original input.

```
In[5]:= Precision[%]
Out[5]= 16
```

When you do high-precision calculations, *Mathematica* keeps track of the precision you have, and tries to make sure that it gives you results only to the precision that can be justified. This means, for example, that when you subtract two nearby high precision numbers, you typically get a result with much lower precision.

In low precision calculations, *Mathematica* does not explicitly keep track of the precision of your results. Instead, it does *all* computations to a fixed machine precision. This means that *Mathematica* can give you results that go beyond the precision that can be justified in a particular case.

For example, if you subtract two nearby low precision numbers, *Mathematica* gives you a result with the same machine precision. The first few digits of this result will be meaningful. Subsequent digits go beyond the precision that can be justified, and are usually quite meaningless. The digits are included only because *Mathematica* is set up to give a result with a fixed precision.

| | |
|---|---|
| The computation is done to the standard machine precision, and the result is 4. to the precision that is printed. | *In[6]:=* **4. + 10^-12 / 3**<br><br>*Out[6]=* **4.** |
| The remainder you get on subtracting 4 is not exactly 10^-12/3. It contains some spurious higher-order digits that go beyond the precision that can be justified. | *In[7]:=* **% - 4**<br><br>*Out[7]=* **3.33067 10**$^{-13}$ |

The fact that you can get spurious digits in low precision numerical calculations with *Mathematica* is in many respects quite unsatisfactory. The ultimate reason, however, that *Mathematica* uses fixed precision for these calculations is a matter of computational efficiency.

*Mathematica* is usually set up to insulate you as much as possible from the details of the computer system you are using. In dealing with low precision numbers, you would lose too much, however, if *Mathematica* did not make use of some specific features of your computer.

The important point is that almost all computers have special hardware or microcode for doing floating point calculations to a particular fixed precision. *Mathematica* makes use of these features when doing low precision numerical calculations.

The typical arrangement is that all low precision numbers in *Mathematica* are represented as "double precision floating point numbers" in the underlying computer system. On most current computers, such numbers contain a total of 64 binary bits, typically yielding 16 decimal digits of mantissa.

The main advantage of using the built-in floating point capabilities of your computer is speed. High precision numerical calculations, which do not make such direct use of these capabilities, are usually many times slower than low precision calculations.

There are several disadvantages of using built-in floating point capabilities. One already mentioned is that it forces all numbers to have a fixed precision, independent of what precision can be justified for them.

A second disadvantage is that the treatment of low precision numbers can vary slightly from one computer system to another. In working with low precision numbers, *Mathematica* is at the mercy of the floating point arithmetic system of each particular computer. If floating point arithmetic is done differently on two computers, you may get slightly different results for low precision *Mathematica* calculations on those computers.

One detail to be aware of is that the floating point numbers implemented on typical computers are restricted not only in their precision, but also in their magnitude. If you give *Mathematica* a number whose magnitude lies outside the range covered by floating point numbers, *Mathematica* will automatically use its own high precision mechanisms to represent and manipulate the number.

When the result of a computation like this cannot be represented at machine precision, *Mathematica* automatically produces a high precision number.

```
In[8]:= Exp[1000.]

Out[8]= 1.970071114017 10^434
```

## ■ 3.1.8 Advanced Topic: Indeterminate and Infinite Results

If you type in an expression like 0/0, *Mathematica* prints a message, and returns the result Indeterminate.

```
In[1]:= 0/0

General::dby0: Division by zero.

Infinity::indt:
        Indeterminate expression 0 ComplexInfinity
        encountered.

Out[1]= Indeterminate
```

An expression like 0/0 is an example of an *indeterminate numerical result*. If you type in 0/0, there is no way for *Mathematica* to know what answer you want. If you got 0/0 by taking the limit of $x/x$ as $x \to 0$, then you might want the answer 1. On the other hand, if you got 0/0 instead as the limit of $2x/x$, then you probably want the answer 2. The expression 0/0 on its own does not contain enough information to choose between these and other cases. As a result, its value must be considered indeterminate.

Whenever an indeterminate result is produced in an arithmetic computation, *Mathematica* prints a warning message, and then returns Indeterminate as the result of the computation. If you ever try to use Indeterminate in an arithmetic computation, you always get the result Indeterminate. A single indeterminate

expression effectively "poisons" any arithmetic computation. (The symbol
`Indeterminate` plays a role in *Mathematica* similar to the "not a number" object
in the IEEE Floating Point Standard.)

The usual laws of arithmetic simplification are suspended in the case of `Indeterminate`.

```
In[2]:= Indeterminate - Indeterminate
Out[2]= Indeterminate
```

`Indeterminate` "poisons" any arithmetic computation, and leads to an indeterminate result.

```
In[3]:= 2 Indeterminate - 7
Out[3]= Indeterminate
```

When you do arithmetic computations inside *Mathematica* programs, it is often important to be able to tell whether indeterminate results were generated in the computations. You can do this by using the function `Check` discussed in Section 2.5.5 to test whether any warning messages associated with indeterminate results were produced.

You can use `Check` inside a program to test whether warning messages are generated in a computation.

```
In[4]:= Check[(7 - 7)/(8 - 8), meaningless]
General::dby0: Division by zero.
Infinity::indt:
        Indeterminate expression 0 ComplexInfinity
            encountered.
Out[4]= meaningless
```

| | |
|---|---|
| `Indeterminate` | an indeterminate numerical result |
| `Infinity` | a positive infinite quantity |
| `-Infinity` | a negative infinite quantity (`DirectedInfinity[-1]`) |
| `DirectedInfinity[r]` | an infinite quantity with complex direction $r$ |
| `ComplexInfinity` | an infinite quantity with an undetermined direction |
| `DirectedInfinity[ ]` | equivalent to `ComplexInfinity` |

Indeterminate and infinite quantities.

There are many situations where it is convenient to be able to do calculations with infinite quantities. The symbol `Infinity` in *Mathematica* represents a positive infinite quantity. You can use it to specify such things as limits of sums and integrals. You can also do some arithmetic calculations with it.

Here is an integral with an infinite limit.

```
In[5]:= Integrate[1/x^3, {x, 1, Infinity}]
```
$$Out[5]= \frac{1}{2}$$

*Mathematica* knows that $1/\infty = 0$.

```
In[6]:= 1/Infinity
```
```
Out[6]= 0
```

If you try to find the difference between two infinite quantities, you get an indeterminate result.

```
In[7]:= Infinity - Infinity
Infinity::indt:
        Indeterminate expression Infinity - Infinity
            encountered.
```
```
Out[7]= Indeterminate
```

There are a number of subtle points that arise in handling infinite quantities. One of them concerns the "direction" of an infinite quantity. When you do an infinite integral, you typically think of performing the integration along a path in the complex plane that goes to infinity in some direction. In this case, it is important to distinguish different versions of infinity that correspond to different directions in the complex plane. $+\infty$ and $-\infty$ are two examples, but for some purposes one also needs $i\infty$ and so on.

In *Mathematica*, infinite quantities can have a "direction", specified by a complex number. When you type in the symbol `Infinity`, representing a positive infinite quantity, this is converted internally to the form `DirectedInfinity[1]`, which represents an infinite quantity in the $+1$ direction. Similarly, `-Infinity` becomes `DirectedInfinity[-1]`, and `I Infinity` becomes `DirectedInfinity[I]`. Although the `DirectedInfinity` form is always used internally, the standard output format for `DirectedInfinity[`$r$`]` as $r$ `Infinity`.

`Infinity` is converted internally to `DirectedInfinity[1]`.

```
In[8]:= Infinity // FullForm
```
```
Out[8]//FullForm= DirectedInfinity[1]
```

Although the notion of a "directed infinity" is often useful, it is not always available. If you type in `1/0`, you get an infinite result, but there is no way to determine the "direction" of the infinity. *Mathematica* represents the result of `1/0` as `DirectedInfinity[ ]`. In standard output form, this undirected infinity is printed out as `ComplexInfinity`.

1/0 gives an undirected form of infinity.

```
In[9]:= 1/0
General::dby0: Division by zero.
Out[9]= ComplexInfinity
```

# ■ 3.2 Mathematical Functions

## ■ 3.2.1 Naming Conventions

Mathematical functions in *Mathematica* are given names according to definite rules. As with most *Mathematica* functions, the names are usually complete English words, fully spelled out. For a few very common functions, *Mathematica* uses the traditional abbreviations. Thus the modulo function, for example, is `Mod`, not `Modulo`.

Mathematical functions that are usually referred to by a person's name have names in *Mathematica* of the form *PersonSymbol*. Thus, for example, the Legendre polynomials $P_n(x)$ are denoted `LegendreP[n, x]`.

Although this convention does lead to longer function names, it avoids any ambiguity or confusion. If you use a particular function a lot, you can always define an alias for its name, as discussed in Section 2.7.1.

When the standard notation for a mathematical function involves both subscripts and superscripts, the subscripts are given *before* the superscripts in the *Mathematica* form. Thus, for example, the associated Legendre polynomials $P_n^m(x)$ are denoted `LegendreP[n, m, x]`.

## ■ 3.2.2 Numerical Functions

| | |
|---|---|
| `Round[x]` | integer $\langle x \rangle$ closest to $x$ |
| `Floor[x]` | greatest integer $\lfloor x \rfloor$ not larger than $x$ |
| `Ceiling[x]` | least integer $\lceil x \rceil$ not smaller than $x$ |
| `Sign[x]` | 1 for $x > 0$, -1 for $x < 0$ |
| `Abs[x]` | absolute value $|x|$ of $x$ |
| `Max[`$x_1$`, `$x_2$`, ...]` or `Max[{`$x_1$`, `$x_2$`, ...}, ...]`<br>the maximum of $x_1$, $x_2$, ... | |
| `Min[`$x_1$`, `$x_2$`, ...]` or `Min[{`$x_1$`, `$x_2$`, ...}, ...]`<br>the minimum of $x_1$, $x_2$, ... | |

Some numerical functions of real variables.

| x | Round[x] | Floor[x] | Ceiling[x] |
|---|---|---|---|
| 2.4 | 2 | 2 | 3 |
| 2.5 | 2 | 2 | 3 |
| 2.6 | 3 | 2 | 3 |
| -2.4 | -2 | -3 | -2 |
| -2.5 | -2 | -3 | -2 |
| -2.6 | -3 | -3 | -2 |

Functions that convert to integers.

| | |
|---|---|
| x + I y | the complex number $x + iy$ |
| Re[z] | the real part $\mathrm{Re}\, z$ |
| Im[z] | the imaginary part $\mathrm{Im}\, z$ |
| Conjugate[z] | the complex conjugate $z^*$ or $\overline{z}$ |
| Abs[z] | the absolute value $|z|$ |
| Arg[z] | the argument $\phi$ such that $z = |z|e^{i\phi}$ |

Numerical functions of complex variables.

# ■ 3.2.3 Pseudorandom Numbers

| | |
|---|---|
| `Random[ ]` | a pseudorandom real between 0 and 1 |
| `Random[Real, xmax]` | a pseudorandom real between 0 and *xmax* |
| `Random[Real, {xmin, xmax}]` | a pseudorandom real between *xmin* and *xmax* |
| `Random[Complex]` | a pseudorandom complex number in unit square |
| `Random[Complex, {zmin, zmax}]` | a pseudorandom complex number in the rectangle defined by *zmin* and *zmax* |
| `Random[type, range, n]` | a pseudorandom number with *n*-digit precision |
| `Random[Integer]` | 0 or 1 with probability $\frac{1}{2}$ |
| `Random[Integer, {imin, imax}]` | a pseudorandom integer between *imin* and *imax*, inclusive |
| `SeedRandom[ ]` | reseed the pseudorandom generator, with the time of day |
| `SeedRandom[s]` | reseed with the integer *s* |

Pseudorandom number generation.

| | |
|---|---|
| This gives a list of three pseudorandom numbers. | *In[1]:=* `Table[Random[ ], {3}]`<br>*Out[1]=* {0.353297, 0.0205034, 0.117374} |
| Here is a 30-digit pseudorandom real number in the range 0 to 1. | *In[2]:=* `Random[Real, {0, 1}, 30]`<br>*Out[2]=* 0.756200220413389091346356107147 |
| This gives a list of eight pseudorandom integers between 100 and 200 (inclusive). | *In[3]:=* `Table[Random[Integer, {100, 200}], {8}]`<br>*Out[3]=* {127, 195, 196, 113, 187, 117, 155, 154} |

If you call **Random[ ]** repeatedly, you should get a "typical" sequence of numbers, with no particular pattern. There are many ways to use such numbers.

One common way to use pseudorandom numbers is in making numerical tests of hypotheses. For example, if you believe that two symbolic expressions are mathematically equal, you can test this by plugging in "typical" numerical values for symbolic parameters, and then comparing the numerical results. (If you do this, you should be careful about functions of complex variables that may not have unique values.)

Here is a symbolic equation.

```
In[4]:= Sin[Cos[x]] == Cos[Sin[x]]
Out[4]= Sin[Cos[x]] == Cos[Sin[x]]
```

Substituting in a random numerical value shows that the equation is not always **True**.

```
In[5]:= % /. x -> Random[ ]
Out[5]= False
```

Other common uses of pseudorandom numbers include simulating probabilistic processes, and sampling large spaces of possibilities. The pseudorandom numbers that *Mathematica* generates are always uniformly distributed over the range you specify.

**Random** is unlike any other *Mathematica* function in that every time you call it, you potentially get a different result. If you use **Random** in a calculation, therefore, you may get different answers on different occasions.

The sequences that you get from **Random[ ]** are not in most senses "truly random", although they should be "random enough" for practical purposes. The sequences are in fact produced by applying a definite mathematical algorithm, starting from a particular "seed". If you give the same seed, then you get the same sequence.

When *Mathematica* starts up, it takes the time of day (measured in small fractions of a second) as the seed for the pseudorandom number generator. Two different *Mathematica* sessions will therefore almost always give different sequences of pseudorandom numbers.

If you want to make sure that you always get the same sequence of pseudorandom numbers, you can explicitly give a seed for the pseudorandom generator, using **SeedRandom**.

This re-seeds the pseudorandom generator.

```
In[6]:= SeedRandom[143]
```

Here are three pseudorandom numbers.

```
In[7]:= Table[Random[ ], {3}]
Out[7]= {0.353297, 0.0205034, 0.117374}
```

If you re-seed the pseudorandom generator with the same seed, you get the same sequence of pseudorandom numbers.

```
In[8]:= SeedRandom[143]; Table[Random[ ], {3}]
Out[8]= {0.353297, 0.0205034, 0.117374}
```

## ■ 3.2.4  Integer and Number Theoretical Functions

| | |
|---|---|
| Mod[$k$, $n$] | $k$ modulo $n$ (positive remainder from dividing $k$ by $n$) |
| Quotient[$m$, $n$] | the quotient of $m$ and $n$ (integer part of $m/n$) |
| GCD[$n_1$, $n_2$, ...] | the greatest common divisor of $n_1$, $n_2$, ... |
| LCM[$n_1$, $n_2$, ...] | the least common multiple of $n_1$, $n_2$, ... |

Some integer functions.

| | |
|---|---|
| The remainder on dividing 17 by 3. | `In[1]:= Mod[17, 3]` |
| | `Out[1]= 2` |
| The integer part of 17/3. | `In[2]:= Quotient[17, 3]` |
| | `Out[2]= 5` |
| Mod also works with real numbers. | `In[3]:= Mod[5.6, 1.2]` |
| | `Out[3]= 0.8` |
| Mod always gives a non-negative result. | `In[4]:= Mod[-5.6, 1.2]` |
| | `Out[4]= 0.4` |

For any integers $a$ and $b$, it is always true that `b*Quotient[a, b] + Mod[a, b]` is equal to $a$.

The **greatest common divisor** function GCD[$n_1$, $n_2$, ...] gives the largest integer that divides all the $n_i$ exactly. When you enter a ratio of two integers, *Mathematica* effectively uses GCD to cancel out common factors, and give a rational number in lowest terms.

The **least common multiple** function LCM[$n_1$, $n_2$, ...] gives the smallest integer that contains all the factors of each of the $n_i$.

| | |
|---|---|
| The largest integer that divides both 24 and 15 is 3. | `In[5]:= GCD[24, 15]` |
| | `Out[5]= 3` |

| | |
|---|---|
| FactorInteger[*n*] | a list of the prime factors of *n*, and their exponents |
| Divisors[*n*] | a list of the integers that divide *n* |
| Prime[*k*] | the $k^{\text{th}}$ prime number |
| PrimeQ[*n*] | give True if *n* is a prime, and False otherwise |

Integer factoring and related functions.

This gives the factors of 24 as $2^3$, $3^1$. The first element in each list is the factor; the second is its exponent.

```
In[6]:= FactorInteger[24]
Out[6]= {{2, 3}, {3, 1}}
```

Here are the factors of a larger integer.

```
In[7]:= FactorInteger[111111111111111111]
Out[7]= {{3, 2}, {7, 1}, {11, 1}, {13, 1}, {19, 1},
   {37, 1}, {52579, 1}, {333667, 1}}
```

You should realize that according to current mathematical thinking, integer factoring is a fundamentally difficult computational problem. As a result, you can easily type in an integer that *Mathematica* will not be able to factor in anything short of an astronomical amount of time. So long as the integers you give are less than about 20 digits long, FactorInteger should have no trouble. Only in special cases, however, will it be able to deal with much longer integers. (You can make some factoring problems go faster by setting the option FactorComplete->False, so that FactorInteger[*n*] tries to pull out only one factor from *n*.)

Here is a rather special long integer.

```
In[8]:= 30!
Out[8]= 265252859812191058636308480000000
```

*Mathematica* can easily factor this special integer.

```
In[9]:= FactorInteger[%]
Out[9]= {{2, 26}, {3, 14}, {5, 7}, {7, 4}, {11, 2},
   {13, 2}, {17, 1}, {19, 1}, {23, 1}, {29, 1}}
```

Although *Mathematica* may not be able to factor a large integer, it can often still test whether or not the integer is a prime. In addition, *Mathematica* has a fast way to find the $k^{\text{th}}$ prime number.

It is often much faster to test whether a number is prime than to factor it.

```
In[10]:= PrimeQ[234242423]
Out[10]= False
```

Here is a plot of the first 100 primes.     *In[11]:=* `ListPlot[ Table[ Prime[n], {n, 100} ] ]`

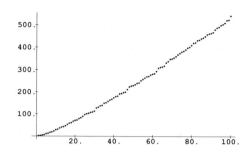

This is the millionth prime.     *In[12]:=* `Prime[1000000]`

*Out[12]=* `15485863`

| | |
|---|---|
| `PowerMod[a, b, n]` | the power $a^b$ modulo $n$ |
| `EulerPhi[n]` | the Euler totient function $\phi(n)$ |
| `MoebiusMu[n]` | the Möbius function $\mu(n)$ |
| `DivisorSigma[k, n]` | the divisor function $\sigma_k(n)$ |
| `JacobiSymbol[n, m]` | the Jacobi symbol $\left(\frac{n}{m}\right)$ |
| `ExtendedGCD[m, n]` | the extended gcd of $m$ and $n$ |
| `LatticeReduce[{v₁, v₂, ...}]` | the reduced lattice basis for the set of integer vectors $v_i$ |

Some functions from number theory.

The **modular power function** `PowerMod[a, b, n]` gives exactly the same results as `Mod[a∧b, n]`. `PowerMod` is much more efficient, however, because it avoids generating the full form of a∧b.

You can use `PowerMod` not only to find positive modular powers, but also to find **modular inverses**. `PowerMod[a, -b, n]` gives, if possible, an integer $k$ such that $(ak)^b \equiv 1 \bmod n$. (Whenever such an integer exists, it is guaranteed to be unique.) If no such integer $k$ exists, *Mathematica* leaves `PowerMod` unevaluated.

`PowerMod` is equivalent to using `Power`, then     *In[13]:=* `PowerMod[2, 13451, 3]`
`Mod`, but is much more efficient.

*Out[13]=* `2`

| | |
|---|---|
| This gives the modular inverse of 3 modulo 7. | $In[14]:=$ `PowerMod[3, -1, 7]` |
| | $Out[14]=$ 5 |

| | |
|---|---|
| Multiplying the inverse by 3 modulo 7 gives 1, as expected. | $In[15]:=$ `Mod[3 %, 7]` |
| | $Out[15]=$ 1 |

The **Euler totient function** $\phi(n)$ gives the number of integers less than $n$ that are relatively prime to $n$. An important relation (Fermat's Little Theorem) is that $a^{\phi(n)} \equiv 1 \bmod n$ for all $a$ relatively prime to $n$.

The **Möbius function** $\mu(n)$ is defined to be $(-1)^k$ if $n$ is a product of $k$ distinct primes, and 0 if $n$ contains a squared factor (other than 1). An important relation is the Möbius inversion formula, which states that if $g(n) = \sum_{d|n} f(d)$, then $f(n) = \sum_{d|n} \mu(d) g(n/d)$, where the sums are over all positive integers $d$ that divide $n$.

The **divisor function** $\sigma_k(n)$ is the sum of the $k^{\text{th}}$ powers of the divisors of $n$. The function $\sigma_0(n)$ gives the total number of divisors of $n$, and is often denoted $d(n)$. The function $\sigma_1(n)$, equal to the sum of the divisors of $n$, is often denoted $\sigma(n)$.

| | |
|---|---|
| For prime $n$, $\phi(n) = n - 1$. | $In[16]:=$ `EulerPhi[17]` |
| | $Out[16]=$ 16 |

| | |
|---|---|
| The result is 1, as guaranteed by Fermat's Little Theorem. | $In[17]:=$ `PowerMod[3, %, 17]` |
| | $Out[17]=$ 1 |

| | |
|---|---|
| This gives a list of all the divisors of 24. | $In[18]:=$ `Divisors[24]` |
| | $Out[18]=$ {1, 2, 3, 4, 6, 8, 12, 24} |

| | |
|---|---|
| $\sigma_0(n)$ gives the total number of distinct divisors of 24. | $In[19]:=$ `DivisorSigma[0, 24]` |
| | $Out[19]=$ 8 |

The **Jacobi symbol** `JacobiSymbol[`$n$`, `$m$`]` reduces to the **Legendre symbol** $\left(\frac{n}{m}\right)$ when $m$ is an odd prime. The Legendre symbol is equal to zero if $n$ is divisible by $m$, otherwise it is equal to 1 if $n$ is a quadratic residue modulo the prime $m$, and to $-1$ if it is not. An integer $n$ relatively prime to $m$ is said to be a quadratic residue modulo $m$ if there exists an integer $k$ such that $k^2 \equiv n \bmod m$. The full Jacobi symbol is a product of the Legendre symbols $\left(\frac{n}{p_i}\right)$ for each of the prime factors $p_i$ such that $m = \prod_i p_i$.

The **extended gcd** `ExtendedGCD[`$m$`, `$n$`]` gives a list {$g$, {$r$, $s$}} where $g$ is the greatest common divisor of $m$ and $n$, and $r$ and $s$ are integers such that $g = rm + sn$.

The extended gcd is important in finding integer solutions to linear (Diophantine) equations.

The first number in the list is the gcd of 105 and 196.

*In[20]:=* **ExtendedGCD[105, 196]**

*Out[20]=* {7, {15, -8}}

The second pair of numbers satisfies $g = rm + sn$.

*In[21]:=* **15 105 - 8 196**

*Out[21]=* 7

The lattice reduction function **LatticeReduce[{$v_1$, $v_2$, ...}]** is used in many modern number theoretical and combinatorial algorithms. The basic idea is to think of the vectors $v_k$ of integers as defining a mathematical *lattice*. The vector representing each point in the lattice can be written as a linear combination of the form $\sum c_k v_k$, where the $c_k$ are integers. For a particular lattice, there are many possible choices of the "basis vectors" $v_k$. What **LatticeReduce** does is to find a reduced set of basis vectors $\bar{v}_k$ for the lattice, with certain special properties.

Three unit vectors along the three coordinate axes already form a reduced basis.

*In[22]:=* **LatticeReduce[{{1,0,0},{0,1,0},{0,0,1}}]**

*Out[22]=* {{1, 0, 0}, {0, 1, 0}, {0, 0, 1}}

This gives the reduced basis for a lattice in four-dimensional space specified by three vectors.

*In[23]:=* **LatticeReduce[{{1,0,0,12345}, {0,1,0,12435}, {0,0,1,12354}}]**

*Out[23]=* {{-1, 0, 1, 9}, {9, 1, -10, 0}, {85, -143, 59, 6}}

Notice that in the last example, **LatticeReduce** replaces vectors that are nearly parallel by vectors that are more perpendicular. In the process, it finds some quite short basis vectors.

## ■ 3.2.5  Combinatorial Functions

| | |
|---|---|
| $n!$ | factorial $n(n-1)(n-2) \times \ldots \times 1$ |
| $n!!$ | double factorial $n(n-2)(n-4) \times \ldots$ |
| Binomial[$n$, $m$] | binomial coefficient $\binom{n}{m} = \frac{n!}{m!(n-m)!}$ |
| Multinomial[$n_1$, $n_2$, ...] | multinomial coefficient $\frac{(n_1+n_2+\ldots)!}{n_1!n_2!\ldots}$ |
| BernoulliB[$n$] | Bernoulli number $B_n$ |
| BernoulliB[$n$, $x$] | Bernoulli polynomial $B_n(x)$ |
| EulerE[$n$] | Euler number $E_n$ |
| EulerE[$n$, $x$] | Euler polynomial $E_n(x)$ |
| StirlingS1[$n$, $m$] | Stirling number of the first kind $S_n^{(m)}$ |
| StirlingS2[$n$, $m$] | Stirling number of the second kind $\mathcal{S}_n^{(m)}$ |
| PartitionsP[$n$] | the number $p(n)$ of unrestricted partitions of the integer $n$ |
| PartitionsQ[$n$] | the number $q(n)$ of partitions of $n$ into distinct parts |

Combinatorial functions.

The **factorial function** $n!$ gives the number of ways of ordering $n$ objects. For non-integer $n$, the numerical value of $n!$ is obtained from the gamma function, discussed in Section 3.2.10.

The **binomial coefficient** Binomial[$n$, $m$] can be written as $\binom{n}{m} = \frac{n!}{m!(n-m)!}$. It gives the number of ways of choosing $m$ objects from a collection of $n$ objects, without regard to order. The **Catalan numbers**, which appear in various tree enumeration problems, are given in terms of binomial coefficients $c_n = \frac{1}{n+1}\binom{2n}{n}$.

The **multinomial coefficient** Multinomial[$n_1$, $n_2$, ...], denoted $(N; n_1, n_2, ..., n_m) = \frac{N!}{n_1!n_2!\ldots n_m!}$, gives the number of ways of partitioning $N$ distinct objects into $m$ sets, each of size $n_i$ (with $N = \sum_{i=1}^{m} n_i$).

*Mathematica* gives the exact integer result for the factorial of an integer.

```
In[1]:= 30!
Out[1]= 265252859812191058636308480000000
```

For non-integers, *Mathematica* evaluates factorials using the gamma function.

```
In[2]:= 3.6!

Out[2]= 13.3813
```

*Mathematica* can give symbolic results for some binomial coefficients.

```
In[3]:= Binomial[n, 2]

          n (-1 + n)
Out[3]= ─────────────
              2
```

This gives the number of ways of partitioning $6 + 5 = 11$ objects into sets containing 6 and 5 objects.

```
In[4]:= Multinomial[6, 5]

Out[4]= 462
```

The result is the same as $\binom{11}{6}$.

```
In[5]:= Binomial[11, 6]

Out[5]= 462
```

The **Bernoulli polynomials** BernoulliB[n, x] satisfy the generating function relation $\frac{te^{xt}}{e^t-1} = \sum_{n=0}^{\infty} B_n(x)\frac{t^n}{n!}$. The **Bernoulli numbers** BernouilliB[n] are given by $B_n = B_n(0)$. The $B_n$ appear as the coefficients of the terms in the Euler-Maclaurin summation formula for approximating integrals.

Numerical values for Bernoulli numbers are needed in many numerical algorithms. You can always get these numerical values by first finding exact rational results using BernoulliB[n], and then applying N. The function NBernoulliB[n] gives the numerical value of $B_n$ directly. NBernoulliB[n, p] gives the value to $p$ digit precision.

The **Euler polynomials** EulerE[n, x] have generating function $\frac{2e^{xt}}{e^t+1} = \sum_{n=0}^{\infty} E_n(x)\frac{t^n}{n!}$, and the **Euler numbers** EulerE[n] are given by $E_n = 2^n E_n(\frac{1}{2})$. The Euler numbers are related to the **Genocchi numbers** by $G_n = 2^{2-2n}nE_{2n-1}$.

This gives the second Bernoulli polynomial $B_2(x)$.

```
In[6]:= BernoulliB[2, x]

          1          2
Out[6]= ─ - x + x
          6
```

You can also get Bernoulli polynomials by explicitly computing the power series for the generating function.

```
In[7]:= Series[t Exp[x t]/(Exp[t] - 1), {t, 0, 4}]

                  1             1    x    x    2
Out[7]= 1 + (-(─) + x) t + (── - ─ + ──) t  +
                  2            12    2    2

           x    x    x     3         1      x    x    x     4
        (── - ── + ──) t  + (-(───) + ── - ── + ──) t  +
          12    4    6              720    24   12   24

           5
        O[t]
```

BernoulliB[$n$] gives exact rational number results for Bernoulli numbers.

*In[8]:=* **BernoulliB[20]**

$$Out[8]= -(\frac{174611}{330})$$

NBernoulliB[$n$] gives numerical values for the $B_n$ directly.

*In[9]:=* **NBernoulliB[20]**

*Out[9]=* -529.124242424242

Stirling numbers show up in many combinatorial enumeration problems. For **Stirling numbers of the first kind** StirlingS1[$n$, $m$], $(-1)^{n-m}S_n^{(m)}$ gives the number of permutations of $n$ elements which contain exactly $m$ cycles. These Stirling numbers satisfy the generating function relation $x(x-1)...(x-n+1) = \sum_{m=0}^{n} S_n^{(m)} x^m$.

**Stirling numbers of the second kind** StirlingS2[$n$, $m$] give the number of ways of partitioning a set of $n$ elements into $m$ non-empty subsets. They satisfy the relation $x^n = \sum_{m=0}^{n} S_n^{(m)} x(x-1)...(x-m+1)$.

The **partition function** PartitionsP[$n$] gives the number of ways of writing the integer $n$ as a sum of positive integers, without regard to order. PartitionsQ[$n$] gives the number of ways of writing $n$ as a sum of positive integers, with the constraint that all the integers in each sum are distinct.

This gives a table of Stirling numbers of the first kind.

*In[10]:=* **Table[StirlingS1[5, i], {i, 5}]**

*Out[10]=* {24, -50, 35, -10, 1}

The Stirling numbers appear as coefficients in this product.

*In[11]:=* **Expand[Product[x - i, {i, 0, 4}]]**

$$Out[11]= 24\ x - 50\ x^2 + 35\ x^3 - 10\ x^4 + x^5$$

This gives the number of partitions of 100, with and without the constraint that the terms should be distinct.

*In[12]:=* **{PartitionsQ[100], PartitionsP[100]}**

*Out[12]=* {444793, 190569292}

The partition function $p(n)$ increases asymptotically like $e^{\sqrt{n}}$. Note that you cannot simply use Plot to generate a plot of a function like PartitionsP because the function can only be evaluated with integer arguments.

*In[13]:=* **ListPlot[ Table[
        N[Log[ PartitionsP[n] ]], {n, 100} ] ]**

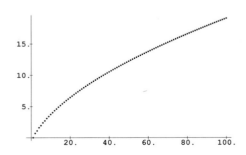

The functions in this section allow you to *enumerate* various kinds of combinatorial objects. Functions like `Permutations`, discussed in Section 1.7.13, allow you instead to *generate* lists of various combinations of elements.

## ■ 3.2.6  Elementary Transcendental Functions

| | |
|---|---|
| `Exp[z]` | exponential function $e^z$ |
| `Log[z]` | logarithm $\log_e(z)$ |
| `Log[b, z]` | logarithm $\log_b(z)$ to base $b$ |
| `Sin[z]`, `Cos[z]`, `Tan[z]`, `Csc[z]`, `Sec[z]`, `Cot[z]` | trigonometric functions (with arguments in radians) |
| `ArcSin[z]`, `ArcCos[z]`, `ArcTan[z]`, `ArcCsc[z]`, `ArcSec[z]`, `ArcCot[z]` | inverse trigonometric functions (giving results in radians) |
| `ArcTan[x, y]` | the argument of $x + iy$ |
| `Sinh[z]`, `Cosh[z]`, `Tanh[z]`, `Csch[z]`, `Sech[z]`, `Coth[z]` | hyperbolic functions |
| `ArcSinh[z]`, `ArcCosh[z]`, `ArcTanh[z]`, `ArcCsch[z]`, `ArcSech[z]`, `ArcCoth[z]` | inverse hyperbolic functions |

Elementary transcendental functions.

*Mathematica* gives exact results for logarithms whenever it can. Here is $\log_2 1024$.

```
In[1]:= Log[2, 1024]
Out[1]= 10
```

You can find the numerical values of mathematical functions to any precision.

```
In[2]:= N[Log[2], 40]
Out[2]= 0.6931471805599453094172321214581765680755
```

$\log(-2)$ gives a complex number result.

```
In[3]:= N[ Log[-2] ]
Out[3]= 0.693147 + 3.14159 I
```

*Mathematica* can evaluate logarithms with complex arguments.

```
In[4]:= N[ Log[2 + 8 I] ]
Out[4]= 2.10975 + 1.32582 I
```

The arguments of trigonometric functions are always given in radians.

```
In[5]:= Sin[Pi/2]
Out[5]= 1
```

You can convert from degrees by explicitly multiplying by the constant `Degree`.

`In[6]:= N[ Sin[30 Degree] ]`

`Out[6]= 0.5`

Here is a plot of the hyperbolic tangent function. It has a characteristic "sigmoidal" form.

`In[7]:= Plot[ Tanh[x], {x, -8, 8} ]`

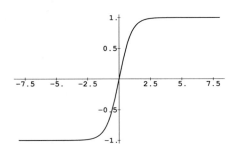

There are a number of additional trigonometric and hyperbolic functions that are sometimes used.

The **versine** function is defined as $\text{vers}(z) = 1 - \cos(z)$. The **haversine** is simply $\text{hav}(z) = \frac{1}{2}\text{vers}(z)$.

The complex exponential $e^{ix}$ is sometimes written as $\text{cis}(x)$.

The **gudermannian function** is defined as $\text{gd}(z) = 2\tan^{-1}(e^z) - \frac{\pi}{2}$. The **inverse gudermannian** is $\text{gd}^{-1}(z) = \log(\sec(z) + \tan(z))$. The gudermannian satisfies such relations as $\sinh(z) = \tan(\text{gd}(x))$.

### ■ 3.2.7  Functions that Do Not Have Unique Values

When you ask for the square root $s$ of a number $a$, you are effectively asking for the solution to the equation $s^2 = a$. This equation, however, in general has two different solutions. Both $s = 2$ and $s = -2$ are, for example, solutions to the equation $s^2 = 4$. When you evaluate the "function" $\sqrt{4}$, however, you usually want to get a single number, and so you have to choose one of these two solutions. A standard choice is that $\sqrt{x}$ should be positive for $x > 0$. This is what the *Mathematica* function `Sqrt[x]` does.

The need to make one choice from two solutions means that `Sqrt[x]` cannot be a true *inverse function* for x∧2. Taking a number, squaring it, and then taking the square root, can give you a different number than you started with.

$\sqrt{4}$ gives $+2$, not $-2$.

`In[1]:= Sqrt[4]`

`Out[1]= 2`

| | |
|---|---|
| Squaring and taking the square root does not necessarily give you the number you started with. | `In[2]:= Sqrt[(-2)^2]`<br><br>`Out[2]= 2` |

When you evaluate $\sqrt{-2i}$, there are again two possible answers: $-1+i$ and $1-i$. In this case, however, it is less clear which one to choose.

There is in fact no way to choose $\sqrt{z}$ so that it is continuous for all complex values of $z$. There has to be a "branch cut" – a line in the complex plane across which the function $\sqrt{z}$ is discontinuous. *Mathematica* adopts the usual convention of taking the branch cut for $\sqrt{z}$ to be along the negative real axis.

| | |
|---|---|
| This gives $1-i$, not $-1+i$. | `In[3]:= N[ Sqrt[-2 I] ]`<br><br>`Out[3]= 1. - 1. I` |

| | |
|---|---|
| The branch cut in `Sqrt` along the negative real axis means that values of `Sqrt[z]` with $z$ just above and below the axis are very different. | `In[4]:= {Sqrt[-2 + 0.1 I], Sqrt[-2 - 0.1 I]}`<br><br>`Out[4]= {0.0353443 + 1.41466 I, 0.0353443 - 1.41466 I}` |

| | |
|---|---|
| Their squares are nevertheless close. | `In[5]:= %^2`<br><br>`Out[5]= {-2. + 0.1 I, -2. - 0.1 I}` |

| | |
|---|---|
| The discontinuity along the negative real axis is quite clear in this three-dimensional picture of the imaginary part of the square root function. | `In[6]:= Plot3D[ Im[Sqrt[x + I y]], {x, -4, 4}, {y, -4, 4},`<br><br>`        Lighting->True ]` |

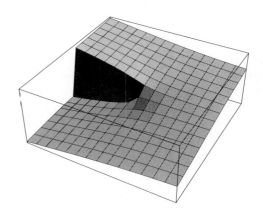

When you find an $n^{\text{th}}$ root using $z^{\frac{1}{n}}$, there are in principle $n$ possible results. To get a single value, you have to choose a particular *principal root*. There is absolutely no guarantee that taking the $n^{\text{th}}$ root of an $n^{\text{th}}$ power will leave you with the same number.

| | |
|---|---|
| This takes the tenth power of a complex number. The result is unique. | `In[7]:= (2.5 + I)^10`<br><br>`Out[7]= -15781.2 - 12335.8 I` |

| | |
|---|---|
| There are ten possible tenth roots. *Mathematica* chooses one of them. In this case it is not the number whose tenth power you took. | `In[8]:= %^(1/10)`<br><br>`Out[8]= 2.61033 - 0.660446 I` |

The complete setup for $n^{\text{th}}$ roots in *Mathematica* involves one further complication. If you take an odd root (say cube root) of a negative real number, *Mathematica* gives you a real number result. However, if you take an odd root of a complex number that has only an approximately zero imaginary part, *Mathematica* gives you a complex number result with phase $e^{i\pi/n}$. (Section 3.1.1 discusses how to set up different kinds of numbers.)

| | |
|---|---|
| Taking the cube root of a negative real number gives a real number result. | `In[9]:= (-2.)^(1/3)`<br><br>`Out[9]= -1.25992` |

| | |
|---|---|
| Taking the cube root of a complex number with only an approximately zero imaginary part gives a complex number result. | `In[10]:= (-2. + 0. I)^(1/3)`<br><br>`Out[10]= 0.629961 + 1.09112 I` |

There are many mathematical functions which, like roots, essentially give solutions to equations. The logarithm function, and inverse trigonometric functions, are examples. In almost all cases, there are many possible solutions to the equations. Unique "principal" values nevertheless have to be chosen for the functions. The choices cannot be made continuous over the whole complex plane. Instead, lines of discontinuity, or branch cuts, must occur. The positions of these branch cuts are often quite arbitrary. *Mathematica* makes the most standard mathematical choices for them.

| | |
|---|---|
| `Sqrt[z]` and $z \wedge n$ | $(-\infty, 0)$ for $\mathrm{Re}\, n \leq 0$, $(-\infty, 0]$ for $\mathrm{Re}\, n > 0$ (*n* not an integer) |
| `Exp[z]` | none |
| `Log[z]` | $(-\infty, 0]$ |
| trigonometric functions | none |
| `ArcSin[z]` and `ArcCos[z]` | $(-\infty, -1)$ and $(+1, +\infty)$ |
| `ArcTan[z]` | $(-i\infty, -i]$ and $[i, i\infty)$ |
| `ArcCsc[z]` and `ArcSec[z]` | $(-1, +1)$ |
| `ArcCot[z]` | $[-i, +i]$ |
| hyperbolic functions | none |
| `ArcSinh[z]` | $(-i\infty, -i)$ and $(+i, +i\infty)$ |
| `ArcCosh[z]` | $(-\infty, +1)$ |
| `ArcTanh[z]` | $(-\infty, -1]$ and $[+1, +\infty)$ |
| `ArcCsch[z]` | $(-i, i)$ |
| `ArcSech[z]` | $(-\infty, 0]$ and $(+1, +\infty)$ |
| `ArcCoth[z]` | $[-1, +1]$ |

Branch cut discontinuities in the complex plane.

ArcSin is a multiple-valued function, so there is no guarantee that it always gives the "inverse" of Sin.

```
In[11]:= ArcSin[Sin[4.5]]
Out[11]= -1.35841
```

Values of `ArcSin[z]` on opposite sites of the branch cut can be very different.

```
In[12]:= {ArcSin[2 + 0.1 I], ArcSin[2 - 0.1 I]}
Out[12]= {1.51316 + 1.31888 I, 1.51316 - 1.31888 I}
```

A three-dimensional picture, showing the two branch cuts for the function $\sin^{-1}(z)$.

```
In[13]:= Plot3D[ Im[ArcSin[x + I y]], {x, -4, 4},
              {y, -4, 4}, Lighting -> True]
```

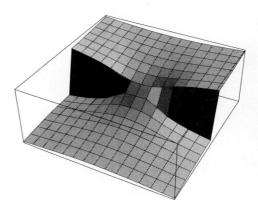

You should realize that the non-uniqueness of functions like square root can have strange consequences for symbolic, as well as numerical, computations. A typical problem is that general symbolic simplification rules give results that are incompatible with specific numerical values.

*Mathematica* simplifies this expression using the built-in rule $\sqrt{x^2} \to x$.

```
In[14]:= Sqrt[(-1 - a)^2]

Out[14]= -1 - a
```

If you now set **a** to 0, you get −1.

```
In[15]:= % /. a -> 0

Out[15]= -1
```

This *first* replaces **a** by 0, then takes the square root. The result is different.

```
In[16]:= Sqrt[ (-1 - a)^2  /. a -> 0 ]

Out[16]= 1
```

## ■ 3.2.8  Mathematical Constants

| | |
|---:|:---|
| I | $i = \sqrt{-1}$ |
| Infinity | $\infty$ |
| Pi | $\pi \simeq 3.14159$ |
| Degree | $\pi/180$: degrees to radians conversion factor |
| GoldenRatio | $\phi = (1 + \sqrt{5})/2 \simeq 1.61803$ |
| E | $e \simeq 2.71828$ |
| EulerGamma | Euler's constant $\gamma \simeq 0.577216$ |
| Catalan | Catalan's constant $\simeq 0.915966$ |

Mathematical constants.

**Euler's constant** EulerGamma is given by the limit $\gamma = \lim_{m \to \infty} \left( \sum_{k=1}^{m} \frac{1}{k} - \log m \right)$. It appears in many integrals, and asymptotic formulae. It is sometimes known as the **Euler-Mascheroni constant**, and denoted $C$.

**Catalan's constant** Catalan is given by the sum $\sum_{k=0}^{\infty} (-1)^k (2k + 1)^{-2}$. It often appears in asymptotic estimates of combinatorial functions.

Mathematical constants can be evaluated to arbitrary precision.

```
In[1]:= N[EulerGamma, 40]
Out[1]= 0.5772156649015328606065120900824024310422
```

# ■ 3.2.9 Orthogonal Polynomials

| | |
|---|---|
| `LegendreP[n, x]` | Legendre polynomials $P_n(x)$ |
| `LegendreP[n, m, x]` | associated Legendre polynomials $P_n^m(x)$ |
| `SphericalHarmonicY[l, m, theta, phi]` | spherical harmonics $Y_l^m(\theta, \phi)$ |
| `GegenbauerC[n, m, x]` | Gegenbauer polynomials $C_n^m(x)$ |
| `ChebyshevT[n, x]`, `ChebyshevU[n, x]` | Chebyshev polynomials $T_n(x)$ and $U_n(x)$ of the first and second kinds |
| `HermiteH[n, x]` | Hermite polynomials $H_n(x)$ |
| `LaguerreL[n, x]` | Laguerre polynomials $L_n(x)$ |
| `LaguerreL[n, a, x]` | generalized Laguerre polynomials $L_n^a(x)$ |
| `JacobiP[n, a, b, x]` | Jacobi polynomials $P_n^{(a,b)}(x)$ |

Orthogonal polynomials.

**Legendre polynomials** `LegendreP[n, x]` arise in studies of systems with three-dimensional spherical symmetry. They satisfy the differential equation $(1 - x^2)\frac{d^2y}{dx^2} - 2x\frac{dy}{dx} + n(n+1)y = 0$, and the orthogonality relation $\int_{-1}^{1} P_m(x)P_n(x)\,dx = 0$ for $m \neq n$.

The **associated Legendre polynomials** `LegendreP[n, m, x]` are obtained from derivatives of the Legendre polynomials according to $P_n^m(x) = (-1)^m(1 - x^2)^{m/2}\frac{d^m}{dx^m}P_n(x)$. Notice that for odd integers $m \leq n$, the $P_n^m(x)$ contain powers of $\sqrt{1 - x^2}$, and are therefore not strictly polynomials. The $P_n^m(x)$ reduce to $P_n(x)$ when $m = 0$.

The **spherical harmonics** `SphericalHarmonicY[l, m, theta, phi]` are related to associated Legendre polynomials. They satisfy the orthogonality relation $\int Y_l^m(\theta, \phi)Y_{l'}^{m'}(\theta, \phi)\,d\Omega = 0$ for $l \neq l'$ or $m \neq m'$, where $d\Omega$ represents integration over the surface of the unit sphere.

This gives the algebraic form of the Legendre polynomial $P_6(x)$.

```
In[1]:= LegendreP[6, x]
```

$$Out[1]= \frac{-5 + 105\,x^2 - 315\,x^4 + 231\,x^6}{16}$$

The integral $\int_{-1}^{1} P_5(x) P_6(x)\, dx$ gives zero by virtue of the orthogonality of the Legendre polynomials.

```
In[2]:= Integrate[LegendreP[5,x] LegendreP[6,x],
                   {x, -1, 1}]

Out[2]= 0
```

Integrating the square of a single Legendre polynomial gives a nonzero result.

```
In[3]:= Integrate[LegendreP[6, x]^2, {x, -1, 1}]

          2
Out[3]= ——
          13
```

High degree Legendre polynomials oscillate rapidly.

```
In[4]:= Plot[LegendreP[10, x], {x, -1, 1}]
```

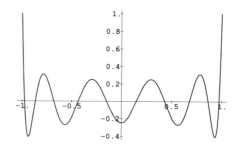

The associated Legendre "polynomials" contain pieces proportional to $\sqrt{1 - x^2}$.

```
In[5]:= LegendreP[6, 3, x]

                         3
                         —
                 2   2   -945 x     3465 x
Out[5]= -((1 - x )    (———————— + ————————))
                           2          2
```

Section 3.2.10 discusses the generalization of Legendre polynomials to Legendre functions, which can have non-integer degrees.

```
In[6]:= LegendreP[6.1, 0]

Out[6]= -0.306319
```

**Gegenbauer polynomials** `GegenbauerC[n, m, x]` can be viewed as generalizations of the Legendre polynomials to systems with $(m + 2)$-dimensional spherical symmetry. They are sometimes known as **ultraspherical polynomials**.

Series of Chebyshev polynomials are often used in making numerical approximations to functions. The **Chebyshev polynomials of the first kind**, `ChebyshevT[n, x]`, are defined by $T_n(\cos\theta) = \cos(n\theta)$. They are normalized so that $T_n(1) = 1$. They satisfy the orthogonality relation $\int_{-1}^{1} T_m(x)T_n(x)(1-x^2)^{-\frac{1}{2}}\, dx = 0$ for $m \neq n$. The $T_n(x)$ also satisfy an orthogonality relation under summation at discrete points in $x$ corresponding to the roots of $T_n(x)$.

The **Chebyshev polynomials of the second kind** `ChebyshevU[n, z]` are defined by $U_n(x) = \frac{\sin(n+1)\theta}{\sin\theta}$. With this definition, $U_n(1) = n + 1$. The $U_n$ satisfy the orthogonality relation $\int_{-1}^{1} U_m(x)U_n(x)(1-x^2)^{\frac{1}{2}}\, dx = 0$ for $m \neq n$.

The name "Chebyshev" is a transliteration from the Cyrillic alphabet; several other English spellings, such as "Tschebyscheff", are sometimes used.

**Hermite polynomials** HermiteH[$n$, x] arise as the quantum mechanical wave functions for a harmonic oscillator. They satisfy the differential equation $\frac{d^2 y}{dx^2} - 2x\frac{dy}{dx} + 2ny = 0$, and the orthogonality relation $\int_{-\infty}^{\infty} H_m(x)H_n(x)e^{-x^2}\,dx = 0$ for $m \neq n$. An alternative form of Hermite polynomials sometimes used is $He_n(x) = H_n(\frac{x}{\sqrt{2}})$ (a different overall normalization of the $He_n(x)$ is sometimes used).

The Hermite polynomials are related to the **parabolic cylinder functions** or **Weber functions** $D_n(x)$ by $D_n(x) = e^{-x^2/4} H_n(\frac{x}{\sqrt{2}})$.

This gives the probability density for an excited state of a quantum mechanical harmonic oscillator. The average of the wiggles is roughly the classical physics result.

$In[7]:=$ `Plot[(HermiteH[6, x] Exp[-x^2/2])^2, {x, -6, 6}]`

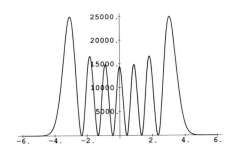

**Generalized Laguerre polynomials** LaguerreL[$n$, a, x] are related to hydrogen atom wave functions in quantum mechanics. They satisfy the differential equation $x\frac{d^2 y}{dx^2} + (a + 1 - x)\frac{dy}{dx} + ny = 0$, and the orthogonality relation $\int_{-\infty}^{\infty} L_m^a(x)L_n^a(x)x^a e^{-x}\,dx = 0$ for $m \neq n$. The **Laguerre polynomials** LaguerreL[$n$, x] correspond to the special case $a = 0$.

**Jacobi polynomials** JacobiP[$n$, a, b, x] occur in studies of the rotation group, particularly in quantum mechanics. They satisfy the orthogonality relation $\int_{-1}^{1} P_m^{(a,b)}(x)P_n(a,b)(x)(1 - x)^a(1 + x)^b\,dx = 0$ for $m \neq n$. Legendre, Gegenbauer and Chebyshev polynomials can all be viewed as special cases of Jacobi polynomials. The Jacobi polynomials are sometimes given in the alternative form $G_n(p, q, x) = \frac{n!\Gamma(n+p)}{\Gamma(2n+p)} P_n^{p-q,q-1}(2x - 1)$.

You can get formulae for generalized Laguerre polynomials with arbitrary values of $a$.

$In[8]:=$ `LaguerreL[2, a, x]`

$Out[8]=$ $\dfrac{x^2}{2} - x\,(2 + a) + \dfrac{(1 + a)\,(2 + a)}{2}$

# ■ 3.2.10 Special Functions

| | |
|---:|:---|
| `AiryAi[z]` | Airy function $\mathrm{Ai}(z)$ |
| `BesselJ[n, z]` and `BesselY[n, z]` | |
| | Bessel functions $J_n(z)$ and $Y_n(z)$ |
| `BesselI[n, z]` and `BesselK[n, z]` | |
| | modified Bessel functions $I_n(z)$ and $K_n(z)$ |
| `Beta[x, y]` | Euler beta function $B(x, y)$ |
| `Beta[a, x, y]` | incomplete beta function $B_a(x, y)$ |
| `Erf[z]` | error function $\mathrm{erf}(z)$ |
| `Erf[z0, z1]` | generalized error function $\mathrm{erf}(z_1) - \mathrm{erf}(z_0)$ |
| `ExpIntegralE[n, z]` | exponential integral $E_n(z)$ |
| `ExpIntegralEi[z]` | exponential integral $\mathrm{Ei}(z)$ |
| `Gamma[z]` | Euler gamma function $\Gamma(z)$ |
| `Gamma[a, z]` | incomplete gamma function $\Gamma(a, z)$ |
| `Gamma[a, z0, z1]` | generalized incomplete gamma function $\Gamma(a, z_1) - \Gamma(a, z_0)$ |
| `Hypergeometric0F1[a, z]` | hypergeometric function ${}_0F_1(; a; z)$ |
| `Hypergeometric1F1[a, b, z]` | Kummer confluent hypergeometric function ${}_1F_1(a; b; z)$ |
| `HypergeometricU[a, b, z]` | confluent hypergeometric function $U(a, b, z)$ |
| `Hypergeometric2F1[a, b, c, z]` | hypergeometric function ${}_2F_1(a, b; c; z)$ |
| `LegendreP[n, z]`, `LegendreQ[n, z]` | |
| | Legendre functions $P_n(z)$ and $Q_n(z)$ of the first and second kinds |
| `LegendreP[n, m, z]`, `LegendreQ[n, m, z]` | |
| | associated Legendre functions $P_n^m(z)$ and $Q_n^m(z)$ |

Special functions, part one.

| | |
|---|---|
| `LerchPhi[z, s, a]` | Lerch's transcendent $\Phi(z, s, a)$ |
| `LogIntegral[z]` | logarithmic integral $\mathrm{li}(z)$ |
| `Pochhammer[a, n]` | Pochhammer symbol $(a)_n$ |
| `PolyGamma[z]` | digamma function $\psi(z)$ |
| `PolyGamma[n, z]` | $n^{\text{th}}$ derivative of the digamma function $\psi^{(n)}(z)$ |
| `PolyLog[n, z]` | polylogarithm function $\mathrm{Li}_n(z)$ |
| `Zeta[s]` | Riemann zeta function $\zeta(s)$ |
| `Zeta[s, a]` | generalized Riemann zeta function $\zeta(s, a)$ |

Special functions, part two.

*Mathematica* includes all the common special functions of mathematical physics. We will discuss each of the functions in turn. You can find more extensive discussions in various handbooks, such as *Handbook of Mathematical Functions*, edited by M. Abramowitz and I. Stegun, (Dover, 1965), *Formulas and Theorems for the Special Functions of Mathematical Physics*, by W. Magnus, F. Oberhettinger and R. P. Soni, (Third edition, Springer-Verlag, 1966), or *Encyclopedic Dictionary of Mathematics*, Volume IV, edited by Kiyosi Itô, (Second Edition, MIT Press, 1987).

There are often several conflicting definitions of any particular special function in the literature. When you use a special function in *Mathematica*, you should look at the definition given below to make sure it is what you want.

| | |
|---|---|
| *Mathematica* gives exact results for some values of special functions. | `In[1]:= Gamma[15/2]` |
| | $Out[1]= \dfrac{135135 \text{ Sqrt[Pi]}}{128}$ |
| No exact result is known here. | `In[2]:= Gamma[15/7]` |
| | $Out[2]= \text{Gamma}[\dfrac{15}{7}]$ |
| A numerical result, to arbitrary precision, can nevertheless be found. | `In[3]:= N[%, 40]` |
| | `Out[3]= 1.0690715000448624397994137689702693267` |
| You can give complex arguments to special functions. | `In[4]:= Gamma[3 + 4I] //N` |
| | `Out[4]= 0.00522554 - 0.172547 I` |

| | |
|---|---|
| Special functions automatically get applied to each element in a list. | $In[5]:=$ `Gamma[{3/2, 5/2, 7/2}]` |

$$Out[5]= \{\frac{\text{Sqrt[Pi]}}{2}, \frac{3\ \text{Sqrt[Pi]}}{4}, \frac{15\ \text{Sqrt[Pi]}}{8}\}$$

| | |
|---|---|
| *Mathematica* knows some analytical properties of special functions, such as derivatives. | $In[6]:=$ `D[Gamma[x], {x, 2}]` |

$$Out[6]= \text{Gamma[x] PolyGamma[x]}^2 + \text{Gamma[x] PolyGamma[1, x]}$$

| | |
|---|---|
| You can use `FindRoot` to find roots of special functions. | $In[7]:=$ `FindRoot[ BesselJ[0, x], {x, 1} ]` |
| | $Out[7]=$ `{x -> 2.40483}` |

Special functions in *Mathematica* can usually be evaluated for arbitrary complex values of their arguments. Often, however, the defining relations given below apply only for some special choices of arguments. In these cases, the full function corresponds to a suitable extension or "analytic continuation" of these defining relations. Thus, for example, integral representations of functions are valid only when the integral exists, but the functions themselves can usually be defined elsewhere by analytic continuation.

As a simple example of how the domain of a function can be extended, consider the function represented by the sum $\sum_{k=0}^{\infty} x^k$. This sum converges only when $|x| < 1$. Nevertheless, it is easy to show analytically that for any $x$, the complete function is equal to $\frac{1}{1-x}$. Using this form, you can easily find a value of the function for any $x$, at least so long as $x \neq 1$.

## Gamma and Related Functions

The **Euler gamma function** `Gamma[z]` is defined by the integral $\Gamma(z) = \int_0^\infty t^{z-1} e^{-t} dt$. For positive integer $n$, $\Gamma(n) = (n-1)!$. $\Gamma(z)$ can be viewed as a generalization of the factorial function, valid for complex arguments $z$.

The **Euler beta function** `Beta[x, y]` is $B(x,y) = \frac{\Gamma(x)\Gamma(y)}{\Gamma(x+y)} = \int_0^1 t^{x-1}(1-t)^{y-1} dt$.

The **Pochhammer symbol** `Pochhammer[a, n]` is $(a)_n = \frac{\Gamma(a+n)}{\Gamma(a)}$. It often appears in series expansions for hypergeometric functions.

The **incomplete gamma function** `Gamma[a, z]` is defined by the integral $\Gamma(a,z) = \int_z^\infty t^{a-1} e^{-t} dt$. *Mathematica* includes a generalized incomplete gamma function `Gamma[a, z0, z1]` defined as $\int_{z_0}^{z_1} t^{a-1} e^{-t} dt$. The alternative incomplete gamma function $\gamma(a,z)$ can therefore be obtained in *Mathematica* as `Gamma[a, 0, z]`.

The **incomplete beta function** `Beta[a, x, y]` is given by $B_a(x,y) = \int_0^a t^{x-1}(1-t)^{y-1} dt$. Notice that the limit of the integral appears as the *first* argument of the incomplete beta function, and the *second* argument of the incomplete gamma functions.

The incomplete beta and gamma functions, and their inverses, are common in statistics.

Derivatives of the gamma function often appear in summing rational series. The **digamma function** PolyGamma[z] is the logarithmic derivative of the gamma function, given by $\psi(z) = \frac{\Gamma'(z)}{\Gamma(z)}$. For integer arguments, the digamma function satisfies the relation $\psi(n) = -\gamma + \sum_{k=1}^{n-1} \frac{1}{k}$, where $\gamma$ is Euler's constant (EulerGamma in *Mathematica*).

The **polygamma functions** PolyGamma[n, z] are given by $\psi^{(n)}(z) = \frac{d^n}{dz^n}\psi(z)$. Notice that the digamma function corresponds to $\psi^{(0)}(z)$: $\psi^{(n)}(z)$ is the $(n+1)^{\text{th}}$, not the $n^{\text{th}}$, logarithmic derivative of the gamma function. The polygamma functions satisfy the relation $\psi^{(n)}(z) = (-1)^{n+1}n! \sum_{k=0}^{\infty} \frac{1}{(z+k)^{n+1}}$.

Many exact results for gamma and polygamma functions are built in to *Mathematica*.

```
In[8]:= PolyGamma[6]

Out[8]= 137
        ---  -  EulerGamma
        60
```

Here is a contour plot of the gamma function in the complex plane. The poles in the function at zero and negative integers are apparent.

```
In[9]:= ContourPlot[ Abs[Gamma[x + I y]], {x, -3, 3},
          {y, -2, 2}, PlotPoints->40 ]
```

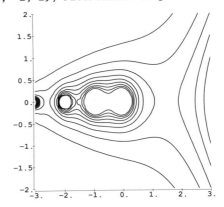

## Zeta and Related Functions

The **Riemann zeta function** Zeta[s] is defined by the relation $\zeta(s) = \sum_{k=1}^{\infty} k^{-s}$ (for $s > 1$). Zeta functions with integer arguments arise in evaluating various sums and integrals. *Mathematica* gives exact results when possible for zeta functions with integer arguments.

There is an analytic continuation of $\zeta(s)$ for arbitrary complex $s \neq 1$. The zeta function for complex argument is central to number theoretical studies of the distribution of primes. Of particular importance are the values on the critical line $\mathrm{Re}\,s = \frac{1}{2}$.

The **generalized Riemann zeta function** or **Hurwitz zeta function** Zeta[s, a] is given by $\zeta(s, a) = \sum_{k=0}^{\infty} (k + a)^{-s}$, where any term with $k + a = 0$ is excluded.

*Mathematica* gives exact results for $\zeta(2n)$.

```
In[10]:= Zeta[6]
```

$$Out[10]= \frac{Pi^6}{945}$$

Here is a three-dimensional picture of the Riemann zeta function in the complex plane. The cover of this book was made from a different view of the same picture.

```
In[11]:= Plot3D[ Abs[ Zeta[x + I y] ], {x, -3, 3},
         {y, 2, 35}, PlotPoints->30 ]
```

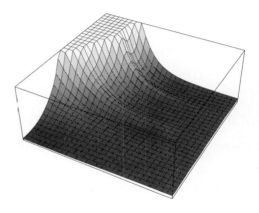

This is a plot of the absolute value of the Riemann zeta function on the critical line $\mathrm{Re}(z) = \frac{1}{2}$. You can see the first few zeroes of the zeta function.

```
In[12]:= Plot[ Abs[ Zeta[ 1/2 + I y ] ], {y, 0, 40} ]
```

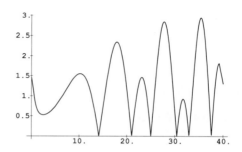

The **polylogarithm functions** PolyLog[n, z] are given by $\mathrm{Li}_n(z) = \sum_{k=1}^{\infty} \frac{z^k}{k^n}$. The **dilogarithm** PolyLog[2, z] satisfies $\mathrm{Li}_2(z) = \int_z^0 \frac{\log(1-t)}{t} dt$. $\mathrm{Li}_2(1 - z)$ is sometimes known as **Spence's integral**. Polylogarithms crop up in Feynman diagram integrals in elementary particle physics. The polylogarithm function is sometimes known as **Jonquière's function**.

The **Lerch transcendent** LerchPhi[z, s, a] is a generalization of the zeta and polylogarithm functions, given by $\Phi(z,s,a) = \sum_{k=0}^{\infty} \frac{z^k}{(a+k)^s}$, where any term with $k+a=0$ is excluded. Many sums of reciprocal powers can be expressed in terms of the Lerch transcendent. For example, the **Catalan beta function** $\beta(s) = \sum_{k=0}^{\infty} (-1)^k (2k+1)^{-s}$ can be obtained as $2^{-s}\Phi(-1, s, \frac{1}{2})$.

The Lerch transcendent is related to integrals of the **Fermi-Dirac** distribution in statistical mechanics by $\int_0^{\infty} \frac{k^s}{e^{k-\mu}+1}\,dk = e^{\mu}\Gamma(s+1)\Phi(-e^{\mu}, s+1, 1)$.

The Lerch transcendent can also be used to evaluate **Dirichlet** $L$ **series** which appear in number theory. The basic $L$ series has the form $L(s, \chi) = \sum_{k=1}^{\infty} \chi(k) k^{-s}$, where the "character" $\chi(k)$ is an integer function with period $m$. $L$ series of this kind can be written as sums of Lerch functions with $z$ a power of $e^{2\pi i/m}$.

LerchPhi[z, s, a, DoublyInfinite->True] gives the doubly-infinite sum $\sum_{k=-\infty}^{\infty} \frac{z^k}{(a+k)^s}$.

## Exponential Integral and Related Functions

*Mathematica* has two forms of exponential integral: ExpIntegralE and ExpIntegralEi.

The **exponential integral function** ExpIntegralE[n, z] is defined by $E_n = \int_1^{\infty} \frac{e^{-zt}}{t^n}\,dt$.

The second **exponential integral function** ExpIntegralEi[z] is defined by $\mathrm{Ei}(z) = -\int_{-z}^{\infty} \frac{e^{-t}}{t}\,dt$, where the principal value of the integral is taken.

The **logarithmic integral function** LogIntegral[z] is given by $\mathrm{li}(z) = \int_0^z \frac{dt}{\log t}$, where the principal value of the integral is taken. $\mathrm{li}(z)$ is central to the study of the distribution of primes in number theory. The logarithmic integral function is sometimes also denoted by $\mathrm{Li}(z)$. In some number-theoretical applications, $\mathrm{li}(z)$ is defined as $\int_2^z \frac{dt}{\log t}$, with no principal value taken. This differs from the definition used in *Mathematica* by the constant $\mathrm{li}(2)$.

The **sine and cosine integral functions** $\mathrm{Si}(z) = \int_0^z \frac{\sin(t)}{t}\,dt$ and $\mathrm{Ci}(z) = -\int_z^{\infty} \frac{\cos(t)}{t}\,dt$ are given in terms of the exponential integral function by $\mathrm{Si}(z) = \frac{1}{2i}[E_1(iz) - E_1(-iz)] + \frac{\pi}{2}$ and $\mathrm{Ci}(z) = -\frac{1}{2}[E_1(iz) + E_1(-iz)]$.

## Error Function

The **error function** `Erf[z]` is the integral of the Gaussian distribution, given   by $\mathrm{erf}(z) = \frac{2}{\sqrt{\pi}} \int_0^z e^{-t^2} dt$.

The generalized error function `Erf[z_0, z_1]` is defined by the integral $\frac{2}{\sqrt{\pi}} \int_{z_0}^{z_1} e^{-t^2} dt$. The **complementary error function** $\mathrm{erfc}(z)$ can be obtained as `Erf[z, Infinity]`.

The error function is central to many calculations in statistics.

Closely related to the error function are the **Fresnel integrals**, $C(z) = \int_0^z \cos\left(\frac{\pi t^2}{2}\right) dt$ and $S(z) = \int_0^z \sin\left(\frac{\pi t^2}{2}\right) dt$. These are given in terms of the error function by $C(z) + iS(z) = \frac{1+i}{2}\mathrm{erf}(\frac{\sqrt{\pi}}{2}(1-i)z)$. Fresnel integrals occur in diffraction theory.

## Bessel Functions

The **Bessel functions** `BesselJ[n, z]` and `BesselY[n, z]` are linearly independent solutions to the differential equation $z^2 \frac{d^2 y}{dz^2} + z \frac{dy}{dz} + (z^2 - n^2)y = 0$. For integer $n$, the $J_n(z)$ are regular at $z = 0$, while the $Y_n(z)$ have a logarithmic divergence at $z = 0$.

Bessel functions arise in solving differential equations for systems with cylindrical symmetry.

$J_n(z)$ is often called the **Bessel function of the first kind**, or simply *the* Bessel function. $Y_n(z)$ is referred to as the **Bessel function of the second kind**, the **Weber function**, or the **Neumann function** (denoted $N_n(z)$).

The **Hankel functions** (or **Bessel functions of the third kind**) $H_n^{(1,2)}(z) = J_n(z) \pm iY_n(z)$ give an alternative pair of solutions to the Bessel differential equation.

In studying systems with spherical symmetry, **spherical Bessel functions** arise, defined by $f_n(z) = \sqrt{\frac{\pi}{2z}} F_{n+\frac{1}{2}}(z)$, where $f$, $F$ can be $j$, $J$, $y$, $Y$, or $h^i$, $H^i$. For integer $n$, *Mathematica* gives exact algebraic formulae for spherical Bessel functions.

The **modified Bessel functions** `BesselI[n, z]` and `BesselK[n, z]` are solutions to the differential equation $z^2 \frac{d^2 y}{dz^2} + z \frac{dy}{dz} - (z^2 + n^2)y = 0$. For integer $n$, $I_n(z)$ is regular at $z = 0$; $K_n(z)$ always has a logarithmic divergence at $z = 0$. The $I_n(z)$ are sometimes known as **hyperbolic Bessel functions**.

Particularly in electrical engineering, one often defines the **Kelvin functions**, according to $\mathrm{ber}_n(z) + i\,\mathrm{bei}(z) = e^{n\pi i} J_n(ze^{-\pi i/4})$, $\mathrm{ker}_n(z) + i\,\mathrm{kei}(z) = e^{-n\pi i/2} K_n(ze^{\pi i/4})$.

The **Airy function** `AiryAi[z]` is a solution to the differential equation $\frac{d^2 y}{dx^2} - xy = 0$.

It is related to Bessel functions with one-third-integer orders.  Ai($z$) appears in electromagnetic theory and quantum mechanics.

Here is a plot of $J_0(\sqrt{x})$. This is a curve that an idealized chain hanging from one end can form when you wiggle it.

`In[13]:= Plot[ BesselJ[0, Sqrt[x]], {x, 0, 50} ]`

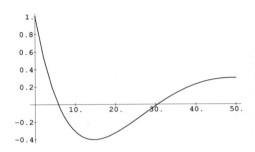

*Mathematica* generates explicit formulae for half-integer-order Bessel functions.

`In[14]:= BesselK[3/2, x]`

$$Out[14]=\ \frac{\text{Sqrt[Pi]} \ (1 + \frac{1}{\text{x}})}{\text{Sqrt[2]} \ \text{E}^{\text{x}} \ \text{Sqrt[x]}}$$

The Airy function plotted here gives the quantum-mechanical amplitude for a particle in a potential that increases linearly from left to right. The amplitude is exponentially damped in the classically inaccessible region on the right.

`In[15]:= Plot[ AiryAi[x], {x, -10, 10} ]`

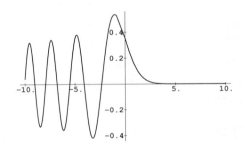

## Legendre and Related Functions

The **Legendre functions** and **associated Legendre functions** satisfy the differential equation $(1 - z^2)\frac{d^2y}{dz^2} - 2z\frac{dy}{dz} + [(n(n + 1) - \frac{m^2}{1-z^2}]y = 0$. The Legendre functions of the first kind, `LegendreP[n, z]` and `LegendreP[n, m, z]`, reduce to Legendre polynomials when $n$ and $m$ are integers. The **Legendre functions of the second kind** `LegendreQ[n, z]` and `LegendreQ[n, m, z]` give the second linearly independent solution to the differential equation. They have logarithmic singularities at $z = \pm1$. The $P_n(z)$ and $Q_n(z)$ solve the differential equation with $m = 0$.

In general, both $P_n^m(z)$ and $Q_n^m(z)$ have a branch cut along the real axis running from $-\infty$ to $+1$. For integer $n$ and even $m$, however, $P_n^m(z)$ is a Legendre polynomial, and has a unique value for all $z$.

It is often necessary to find values for Legendre functions with $z$ a real number in the range $-1 < z < +1$. In this case, the different values from the two sides of the branch cut are conventionally combined to give a unique result using the formulae $P_n^m(x) = [e^{im\pi/2}P_n^m(x + i0) + e^{-im\pi/2}P_n^m(x - i0)]/2$ and $Q_n^m(x) = e^{-im\pi}[e^{-im\pi/2}Q_n^m(x + i0) + e^{im\pi/2}P_n^m(x - i0)]/2$.

The two versions of Legendre functions are distinguished by settings for the option `LegendreType`. `LegendreType->Complex` gives Legendre functions with a branch cut from $-\infty$ to $+1$. `LegendreType->Real` combines values from the two sides of the branch cut to give functions with branch cuts from $-\infty$ to $-1$, and $+1$ to $+\infty$. These functions are continuous on the interval $(-1, 1)$.

The Legendre functions crop up in studies of quantum mechanical scattering processes.

**Toroidal functions** or **ring functions**, which arise in studying systems with toroidal symmetry, can be expressed in terms of the Legendre functions $P_{\nu-\frac{1}{2}}^{\mu}(\cosh\eta)$ and $Q_{\nu-\frac{1}{2}}^{\mu}(\cosh\eta)$.

**Conical functions** can be expressed in terms of $P_{-\frac{1}{2}+ip}^{\mu}(\cos\theta)$ and $Q_{-\frac{1}{2}+ip}^{\mu}(\cos\theta)$.

When you use the function `LegendreP[n, x]` with an integer $n$, you get a Legendre polynomial. If you take $n$ to be an arbitrary complex number, you get in general a Legendre function.

In the same way, you can use the functions `GegenbauerC` and so on with arbitrary complex indices to get **Gegenbauer functions**, **Chebyshev functions**, **Hermite functions**, **Jacobi functions** and **Laguerre functions**.

## Confluent Hypergeometric Functions

Many of the special functions that we have discussed so far can be viewed as special cases of the **confluent hypergeometric function** `Hypergeometric1F1[a, b, z]`.

The confluent hypergeometric function can be obtained from the series expansion $_1F_1(a; b; z) = 1 + \frac{az}{b} + \frac{a(a+1)}{b(b+1)}\frac{z^2}{2!} + \ldots = \sum_{k=0}^{\infty}\frac{(a)_k}{(b)_k}\frac{z^k}{k!}$. Some special results are obtained when $a$ and $b$ are both integers. If $a < 0$, and either $b > 0$ or $b < a$, the series yields a polynomial with a finite number of terms. If integer $b \leq 0$, $_1F_1(a; b; z)$ is undefined.

Among the functions that can be obtained from $_1F_1$ are the Bessel functions, error function, incomplete gamma function, and Hermite and Laguerre polynomials.

The function $_1F_1(a; b; z)$ is sometimes denoted $\mathbf{\Phi}(a; b; z)$ or $M(a, b, z)$. It is often known as the **Kummer function**.

The $_1F_1$ function can be written in the integral representation
$_1F_1(a; b; z) = \frac{\Gamma(b)}{\Gamma(b-a)\Gamma(a)} \int_0^1 e^{zt} t^{a-1} (1-t)^{b-a-1} \, dt$.

The $_1F_1$ confluent hypergeometric function is a solution to Kummer's differential equation $z\frac{d^2y}{dz^2} + (b - z)\frac{dy}{dz} - ay = 0$, with the boundary conditions $_1F_1(a; b; 0) = 1$ and $\frac{\partial}{\partial z} {}_1F_1(a; b; z)|_{z=0} = \frac{a}{b}$.

The function `HypergeometricU[a, b, z]` gives a second linearly independent solution to Kummer's equation. This function behaves like $z^{1-b}$ for small $z$. It has a branch cut along the negative real axis in the complex $z$ plane.

The function $U(a, b, z)$ has the integral representation
$U(a, b, z) = \frac{1}{\Gamma(a)} \int_0^\infty e^{-zt} t^{a-1} (1+t)^{b-a-1} \, dt$.

Special cases of $U$ give such functions as the exponential and logarithmic integral functions, and modified Bessel functions.

$U(a, b, z)$, like $_1F_1(a; b; z)$, is sometimes known as the **Kummer function**, and sometimes denoted by $\mathbf{\Psi}$.

The **Whittaker functions** give an alternative pair of solutions to Kummer's differential equation. The Whittaker function $M_{\kappa, \mu}$ is related to $_1F_1$ by $M_{\kappa, \mu}(z) = e^{-z/2} z^{\frac{1}{2}+\mu} {}_1F_1(\frac{1}{2} + \mu - \kappa; 1 + 2\mu; z)$. The second Whittaker function $W_{\kappa, \mu}$ obeys the same relation, with $_1F_1$ replaced by $U$.

The **parabolic cylinder functions** are related to Whittaker functions by $D_\nu(z) = 2^{\frac{1}{4}+\frac{\nu}{2}} z^{-\frac{1}{2}} W_{\frac{1}{4}+\frac{\nu}{2}, -\frac{1}{4}}(\frac{z^2}{2})$. For integer $\nu$, the parabolic cylinder functions reduce to Hermite polynomials.

The **Coulomb wave functions** are also special cases of the confluent hypergeometric function. Coulomb wave functions give solutions to the radial Schrödinger equation in the Coulomb potential of a point nucleus. The regular Coulomb wave function is given by $F_L(\eta, \rho) = C_L(\eta)\rho^{L+1}e^{-i\rho} {}_1F_1(L + 1 - i\eta; 2L + 2; 2i\rho)$, where $C_L(\eta) = [2^L e^{-\pi\eta/2} \mid \Gamma(L + 1 + i\eta) \mid]/\Gamma(2L + 2)$.

Other special cases of the confluent hypergeometric function include the **Toronto functions** $T(m, n, r)$, **Poisson-Charlier polynomials** $\rho_n(\nu, x)$, **Cunningham functions** $\omega_{n,m}(x)$ and **Bateman functions** $k_\nu(x)$.

A limiting form of the confluent hypergeometric function which often appears is `HypergeometricOF1[a, z]`. This function is obtained as the limit $_0F_1(; a; z) = \lim_{q \to \infty} {}_1F_1(q; a; \frac{z}{q})$.

The $_0F_1$ function has the series expansion $_0F_1(;a;z) = \sum_{k=0}^{\infty} \frac{z^k}{(a)_k k!}$ and satisfies the differential equation $z\frac{d^2y}{dz^2} + a\frac{dy}{dz} - y = 0$.

Bessel functions of the first kind can be expressed in terms of the $_0F_1$ function.

## Hypergeometric Functions

The **hypergeometric function** `Hypergeometric2F1[a, b, c, z]` has series expansion $_2F_1(a,b;c;z) = \sum_{k=0}^{\infty} \frac{(a)_k (b)_k}{(c)_k} \frac{z^k}{k!}$. The function is a solution of the hypergeometric differential equation $z(1-z)\frac{d^2y}{dz^2} + [c - (a+b+1)z]\frac{dy}{dz} - aby = 0$.

The hypergeometric function can also be written as an integral: $_2F_1(a,b;c;z) = \frac{\Gamma(c)}{\Gamma(b)\Gamma(c-b)} \int_0^1 t^{b-1}(1-t)^{c-b-1}(1-tz)^{-a}\, dt$.

The hypergeometric function is also sometimes denoted by $F$, and is known as the **Gauss series** or the **Kummer series**.

The Legendre functions, and the functions which give generalizations of other orthogonal polynomials, can be expressed in terms of the hypergeometric function. Complete elliptic integrals can also be expressed in terms of the $_2F_1$ function.

The **Riemann *P* function**, which gives solutions to Riemann's differential equation, is also a $_2F_1$ function.

## ■ 3.2.11  Elliptic Integrals and Elliptic Functions

| | |
|---:|---|
| `EllipticK[`$m$`]` | complete elliptic integral of the first kind $K(m)$ |
| `EllipticF[`$phi$`, `$m$`]` | elliptic integral of the first kind $F(\phi\|m)$ |
| `EllipticE[`$m$`]` | complete elliptic integral of the second kind $E(m)$ |
| `EllipticE[`$phi$`, `$m$`]` | elliptic integral of the second kind $E(\phi\|m)$ |
| `EllipticPi[`$n$`, `$m$`]` | complete elliptic integral of the third kind $\Pi(n\|m)$ |
| `EllipticPi[`$n$`, `$phi$`, `$m$`]` | elliptic integral of the third kind $\Pi(n;\phi\|m)$ |
| `JacobiAmplitude[`$u$`, `$m$`]` | amplitude function $\mathrm{am}(u\|m)$ |
| `JacobiSN[`$u$`, `$m$`]`, `JacobiCN[`$u$`, `$m$`]`, etc. | Jacobi elliptic functions $\mathrm{sn}(u\|m)$, etc. |
| `InverseJacobiSN[`$v$`, `$m$`]`, `InverseJacobiCN[`$v$`, `$m$`]`, etc. | inverse Jacobi elliptic functions $\mathrm{sn}^{-1}(v\|m)$, etc. |
| `EllipticTheta[`$a$`, `$u$`, `$q$`]` | elliptic theta functions $\theta_a(u\|q)$ $(a = 1, ..., 4)$ |
| `EllipticLog[{`$x$`, `$y$`}, {`$a$`, `$b$`}]` | generalized logarithm associated with the elliptic curve $y^2 = x^3 + ax^2 + bx$ |
| `EllipticExp[`$u$`, {`$a$`, `$b$`}]` | generalized exponential associated with the elliptic curve $y^2 = x^3 + ax^2 + bx$ |
| `ArithmeticGeometricMean[`$a$`, `$b$`]` | the arithmetic-geometric mean of $a$ and $b$ |

Elliptic integrals and elliptic functions.

You should be very careful about the arguments you give to elliptic integrals and elliptic functions in *Mathematica*. There are several incompatible conventions in common mathematical use. You will often have to convert from a particular convention to the one that *Mathematica* uses.

In mathematical usage, the different argument conventions are sometimes distinguished by the use of separators other than commas between the arguments. Often, however, there is no clue about which notation is used, other than perhaps the specific names given to the arguments. In addition, in many cases, some arguments are not explicitly given.

Amplitude $\phi$ (used by *Mathematica*, in radians)

Delta amplitude $\Delta(\phi)$: $\Delta(\phi) = \sqrt{1 - m \sin^2(\phi)}$

Coordinate $x$: $x = \sin(\phi)$

Parameter $m$ (used by *Mathematica*): preceded by |, as in $I(\phi|m)$

Complementary parameter $m_1$: $m_1 = 1 - m$

Modular angle $\alpha$: preceded by \, as in $I(\phi \backslash \alpha)$; $m = \sin^2(\alpha)$

Modulus $k$: preceded by comma, as in $I(\phi, k)$; $m = k^2$

Nome $q$: preceded by comma in $\theta$ functions; $q = \exp(-\pi K(1 - m)/K(m))$

Characteristic $n$ (used by *Mathematica* in elliptic integrals of the third kind)

Argument $u$ (used by *Mathematica*): related to the amplitude by $\phi = \mathrm{am}(u)$

Invariants $g_2$, $g_3$ (used by *Mathematica*)

Periods $\omega$, $\omega'$: $g_2 = 60 \sum_{r,s} \frac{1}{w^4}$, $g_3 = 140 \sum_{r,s} \frac{1}{w^6}$, where $w = 2r\omega + 2s\omega'$

Parameters of curve $a$, $b$ (used by *Mathematica*)

Coordinate $y$ (used by *Mathematica*): related by $y^2 = x^3 + ax^2 + bx$

Arguments for elliptic integrals and elliptic functions.

## Elliptic Integrals

Integrals of the form $\int R(x, y)\, dx$, where $R$ is a rational function, and $y^2$ is a cubic or quartic polynomial in $x$, are known as **elliptic integrals**. Any elliptic integral can be expressed in terms of the three standard kinds of **Legendre-Jacobi elliptic integrals**.

The **elliptic integral of the first kind** EllipticF[*phi*, *m*] is given by $F(\phi|m) = \int_0^\phi (1 - m \sin^2(\theta))^{-\frac{1}{2}} d\theta = \int_0^{\sin(\phi)} [(1 - t^2)(1 - mt^2)]^{-\frac{1}{2}} dt$. This elliptic integral arises in solving the equations of motion for a simple pendulum. It is sometimes known as an **incomplete elliptic integral of the first kind**.

Note that the arguments of the elliptic integrals are sometimes given in the opposite order from what is used in *Mathematica*.

The **complete elliptic integral of the first kind** EllipticK[*m*] is given by $K(m) = F(\frac{\pi}{2}|m)$. Note that $K$ is used to denote the *complete* elliptic integral of the first kind, while $F$ is used for its incomplete form. In many applications, the parameter

$m$ is not given explicitly, and $K(m)$ is denoted simply by $K$. The **complementary complete elliptic integral of the first kind** $K'(m)$ is given by $K(1 - m)$. It is often denoted $K'$. $K$ and $iK'$ give the "real" and "imaginary" quarter-periods of the corresponding Jacobi elliptic functions discussed below. The **nome** $q$ is given by $q(m) = \exp[-\pi K'(m)/K(m)]$.

The **elliptic integral of the second kind** `EllipticE[phi, m]` is given by $E(\phi|m) = \int_0^\phi (1 - m \sin^2(\theta))^{\frac{1}{2}} \, d\theta = \int_0^{\sin(\phi)} (1 - t^2)^{\frac{1}{2}} (1 - mt^2)^{-\frac{1}{2}} \, dt$.

The **complete elliptic integral of the second kind** `EllipticE[m]` is given by $E(m) = E(\frac{\pi}{2}|m)$. It is often denoted $E$. The complementary form is $E'(m) = E(1 - m)$.

The **Jacobi zeta function** is given in terms of the elliptic integrals $E$, $F$ and $K$ by $Z(\phi|m) = E(\phi|m) - E(m)F(\phi|m)/K(m)$.

The **Heuman lambda function** is given by $\Lambda_0(\phi|m) = F(\phi|1 - m)/K(1 - m) + \frac{2}{\pi} K(m) Z(\phi|1 - m)$.

The **elliptic integral of the third kind** `EllipticPi[n, phi, m]` is given by $\Pi(n; \phi|m) = \int_0^\phi (1 - n \sin^2(\theta))^{-1} [1 - \sin^2(\alpha) \sin^2(\theta)]^{-\frac{1}{2}} \, d\theta$.

The **complete elliptic integral of the third kind** `EllipticPi[n, m]` is given by $\Pi(n|m) = \Pi(n; \frac{\pi}{2}|m)$.

Here is a plot of the complete elliptic integral of the second kind $E(m)$.

*In[1]:=* `Plot[EllipticE[m], {m, 0, 1}]`

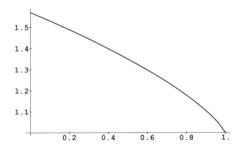

Here is $K(\alpha)$ with $\alpha = 30°$.

*In[2]:=* `EllipticK[Sin[30 Degree]^2] // N`

*Out[2]=* `1.68575`

The elliptic integrals have a complicated structure in the complex plane.

*In[3]:=* `Plot3D[Abs[EllipticF[px + I py, 1/2]],`
`{px, -Pi, Pi}, {py, -2, 2}]`

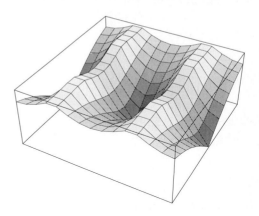

## Elliptic Functions

Rational functions involving square roots of quadratic forms can be integrated in terms of inverse trigonometric functions. The trigonometric functions can thus be defined as inverses of the functions obtained from these integrals.

By analogy, **elliptic functions** are defined as inverses of the functions obtained from elliptic integrals.

The **amplitude** for Jacobi elliptic functions `JacobiAmplitude[`$u$`, `$m$`]` is the inverse of the elliptic integral of the first kind. If $u = F(\phi|m)$, then $\phi = \mathrm{am}(u|m)$. In working with Jacobi elliptic functions, the argument $m$ is often dropped, so $\mathrm{am}(u|m)$ is written as $\mathrm{am}(u)$.

The **Jacobi elliptic functions** `JacobiSN[`$u$`, `$m$`]` and `JacobiCN[`$u$`, `$m$`]` are given respectively by $\mathrm{sn}(u) = \sin(\phi)$ and $\mathrm{cn}(u) = \cos(\phi)$, where $\phi = \mathrm{am}(u|m)$. In addition, `JacobiDN[`$u$`, `$m$`]` is given by $\mathrm{dn}(u) = \sqrt{1 - m\sin^2(\phi)} = \Delta(\phi)$.

There are a total of twelve Jacobi elliptic functions `Jacobi`$PQ$`[`$u$`, `$m$`]`, with the letters $P$ and $Q$ chosen from the set `S`, `C`, `D` and `N`. Each Jacobi elliptic function `Jacobi`$PQ$`[`$u$`, `$m$`]` satisfies the relation $\mathrm{pq}(u) = \mathrm{pr}(u)/\mathrm{qr}(u)$, where for these purposes $\mathrm{pp}(u) = 1$.

There are many relations between the Jacobi elliptic functions, somewhat analogous to those between trigonometric functions.

The notation $\mathrm{Pq}(u)$ is often used for the integrals $\int_0^u \mathrm{pq}^2(t)\,dt$. These integrals can be expressed in terms of the Jacobi zeta function defined above.

The first complete period of $\operatorname{sn}(u|\frac{1}{2})$ and $\operatorname{cn}(u|\frac{1}{2})$.

```
In[4]:= Plot[{JacobiSN[u, 1/2], JacobiCN[u, 1/2]},
             {u, 0, 4 EllipticK[1/2]}]
```

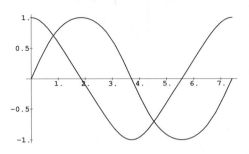

The Jacobi elliptic function $\operatorname{am}(u)$ has a complicated structure in the complex plane.

```
In[5]:= Plot3D[Abs[JacobiAmplitude[ux + I uy, 1/2]],
              {ux, -4, 2}, {uy, 0, 2}]
```

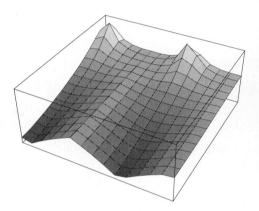

One of the most important properties of elliptic functions is that they are *doubly periodic* in the complex values of their arguments. Ordinary trigonometric functions are singly periodic, in the sense that $f(z + s\omega) = f(z)$ for any integer $s$. The elliptic functions are doubly periodic, so that $f(z + r\omega + s\omega') = f(z)$ for any pair of integers $r$ and $s$.

The Jacobi elliptic functions $\operatorname{sn}(u|m)$ etc. are doubly periodic in the complex $u$ plane. Their periods include $\omega = 4K(m)$ and $\omega' = 4iK(1 - m)$, where $K$ is the complete elliptic integral of the first kind.

The choice of p and q in the notation $\operatorname{pq}(u|m)$ for Jacobi elliptic functions can be understood in terms of the values of the functions at the quarter periods $K$ and $iK'$.

This shows one complete period in each direction of the Jacobi elliptic function $\mathrm{sn}(u|\frac{1}{3})$.

```
In[6]:= ContourPlot[Abs[JacobiSN[ux + I uy, 1/3]],
          {ux, 0, 4 EllipticK[1/3]},
          {uy, 0, 4 EllipticK[2/3]},
          PlotPoints->40 ]
```

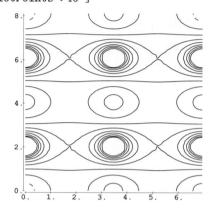

Also built into *Mathematica* are the **inverse Jacobi elliptic functions** `InverseJacobiSN[v, m]`, `InverseJacobiCN[v, m]`, etc. The inverse function $\mathrm{sn}^{-1}(v|m)$ gives for example the value of $u$ for which $v = \mathrm{sn}(u|m)$. The inverse Jacobi elliptic functions are related to elliptic integrals.

The four **elliptic theta functions** $\theta_a(u|m)$ are obtained from `EllipticTheta[a, u, m]` by taking a to be 1, 2, 3 or 4. The functions are defined by: $\theta_1(u,q) = 2q^{\frac{1}{4}} \sum_{n=0}^{\infty} (-1)^n q^{n(n+1)} \sin((2n+1)u)$, $\theta_2(u,q) = 2q^{\frac{1}{4}} \sum_{n=0}^{\infty} q^{n(n+1)} \cos((2n+1)u)$, $\theta_3(u,q) = 1 + 2 \sum_{n=1}^{\infty} q^{n^2} \cos(2nu)$, $\theta_4(u,q) = 1 + 2 \sum_{n=1}^{\infty} (-1)^n q^{n^2} \cos(2nu)$. The theta functions are sometimes given in the form $\theta(u|m)$, where $m$ is related to $q$ by $q = \exp(-\pi K(1-m)/K(m))$. In addition, $q$ is sometimes replaced by $\tau$, given by $q = e^{i\pi\tau}$. All the theta functions satisfy a diffusion-like differential equation $\frac{\delta^2 \theta(u,\tau)}{\partial u^2} = 4\pi i \frac{\partial \theta(u,\tau)}{\partial \tau}$.

The Jacobi elliptic function can be expressed as ratios of the theta functions.

An alternative notation for theta functions is $\Theta(u|m) = \theta_4(v|m)$, $\Theta_1(u|m) = \theta_3(v|m)$, $\mathrm{H}(u|m) = \theta_1(v)$, $\mathrm{H}_1(u|m) = \theta_2(v)$, where $v = \frac{\pi u}{2K(m)}$.

In terms of $\Theta$ and $\mathrm{H}$, the **Neville theta functions** can be written $\theta_s(u) = \mathrm{H}(u)/\mathrm{H}_1(0)$, $\theta_c(u) = \mathrm{H}_1(u)/\mathrm{H}(u)$, $\theta_d(u) = \Theta_1(u)/\Theta(u)$, $\theta_n(u) = \Theta(u)/\Theta(0)$.

The **Weierstrass elliptic function** `WeierstrassP[u, g2, g3]` can be considered as the inverse of an elliptic integral. The Weierstrass function $\wp(u; g_2, g_3)$ gives the value of $x$ for which $u = \int_{\infty}^{x} (4t^3 - g_2 t - g_3)^{-\frac{1}{2}} dt$. The function `WeierstrassPPrime[u, g2, g3]` is given by $\wp'(u; g_2, g_3) = \frac{\partial}{\partial u} \wp(u; g_2, g_3)$.

The Weierstrass functions are also sometimes written in terms of their *fundamental periods* $\omega$ and $\omega'$.

## Generalized Elliptic Integrals and Functions

The definitions for elliptic integrals and functions given above are based on traditional usage. For modern algebraic geometry, it is convenient to use slightly more general definitions.

The function `EllipticLog[{x, y}, {a, b}]` is defined as the value of the integral $\int_\infty^x (t^3 + at^2 + bt)^{-\frac{1}{2}} \, dt$, where the sign of the square root is specified by giving the value of $y$ such that $y = \sqrt{x^3 + ax^2 + bx}$. Integrals of the form $\int_\infty^x (t^2 + at)^{-\frac{1}{2}} \, dt$ can be expressed in terms of the ordinary logarithm (and inverse trigonometric functions). You can think of `EllipticLog` as giving a generalization of this, where the polynomial under the square root is now of degree three.

The function `EllipticExp[u, {a, b}]` is the inverse of `EllipticLog`. It returns the list `{x, y}` that appears in `EllipticLog`. `EllipticExp` is an elliptic function, doubly periodic in the complex $u$ plane.

`ArithmeticGeometricMean[a, b]` gives the **arithmetic-geometric mean** (**AGM**) of two numbers $a$ and $b$. This quantity is central to many numerical algorithms for computing elliptic integrals and other functions. The AGM is obtained by starting with $a_0 = a$, $b_0 = b$, then iterating the transformation $a_{n+1} = \frac{1}{2}(a_n + b_n)$, $b_{n+1} = \sqrt{a_n b_n}$ until $a_n = b_n$ to the precision required.

# ■ 3.3  Polynomials and Rational Functions

## ■ 3.3.1  Structural Operations on Polynomials

| | |
|---|---|
| Expand[*poly*] | expand out products and powers |
| Factor[*poly*] | factor completely |
| FactorTerms[*poly*] | pull out common factors that appear in each term |
| Collect[*poly*, *x*] | arrange a polynomial as a sum of powers of *x* |
| Collect[*poly*, {*x*, *y*, ...}] | arrange a polynomial as a sum of powers of *x*, *y*, ... |

Structural operations on polynomials.

Here is a polynomial in one variable.

$In[1]:= (2 + 4 x^2)^2 (1 - x)^3$

$Out[1]= (1 - x)^3 (2 + 4 x^2)^2$

Expand expands out products and powers, writing the polynomial as a simple sum of terms.

$In[2]:= t = Expand[\%]$

$Out[2]= 4 - 12 x + 28 x^2 - 52 x^3 + 64 x^4 - 64 x^5 + 48 x^6 - 16 x^7$

Factor performs complete factoring of the polynomial.

$In[3]:= Factor[ t ]$

$Out[3]= -4 (-1 + x)^3 (1 + 2 x^2)^2$

FactorTerms pulls out common factors from each term, but does not do complete factoring.

$In[4]:= FactorTerms[ t ]$

$Out[4]= -4 (-1 + 3 x - 7 x^2 + 13 x^3 - 16 x^4 + 16 x^5 - 12 x^6 + 4 x^7)$

There are several ways to write any polynomial. The functions Expand, FactorTerms and Factor give three common ways. Expand writes a polynomial as a simple sum of terms, with all products expanded out. FactorTerms pulls out common factors from each term. Factor does complete factoring, writing the polynomial as a product of terms, each as small as possible.

When you have a polynomial in more than one variable, you can put the polynomial in different forms by essentially choosing different variables to be "dominant". Collect[*poly*, *x*] takes a polynomial in several variables and rewrites it as a sum of terms containing different powers of the "dominant variable" $x$.

Here is a polynomial in two variables.

$In[5]:=$ **Expand[ (1 + 2x + y)^3 ]**

$Out[5]=$ $1 + 6 x + 12 x^2 + 8 x^3 + 3 y + 12 x y + 12 x^2 y +$

$3 y^2 + 6 x y^2 + y^3$

`Collect` reorganizes the polynomial so that $x$ is the "dominant variable".

$In[6]:=$ **Collect[% ,x]**

$Out[6]=$ $1 + 8 x^3 + 3 y + 3 y^2 + y^3 + x^2 (12 + 12 y) +$

$x (6 + 12 y + 6 y^2)$

If you specify a list of variables, `Collect` will effectively write the expression as a polynomial in these variables.

$In[7]:=$ **Collect[ Expand[ (1 + x + 2y + 3z)^3 ], {x, y} ]**

$Out[7]=$ $1 + x^3 + 6 x^2 y + 12 x y^2 + 8 y^3 + 9 z + 27 z^2 +$

$27 z^3 + x^2 (3 + 9 z) + x y (12 + 36 z) +$

$y^2 (12 + 36 z) + x (3 + 18 z + 27 z^2) +$

$y (6 + 36 z + 54 z^2)$

## ■ 3.3.2 Finding the Structure of a Polynomial

| | |
|---|---|
| PolynomialQ[*expr*, *x*] | test whether *expr* is a polynomial in *x* |
| PolynomialQ[*expr*, {*x₁*, *x₂*, ...}] | |
| | test whether *expr* is a polynomial in the $x_i$ |
| Variables[*poly*] | a list of the variables in *poly* |
| Length[*poly*] | the total number of terms in *poly* |
| Exponent[*poly*, *x*] | the maximum exponent with which *x* appears in *poly* |
| Coefficient[*poly*, *expr*] | the coefficient of *expr* in *poly* |
| Coefficient[*poly*, *expr*, *n*] | the coefficient of *expr*∧*n* in *poly* |
| Coefficient[*poly*, *expr*, 0] | the term in *poly* not proportional to *expr* |
| CoefficientList[*poly*, {*x₁*, *x₂*, ...}] | |
| | generate an array of the coefficients of the $x_i$ in *poly* |

Finding the structure of polynomials written in expanded form.

Here is a polynomial in two variables, written in expanded form.

```
In[1]:= t = Expand[ (1 + x)^3 (1 - y - x)^2 ]
```
$$Out[1]= 1 + x - 2 x^2 - 2 x^3 + x^4 + x^5 - 2 y - 4 x y +$$
$$4 x^3 y + 2 x^4 y + y^2 + 3 x y^2 + 3 x^2 y^2 + x^3 y^2$$

PolynomialQ reports that t is not a polynomial in the single variable x.

```
In[2]:= PolynomialQ[t, x]
```
```
Out[2]= False
```

t is, however, a polynomial in the two variables x and y.

```
In[3]:= PolynomialQ[t, {x, y}]
```
```
Out[3]= True
```

Variables gives a list of the variables in the polynomial.

```
In[4]:= Variables[t]
```
```
Out[4]= {x, y}
```

The polynomial t has the form of a sum of terms. Length[t] gives the number of terms in this sum.

```
In[5]:= Length[t]
```
```
Out[5]= 14
```

This gives the maximum exponent with which x appears in the polynomial t. For a polynomial in one variable, Exponent gives the degree of the polynomial.

```
In[6]:= Exponent[t, x]
```
```
Out[6]= 5
```

Coefficient[*poly*, *expr*] gives the total coefficient with which *expr* appears in *poly*. In this case, the result is a sum of two terms.

```
In[7]:= Coefficient[t, x^2]

            2
Out[7]= -2 + 3 y
```

This is equivalent to Coefficient[t, x^2].

```
In[8]:= Coefficient[t, x, 2]

            2
Out[8]= -2 + 3 y
```

This picks out the coefficient of $x^0$ in t.

```
In[9]:= Coefficient[t, x, 0]

                 2
Out[9]= 1 - 2 y + y
```

CoefficientList gives a list of the coefficients of each power of $x$, starting with $x^0$.

```
In[10]:= CoefficientList[1 + 3x^2 + 4x^4, x]

Out[10]= {1, 0, 3, 0, 4}
```

For multivariate polynomials, CoefficientList gives an array of the coefficients for each power of each variable.

```
In[11]:= CoefficientList[t, {x, y}]

Out[11]= {{1, -2, 1}, {1, -4, 3}, {-2, 0, 3}, {-2, 4, 1},
          {1, 2, 0}, {1, 0, 0}}
```

It is important to realize that the functions in this section will work as shown above only on polynomials that are given in expanded form. If, for example, you apply **Length** to a factored polynomial, you will get the number of factors, rather than the number of terms in the expanded polynomial.

Many of the functions in this section also work on expressions that are not strictly polynomials.

Without giving specific integer values to a, b and c, this expression cannot strictly be considered a polynomial.

```
In[12]:= x^a + x^b + y^c

            a    b    c
Out[12]= x  + x  + y
```

Exponent[*expr*, x] still gives the maximum exponent of x in *expr*, but here has to write the result in symbolic form.

```
In[13]:= Exponent[%, x]

Out[13]= Max[a, b, 0]
```

## ■ 3.3.3 Structural Operations on Rational Expressions

For ordinary polynomials, **Factor** and **Expand** give the most important forms. For rational expressions, there are many different forms that can be useful.

| | |
|---|---|
| ExpandNumerator[*expr*] | expand numerators only |
| ExpandDenominator[*expr*] | expand denominators only |
| Expand[*expr*] | expand numerators, dividing the denominator into each term |
| ExpandAll[*expr*] | expand numerators and denominators completely |

Different kinds of expansion for rational expressions.

Here is a rational expression.

$$In[1]:= \mathbf{t =}$$
$$\mathbf{(1 + x)\wedge 2 \ / \ (1 - x) + 3 \ x\wedge 2 \ / \ (1 + x)\wedge 2 + (2 - x)\wedge 2}$$

$$Out[1]= \frac{3 \ x^2}{(1 + x)^2} + \frac{(1 + x)^2}{1 - x} + (2 - x)^2$$

ExpandNumerator writes the numerator of each term in expanded form.

$$In[2]:= \mathbf{ExpandNumerator[t]}$$

$$Out[2]= 4 - 4 \ x + x^2 + \frac{3 \ x^2}{(1 + x)^2} + \frac{1 + 2 \ x + x^2}{1 - x}$$

Expand expands the numerator of each term, and divides all the terms by the appropriate denominators.

$$In[3]:= \mathbf{Expand[t]}$$

$$Out[3]= 4 - 4 \ x + x^2 + \frac{1}{1 - x} + \frac{2 \ x}{1 - x} + \frac{x^2}{1 - x} + \frac{3 \ x^2}{(1 + x)^2}$$

ExpandDenominator expands out the denominator of each term.

$$In[4]:= \mathbf{ExpandDenominator[t]}$$

$$Out[4]= \frac{(1 + x)^2}{1 - x} + (2 - x)^2 + \frac{3 \ x^2}{1 + 2 \ x + x^2}$$

ExpandAll does all possible expansions in the numerator and denominator of each term.

$$In[5]:= \mathbf{ExpandAll[t]}$$

$$Out[5]= 4 - 4 \ x + x^2 + \frac{1}{1 - x} + \frac{2 \ x}{1 - x} + \frac{x^2}{1 - x} +$$

$$\frac{3 \ x^2}{1 + 2 \ x + x^2}$$

| Together[*expr*] | combine all terms over a common denominator |
| Apart[*expr*] | write an expression as a sum of terms with simple denominators |
| Cancel[*expr*] | cancel common factors between numerators and denominators |
| Factor[*expr*] | perform a complete factoring |

Structural operations on rational expressions.

Here is a rational expression.

$In[6]:= $ u =
(1 + x)^2/((1 - x)(2 - x)) + (1 - x^2)/((1 + x)(2 - x))

$$Out[6]= \frac{(1 + x)^2}{(1 - x)\ (2 - x)} + \frac{1 - x^2}{(1 + x)\ (2 - x)}$$

Together puts all terms over a common denominator.

$In[7]:= $ Together[u]

$$Out[7]= \frac{2 + 2\ x^2}{2 - 3\ x + x^2}$$

You can use Factor to factor the numerator and denominator of the resulting expression.

$In[8]:= $ Factor[%]

$$Out[8]= \frac{2\ (1 + x^2)}{(-2 + x)\ (-1 + x)}$$

Apart writes the expression as a sum of terms, with each term having as simple a denominator as possible.

$In[9]:= $ Apart[u]

$$Out[9]= 2 + \frac{10}{-2 + x} - \frac{4}{-1 + x}$$

Cancel cancels any common factors between numerators and denominators. In this case, this leads to a simplification in the second term.

$In[10]:= $ Cancel[u]

$$Out[10]= \frac{1 - x}{2 - x} + \frac{1 + 2\ x + x^2}{2 - 3\ x + x^2}$$

Factor first puts all terms over a common denominator, then factors the result.

$In[11]:= $ Factor[%]

$$Out[11]= \frac{2\ (1 + x^2)}{(-2 + x)\ (-1 + x)}$$

In mathematical terms, Apart decomposes a rational expression into "partial fractions".

In expressions with several variables, you can use `Apart[`*expr,  var*`]` to do partial fraction decompositions with respect to different variables.

Here is a rational expression in two variables.

$$In[12]:= \text{v} = \text{(x^2+y^2)/(x + x y)}$$

$$Out[12]= \frac{x^2 + y^2}{x + x\ y}$$

This gives the partial fraction decomposition with respect to x.

$$In[13]:= \text{Apart[v, x]}$$

$$Out[13]= \frac{y^2}{x\ (1 + y)} + \frac{x\ (1 + y)}{1 + 2\ y + y^2}$$

Here is the partial fraction decomposition with respect to y.

$$In[14]:= \text{Apart[v, y]}$$

$$Out[14]= -\left(\frac{1}{x}\right) + \frac{y}{x} + \frac{1 + x^2}{x\ (1 + y)}$$

## ■ 3.3.4  Algebraic Operations on Polynomials

For many kinds of practical calculations, the only operations you will need to perform on polynomials are essentially the structural ones discussed in the preceding sections.

If you do more advanced algebra with polynomials, however, you will have to use the algebraic operations discussed in this section.

You should realize that most of the operations discussed in this section work only on ordinary polynomials, with integer exponents, and rational number coefficients for each term.

| `PolynomialQuotient[p, q, x]` | find the result of dividing the polynomials $p$ and $q$ in $x$, dropping any remainder term |
|---|---|
| `PolynomialRemainder[p, q, x]` | find the remainder from dividing the polynomials $p$ and $q$ in $x$ |
| `GCD[poly_1, poly_2, ...]` | find the greatest common divisor of the polynomials $poly_i$ |
| `Resultant[poly_1, poly_2, x]` | find the resultant of two polynomials |
| `Factor[poly]` | factor a polynomial |
| `FactorTerms[poly]` | factor out the gcd of all terms |
| `FactorSquareFree[poly]` | write a polynomial as a product of powers of square-free factors |
| `FactorList[poly]`, `FactorTermsList[poly]`, `FactorSquareFreeList[poly]` | give results as lists of factors |
| `Cyclotomic[n, x]` | give the cyclotomic polynomial of order $n$ in $x$ |
| `Decompose[poly, x]` | decompose *poly*, if possible, into a composition of a list of simpler polynomials |

Algebraic operations on polynomials.

Given two polynomials $p(x)$ and $q(x)$, one can always uniquely write $\frac{p(x)}{q(x)} = a(x) + \frac{b(x)}{q(x)}$, where the degree of $b(x)$ is less than the degree of $q(x)$. `PolynomialQuotient` gives the quotient $a(x)$, and `PolynomialRemainder` gives the remainder $b(x)$.

This gives the remainder from dividing $x^2$ by $1 + x$.

```
In[1]:= PolynomialRemainder[x^2, x+1, x]
Out[1]= 1
```

Here is the quotient of $x^2$ and $x + 1$, with the remainder dropped.

```
In[2]:= PolynomialQuotient[x^2, x+1, x]
Out[2]= -1 + x
```

This gives back the original expression.

```
In[3]:= Factor[ % + %% / (x + 1) ]

           2
          x
Out[3]= ------
        1 + x
```

`GCD[poly_1, poly_2, ...]` finds the largest polynomial that divides all the $poly_i$

exactly. Notice that the function GCD used for polynomials is the same one that we discussed for numbers in Section 3.2.4.

GCD gives the greatest common divisor of the two polynomials, and writes the result in expanded form.

```
In[4]:= GCD[ (1-x)^2 (1+x) (2+x), (1-x) (2+x) (3+x) ]

Out[4]= -2 + x + x
                   2
```

Factor writes the result in a form that makes its origin clear.

```
In[5]:= Factor[%]

Out[5]= (-1 + x) (2 + x)
```

The function Resultant[$poly_1$, $poly_2$, x] is needed in various algebraic algorithms. The resultant of two polynomials $a$ and $b$, both with leading coefficient one, is given by the product of all the differences $a_i - b_j$ between the roots of the polynomials. It turns out that for any pair of polynomials, the resultant is also a polynomial. The resultant of two polynomials is zero if and only if the two polynomials have a common root, or if the leading coefficients simultaneously vanish.

Here is the resultant with respect to $y$ of two polynomials in $x$ and $y$. The original polynomials have a common root in $y$ only for values of $x$ at which the resultant vanishes.

```
In[6]:= Resultant[(x-y)^2-2, y^2-3, y]

Out[6]= 1 - 10 x  + x
                2    4
```

The functions Factor, FactorTerms and FactorSquareFree perform various degrees of factoring on polynomials. Factor does full factoring over the integers. FactorTerms extracts the GCD or "content" of all the terms. FactorSquareFree pulls out any factors that appear squared, and then writes the polynomial as a product of powers of square-free factors.

Here is a polynomial, in expanded form.

```
In[7]:= t = Expand[ 2 (1 + x)^2 (2 + x) (3 + x) ]

Out[7]= 12 + 34 x + 34 x  + 14 x  + 2 x
                        2       3      4
```

FactorTerms just pulls out the factor of 2 that is common to all the terms.

```
In[8]:= FactorTerms[t]

Out[8]= 2 (6 + 17 x + 17 x  + 7 x  + x )
                          2      3     4
```

FactorSquareFree factors out the term (1 + x)^2, but leaves the rest unfactored.

```
In[9]:= FactorSquareFree[t]

Out[9]= 2 (1 + x)  (6 + 5 x + x )
                  2              2
```

Factor does full factoring, recovering the original form.

```
In[10]:= Factor[t]

Out[10]= 2 (1 + x)  (2 + x) (3 + x)
                   2
```

Particularly when you write programs that work with polynomials, you will often find it convenient to pick out pieces of polynomials in a standard form. The function `FactorList` gives a list of all the factors of a polynomial, together with their exponents. The first element of the list is always the overall numerical factor for the polynomial.

The form that `FactorList` returns is the analog for polynomials of the form produced by `FactorInteger` for integers.

Here is a list of the factors of the polynomial in the previous set of examples. Each element of the list gives the factor, together with its exponent.

```
In[11]:= FactorList[t]
Out[11]= {{2, 1}, {2 + x, 1}, {3 + x, 1}, {1 + x, 2}}
```

The function `Cyclotomic[n, x]` gives the cyclotomic polynomial of order $n$ in x. Cyclotomic polynomials arise as "elementary polynomials" in various algebraic algorithms. The cyclotomic polynomials are defined by $C_n(x) = \prod_k (x - e^{2\pi i k/n})$, where $k$ runs over all positive integers less than $n$ that are relatively prime to $n$.

This is the cyclotomic polynomial $C_6(x)$.

```
In[12]:= Cyclotomic[6, x]
Out[12]= 1 - x + x
```

$C_6(x)$ appears in the factors of $x^6 - 1$.

```
In[13]:= Factor[x^6 - 1]
                                    2          2
Out[13]= (-1 + x) (1 + x) (1 - x + x ) (1 + x + x )
```

Factorization is one important way of breaking down polynomials into simpler parts. Another, quite different, way is *decomposition*. When one factors a polynomial $P(x)$, one writes it as a product $p_1(x)p_2(x)...$ of polynomials $p_i(x)$. Decomposing a polynomial $Q(x)$ consists in writing it as a *composition* of polynomials of the form $q_1(q_2(...(x)...))$.

Here is a simple example of Decompose. The original polynomial $x^4 + x^2 + 1$ can be written as the polynomial $\bar{x}^2 + \bar{x} + 1$, where $\bar{x}$ is the polynomial $x^2$.

```
In[14]:= Decompose[x^4 + x^2 + 1, x]
                       2    2
Out[14]= {1 + x + x , x }
```

Here are two polynomial functions.

```
In[15]:= ( q1[x_] = 1 - 2x + x^4 ;
           q2[x_] = 5x + x^3 ; )
```

This gives the composition of the two functions.

```
In[16]:= Expand[ q1[ q2[ x ] ] ]
```

$$Out[16]= 1 - 10 x - 2 x^3 + 625 x^4 + 500 x^6 + 150 x^8 + 20 x^{10} + x^{12}$$

Decompose recovers the original functions.

```
In[17]:= Decompose[%, x]
```

$$Out[17]= \{1 - 2 x + x^4, \ x (5 + x^2)\}$$

Decompose[*poly*, x] is set up to give a list of polynomials in x, which, if composed, reproduce the original polynomial. The original polynomial can contain variables other than x, but the sequence of polynomials that Decompose produces are all intended to be considered as functions of x.

Unlike factoring, the decomposition of polynomials is not completely unique. For example, the two sets of polynomials $q_i$ and $q_i'$, related by $q_1'(x) = q_1(x - a)$ and $q_2'(x) = q_2(x) + a$ give the same result on composition, so that $q_1(q_2(x)) = q_1'(q_2'(x))$. *Mathematica* follows the convention of absorbing any constant terms into the first polynomial in the list produced by Decompose.

## ■ 3.3.5  Polynomials Modulo Primes

*Mathematica* can work with polynomials whose coefficients are in the finite field $Z_p$ of integers modulo a prime $p$.

| | |
|---|---|
| Mod[*poly*, n] | reduce the coefficients in a polynomial modulo n |
| Factor[*poly*, Modulus->p] | factor *poly* modulo p |
| GCD[*poly*₁, *poly*₂, ..., Modulus->p] | |
| | find the gcd of the *poly*$_i$ modulo p |

Functions for manipulating polynomials over finite fields.

Here is an ordinary polynomial.

```
In[1]:= Expand[ (1 + x)^6 ]
```

$$Out[1]= 1 + 6 x + 15 x^2 + 20 x^3 + 15 x^4 + 6 x^5 + x^6$$

This reduces the coefficients modulo two.

```
In[2]:= Mod[%, 2]
```

$$Out[2]= 1 + x^2 + x^4 + x^6$$

Here are the factors of the resulting polynomial over the integers.

$In[3]:=$ `Factor[%]`

$Out[3]=$ $(1 + x^2) (1 + x^4)$

If you work modulo two, further factoring becomes possible.

$In[4]:=$ `Factor[%, Modulus->2]`

$Out[4]=$ $(1 + x)^6$

# ■ 3.4  Manipulating Equations

## ■ 3.4.1  The Representation of Equations and Solutions

*Mathematica* treats equations as logical statements. If you type in an equation like
`x^2 + 3x == 2`, *Mathematica* interprets this as a logical statement which asserts
that `x^2 + 3x` is equal to 2. If you have assigned an explicit value to `x`, say
`x = 4`, then *Mathematica* can explicitly determine that the logical statement
`x^2 + 3x == 2` is `False`.

If you have not assigned any explicit value to `x`, however, *Mathematica* cannot
work out whether `x^2 + 3x == 2` is `True` or `False`. As a result, it leaves the
equation in the symbolic form `x^2 + 3x == 2`.

You can manipulate symbolic equations in *Mathematica* in many ways. One
common goal is to rearrange the equations so as to "solve" for a particular set of
variables.

<table>
<tr>
<td>Here is a symbolic equation.</td>
<td>

`In[1]:= x^2 + 3x == 2`

$Out[1]= 3\ x + x^2 == 2$

</td>
</tr>
<tr>
<td>You can use the function `Roots` to rearrange the equation so as to give "solutions" for x. The result, like the original equation, can be viewed as a logical statement.</td>
<td>

`In[2]:= Roots[%, x]`

$Out[2]= x == \dfrac{-3 + Sqrt[17]}{2}\ ||\ x == \dfrac{-3 - Sqrt[17]}{2}$

</td>
</tr>
</table>

The quadratic equation `x^2 + 3x == 2` can be thought of as an implicit statement about the value of `x`. As shown in the example above, you can use the function
`Roots` to get a more explicit statement about the value of `x`. The expression pro-
duced by `Roots` has the form `x == `$r_1$` || x == `$r_2$. This expression is again a
logical statement, which asserts that either `x` is equal to $r_1$, or `x` is equal to $r_2$.
The values of `x` that are consistent with this statement are exactly the same as the
ones that are consistent with the original quadratic equation. For many purposes,
however, the form that `Roots` gives is much more useful than the original equation.

You can combine and manipulate equations just like other logical statements.
You can use logical connectives such as `||` and `&&` to specify alternative or simulta-
neous conditions. You can use functions like `LogicalExpand` to simplify collections
of equations.

For many purposes, you will find it convenient to manipulate equations simply
as logical statements. Sometimes, however, you will actually want to use explicit
solutions to equations in other calculations. In such cases, it is convenient to convert

equations that are stated in the form *lhs* == *rhs* into transformation rules of the form *lhs* -> *rhs*. Once you have the solutions to an equation in the form of explicit transformation rules, you can substitute the solutions into expressions by using the /. operator.

Roots produces a logical statement about the values of x corresponding to the roots of the quadratic equation.

```
In[3]:= Roots[ x^2 + 3x == 2, x ]
```

$$Out[3]= x == \frac{-3 + Sqrt[17]}{2} \; || \; x == \frac{-3 - Sqrt[17]}{2}$$

ToRules converts the logical statement into an explicit list of transformation rules.

```
In[4]:= {ToRules[ % ]}
```

$$Out[4]= \{\{x \rightarrow \frac{-3 + Sqrt[17]}{2}\}, \{x \rightarrow \frac{-3 - Sqrt[17]}{2}\}\}$$

You can now use the transformation rules to substitute the solutions for x into expressions involving x.

```
In[5]:= x^2 + a x /. %
```

$$Out[5]= \{\frac{a\,(-3 + Sqrt[17])}{2} + \frac{(-3 + Sqrt[17])^2}{4},$$

$$\frac{a\,(-3 - Sqrt[17])}{2} + \frac{(-3 - Sqrt[17])^2}{4}\}$$

The function Solve produces transformation rules for solutions directly.

```
In[6]:= Solve[ x^2 + 3x == 2, x ]
```

$$Out[6]= \{\{x \rightarrow \frac{-3 + Sqrt[17]}{2}\}, \{x \rightarrow \frac{-3 - Sqrt[17]}{2}\}\}$$

When Solve cannot find explicit solutions, it leaves the result in a symbolic form in terms of the functions Roots and ToRules.

```
In[7]:= Solve[ x^5 + 5x + 1 == 0, x ]
```

$$Out[7]= \{ToRules[Roots[5 x + x^5 == -1, x]]\}$$

If you apply N, Roots finds numerical roots, and ToRules converts the result into transformation rules.

```
In[8]:= N[ % ]
Out[8]= {{x -> -1.0045 - 1.06095 I},
         {x -> -1.0045 + 1.06095 I}, {x -> -0.199936},
         {x -> 1.10447 - 1.05983 I},
         {x -> 1.10447 + 1.05983 I}}
```

## ■ 3.4.2 Equations in One Variable

The main class of equations that Solve and related *Mathematica* functions deal with are *polynomial equations*.

It is easy to solve a linear equation in x.

```
In[1]:= Solve[ a x + b == c , x ]
```

$$Out[1] = \{\{x \rightarrow -(\frac{b-c}{a})\}\}$$

One can also solve quadratic equations just by applying a simple formula.

```
In[2]:= Solve[ x^2 + a x + 2 == 0 , x ]
```

$$Out[2] = \{\{x \rightarrow \frac{-a + \text{Sqrt}[-8 + a^2]}{2}\},$$

$$\{x \rightarrow \frac{-a - \text{Sqrt}[-8 + a^2]}{2}\}\}$$

*Mathematica* can also find the exact solution to an arbitrary cubic equation. The results are however often very complicated. Here is the first solution to a comparatively simple cubic equation.

```
In[3]:= Solve[ x^3 + 34 x + 1 == 0 , x ] [[1]]
Out[3]= {x ->
```

$$\frac{-34}{3 \; (-(\frac{1}{2}) + \frac{\text{Sqrt}[157243]}{6 \; \text{Sqrt}[3]})^{\frac{1}{3}}} + (-(\frac{1}{2}) + \frac{\text{Sqrt}[157243]}{6 \; \text{Sqrt}[3]})^{\frac{1}{3}} \}$$

*Mathematica* can always find exact solutions to polynomial equations of degree four or less. For cubic and quartic equations, however, the results can be extremely complicated. If the parameters in equations like these are symbolic, there can also be some subtlety in what the solutions mean. The result you get by substituting specific values for the symbolic parameters into the final solution may not be the same as what you would get by doing the substitutions in the original equation.

This generates the first solution to a cubic equation with symbolic parameters.

```
In[4]:= Solve[ x^3 + a x^2 + b x + 2 == 0 , x ] [[1]] ;
```

If you try substituting specific numerical values for the symbolic parameters, you end up dividing by zero, and getting a meaningless result.

```
In[5]:= % /. {a->3, b->3}
```

```
Power::infy: Infinite expression 0^{-(\frac{1}{3})} encountered.

Infinity::indt:
        Indeterminate expresssion -(0 ComplexInfinity)
          encountered.

Out[5]= {x -> Indeterminate}
```

If you use specific values for the parameters in the original equation, then you get the correct result.

```
In[6]:= Solve[ x^3 + 3 x^2 + 3 x + 2 == 0 , x ]
```

$$Out[6]= \{\{x \rightarrow -2\}, \{x \rightarrow \frac{-1 + Sqrt[-3]}{2}\},$$

$$\{x \rightarrow \frac{-1 - Sqrt[-3]}{2}\}\}$$

In trying to solve polynomial equations with degrees higher than four, *Mathematica* runs into some fundamental mathematical difficulties.

The main mathematical result is that the solutions to an arbitrary polynomial equation of degree five or more cannot necessarily be written as algebraic expressions. More specifically, the solutions cannot be written as combinations of arithmetic functions and $k^{\text{th}}$ roots.  (It turns out that for equations with degree exactly five, the solutions can in principle be written in a complicated way in terms of elliptic functions; for higher degree equations, even this is not possible.)

There are nevertheless two large classes of higher degree equations which can be solved. The first are those in which the polynomial can be written using **Factor** as product of polynomials with low degrees. The second class are those where the polynomial can be written using **Decompose** as a composition of polynomials with low degrees. When you give a high degree polynomial to **Solve** it successively tries to use **Factor** and **Decompose**, together with some other tricks, to simplify the polynomial. As a result, **Solve** is able to give explicit algebraic solutions to many high degree polynomial equations.

Here is a factorizable polynomial of degree 5.

```
In[7]:= Expand[ Product[ x - i, {i, 5} ] ]
```

$$Out[7]= -120 + 274 x - 225 x^2 + 85 x^3 - 15 x^4 + x^5$$

*Mathematica* solves the equation by factoring the polynomial.

```
In[8]:= Solve[ % == 0, x ]
```

$$Out[8]= \{\{x \rightarrow 5\}, \{x \rightarrow 4\}, \{x \rightarrow 3\}, \{x \rightarrow 2\}, \{x \rightarrow 1\}\}$$

**Solve** gives the solution to an equation like this in terms of complex exponentials.

```
In[9]:= Solve[x^6 == 1, x]
```

$$Out[9]= \{\{x \rightarrow 1\}, \{x \rightarrow E^{\frac{I}{3} Pi}\}, \{x \rightarrow E^{\frac{2 I}{3} Pi}\},$$

$$\{x \rightarrow -1\}, \{x \rightarrow E^{\frac{4 I}{3} Pi}\}, \{x \rightarrow E^{\frac{5 I}{3} Pi}\}\}$$

Here is an equation for which explicit algebraic solutions cannot be found. *Mathematica* leaves the result in a symbolic form.

```
In[10]:= Solve[x^5 - 1331 x + 11 == 0 , x]

Out[10]= {ToRules[Roots[-1331 x + x  == -11, x]]}
                                      5
```

Applying N gives the numerical result.

```
In[11]:= N[ % ]
Out[11]= {{x -> -6.04217},
          {x -> -0.00206611 - 6.04011 I},
          {x -> -0.00206611 + 6.04011 I}, {x -> 0.00826446},
          {x -> 6.03804}}
```

Here is a complicated polynomial.

```
In[12]:= p = 3 + 3 x - 7 x^2 - x^3 + 2 x^4 +
              3 x^7 - 3 x^8 - x^9 + x^10
                              2     3       4       7       8     9
Out[12]= 3 + 3 x - 7 x  - x  + 2 x  + 3 x  - 3 x  - x  +
          10
         x
```

*Mathematica* finds some of the solutions, and leaves the rest in a symbolic form. Applying N would give the numerical solutions.

```
In[13]:= Solve[ % == 0 , x ]
Out[13]= {{x -> 1}, {x -> Sqrt[3]}, {x -> -Sqrt[3]},
                                      7
          ToRules[Roots[1 + 2 x + x  == 0, x]]}
```

If you ultimately need only the numerical solution, it is usually a lot faster to use NRoots to ask for numerical results from the outset.

```
In[14]:= NRoots[ p == 0 , x ]
Out[14]= x == -1.73205 || x == -0.868688 - 0.585282 I ||
          x == -0.868688 + 0.585282 I || x == -0.496292 ||
          x == 0.0763556 - 1.14095 I ||
          x == 0.0763556 + 1.14095 I || x == 1. ||
          x == 1.04048 - 0.56735 I ||
          x == 1.04048 + 0.56735 I || x == 1.73205
```

If there are approximate numbers in your original equation, Solve will immediately get a numerical solution.

```
In[15]:= Solve[x^3 + 7.8 x + 1 == 0, x]
Out[15]= {{x -> -0.127937}, {x -> 0.0639683 - 2.79504 I},
          {x -> 0.0639683 + 2.79504 I}}
```

If Solve cannot find an algebraic solution to a high degree polynomial equation, then it is a good guess that no such solution exists. However, you should realize that one can construct complicated equations that have algebraic solutions which the procedures built into *Mathematica* do not find. The simplest example of such an equation that we know is $-23 - 36x + 27x^2 - 4x^3 - 9x^4 + x^6 = 0$, which has a solution $x = 2^{\frac{1}{3}} + 3^{\frac{1}{2}}$ that Solve does not find.

When *Mathematica* can find solutions to an $n^{\text{th}}$ degree polynomial equation, it always gives exactly *n* solutions.  The number of times that each root of the polynomial appears is equal to its multiplicity.

| | |
|---|---|
| Solve gives two identical solutions to this equation. | `In[16]:= Solve[(x-1)^2 == 0, x]` |
| | `Out[16]= {{x -> 1}, {x -> 1}}` |

*Mathematica* knows how to solve some equations which are not explicitly in the form of polynomials.

Here is an equation that is not explicitly of polynomial form.

`In[17]:= Solve[ Sqrt[1-x] + Sqrt[1+x] == a, x ]`

$$Out[17]= \{\{x \rightarrow \frac{a \; Sqrt[4 - a^2]}{2}\}, \{x \rightarrow \frac{-(a \; Sqrt[4 - a^2])}{2}\}\}$$

*Mathematica* can always give you numerical approximations to the solutions of a polynomial equation.  For more general equations, involving say transcendental functions, there is often no systematic procedure even for finding numerical solutions.  Section 3.9.6 discusses approaches to this problem in *Mathematica*.

This finds a numerical solution to the equation $x \sin(x) = \frac{1}{2}$, close to $x = 1$.

`In[18]:= FindRoot[ x Sin[x] - 1/2 == 0 , {x, 1} ]`

`Out[18]= {x -> 0.740841}`

Plotting a graph of $x \sin(x) - \frac{1}{2}$ makes it pretty clear that there are in fact an infinite number of solutions to the equation.

`In[19]:= Plot[ x Sin[x] - 1/2 , {x, 0, 30} ]`

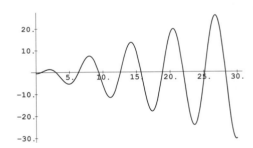

### ■ 3.4.3  Simultaneous Equations

You can give `Solve` a list of simultaneous equations to solve.  `Solve` can find explicit solutions for a large class of simultaneous polynomial equations.

Here is a simple linear equation with two unknowns.

```
In[1]:= Solve[ { a x + b y == 1, x - y == 2 } ,
          {x, y} ]
```

$$Out[1]= \{\{x \rightarrow -(\frac{1}{-a - b}) - \frac{2\ b}{-a - b},$$

$$y \rightarrow -(\frac{1}{-a - b}) + \frac{2\ a}{-a - b}\}\}$$

Here is a more complicated example. The result is a list of solutions, with each solution consisting of a list of transformation rules for the variables.

```
In[2]:= Solve[{x^2 + y^2 == 1, x + y == a}, {x, y}]
```

$$Out[2]= \{\{x \rightarrow \frac{2\ a - \text{Sqrt}[4\ a^2 - 8\ (-1 + a^2)]}{4},$$

$$y \rightarrow \frac{2\ a + \text{Sqrt}[4\ a^2 - 8\ (-1 + a^2)]}{4}\},$$

$$\{x \rightarrow \frac{2\ a + \text{Sqrt}[4\ a^2 - 8\ (-1 + a^2)]}{4},$$

$$y \rightarrow \frac{2\ a - \text{Sqrt}[4\ a^2 - 8\ (-1 + a^2)]}{4}\}\}$$

You can use the list of solutions with the /. operator.

```
In[3]:= x^3 + y^3 /. % /. a -> 0.7
Out[3]= {0.8785, 0.8785}
```

Even when **Solve** cannot find explicit solutions, it often can "unwind" simultaneous equations to produce a symbolic result in terms of nested **Roots** functions.

```
In[4]:= Solve[{x^3 + y^3 == x y, x + y + x y == 1},
          {x, y}]
Out[4]= {ToRules[Roots[4 x ==
```

$$3 - 3\ y + y^2 - 2\ y^3 - 2\ y^4 - y^5,\ x,$$

$$\text{Using} \rightarrow$$

$$\text{Roots}[-4\ y + 2\ y^2 + y^3 + 4\ y^4 + 3\ y^5 + y^6$$

$$== -1,\ y]]]\}$$

You can then use N to get a numerical
result.

```
In[5]:= N[ % ]
Out[5]= {{x -> -1.74543 + 1.2018 I,
            y -> -1.74543 - 1.2018 I},
          {x -> -1.74543 - 1.2018 I, y -> -1.74543 + 1.2018 I},
            {x -> -0.17169 + 1.14626 I,
            y -> -0.17169 - 1.14626 I},
          {x -> -0.17169 - 1.14626 I,
            y -> -0.17169 + 1.14626 I},
          {x -> 0.507861, y -> 0.326382},
          {x -> 0.326382, y -> 0.507861}}
```

The variables that you use in `Solve` do not need to be single symbols. Often when you set up large collections of simultaneous equations, you will want to use expressions like $a[i]$ as variables.

Here is a list of three equations for the
$a[i]$.

```
In[6]:= Table[ 2 a[i] + a[i-1] == a[i+1], {i, 3} ]
Out[6]= {a[0] + 2 a[1] == a[2], a[1] + 2 a[2] == a[3],
          a[2] + 2 a[3] == a[4]}
```

This solves for some of the $a[i]$.

```
In[7]:= Solve[ % , {a[1], a[2], a[3]} ]
```

$$Out[7]= \left\{\left\{a[1] \to \frac{-5\ a[0]}{12} + \frac{a[4]}{12},\ a[2] \to \frac{a[0]}{6} + \frac{a[4]}{6},\right.\right.$$
$$\left.\left. a[3] \to \frac{-a[0]}{12} + \frac{5\ a[4]}{12}\right\}\right\}$$

| | |
|---|---|
| `Solve[`*eqns*`, {`$x_1$`, `$x_2$`, ...}]` | solve *eqns* for the specific objects $x_i$ |
| `Solve[`*eqns*`]` | try to solve *eqns* for all the objects that appear in them |

Solving simultaneous equations.

If you do not explicitly specify objects to
solve for, `Solve` will try to solve for all the
variables.

```
In[8]:= Solve[ { x + y == 1, x - 3 y == 2 } ]
```

$$Out[8]= \left\{\left\{x \to \frac{5}{4},\ y \to -\left(\frac{1}{4}\right)\right\}\right\}$$

> ```
> Solve[{lhs₁==rhs₁, lhs₂==rhs₂, ...}, vars]
>
> Solve[lhs₁==rhs₁ && lhs₂==rhs₂ && ..., vars]
>
> Solve[{lhs₁, lhs₂, ...} == {rhs₁, rhs₂, ...}, vars]
> ```

Ways to present simultaneous equations to `Solve`.

If you construct simultaneous equations from matrices, you typically get equations between lists of expressions.

```
In[9]:= {{3,1},{2,-5}}.{x,y}=={7,8}
Out[9]= {3 x + y, 2 x - 5 y} == {7, 8}
```

`Solve` converts equations involving lists to lists of equations.

```
In[10]:= Solve[%, {x, y}]
               43          10
Out[10]= {{x -> --, y -> -(--)}}
               17          17
```

You can use `LogicalExpand` to do the conversion explicitly.

```
In[11]:= LogicalExpand[%%]
Out[11]= 3 x + y == 7 && 2 x - 5 y == 8
```

## ■ 3.4.4  Getting Full Solutions

If you have an equation like `2 x == 0`, it is perfectly clear that the only possible solution is `x -> 0`. However, if you have an equation like `a x == 0`, things are not so clear. If `a` is not equal to zero, then `x -> 0` is again the only solution. However, if `a` is in fact equal to zero, then *any* value of `x` is a solution.

`Solve` implicitly assumes that the parameter `a` does not have the special value 0.

```
In[1]:= Solve[ a x == 0 , x ]
Out[1]= {{x -> 0}}
```

`Roots` makes the same assumption.

```
In[2]:= Roots[ a x == 0 , x ]
Out[2]= x == 0
```

`Reduce`, on the other hand, gives you all the possibilities, without assuming anything about the value of `a`.

```
In[3]:= Reduce[ a x == 0 , x ]
Out[3]= a != 0 && x == 0 || a == 0
```

The results that `Reduce` gives are logical statements representing all possible solutions to an equation, allowing for special values of parameters.

A result like `a != 0 && x == 0 || a == 0` is interpreted as follows. The `&&` stands for AND; `||` stands for OR. Since in *Mathematica* the `||` operator has lower precedence than `&&`, the expression is equivalent to (a != 0 && x == 0) || (a == 0). The two pieces then represent alternative solutions. The first alternative is that a is not equal to 0, and x equals 0. This is the solution that `Solve` finds. The second alternative is that a is equal to 0, but there is no restriction on x.

| | |
|---|---|
| *lhs* == *rhs* | an equation asserting that two quantities are equal |
| *lhs* != *rhs* | an inequation asserting that two quantities are unequal |
| *eqn$_1$* && *eqn$_2$* | equations that must simultaneously be satisfied |
| *eqn$_1$* \|\| *eqn$_2$* | alternative equations, only one of which need be satisfied |

Logical forms associated with equations.

This is the solution to an arbitrary linear equation given by `Roots` and `Solve`.

```
In[4]:= Roots[a x + b == 0, x]
```

$$Out[4]= x == -\left(\frac{b}{a}\right)$$

`Reduce` gives the full version, which includes the possibility a==b==0.

```
In[5]:= Reduce[a x + b == 0, x]
```

$$Out[5]= a \;!= 0 \;\&\& \;x == -\left(\frac{b}{a}\right) \;||\; a == 0 \;\&\& \;b == 0$$

Here is the full solution to a general quadratic equation. There are three alternatives. If a is nonzero, then there are two solutions for x, given by the standard quadratic formula. If a is zero, however, the equation reduces to a linear one. Finally, if a, b and c are all zero, there is no restriction on x.

```
In[6]:= Reduce[a x^2 + b x + c == 0, x]
```

$$Out[6]= a \;!= 0 \;\&\& \;\left(x == \frac{-\left(\frac{b}{a}\right) + \mathrm{Sqrt}\left[\frac{b^2}{a^2} - \frac{4\,c}{a}\right]}{2}\right. \;||$$

$$\left. x == \frac{-\left(\frac{b}{a}\right) - \mathrm{Sqrt}\left[\frac{b^2}{a^2} - \frac{4\,c}{a}\right]}{2}\right) \;||$$

$$b \;!= 0 \;\&\& \;a == 0 \;\&\& \;x == -\left(\frac{c}{b}\right) \;||$$

$$a == 0 \;\&\& \;b == 0 \;\&\& \;c == 0$$

The most important difference between `Reduce` and `Solve` is that `Reduce` gives *all* the possible solutions to a set of equations, while `Solve` gives only the *generic* ones. Solutions are considered "generic" if they involve conditions only on the variables that you explicitly solve for, and not on other parameters in the equations. `Reduce` and `Solve` also differ in that `Reduce` always returns combinations of equations, while `Solve` gives results in the form of transformation rules.

| | |
|---|---|
| `Solve[eqns, vars]` | find generic solutions to equations |
| `Reduce[eqns, vars]` | reduce equations, maintaining all solutions |

Solving equations.

## ■ 3.4.5  Advanced Topic: Existence of Solutions

Using `Reduce`, you can find out under exactly what conditions a particular set of equations has solutions. `Solve` tells you whether any generic solutions exist.

There is no value of x which solves these simultaneous equations. `Reduce` thus simplifies the logical statement x==1 && x==2 to the explicit value `False`.

```
In[1]:= Reduce[ x == 1 && x == 2 , x ]
Out[1]= False
```

There is a solution to these equations, but only when a has the special value 1.

```
In[2]:= Reduce[ x == 1 && x == a , x ]
Out[2]= a == 1 && x == 1
```

The solution is not generic, and is rejected by `Solve`.

```
In[3]:= Solve[ x == 1 && x == a , x ]
Out[3]= {}
```

This equation is true for any value of x.

```
In[4]:= Reduce[ x == x , x ]
Out[4]= True
```

This is the kind of result `Solve` returns when you give an equation that is always true.

```
In[5]:= Solve[ x == x , x ]
Out[5]= {{}}
```

When you work with systems of linear equations, you can use `Solve` to get generic solutions, and `Reduce` to find out for what values of parameters solutions exist.

Here is a matrix whose $i, j^{\text{th}}$ element is $i + j$.

```
In[6]:= m = Table[i + j, {i, 3}, {j, 3}]
Out[6]= {{2, 3, 4}, {3, 4, 5}, {4, 5, 6}}
```

The matrix has determinant zero.

```
In[7]:= Det[ m ]
Out[7]= 0
```

This makes a set of three simultaneous equations.

```
In[8]:= eqn =  m . {x, y, z} == {a, b, c}
Out[8]= {2 x + 3 y + 4 z, 3 x + 4 y + 5 z,
           4 x + 5 y + 6 z} == {a, b, c}
```

Solve reports that there are no generic solutions.

```
In[9]:= Solve[eqn, {x, y, z}]
Out[9]= {}
```

Reduce, however, shows that there *would* be a solution if the parameters satisfied the special condition c == -a + 2b.

```
In[10]:= Reduce[eqn, {x, y, z}]
Out[10]= c == -a + 2 b && x == -4 a + 3 b + z &&
           y == 3 a - 2 b - 2 z
```

For nonlinear equations, the conditions for the existence of solutions may be very complicated.

Here is a very simple pair of nonlinear equations.

```
In[11]:= eqn = {x y == a, x^2 y^2 == b}
                                 2  2
Out[11]= {x y == a, x  y  == b}
```

Solve shows that the equations have no generic solutions.

```
In[12]:= Solve[eqn, {x, y}]
Out[12]= {}
```

Reduce gives the complete conditions for a solution to exist.

```
In[13]:= Reduce[eqn, {x, y}]
                              2           a
Out[13]= y != 0 && b == a  && x == - ||
                                          y

           a == 0 && b == 0 && y == 0
```

## ■ 3.4.6 Eliminating Variables

When you write down a set of simultaneous equations in *Mathematica*, you are specifying a collection of constraints between variables. When you use `Solve`, you are finding values for some of the variables in terms of others, subject to the constraints represented by the equations.

| | |
|---|---|
| `Solve[eqns, vars, elims]` | find solutions for *vars*, eliminating the variables *elims* |
| `Eliminate[eqns, elims]` | rearrange equations to eliminate the variables *elims* |

Eliminating variables.

Here are two equations involving x, y and the "parameter" a.

```
In[1]:= eqn = {x == 1 + 2 a, y == 9 + 2 x}
Out[1]= {x == 1 + 2 a, y == 9 + 2 x}
```

If you solve for both x and y, you get results in terms of a.

```
In[2]:= Solve[eqn, {x, y}]
Out[2]= {{x -> 1 + 2 a, y -> 9 - 2 (-1 - 2 a)}}
```

Similarly, if you solve for x and a, you get results in terms of y.

```
In[3]:= Solve[eqn, {x, a}]
```
$$Out[3]= \{\{x \to \frac{-9 + y}{2}, \ a \to -(\frac{1}{2}) + \frac{-9 + y}{4}\}\}$$

If you only want to solve for x, however, you have to specify whether you want to eliminate y or a. This eliminates y, and so gives the result in terms of a.

```
In[4]:= Solve[eqn, x, y]
Out[4]= {{x -> 1 + 2 a}}
```

If you eliminate a, then you get a result in terms of y.

```
In[5]:= Solve[eqn, x, a]
```
$$Out[5]= \{\{x \to \frac{-9 + y}{2}\}\}$$

In some cases, you may want to construct explicitly equations in which variables have been eliminated. You can do this using `Eliminate`.

This combines the two equations in the list eqn, by eliminating the variable a.

```
In[6]:= Eliminate[eqn, a]
Out[6]= y == 9 + 2 x
```

This is what you get if you eliminate y instead of a.

```
In[7]:= Eliminate[eqn, y]
Out[7]= 2 a == -1 + x
```

As a more sophisticated example of `Eliminate`, consider the problem of writing $x^5 + y^5$ in terms of the "symmetric polynomials" $x + y$ and $xy$.

To solve the problem, we simply have to write f in terms of a and b, eliminating the original variables x and y.

```
In[8]:= Eliminate[ {f == x^5 + y^5, a == x + y, b == x y},
                   {x, y} ]
```
$$Out[8]= -5 a^3 b + 5 a b^2 == -a^5 + f$$

## ■ 3.4.7  Solving Equations with Subsidiary Conditions

In doing calculations with equations, you will often find it convenient to think of a particular set of equations as the "main" ones you are working with, and to think of other equations as "subsidiary conditions" that must also be satisfied.

A typical thing to do is to assign a name to the list of subsidiary conditions, and then to include them by name in each list of equations you give to `Solve`.

| | |
|---|---|
| `sincos` is defined to be the equation $\sin^2(x) + \cos^2(x) = 1$. | `In[1]:= sincos = Sin[x]^2 + Cos[x]^2 == 1`<br><br>`Out[1]= Cos[x]` $^2$ `+ Sin[x]` $^2$ `== 1` |

This solves the equation $\sin(x) + 2\cos(x) = 1$, with the "subsidiary condition" $\sin^2(x) + \cos^2(x) = 1$.

```
In[2]:= Solve[ { Sin[x] + 2 Cos[x] == 1, sincos } ,
                 { Sin[x], Cos[x] } ]
```

$$Out[2]= \{\{Sin[x] \rightarrow -(\frac{3}{5}), Cos[x] \rightarrow \frac{4}{5}\},$$

$$\{Sin[x] \rightarrow 1, Cos[x] \rightarrow 0\}\}$$

Here is another equation, solved with the same "subsidiary condition".

```
In[3]:= Solve[ { Sin[x] == Cos[x], sincos } ,
                 { Sin[x], Cos[x] } ]
```

$$Out[3]= \{\{Sin[x] \rightarrow \frac{1}{Sqrt[2]}, Cos[x] \rightarrow \frac{1}{Sqrt[2]}\},$$

$$\{Sin[x] \rightarrow -(\frac{1}{Sqrt[2]}), Cos[x] \rightarrow -(\frac{1}{Sqrt[2]})\}\}$$

Section 3.4.10 discusses another way to set up and use algebraic subsidiary conditions.

## ■ 3.4.8 Advanced Topic: Solving Logical Combinations of Equations

When you give a list of equations to `Solve`, it assumes that you want all the equations to be satisfied simultaneously. It is also possible to give `Solve` more complicated logical combinations of equations.

Solve assumes that the equations `x + y == 1` and `x - y == 2` are simultaneously valid.

```
In[1]:= Solve[{x + y == 1, x - y == 2}, {x, y}]
```

$$Out[1]= \{\{x \rightarrow \frac{3}{2}, y \rightarrow -(\frac{1}{2})\}\}$$

Here is an alternative form, using the logical connective `&&` explicitly.

```
In[2]:= Solve[ x + y == 1 && x - y == 2, {x, y}]
```

$$Out[2]= \{\{x \rightarrow \frac{3}{2}, y \rightarrow -(\frac{1}{2})\}\}$$

This specifies that *either* `x + y == 1` *or* `x - y == 2`. Solve gives two solutions for `x`, corresponding to these two possibilities.

```
In[3]:= Solve[ x + y == 1 || x - y == 2, x ]

Out[3]= {{x -> 1 - y}, {x -> 2 + y}}
```

Solve gives three solutions to this equation.

```
In[4]:= Solve[x^3 == x, x]
Out[4]= {{x -> 1}, {x -> -1}, {x -> 0}}
```

If you explicitly include the assertion that x != 0, one of the solutions is suppressed.

```
In[5]:= Solve[x^3 == x && x != 0, x]
Out[5]= {{x -> 1}, {x -> -1}}
```

Here is a slightly more complicated example. Note that the precedence of || is lower than the precedence of &&, so the equation is interpreted as (x^3 == x && x != 1) || x^2 == 2, not x^3 == x && (x != 1 || x^2 == 2).

```
In[6]:= Solve[x^3 == x && x != 1 || x^2 == 2 , x]
Out[6]= {{x -> -1}, {x -> 0}, {x -> Sqrt[2]},
         {x -> -Sqrt[2]}}
```

When you use `Solve`, the final results you get are in the form of transformation rules. If you use `Reduce` or `Eliminate`, on the other hand, then your results are logical statements, which you can manipulate further.

This gives a logical statement representing the solutions of the equation x^2 == x.

```
In[7]:= Reduce[x^2 == x, x]
Out[7]= x == 1 || x == 0
```

This finds values of x which satisfy x^5 == x but do not satisfy the statement representing the solutions of x^2 == x.

```
In[8]:= Reduce[x^5 == x && !%, x]
Out[8]= x == -1 || x == I || x == -I
```

The logical statements produced by `Reduce` can be thought of as representations of the solution set for your equations. The logical connectives &&, || and so on then correspond to operations on these sets.

| | |
|---|---|
| *eqns₁* || *eqns₂* | union of solution sets |
| *eqns₁* && *eqns₂* | intersection of solution sets |
| !*eqns* | complement of solution set |
| Implies[*eqns₁*, *eqns₂*] | the part of *eqns₁* that contains *eqns₂* |

Operations on solution sets.

In dealing with sets of equations, it is common to consider some of the objects that appear as true "variables", and others as "parameters". In some cases, you may need to know for what values of parameters a particular relation between the variables is *always* satisfied.

| `SolveAlways[eqns, vars]` | solve for the values of parameters for which the *eqns* are satisfied for all values of the *vars* |
|---|---|

Solving for parameters that make relations always true.

| | |
|---|---|
| This finds the values of a, b and c for which the relation x + y == 1 implies a x^2 + b x y + c y^2 == 1 for all x and y. | `In[9]:= SolveAlways[`<br>`    Implies[ x + y == 1, a x^2 + b x y + c y^2 == 1 ] ,`<br>`        { x, y } ]`<br>`Out[9]= {{a -> 1, b -> 2, c -> 1}}` |

## ■ 3.4.9  Advanced Topic: Equations Modulo Integers

When you write an equation like *lhs* == *rhs*, you usually want to assert that the expressions *lhs* and *rhs* are exactly equal. For some purposes, however, it is convenient to use a weaker notion of equality, and to interpret *lhs* == *rhs* as meaning that two integer expressions are equal modulo some fixed integer. Solving equations that use this weaker notion of equality is important in many problems in number theory.

| `Solve[eqns, vars, ..., Mode->Modular]` | solve equations with equality required only modulo an integer |
|---|---|
| `Modulus == p` | a special equation specifying the modulus used to determine equality |

Solving equations modulo integers.

There are two ways to work with equations modulo integers. The first is explicitly to specify the modulus you want to use. The second is to let `Solve` find a modulus for which your equations are satisfied.

| | |
|---|---|
| *Mathematica* cannot find a closed form solution for this equation over complex numbers. | `In[1]:= Solve[5 + 11x + 17x^2 + 7x^3 + 16x^4 + x^5==0, x]`<br>`Out[1]= {ToRules[Roots[11 x + 17 x^2 + 7 x^3 + 16 x^4 + x^5 ==`<br>`                -5, x]]}` |

| | |
|---|---|
| The equation does, however, have simple solutions over integers modulo 19. Notice that if you include an equation for Modulus, you do not have to set Mode->Modular explicitly. | `In[2]:= Solve[5 + 11x + 17x^2 + 7x^3 + 16x^4 + x^5==0 &&`<br>`            Modulus==19, x]`<br>`Out[2]= {{Modulus -> 19, x -> -1},`<br>`    {Modulus -> 19, x -> -7}, {Modulus -> 19, x -> -12},`<br>`    {Modulus -> 19, x -> -16}, {Modulus -> 19, x -> -18}}` |

If you use `Mode->Modular`, but do not explicitly include an equation for the modulus you want to use, *Mathematica* will try to find a modulus for which your set of equations can be satisfied.

The result shows that these equations are satisfied modulo two when $x$ is odd.

```
In[3]:= Solve[{x^2 + 1 == 0, x^3 + 1 == 0}, x,
                                        Mode->Modular]

Out[3]= {{Modulus -> 2, x -> -1}}
```

When you solve equations in the usual way over complex numbers, it takes $n$ equations to determine the values of $n$ complex variables. When you do not specify the modulus in advance, however, you can expect to get a finite number of solutions for $n$ integer variables only by giving $n + 1$ equations. You can think of the extra equation as being what is needed to determine the modulus.

Here is a polynomial of degree three.

```
In[4]:= f = x^3 + 4x + 17
                              3
Out[4]= 17 + 4 x + x
```

This finds the value of x and the modulus for which both f and its derivative vanish.

```
In[5]:= Solve[ f == D[f,x] == 0, x, Mode->Modular ]
Out[5]= {{Modulus -> 8059, x -> 1001}}
```

Here are the corresponding values of f and D[f,x].

```
In[6]:= {f, D[f,x]} /. %
Out[6]= {{1003007022, 3006007}}
```

They indeed do vanish modulo 8059.

```
In[7]:= Mod[%, 8059]
Out[7]= {{0, 0}}
```

Here is another example, based on a polynomial in two variables.

```
In[8]:= f = y^2 - y - x^3 + x^2
             2   3       2
Out[8]= x  - x  - y + y
```

In the language of arithmetic geometry, this shows that the curve defined by $f = 0$ has a singular point modulo the prime number 11.

```
In[9]:= Solve[ f == D[f,x] == D[f,y] == 0, {x, y},
                            Mode->Modular ]
Out[9]= {{Modulus -> 11, y -> -5, x -> -3}}
```

## ■ 3.4.10  Setting Up Algebraic Transformation Rules

Transformation rules in *Mathematica* are usually based on the *structure* of expressions, not their algebraic meaning. Using `Solve` and related functions, however, you can effectively carry out true algebraic transformations on expressions.

The transformation rule replaces the specific object x^2 by a. The rule says nothing about objects like x^4 that are algebraically related to x^2.

```
In[1]:= 1 + x^2 + x^4 /. x^2 -> a

Out[1]= 1 + a + x^4
```

By calling Solve with the equation x^2 == a, and asking it to eliminate x, you can effectively carry out a true algebraic transformation.

```
In[2]:= Solve[{ f == 1 + x^2 + x^4, x^2 == a } , f , x ]

Out[2]= {{f -> 1 + a + a^2}}
```

Often, you need to perform the same algebraic transformation several times. *Mathematica* therefore allows you to construct a set of *algebraic rules*, which embody the transformations you specify, and which you can apply simply by using the standard /. operator.

| | |
|---|---|
| AlgebraicRules[*eqns, vars*] | generate a set of algebraic rules which replace variables earlier in the list *vars* by ones later in the list, according to the equations *eqns* |
| *expr* /. *algrules* | apply algebraic rules to a particular expression |

Algebraic transformation rules.

This sets up algebraic transformation rules which try to replace x by a according to the equation x^2 == a.

```
In[3]:= ar = AlgebraicRules[x^2 == a, {x, a}]

Out[3]= {x^2 -> a}
```

You can apply the algebraic rules using the /. operator.

```
In[4]:= 1 + x^2 + x^4 /. ar

Out[4]= 1 + a + a^2
```

The algebraic rules replace as many powers of x^2 as possible.

```
In[5]:= 1 + x^3 + x^7 /. ar

Out[5]= 1 + a x + a^3 x
```

Algebraic rules in *Mathematica* are set up using mathematical objects known as *Gröbner bases*. Although the output from AlgebraicRules is usually displayed as a simple list of rules, it is in fact a representation of a Gröbner basis.

This is the internal form of the object produced by AlgebraicRules. It is a representation of a Gröbner basis.

```
In[6]:= InputForm[ar]

Out[6]//InputForm=
     AlgebraicRulesData[{x, a}, {x, a}, True,
       {{{2, {{0, 1}}}, {0, {{1, -1}}}}}, {x, a},
       {x^2 -> a}, Rational]
```

Many of *Mathematica*'s internal equation manipulation algorithms use Gröbner bases in the form produced by `AlgebraicRules`. If you need the explicit form of a Gröbner basis, you can find it by pulling out the appropriate part of the expression you get from `AlgebraicRules`.

You can use `AlgebraicRules` to set up algebraic rules involving several variables.

| | |
|---|---|
| This sets up algebraic rules which try to replace x and y by a and b using the equations given. | `In[7]:= ar = AlgebraicRules[{a == x+y, b == x y},`<br>`               {x, y, a, b}]`<br><br>`Out[7]= {-y^2 -> b - a y, -x -> -a + y}` |
| By applying the algebraic rules ar, you can rewrite x^3 + y^3 in terms of a and b. | `In[8]:= x^3 + y^3 /. ar`<br><br>`Out[8]= a^3 - 3 a b` |
| You can apply the same rules to x^4 + y^4. | `In[9]:= x^4 + y^4 /. ar`<br><br>`Out[9]= a^4 - 4 a^2 b + 2 b^2` |
| In this case, it is not possible to eliminate x and y entirely. Following the order of variables you specified in `AlgebraicRules`, *Mathematica* nevertheless tries to eliminate x in favor of y. | `In[10]:= x^3 + y^4 /. ar`<br><br>`Out[10]= a^3 - 2 a b - a^2 b + b^2 - a^2 y + a^2 y - 2 a b y + b y` |

# ■ 3.5  Calculus

## ■ 3.5.1  Differentiation

| | |
|---|---|
| `D[f, x]` | partial derivative $\frac{\partial}{\partial x} f$ |
| `D[f, x_1, x_2, ...]` | multiple derivative $\frac{\partial}{\partial x_1} \frac{\partial}{\partial x_2} ... f$ |
| `D[f, {x, n}]` | $n^{\text{th}}$ derivative $\frac{\partial^n}{\partial x^n} f$ |
| `D[f, x, NonConstants -> {v_1, v_2, ...}]` | |
| | $\frac{\partial}{\partial x} f$ with the $v_i$ taken to depend on $x$ |

Partial differentiation operations.

This gives $\frac{\partial}{\partial x} x^n$.

```
In[1]:= D[x^n, x]
                -1 + n
Out[1]= n x
```

This gives the third derivative.

```
In[2]:= D[x^n, {x, 3}]
                -3 + n
Out[2]= n x          (-2 + n) (-1 + n)
```

You can differentiate with respect to any expression.

```
In[3]:= D[ x[1]^2 + x[2]^2, x[1] ]
Out[3]= 2 x[1]
```

D does *partial differentiation*. It assumes here that y is independent of x.

```
In[4]:= D[x^2 + y^2, x]
Out[4]= 2 x
```

If $y$ does in fact depend on $x$, you can use the explicit functional form y[x]. Section 3.5.4 describes how objects like y'[x] work.

```
In[5]:= D[x^2 + y[x]^2, x]
Out[5]= 2 x + 2 y[x] y'[x]
```

Instead of giving an explicit function y[x], you can tell D that y *implicitly* depends on x. D[y, x, NonConstants->{y}] then represents $\frac{\partial y}{\partial x}$, with $y$ implicitly depending on $x$.

```
In[6]:= D[x^2 + y^2, x, NonConstants -> {y}]
Out[6]= 2 x + 2 y D[y, x, NonConstants -> {y}]
```

## ■ 3.5.2 Total Derivatives

| | |
|---:|:---|
| Dt[*f*] | total differential $df$ |
| Dt[*f*, *x*] | total derivative $\frac{df}{dx}$ |
| Dt[*f*, *x₁*, *x₂*, ...] | multiple total derivative $\frac{d}{dx_1}\frac{d}{dx_2}...f$ |
| Dt[*f*, *x*, Constants -> {*c₁*, *c₂*, ...}] | |
| | total derivative with $c_i$ constant (i.e. $dc_i = 0$) |
| *y*/: Dt[*y*, *x*] = 0 | set $\frac{dy}{dx} = 0$ |
| SetAttributes[*c*, Constant] | define $c$ to be a constant in all cases |

Total differentiation operations.

When you find the derivative of some expression $f$ with respect to $x$, you are effectively finding out how fast $f$ changes as you vary $x$. Often $f$ will depend not only on $x$, but also on other variables, say $y$ and $z$. The results that you get then depend on how you assume that $y$ and $z$ vary as you change $x$.

There are two common cases. Either $y$ and $z$ are assumed to stay fixed when $x$ changes, or they are allowed to vary with $x$. In a standard *partial derivative* $\frac{\partial f}{\partial x}$, all variables other than $x$ are assumed fixed. On the other hand, in the *total derivative* $\frac{df}{dx}$, all variables are allowed to change with $x$.

In *Mathematica*, D[*f*, *x*] gives a partial derivative, with all other variables assumed independent of $x$. Dt[*f*, *x*] gives a total derivative, in which all variables are assumed to depend on $x$. In both cases, you can add an argument to give more information on dependencies.

This gives the *partial derivative* $\frac{\partial}{\partial x}(x^2 + y^2)$. $y$ is assumed to be independent of $x$.

```
In[1]:= D[x^2 + y^2, x]
Out[1]= 2 x
```

This gives the *total derivative* $\frac{d}{dx}(x^2 + y^2)$. Now $y$ is assumed to depend on $x$.

```
In[2]:= Dt[x^2 + y^2, x]
Out[2]= 2 x + 2 y Dt[y, x]
```

You can make a replacement for $\frac{dy}{dx}$.

```
In[3]:= % /. Dt[y, x] -> yx
Out[3]= 2 x + 2 y yx
```

You can also make an explicit definition for $\frac{dy}{dx}$. You need to use y/: to make sure that the definition is associated with y.

```
In[4]:= y/: Dt[y, x] = 0
Out[4]= 0
```

With this definition made, Dt treats y as independent of x.

```
In[5]:= Dt[x^2 + y^2 + z^2, x]
Out[5]= 2 x + 2 z Dt[z, x]
```

This removes your definition for the derivative of y.

```
In[6]:= Clear[y]
```

This takes the total derivative, with z held fixed.

```
In[7]:= Dt[x^2 + y^2 + z^2, x, Constants->{z}]
Out[7]= 2 x + 2 y Dt[y, x]
```

This specifies that c is a constant under differentiation.

```
In[8]:= SetAttributes[c, Constant]
```

The variable c is taken as a constant.

```
In[9]:= Dt[a^2 + c x^2, x]
Out[9]= 2 c x + 2 a Dt[a, x]
```

The *function* c is also assumed to be a constant.

```
In[10]:= Dt[a^2 + c[x] x^2, x]
Out[10]= 2 a Dt[a, x] + 2 x c[x]
```

This gives the total differential $d(x^2 + cy^2)$.

```
In[11]:= Dt[x^2 + c y^2]
Out[11]= 2 x Dt[x] + 2 c y Dt[y]
```

You can make replacements and assignments for total differentials.

```
In[12]:= % /. Dt[y] -> dy
Out[12]= 2 c dy y + 2 x Dt[x]
```

## ■ 3.5.3  Derivatives of Unknown Functions

Differentiating a known function gives an explicit result.

```
In[1]:= D[Log[x]^2, x]
```
$$Out[1]= \frac{2 \ Log[x]}{x}$$

Differentiating an unknown function f gives a result in terms of f′.

```
In[2]:= D[f[x]^2, x]
Out[2]= 2 f[x] f'[x]
```

*Mathematica* applies the chain rule for differentiation, and leaves the result in terms of f′.

```
In[3]:= D[x f[x^2], x]
Out[3]= f[x^2] + 2 x^2 f'[x^2]
```

Differentiating again gives a result in terms of f, f′ and f′′.

```
In[4]:= D[%, x]
Out[4]= 6 x f'[x^2] + 4 x^3 f''[x^2]
```

When a function has more than one argument, superscripts are used to indicate how many times each argument is being differentiated.

```
In[5]:= D[g[x^2, y^2], x]
                (1,0)  2    2
Out[5]= 2 x g       [x , y ]
```

This represents $\frac{\partial}{\partial x}\frac{\partial}{\partial x}\frac{\partial}{\partial y}g(x,y)$. *Mathematica* assumes that the order in which derivatives are taken with respect to different variables is irrelevant.

```
In[6]:= D[g[x, y], x, x, y]
            (2,1)
Out[6]= g       [x, y]
```

You can find the value of the derivative when $x = 0$ by replacing x with 0.

```
In[7]:= % /. x->0
            (2,1)
Out[7]= g       [0, y]
```

|  |  |
|---|---|
| $f'[x]$ | first derivative of a function of one variable |
| $f^{(n)}[x]$ | $n^{\text{th}}$ derivative of a function of one variable |
| $f^{(n_1, n_2, \ldots)}[x]$ | derivative of a function of several variables, $n_i$ times with respect to variable $i$ |

Output forms for derivatives of unknown functions.

### ■ 3.5.4  Advanced Topic: The Representation of Derivatives

Derivatives in *Mathematica* work essentially the same as in standard mathematics. The usual mathematical notation, however, often hides many details. To understand how derivatives are represented in *Mathematica*, we must look at these details.

The standard mathematical notation $f'(0)$ is really a short hand for $\frac{d}{dt}f(t)\,|_{t=0}$, where $t$ is a "dummy variable". Similarly, $f'(x^2)$ is a short hand for $\frac{d}{dt}f(t)\,|_{t=x^2}$. As suggested by the notation $f'$, the object $\frac{d}{dt}f(t)$ can in fact be viewed as a "pure function", to be evaluated with a particular choice of its parameter $t$. You can in fact think of the operation of differentiation as acting on a *function* $f$, to give a new *function*, usually called $f'$.

With functions of more than one argument, the simple notation based on primes breaks down. You cannot tell for example whether $g'(0, 1)$ stands for $\frac{d}{dt}g(t, 1)\,|_{t=0}$ or $\frac{d}{dt}g(0, t)\,|_{t=1}$, and for almost any $g$, these will have totally different values. Once again, however, $t$ is just a dummy variable, whose sole purpose is to show with respect to which "slot" $g$ is to be differentiated.

In *Mathematica*, as in some branches of mathematics, it is convenient to think about a kind of differentiation that acts on *functions*, rather than on expressions. We need an operation that takes the function $f$, and gives us the *derivative function* $f'$. Operations such as this that act on *functions*, rather than variables, are known in mathematics as *functionals*.

The object `f'` in *Mathematica* is the result of applying the differentiation functional to the function `f`. The full form of `f'` is in fact `Derivative[1][f]`. `Derivative[1]` is the *Mathematica* differentiation functional.

The arguments in the functional `Derivative[`$n_1$`, `$n_2$`, ...]` specify how many times to differentiate with respect to each "slot" of the function on which it acts. By using functionals to represent differentiation, *Mathematica* avoids any need to introduce explicit "dummy variables".

| | |
|---|---|
| This is the full form of the derivative of the function f. | `In[1]:= f' // FullForm`<br><br>`Out[1]//FullForm= Derivative[1][f]` |
| Here an argument x is supplied. | `In[2]:= f'[x] // FullForm`<br><br>`Out[2]//FullForm= Derivative[1][f][x]` |
| This is the second derivative. | `In[3]:= f''[x] // FullForm`<br><br>`Out[3]//FullForm= Derivative[2][f][x]` |
| This gives a derivative of the function g with respect to its second "slot". | `In[4]:= D[g[x, y], y]`<br><br>`Out[4]= g`$^{(0,1)}$`[x, y]` |
| Here is the full form. | `In[5]:= % // FullForm`<br><br>`Out[5]//FullForm= Derivative[0, 1][g][x, y]` |
| Here is the second derivative with respect to the variable y, which appears in the second slot of g. | `In[6]:= D[g[x, y], {y, 2}] // FullForm`<br><br>`Out[6]//FullForm= Derivative[0, 2][g][x, y]` |
| This is a mixed derivative. | `In[7]:= D[g[x, y], x, y, y] // FullForm`<br><br>`Out[7]//FullForm= Derivative[1, 2][g][x, y]` |
| Since `Derivative` only specifies how many times to differentiate with respect to each slot, the order of the derivatives is irrelevant. | `In[8]:= D[g[x, y], y, y, x] // FullForm`<br><br>`Out[8]//FullForm= Derivative[1, 2][g][x, y]` |
| Here is a more complicated case, in which both arguments of g depend on the differentiation variable. | `In[9]:= D[g[x, x], x]`<br><br>`Out[9]= g`$^{(0,1)}$`[x, x] + g`$^{(1,0)}$`[x, x]` |

This is the full form of the result.

```
In[10]:= % // FullForm
Out[10]//FullForm=
        Plus[Derivative[0, 1][g][x, x],
          Derivative[1, 0][g][x, x]]
```

The object **f'** behaves essentially like any other function in *Mathematica*. You can evaluate the function with any argument, and you can use standard *Mathematica* **/.** operations to change the argument. (This would not be possible if explicit dummy variables had been introduced in the course of the differentiation.)

This is the *Mathematica* representation of the derivative of a function **f**, evaluated at the origin.

```
In[11]:= f'[0] // FullForm
Out[11]//FullForm= Derivative[1][f][0]
```

The result of this derivative involves **f'** evaluated with the argument **x^2**.

```
In[12]:= D[f[x^2], x]
                      2
Out[12]= 2 x f'[x ]
```

You can evaluate the result at the point $x = 2$ by using the standard *Mathematica* replacement operation.

```
In[13]:= % /. x->2
Out[13]= 4 f'[4]
```

There is some slight subtlety when you need to deduce the value of **f'** based on definitions for objects like **f[x_]**.

Here is a definition for a function **h**.

```
In[14]:= h[x_] := x^4
```

When you take the derivative of **h[x]**, *Mathematica* first evaluates **h[x]**, then differentiates the result.

```
In[15]:= D[h[x], x]
                3
Out[15]= 4 x
```

You can get the same result by applying the function **h'** to the argument **x**.

```
In[16]:= h'[x]
                3
Out[16]= 4 x
```

Here is the function **h'** on its own.

```
In[17]:= h'
                3
Out[17]= 4 #1  &
```

The function **f'** is completely determined by the form of the function **f**. Definitions for objects like **f[x_]** do not immediately apply however to expressions like **f'[x_]**. The problem is that **f'[x]** has the full form **Derivative[1][f][x]**, which nowhere contains anything that explicitly matches the pattern **f[x_]**. In addition, for many purposes it is convenient to have a representation of the function **f'** itself, without necessarily applying it to any arguments.

What *Mathematica* does is to try and find the explicit form of a *pure function* which represents the object **f'**. When *Mathematica* gets an expression like `Derivative[1][f]`, it effectively converts it to the explicit form `D[f[#], #]&` and then tries to evaluate the derivative. In the explicit form, *Mathematica* can immediately use values that have been defined for objects like **f[x_]**. If *Mathematica* succeeds in doing the derivative, it returns the explicit pure function result. If it does not succeed, it leaves the derivative in the original **f'** form.

| | |
|---|---|
| This gives the derivative of **Tan** in pure function form. | *In[18]:=* **Tan'**  <br><br> *Out[18]=* Cos[#1]$^{-2}$ & |
| Here is the result of applying the pure function to the specific argument **y**. | *In[19]:=* **%[y]** <br><br> *Out[19]=* Cos[y]$^{-2}$ |

### ■ 3.5.5  Defining Derivatives

You can define the derivative in *Mathematica* of a function **f** of one argument simply by an assignment like **f'[x_] = fp[x]**.

| | |
|---|---|
| This defines the derivative of $f(x)$ to be $fp(x)$. In this case, you could have used = instead of :=. | *In[1]:=* **f'[x_] := fp[x]** |
| The rule for **f'[x_]** is used to evaluate this derivative. | *In[2]:=* **D[f[x^2], x]** <br><br> *Out[2]=* 2 x fp[x$^2$] |
| Differentiating again gives derivatives of *fp*. | *In[3]:=* **D[%, x]** <br><br> *Out[3]=* 2 fp[x$^2$] + 4 x$^2$ fp'[x$^2$] |
| This defines a value for the derivative of $g$ at the origin. | *In[4]:=* **g'[0] = g0** <br><br> *Out[4]=* g0 |
| The value for **g'[0]** is used. | *In[5]:=* **D[g[x]^2, x]  /. x->0** <br><br> *Out[5]=* 2 g0 g[0] |

This defines the second derivative of g, with any argument.

```
In[6]:= g''[x_] = gpp[x]
Out[6]= gpp[x]
```

The value defined for the second derivative is used.

```
In[7]:= D[g[x]^2, {x, 2}]
```

$$Out[7]= 2 \text{ g[x] gpp[x] } + 2 \text{ g'[x]}^2$$

To define derivatives of functions with several arguments, you have to use the general representation of derivatives in *Mathematica*.

| | |
|---|---|
| `f'[x] := rhs` | define the first derivative of $f$ |
| `Derivative[n][f][x] := rhs` | define the $n^{th}$ derivative of $f$ |
| `Derivative[n1, n2, ...][g][x1, x2, ...] := rhs` | define derivatives of $g$ with respect to various arguments |

Defining derivatives.

This defines the second derivative of g with respect to its second argument.

```
In[8]:= Derivative[0, 2][g][x_, y_] := g2p[x, y]
```

## ■ 3.5.6 Indefinite Integrals

The *Mathematica* function `Integrate[f, x]` gives you the *indefinite integral* $\int f \, dx$. You can think of the process of indefinite integration as like an inverse of differentiation. If you take the result from `Integrate[f, x]`, and then differentiate it, you always get a result that is mathematically equal to the original expression $f$.

In general, however, there is a whole family of results which have the property that their derivative is $f$. `Integrate[f, x]` gives you *an* expression whose derivative is $f$. You can get other expressions by adding an arbitrary constant of integration.

When you fill in explicit limits for your integral, any such constants of integration must cancel out. Even though the indefinite integral contains arbitrary constants, it is still often very convenient to manipulate it before filling in the limits.

*Mathematica* applies standard rules to find indefinite integrals.

```
In[1]:= Integrate[x^2, x]
```

$$Out[1]= \frac{x^3}{3}$$

You can add an arbitrary constant to the indefinite integral, and still get the same derivative. `Integrate` simply gives you *an* expression with the required derivative.

```
In[2]:= D[ % + c , x]

       2
Out[2]= x
```

This gives the indefinite integral $\int \frac{dx}{x^2-1}$.

```
In[3]:= Integrate[1/(x^2 - 1), x]

        Log[-1 + x]   Log[1 + x]
Out[3]= ----------- - ----------
             2             2
```

Differentiating should give the original function back again.

```
In[4]:= D[%, x]

             1             1
Out[4]= ----------- - -----------
        2 (-1 + x)    2 (1 + x)
```

You need to manipulate it to get it back into the original form.

```
In[5]:= Simplify[%]

             1
Out[5]= ---------
               2
        -1 + x
```

The `Integrate` function assumes that any object that does not explicitly contain the integration variable is independent of it, and can be treated as a constant. As a result, `Integrate` is like an inverse of the *partial differentiation* function D.

The variable `a` is assumed to be independent of `x`

```
In[6]:= Integrate[a x^2, x]

            3
        a x
Out[6]= ----
         3
```

The integration variable can be any expression.

```
In[7]:= Integrate[x b[x]^2, b[x]]

             3
        x b[x]
Out[7]= ------
          3
```

Another assumption that `Integrate` implicitly makes is that all the symbolic quantities in your integrand have "generic" values. Thus, for example, *Mathematica* will tell you that $\int x^n \, dx$ is $\frac{x^{n+1}}{n+1}$ even though this is not true in the special case $n = -1$.

*Mathematica* gives the standard result for this integral, implicitly assuming that n is not equal to -1.

```
In[8]:= Integrate[x^n, x]

         1 + n
        x
Out[8]= ------
        1 + n
```

| If you specifically give an exponent of –1, *Mathematica* produces a different result. | `In[9]:= Integrate[x^-1, x]` |
| | `Out[9]= Log[x]` |

The results you get by doing integrals can often be written in many different forms. *Mathematica* follows various principles in deciding which form to use in each particular case. One principle is that if your input does not contain complex numbers, then neither should your output. Thus, for example, *Mathematica* tries to choose between forms involving logarithms and arc tangents in such a way as to avoid unnecessary complex numbers.

*Mathematica* writes this integral in terms of logarithms.

```
In[10]:= Integrate[1/(x^2 - 8), x]

               4 Sqrt[2] - 2 x
           Log[---------------]
               4 Sqrt[2] + 2 x
Out[10]= -----------------------
                4 Sqrt[2]
```

If you reverse the sign of the denominator term, *Mathematica* gives a result in terms of arc tangents.

```
In[11]:= Integrate[1/(x^2 + 8), x]

                     x
             ArcTan[---------]
                    2 Sqrt[2]
Out[11]= ----------------------
               2 Sqrt[2]
```

If your integral involves symbolic parameters with unspecified signs, it is not so clear how to avoid complex numbers. In this case, *Mathematica* gives the result appropriate for positive a.

```
In[12]:= Integrate[1/(x^2 + a), x]

                    x
            ArcTan[-------]
                   Sqrt[a]
Out[12]= -------------------
              Sqrt[a]
```

In the course of evaluating the integral, *Mathematica* explicitly calls `Sign` to try and determine the sign of a. You can add your own definition for `Sign[a]`.

```
In[13]:= a/: Sign[a] = -1
Out[13]= -1
```

Now *Mathematica* will instead assume that a is negative, and will give the result in the appropriate form.

```
In[14]:= Integrate[1/(x^2 + a), x]

          -I      -I Sqrt[a] + x
          -- Log[----------------]
          2       I Sqrt[a] + x
Out[14]= --------------------------
                 Sqrt[a]
```

## ■ 3.5.7  Integrals that *Mathematica* Can and Cannot Do

Evaluating integrals is much more difficult than evaluating derivatives. For derivatives, there is a systematic procedure involving the chain and product rules that allows one to work out any derivative. For integrals, however, there is no such systematic procedure. There are some general principles, but there are many integrals that cannot be done using these principles.

Before going any further, one must address the important question of exactly what it means to "do" an integral. As an operational matter, the important issue is usually whether one can write down a definite formula for the integral, which one can then easily manipulate or evaluate. The most useful formulae are typically ones that involve only rather simple functions, such as logarithms and exponentials.

The class of integrals that can be done in terms of "simple functions" is an important one, albeit in many respects not a particularly large one. One of the main capabilities of the built-in *Mathematica* `Integrate` function is being able to take essentially any integrand that involves only a particular set of "simple functions", and find the integral if it can be expressed in terms of the same set of simple functions. The relevant set of "simple functions" includes rational functions, exponentials and logarithms, as well as trigonometric and inverse trigonometric functions.

Integrals of rational functions are usually quite easy to evaluate. The answers come out in terms of rational functions, together with logarithms and inverse trigonometric functions.

$$In[1]:= \text{Integrate}[x/((x - 1)(x + 2)), x]$$

$$Out[1]= \frac{\text{Log}[-1 + x]}{3} + \frac{2\,\text{Log}[2 + x]}{3}$$

If *Mathematica* cannot get explicit formulae for the roots of the denominator polynomial, however, it cannot give you an explicit formula for the integral.

$$In[2]:= \text{Integrate}[1/(1 + 3x + x^5), x]$$

$$Out[2]= \text{Integrate}\left[\frac{1}{1 + 3\,x + x^5}, x\right]$$

Integrals involving logarithms and powers can be done in terms of logarithms and powers.

$$In[3]:= \text{Integrate}[x^4\,\text{Log}[x]^2, x]$$

$$Out[3]= \frac{2\,x^5}{125} - \frac{2\,x^5\,\text{Log}[x]}{25} + \frac{x^5\,\text{Log}[x]^2}{5}$$

Integrals of trigonometric functions usually come out in terms of other trigonometric functions.

$$In[4]:= \text{Integrate}[\text{Sin}[x]^3\,\text{Cos}[x]^2, x]$$

$$Out[4]= \frac{-2\,\text{Cos}[x]}{15} - \frac{\text{Cos}[x]\,\text{Sin}[x]^2}{15} + \frac{\text{Cos}[x]\,\text{Sin}[x]^4}{5}$$

When you combine "simple functions", you sometimes get integrals that can be done.

```
In[5]:= Integrate[Sin[Log[x]], x]

Out[5]= -(x Cos[Log[x]])     x Sin[Log[x]]
        ----------------- + ---------------
                2                  2
```

Often, however, you get integrals that cannot be done in terms of simple functions.

```
In[6]:= Integrate[Sin[Sin[x]], x]

Out[6]= Integrate[Sin[Sin[x]], x]
```

It is remarkable what simple integrands can lead to integrals that cannot be done, say in terms of "simple functions". In fact, if you were randomly to combine simple functions together, most of the integrals you would get could probably not be done in terms of simple functions.

In practical usage, however, there are certain integrals that occur much more often than others. These integrals can sometimes be expressed in terms of "special functions", which were often defined specifically as a way to represent the integrals. Most of the standard special functions are built into *Mathematica*, as discussed in Section 3.2. If you give an integral which can be done in terms of these special functions, *Mathematica* will often recognize it.

The integral $\int \frac{\log(1-x)}{x}\,dx$ comes out in terms of a special function known as the dilogarithm.

```
In[7]:= Integrate[Log[1-x]/x, x]

Out[7]= -PolyLog[2, x]
```

$\int \log(\log(x))\,dx$ can be written in terms of the logarithmic integral function.

```
In[8]:= Integrate[Log[Log[x]], x]

Out[8]= x Log[Log[x]] - LogIntegral[x]
```

Although it may be entertaining to try and construct integrals which work out in particularly subtle ways, it is worth realizing that in practical applications, such integrals are usually quite rare. The integrals that crop up in practice can usually be divided into three classes:

- Simple integrals that can be done by simple methods.

- Integrals whose form is close to the definition of a particular special function.

- Integrals that cannot be done at all in terms of standard simple or special functions.

The rules that are built into *Mathematica* should allow you to do most of the *indefinite* integrals that are found in books of mathematical tables. Sometimes, however, you may want to add your own rules for certain kinds of integrals. Section 3.5.9 describes how to do this.

*Mathematica* could make the best use of rules that you add, if it could put all integrals into standard forms that it can recognize. The chain rule makes it possible to put all derivatives into standard forms, in terms of the *Mathematica* function `Derivative`, as discussed in Section 3.5.4. For integrals, however, there is no such systematic way to produce a standard form. Instead, *Mathematica* uses some simple transformations to try and produce easily-recognizable forms.

*Mathematica* makes simple transformations to try and put integrals it cannot do into standard forms.

```
In[9]:= Integrate[Sin[Sin[x]] + Cos[Cos[x]], x]

Out[9]= Integrate[Cos[Cos[x]], x] +
            Integrate[Sin[Sin[x]], x]
```

*Mathematica* will sometimes do part of an integral, then leave the part it cannot do in a standard form.

```
In[10]:= Integrate[(1 + Log[x]^2)/(1 - Log[x]), x]
                         -2
Out[10]= Integrate[-----------, x] - x Log[x]
                     -1 + Log[x]
```

There are some general transformations on integrals that *Mathematica* tries, regardless of the functions that the integrals involve.

Integrating $f'(x)$ for any $f$ gives $f(x)$.

```
In[11]:= Integrate[f'[x], x]

Out[11]= f[x]
```

*Mathematica* can also deal with slightly more complicated cases.

```
In[12]:= Integrate[f'[x] f[x]^2, x]
              3
          f[x]
Out[12]= ------
            3
```

Here is a derivative.

```
In[13]:= D[Log[Log[Log[x]]], x]
                    1
Out[13]= ---------------------------
          x Log[x] Log[Log[x]]
```

The general transformations that *Mathematica* applies often allow it to do integrals like this.

```
In[14]:= Integrate[%, x]

Out[14]= Log[Log[Log[x]]]
```

# ■ 3.5.8 Definite Integrals

| | |
|---|---|
| Integrate[f, x] | the indefinite integral $\int f\,dx$ |
| Integrate[f, {x, xmin, xmax}] | the definite integral $\int_{xmin}^{xmax} f\,dx$ |
| Integrate[f, {x, xmin, xmax}, {y, ymin, ymax}] | |
| | the multiple integral $\int_{xmin}^{xmax} dx \int_{ymin}^{ymax} dy\ f$ |

Integration functions.

Here is the integral $\int_a^b x^2\,dx$.

```
In[1]:= Integrate[x^2, {x, a, b}]
```

$$Out[1]= \frac{-a^3}{3} + \frac{b^3}{3}$$

This gives the multiple integral $\int_0^a dx \int_0^b dy\,(x^2 + y^2)$.

```
In[2]:= Integrate[x^2 + y^2, {x, 0, a}, {y, 0, b}]
```

$$Out[2]= \frac{a^3 b}{3} + \frac{a b^3}{3}$$

The y integral is done first. Its limits can depend on the value of x. This ordering is the same as is used in functions like Sum and Table.

```
In[3]:= Integrate[x^2 + y^2, {x, 0, a}, {y, 0, x}]
```

$$Out[3]= \frac{a^4}{3}$$

You can often do a definite integral by first finding the indefinite one, and then explicitly substituting in the limits. You have to be careful, however, when the integration region contains a singularity. The integral $\int_{-1}^{1} x^{-2}\,dx$, for example, has an indefinite form which is finite at each end point. Nevertheless, the integrand has a double pole at $x = 0$, and the true integral is infinite.

# ■ 3.5.9 Defining Integrals

You can supplement the built-in integration functions of *Mathematica* by defining transformation rules for other integrals. You can, for example, enter some of the long lists of particular definite integrals that can be done.

The lack of a definite standard form for all integrals means that you sometimes have to give several different versions of the same integral: there is no guarantee that the appropriate changes of variable will automatically be done.

| | |
|---|---|
| This integral cannot be done by the built-in *Mathematica* integration algorithm. | `In[1]:= Integrate[Sin[Sin[x]], x]`<br><br>`Out[1]= Integrate[Sin[Sin[x]], x]` |
| Before you add your own rules for integration, you have to remove write protection. | `In[2]:= Unprotect[Integrate]`<br><br>`Out[2]= {Integrate}` |
| You can, however, set up your own rule to define the integral to be, say, a "Jones" function. | `In[3]:= Integrate[Sin[Sin[a_. + b_. x]], x] :=`<br>`                Jones[a, x]/b` |
| Now *Mathematica* can do integrals that give Jones functions. | `In[4]:= Integrate[Sin[Sin[3x]], x]`<br><br>`Out[4]= `$\dfrac{\texttt{Jones[0, x]}}{3}$ |

## ■ 3.5.10  Manipulating Integrals in Symbolic Form

When *Mathematica* cannot give you an explicit result for an integral, it leaves the integral in a symbolic form. It is often useful to manipulate this symbolic form.

| | |
|---|---|
| *Mathematica* cannot give an explicit result for this integral, so it leaves the integral in symbolic form. | `In[1]:= Integrate[x^2 f[x], x]`<br><br>`Out[1]= Integrate[x`$^2$` f[x], x]` |
| Differentiating the symbolic form gives the integrand back again. | `In[2]:= D[%, x]`<br><br>`Out[2]= x`$^2$` f[x]` |
| Here is a definite integral which cannot be done explicitly. | `In[3]:= Integrate[f[x], {x, a[x], b[x]}]`<br><br>`Out[3]= Integrate[f[x], {x, a[x], b[x]}]` |
| This gives the derivative of the definite integral. | `In[4]:= D[%, x]`<br><br>`Out[4]= -(f[a[x]] a'[x]) + f[b[x]] b'[x]` |
| Here is a definite integral with end points that do not explicitly depend on x. | `In[5]:= defint = Integrate[f[x], {x, a, b}]`<br><br>`Out[5]= Integrate[f[x], {x, a, b}]` |
| The partial derivative of this with respect to x is zero. | `In[6]:= D[defint, x]`<br><br>`Out[6]= 0` |
| There is a non-trivial total derivative, however. | `In[7]:= Dt[defint, x]`<br><br>`Out[7]= -(Dt[a, x] f[a]) + Dt[b, x] f[b]` |

# ■ 3.6  Power Series and Limits

## ■ 3.6.1  Making Power Series Expansions

| | |
|---|---|
| Series[*expr*, {x, x$_0$, n}] | find the power series expansion of *expr* about the point $x = x_0$ to order at most $(x - x_0)^n$ |
| Series[*expr*, {x, x$_0$, n$_x$}, {y, y$_0$, n$_y$}] | find series expansions with respect to y then x |

Functions for creating power series.

Here is the power series expansion for $\exp(x)$ about the point $x = 0$ to order $x^4$.

*In[1]:=* **Series[ Exp[x], {x, 0, 4} ]**

$$Out[1]= 1 + x + \frac{x^2}{2} + \frac{x^3}{6} + \frac{x^4}{24} + O[x]^5$$

Here is the series expansion of $\exp(x)$ about the point $x = 1$.

*In[2]:=* **Series[ Exp[x], {x, 1, 4} ]**

$$Out[2]= E + E (-1 + x) + \frac{E (-1 + x)^2}{2} + \frac{E (-1 + x)^3}{6} +$$

$$\frac{E (-1 + x)^4}{24} + O[-1 + x]^5$$

If it does not know the series expansion of a particular function, it writes the result symbolically in terms of derivatives.

*In[3]:=* **Series[ f[x], {x, 0, 3} ]**

$$Out[3]= f[0] + f'[0] \ x + \frac{f''[0] \ x^2}{2} + \frac{f^{(3)}[0] \ x^3}{6} + O[x]^4$$

In mathematical terms, **Series** can be viewed as a way of constructing Taylor series for functions.

The standard formula for the Taylor series expansion about the point $x = x_0$ of a function $g(x)$ with $k^{\text{th}}$ derivative $g^{(k)}(x)$ is $g(x) = \sum_{k=0} g^{(k)}(x_0)\frac{(x-x_0)^k}{k!}$. Whenever this formula applies, it gives the same results as **Series**. (For common functions, **Series** nevertheless internally uses somewhat more efficient algorithms.)

**Series** can also generate some power series that involve fractional and negative powers, not directly covered by the standard Taylor series formula.

Here is a power series that contains negative powers of $x$.

$In[4]:=$ `Series[ Exp[x]/x^2, {x, 0, 4} ]`

$$Out[4]= x^{-2} + \frac{1}{x} + \frac{1}{2} + \frac{x}{6} + \frac{x^2}{24} + \frac{x^3}{120} + \frac{x^4}{720} + O[x]^5$$

Here is a power series involving fractional powers of $x$.

$In[5]:=$ `Series[ Exp[Sqrt[x]], {x, 0, 2} ]`

$$Out[5]= 1 + Sqrt[x] + \frac{x}{2} + \frac{x^{\frac{3}{2}}}{6} + \frac{x^2}{24} + O[x]^{\frac{5}{2}}$$

`Series` can also handle series that involve logarithmic terms.

$In[6]:=$ `Series[ Exp[2x] Log[x], {x, 0, 2} ]`

$$Out[6]= Log[x] + 2\ Log[x]\ x + 2\ Log[x]\ x^2 + O[x]^3$$

There are, of course, mathematical functions for which no standard power series exist. *Mathematica* recognizes many such cases.

`Series` sees that $\exp(\frac{1}{x})$ has an essential singularity at $x = 0$, and does not produce a power series.

$In[7]:=$ `Series[ Exp[1/x], {x, 0, 2} ]`

`Exp::esss: Essential singularity encountered in`
$$Exp[\frac{1}{x} + O[x]].$$

$$Out[7]= Series[E^{\frac{1}{x}}, \{x, 0, 2\}]$$

`Series` can nevertheless give you the power series for $\exp(\frac{1}{x})$ about the point $x = \infty$.

$In[8]:=$ `Series[ Exp[1/x], {x, Infinity, 3} ]`

$$Out[8]= 1 + \frac{1}{x} + \frac{1}{2\ x^2} + \frac{1}{6\ x^3} + O[\frac{1}{x}]^4$$

Especially when negative powers occur, there is some subtlety in exactly how many terms of a particular power series the function `Series` will generate.

One way to understand what happens is to think of the analogy between power series taken to a certain order, and real numbers taken to a certain precision. Power series are "approximate formulae" in much the same sense as finite-precision real numbers are approximate numbers.

The procedure that `Series` follows in constructing a power series is largely analogous to the procedure that `N` follows in constructing a real number approximation. Both functions effectively start by replacing the smallest pieces of your expression by finite order, or finite precision, approximations, and then evaluating the resulting expression. If there are, for example, cancellations, this procedure may give a final result whose order or precision is less than the order or precision that you originally asked for.   Unlike N, however, Series has some ability to retry its computations so as to get results to the order you ask for. In cases where it does not succeed, you can usually still get results to a particular order by asking for a higher order than you need.

Series compensates for cancellations in this computation, and succeeds in giving you a result to order $x^3$.

$In[9]:=$ **Series[ Sin[x]/x^2, {x, 0, 3} ]**

$$Out[9]= \frac{1}{x} - \frac{x}{6} + \frac{x^3}{120} + O[x]^4$$

When you make a power series expansion in a variable $x$, *Mathematica* assumes that all objects that do not explicitly contain $x$ are in fact independent of $x$. Series thus does partial derivatives (effectively using D) to build up Taylor series.

Both a and n are assumed to be independent of x.

$In[10]:=$ **Series[ (a + x)^n , {x, 0, 2} ]**

$$Out[10]= a^n + a^{-1 + n} n x + \frac{a^{-2 + n} n (-1 + n) x^2}{2} + O[x]^3$$

a[x] is now given as an explicit function of x.

$In[11]:=$ **Series[ (a[x] + x)^n, {x, 0, 2} ]**

$$Out[11]= a[0]^n + n (1 + a'[0]) a[0]^{-1 + n} x +$$
$$(\frac{n (-1 + n) (1 + a'[0])^2 a[0]^{-2 + n}}{2} +$$
$$\frac{n a[0]^{-1 + n} a''[0]}{2}) x^2 + O[x]^3$$

You can use Series to generate power series in a sequence of different variables. Series works like Integrate, Sum and so on, and expands first with respect to the last variable you specify.

Series performs a series expansion successively with respect to each variable. The result in this case is a series in x, whose coefficients are series in y.

$In[12]:=$ **Series[Exp[x y], {x, 0, 3}, {y, 0, 3}]**

$$Out[12]= 1 + (y + O[y]^4) x + (\frac{y^2}{2} + O[y]^5) x^2 +$$
$$(\frac{y^3}{6} + O[y]^6) x^3 + O[x]^4$$

## ■ 3.6.2  Advanced Topic: The Representation of Power Series

Power series are represented in *Mathematica* as `SeriesData` objects.

<table>
<tr>
<td>The power series is printed out as a sum of terms, ending with O[x] raised to a power.</td>
<td>

`In[1]:= Series[Cos[x], {x, 0, 4}]`

$$Out[1]= 1 - \frac{x^2}{2} + \frac{x^4}{24} + O[x]^5$$

</td>
</tr>
<tr>
<td>Internally, however, the series is stored as a SeriesData object.</td>
<td>

`In[2]:= InputForm[%]`

`Out[2]//InputForm=`
`    SeriesData[x, 0, {1, 0, -1/2, 0, 1/24}, 0, 5, 1]`

</td>
</tr>
</table>

By using `SeriesData` objects, rather than ordinary expressions, to represent power series, *Mathematica* can keep track of the order and expansion point, and do operations on the power series appropriately. You should not normally need to know the internal structure of `SeriesData` objects.

You can recognize a power series that is printed out in standard output form by the presence of an `O[x]` term. This term mimics the standard mathematical notation $O(x)$, and represents omitted terms of order $x$. For various reasons of consistency, *Mathematica* uses the notation `O[x]^n` for omitted terms of order $x^n$, corresponding to the mathematical notation $O(x)^n$, rather than the slightly more familiar, though equivalent, form $O(x^n)$.

Any time that an object like `O[x]` appears in a sum of terms, *Mathematica* will in fact convert the whole sum into a power series.

<table>
<tr>
<td>The presence of O[x] makes *Mathematica* convert the whole sum to a power series.</td>
<td>

`In[3]:= a x + Exp[x] + O[x]^3`

$$Out[3]= 1 + (1 + a)\ x + \frac{x^2}{2} + O[x]^3$$

</td>
</tr>
</table>

## ■ 3.6.3  Operations on Power Series

*Mathematica* allows you to perform many operations on power series. In all cases, *Mathematica* gives results only to as many terms as can be justified from the accuracy of your input.

<table>
<tr>
<td>Here is a power series with four terms.</td>
<td>

`In[1]:= Series[ Exp[x], {x, 0, 4} ]`

$$Out[1]= 1 + x + \frac{x^2}{2} + \frac{x^3}{6} + \frac{x^4}{24} + O[x]^5$$

</td>
</tr>
</table>

When you square the power series, you get another power series, also with four terms.

$In[2]:=$ `%^2`

$$Out[2]= 1 + 2 x + 2 x^2 + \frac{4 x^3}{3} + \frac{2 x^4}{3} + O[x]^5$$

Taking the logarithm gives you the result $2x$, but only to order $x^4$.

$In[3]:=$ `Log[%]`

$$Out[3]= 2 x + O[x]^5$$

*Mathematica* keeps track of the orders of power series in much the same way as it keeps track of the precision of approximate real numbers. Just as with numerical calculations, there are operations on power series which can increase, or decrease, the precision (or order) of your results.

Here is a power series accurate to order $x^4$.

$In[4]:=$ `Series[ Exp[x], {x, 0, 4} ]`

$$Out[4]= 1 + x + \frac{x^2}{2} + \frac{x^3}{6} + \frac{x^4}{24} + O[x]^5$$

This gives a power series that is accurate only to order $x^2$.

$In[5]:=$ `1 / (1 - %)`

$$Out[5]= -\left(\frac{1}{x}\right) + \frac{1}{2} - \frac{x}{12} + O[x]^3$$

*Mathematica* also allows you to do calculus with power series.

Here is a power series for $\cos(x)$.

$In[6]:=$ `Series[Cos[x], {x, 0, 6}]`

$$Out[6]= 1 - \frac{x^2}{2} + \frac{x^4}{24} - \frac{x^6}{720} + O[x]^7$$

Here is its derivative with respect to x.

$In[7]:=$ `D[%, x]`

$$Out[7]= -x + \frac{x^3}{6} - \frac{x^5}{120} + O[x]^6$$

Integrating with respect to x gives back a power series with the same dependence on x as the original one, but with a different constant of integration.

$In[8]:=$ `Integrate[%, x]`

$$Out[8]= \frac{-x^2}{2} + \frac{x^4}{24} - \frac{x^6}{720} + O[x]^7$$

When you perform an operation that involves both a normal expression and a power series, *Mathematica* "absorbs" the normal expression into the power series whenever possible.

The 1 is automatically absorbed into the power series.

```
In[9]:= 1 + Series[Exp[x], {x, 0, 4}]
```

$$Out[9]= 2 + x + \frac{x^2}{2} + \frac{x^3}{6} + \frac{x^4}{24} + O[x]^5$$

The x^2 is also absorbed into the power series.

```
In[10]:= % + x^2
```

$$Out[10]= 2 + x + \frac{3\,x^2}{2} + \frac{x^3}{6} + \frac{x^4}{24} + O[x]^5$$

If you add `Sin[x]`, *Mathematica* generates the appropriate power series for `Sin[x]`, and combines it with the power series you have.

```
In[11]:= % + Sin[x]
```

$$Out[11]= 2 + 2\,x + \frac{3\,x^2}{2} + \frac{x^4}{24} + O[x]^5$$

*Mathematica* also absorbs expressions that multiply power series. The symbol `a` is assumed to be independent of `x`.

```
In[12]:= (a + x) %^2
```

$$Out[12]= 4\,a + (4 + 8\,a)\,x + (8 + 10\,a)\,x^2 +$$
$$(10 + 6\,a)\,x^3 + (6 + \frac{29\,a}{12})\,x^4 + O[x]^5$$

*Mathematica* knows how to apply a wide variety of functions to power series. However, if you apply an arbitrary function to a power series, it is impossible for *Mathematica* to give you anything but a symbolic result.

*Mathematica* does not apply the function `f` to a power series, so it just leaves the symbolic result.

```
In[13]:= f[ Series[ Exp[x], {x, 0, 3} ] ]
```

$$Out[13]= f[1 + x + \frac{x^2}{2} + \frac{x^3}{6} + O[x]^4]$$

## ■ 3.6.4 Advanced Topic: Composition and Inversion of Power Series

When you manipulate power series, it is sometimes convenient to think of the series as representing *functions*, which you can, for example, compose or invert.

| | |
|---|---|
| *series₁* `/.` x->*series₂* | compose two power series |
| `InverseSeries[`*series*`]` | invert a power series |

Composition and inversion of power series.

Here is the power series for $\sin(x)$ to $O(x^5)$.

*In[1]:=* **Series[Sin[x], {x, 0, 5}]**

$$Out[1]= x - \frac{x^3}{6} + \frac{x^5}{120} + O[x]^6$$

The variable in the original power series is now replaced by the power series for $\sin(x)$.

*In[2]:=* **% /. x -> Series[Sin[x], {x, 0, 5}]**

$$Out[2]= x - \frac{x^3}{3} + \frac{x^5}{10} + O[x]^6$$

The result is the power series for $\sin(\sin(x))$.

*In[3]:=* **Series[Sin[Sin[x]], {x, 0, 5}]**

$$Out[3]= x - \frac{x^3}{3} + \frac{x^5}{10} + O[x]^6$$

If you think of a power series in $x$ as approximating a function $f(x)$, then substituting for $x$ a power series for another function $g(y)$ gives a power series for the composed function $f(g(y))$. This power series can only be constructed if the first term in the power series for the inner function $g(y)$ involves a positive power of $y$.

If you have a power series for a function $f(x)$ where the first term is proportional to $x$, then it is possible to find the power series for the inverse function $f^{-1}(x)$ such that $f(f^{-1}(x)) = x$. The operation of finding the power series for an inverse function is sometimes known as *reversion* of power series.

Here is the series for $\sin(x)$.

*In[4]:=* **Series[Sin[x], {x, 0, 5}]**

$$Out[4]= x - \frac{x^3}{6} + \frac{x^5}{120} + O[x]^6$$

Inverting the series gives the series for $\sin^{-1}(x)$.

*In[5]:=* **InverseSeries[%]**

$$Out[5]= x + \frac{x^3}{6} + \frac{3 x^5}{40} + O[x]^6$$

Composing the two series gives the identity function.

*In[6]:=* **% /. x -> %%**

$$Out[6]= x + O[x]^6$$

## ■ 3.6.5 Converting Power Series to Normal Expressions

| | |
|---|---|
| Normal[*expr*] | convert a power series to a normal expression. |

Converting power series to normal expressions.

As discussed above, power series in *Mathematica* are represented in a special internal form, which keeps track of such attributes as their expansion order.

For some purposes, you may want to convert power series to normal expressions. From a mathematical point of view, this corresponds to truncating the power series, and assuming that all higher order terms are zero.

This generates a power series, with four terms.

$$In[1]:= \texttt{t = Series[ Exp[x], \{x, 0, 4\} ]}$$

$$Out[1]= 1 + x + \frac{x^2}{2} + \frac{x^3}{6} + \frac{x^4}{24} + O[x]^5$$

Squaring the power series gives you another power series, with the appropriate number of terms.

$$In[2]:= \texttt{t\^{}2}$$

$$Out[2]= 1 + 2 x + 2 x^2 + \frac{4 x^3}{3} + \frac{2 x^4}{3} + O[x]^5$$

Normal truncates the power series, giving a normal expression.

$$In[3]:= \texttt{Normal[\%]}$$

$$Out[3]= 1 + 2 x + 2 x^2 + \frac{4 x^3}{3} + \frac{2 x^4}{3}$$

You can now apply standard algebraic operations.

$$In[4]:= \texttt{Factor[\%]}$$

$$Out[4]= \frac{3 + 6 x + 6 x^2 + 4 x^3 + 2 x^4}{3}$$

## ■ 3.6.6  Solving Equations Involving Power Series

> LogicalExpand[*series₁* == *series₂*]
>
> > give the equations obtained by equating corresponding coefficients in the power series
>
> Solve[*series₁* == *series₂*, {*a₁*, *a₂*, ...}]
>
> > solve for coefficients in power series

Solving equations involving power series.

Here is a power series.

$In[1]:= $ y = 1 + Sum[a[i] x^i, {i, 3}] + O[x]^4

$Out[1]= $ 1 + a[1] x + a[2] x$^2$ + a[3] x$^3$ + O[x]$^4$

This gives an equation involving the power series.

$In[2]:= $ D[y, x]^2 - y == x

$Out[2]= $ (-1 + a[1]$^2$) + (-a[1] + 4 a[1] a[2]) x +

(-a[2] + 4 a[2]$^2$ + 6 a[1] a[3]) x$^2$ + O[x]$^3$ == x

LogicalExpand generates a sequence of equations for each power of x.

$In[3]:= $ LogicalExpand[ % ]

$Out[3]= $ -1 + a[1]$^2$ == 0 &&

-1 - a[1] + 4 a[1] a[2] == 0 &&

-a[2] + 4 a[2]$^2$ + 6 a[1] a[3] == 0

This solves the equations for the coefficients a[i]. You can also feed equations involving power series directly to Solve.

$In[4]:= $ Solve[ % ]

$Out[4]= $ {{a[3] -> -($\frac{1}{12}$), a[2] -> $\frac{1}{2}$, a[1] -> 1},

{a[3] -> 0, a[2] -> 0, a[1] -> -1}}

Some equations involving power series can also be solved using the InverseSeries function discussed on page 433.

## ■ 3.6.7  Finding Limits

In doing many kinds of calculations, you need to evaluate expressions when variables take on particular values. In many cases, you can do this simply by applying transformation rules for the variables using the /. operator.

You can get the value of $\cos(x^2)$ just by explicitly replacing $x$ with 0, and then evaluating the result.

```
In[1]:= Cos[x^2] /. x -> 0
Out[1]= 1
```

In some cases, however, you have to be more careful.

Consider, for example, finding the value of the expression $\frac{\sin(x)}{x}$ when $x = 0$. If you simply replace $x$ by 0 in this expression, you get the indeterminate result $\frac{0}{0}$. To find the correct value of $\frac{\sin(x)}{x}$ when $x = 0$, you need to take the *limit*, in this case using L'Hospital's rule.

| | |
|---|---|
| `Limit[expr, x -> `$x_0$`]` | find the limit of *expr* when *x* approaches $x_0$ |

Finding limits.

This gives the correct value for the limit of $\frac{\sin(x)}{x}$ as $x \to 0$.

```
In[2]:= Limit[ Sin[x]/x, x -> 0 ]
Out[2]= 1
```

No finite limit exists in this case.

```
In[3]:= Limit[ Sin[x]/x^2, x -> 0 ]
Out[3]= ComplexInfinity
```

Limit can find this limit, even though you cannot get an ordinary power series for $x \log(x)$ at $x = 0$.

```
In[4]:= Limit[ x Log[x], x -> 0 ]
Out[4]= 0
```

$\exp(\frac{1}{x})$ has an essential singularity at $x = 0$, so no limit exists.

```
In[5]:= Limit[ Exp[1/x], x -> 0 ]
Limit::nlm: Could not find definite limit.
                        1
                        -
                        x
Out[5]= Limit[E , x -> 0]
```

If you give Limit a function it does not know, it assumes that the function is continuous at the limit point.

```
In[6]:= Limit[ f[x], x -> 0 ]
Out[6]= f[0]
```

# ■ 3.7 Linear Algebra

## ■ 3.7.1 Constructing Matrices

| | |
|---|---|
| Table[f, {i, m}, {j, n}] | build an $m \times n$ matrix where $f$ is a function of $i$ and $j$ that gives the value of $i, j^{\text{th}}$ entry |
| Array[f, {m, n}] | build an $m \times n$ matrix whose $i, j^{\text{th}}$ entry is f[i, j] |
| DiagonalMatrix[*list*] | generate a diagonal matrix with the elements of *list* on the diagonal |
| IdentityMatrix[*n*] | generate an $n \times n$ identity matrix |

Functions for constructing matrices.

This generates a $2 \times 2$ matrix whose $i, j^{\text{th}}$ entry is a[i, j].

```
In[1]:= Table[a[i, j], {i, 2}, {j, 2}]
Out[1]= {{a[1, 1], a[1, 2]}, {a[2, 1], a[2, 2]}}
```

Here is another way to produce the same matrix.

```
In[2]:= Array[a, {2, 2}]
Out[2]= {{a[1, 1], a[1, 2]}, {a[2, 1], a[2, 2]}}
```

DiagonalMatrix makes a matrix with zeroes everywhere except on the leading diagonal.

```
In[3]:= DiagonalMatrix[{a, b, c}]
Out[3]= {{a, 0, 0}, {0, b, 0}, {0, 0, c}}
```

IdentityMatrix[*n*] produces an $n \times n$ identity matrix.

```
In[4]:= IdentityMatrix[3]
Out[4]= {{1, 0, 0}, {0, 1, 0}, {0, 0, 1}}
```

Of the functions for constructing matrices mentioned above, Table is the most general. You can use Table to produce many kinds of matrices.

Table[0, {*m*}, {*n*}]     a zero matrix

Table[Random[ ], {*m*}, {*n*}]     a matrix with random numerical entries

Table[If[*i* >= *j*, 1, 0], {*i*, *m*}, {*j*, *n*}]
                            a lower triangular matrix

Table[If[*i* <= *j*, 1, 0], {*i*, *m*}, {*j*, *n*}]
                            an upper triangular matrix

Table[Switch[*i*-*j*,-1,*a*[[*i*]],0,*b*[[*i*]],1,*c*[[*i*-1]],_,0], {*i*, *m*}, {*j*, *n*}]
                            a tridiagonal matrix

Some special types of matrices.

Table evaluates Random[ ] separately for each element, to give a different pseudorandom number in each case.

```
In[5]:= Table[Random[ ], {2}, {2}]
Out[5]= {{0.353297, 0.0205034}, {0.117374, 0.546051}}
```

This gives a tridiagonal matrix.

```
In[6]:= Table[Switch[i-j, -1, a, 0, b, 1, c, _, 0],
            {i, 5}, {j, 5}]
Out[6]= {{b, a, 0, 0, 0}, {c, b, a, 0, 0},
        {0, c, b, a, 0}, {0, 0, c, b, a}, {0, 0, 0, c, b}}
```

MatrixForm prints the matrix in a two-dimensional array, and makes the structure in this case clearer.

```
In[7]:= MatrixForm[%]
                    b  a  0  0  0
                    c  b  a  0  0
                    0  c  b  a  0
                    0  0  c  b  a
Out[7]//MatrixForm= 0  0  0  c  b
```

# ■ 3.7.2 Getting Pieces of Matrices

$$m[[i, j]] \quad \text{the } i, j^{\text{th}} \text{ entry}$$

$$m[[i]] \quad \text{the } i^{\text{th}} \text{ row}$$

$\texttt{Transpose}[m] \ [[i]] \ \text{or} \ \texttt{Map}[\#[[i]]\&, \ m]$
$$\text{the } i^{\text{th}} \text{ column}$$

$m[[\{i_1, \ ..., \ i_r\}, \ \{j_1, \ ..., \ j_s\}]]$  the $r \times s$ submatrix of $m$ with elements having row indices $i_k$ and column indices $j_k$

$m[[ \ \texttt{Range}[i_0, \ i_1], \ \texttt{Range}[j_0, \ j_1] \ ]]$

a submatrix with elements having row and column indices respectively in the ranges $i_0$ through $i_1$ and $j_0$ through $j_1$

Ways to get pieces of matrices.

Matrices in *Mathematica* are represented as lists of lists. You can use all the standard *Mathematica* list manipulation operations on matrices.

Here is a sample $3 \times 3$ matrix.

```
In[1]:= t = Array[a, {3,3}]
Out[1]= {{a[1, 1], a[1, 2], a[1, 3]},
         {a[2, 1], a[2, 2], a[2, 3]},
         {a[3, 1], a[3, 2], a[3, 3]}}
```

This picks out the second row of the matrix.

```
In[2]:= t[[2]]
Out[2]= {a[2, 1], a[2, 2], a[2, 3]}
```

Here is the second column of the matrix.

```
In[3]:= Map[#[[2]]&, t]
Out[3]= {a[1, 2], a[2, 2], a[3, 2]}
```

This picks out a submatrix.

```
In[4]:= t[[ {1, 2}, {2, 3} ]]
Out[4]= {{a[1, 2], a[1, 3]}, {a[2, 2], a[2, 3]}}
```

Here is another way to specify the submatrix, convenient when you deal with bigger matrices.

```
In[5]:= t[[ Range[1,2], Range[2,3] ]]
Out[5]= {{a[1, 2], a[1, 3]}, {a[2, 2], a[2, 3]}}
```

# ■ 3.7.3 Scalars, Vectors and Matrices

*Mathematica* represents matrices and vectors using lists. Anything that is not a list

*Mathematica* considers as a scalar.

A vector in *Mathematica* consists of a list of scalars. A matrix consists of a list of vectors, representing each of its rows. In order to be a valid matrix, all the rows must be the same length, so that the elements of the matrix effectively form a rectangular array.

| | |
|---|---|
| `VectorQ[`*expr*`]` | give `True` if *expr* has the form of a vector, and `False` otherwise |
| `MatrixQ[`*expr*`]` | give `True` if *expr* has the form of a matrix, and `False` otherwise |
| `Dimensions[`*expr*`]` | a list of the dimensions of a vector or matrix |

Functions for testing the structure of vectors and matrices.

The list `{a, b, c}` has the form of a vector.

```
In[1]:= VectorQ[ {a, b, c} ]
Out[1]= True
```

Anything that is not manifestly a list is treated as a scalar, so applying `VectorQ` gives `False`.

```
In[2]:= VectorQ[ x + y ]
Out[2]= False
```

This is a $3 \times 2$ matrix.

```
In[3]:= Dimensions[ {{a, b, c}, {ap, bp, cp}} ]
Out[3]= {2, 3}
```

For a vector, `Dimensions` gives a list with a single element equal to the result from `Length`.

```
In[4]:= Dimensions[ {a, b, c} ]
Out[4]= {3}
```

This object does not count as a matrix because its rows are of different lengths.

```
In[5]:= MatrixQ[ {{a, b, c}, {ap, bp}} ]
Out[5]= False
```

## ■ 3.7.4 Operations on Scalars, Vectors and Matrices

Most mathematical functions in *Mathematica* are set up to apply themselves separately to each element in a list. This is true in particular of all functions that carry the attribute `Listable`.

A consequence is that most mathematical functions are applied element-by-element to matrices and vectors.

The Log applies itself separately to each element in the vector.

```
In[1]:= Log[ {a, b, c} ]
Out[1]= {Log[a], Log[b], Log[c]}
```

The same is true for a matrix, or, for that matter, for any nested list.

```
In[2]:= Log[ {{a, b}, {c, d}} ]
Out[2]= {{Log[a], Log[b]}, {Log[c], Log[d]}}
```

The differentiation function D also applies separately to each element in a list.

```
In[3]:= D[ {x, x^2, x^3}, x ]
                        2
Out[3]= {1, 2 x, 3 x }
```

The sum of two vectors is carried out element-by-element.

```
In[4]:= {a, b} + {ap, bp}
Out[4]= {a + ap, b + bp}
```

If you try to add two vectors with different lengths, you get an error.

```
In[5]:= {a, b, c} + {ap, bp}
Thread::badlen:
        Objects of unequal length in {a, b, c} + {ap, bp}
           cannot be combined.
Out[5]= {ap, bp} + {a, b, c}
```

This adds the scalar 1 to each element of the vector.

```
In[6]:= 1 + {a, b}
Out[6]= {1 + a, 1 + b}
```

Any object that is not manifestly a list is treated as a scalar. Here c is treated as a scalar, and added separately to each element in the vector.

```
In[7]:= {a, b} + c
Out[7]= {a + c, b + c}
```

This multiplies each element in the vector by the scalar k.

```
In[8]:= k {a, b}
Out[8]= {a k, b k}
```

It is important to realize that *Mathematica* treats an object as a vector in a particular operation only if the object is explicitly a list at the time when the operation is done. If the object is not explicitly a list, *Mathematica* always treats it as a scalar. This means that you can get different results, depending on whether you assign a particular object to be a list before or after you do a particular operation.

The object p is treated as a scalar, and added separately to each element in the vector.

```
In[9]:= {a, b} + p
Out[9]= {a + p, b + p}
```

This is what happens if you now replace p by the list {c, d}.

```
In[10]:= % /. p -> {c, d}
Out[10]= {{a + c, a + d}, {b + c, b + d}}
```

| | |
|---|---|
| You would have got a different result if you had replaced p by {c, d} before you did the first operation. | *In[11]:=* {a, b} + {c, d}<br>*Out[11]=* {a + c, b + d} |

## ■ 3.7.5 Multiplying Vectors and Matrices

| | |
|---|---|
| $c\ v,\ c\ m$, etc. | multiply each element by a scalar |
| $v.v,\ v.m,\ m.v,\ m.m$, etc. | vector and matrix multiplication |
| Outer[Times, $t_1$, $t_2$, ...] | outer product |

Different kinds of vector and matrix multiplication.

| | |
|---|---|
| This multiplies each element of the vector by the scalar k. | *In[1]:=* k {a, b, c}<br>*Out[1]=* {a k, b k, c k} |
| The "dot" operator gives the scalar product of two vectors. | *In[2]:=* {a, b, c} . {ap, bp, cp}<br>*Out[2]=* a ap + b bp + c cp |
| You can also use dot to multiply a matrix by a vector. | *In[3]:=* {{a, b}, {c, d}} . {x, y}<br>*Out[3]=* {a x + b y, c x + d y} |
| Dot is also the notation for matrix multiplication in *Mathematica*. | *In[4]:=* {{a, b}, {c, d}} . {{1, 2}, {3, 4}}<br>*Out[4]=* {{a + 3 b, 2 a + 4 b}, {c + 3 d, 2 c + 4 d}} |

It is important to realize that you can use "dot" for both left- and right-multiplication of vectors by matrices. *Mathematica* makes no distinction between "row" and "column" vectors. Dot carries out whatever operation is possible. (In formal terms, $a.b$ contracts the last index of the tensor $a$ with the first index of $b$.)

| | |
|---|---|
| Here are definitions for a matrix m and a vector v. | *In[5]:=* m = {{a, b}, {c, d}} ;  v = {x, y}<br>*Out[5]=* {x, y} |
| This left multiplies the vector v by m. The object v is effectively treated as a column vector in this case. | *In[6]:=* m . v<br>*Out[6]=* {a x + b y, c x + d y} |
| You can also use dot to right multiply v by m. Now v is effectively treated as a row vector. | *In[7]:=* v . m<br>*Out[7]=* {a x + c y, b x + d y} |

You can multiply m by v on both sides, to
get a scalar.

*In[8]:=* **v . m . v**

*Out[8]=* x (a x + c y) + y (b x + d y)

For some purposes, you may need to represent vectors and matrices symbolically, without explicitly giving their elements. You can use dot to represent multiplication of such symbolic objects.

Dot effectively acts here as a
non-commutative form of multiplication.

*In[9]:=* **a . b . a**

*Out[9]=* a . b . a

It is, nevertheless, associative.

*In[10]:=* **(a . b) . (a . b)**

*Out[10]=* a . b . a . b

Dot products of sums are not automatically
expanded out.

*In[11]:=* **(a + b) . c . (d + e)**

*Out[11]=* (a + b) . c . (d + e)

You can apply the distributive law in this
case using the function **Distribute**, as
discussed in Section 2.4.5.

*In[12]:=* **Distribute[ % ]**

*Out[12]=* a . c . d + a . c . e + b . c . d + b . c . e

The "dot" operator gives "inner products" of vectors, matrices, and so on. In more advanced calculations, you may also need to construct outer or Kronecker products of vectors and matrices. You can use the general function **Outer** to do this.

The outer product of two vectors is a
matrix.

*In[13]:=* **Outer[Times, {a, b}, {c, d}]**

*Out[13]=* {{a c, a d}, {b c, b d}}

The outer product of a matrix and a vector
is a rank three tensor.

*In[14]:=* **Outer[Times, {{1, 2}, {3, 4}}, {x, y, z}]**

*Out[14]=* {{{x, y, z}, {2 x, 2 y, 2 z}},

{{3 x, 3 y, 3 z}, {4 x, 4 y, 4 z}}}

Outer products will be discussed in more detail in Section 3.7.12 below.

## ■ 3.7.6  Matrix Inversion

| | |
|---|---|
| **Inverse[*m*]** | find the inverse of a square matrix |

Matrix inversion.

Here is a simple $2 \times 2$ matrix.

```
In[1]:= m = {{a, b}, {c, d}}
Out[1]= {{a, b}, {c, d}}
```

This gives the inverse of m. In producing this formula, *Mathematica* implicitly assumes that the determinant a d – b c is nonzero.

```
In[2]:= Inverse[ m ]
```

$$Out[2]= \{\{\frac{d}{-(b\ c) + a\ d}, -(\frac{b}{-(b\ c) + a\ d})\},$$
$$\{-(\frac{c}{-(b\ c) + a\ d}), \frac{a}{-(b\ c) + a\ d}\}\}$$

Multiplying the inverse by the original matrix should give the identity matrix.

```
In[3]:= % . m
```

$$Out[3]= \{\{-(\frac{b\ c}{-(b\ c) + a\ d}) + \frac{a\ d}{-(b\ c) + a\ d}, 0\},$$
$$\{0, -(\frac{b\ c}{-(b\ c) + a\ d}) + \frac{a\ d}{-(b\ c) + a\ d}\}\}$$

You have to use **Together** to clear the denominators, and get back a standard identity matrix.

```
In[4]:= Together[ % ]
Out[4]= {{1, 0}, {0, 1}}
```

Here is a matrix of rational numbers.

```
In[5]:= hb = Table[1/(i + j), {i, 4}, {j, 4}]
```

$$Out[5]= \{\{\frac{1}{2}, \frac{1}{3}, \frac{1}{4}, \frac{1}{5}\}, \{\frac{1}{3}, \frac{1}{4}, \frac{1}{5}, \frac{1}{6}\}, \{\frac{1}{4}, \frac{1}{5}, \frac{1}{6}, \frac{1}{7}\},$$
$$\{\frac{1}{5}, \frac{1}{6}, \frac{1}{7}, \frac{1}{8}\}\}$$

*Mathematica* finds the exact inverse of the matrix.

```
In[6]:= Inverse[hb]
Out[6]= {{200, -1200, 2100, -1120},
        {-1200, 8100, -15120, 8400},
        {2100, -15120, 29400, -16800},
        {-1120, 8400, -16800, 9800}}
```

Multiplying by the original matrix gives the identity matrix.

```
In[7]:= % . hb
Out[7]= {{1, 0, 0, 0}, {0, 1, 0, 0}, {0, 0, 1, 0},
        {0, 0, 0, 1}}
```

If you try to invert a singular matrix, *Mathematica* prints a warning message, and returns the inverse undone.

```
In[8]:= Inverse[ {{1, 2}, {1, 2}} ]
Inverse::sing: Matrix {{1, 2}, {1, 2}} is singular.
Out[8]= Inverse[{{1, 2}, {1, 2}}]
```

If you give a matrix with exact symbolic or numerical entries, *Mathematica* gives the exact inverse. If, on the other hand, some of the entries in your matrix are approximate real numbers, then *Mathematica* finds an approximate numerical result.

| | |
|---|---|
| Here is a matrix containing approximate real numbers. | `In[9]:= m = {{1.2, 5.7}, {4.2, 5.6}}`<br>`Out[9]= {{1.2, 5.7}, {4.2, 5.6}}` |
| This finds the numerical inverse. | `In[10]:= Inverse[ % ]`<br>`Out[10]= {{-0.325203, 0.33101}, {0.243902, -0.0696864}}` |

Multiplying by the original matrix gives you an identity matrix with small numerical errors.

`In[11]:= % . m`

$$Out[11]= \{\{1., 2.22045\ 10^{-16}\}, \{-1.11022\ 10^{-16}, 1.\}\}$$

You can get rid of the small off-diagonal terms using Chop.

`In[12]:= Chop[ % ]`
`Out[12]= {{1., 0}, {0, 1.}}`

When you try to invert a matrix with exact entries, *Mathematica* can always tell whether or not the matrix is singular. When you invert a numerical matrix, *Mathematica* can never tell for certain whether or not the matrix is singular: all it can tell is for example that the determinant is small compared to the entries of the matrix. When *Mathematica* suspects that you are trying to invert a singular numerical matrix, it prints a warning.

*Mathematica* prints a warning if you invert a numerical matrix that it suspects is singular.

```
In[13]:= Inverse[ {{1., 2.}, {1., 2.}} ]
Inverse::cond:
       Result for inverse of badly conditioned matrix
       {{1., 2.}, {1., 2.}} may be meaningless.
```

$$Out[13]= \{\{1.42972\ 10^{33}, -1.42972\ 10^{33}\},$$
$$\{-7.14862\ 10^{32}, 7.14862\ 10^{32}\}\}$$

If you work with high precision approximate numbers, *Mathematica* will keep track of the precision of matrix inverses that you generate.

This generates a $6 \times 6$ numerical matrix with entries of 50-digit precision.

`In[14]:= m = N [ Table[ Exp[i j], {i, 6}, {j, 6} ], 50 ] ;`

This takes the matrix, multiplies it by its inverse, and shows the first row of the result. The off-diagonal terms are zero to a precision of nearly 50 digits.

```
In[15]:= (m . Inverse[m]) [[1]]
Out[15]= {1., 0., -1. 10^-53, 1. 10^-57, -2. 10^-58,
         -1. 10^-61}
```

This generates a 50-digit numerical approximation to a $6 \times 6$ Hilbert matrix. Hilbert matrices are notoriously hard to invert numerically.

```
In[16]:= m = N[Table[1/(i + j - 1), {i, 6}, {j, 6}], 50] ;
```

In this case, the off-diagonal terms are zero to an accuracy of less than 50 digits. The larger off-diagonal terms are a reflection of the "bad numerical conditioning" of this matrix.

```
In[17]:= (m . Inverse[m]) [[1]]
Out[17]= {1., 0., -3. 10^-39, 0., 0., -3. 10^-39}
```

Inverse works only on square matrices. Section 3.7.11 discusses the function PseudoInverse, which can also be used with non-square matrices.

## ■ 3.7.7  Basic Matrix Operations

| | |
|---|---|
| Transpose[$m$] | transpose |
| Inverse[$m$] | matrix inverse |
| Det[$m$] | determinant |
| Minors[$m$, $k$] | a list of the $k \times k$ minors of $m$ |
| Sum[$m$[[$i$, $i$]], {$i$, Length[$m$]}] | trace |

Some basic matrix operations.

Transposing a matrix interchanges the rows and columns in the matrix. If you transpose an $m \times n$ matrix, you get an $n \times m$ matrix as the result.

Transposing a $2 \times 3$ matrix gives a $3 \times 2$ result.

```
In[1]:= Transpose[ {{a, b, c}, {ap, bp, cp}} ]
Out[1]= {{a, ap}, {b, bp}, {c, cp}}
```

Det[$m$] gives the determinant of a square matrix $m$. Minors[$m$, $k$] gives a list of the determinants of all the $k \times k$ submatrices of $m$. You can apply Minors to rectangular, as well as square, matrices.

| | |
|---|---|
| Here is the determinant of a simple $2 \times 2$ matrix. | `In[2]:= Det[ {{a, b}, {c, d}} ]`<br>`Out[2]= -(b c) + a d` |

This generates a $3 \times 3$ matrix, whose $i, j^{\text{th}}$ entry is a[$i$, $j$].

```
In[3]:= m = Array[a, {3, 3}]
Out[3]= {{a[1, 1], a[1, 2], a[1, 3]},
         {a[2, 1], a[2, 2], a[2, 3]},
         {a[3, 1], a[3, 2], a[3, 3]}}
```

Here is the determinant of m.

```
In[4]:= Det[ m ]
Out[4]= -(a[1, 3] a[2, 2] a[3, 1]) +
         a[1, 2] a[2, 3] a[3, 1] + a[1, 3] a[2, 1] a[3, 2] -
         a[1, 1] a[2, 3] a[3, 2] - a[1, 2] a[2, 1] a[3, 3] +
         a[1, 1] a[2, 2] a[3, 3]
```

This gives the list of all $2 \times 2$ minors of m.

```
In[5]:= Minors[m, 2]
Out[5]= {{-(a[1, 2] a[2, 1]) + a[1, 1] a[2, 2],
          -(a[1, 3] a[2, 1]) + a[1, 1] a[2, 3],
          -(a[1, 3] a[2, 2]) + a[1, 2] a[2, 3]},
         {-(a[1, 2] a[3, 1]) + a[1, 1] a[3, 2],
          -(a[1, 3] a[3, 1]) + a[1, 1] a[3, 3],
          -(a[1, 3] a[3, 2]) + a[1, 2] a[3, 3]},
         {-(a[2, 2] a[3, 1]) + a[2, 1] a[3, 2],
          -(a[2, 3] a[3, 1]) + a[2, 1] a[3, 3],
          -(a[2, 3] a[3, 2]) + a[2, 2] a[3, 3]}}
```

You can use `Det` to find the characteristic polynomial for a matrix. Section 3.7.10 discusses ways to find eigenvalues and eigenvectors directly.

Here is a $3 \times 3$ matrix.

```
In[6]:= m = Table[ 1/(i + j), {i, 3}, {j, 3} ]
```
$$Out[6]= \{\{\frac{1}{2}, \frac{1}{3}, \frac{1}{4}\}, \{\frac{1}{3}, \frac{1}{4}, \frac{1}{5}\}, \{\frac{1}{4}, \frac{1}{5}, \frac{1}{6}\}\}$$

Following precisely the standard mathematical definition, this gives the characteristic polynomial for m.

```
In[7]:= Det[ m - x IdentityMatrix[3] ]
```
$$Out[7]= \frac{1}{43200} - \frac{131\ x}{3600} + \frac{11\ x^2}{12} - x^3$$

There are many other operations on matrices that can be built up from standard *Mathematica* functions. One example is the *trace* or *spur* of a matrix, given by the sum of the terms on the leading diagonal.

| | |
|---|---|
| Here is a simple $2 \times 2$ matrix. | *In[8]:=* `m = {{a, b}, {c, d}}` |
| | *Out[8]=* `{{a, b}, {c, d}}` |
| You can get the trace of the matrix by explicitly constructing a sum of the elements on its leading diagonal. | *In[9]:=* `Sum[ m[[i, i]], {i, 2} ]` |
| | *Out[9]=* `a + d` |

## ■ 3.7.8 Solving Linear Systems

Many calculations involve solving systems of linear equations. In many cases, you will find it convenient to write down the equations explicitly, and then solve them using `Solve`.

In some cases, however, you may prefer to convert the system of linear equations into a matrix equation, and then apply matrix manipulation operations to solve it. This approach is often useful when the system of equations arises as part of a general algorithm, and you do not know in advance how many variables will be involved.

A system of linear equations can be stated in matrix form as **m.x** = **b**, where **x** is the vector of variables.

| | |
|---|---|
| `LinearSolve[`*m, b*`]` | give the vector *x* which solves the matrix equation `m.x == ` *b* |
| `NullSpace[`*m*`]` | a list of basis vectors whose linear combinations satisfy the matrix equation `m.x == 0` |
| `RowReduce[`*m*`]` | a simplified form of *m* obtained by making linear combinations of rows |

Functions for solving linear systems.

| | |
|---|---|
| Here is a $2 \times 2$ matrix. | *In[1]:=* `m = {{1, 5}, {2, 1}}` |
| | *Out[1]=* `{{1, 5}, {2, 1}}` |
| This gives two linear equations. | *In[2]:=* `m . {x, y} == {a, b}` |
| | *Out[2]=* `{x + 5 y, 2 x + y} == {a, b}` |
| You can use `Solve` directly to solve these equations. | *In[3]:=* `Solve[ %, {x, y} ]` |
| | *Out[3]=* $\{\{x \rightarrow \frac{-a}{9} + \frac{5\ b}{9},\ y \rightarrow \frac{2\ a}{9} - \frac{b}{9}\}\}$ |

You can also get the vector of solutions by calling `LinearSolve`. The result is equivalent to the one you get from `Solve`.

```
In[4]:= LinearSolve[m, {a, b}]
```

$$Out[4]= \{-(\frac{a}{9} - \frac{5\,b}{9}),\ -(\frac{-2\,a}{9} + \frac{b}{9})\}$$

Another way to solve the equations is to invert the matrix m, and then multiply {a, b} by the inverse. This is not as efficient as using `LinearSolve`.

```
In[5]:= Inverse[m] . {a, b}
```

$$Out[5]= \{\frac{-a}{9} + \frac{5\,b}{9},\ \frac{2\,a}{9} - \frac{b}{9}\}$$

Particularly when you have large, sparse, matrices, `LinearSolve` is the most efficient method to use.

If you have a square matrix **m** with a nonzero determinant, then you can always find a unique solution to the matrix equation **m.x** = **b** for any **b**. If, however, the matrix **m** has determinant zero, then there can be no vector **x** which satisfies **m.x** = **b** for a particular **b**. This situation corresponds to the case in which the linear equations embodied in **m** are not independent.

When **m** has determinant zero, it is nevertheless always possible to find vectors **x** that satisfy **m.x** = **0**. The set of vectors **x** satisfying this equation form the *null space* or *kernel* of the matrix **m**.    Any of the vectors can be expressed as a linear combination of a particular set of basis vectors, which can be obtained using `NullSpace[`*m*`]`.

Here is a simple matrix, corresponding to two identical linear equations.

```
In[6]:= m = {{1, 2}, {1, 2}}
```
```
Out[6]= {{1, 2}, {1, 2}}
```

The matrix has determinant zero.

```
In[7]:= Det[ m ]
```
```
Out[7]= 0
```

`LinearSolve` cannot find a solution to the equation **m.x** = **b** in this case.

```
In[8]:= LinearSolve[m, {a, b}]
LinearSolve::nsl:
     Linear equation encountered which has no solution.
```
```
Out[8]= LinearSolve[{{1, 2}, {1, 2}}, {a, b}]
```

There is a single basis vector for the null space of m.

```
In[9]:= NullSpace[ m ]
```
```
Out[9]= {{-2, 1}}
```

Multiplying the basis vector for the null space by m gives the zero vector.

```
In[10]:= m . %[[1]]
```
```
Out[10]= {0, 0}
```

Here is a simple symbolic matrix with determinant zero.

```
In[11]:= m = {{a, b, c}, {2 a, 2 b, 2 c}, {3 a, 3 b, 3 c}}

Out[11]= {{a, b, c}, {2 a, 2 b, 2 c}, {3 a, 3 b, 3 c}}
```

The basis for the null space of m contains two vectors. Any linear combination of these vectors gives zero when multiplied by m.

```
In[12]:= NullSpace[ m ]
                    c                  b
Out[12]= {{-(-), 0, 1}, {-(-), 1, 0}}
                    a                  a
```

An important feature of **LinearSolve** and **NullSpace** is that they work with *rectangular*, as well as *square*, matrices.

When you represent a system of linear equations by a matrix equation of the form $\mathbf{m.x} = \mathbf{b}$, the number of columns in $\mathbf{m}$ gives the number of variables, and the number of rows give the number of equations. There are a number of cases.

| | |
|---|---|
| *Underdetermined* | number of independent equations less than the number of variables; many solutions may exist |
| *Overdetermined* | number of independent equations more than the number of variables; solutions may not exist |
| *Nonsingular* | number of independent equations equal to the number of variables, and determinant nonzero; a unique solution exists |
| *Consistent* | at least one solution exists |
| *Inconsistent* | no solutions exist |

Classes of linear systems represented by rectangular matrices.

This asks for the solution to the inconsistent set of equations $x = 1$ and $x = 0$.

```
In[13]:= LinearSolve[{{1}, {1}}, {1, 0}]

LinearSolve::nsl:
     Linear equation encountered which has no solution.

Out[13]= LinearSolve[{{1}, {1}}, {1, 0}]
```

This matrix represents two equations, for three variables.

```
In[14]:= m = {{1, 3, 4}, {2, 1, 3}}

Out[14]= {{1, 3, 4}, {2, 1, 3}}
```

**LinearSolve** gives one of the possible solutions to this underdetermined set of equations.

```
In[15]:= v = LinearSolve[m, {1, 1}]
                  2  1
Out[15]= {-, -, 0}
                  5  5
```

When a matrix represents an underdetermined system of equations, the matrix has a non-trivial null space. In this case, the null space is spanned by a single vector.

```
In[16]:= NullSpace[m]
Out[16]= {{-1, -1, 1}}
```

If you take the solution you get from `LinearSolve`, and add any linear combination of the basis vectors for the null space, you still get a solution.

```
In[17]:= m . (v + 4 %[[1]])
Out[17]= {1, 1}
```

You can find out the number of redundant equations corresponding to a particular matrix by evaluating `Length[NullSpace[m]]`. Subtracting this quantity from the number of columns in $m$ gives the *rank* of the matrix $m$.

## ■ 3.7.9 Advanced Topic: Generalized Linear Algebra

The matrix operations discussed in the previous section work by trying to find combinations of matrix elements which give zero. By default, a simple test of the form $e==0$ is effectively applied to each combination that is generated to see if it is in fact zero.

Sometimes you may want to apply more complicated tests to determine whether combinations of matrix elements should be considered to be zero. The option `ZeroTest` allows you to specify a function which is applied to each combination that is generated to determine whether the combination should be considered to be zero.

| | |
|---|---|
| `LinearSolve[`$m$`, `$b$`, ZeroTest -> `$f$`]`, etc. | apply $f$ to determine whether combinations of matrix elements are zero |

Generalized linear algebra.

Here is a 2 × 2 matrix.

```
In[1]:= m = {{1, 1, 0}, {0, 1, 1}, {1, 0, 1}}
Out[1]= {{1, 1, 0}, {0, 1, 1}, {1, 0, 1}}
```

In the usual case, m has no null space.

```
In[2]:= NullSpace[m]
Out[2]= {}
```

If, however, combinations of matrix elements need only be zero modulo two, m does have a non-trivial null space.

```
In[3]:= NullSpace[m, ZeroTest -> (Mod[#, 2]==0 &)]
Out[3]= {{1, -1, 1}}
```

You can use `ZeroTest` to do linear algebra with matrices whose elements are not necessarily ordinary real numbers. One important application is in working with matrices whose elements are symbolic expressions. When complicated symbolic expressions are involved, it may be necessary to apply various transformations in order to find out whether particular combinations of expressions are in fact zero. You can use `ZeroTest` to specify such transformations.

## ■ 3.7.10 Eigenvalues and Eigenvectors

| | |
|---|---|
| `Eigenvalues[`*m*`]` | a list of the eigenvalues of *m* |
| `Eigenvectors[`*m*`]` | a list of the eigenvectors of *m* |
| `Eigensystem[`*m*`]` | a list of the form *{eigenvalues, eigenvectors}* |
| `Eigenvalues[ N[`*m*`] ]`, etc. | numerical eigenvalues |
| `Eigenvalues[ N[`*m, k*`] ]`, etc. | numerical eigenvalues, starting with *k*-digit precision |

Eigenvalues and eigenvectors.

The eigenvalues of a matrix **m** are the values $\lambda_i$ for which one can find vectors $\mathbf{x}_i$ such that $\mathbf{m}.\mathbf{x}_i = \lambda_i \mathbf{x}_i$. The eigenvectors are the vectors $\mathbf{x}_i$.

Finding the eigenvalues of an $n \times n$ matrix in general involves solving an $n^{\text{th}}$ degree polynomial equation. Since for $n \geq 5$ explicit algebraic solutions cannot in general be found, it is impossible to give explicit algebraic results for the eigenvalues and eigenvectors of all but the simplest or sparsest matrices.

Even for a matrix as simple as this, the explicit form of the eigenvalues is quite complicated.

$In[1]:=$ `Eigenvalues[ {{a, b}, {-b, 2a}} ]`

$$Out[1]= \left\{ \frac{3\,a + \text{Sqrt}[9\,a^2 - 4\,(2\,a^2 + b^2)]}{2}, \right.$$

$$\left. \frac{3\,a - \text{Sqrt}[9\,a^2 - 4\,(2\,a^2 + b^2)]}{2} \right\}$$

If you give a matrix of approximate real numbers, *Mathematica* will find the approximate numerical eigenvalues and eigenvectors.

Here is a $2 \times 2$ numerical matrix.

$In[2]:=$ `m = {{2.3, 4.5}, {6.7, -1.2}}`

$Out[2]=$ `{{2.3, 4.5}, {6.7, -1.2}}`

The matrix has two eigenvalues, in this case both real.

```
In[3]:= Eigenvalues[ m ]
Out[3]= {6.31303, -5.21303}
```

Here are the two eigenvectors of m.

```
In[4]:= Eigenvectors[ m ]
Out[4]= {{0.746335, 0.66557}, {-0.523116, 0.873374}}
```

**Eigensystem** computes the eigenvalues and eigenvectors at the same time. The assignment sets **vals** to the list of eigenvalues, and **vecs** to the list of eigenvectors.

```
In[5]:= {vals, vecs} = Eigensystem[m]
Out[5]= {{6.31303, -5.21303},
         {{0.746335, 0.66557}, {-0.523116, 0.873374}}}
```

This verifies that the first eigenvalue and eigenvector satisfy the appropriate condition.

```
In[6]:= m . vecs[[1]] == vals[[1]] vecs[[1]]
Out[6]= True
```

This finds the eigenvalues of a random $4 \times 4$ matrix. For non-symmetric matrices, the eigenvalues can have imaginary parts.

```
In[7]:= Eigenvalues[ Table[Random[ ],{i,4},{j,4}] ]
Out[7]= {1.76797, -0.235343 + 0.433364 I,
         -0.235343 - 0.433364 I, 0.432073}
```

The function **Eigenvalues** always gives you a list of $n$ eigenvalues for an $n \times n$ matrix. The eigenvalues correspond to the roots of the characteristic polynomial for the matrix, and may not necessarily be distinct. **Eigenvectors**, on the other hand, gives a list of eigenvectors with are guaranteed to be independent. The number of such eigenvectors may be less than $n$.

Here is a $3 \times 3$ matrix.

```
In[8]:= mz = {{0, 1, 0}, {0, 0, 1}, {0, 0, 0}}
Out[8]= {{0, 1, 0}, {0, 0, 1}, {0, 0, 0}}
```

The matrix has three eigenvalues, all equal to zero.

```
In[9]:= Eigenvalues[mz]
Out[9]= {0, 0, 0}
```

There is, however, only one independent eigenvector for the matrix.

```
In[10]:= Eigenvectors[mz]
Out[10]= {{1, 0, 0}, {0, 0, 0}, {0, 0, 0}}
```

## ■ 3.7.11  Advanced Topic: Singular Value Decomposition

| | |
|---|---|
| SingularValues[*m*] | find the singular value decomposition of a numerical matrix |
| PseudoInverse[*m*] | compute the pseudoinverse of a numerical matrix |

Some advanced numerical matrix operations.

Singular value decomposition is an important element of many numerical matrix algorithms. The basic idea is to write any matrix **m** in the form $\mathbf{u}^T \mathbf{m}_D \mathbf{v}$, where $\mathbf{m}_D$ is a diagonal matrix, and **u** and **v** are respectively row and column orthogonal matrices. The function SingularValues[*m*] returns a list containing the matrix **u**, the list of diagonal elements of $\mathbf{m}_D$, and the matrix **v**.

The diagonal elements of $\mathbf{m}_D$ are known as the *singular values* of the matrix **m**. One interpretation of the singular values is as follows. If you take a sphere in $n$-dimensional space, and multiply each vector in it by an $m \times n$ matrix **m**, you will get an ellipsoid in $m$-dimensional space. The singular values give the lengths of the principal axes of the ellipsoid. If the matrix **m** is singular in some way, this will be reflected in the shape of the ellipsoid. In fact, the ratio of the largest singular value of a matrix to the smallest one gives the *condition number* of the matrix, which determines, for example, the accuracy of numerical matrix inverses.

In general, very small singular values are numerically meaningless. SingularValues removes any singular values that are smaller than a certain *tolerance* multiplied by the largest singular value. The option Tolerance specifies the tolerance to use. The default tolerance is ten times the precision of the numbers in the original matrix **m**.

Here is the singular value decomposition for a non-singular $2 \times 2$ matrix.

```
In[1]:= SingularValues[N[{{1, 3}, {-4, 3}}]]
Out[1]= {{{-0.957092, 0.289784}, {-0.289784, -0.957092}},
          {2.91309, 5.14916},
          {{-0.726454, -0.687215}, {0.687215, -0.726454}}}
```

Here is a convenient way to pick out the pieces of the result.

```
In[2]:= {u, md, v} = %
Out[2]= {{{-0.957092, 0.289784}, {-0.289784, -0.957092}},
          {2.91309, 5.14916},
          {{-0.726454, -0.687215}, {0.687215, -0.726454}}}
```

This gives something close to the original matrix.

```
In[3]:= Transpose[u] . DiagonalMatrix[md] . v
Out[3]= {{1., 3.}, {-4., 3.}}
```

Here is the singular value decomposition of a singular matrix. Only one singular value is given.

```
In[4]:= SingularValues[N[{{1, 2}, {1, 2}}]]
Out[4]= {{{0.707107, 0.707107}}, {3.16228},
           {{0.447214, 0.894427}}}
```

The standard definition for the inverse of a matrix fails if the matrix is not square. Using singular value decomposition, however, it is possible to define a *pseudoinverse* even for non-square matrices, or for singular square ones. The pseudoinverse is defined in terms of the objects $\mathbf{u}$, $\mathbf{m}_D$ and $\mathbf{v}$ as $\mathbf{m}^{(-1)} = \mathbf{v}^T \mathbf{m}_D^{-1} \mathbf{u}$. The pseudoinverse has the property that the sum of the squares of all the entries in $\mathbf{m}.\mathbf{m}^{(-1)} - \mathbf{I}$, where $\mathbf{I}$ is an identity matrix, is minimized. The pseudoinverse found in this way is important, for example, in carrying out fits to numerical data. The pseudoinverse is sometimes known as the generalized inverse, or the Moore-Penrose inverse.

■ **3.7.12 Advanced Topic: Tensors**

*Tensors* are mathematical objects that give generalizations of vectors and matrices. In *Mathematica*, a tensor is represented as a set of lists, nested to a certain number of levels. The nesting level is the *rank* of the tensor.

| | |
|---|---|
| rank 0 | scalar |
| rank 1 | vector |
| rank 2 | matrix |
| rank $k$ | rank $k$ tensor |

Interpretations of nested lists.

A tensor of rank $k$ is essentially a $k$-dimensional table of values. To be a true rank $k$ tensor, it must be possible to arrange the elements in the table in a $k$-dimensional cuboidal array. There can be no holes or protrusions in the cuboid.

The *indices* that specify a particular element in the tensor correspond to the coordinates in the cuboid. The *dimensions* of the tensor correspond to the side lengths of the cuboid.

One simple way that a rank $k$ tensor can arise is in giving a table of values for a function of $k$ variables. In physics, the tensors that occur typically have indices which run over the possible directions in space or spacetime. Notice, however, there is no built-in notion of covariant and contravariant tensor indices in *Mathematica*: you have to set these up explicitly using metric tensors.

Table[*f*, {*i₁*, *n₁*}, {*i₂*, *n₂*}, ..., {*iₖ*, *nₖ*}]

$\qquad$ create an $n_1 \times n_2 \times ... \times n_k$ tensor whose elements are the values of $f$

Array[*a*, {*n₁*, *n₂*, ..., *nₖ*}]
$\qquad$ create an $n_1 \times n_2 \times ... \times n_k$ tensor with elements given by applying $a$ to each set of indices

Dimensions[*t*] $\qquad$ give a list of the dimensions of a tensor

TensorRank[*t*] $\qquad$ find the rank of a tensor

MatrixForm[*t*] $\qquad$ print with the elements of $t$ arranged in a two-dimensional array

Functions for creating and testing the structure of tensors.

| | |
|---|---|
| Here is a $2 \times 3 \times 2$ tensor. | *In[1]:=* t = Table[i1+i2 i3, {i1, 2}, {i2, 3}, {i3, 2}]<br>*Out[1]=* {{{2, 3}, {3, 5}, {4, 7}},<br>$\qquad$ {{3, 4}, {4, 6}, {5, 8}}} |
| This is another way to produce the same tensor. | *In[2]:=* Array[(#1 + #2 #3)&, {2, 3, 2}]<br>*Out[2]=* {{{2, 3}, {3, 5}, {4, 7}},<br>$\qquad$ {{3, 4}, {4, 6}, {5, 8}}} |
| MatrixForm displays the elements of the tensor in a two-dimensional array. You can think of the array as consisting of two $3 \times 2$ matrices arranged side by side. | *In[3]:=* MatrixForm[ t ]<br>$\qquad$ 2   3   3   4<br>$\qquad$ 3   5   4   6<br>*Out[3]//MatrixForm=* 4   7   5   8 |
| Dimensions gives the dimensions of the tensor. | *In[4]:=* Dimensions[ t ]<br>*Out[4]=* {2, 3, 2} |
| Here is the 111 element of the tensor. | *In[5]:=* t[[1, 1, 1]]<br>*Out[5]=* 2 |
| TensorRank gives the rank of the tensor. | *In[6]:=* TensorRank[ t ]<br>*Out[6]=* 3 |

The rank of a tensor is equal to the number of indices needed to specify each element. You can pick out subtensors by using a small number of indices.

| | |
|---|---|
| Transpose[*t*] | transpose the first two indices in a tensor |
| Transpose[*t*, {*p₁*, *p₂*, ...}] | transpose the indices in a tensor so that the $p_k^{\text{th}}$ becomes the $k^{\text{th}}$ |
| Outer[*f*, *t₁*, *t₂*, ...] | form the generalized outer product of the tensors $t_i$ with "multiplication operator" $f$ |
| *t₁* . *t₂* | form the dot product of $t_1$ and $t_2$ (last index of $t_1$ contracted with first index of $t_2$) |
| Inner[*f*, *t₁*, *t₂*, *g*] | form the generalized inner product, with "multiplication operator" $f$ and "addition operator" $g$ |

Tensor manipulation operations.

You can think of a rank $k$ tensor as having $k$ "slots" into which you insert indices. Applying Transpose is effectively a way of reordering these slots. If you think of the elements of a tensor as forming a $k$-dimensional cuboid, you can view Transpose as effectively rotating (and possibly reflecting) the cuboid.

In the most general case, Transpose allows you to specify an arbitrary reordering to apply to the indices of a tensor. The function
Transpose[*T*, {*p₁*, *p₂*, ..., *pₖ*}], gives you a new tensor $T'$ such that the value of $T'_{i_1 i_2 \ldots i_k}$ is given by $T_{i_{p_1} i_{p_2} \ldots i_{p_k}}$.

If you originally had a $n_1 \times n_2 \times \ldots \times n_k$ tensor, then by applying Transpose, you will get a $n_{p_1} \times n_{p_2} \times \ldots \times n_{p_k}$ tensor.

| | |
|---|---|
| Here is a matrix, that you can also think of as a $2 \times 3$ tensor. | *In[7]:=* m = {{a, b, c}, {ap, bp, cp}} <br><br> *Out[7]=* {{a, b, c}, {ap, bp, cp}} |
| Applying Transpose gives you a $3 \times 2$ tensor. Transpose effectively interchanges the two "slots" for tensor indices. | *In[8]:=* mt = Transpose[m] <br><br> *Out[8]=* {{a, ap}, {b, bp}, {c, cp}} |
| The element m[[2, 3]] in the original tensor becomes the element m[[3, 2]] in the transposed tensor. | *In[9]:=* { m[[2, 3]], mt[[3, 2]] } <br><br> *Out[9]=* {cp, cp} |

This produces a $2 \times 3 \times 1 \times 2$ tensor.

```
In[10]:= t = Array[a, {2, 3, 1, 2}]
Out[10]= {{{{a[1, 1, 1, 1], a[1, 1, 1, 2]}},
         {{a[1, 2, 1, 1], a[1, 2, 1, 2]}},
         {{a[1, 3, 1, 1], a[1, 3, 1, 2]}}},
        {{{a[2, 1, 1, 1], a[2, 1, 1, 2]}},
         {{a[2, 2, 1, 1], a[2, 2, 1, 2]}},
         {{a[2, 3, 1, 1], a[2, 3, 1, 2]}}}}
```

This transposes the first two levels of t.

```
In[11]:= tt1 = Transpose[t]
Out[11]= {{{{a[1, 1, 1, 1], a[1, 1, 1, 2]}},
         {{a[2, 1, 1, 1], a[2, 1, 1, 2]}}},
        {{{a[1, 2, 1, 1], a[1, 2, 1, 2]}},
         {{a[2, 2, 1, 1], a[2, 2, 1, 2]}}},
        {{{a[1, 3, 1, 1], a[1, 3, 1, 2]}},
         {{a[2, 3, 1, 1], a[2, 3, 1, 2]}}}}
```

The result is a $3 \times 2 \times 1 \times 2$ tensor.

```
In[12]:= Dimensions[ tt1 ]
Out[12]= {3, 2, 1, 2}
```

Outer products, and their generalizations, are a way of building higher-rank tensors from lower-rank ones. Outer products are also sometimes known as direct, tensor or Kronecker products.

From a structural point of view, the tensor you get from Outer[$f$, $t$, $u$] has a copy of the structure of $u$ inserted at the "position" of each element in $t$. The elements in the resulting structure are obtained by combining elements of $t$ and $u$ using the function $f$.

This gives the "outer f" of two vectors. The result is a matrix.

```
In[13]:= Outer[ f, {a, b}, {ap, bp} ]
Out[13]= {{f[a, ap], f[a, bp]}, {f[b, ap], f[b, bp]}}
```

If you take the "outer f" of a length 3 vector with a length 2 vector, you get a $3 \times 2$ matrix.

```
In[14]:= Outer[ f, {a, b, c}, {ap, bp} ]
Out[14]= {{f[a, ap], f[a, bp]}, {f[b, ap], f[b, bp]},
         {f[c, ap], f[c, bp]}}
```

The result of taking the "outer f" of a $2 \times 2$ matrix and a length 3 vector is a $2 \times 2 \times 3$ tensor.

```
In[15]:= Outer[ f, {{m11, m12}, {m21, m22}}, {a, b, c} ]
Out[15]= {{{f[m11, a], f[m11, b], f[m11, c]},
         {f[m12, a], f[m12, b], f[m12, c]}},
        {{f[m21, a], f[m21, b], f[m21, c]},
         {f[m22, a], f[m22, b], f[m22, c]}}}
```

Here are the dimensions of the tensor.

```
In[16]:= Dimensions[ % ]
Out[16]= {2, 2, 3}
```

If you take the generalized outer product of a $m_1 \times m_2 \times \ldots \times m_r$ tensor and a $n_1 \times n_2 \times \ldots \times n_s$ tensor, you get a $m_1 \times \ldots \times m_r \times n_1 \times \ldots \times n_s$ tensor. If the original tensors have ranks $r$ and $s$, your result will be a rank $r + s$ tensor.

In terms of indices, the result of applying **Outer** to two tensors $T_{i_1 i_2 \ldots i_r}$ and $U_{j_1 j_2 \ldots j_s}$ is the tensor $V_{i_1 i_2 \ldots i_r j_1 j_2 \ldots j_s}$ with elements $f[T_{i_1 i_2 \ldots i_r}, U_{j_1 j_2 \ldots j_s}]$.

In doing standard tensor calculations, the most common function $f$ to use in **Outer** is **Times**, corresponding to the standard outer product.

Particularly in doing combinatorial calculations, however, it is often convenient to take $f$ to be **List**. Using **Outer**, you can then get combinations of all possible elements in one tensor, with all possible elements in the other.

In constructing **Outer[f, t, u]** you effectively insert a copy of $u$ at every point in $t$. To form **Inner[f, t, u]**, you effectively "glue" edges of $u$ on to edges of $t$. The idea is to take a $m_1 \times m_2 \times \ldots \times m_r$ tensor and a $n_1 \times n_2 \times \ldots \times n_s$ tensor, with $m_r = n_1$, and get a $m_1 \times m_2 \times \ldots \times m_{r-1} \times n_2 \times \ldots \times n_s$ tensor as the result.

The simplest examples are with vectors. If you apply **Inner** to two vectors of equal length, you get a scalar. **Inner[f, $v_1$, $v_2$, g]** gives a generalization of the usual scalar product, with $f$ playing the role of multiplication, and $g$ playing the role of addition.

This gives a generalization of the standard scalar product of two vectors.

```
In[17]:= Inner[f, {a, b, c}, {ap, bp, cp}, g]
Out[17]= g[f[a, ap], f[b, bp], f[c, cp]]
```

This gives a generalization of a matrix product.

```
In[18]:= Inner[f, {{1, 2}, {3, 4}}, {{a, b}, {c, d}}, g]
Out[18]= {{g[f[1, a], f[2, c]], g[f[1, b], f[2, d]]},
          {g[f[3, a], f[4, c]], g[f[3, b], f[4, d]]}}
```

Here is a $3 \times 2 \times 2$ tensor.

```
In[19]:= a = Array[1&, {3, 2, 2}]
Out[19]= {{{1, 1}, {1, 1}}, {{1, 1}, {1, 1}},
          {{1, 1}, {1, 1}}}
```

Here is a $2 \times 3 \times 1$ tensor.

```
In[20]:= b = Array[2&, {2, 3, 1}]
Out[20]= {{{2}, {2}, {2}}, {{2}, {2}, {2}}}
```

| | |
|---|---|
| This gives a $3 \times 2 \times 3 \times 1$ tensor. | `In[21]:= a . b` |
| | `Out[21]= {{{{4}, {4}, {4}}, {{4}, {4}, {4}}},` |
| | `          {{{4}, {4}, {4}}, {{4}, {4}, {4}}},` |
| | `          {{{4}, {4}, {4}}, {{4}, {4}, {4}}}}` |
| | |
| Here are the dimensions of the result. | `In[22]:= Dimensions[ % ]` |
| | `Out[22]= {3, 2, 3, 1}` |

You can think of **Inner** as performing a "contraction" of the last index of one tensor with the first index of another. If you want to perform contractions across other pairs of indices, you can do this by first transposing the appropriate indices into the first or last position, then applying **Inner**, and then transposing the result back.

In many applications of tensors, you need to insert signs to implement anti-symmetry. The function **Signature**$[\{i_1, i_2, ...\}]$, which gives the signature of a permutation, is often useful for this purpose.

# ■ 3.8 Numerical Operations on Data

## ■ 3.8.1 Curve Fitting

Built into *Mathematica* are various facilities for finding least-squares fits to data. The basic idea of the fits is to take a list of functions that you specify, and try to find a linear combination of them which approximates your data as well as possible. The goodness of fit is measured by the quantity $\chi^2 = \sum_i |F_i - f_i|^2$, where $F_i$ is the value of your $i^{\text{th}}$ data point, and $f_i$ is the value obtained from the fit. The best fit is the one which minimizes $\chi^2$.

| | |
|---|---|
| Fit[*data*, *funs*, *vars*] | fit a list of data points using the functions *funs* of variables *vars* |

The basic form of the Fit function.

| | |
|---|---|
| Fit[{$f_1$, $f_2$, ...}, {1, x}, x] | linear fit |
| Fit[{$f_1$, $f_2$, ...}, {1, x, x∧2}, x] | |
| | quadratic fit |
| Fit[*data*, Table[x∧i, {i, 0, n}], x] | |
| | $n^{\text{th}}$ degree polynomial fit |
| Exp[ Fit[Log[*data*], {1, x}, x] ] | |
| | fit to $e^{a+bx}$ |

Some fits to lists of data.

Here is a table of the first 20 primes.

```
In[1]:= fp = Table[Prime[x], {x, 20}]
Out[1]= {2, 3, 5, 7, 11, 13, 17, 19, 23, 29, 31, 37, 41,
         43, 47, 53, 59, 61, 67, 71}
```

Here is a plot of this "data".

```
In[2]:= gp = ListPlot[ fp ]
```

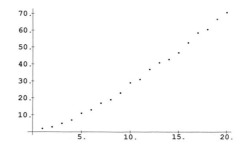

This gives a linear fit to the list of primes. The result is the best linear combination of the functions 1 and x.

`In[3]:= Fit[fp, {1, x}, x]`

`Out[3]= -7.67368 + 3.77368 x`

Here is a plot of the fit.

`In[4]:= Plot[%, {x, 0, 20}]`

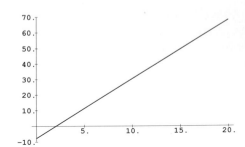

Here is the fit superimposed on the original data.

`In[5]:= Show[%, gp]`

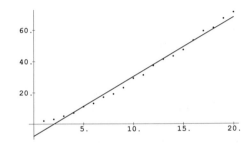

This gives a quadratic fit to the data.

`In[6]:= Fit[fp, {1, x, x^2}, x]`

`Out[6]= -1.92368 + 2.2055 x + 0.0746753 x^2`

Here is a plot of the quadratic fit.

`In[7]:= Plot[%, {x, 0, 20}]`

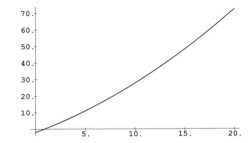

This shows the fit superimposed on the
original data. The quadratic fit is better
than the linear one.

`In[8]:= Show[%, gp]`

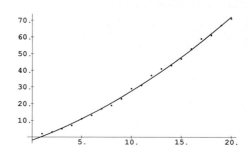

Polynomial fits are the most common kind to use. However, if you have a reason
to believe that your data follows some other functional form, you can include the
appropriate functions in the list you give to `Fit`.

This gives a table of the values of $1 + 2e^{\frac{x}{3}}$
for $x$ from 1 to 10 in steps of 1.

`In[9]:= ft = Table[ N[1 + 2 Exp[-x/3]] , {x, 10}]`

`Out[9]= {2.43306, 2.02683, 1.73576, 1.52719, 1.37775,`

`           1.27067, 1.19394, 1.13897, 1.09957, 1.07135}`

This fit recovers the original functional
form.

`In[10]:= Fit[ ft, {1, Exp[-x/3]}, x ]`

$$Out[10]= 1. + \frac{2.}{E^{\frac{x}{3}}}$$

If you include other functions in the list,
`Fit` determines that they occur with small
coefficients.

`In[11]:= Fit[ ft, {1, Sin[x], Exp[-x/3], Exp[-x]}, x ]`

$$Out[11]= 1. - \frac{9.76996\ 10^{-15}}{E^{x}} + \frac{2.}{E^{\frac{x}{3}}} + 0.\ Sin[x]$$

You can use `Chop` to get rid of the terms
with small coefficients.

`In[12]:= Chop[%]`

$$Out[12]= 1. + \frac{2.}{E^{\frac{x}{3}}}$$

There are several common reasons for doing fits.

If you have a particular model for some data, you can do a fit to try and determine the parameters of the model.

Another common use of fits is in finding approximate formulae to describe a particular set of data. You can use the form you get from a **Fit** as a summary of your actual data.

If you have only a few data points, then by including enough functions, you can get a fit which *exactly* reproduces the data you have. You can then interpolate or extrapolate from your data just by evaluating the fit at other points. If you use polynomial fits, you will find that you can always reproduce $n$ data points with a polynomial of degree $n - 1$.

Here is a list of the first five factorials.

```
In[13]:= Table[x!, {x, 5}]
Out[13]= {1, 2, 6, 24, 120}
```

This gives a fourth degree polynomial fit to the data.

```
In[14]:= fti = Fit[%, Table[x^i, {i, 0, 4}], x]
Out[14]= 45. - 93.75 x + 67.7917 x^2 - 20.25 x^3 +
          2.20833 x^4
```

Evaluating the fit for integer x between 1 and 5 reproduces your exact data.

```
In[15]:= fti /. x->3
Out[15]= 6.
```

Here is the interpolated value at $x = 2.5$.

```
In[16]:= fti /. x->2.5
Out[16]= 4.17969
```

This gives an extrapolation of your data, based on your fit.

```
In[17]:= fti /. x->8
Out[17]= 2311.
```

Like many extrapolations, it does not give a terribly accurate result.

```
In[18]:= 8!
Out[18]= 40320
```

In all the examples of **Fit** so far, the data points you give are assumed to correspond to the results of evaluating a function of one variable when the variable successively takes on values 1, 2, .... You can also specify data that depends on several variables, each given an arbitrary sequence of values, not necessarily arranged in any kind of regular array.

| | |
|---|---|
| $\{f_1,\ f_2,\ ...\}$ | data points obtained when a single coordinate takes on values 1, 2, ... |
| $\{\{x_1,\ y_1,\ ...,\ f_1\},\ \{x_2,\ y_2,\ ...,\ f_2\},\ ...\}$ | data points obtained with values $x_i,\ y_i,\ ...$ of a sequence of coordinates |

Ways of specifying data in `Fit`.

This gives a table of the values of $x$, $y$ and $1 + 2x + 3x - xy$. You need to use `Flatten` to get it in the right form for `Fit`.

```
In[19]:= Flatten[ Table[ {x, y, 1 + 5x - x y},
    {x, 0, 1, .4}, {y, 0, 1, .4} ], 1]
Out[19]= {{0, 0, 1}, {0, 0.4, 1}, {0, 0.8, 1},
    {0.4, 0, 3.}, {0.4, 0.4, 2.84}, {0.4, 0.8, 2.68},
    {0.8, 0, 5.}, {0.8, 0.4, 4.68}, {0.8, 0.8, 4.36}}
```

This produces a fit to a function of two variables.

```
In[20]:= Fit[ % , {1, x, y, x y}, {x, y} ]
Out[20]= 1. + 5. x + 1.55431 10^-15 y - 1. x y
```

Fit takes the list of functions you give, and finds the best fit to your data, according to the least squares criterion, using these functions. There is absolutely no guarantee that the fit you get will in fact accurately reproduce your data. To find out whether it can, you should use statistical testing functions, such as those in the statistics section of the *Mathematica* library.

## ■ 3.8.2  Fourier Transforms

A common operation in analyzing various kinds of data is to find the Fourier transform, or spectrum, of a list of values. The idea is typically to pick out components of the data with particular frequencies, or ranges of frequencies.

| | |
|---|---|
| `Fourier[`$\{y_0,\ y_1,\ ...\}$`]` | Fourier transform |
| `InverseFourier[`$\{y_0,\ y_1,\ ...\}$`]` | inverse Fourier transform |

Fourier transforms.

*Mathematica* uses the standard complex Fourier transform. The Fourier transform $b_s$ of a list $a_r$ of length $n$ is defined to be $\frac{1}{\sqrt{n}} \sum_{r=1}^{n} a_r e^{2\pi i(r-1)(s-1)/n}$. Notice that the zero frequency term appears at position 1 in the resulting list.

The Fourier transform takes you from a time series of data to the frequency components of the data. You can use the inverse Fourier transform to get back to the time series.

The inverse Fourier transform $a_r$ of a list $b_s$ of length $n$ is defined to be $\frac{1}{\sqrt{n}} \sum_{s=1}^{n} b_s e^{-2\pi i(r-1)(s-1)/n}$.

| | |
|---|---|
| Here is some data, corresponding to a square pulse. | `In[1]:= {-1, -1, -1, -1, 1, 1, 1, 1}`<br><br>`Out[1]= {-1, -1, -1, -1, 1, 1, 1, 1}` |
| Here is the Fourier transform of the data. It is involves complex numbers. | `In[2]:= fft = Fourier[%]`<br><br>`Out[2]= {0., -0.707107 - 1.70711 I, 0.,`<br>`        -0.707107 - 0.292893 I, 0., -0.707107 + 0.292893 I,`<br>`        0., -0.707107 + 1.70711 I}` |

Here is the inverse Fourier transform.

`In[3]:= InverseFourier[%]`

$$Out[3]= \{-1., -1., -1. + 2.7477\ 10^{-16}\ I, -1., 1., 1.,$$
$$1. - 2.7477\ 10^{-16}\ I, 1.\}$$

| | |
|---|---|
| After using `Chop`, this gives back exactly your original data. | `In[4]:= Chop[%]`<br><br>`Out[4]= {-1., -1., -1., -1., 1., 1., 1., 1.}` |
| `Fourier` works whether or not your list of data has a length which is a power of two. | `In[5]:= Fourier[{1, -1, 1}]`<br><br>`Out[5]= {0.57735, 0.57735 - 1. I, 0.57735 + 1. I}` |

# ■ 3.9  Numerical Operations on Functions

## ■ 3.9.1  Numerical Mathematics in *Mathematica*

One of the most important features of *Mathematica* is its ability to give you exact, symbolic, results for computations. There are, however, computations where it is just mathematically impossible to get exact "closed form" results. In such cases, you can still often get approximate numerical results.

| | |
|---|---|
| There is no "closed form" result for $\int_0^1 \sin(\exp(x))\,dx$. *Mathematica* returns the integral in its original symbolic form. | `In[1]:= Integrate[Sin[Exp[x]], {x, 0, 1}]`<br><br>`Out[1]= Integrate[Sin[E`$^x$`], {x, 0, 1}]` |
| You can now take the symbolic form of the integral, and ask for its approximate numerical value. | `In[2]:= N[%]`<br><br>`Out[2]= 0.874957` |

When *Mathematica* cannot find an explicit result for something like a definite integral, it returns a symbolic form. You can take this symbolic form, and try to get an approximate numerical value by applying N.

| | |
|---|---|
| By giving a second argument to N, you can specify the numerical precision to use. | `In[3]:= N[ Integrate[Sin[Exp[x]], {x, 0, 1}], 40 ]`<br><br>`Out[3]= 0.8749571987803839994388329808353131568824` |

If you want to evaluate an integral numerically in *Mathematica*, then using `Integrate` and applying N to the result is not the most efficient way to do it. It is better instead to use the function `NIntegrate`, which immediately gives a numerical answer, without first trying to get an exact, symbolic, result. You should realize that even when `Integrate` does not in the end manage to give you an exact result, it may spend a lot of time trying to do so.

| | |
|---|---|
| `NIntegrate` evaluates numerical integrals directly, without first trying to get a symbolic result. | `In[4]:= NIntegrate[ Sin[Exp[x]], {x, 0, 1} ]`<br><br>`Out[4]= 0.874957` |

| Integrate | NIntegrate | definite integrals |
|-----------|-----------|--------------------|
| Sum | NSum | sums |
| Product | NProduct | products |
| Roots | NRoots | roots of polynomials |

Symbolic and numerical versions of some *Mathematica* functions.

## ■ 3.9.2  The Uncertainties of Numerical Mathematics

*Mathematica* does operations like numerical integration very differently from the way it does their symbolic counterparts.

When you do a symbolic integral, *Mathematica* takes the functional form of the integrand you have given, and applies a sequence of exact symbolic transformation rules to it, to try and evaluate the integral.

When you do a numerical integral, however, *Mathematica* does not look directly at the functional form of the integrand you have given. Instead, it simply finds a sequence of numerical values of the integrand at particular points, then takes these values and tries to deduce from them a good approximation to the integral.

An important point to realize is that when *Mathematica* does a numerical integral, the *only* information it has about your integrand is a sequence of numerical values for it. To get a definite result for the integral, *Mathematica* then effectively has to make certain assumptions about the smoothness and other properties of your integrand. If you give a sufficiently pathological integrand, these assumptions may not be valid, and as a result, *Mathematica* may simply give you the wrong answer for the integral.

This problem may occur, for example, if you try to integrate numerically a function which has a very thin spike at a particular position. *Mathematica* samples your function at a number of points, and then assumes that the function varies smoothly between these points. As a result, if none of the sample points come close to the spike, then the spike will go undetected, and its contribution to the numerical integral will not be correctly included.

Here is a plot of the function $\exp(-x^2)$.

`In[1]:= Plot[Exp[-x^2], {x, -10, 10}, PlotRange->All]`

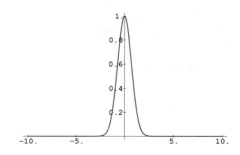

NIntegrate gives the correct answer for the numerical integral of this function from -10 to +10.

`In[2]:= NIntegrate[Exp[-x^2], {x, -10, 10}]`

`Out[2]= 1.77245`

If, however, you ask for the integral from $-10^6$ to $+10^6$, NIntegrate will miss the peak near $x = 0$, and give the wrong answer.

`In[3]:= NIntegrate[Exp[-x^2], {x, -10^6, 10^6}]`

`Out[3]= 0.`

Although **NIntegrate** follows the principle of looking only at the numerical values of your integrand, it nevertheless tries to make the best possible use of the information that it can get. Thus, for example, if **NIntegrate** notices that your integrand is changing rapidly in a particular region, it will take more samples in that region. In this way, **NIntegrate** tries to "adapt" its operation to the particular integrand you have given.

The kind of adaptive procedure that **NIntegrate** uses is similar, at least in spirit, to what **Plot** does in trying to draw smooth curves for functions. In both cases, *Mathematica* tries to go on taking more samples in a particular region until it has effectively found a smooth approximation to the function in that region.

The kinds of problems that can appear in numerical integration can also arise in doing other numerical operations on functions.

For example, if you ask for a numerical approximation to the sum of an infinite series, *Mathematica* samples a certain number of terms in the series, and then does an extrapolation to estimate the contributions of other terms. If you insert large terms far out in the series, they may not be detected when the extrapolation is done, and the result you get for the sum may be incorrect.

A similar problem arises when you try to find a numerical approximation to the minimum of a function. *Mathematica* samples only a finite number of values, then effectively assumes that the actual function interpolates smoothly between these values. If in fact the function has a sharp dip in a particular region, then *Mathematica* may miss this dip, and you may get the wrong answer for the minimum.

If you work only with numerical values of functions, there is simply no way to avoid the kinds of problems we have been discussing. Exact symbolic computation, of course, allows you to get around these problems.

In many calculations, it is therefore worthwhile to go as far as you can symbolically, and then resort to numerical methods only at the very end. This gives you the best chance of avoiding the problems that can arise in purely numerical computations.

One might imagine that you could use symbolic methods to check for any features, say in the integrand of a numerical integral, that would give rise to problems in numerical computation. As soon as your integrand contains conditionals, control structures or nested function calls, there can be no general procedure, however, to do the tests that are needed. Nevertheless, for specific classes of integrands, it may be possible to perform some such tests. You can always implement these tests by defining special rules for `NIntegrate` in certain cases.

## ■ 3.9.3 Numerical Integration

| | |
|---|---|
| `N[Integrate[`*expr*`, {`*x*`, `*xmin*`, `*xmax*`}]]` | try to perform an integral exactly, then find numerical approximations to the parts that remain |
| `NIntegrate[`*expr*`, {`*x*`, `*xmin*`, `*xmax*`}]` | find a numerical approximation to an integral |
| `NIntegrate[`*expr*`, {`*x*`, `*xmin*`, `*xmax*`}, {`*y*`, `*ymin*`, `*ymax*`}, ...]` | multidimensional numerical integral $\int_{xmin}^{xmax} dx \int_{ymin}^{ymax} dy \ldots expr$ |
| `NIntegrate[`*expr*`, {`*x*`, `*xmin*`, `*x₁*`, `*x₂*`, ..., `*xmax*`}]` | do a numerical integral along a line, starting at *xmin*, going through the points $x_i$, and ending at *xmax* |

Numerical integration functions.

This finds a numerical approximation to the integral $\int_0^\infty e^{-x^3} \, dx$.

```
In[1]:= NIntegrate[Exp[-x^3], {x, 0, Infinity}]
Out[1]= 0.89298
```

Here is the numerical value of the double integral $\int_{-1}^1 dx \int_{-1}^1 dy \, (x^2 + y^2)$.

```
In[2]:= NIntegrate[x^2 + y^2, {x, -1, 1}, {y, -1, 1}]
Out[2]= 2.66667
```

An important feature of `NIntegrate` is its ability to deal with functions that "blow up" at known points. `NIntegrate` automatically checks for such problems at the end points of the integration region.

| | |
|---|---|
| The function $1/\sqrt{x}$ blows up at $x = 0$, but `NIntegrate` still succeeds in getting the correct value for the integral. | `In[3]:= NIntegrate[1/Sqrt[x], {x, 0, 1}]`<br><br>`Out[3]= 2.` |

| | |
|---|---|
| *Mathematica* can find the integral of $1/\sqrt{x}$ exactly. | `In[4]:= Integrate[1/Sqrt[x], {x, 0, 1}]`<br><br>`Out[4]= 2` |

| | |
|---|---|
| `NIntegrate` detects that the singularity in $\frac{1}{x}$ at $x = 0$ is not integrable. | `In[5]:= NIntegrate[1/x, {x, 0, 1}]`<br><br>`NIntegrate::conv:`<br>    `Numerical integral failed to reach specified`<br>      `accuracy after 7 recursive subdivisions near`<br>                     `-13`<br>      `9.394176720306658 10`    `for variable number 1.`<br><br>`Out[5]= 111.92` |

`NIntegrate` does not automatically look for singularities except at the end points of your integration region. When other singularities are present, `NIntegrate` may not give you the right answer for the integral. Nevertheless, in following its adaptive procedure, `NIntegrate` will often detect the presence of potentially singular behavior, and will warn you about it.

| | |
|---|---|
| `NIntegrate` does not handle the singularity in $1/\sqrt{\lvert x \rvert}$ in the middle of the integration region. However, it warns you of a possible problem. In this case, the final result is numerically quite close to the correct answer. | `In[6]:= NIntegrate[1/Sqrt[Abs[x]], {x, -1, 1}]`<br><br>`NIntegrate::conv:`<br>    `Numerical integral failed to reach specified`<br>      `accuracy after 7 recursive subdivisions near`<br>      `-0.015625 for variable number 1.`<br><br>`NIntegrate::conv:`<br>    `Numerical integral failed to reach specified`<br>      `accuracy after 7 recursive subdivisions near`<br>      `0.015625 for variable number 1.`<br><br>`Out[6]= 3.97439` |

If you know that your integrand has singularities at particular points, you can explicitly tell `NIntegrate` to deal with them.
`NIntegrate[`*expr*`, {x,` *xmin*`,` $x_1$`,` $x_2$`, ...,` *xmax*`}]` integrates *expr* from *xmin* to *xmax*, looking for possible singularities at each of the intermediate points $x_i$.

| | |
|---|---|
| This again gives the integral $\int_{-1}^{1} \frac{1}{\sqrt{\lvert x \rvert}}\, dx$, but now explicitly deals with the singularity at $x = 0$. | `In[7]:= NIntegrate[1/Sqrt[Abs[x]], {x, -1, 0, 1}]`<br><br>`Out[7]= 4.` |

You can also use the list of intermediate points $x_i$ in `NIntegrate` to specify an integration contour to follow in the complex plane. The contour is taken to consist of a sequence of line segments, starting at *xmin*, going through each of the $x_i$, and ending at *xmax*.

| | |
|---|---|
| This integrates $\frac{1}{x}$ around the closed contour in the complex plane, going from -1, through the points $-i$, 1 and $i$, then back to -1. | `In[8]:= NIntegrate[1/x, {x, -1, -I, 1, I, -1}]`<br><br>`Out[8]= 6.28319 I` |
| The integral gives $2\pi i$, as expected from Cauchy's theorem. | `In[9]:= N[ 2 Pi I ]`<br><br>`Out[9]= 6.28319 I` |

There are a number of ways you can control the operation of `NIntegrate`. First, you may want to specify the accuracy of the answers you are trying to get. If you use `Integrate`, and then apply N to get numerical results, then the second argument you give to N specifies the precision to use in the internal computations used to do the numerical integral. You can also specify this precision using the option `WorkingPrecision -> n` for `NIntegrate`.

You should realize, however, that the option `WorkingPrecision` specifies only the precision to use for internal computations done by `NIntegrate`. The final answer that `NIntegrate` gives will almost always have a lower precision. You can nevertheless use `NIntegrate` to try and get an answer with a particular *accuracy* by setting the option `AccuracyGoal -> n`. The setting for `AccuracyGoal` gives the number of digits to the right of the decimal point that `NIntegrate` tries to get. In almost all cases, you should set `WorkingPrecision` to be at least as large as `AccuracyGoal`.

| | |
|---|---|
| This evaluates $\int_1^2 \frac{1}{x}\, dx$ using 40 digit precision for internal computations. | `In[10]:= NIntegrate[1/x, {x, 1, 2}, WorkingPrecision->40]`<br>`Out[10]= 0.6931471805599453236737079617308134480957691` |
| The result differs from the exact value of $\log(2)$ by about 1 part in $10^{20}$. | `In[11]:= % - N[Log[2], 40]`<br><br>`Out[11]= -7.268015250415004175849859 10`$^{-17}$ |
| You can use the option `AccuracyGoal` to specify the number of digits of accuracy you want in the final answer. You often need to specify a slightly higher precision for internal computations in order to get a particular accuracy for the final result. | `In[12]:= NIntegrate[1/x, {x, 1, 2}, WorkingPrecision->40,`<br>`                  AccuracyGoal->30]`<br>`Out[12]= 0.693147180559945309417232121458176566990973` |

Now the result is accurate to the full 30 digits you asked for.

```
In[13]:= % - N[Log[2], 30]

Out[13]= -2. 10
                -34
```

| AccuracyGoal | 6 | number of digits of accuracy to try and get in the final answer |
| MinRecursion | 1 | minimum number of recursive subdivisions of the integration region |
| MaxRecursion | 6 | maximum number of recursive subdivisions |
| SingularityDepth | 3 | number of recursive subdivisions to use before doing a change of variables |
| Points | Automatic | number of sample points in each direction to use at first |
| WorkingPrecision | Precision[1.] | number of digits to use in internal computations |

Options for `NIntegrate`.

When `NIntegrate` tries to evaluate a numerical integral, it samples the integrand at a sequence of points. If it finds that the integrand changes rapidly in a particular region, then it recursively takes more sample points in that region. The parameters `MinRecursion` and `MaxRecursion` specify the minimum and maximum number of levels of recursive subdivision to use. Increasing the value of `MinRecursion` guarantees that `NIntegrate` will use a larger number of sample points. `MaxRecursion` limits the number of sample points which `NIntegrate` will ever try to use. Increasing `MinRecursion` or `MaxRecursion` will make `NIntegrate` work more slowly. The option `Points` specifies how many sample points `NIntegrate` should use before it starts recursive subdivision. `SingularityDepth` specifies how many levels of recursive subdivision `NIntegrate` should try before it concludes that the integrand is "blowing up", and does a change of variables.

With the default settings for all options, `NIntegrate` misses the peak in $\exp(-x^2)$ near $x = 0$, and gives the wrong answer for the integral.

```
In[14]:= NIntegrate[Exp[-x^2], {x, -500, 500}]
                             -42
Out[14]= 7.97921 10
```

With the option `MinRecursion->2`, `NIntegrate` samples enough points that it notices the peak around $x = 0$. With the default setting of `MaxRecursion`, however, `NIntegrate` cannot use enough sample points to guarantee an accurate answer.

```
In[15]:= NIntegrate[Exp[-x^2], {x, -500, 500},
            MinRecursion->2]
NIntegrate::conv:
     Numerical integral failed to reach specified
        accuracy after 7 recursive subdivisions near
        -7.8125 for variable number 1.

NIntegrate::conv:
     Numerical integral failed to reach specified
        accuracy after 7 recursive subdivisions near
        7.8125 for variable number 1.

Out[15]= 1.77563
```

With this setting of `MaxRecursion`, `NIntegrate` can get an accurate answer for the integral.

```
In[16]:= NIntegrate[Exp[-x^2], {x, -500, 500},
            MinRecursion->2, MaxRecursion->10]
Out[16]= 1.77245
```

Another way to solve the problem is to make `NIntegrate` break the integration region into several pieces, with a small piece that explicitly covers the neighborhood of the peak.

```
In[17]:= NIntegrate[Exp[-x^2], {x, -500, -10, 10, 500}]
Out[17]= 1.77245
```

## ■ 3.9.4  Numerical Evaluation of Sums and Products

| | |
|---|---|
| `NSum[f, {i, imin, imax}]` | find a numerical approximation to the sum $\sum_{i=imin}^{imax} f$ |
| `NSum[f, {i, imin, imax, di}]` | use step $di$ in the sum |
| `NProduct[f, {i, imin, imax}]` | find a numerical approximation to the product $\prod_{i=imin}^{imax} f$ |

Numerical sums and products.

This gives a numerical approximation to $\sum_{i=1}^{\infty} \frac{1}{i^3}$.

```
In[1]:= NSum[1/i^3, {i, 1, Infinity}]
Out[1]= 1.20206
```

*Mathematica* does not know the exact result for this sum, so leaves it in symbolic form.

```
In[2]:= Sum[1/i^3, {i, 1, Infinity}]
              -3
Out[2]= Sum[i  , {i, 1, Infinity}]
```

You can apply `N` explicitly to get a numerical result.

```
In[3]:= N[%]
Out[3]= 1.20206
```

The way `NSum` works is to include a certain number of terms explicitly, and then to try and estimate the contribution of the remaining ones. There are two approaches to estimating this contribution. The first uses the Euler-Maclaurin method, and is based on approximating the sum by an integral. The second method, known as Wynn's epsilon method, samples a number of additional terms in the sum, and then tries to fit them to a polynomial multiplied by a decaying exponential.

| | | |
|---|---|---|
| WorkingPrecision | Precision[1.] | number of digits of precision to use in internal computations |
| Method | Automatic | Integrate (Euler-Maclaurin method) or Fit (Wynn epsilon method) |
| Terms | 15 | number of terms to include explicitly |
| ExtraTerms | 11 | number of terms to use for extrapolation in the Wynn epsilon method |
| AccuracyGoal | 6 | number of digits of accuracy to try and get in the Euler-Maclaurin method |

Options for NSum.

If you do not explicitly specify the method to use, NSum will try to choose between the methods it knows. In any case, some implicit assumptions about the functions you are summing have to be made. If these assumptions are not correct, you may get inaccurate answers.

The most common place to use NSum is in evaluating sums with infinite limits. You can, however, also use it for sums with finite limits. By making implicit assumptions about the objects you are evaluating, NSum can often avoid doing as many function evaluations as an explicit Sum computation would require.

This finds the numerical value of $\sum_{n=0}^{100} e^{-n}$ by extrapolation techniques.

```
In[4]:= NSum[Exp[-n], {n, 0, 100}]
Out[4]= 1.58198
```

You can also get the result, albeit much less efficiently, by constructing the symbolic form of the sum, then evaluating it numerically.

```
In[5]:= Sum[Exp[-n], {n, 0, 100}] //N
Out[5]= 1.58198
```

NProduct works in essentially the same way as NSum, except that only the Wynn epsilon method can be used: there is no way to approximate a product directly by an integral. (If necessary, you can nevertheless form a product from an exponential of a sum of logarithms.)

## ■ 3.9.5 Numerical Solution of Polynomial Equations

When `Solve` cannot find explicit solutions to polynomial equations, it returns a symbolic form of the result.

```
In[1]:= Solve[x^5 + 7x + 1 == 0, x]
                            5
Out[1]= {ToRules[Roots[7 x + x  == -1, x]]}
```

You can get numerical solutions by applying `N`.

```
In[2]:= N[%]
Out[2]= {{x -> -1.11308 - 1.15173 I},
    {x -> -1.11308 + 1.15173 I}, {x -> -0.142849},
    {x -> 1.1845 - 1.15139 I}, {x -> 1.1845 + 1.15139 I}}
```

This gives the numerical solutions to 16-digit precision.

```
In[3]:= N[%%, 16]
Out[3]= {{x -> -1.11307797654771 - 1.151734362151675 I},
    {x -> -1.11307797654771 + 1.151734362151675 I},
    {x -> -0.1428486455250044},
    {x -> 1.184502299310213 - 1.151390075408837 I},
    {x -> 1.184502299310213 + 1.151390075408837 I}}
```

You can use `NRoots` to get numerical solutions to polynomial equations directly, without first trying to find exact results.

```
In[4]:= NRoots[x^7 + x + 1 == 0, x]
Out[4]= x == -0.796544 || x == -0.705298 - 0.637624 I ||
    x == -0.705298 + 0.637624 I ||
    x == 0.123762 - 1.05665 I ||
    x == 0.123762 + 1.05665 I ||
    x == 0.979808 - 0.516677 I ||
    x == 0.979808 + 0.516677 I
```

This converts the solutions to a sequence of transformation rules.

```
In[5]:= {ToRules[%]}
Out[5]= {{x -> -0.796544}, {x -> -0.705298 - 0.637624 I},
    {x -> -0.705298 + 0.637624 I},
    {x -> 0.123762 - 1.05665 I},
    {x -> 0.123762 + 1.05665 I},
    {x -> 0.979808 - 0.516677 I},
    {x -> 0.979808 + 0.516677 I}}
```

| | |
|---|---|
| NRoots[*poly*==0, x] | get approximate numerical solutions to a polynomial equation |
| NRoots[*poly*==0, x, *n*] | get solutions to *n* digit precision |
| {ToRules[*eqns*]} | write solutions from Roots or NRoots in the form of transformation rules |

Numerical solution of polynomial equations.

NRoots will always give you the complete set of numerical solutions to any polynomial equation in one variable.

You can also get numerical solutions to sets of simultaneous polynomial equations. You can use Solve to "unwind" the simultaneous equations, and then apply N to get numerical results.

Solve writes these equations as a composition of simpler equations.

```
In[6]:= Solve[{x^2 + y^2 == 1, x^3 + y^3 == 2}, {x, y}]
```
$$Out[6]= \{ToRules[Roots[3\ x ==$$
$$y\ (-3 - 6\ y - y^2 + 4\ y^3 + 2\ y^4),\ x,$$
$$Using ->$$
$$Roots[3\ y^2 - 4\ y^3 - 3\ y^4 + 2\ y^6 == -3,\ y]]]\}$$

You can apply N to get a numerical result.

```
In[7]:= N[%]
```
$$Out[7]= \{\{x\ ->\ -1.09791 + 0.839887\ I,$$
$$y\ ->\ -1.09791 - 0.839887\ I\},$$
$$\{x\ ->\ -1.09791 - 0.839887\ I,$$
$$y\ ->\ -1.09791 + 0.839887\ I\},$$
$$\{x\ ->\ 1.22333 - 0.0729987\ I,$$
$$y\ ->\ -0.125423 - 0.712005\ I\},$$
$$\{x\ ->\ 1.22333 + 0.0729987\ I,$$
$$y\ ->\ -0.125423 + 0.712005\ I\},$$
$$\{x\ ->\ -0.125423 - 0.712005\ I,$$
$$y\ ->\ 1.22333 - 0.0729987\ I\},$$
$$\{x\ ->\ -0.125423 + 0.712005\ I,$$
$$y\ ->\ 1.22333 + 0.0729987\ I\}\}$$

## ■ 3.9.6  Numerical Root Finding

NRoots gives you a general way to find numerical approximations to the solutions of polynomial equations. Finding numerical solutions to more general equations, however, can be much more difficult, as discussed in Section 3.4.2. `FindRoot` gives you a way to search for a numerical solution to an arbitrary equation, or set of equations.

| | |
|---|---|
| `FindRoot[`*lhs*`==`*rhs*`, {`*x*`, `*x₀*`}]` | search for a numerical solution to the equation *lhs*`==`*rhs*, starting with $x=x_0$ |
| `FindRoot[`*lhs*`==`*rhs*`, {`*x*`, {`*x₀*`, `*x₁*`}}]` | |
| | search for a solution using $x_0$ and $x_1$ as the first two values of $x$ (this form must be used if symbolic derivatives of the equation cannot be found) |
| `FindRoot[`*lhs*`==`*rhs*`, {`*x*`, `*xstart*`, `*xmin*`, `*xmax*`}]` | |
| | search for a solution, stopping the search if $x$ ever gets outside the range *xmin* to *xmax* |
| `FindRoot[{`*eqn₁*`, `*eqn₂*`, ...}, {`*x*`, `*x₀*`}, {`*y*`, `*y₀*`}, ...]` | |
| | search for a numerical solution to the simultaneous equations $eqn_i$ |

Numerical root finding.

The curves for $\cos(x)$ and $x$ intersect at one point.

*In[1]:=* `Plot[{Cos[x], x}, {x, -1, 1}]`

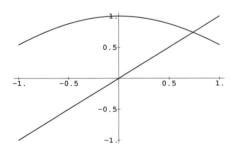

This finds a numerical approximation to the value of $x$ at which the intersection occurs. The 0 tells `FindRoot` what value of $x$ to try first.

*In[2]:=* `FindRoot[Cos[x] == x, {x, 0}]`

*Out[2]=* `{x -> 0.739085}`

In trying to find a solution to your equation, `FindRoot` starts at the point you specify, and then progressively tries to get closer and closer to a solution. Even if your equations have several solutions, `FindRoot` always returns the first solution it finds. Which solution this is will depend on what starting point you chose. So long as you start sufficiently close to a particular solution, `FindRoot` will always return that solution.

| | |
|---|---|
| The equation $\sin(x) = 0$ has an infinite number of solutions of the form $x = n\pi$. If you start sufficiently close to a particular solution, `FindRoot` will give you that solution. | `In[3]:= FindRoot[Sin[x] == 0, {x, 3}]`<br><br>`Out[3]= {x -> 3.14159}` |

If you start with $x = 6$, you get a numerical approximation to the solution $x = 2\pi$.

`In[4]:= FindRoot[Sin[x] == 0, {x, 6}]`

`Out[4]= {x -> 6.28319}`

This is what happens if `FindRoot` cannot find a solution to your equation.

`In[5]:= FindRoot[Sin[x] == 2, {x, 1}]`

```
FindRoot::convNewt:
      Newton's method failed to converge to the prescribed
         accuracy after 15 iterations.
```

`Out[5]= {x -> 2.06095}`

If you want `FindRoot` to search for complex solutions to this equation, then you have to give a complex starting value.

`In[6]:= FindRoot[Sin[x] == 2, {x, I}]`

`Out[6]= {x -> 1.5708 + 1.31696 I}`

You can give `FindRoot` bounds on the region in which you want it to look for solutions.

This tells `FindRoot` to try values of x starting at 1, but never going outside the region 0.5 to 1.5. In this case, `FindRoot` finds no solutions in the region you specified.

`In[7]:= FindRoot[Sin[x] == 0, {x, 1, 0.5, 1.5}]`

```
FindRoot::regext:
      Reached the point {-0.557408}
         which is outside the region {{0.5, 1.5}}.
```

`Out[7]= FindRoot[Sin[x] == 0, {x, 1, 0.5, 1.5}]`

Picking good starting points is crucial in getting useful answers from `FindRoot`. To know how to pick good starting points, you need to understand a little about how `FindRoot` actually works.

In the simplest case, `FindRoot` uses *Newton's method*. To find a solution to an equation of the form $f(x) = 0$, the method starts at $x_0$, then uses knowledge of the derivative $f'$ to take a sequence of steps towards a solution. Each new point $x_n$ that it tries is found from the previous point $x_{n-1}$ by the formula $x_n = x_{n-1} - f(x_{n-1})/f'(x_{n-1})$.

One important limitation of Newton's method is that it "gets stuck" if it ever gets to a point where the derivative of the function vanishes. You can usually avoid this problem by choosing starting points that have no special properties with respect to the equations you are trying to solve.

The derivative of $x^2 - 1$ is zero at the starting point $x = 0$. As a result FindRoot cannot decide whether to take its first step in the positive or the negative direction.

```
In[8]:= FindRoot[x^2 - 1 == 0, {x, 0}]
FindRoot::jsing:
        Encountered a singular Jacobian at the point {0.}
        . Try perturbing the initial point.

              2
Out[8]= FindRoot[x  - 1 == 0, {x, 0}]
```

If you start at a random point, however, FindRoot will usually succeed in finding a solution.

```
In[9]:= FindRoot[x^2 - 1 == 0, {x, Random[ ]}]
Out[9]= {x -> 1.}
```

**FindRoot** uses versions of Newton's method in many cases. Especially when there are several variables, the precise set of starting points which lead to a particular solution can become extremely complicated. The best policy is to try and start as close to the solution as possible, and to avoid any "special points".

This finds a solution to a set of simultaneous equations. It is a good idea to avoid taking the starting values for x and y to be equal, or in any other way "special".

```
In[10]:= FindRoot[{Sin[x] == Cos[y], x + y == 1},
            {x, .1}, {y, .2}]
Out[10]= {x -> 1.2854, y -> -0.285398}
```

If the functions that appear in your equations are sufficiently simple, then *Mathematica* will be able to find their derivatives symbolically. In all the examples of **FindRoot** that we have used so far, this is possible. As a result, **FindRoot** can use the formula for Newton's method directly.

If, on the other hand, **FindRoot** has to estimate the derivative of your functions numerically, then it must take another approach. In simple cases, the approach it uses is based on the "secant method". One feature of this method is that to get it started, you have to specify not just the first value to try, but rather the first *two* values.

This specifies the first two values of x to try.

```
In[11]:= FindRoot[Cos[x] == x, {x, {0, 1}}]
Out[11]= {x -> 0.739085}
```

If *Mathematica* cannot get an explicit formula for the function that appears in your equation, you *have to* specify the first two values to try. Here FindRoot finds a zero of the Riemann zeta function.

```
In[12]:= FindRoot[Zeta[1/2 + I t] == 0, {t, {12, 13}}]
                                       -7
Out[12]= {t -> 14.1347 - 4.42626 10   I}
```

If you are finding a root of a function of one variable, and the first two points you tell **FindRoot** to try give values of the function with opposite signs, then **FindRoot** is guaranteed to find a root. (This is true so long as your function satisfies some basic continuity conditions.)

| AccuracyGoal | 6 | the accuracy with which functions must be zero in order to accept a candidate solution |
| WorkingPrecision | Precision[1.] | the number of digits of precision to keep in internal computations |
| MaxIterations | 15 | the maximum number of steps to take in trying to find a solution |

Options for `FindRoot`.

There are several options you can use to control the operation of `FindRoot`. First, you can set `MaxIterations` to specify the maximum number of steps that `FindRoot` should use in attempting to find a solution. Even if `FindRoot` does not successfully find a solution in the number of steps you specify, it returns the most recent values it has tried. If you want to continue the search, you can then give these values as starting points.

To work out whether it has found an acceptable root, `FindRoot` evaluates your function and sees whether the result is zero to within the accuracy specified by the option `AccuracyGoal`. `FindRoot` will always print a warning message if it does not find a solution to within the specified accuracy. In doing internal computations, `FindRoot` uses the precision specified by the option `WorkingPrecision`.

This specifies that the zeta function needs to be zero to 10 digit accuracy at the solution. The Riemann hypothesis asserts that the imaginary part of **t** should be exactly zero at a root.

```
In[13]:= FindRoot[Zeta[1/2 + I t] == 0, {t, {12, 13}},
                   AccuracyGoal -> 10]

Out[13]= {t -> 14.1347 + 1.79056 10^{-11} I}
```

## ■ 3.9.7  Numerical Minimization

`FindRoot` gives you a way to find points at which a particular function is equal to zero. It is also often important to be able to find points at which a function has its minimum value. In principle, you could do this by applying `FindRoot` to the derivative of the function. In practice, however, there are much more efficient approaches.

`FindMinimum` gives you a way to find a minimum value for a function. As in `FindRoot`, you specify the first one or two points to try, and then `FindMinimum` tries to get progressively more accurate approximations to a minimum. If `FindMinimum` returns a definite result, then the result is guaranteed to correspond to at least a local minimum of your function. However, it is important to understand that the result may not be the global minimum point.

You can understand something about how `FindMinimum` works by thinking of the values of your function as defining the height of a surface. What `FindMinimum` does is essentially to start at the points you specify, then follow the path of steepest descent on the surface. Except in very pathological cases, this path always leads to at least a local minimum on the surface. In many cases, however, the minimum will not be a global one. As a simple analogy which illustrates this point, consider a physical mountain. Any water that falls on the mountain takes the path of steepest descent down the side of the mountain. Yet not all the water ends up at the bottom of the valleys; much of it gets stuck in mountain lakes which correspond to local minima of the mountain height function.

You should also realize that because `FindMinimum` does not take truly infinitesimal steps, it is still possible for it to overshoot even a local minimum.

<table>
<tr><td>This finds the value of $x$ which minimizes $\Gamma(x)$, starting from $x = 2$.</td><td>

```
In[1]:= FindMinimum[Gamma[x], {x, 2}]
Out[1]= {0.885603, {x -> 1.46161}}
```
</td></tr>
<tr><td>Here is a function with many local minima.</td><td>

```
In[2]:= Plot[Sin[x] + x/5, {x, -10, 10}]
```
</td></tr>
</table>

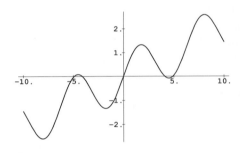

<table>
<tr><td>`FindMinimum` finds the local minimum closest to $x = 1$. This is not the global minimum for the function.</td><td>

```
In[3]:= FindMinimum[Sin[x] + x/5, {x, 1}]
Out[3]= {-1.33423, {x -> -1.77211}}
```
</td></tr>
<tr><td>This finds the local minimum of a function of two variables. As in `FindRoot`, it is a good idea to choose starting values that are not too "special".</td><td>

```
In[4]:= FindMinimum[x^4 + 3 x^2 y + 5 y^2 + x + y,
            {x, 0.1}, {y, 0.2}]
Out[4]= {-0.832579, {x -> -0.886325, y -> -0.335672}}
```
</td></tr>
</table>

| | |
|---|---|
| FindMinimum[$f$, {$x$, $x_0$}] | search for a local minimum in the function $f$, starting from the point $x$=$x_0$ |
| FindMinimum[$f$, {$x$, {$x_0$, $x_1$}}] | search for a local minimum using $x_0$ and $x_1$ as the first two values of $x$ (this form must be used if symbolic derivatives of $f$ cannot be found) |
| FindMinimum[$f$, {$x$, $xstart$, $xmin$, $xmax$}] | search for a local minimum, stopping the search if $x$ ever gets outside the range $xmin$ to $xmax$ |
| FindMinimum[$f$, {$x$, $x_0$}, {$y$, $y_0$}, ...] | search for a local minimum in a function of several variables |

Numerical minimization.

# Chapter Four:
## *Mathematica as a Computer Language*

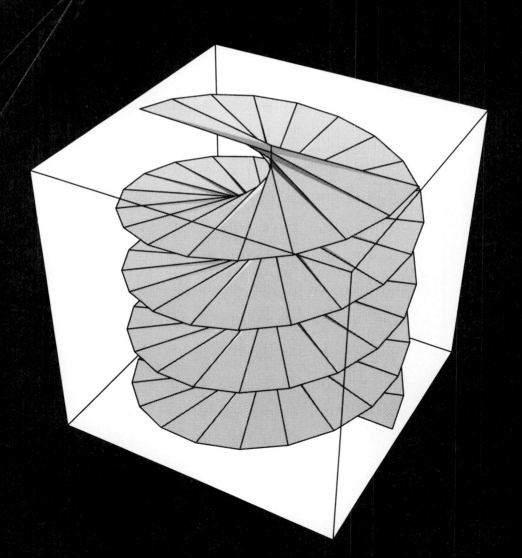

This chapter is intended to develop your understanding of *Mathematica* as a computer language. The chapter assumes that you have a general knowledge of how to *use Mathematica*. It concentrates on explaining some of the strategies and styles of *Mathematica* usage.

If you are familiar with other computer languages, reading this chapter should help you to understand the analogies, and differences, with *Mathematica*.

If *Mathematica* is your first computer language, you will probably not find this chapter particularly useful. If *Mathematica* is your second computer language, you should look at the section that compares *Mathematica* with your first language.

**About the illustration overleaf:**

This is a picture of a double helix, generated by the *Mathematica* command `Show[ Graphics3D[DoubleHelix[ ]] ]`. The function `DoubleHelix` is defined in the package `Shapes.m`. It returns a list of polygons which form a double helix.

# ■ 4.1  Programming Methodologies

## ■ 4.1.1  Approaches to Programming

There are several different approaches to "programming" in *Mathematica*. Which approach you choose in a particular case will depend on your computational background, and on the problems you are trying to solve.

All the approaches are in a sense ultimately equivalent, but one of them may be vastly more efficient for a particular problem, or may simply fit better with your way of thinking about the problem.

What this section does is to go through a number of different common programming methodologies, and explains how you can use them in *Mathematica*.

| | |
|---|---|
| Procedural programming | specify step-by-step algorithms |
| Functional programming | specify a collection of functions to apply |
| Mathematical programming | specify mathematical relations |

Three common approaches to *Mathematica* programming.

## ■ 4.1.2  Procedural Programming

Procedural programming is the standard approach used in traditional computer languages such C, Pascal, FORTRAN and BASIC. The basic idea is to have a program specify the sequence of steps that implements a particular algorithm.

```
BitCount[n_Integer] :=
      Block[ { ct = 0, m = n } ,
            While[ m != 0 ,
                  If[ Mod[m, 2] != 0, ct++ ] ;
                  m = Quotient[m, 2] ;
            ] ;
            Return[ ct ]
      ]
```

A procedural program to count the number of ones in the binary representation of an integer.

The simplest procedural programs consist of a sequence of commands which are executed in order. The commands typically set values for variables, which are then used later in the program. The "state" of the program at a particular point is determined by the values of the various variables that are in use.

You can think of the sequence of input lines in a particular *Mathematica* session as being like the steps in this kind of simple procedural program.

In the next level of procedural programming, one introduces the notion of *conditionals*. The *Mathematica* expression If[*predicate*, *branch$_T$*, *branch$_F$*] is a *conditional* which executes the commands *branch$_T$* if the predicate is True, and the commands *branch$_F$* if it is false. Conditionals are the simplest way to control the *flow* of a procedural program. When you get to a particular point in your program, you can explicitly test a given condition, and decide on the basis of it what commands to execute.

Sequences of commands in procedural programs form *blocks*. In *Mathematica*, the commands in a block are separated by semicolons. The *Mathematica* function Block lets you introduce variables that are "local" to a particular block.

Using blocks is important in producing structured programs. Each block can correspond to a "module" of your program, with a certain degree of independence from other modules.

Another important element of procedural programming is *iteration*. You can create loops that are executed repeatedly using *Mathematica* iteration functions like While and For. In the simplest cases, you know how many times a particular set of commands has to be executed. In more complicated cases, you can use iteration functions to execute a sequence of commands repeatedly, until, for example, a particular condition stops being true. At each step in the iteration, you typically increment or otherwise update some particular set of variables that you are using.

Conditionals and iteration give you two ways to control the *flow* of your program. Conditionals let you choose to execute different branches in your code; iteration lets you loop over a single piece of code. Sometimes the flow of control in your programs may become sufficiently complicated that it can no longer be specified just by conditionals and iteration. Often this is a sign of inadequate structure in your program. Sometimes, however, it is inevitable. In such cases, you can use the *Mathematica* function Goto to "transfer control" to a Label at a specific point in your program.

Procedural programming is the traditional approach to computer programming, embodied in the traditional programming languages. It has had the historical advantage of being easy to implement on standard computer hardware.

Most of the computer algorithms you find now written out in books are given as procedural programs, often in a pseudo-Pascal language. The procedural programming functions in *Mathematica* allow you to implement these kinds of programs almost directly in *Mathematica*.

There are nevertheless many kinds of problems that are ill-suited to procedural programming. The constraints of traditional programming languages have often led people to formulate even these problems as procedural programs. But with a language like *Mathematica*, you have a wider range of choices.

If you are used to a procedural programming language like FORTRAN, you will often find that you instinctively try to create *Mathematica* programs that look like FORTRAN. It is certainly possible to use *Mathematica* in this way, but you will not get the best out of it.

Procedural programming is in many respects the lowest-level form of programming that *Mathematica* supports. When you write a procedural program, you have to specify explicitly many details about the exact flow of control, and so on. When you use higher-level forms of programming, you do not see these kinds of details, and it is easier for you to concentrate on the main issues in your program.

In fact, you will often find that the best way to create a *Mathematica* program is to start from the original mathematical description of your problem, and try to implement that as directly as possible. Thinking about your problems in terms of procedural programs is often a handicap in creating the most efficient and clear *Mathematica* programs.

### ■ 4.1.3  Recursive Programming

Recursion is an important technique in formulating many kinds of problems. The basic idea is to break your problem up into many equivalent steps. Then your program can simply carry out one of these steps, and call itself "recursively" to have subsequent steps done.

Recursion is often used in languages like C, Pascal and LISP. Until recently, however, standard versions of FORTRAN did not allow recursion. As a result, many algorithms which would most naturally be formulated as recursive programs, were instead implemented as much more complicated non-recursive programs. The algorithms can often be made much clearer and more general by using recursion.

```
BitCount[n_Integer] := Mod[n,2] + BitCount[Quotient[n,2]]

BitCount[0] = 0
```

A recursive program to calculate the number of ones in the binary decomposition of an integer.

Recursion can take some getting used to. Recursive programs often look deceptively simple. It is hard to imagine how such small programs can do the things they do. The point is that each step may not do very much, but the steps are executed many times. In looking at recursive programs, it is often difficult to see exactly what sequence of steps will be followed when the program runs.

You can think of recursion as just another way to execute commands repeatedly. Any recursive program can always in principle be written using iteration. The recursive version is nevertheless usually much shorter and clearer. The main reasons are that when you use recursion, you do not have to specify the explicit "flow of control", nor do you have to define so many explicit intermediate variables.

```
log[x_ y_] := log[x] + log[y]
```

A rule that is used recursively to expand out logarithms.

Many kinds of mathematical transformation rules that you specify in *Mathematica* implicitly involve recursion. One example is the rule `log[x_ y_] := log[x] + log[y]` for expanding out logarithms of products. When you type in `log[a b c]`, the rule is applied once to give `log[a] + log[b c]`. The same rule is then applied again to expand out `log[b c]`.

In writing a recursive program, you have to provide two things. First, you have to specify the operations that are to be performed at each step. And second, you have to give some kind of "end conditions" that tell the system when to stop taking more steps. In the `BitCount` example above, the first rule specifies how `BitCount[n]` should be calculated in terms of `BitCount[Quotient[n,2]]`. We want this rule to be applied many times, until the argument of `BitCount` is 0. The appropriate end condition in this case is therefore `BitCount[0] = 0`.

When you create a recursive program like `BitCount`, *Mathematica* can usually recognize which rules correspond to special-case end conditions, and which ones are general steps in the recursion. It tries to arrange the special cases first in its list, so that they are checked before the general rules are applied.

There are many mathematical functions that can be computed using "recurrence" or "recursion" relations. One classic example is the factorial function.

```
factorial[n_Integer] := n factorial[n - 1]

factorial[1] = 1
```

The factorial function; a classic example of recursion.

The recursive program for the factorial function is certainly elegant. Nevertheless, on almost all computer systems, it is much less efficient than the obvious iterative program. For problems as simple as computing factorials, it is not difficult to devise iterative procedures, and avoid using recursion. Nevertheless, with more complicated problems, recursion often rapidly becomes overwhelmingly the most convenient approach. There may well be an iterative program that would solve a particular problem. But the complications involved in creating the iterative program may be so great that they would become the predominant factor in formulating the algorithm to be used. It is almost always much better to use a recursive program with a better algorithm, than an iterative program with a worse algorithm.

When you write an iterative program, you explicitly specify which commands are to be executed repeatedly. As a result, it is comparatively easy to foresee how many times your commands will be executed. In a recursion program, on the other hand, the mechanism by which commands are repeated is less explicit. As a result, it is often more difficult to foresee just how much computation will be involved in running a recursive program.

```
fibonacci[n_Integer] := fibonacci[n - 1] + fibonacci[n - 2]

fibonacci[0] = fibonacci[1] = 1
```

The Fibonacci function; another classic recursive program.

Computing the Fibonacci function is another example of a problem that can be formulated elegantly in terms of recursion. It reveals, however, one of the potential pitfalls of recursive programs, that is particularly common with simple functions of integers. The issue is that when you are calculating say `fibonacci[20]`, the value of say `fibonacci[8]` will be needed many times. In fact, you can see that in calculating `fibonacci[`$n$`]`, the values of `fibonacci[0]` and `fibonacci[1]` must be needed `fibonacci[`$n$`]` times. This means that the time needed to calculate `fibonacci[`$n$`]` by this method must grow exponentially with the size of `fibonacci[`$n$`]`.

There are several ways to avoid this problem. The clearest one to use in *Mathematica* is to store all the values of `fibonacci[`$m$`]` that you calculate.

```
fibonacci[n_Integer] := fibonacci[n] = fibonacci[n - 1] + fibonacci[n - 2]

fibonacci[0] = fibonacci[1] = 1
```

A program for the Fibonacci function that saves the values it has calculated.

If you store the values of `fibonacci` that you have already computed, then you simply have to look them up each time you need them, and you do not have to recompute them. As a result, you can compute the Fibonacci function with very few steps of recursion.

Here is the standard recursive definition of the Fibonacci function, with a piece added to print out the arguments that occur.

*In[1]:=* `fib[n_] := (Print[n]; fib[n-1] + fib[n-2])`

Here are the end conditions for the recursion.

*In[2]:=* `fib[0] = fib[1] = 1`

*Out[2]=* 1

This computes `fib[6]`, printing out the intermediate cases it uses. Many cases appear several times.

*In[3]:=* `fib[6]`

```
6
5
4
3
2
2
3
2
4
3
2
2
```

*Out[3]=* 13

This defines a Fibonacci function which remembers the values you have computed.

*In[4]:=* `mfib[n_] :=`
`(Print[n]; mfib[n] = mfib[n-1] + mfib[n-2])`

Here are the end conditions.

*In[5]:=* `mfib[0] = mfib[1] = 1`

*Out[5]=* 1

Many fewer cases are used in computing `mfib[6]`.

*In[6]:=* `mfib[6]`

```
6
5
4
3
2
```

*Out[6]=* 13

mfib saves all the intermediate values.

```
In[7]:= ?mfib
mfib

mfib/: mfib[1] = 1
mfib/: mfib[0] = 1
mfib/: mfib[2] = 2
mfib/: mfib[3] = 3
mfib/: mfib[4] = 5
mfib/: mfib[5] = 8
mfib/: mfib[6] = 13
mfib/: mfib[n_] :=
        (Print[n]; mfib[n] = mfib[n - 1] + mfib[n - 2])
```

The approach of remembering values you have calculated (sometimes called "dynamic programming") is a good one in writing programs to evaluate simple integer functions. However, if the arguments to your functions are more general symbolic expressions, the approach is usually not useful, since it is rather rare that the exact same argument occurs many times.

Specifying end conditions for recursion is often more complicated when the arguments to your functions are symbolic expressions. The general principle that *Mathematica* uses is to continue to apply whatever rules you have given until it reaches a "fixed point", and there are no more rules to apply. A recursive rule like `log[x_ y_] := log[x] + log[y]` has no explicit end condition. The rule stops being applied when none of the logarithms in your expression contain products.

Making sure that there is an appropriate end condition, whether implicit or explicit, is crucial in creating recursive programs. One common way to set up a recursive program is to compute the value of a function with some number of objects in its argument in terms of the same function with fewer objects. You can do this in *Mathematica* by giving definitions like `f[x_ y__] := h[x, f[y]]`. Particularly if you use x___, it is very important that you specify the appropriate end conditions. If you do not, *Mathematica* will apply the rules you have given to the case of zero objects forever.

Recursive programs often work by evaluating functions with a sequence of arguments along a particular "track". You specify end conditions which stop evaluation along that track at some point. Thus, for example, the `factorial` function is evaluated with a sequence of integer arguments, stopping when the end condition at 1 is reached. However, if you try to use the recursive rules for `factorial` with something other than an integer argument, you will get "off the track", and never run

into the end condition that you specified. Instead, *Mathematica* will go on trying
to evaluate `factorial` with more and more negative arguments forever. To avoid
this kind of thing, it is important to constrain the original arguments to recursive
functions so that they do indeed stay on the "track" that leads to the end conditions
that you have specified.

## ■ 4.1.4 Functional Programming

An interactive system like *Mathematica* gives you the possibility of building up
your programs in stages, rather than having to write a whole program in one go.
Some styles of programming make this kind of incremental development easier than
others.

Procedural programs, for example, are not particularly easy to build in stages.
At any given point in a procedural program, there will usually be many local variables defined, and various control structures in use. As a result, it is not particularly
easy to just "slot in" another piece of code.

One approach that works well for building up programs in stages is *functional
programming*. The basic idea is to have your program consist of many nested
functions, each one acting on results from previous ones. Instead of defining local
variables to store your intermediate results, you just pass the results immediately
to other functions.

```
exprod[n_Integer] :=
       Block[ { t, i } ,
              t = 1 ;
              For [ i = 0, i < n, i++,
                    t = ( x + i ) t
              ] ;
              t = Expand[t] ;
              Return[t] ;
       ]
```

A procedural program for expanding out a product of terms.

```
exprod[n_Integer] := Expand[ Product[x + i, {i, n}] ]
```

A functional program for expanding out a product of terms.

In simple cases, you can think of functional programs as just applying sequences
of functions to a single "current expression". All the "state" of your program is
encapsulated in the current expression. If you want to add a new piece to your program, you simply have to insert another function to apply to the current expression.

If you want to know the intermediate results of a functional program, all you need do is to print out the "current expression" at a particular stage in the execution of the program. Unlike procedural programs, functional programs have no "hidden state" associated with the values of local variables in use, or the control structures being executed.

In building up a functional program, it is important that the current expression can have a nontrivial structure. In the classic example of APL, the "current expression" is a nested list of numbers. In the pure LISP language, the current expression is an arbitrary list structure.

If you follow the functional programming style, you should rarely need to use local variables or control structures. You can often avoid control structures by using iteration functions like **Sum**. You can take a function that you have built up, and then apply a function like **Sum** to iterate over different instances of it.

When you write complicated programs in the functional programming style, you will find that you need to nest functions many levels deep. It is important to format your code so that the nesting is clear. One way to do this is simply to indent blocks at successively higher nesting levels.

## Pure Functions

When you build up a functional program, you will often need to use *Mathematica* functions like **Apply**, **Map** and **Array** which take *functions* as arguments, and apply them in various ways to the current expressions. There are various ways to specify the functions you give as arguments. If they are built-in functions, or are functions that you have explicitly defined, then you can refer to them simply by giving their names. In many cases, however, it is more convenient to be able to build up "pure functions" to which you do not have to give specific names.

You can create pure functions in *Mathematica* using **Function** (abbreviated **&**). An expression like **Function[x, x^2 + 3]** represents a pure function which takes its argument, squares it, and adds 3 to the result. This kind of *Mathematica* expression is directly analogous to the $\lambda$ expressions that are used in LISP or in formal logic.

When you write large functional programs, they usually contain many pure functions. *Mathematica* has various short-hand notations for pure functions. You can, for example, write **Function[x, x^2 + 3]** as **Function[#^2 + 3]** or even **(#^2 + 3)&**.

One goal of functional programming is completely to eliminate named variables. When you use a function like **Sum** to implement iteration, you still have to give an explicit name to the iteration variable that you use. You can do iteration without introducing any variables at all by using `Nest` and `NestList`.

| | |
|---|---|
| Here is a pure function for building up products of the form $x(x+1)(x+2)$.... | `In[1]:= prod = {1 + First[#], Apply[Times, #]} &`<br><br>`Out[1]= {1 + First[#1], Apply[Times, #1]} &` |
| This is the result from one application of `prod`. | `In[2]:= prod[{x, 1}]`<br><br>`Out[2]= {1 + x, x}` |
| This is the result of applying `prod` again. | `In[3]:= prod[%]`<br><br>`Out[3]= {2 + x, x (1 + x)}` |
| Here is a functional program that involves no explicit variables. | `In[4]:= exprod[n_Integer] :=`<br>`            Expand[ Last[ Nest[ prod, {x, 1}, n ] ] ]` |
| Here a result from running the program. | `In[5]:= exprod[3]`<br><br>`Out[5]= 2 x + 3 x$^2$ + x$^3$` |

Correction for math: `Out[5]= 2 x + 3 x^2 + x^3`

## ■ 4.1.5 Data Types

Many programming languages make you declare the "types" of all the variables or functions you use. There are several reasons for this. Historically, the main reason was that operations on integers could usually be performed much more efficiently on standard computer hardware than the corresponding operations on floating point numbers. As a result, it was important for you to specify whether a particular variable could be taken to be an integer, and therefore manipulated with more efficient operations.

Another reason to use data types is to allow you to understand and check the structure of your program more easily. If a particular variable is supposed to be of a particular type, and you try to use it in a way that is inconsistent with its type, it is worthwhile for the programming language to tell you. This is especially valuable for *compiled* languages such as C and Pascal where such errors can be recognized at the compilation stage.

The major disadvantage of requiring you to declare the types of all your variables is that any program you write must start with lines of declarations which, in and of themselves, perform no useful operations.

At a fundamental level, there are no data types in *Mathematica*. Every object you use is an *expression*, and every function can take any expression as an argument.

Of course, there may only be rules for the value of a function when its arguments have a particular form. If the arguments do not have that form, the function is left unevaluated.

*Mathematica* allows you to check the form of arguments to functions in several ways. At the simplest level, you can define a function by giving a transformation rule for a pattern that involves something like `n_Integer`. This object only *matches* expressions that are integers. As a result, you can think of the variable `n` in this particular pattern as being required to be of "type" `Integer`.

You can also use `?` and `/;` to specify constraints on the arguments to functions. You need not just say that `n` must be an integer; you can use `?` or `/;` to specify explicitly that it must be an integer, say, between `0` and `5`.

It is often convenient to create objects that act like "packets" of data. Lists are probably the most common example. The only role of the *Mathematica* function `List` is to "tag" a collection of objects. You can think of this "tag", as specifying that the collection is of "type" `List`. There are then many *Mathematica* functions which act only on this particular type of data. The functions are defined by giving transformation rules for patterns in which their arguments are lists. No transformation rules are given when their arguments are not lists, and so no values can be found in these cases.

You can easily create your own "types" of data in *Mathematica*. For example, if you want to create a type that represents an integer modulo $n$, you can just start using objects of the form `ModularInteger[`$i$`, `$n$`]`. The function `ModularInteger` itself may do nothing. But you can use it as a "tag" to indicate to other functions that the object you are using is of "type" `ModularInteger`. You can then define functions that act on `ModularInteger` objects just by specifying rules in which the arguments of functions are patterns involving `ModularInteger`. So, for example, you could give a rule for `negate[ModularInteger[i_, n_]]` to specify how to negate modular integers.

## ■ 4.1.6  Object-Oriented Programming

When you write programs that involve many different functions, it is important to have some kind of general scheme for organizing your code. One traditional approach is to break your program into different "modules", with each module containing all the functions that do a particular kind of thing.

Object-oriented programming is another approach to organizing code. The basic idea is to collect together not functions that do the same kinds of things, but rather functions that act on the same kinds of objects. Object-oriented programming is becoming very popular for organizing large software systems. In fact, the internal code of *Mathematica* itself was written using an object-oriented extension of the C programming language.

In the object-oriented approach, you introduce various types of object, and then specify "methods" for carrying out different operations on these objects. You can see how this works by thinking about writing a program to print out objects. The traditional approach would be to have one "print" function, which contains code for many different kinds of objects. The object-oriented approach is instead to associate with each type of object a function that gives the "method" for printing the object.

It is very easy to do object-oriented programming in *Mathematica*. The basic idea is to associate *Mathematica* transformation rules with the "objects" they act on, rather than with the functions they perform.

If you specify a rule for the pattern f[x_], the rule will be associated with the symbol f. However, if you give a rule for f[g[x_]], the rule can be associated either with f or with g.

| | |
|---|---|
| This defines a rule for the "function" f. | *In[1]:=* f[x_] := x^2 |

| | |
|---|---|
| This rule is also associated with f. | *In[2]:=* f[g[x_]] := -g[-x] |

| | |
|---|---|
| Here are the two rules you have given for f. | *In[3]:=* ?f |

```
f
f/: f[g[x_]] := -g[-x]

                    2
f/: f[x_] := x
```

| | |
|---|---|
| The h/:  tells *Mathematica* to associate this rule with h, rather than f. | *In[3]:=* h/: f[h[x_]] := p[x] |

| | |
|---|---|
| This shows the rule you have given for the "object" h. | *In[4]:=* ?h |

```
h
h/: f[h[x_]] := p[x]
```

You can set up different "types" of objects in *Mathematica* just by giving them different symbols as heads. Then you can associate rules or "methods" with these objects by including the appropriate /: in the definitions you make.

```
ModularInteger/: Format[ModularInteger[i_, n_]] :=
                              SequenceForm[i, " mod ", n]

ModularInteger/: Minus[ModularInteger[i_, n_]] := ModularInteger[Mod[-i, n], n]
```

Some rules for `ModularInteger` objects.

Object-oriented programming lets us organize definitions of mathematical objects in *Mathematica* in much the same way as the definitions might be organized in a mathematics textbook. You can have different "sections" of your code that give all the definitions associated with a particular kind of object. Using /:, you can keep the definitions for each new kind of object separate.

```
ModularInteger/: ModularInteger[i_, n_] + ModularInteger[j_, n_] :=
                              ModularInteger[Mod[i + j, n], n]
```

A rule for calculating sums of `ModularInteger` objects.

## Operator Overloading

One important aspect of object-oriented programming in *Mathematica* is that it lets you "overload" operators like +. You can use the familiar + notation to represent any kind of addition. But exactly what the addition does can depend on the types of objects that are involved.

Associating definitions with types of objects rather than operations not only makes your code better organized, but can also make it much more efficient. The standard addition function `Plus` is used very often in *Mathematica*. If you gave additional definitions for `Plus` itself, then *Mathematica* would have to test these definitions every time it used the function `Plus`. The presence of your definitions would then slow down every single addition operation in *Mathematica*. On the other hand, if you associate your definitions with a particular type of object, *Mathematica* tests your definitions only when that particular object occurs. *Mathematica* would therefore usually not look at your definitions when it does additions, except in the specific cases where the arguments are of a particular type.

*Mathematica* always follows the general principle of looking at more specific definitions before more general ones. One consequence of this principle is that when *Mathematica* does an operation like addition, it looks at definitions that apply to the particular types of arguments used, before it looks at general definitions for addition with arbitrary types of arguments. As a result, your definitions for addition of a particular kind of object will always be tried before the standard built-in *Mathematica* addition function is used. You can effectively "override" the built-in addition function when a particular kind of object occurs.

The same mechanism allows you to insert your own definitions to specify how a particular kind of object should be printed. *Mathematica* tries your definitions before it uses its own standard built-in print functions.

In general, you can extend the way that *Mathematica*'s built-in functions work by adding definitions for how they should act on new kinds of objects that you introduce.

Sometimes you will need to introduce both new kinds of objects and new operations. You can give definitions for how your new operations act on various kinds of objects. Then you can give a more general definition for how your new operations act on other objects, for which you have not given more specific definitions. *Mathematica* will then first try to use the definitions you have given for specific types of objects; if it finds none that apply, then it will use the more general definition you have given for the operation.

## Functions with Several Arguments

In object-oriented programming, each definition you make is associated with a particular kind of object. This approach works very well if each of your definitions involves only one kind of object. This is certainly true when you are dealing with functions like `Format` and `Minus` that take just one argument. However, things become more complicated when you need to deal with functions that take several arguments.

So long as all the arguments to a particular function are of the same type, things are still quite simple. The real problem comes when the arguments are of different types. What should *Mathematica* do when you ask to add a `ModularInteger` and a `PAdicInteger`? Should the result be a `ModularInteger` or a `PAdicInteger`? Sometimes you will just want to say that the objects you are trying to add together have incompatible types. But often, you will want to produce a definite result.

A common example that arises in many programming languages is the problem of combining different types of numbers. If you add an integer to a real number, you should get a real number as the result. If you add a rational number to an integer, you should get a rational number. You can think of the different types of numbers as being arranged in the hierarchy: `Integer` $\rightarrow$ `Rational` $\rightarrow$ `Real`. Whenever you combine two numbers, they are both converted to the type that is higher on the hierarchy. If you add an integer to a real number, the integer is converted into a real number, and then the rule for adding two real numbers is used.

When several different kinds of objects appear in a particular definition, you can associate the definition with any of the kinds of objects. *Mathematica* will check all the objects in a particular expression to see if there are definitions associated with them.

Often you will want to associate your definitions with the least common object that appears. If you do this, *Mathematica* will test the definition as infrequently as possible.

By allowing you simply to associate transformation rules with any type of object, *Mathematica* gives you a flexible mechanism for dealing with expressions involving several different kinds of objects. One can imagine, however, developing a more structured approach to dealing with such expressions. At the simplest level, one might have a hierarchy of types of objects, and demand that when two objects occur together, they are always converted to the type that appears highest on the hierarchy. In practice, however, types of mathematical objects do not form any kind of strict hierarchy. In some respects, they form a network, or directed graph, and one could imagine always converting objects to the type of their "common ancestor" in the network. But even this much more elaborate mechanism does not adequately capture actual mathematical usage. Different forms of algebraic expressions, say factored and expanded out, can be thought of as different types. In most cases, the rules for when to convert between these types are much more complicated than you can represent by a simple fixed network of type conversions.

### ■ 4.1.7  Rule-Based Programming

One of the most powerful, and unique, features of *Mathematica* is the ability to set up calculations by specifying collections of transformation rules. The basic idea is to say that whenever *Mathematica* sees an expression that matches a particular pattern, it should transform it in a particular way.

This approach allows you to write out a sequence of rules that mimic quite closely the tables of mathematical relations that you find in books.

```
diff[x_^n_., x]  := n x^(n-1)

diff[Log[x], x]  := 1/x
```

Two simple rules for differentiation.

```
diff[y_, x_] :=
      Block[ { n } ,
             If[ TrueQ [ Length[y] == 2 && y[[0]] == Power && y[[1]] == x ] ,
                 n = y[[2]] ; n x^(n-1) ,
```

```
If[ TrueQ[ y == x ] , 1 ,
    If[ TrueQ[ Length[y] == 1 && y[[0]] == Log && y[[1]] == x ] ,
        1/x ]
    ]
    ]
]
```

An ugly program that implements the simple differentiation rules using conditionals.

If you are trying to implement a sequence of mathematical rules or relations, rule-based programming is overwhelmingly the best method to use. The example above shows how complicated it is to imitate even a simple set of rules using explicit conditionals.

It is also worth realizing that the internal *Mathematica* code for transformation rules is highly optimized, and will usually work much faster than, for example, a collection of explicit conditionals.

There are many problems that are most naturally formulated in terms of transformation rules. When you analyze a problem, you will often find it better to start from scratch and build up a set of *Mathematica* rules than to take an existing procedural program, and adapt it to *Mathematica*.

A great advantage of rule-based programming is that it makes it easy for you to build up "programs" in stages. You start off with a small number of rules, and then progressively add more rules, to deal with wider and wider ranges of cases.

```
bubble[{}] := {}

bubble[{single_}] := {single}

bubble[{first_, rest__}] := bubble1[{}, {first, rest}]


bubble1[head_, {last_}] := bubble2[bubble[head], last]

bubble1[{head___}, {first_, second_, rest___}] :=
     bubble1[{head, first}, {second, rest}] /; OrderedQ[{first, second}]

bubble1[{head___}, {first_, second_, rest___}] :=
     bubble1[{head, second}, {first, rest}]


bubble2[{head___}, last_] := {head, last}
```

A bubble sort program, written entirely with transformation rules.

As a matter of principle, it is not difficult to prove that *any Mathematica* program can in fact be implemented using transformation rules alone. In practice, not all programs are best formulated like this.

One guideline is that rule-based programming is appropriate when you can set up a large number of rules, but need to use only a few of them in any particular instance. If all the rules have to be used all the time, you may do better to write a more traditional procedural or functional program.

## ■ 4.1.8  Programming by Constraint Propagation

One important feature of transformation rules in *Mathematica* is that they are *directed*. You give a pattern, and specify how it should be transformed.

For some kinds of problems, a better approach is to specify a set of *constraints* that quantities should satisfy. Making an *assignment* like x = y + 5p specifies that x should be *replaced* by y + 5p whenever it appears. On the other hand, the *equation* x == y + 5p merely represents the *constraint* that x should be equal to y + 5p.

One way to create a "program" is simply to build up a collection of constraints between different quantities. Then you can find values of quantities consistent with these constraints by explicitly using `Solve`.

```
va == vo r1 / (r1 + r2)

va == vi

g == vo / vi
```

Some equations giving constraints between various quantities.

Here are the constraint equations.

```
In[1]:= eqns = {
            va == vo r1 / (r1 + r2) ,
            va == vi ,
            g == vo / vi
        }
```

$$Out[1]= \{va == \frac{r1\ vo}{r1 + r2},\ va == vi,\ g == \frac{vo}{vi}\}$$

This solves the equations for g in terms of r1 and r2.

```
In[2]:= Solve[eqns, g, {r1, r2}]
```

$$Out[2]= \{\{g \to \frac{vo}{va}\}\}$$

This solves for `r1` in terms of `g`.          $In[3]:=$ `Solve[eqns, r1, g]`

$$Out[3]= \{\{r1 \rightarrow -(\frac{r2\ va}{va - vo})\}\}$$

If you set up a calculation using assignments, you are essentially giving a specific set of "inputs", from which you compute a specific set of "outputs". When you use equations, instead of assignments, you are giving relations with no definite "direction". It is only when you use `Solve` to find the value of a particular variable that you are imposing a definite direction.

Setting up calculations using equations, rather than assignments, is particularly convenient if you need to "work backwards" from your output, to find appropriate "inputs". You can use `Solve` equally well to find the "outputs" in terms of the "inputs", or the "inputs" in terms of the "outputs".

Building up a large collection of equations in *Mathematica* is something like setting up a spreadsheet. Each one of your variables corresponds to the value in a cell of the spreadsheet. Your equations specify the relations between values in different cells. You can use `Solve` to find the value of *any* cell in terms of others.

Whether an arrangement like this really works depends on how complicated the relations between different variables are. Essentially all traditional spreadsheet programs require all the relations to be *linear*. In this case, it is always possible to find a formula for the value of a particular variable, so long as the value is uniquely determined.

*Mathematica* allows you to give more complicated relations between variables. You can introduce non-linear dependencies by giving polynomial equations for one variable in terms of others. With equations like these, you cannot always get explicit formulae for one variable in terms of others.

### ■ 4.1.9  Logic Programming

The basic way that *Mathematica* works is to take an expression you give as input, and then generate from it a chain of expressions by applying various transformation rules. At each step, *Mathematica* tries rules in order, using the first one that applies.

Logic programming systems such as Prolog are, like *Mathematica*, based on transformation rules. But, unlike *Mathematica*, such systems emphasize applying many transformation rules in parallel. Instead of producing a single chain of expressions by applying one rule at each step, logic programming systems typically apply many different rules at each step, thereby generating many different chains of possible expressions. Whereas *Mathematica* typically "commits" to a particular rule at each step, logic programming systems try out many different possibilities, committing to a particular one only when they get the result of the whole calculation.

One of the advantages of logic programming is that you do not have to define a particular "path" for a calculation to take. The system tries out all possible paths, keeping only the ones that give desired result. While potentially flexible, this approach has the serious problem, however, that it is impossible to predict in advance even approximately how long any given calculation will take. Depending on exactly what rules have been given, the system could spend a very long time checking out many chains of transformations that do not work out.

*Mathematica* is designed to be more predictable in its operation. It simply tries the rules it knows, in a particular order, and uses the first one that applies.

There are some circumstances, however, when *Mathematica* does effectively try out several possibilities, much like a logic programming system.

The "test" in this transformation rule prints the forms of x, y and z that *Mathematica* is trying. Since the **Print** does not return **True**, *Mathematica* goes on trying other possibilities.

```
In[1]:= f[x__, y__, z__] := none /; Print[{x}, {y}, {z}]
```

This shows all the possible partitions of arguments that *Mathematica* uses in trying to use the transformation rule for f.

```
In[2]:= f[1,2,3,4,5]

{1}{2}{3, 4, 5}
{1}{2, 3}{4, 5}
{1, 2}{3}{4, 5}
{1}{2, 3, 4}{5}
{1, 2}{3, 4}{5}
{1, 2, 3}{4}{5}

Out[2]= f[1, 2, 3, 4, 5]
```

When *Mathematica* is trying to match a pattern, there are sometimes several possible ways that it can fill in blanks. If, for example, the pattern contains several __ or ___, *Mathematica* may have to try several different partitionings of function arguments. Similarly, if the pattern involves an **Orderless** function, *Mathematica* may have to try the arguments in all possible orders. Whether a particular way of filling in blanks works is sometimes determined by consistency with other parts of the pattern, but may also be determined by the results of /; conditions.

By giving many rules with different /; conditions, you can force *Mathematica* to test out several transformations. In fact, you could in principle implement a full logic programming system in *Mathematica* using large collection of rules with /; conditions.

# ■ 4.2  Correspondences with Other Languages

## ■ 4.2.1  Introduction

Knowing another programming language should make it easier for you to learn *Mathematica*. This section discusses some of the correspondences between *Mathematica* and various common programming languages. You should read the parts on programming languages you know.

There are two rather different kinds of computer languages: those that are *interpreted*, and those that are *compiled*. *Mathematica* is an example of an interpreted language. The *Mathematica* system reads your input, "interprets" it, and immediately gives you a result. The immediate feedback that this provides is what makes it possible to do calculations *interactively* with *Mathematica*.

Languages like FORTRAN are *compiled*. When you use FORTRAN, you always have to create a complete program. Before you run the program, you first have to "compile" it into machine language. It is effectively impossible to use compiled languages interactively. The traditional advantage of compiled languages has been that they can potentially produce highly efficient code that runs directly on your computer hardware, without the need for an interpreter.

There are two points to realize about interpreted languages like *Mathematica*. First, when you need to solve a problem, there are two parts that take time: formulating the problem on the computer, and actually running the program. For all but the very largest problems, today's computers make the time you spend running your program negligible compared to the time you spend writing the program. As a result, it will take you less time altogether if you use a system that makes formulating your problem as easy as possible, even if it takes longer to run the program in the end. This is one reason that interpreted languages have become very popular.

Even though simple operations may be slower in an interpreted language than a compiled one, programs you write in *Mathematica* may nevertheless end up being faster than those you write in compiled languages. The main reason is that in most problems it is primarily the algorithm you use, rather than the speed of each step, which determines how fast your whole program will run. When you write a program in *Mathematica*, you automatically get the benefit of the sophisticated algorithms that *Mathematica* contains. The speed of these algorithms often more than makes up for the overhead associated with the interpreter aspects of *Mathematica*.

In some respects, *Mathematica* actually also acts as a compiler. When you enter a program, *Mathematica* converts it to an internal form, which can more efficiently be executed. When you set up transformation rules, *Mathematica* "compiles" them into a specially encoded form, which allows them to be tested and used as quickly as possible.

## ■ 4.2.2  BASIC

One similarity between BASIC and *Mathematica* is that both are primarily interpreted languages. You type input, and they immediately process it.

*Mathematica* is, of course, a much more sophisticated language than BASIC. However, at a simple level, you can use *Mathematica* a bit like a version of BASIC that does symbolic, as well numerical, computations.

One immediate difference is that *Mathematica* prints the result from every input line you give. You do not have to include a notation like ? to get your results printed out.

| BASIC | *Mathematica* |
|---:|:---|
| $f(x)$ | $f[x]$ |
| $x * y$ | $x * y$ or $x\ y$ |
| `let` $x = y$ (assignment) | $x = y$ |
| $x = y$ (equality test) | $x == y$ |
| $x <> y$ | $x$ != $y$ |
| $x$ `and` $y$ | $x$ && $y$ |
| $x$ `or` $y$ | $x$ \|\| $y$ |
| $\text{sqr}(x)$ | $\text{Sqrt}[x]$ |
| $\text{fix}(x)$ | $\text{Floor}[x]$ |
| $\text{int}(x)$ | $\text{If}[x>=0, \text{Floor}[x], \text{Ceiling}[x]]$ |
| $\text{rnd}()$ | $\text{Random}[\ ]$ |
| $\text{abs}(x), \log(x)$ etc. | $\text{Abs}[x], \text{Log}[x]$, etc. |
| $a(i)$ (array reference) | $a[[i]]$ |
| `rem` *text* | (* *text* *) |
| `if` *predicate* `then` $t$ `else` $f$ | $\text{If}[\textit{predicate},\ t,\ f]$ |
| `for` $i = imin$ `to` $imax$ ↩ *statement* ↩ `next` $i$ | $\text{Do}[\textit{statement}, \{i,\ imin,\ imax\}]$ |

Some correspondences between BASIC and *Mathematica*.

### ■ 4.2.3  FORTRAN

*Mathematica* and FORTRAN differ in many ways. Nevertheless, some superficial features, such as the way you enter basic arithmetic operations, are quite similar.

Like any modern computer language, *Mathematica* does not care what column you enter your input in. Nor does it care how many letters are in your variable names.

| FORTRAN | *Mathematica* |
|---|---|
| $f(x)$ | $f[x]$ |
| $x*y$ | $x*y$ or $x\ y$ |
| $x**y$ | $x\wedge y$ |
| $\mathtt{sqrt}(x), \mathtt{alog}(x)$ etc. | $\mathtt{Sqrt}[x], \mathtt{Log}[x]$ etc. |
| $a(i)$ (array reference) | $a[[i]]$ |
| do *label* $i$ = *imin*, *imax* ↩ *statement* ↩ *label* continue | Do[*statement*, {$i$, *imin*, *imax*}] |
| if($i$.eq.$j$) *statement* | If[$i$ == $j$, *statement*] |

Some correspondences between FORTRAN and *Mathematica*.

You can get *Mathematica* output in FORTRAN input form using the *Mathematica* function `FortranForm`.

## ■ 4.2.4   C

The procedural programming aspects of *Mathematica* are quite similar to C.

The following operators work essentially the same in *Mathematica* as in C: ! (Not), ++ (Increment and PreIncrement), -- (Decrement and PreDecrement), < (Less), etc., == (Equal), != (Unequal), && (And), || (Or), = (Set), += (AddTo), -= (SubtractFrom), *= (TimesBy), /= (DivideBy). There are no bitwise operators built in to *Mathematica*.

| C | *Mathematica* |
|---|---|
| $f(x)$ | $f[x]$ |
| $x$ % $y$ | Mod[$x$, $y$] |
| floor($x$), ceil($x$), sqrt($x$), etc. | Floor[$x$], Ceiling[$x$], Sqrt[$x$], etc. |
| a[$i$] | a[[$i$]] |
| /* *text* */ | (* *text* *) |
| if(*predicate*) $t$ else $f$ | If[*predicate*, $t$, $f$] |
| switch(*value*) { case $a$: *va* ; case $b$: *vb* ; default: *vdef* ; } | Switch[$a$, *va*, $b$, *vb*, _, *vdef*] |
| while(*predicate*) *statement* | While[*predicate*, *statement*] |
| for(*start*; *test*; *increment*) *body* | For[*start*, *test*, *increment*, *body*] |
| continue | Continue[ ] |
| break | Break[ ] |
| *identifier*: *statement* | Label[*identifier*]; *statement* |
| return *result* | Return[*result*] |

Some correspondences between C and *Mathematica*.

The control structures in *Mathematica* are quite similar to those in C. One important difference is that in *Mathematica* there is no distinction between expressions and statements; every object returns a value. As a result, semicolons in *Mathematica* play the role of both semicolons and commas in C. Commas in *Mathematica* are used only as separators for function arguments.

This has the consequence that in the specification of a For loop, the roles of ; and , in *Mathematica* and C are *reversed*. The C code
for(i=0, j=1; i<10; i++) *statement*; becomes the *Mathematica* code
For[ i=0; j=1, i<10, i++, *statement* ]. Note that a null condition in a *Mathematica* For is interpreted as *false*, whereas in C a null condition is interpreted as *true*.

You can set up blocks of code with their own local variables in *Mathematica* much as you do in C. However, since every *Mathematica* variable can represent any expression, you do not have to declare the "types" of variables in *Mathematica*.

`Block[{x, y, z = `$z_0$`}, `*code*`]` represents a block of code with local variables $x$, $y$ and $z$. In this case, the variable $z$ is set to have initial value $z_0$. Notice that in *Mathematica* there is a *comma* after the list that specifies local variables, whereas in C variable declarations end with semicolons.

Another difference between C and *Mathematica* concerns Boolean tests. True and false are represented in *Mathematica* by the symbols `True` and `False`, rather than `1` and `0`. In addition, symbolic expressions like `x==y` may have undetermined truth value; as a result, functions like `If` have an extra element that specifies what to do in this case.

Lists in *Mathematica* are largely analogous to arrays in C. One important difference is that *Mathematica* arrays have index origin 1, rather than 0.

You can output *Mathematica* expressions and code in C format using the function `CForm[`*expr*`]`.

## ■ 4.2.5 Pascal

| Pascal | *Mathematica* |
|---:|:---|
| $f(x)$ | `f[x]` |
| $x$ `:=` $y$ | $x$ `=` $y$ |
| $x$ `=` $y$ | $x$ `==` $y$ |
| $x$ `<>` $y$ | $x$ `!=` $y$ |
| $x$ `and` $y$ | $x$ `&&` $y$ |
| $x$ `or` $y$ | $x$ `||` $y$ |
| `trunc(`$x$`)` | `Floor[`$x$`]` |
| `mod(`$x$`, `$y$`)`, `div(`$x$`, `$y$`)` | `Mod[`$x$`, `$y$`]`, `Quotient[`$x$`, `$y$`]` |
| `sqrt(`$x$`)`, `ln(`$x$`)`, etc. | `Sqrt[`$x$`]`, `Log[`$x$`]`, etc. |
| `a[`$i$`]` | `a[[`$i$`]]` |
| `for` $i$`:=`*imin* `to` *imax* `do` *statement* | |
| | `Do[`*statement*`, {`$i$`, `*imin*`, `*imax*`}]` |

Some correspondences between Pascal and *Mathematica*.

# ■ 4.2.6  APL

You can use *Mathematica* very much like APL. You can represent APL arrays as nested *Mathematica* lists. Most mathematical operations in *Mathematica*, as in APL, can operate on arrays of elements as well as on single elements.

| *APL operation* | *related Mathematica function* |
|---:|:---|
| subscripting $a[i]$ | `a[[i]]` ($i$ can be a list) |
| index ($\iota$) | `Range` |
| shape ($\rho$) | `Dimensions` |
| ravel ($,$) | `Flatten` |
| reshape ($\rho$) | `Partition` |
| catenate ($,$) | `Join` |
| membership ($\epsilon$) | `MemberQ` |
| take ($\uparrow$) and drop ($\downarrow$) | `Take` and `Drop` |
| reverse and rotate | `Reverse` and `RotateLeft` |
| transpose (monadic and dyadic) | `Transpose` |
| grade up | roughly like `Sort` |
| encode and decode | roughly like `^^` and `BaseForm` |
| compress ($/$) | `Select` |
| outer product ($\circ.f$) | `Outer[f, ...]` |
| inner product ($f.g$) | `Inner[g, ..., f]` |
| reduce ($f/$) | `Apply[f, ...]` |

Some correspondences between APL and *Mathematica*.

The symbolic nature of *Mathematica* allows you to give "operations" or "functions" as arguments to other functions. In this way, you can effectively create composite operators. Thus, for example, the APL composite operator `+.`$\times$ becomes `Inner[Times, ` $a$`, ` $b$`, Plus]` in *Mathematica*.

# ■ 4.2.7  LISP

The main similarity between *Mathematica* and LISP is that both are fundamentally symbolic languages. *Mathematica* is, however, in most respects a much higher level language than LISP.

*Mathematica* expressions are in many respects like LISP lists. In *Mathematica*, however, expressions are the lowest-level objects accessible to the user. LISP allows you to go below lists, and access the binary trees from which they are built. *Mathematica* hides such implementation details (in fact, *Mathematica* expressions are effectively implemented as vectors). In LISP, there are also functions like `eq`, `rplaca` and `copy` which allow you to test and modify the actual representations of objects in computer memory. *Mathematica* has no such low-level functions. All manipulation of *Mathematica* expressions is done without specific reference to their actual representation and location in computer memory. In this way, *Mathematica* can exert more control over internal details. For example, the fact that *Mathematica* does not allow user-level destructive functions means that meaningful circular internal data structures cannot be created, so that *Mathematica* can safely use more efficient reference count memory management schemes.

One fundamental difference between LISP and *Mathematica* is the way in which evaluation is done. LISP is essentially a one-step evaluation system; *Mathematica* is an infinite evaluation system. In both systems, you can define values for symbols and functions. In LISP, each evaluation (or call to `eval`) replaces any symbol or function in an expression by the value you have defined, but does not go on to perform any further evaluation on this value. In *Mathematica*, on the other hand, the evaluation goes on until the results you get no longer change.

In LISP, every object that you use must have a value defined, unless it is explicitly "quoted". In *Mathematica*, objects are simply left unevaluated if no values are known for them.

The *Mathematica* object `Function` is a direct analog of `lambda` in LISP. In *Mathematica*, as in LISP, you can define pure functions which can be applied to expressions. For most purposes, however, it is better to define functions in *Mathematica* using transformation rules, rather than by directly creating pure functions. There are some differences between the way function arguments are treated in *Mathematica* and in LISP. When you make a call to a function in *Mathematica*, all occurrences of the function arguments that appear in the body of the function are *replaced* by the values that you give for the arguments. In LISP, on the other hand, the values of function arguments are effectively inserted by making temporary assignments, and then evaluating the body of the function.

## ■ 4.2.8 PostScript

*Mathematica* generates all its graphics output in PostScript. The two-dimensional graphics primitives that *Mathematica* uses are quite similar to those in PostScript.

| PostScript | *Mathematica* |
|---|---|
| gsave *primitives* grestore | { *primitives* } |
| $x$ $y$ moveto 0 0 rlineto stroke | Point[{$x$, $y$}] |
| $x_1$ $y_1$ moveto $x_2$ $y_2$ lineto ... stroke | |
| | Line[{{$x_1$, $y_1$}, {$x_2$, $y_2$}, ...}] |
| newpath $x_1$ $y_1$ moveto $x_2$ $y_2$ moveto ... fill | |
| | Polygon[{{$x_1$, $y_1$}, {$x_2$, $y_2$}, ...}] |
| ... image | CellArray[{{...}, ...}] |
| $dx$ setlinewidth | Thickness[$dx$] |
| *level* setgray | GrayLevel[*level*] |
| $r$ $g$ $b$ setrgbcolor | RGBColor[$r$, $g$, $b$] |
| ... setdash | Dashing[{...}] |

Some correspondences between PostScript and *Mathematica* Graphics primitives.

The choice of coordinate system in *Mathematica* is specified by the option PlotRange. It is often based on the actual objects you are plotting.

Most *Mathematica* graphics is specified at a much higher level than PostScript. So, for example, the option Axes determines whether a complete set of axes should be drawn. In addition, when you plot a function using Plot, *Mathematica* chooses sample points using an adaptive algorithm, so it does not have to resort to splines to get a smooth curve. (ContourPlot nevertheless does use Bézier curves for contour lines.)

*Mathematica* primitives such as Thickness and Dashing specify distances as fractions of the width of the whole plot. The *Mathematica* primitive PointSize[*size*] specifies the diameter of a single dot or point in these units.

# Appendix A:
# *Some Examples of Mathematica Packages*

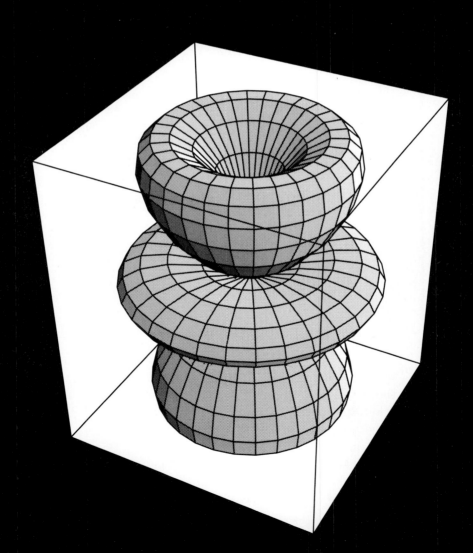

One of the most important things about *Mathematica* is that it is highly extensible. As well as using the functions that are already built into *Mathematica*, you can define your own functions, to customize *Mathematica* to your particular needs.

This Appendix contains examples from packages that give various kinds of *Mathematica* definitions. Most of the examples are just fragments of packages, but are nevertheless chosen to be representative of the style used in the whole packages.

The examples are "real", in the sense that they come from actual *Mathematica* packages distributed with many versions of *Mathematica*.

The topics for the packages in this Appendix have been chosen to be of comparatively widespread applicability. Many actual *Mathematica* packages will address much more specific application areas.

One important point about the packages in this Appendix is that they are all plain *Mathematica* input files, not "notebooks". Notebooks can include not only *Mathematica* definitions, but also explanatory text and other material, as discussed briefly in Section 1.3. The details of writing notebooks for *Mathematica* on various computers will be described elsewhere.

**About the illustration overleaf:**

This is a parametric plot of the spherical harmonic $Y_3^1(\theta, \phi)$. The spherical harmonic is represented in *Mathematica* by the function `SphericalHarmonicY[3, 1, theta, phi]`. With this function assigned as the value of `y`, the plot was generated by the command
`ParametricPlot3D[`*list*`,` *thetarange*`,` *phirange*`]`, where *list* is
`{Abs[y] Sin[theta] Cos[phi], Abs[y] Sin[theta] Sin[phi], Abs[y] Cos[theta]}`,
*thetarange* is `{theta, Pi/30, Pi-Pi/30, Pi/30}` and *phirange* is `{phi, 0, 2Pi, Pi/15}`. The function `ParametricPlot3D` is defined in the package `ParametricPlot.m`.

# ■ A.1 Defining Mathematical Functions

## ■ A.1.1 Some Combinatorial Functions

Probably the simplest kinds of *Mathematica* packages are ones that define simple mathematical functions in terms of mathematical functions that are built into *Mathematica*.

As a first example, we consider the definition of Catalan numbers. These arise, for example, in counting the number of possible tree structures of a certain size. Here is the definition of Catalan numbers given in the package CombinatorialFunctions.m. Following standard *Mathematica* conventions, the function that gives Catalan numbers is named `CatalanNumber`.

```
CatalanNumber::usage = "CatalanNumber[n] gives the nth Catalan number."

CatalanNumber[n_Integer] := Binomial[2n, n]/(n + 1)
```

The definition of Catalan numbers.

Notice that in addition to the actual *Mathematica* definition for `CatalanNumber`, the package gives a `usage` message. This is retrieved when you ask for information using ? in *Mathematica*.

```
Subfactorial::usage =
      "Subfactorial[n] gives the number of permutations of n objects
      which leave no object fixed."

Subfactorial[n_Integer?Positive] := n! Block[{k}, Sum[(-1)^k/k!, {k, 0, n}]]
```

The subfactorial function.

The `Subfactorial` function is defined using `Sum`. Notice that the dummy variable `k` in the sum is specified as being local to a block. This ensures that the variable used in this definition will not get confused with other variables named `k`.

```
Fibonacci::usage = "Fibonacci[n] gives the nth Fibonacci number."

Fibonacci[n_Integer?Positive] := Fibonacci[n] = Fibonacci[n-1] + Fibonacci[n-2]

Fibonacci[0] = Fibonacci[1] = 1
```

The Fibonacci numbers.

Fibonacci numbers are defined here using recursion. Notice that the argument to

`Fibonacci` is specified to be positive. It is important to put in constraints like this to make that recursive procedure terminate properly. Notice also that `Fibonacci` stores each value that it generates. This is a common method for optimizing the evaluation of recursive functions.

| | |
|---|---|
| This reads in the package `CombinatorialFunctions.m`. This package may or not exist on your particular computer system. | `In[1]:= <<CombinatorialFunctions.m` |
| Typing ? gives you the usage message for a particular object. | `In[2]:= ?CatalanNumber`<br>`CatalanNumber[n] gives the nth Catalan number.` |
| Here is the 20$^{\text{th}}$ Catalan number. | `In[2]:= CatalanNumber[20]`<br>`Out[2]= 6564120420` |

The definitions give above are in fact fragments from *Mathematica* packages. A complete *Mathematica* package contains in addition context specifications. Some packages also write protect the objects they define.

```
BeginPackage["Hofstadter`"]

Hofstadter::usage = "Hoftstadter[n] gives Hoftstadter's function."

(* Recursive definition of the Hofstader function *)

Hofstadter[n_Integer?Positive] :=
        Hofstadter[n] =
                Hofstadter[n - Hofstadter[n-1]] + Hofstadter[n - Hofstadter[n-2]]

Hofstadter[1] = Hofstadter[2] = 1

EndPackage[ ]
```

A complete package for the Hofstadter function.

## ■ A.1.2  Clebsch-Gordan Coefficients

Clebsch-Gordan coefficients arise in various group-theoretical calculations, particularly those involving addition of angular momenta in quantum mechanics.

```
BeginPackage["Clebsch`"]

Clebsch::usage =
```

```
        "Clebsch[{j1,m1},{j2,m2},{j,m}] gives the Clebsch-Gordan coefficient
        for the addition of angular momenta."

Begin["Clebsch`private`"]

C1[j_,j1_,j2_,m1_,m2_] :=
        Block[{k},
            Sum[ (-1)^k
            (k! (j1+j2-j-k)! (j1-m1-k)! (j2+m2-k)! (j-j2+m1+k)! (j-j1-m2+k)!)^-1,
                {k, Max[0,j2-j-m1,j1-j+m2], Min[j1+j2-j,j1-m1,j2+m2]} ]
        ]

C2[j_,j1_,j2_] := (-j+j1+j2)! (j-j1+j2)! (j+j1-j2)! (1+2j) / (1+j+j1+j2)!

C3[j_,j1_,j2_,m_,m1_,m2_] := (j-m)! (j+m)! (j1-m1)! (j1+m1)! (j2-m2)! (j2+m2)!

Clebsch[ {j1_, m1_}, {j2_, m2_}, {j_, m_} ] :=
                If[ m!=m1+m2 , 0 ,
                    Block[ {t},
                        t = C1[j,j1,j2,m1,m2] ;
                        Sign[t] Sqrt[t^2 C2[j,j1,j2] C3[j,j1,j2,m,m1,m2]]
                    ]
                ]

End[ ]

EndPackage[ ]
```

Definitions of Clebsch-Gordan coefficients.

Notice the use of a private context inside the main `Clebsch`` context, for defining subsidiary functions used by the main `Clebsch` function.

| | |
|---|---|
| Read in the Clebsch-Gordan coefficient package. | `In[1]:= <<Clebsch.m` |
| This evaluates a particular Clebsch-Gordan coefficient. | `In[2]:= Clebsch[{2, 0}, {2, 0}, {2, 0}]` |

$$Out[2]= -(\frac{Sqrt[2]}{Sqrt[7]})$$

## ■ A.1.3  Statistics

Here is part of a package that evaluates various simple statistical quantities for lists of numbers.

```
BeginPackage["Statistics`"]

Mean[list_List] := Apply[Plus, list] / Length[list]

GeometricMean[list_List] := Apply[Times, list]^(1/Length[list])

Median[list_List] :=
        Block[{sl,len},
        len = Length[list];
        sl = Sort[list];
        If[OddQ[Length[sl]],
                sl[[len/2]],
                (sl[[len/2]] + sl[[len/2+1]])/2 ]
        ]

Variance[list_List] := Mean[ (list - Mean[list])^2 ]

`Range[list_List] := Apply[Max, list] - Apply[Min, list]
(* `Range hides System`Range *)

EndPackage[ ]
```

Simple statistics.

| | |
|---|---|
| Read in the simple statistics package. | *In[1]:=* **<<Statistics.m** |
| Generate a list of ten pseudorandom numbers. | *In[2]:=* **d = Table[Random[ ], {10}]**<br>*Out[2]=* {0.353297, 0.0205034, 0.117374, 0.546051,<br>          0.417205, 0.704711, 0.559345, 0.247266, 0.133088,<br>          0.49174} |
| Here is the mean of the list of numbers. | *In[3]:=* **Mean[d]**<br>*Out[3]=* 0.359058 |
| This evaluates the range of the list of numbers. | *In[4]:=* **Range[d]**<br>*Out[4]=* 0.684207 |
| The function **Range** in the statistics package hides the built-in **Range** function. This is how you access the built-in **Range** function. | *In[5]:=* **System`Range[4]**<br>*Out[5]=* {1, 2, 3, 4} |

# ■ A.2  Implementing Mathematical Algorithms

## ■ A.2.1  Runge-Kutta Methods

Runge-Kutta methods are used to find numerical approximations to the solutions of ordinary differential equations. The version we give here can be used to solve first-order equations of the form $y' = f(x, y)$.     An important feature of the *Mathematica* implementation of Runge-Kutta methods is that you can give the function $f(x, y)$ in an explicit symbolic form.

```
RungeKutta::usage = "RungeKutta[f, {x, y}, {x0, y0}, h, ntot] gives
        ntot {x, y} pairs obtained by integrating the differential
        equation y'==f by the fourth order Runge-Kutta method."

RungeKutta[f_, {x_, y_}, {x0_, y0_}, h_, ntot_] :=
        NestList[RKStep[f, {x, y}, #, h]&, {x0, y0}, ntot]

RKStep[f_, {x_, y_}, {xn_, yn_}, h_] :=
        Block[{k1, k2, k3, k4},
        k1 = h f /. {x->xn, y->yn} ;
        k2 = h f /. {x->xn+h/3, y->yn+k1/3} ;
        k3 = h f /. {x->xn+2h/3, y->yn-k1/3+k2} ;
        k4 = h f /. {x->xn+h, y->yn+k1-k2+k3} ;
        { xn + h, yn + (k1 + 3k2 + 3k3 + k4)/8 }
        ]
```

Runge-Kutta methods.

The Runge-Kutta method works by taking a sequence of steps. The function `RKStep` does one step. `RungeKutta` itself applies `RKStep` many times using the functional iteration operation `NestList`.

Read in the package that implements Runge-Kutta methods.

```
In[1]:= <<RungeKutta.m
```

This finds a numerical approximation to the solution of the equation $y' = 2y$. As expected, the result approximates an exponential in $x$

```
In[2]:= RungeKutta[2 y, {x, y}, {0, 1}, .1, 5]
Out[2]= {{0, 1}, {0.1, 1.2214}, {0.2, 1.49182},
        {0.3, 1.82211}, {0.4, 2.22552}, {0.5, 2.71825}}
```

This generates a numerical approximation to the solution of the equation $y' = 1 - xy^2$, with $y(0) = 0$.

```
In[3]:= s = RungeKutta[1 - x y^2, {x, y}, {0, 0}, .1, 40];
```

Here is a plot of the solution.          $In[4]:=$ `ListPlot[%, PlotJoined->True]`

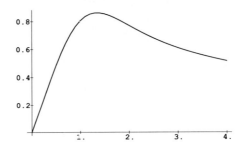

## ■ A.2.2  Continued Fractions

In number theory and dynamical systems theory it is often convenient to represent numbers as "continued fractions", of the form $\dfrac{1}{a_1+\frac{1}{a_2+\frac{1}{a_3+...}}}$. The following *Mathematica* package takes a number, and generates a list of the quantities $a_i$ in the continued fraction expansion. To show what kind of object the resulting list is, the package tags it with the head `ContinuedFractionForm`.

```
ContinuedFraction[x_Real, n_Integer?Positive] :=
      Block[ {
              xi, xp = x, r = {}
              },
              Do[
                      xi = Floor[xp] ;
                      AppendTo[r, xi] ;
                      xp = 1 / (xp - xi) ,
              {n} ] ;
              Return [ ContinuedFractionForm[r] ]
      ]


ContinuedFractionForm/: Normal[ContinuedFractionForm[a_List]] :=
      Block[ {
              x, ar = Reverse[a]
              },

              x = ar[[1]] ;
              Do [ x = 1/x + ar[[i]], {i, 2, Length[ar]} ] ;
              Return [ x ]
      ]
```

Continued fractions.

Read in the continued fractions package.

*In[1]:=* **<<ContinuedFractions.m**

Here is $\sqrt{7}$ to 40 decimal places.

*In[2]:=* **N[Sqrt[7], 40]**

*Out[2]=* 2.645751311064590590501615753639260425 71

This finds the first twenty continued fraction coefficients. Notice that the sequence becomes periodic, as it does for any irrational root of a quadratic equation with rational coefficients.

*In[3]:=* **ContinuedFraction[%, 20]**

*Out[3]=* ContinuedFractionForm[{2, 1, 1, 1, 4, 1, 1, 1, 4, 1, 1, 1, 4, 1, 1, 1, 4, 1, 1, 1}]

The package also specifies that when **Normal** is applied to a **ContinuedFractionForm**, it is converted to an ordinary number. This is a rational number approximation to $\sqrt{7}$.

*In[4]:=* **Normal[%]**

*Out[4]=* $\dfrac{514088}{194307}$

It is very close to $\sqrt{7}$.

*In[5]:=* **N[%, 20]**

*Out[5]=* 2.6457513110695960516

## ■ A.2.3  Permutations

You can represent a permutation in *Mathematica* as a list of integers. The built-in function **Permutations** gives all possible permutations of lists of objects.

```
PermutationQ::usage = "PermutationQ[e] yields True if e represents a permutation."

PermutationQ[e_] := TrueQ[ Sort[e] == Range[Length[e]] ]

RandomPermutation::usage =
      "RandomPermutation[n] gives a random permutation of n elements."

RandomPermutation[n_Integer?Positive] :=
      Block[{t, i},
            t = Table[{Random[], i}, {n}] ;
            t = Sort[t];
            Map[ Last, t ]
      ]
```

Functions for checking permutations, and generating random ones.

Read in the permutations package.

*In[1]:=* **<<Permutations.m**

The number 2 appears twice, so this is not considered a legal permutation.

```
In[2]:= PermutationQ[{3, 1, 2, 2}]
Out[2]= False
```

Here is a random permutation of eight elements.

```
In[3]:= RandomPermutation[8]
Out[3]= {2, 3, 8, 1, 5, 4, 7, 6}
```

In many algorithms, it is necessary to write permutations as compositions of special cyclic permutations. Here are some functions that convert into and out of this form.

```
ToCycles::usage =
      "ToCycles[p] writes the permutation p as a list of cyclic permutations."

ToCycles[perm_?PermutationQ] :=
      Block[{a, t, n, l, i, len},
              len = Length[perm];
              a = {} ;
              t = Table[True, {len}];
              For[i=1, i<=len, i++,
                      If[t[[i]],
                              For[n = perm[[i]]; l = {},
                                      t[[n]],
                                      n = perm[[n]],
                                      t[[n]] = False; AppendTo[l, n]
                              ];
                              AppendTo[a, l]
                      ]
              ] ;
              Return[a]
      ]

FromCycles::usage =
      "FromCycles[{p1,p2,..}] gives the permutation that corresponds to
      a list of cycles."

FromCycles[cyc_List] :=
      Block[{list},
      Scan[ FromCycles0[list, #] &, cyc, 1] ;
      Array[list, Length[Flatten[cyc]]]
      ]

FromCycles0[list_, c_] :=
      Block[{c1, i},
              c1 = RotateRight[c];
              Table[ list[ c1[[i]] ] = c[[i]], {i, Length[c]} ]
```

```
        ]
```

Cycle forms of permutations.

| | |
|---|---|
| Here is a random permutation of ten elements. | *In[4]:=* `RandomPermutation[10]`<br>*Out[4]=* {7, 1, 3, 8, 2, 9, 4, 10, 5, 6} |
| Here is the permutation written as a composition of cyclic permutations. | *In[5]:=* `ToCycles[%]`<br>*Out[5]=* {{7, 4, 8, 10, 6, 9, 5, 2, 1}, {3}} |
| This converts back from the cycle representation. | *In[6]:=* `FromCycles[%]`<br>*Out[6]=* {7, 1, 3, 8, 2, 9, 4, 10, 5, 6} |

## ■ A.2.4  Counting Roots of Polynomials

The packages we have discussed so far implement algorithms that basically involve only numbers or lists of numbers. You can also write *Mathematica* programs that implement symbolic and algebraic algorithms.

Here is an example of a package that implements Sturm's method for counting the real roots of a polynomial in an interval.

```
CountRoots::usage =
        "CountRoots[f,{x,a,b}] computes the number of zeroes of the real polynomial
        f on the interval a <= x <= b.  The endpoints may be infinite."

OmitZeroes[m_] := Select[m, #!=0&]

CountChanges[m_] := Block[{i,len=Length[m],num=0} ,
        Do[ If[m[[i]] != m[[i+1]], num++], {i,len-1} ];
        num]

CountSignChanges[m_] := CountChanges[OmitZeroes[Sign[m]]]

SturmSequence[f_,g_,x_] := Block[ { seq = {f}, p=f, q=g} ,
        While[ If[q!=0,True,False,True] ,
                AppendTo[seq,q];
                {p,q} = {q,Expand[-PolynomialRemainder[p,q,x]]};
                ];
        seq
        ]

SturmSequence[f_,x_] := SturmSequence[f,D[f,x],x]
```

```
CountRoots[f_,{x_,a_,b_}] := Block[{seq = SturmSequence[f,x]} ,
        CountSignChanges[ seq/.x->a ]
        - CountSignChanges[ seq/.x->b ]]
```

Counting roots of polynomials.

| | |
|---|---|
| Read in the package. | *In[1]:=* <<CountRoots.m |
| Here is a polynomial. | *In[2]:=* poly := x^5 - 3x^3 + 2 |
| This shows that the polynomial has three real roots in the range -2 to 2. | *In[3]:=* Plot[poly, {x, -2, 2}] |

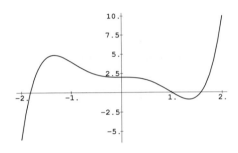

| | |
|---|---|
| You can check this result using CountRoots. | *In[4]:=* CountRoots[poly, {x, -2, 2}] |
| | *Out[4]=* 3 |

## ■ A.2.5  Recognizing Algebraic Numbers

If you are told that a particular number is the square root of an integer, then given a sufficiently accurate numerical approximation, you can easily recognize what integer the number is the square root of. It is possible to generalize this kind of "number recognizing" to work for numbers that appear as the roots of arbitrary polynomial equations. Here is a package that finds the minimal polynomial equation for which a particular number is a good approximation to a solution.

The heart of the package is a single call to the lattice reduction function LatticeReduce. Wrapped around this call are a variety of other functions, which prepare the input, and process the output. Notice the use of indentation to make a sequence of deeply-nested functions slightly easier to read.

```
Recognize::usage = "Recognize[x,n,t] finds a polynomial cf degree at
              most n in the variable t which is satisfied by the number x."

Recognize[x_Real,n_Integer?Positive,t_] :=
     Block[ {i},
     Table[t^i, {i, 0, n}] .
             Drop[ LatticeReduce[
                             Transpose[
                                  Append[
                                       IdentityMatrix[n+1],
                                         Round[
                                           Table[x^i, {i, 0, n}]
                                             10^Precision[x]
                                         ]
                                  ]
                             ]
                       ] [[1]],
                       -1
                 ]
           ]
```

Recognizing algebraic numbers.

| | |
|---|---|
| Read in the number recognizer. | `In[1]:= <<Recognize.m` |
| This gives the numerical value of $\sqrt{2} + \sqrt{5}$ to 30 decimal places. | `In[2]:= N[Sqrt[2] + Sqrt[5], 30]`<br>`Out[2]= 3.65028153987288474521086239294` |
| Recognize finds that this number is a root of a simple fourth-degree polynomial. | `In[3]:= Recognize[%, 4, x]`<br>`Out[3]= 9 - 14 x^2 + x^4` |
| NRoots verifies the result. | `In[4]:= NRoots[%==0, x]`<br>`Out[4]= x == -3.65028 || x == -0.821854 ||`<br>`           x == 0.821854 || x == 3.65028` |

## ■ A.2.6  Symbolic Summation

As a final example of the implementation of mathematical algorithms in *Mathematica*, we consider a somewhat more complicated example: Gosper's algorithm for finding closed-form results for symbolic sums.

This algorithm can take sums whose successive terms have ratios which are rational functions, and can find explicit formulae for sums in terms of rational and other functions. The algorithm is in some respects analogous to the Risch algorithm that *Mathematica* uses for indefinite integration.

```
Gosper::usage =
        "Gosper[term, {var, n0, n1}] finds the value of
        Sum[term, {var, n0, n1}] for symbolic n0, n1."

(* linearity *)
Gosper[an_ + bn_, {var_, n0_, n1_, inc_}] :=
        Gosper[an, {var, n0, n1, inc}] + Gosper[bn, {var, n0, n1, inc}]

(* default increment *)
Gosper[an_, {var_, n0_, n1_}] := Gosper[an, {var, n0, n1, 1}]

(* default startvalue *)
Gosper[an_, {var_, n1_}] := Gosper[an, {var, 1, n1, 1}]

(* trivial cases *)
Gosper[an_, {var_, n0_, n1_, 1}] := an (n1 - n0 + 1) /; FreeQ[an, var]
Gosper[an_, {var_, n0_, n0_, _}] := an /. var -> n0

Begin["Gosper`private`"]

Subvar[expr_, old_Symbol, new_] := expr /. old -> new

Gosper[an_, {var_, n0_, n1_, 1}] :=
Block[{pn, qn, rn, an1, rnj, jj, res, resn, resp, rat, ann, qrpos, ii,
        qrneg, dqrpos, dqrneg, dk, dp, fn, sn, k0, fn, eq, i, s0, s1},
        ann = an;
        an1 = Subvar[ann, var, var-1];
        rat = ann/an1; (* user-defined rules take effect here *)
        rat = Together[rat];
        qn = Numerator[rat];
        rn = Denominator[rat];
        If[!PolynomialQ[qn, var] || !PolynomialQ[rn, var],
                (* not a rational function *)
                Return[Sum[an, {var, n0, n1, 1}]]];
        pn = 1;
        rnj = Expand[Subvar[rn, var, var+jj]];
        res = Resultant[qn, rnj, var];
        res = FactorList[res];
        res = Map[#[[1]]&, res];
        (* find factors linear in jj *)
        resp = Cases[res, jj+_Integer];
        resn = Cases[res, -jj+n_Integer];
```

```
    res = Join[-(resp - jj), resn + jj];
    res = Select[res, Positive];
    (* adjust for positive integer zeros *)
    For[resn = Length[res],resn > 0, resn--, Block[{gn, gnj},
            gn = GCD[qn, Expand[Subvar[rn, var, var+res[[resn]]]], var];
            qn = Cancel[qn/gn];
            gnj = gn;
            For[i = 1, i <= res[[resn]], i++,
                    pn = Expand[pn gnj];
                    gnj = Expand[Subvar[gn, var, var-i]]
            ];
            rn = Cancel[rn/gnj]]
    ];
    (* find degree bound *)
    qn = Expand[Subvar[qn, var, var+1]];
    dp = Exponent[pn, var];
    qrpos = Expand[qn+rn]; dqrpos = Exponent[qrpos, var];
    qrneg = Expand[qn-rn]; dqrneg = Exponent[qrneg, var];
    If[dqrpos <= dqrneg, dk = dp - dqrneg,
            If[dqrneg < dqrpos - 1 || dqrneg == -1, dk = dp - dqrpos + 1,
            (* else *)
                k0 = - Cancel[Coefficient[qrneg, var^dqrneg]/
                    Coefficient[qrpos, var^dqrpos]];
                dk = If[IntegerQ[k0], Max[k0, dp - dqrpos + 1],
                            dp - dqrpos + 1]
            ]
    ];
    If[dk >= 0, (* solution possible *)
            fn = Sum[f[ii] var^ii, {ii, 0, dk}];
            eq = Expand[pn - qn fn + rn Subvar[fn, var, var-1]];
            eq = CoefficientList[eq, var];
            eq = Solve[Thread[eq == 0], Array[f, dk+1, 0]];
            If[Length[eq] > 0,
                fn = fn /. eq[[1]];
                fn = fn /. f[0] -> 0; (* summation constant *)
                sn = Cancel[qn/pn fn] ann;
                (* crude test for infinity *)
                s1 = sn /. var -> n1;
                s0 = (sn /. var -> n0) - (ann /. var -> n0);
                Return[s1 - s0],
            (* else fail *)
                Return[Sum[an, {var, n0, n1, 1}]]
            ],
    (* else fail *)
            Return[Sum[an, {var, n0, n1, 1}]]
    ]
]
```

```
End[]
```

Gosper's summation algorithm.

This reads in the symbolic summation package.

$In[1]:=$ `<<Gosper.m`

Here is the result for $\sum_{k=1}^{n} k^2(1+k)$.

$In[2]:=$ `Gosper[k^2 (1+k), {k, 1, n}]`

$$Out[2]= \frac{n\ (1+n)\ (2+7\ n+3\ n^2)}{12}$$

# ■ A.3  Mathematical Operations and Objects

## ■ A.3.1  Vector Analysis

Vector analysis is used in many areas of applied mathematics. This section gives part of a simple package for doing vector analysis in three dimensions, with some specific coordinate systems.

```
Coordinates[Cartesian] ^:= {x, y, z}
ScaleFactors[Cartesian] ^:= {1, 1, 1}

Coordinates[Cylindrical] ^:= {r, phi, z}
ScaleFactors[Cylindrical] ^:= {1, r, 1}

Coordinates[Spherical] ^:= {r, theta, phi}
ScaleFactors[Spherical] ^:= {1, r, r Sin[theta]}

VolumeElement[system_:$CoordinateSystem] :=
        Block[{i, s=ScaleFactors[system], c=Coordinates[system]},
        Product[s[[i]] Dt[c[[i]]], {i, 3}]
        ]

Grad[f_, system_:$CoordinateSystem] :=
        Block[{i, s=ScaleFactors[system], c=Coordinates[system]},
        Table[ D[ f, c[[i]] ] / s[[i]], {i, 3}]
        ]

Div[f_?VectorQ, system_:$CoordinateSystem] :=
        Block[{i, s=ScaleFactors[system], c=Coordinates[system], v},
        v = Product[s[[i]], {i, 3}] ;
        Sum[ D[f[[i]] v/s[[i]], c[[i]]], {i, 3} ] / v
        ]
```

Some operations for vector analysis.

| | |
|---|---|
| Read in the vector analysis package. | `In[1]:= <<VectorAnalysis.m` |
| Here is the volume element in spherical coordinates. | `In[2]:= VolumeElement[Spherical]`<br><br>`Out[2]= r` $^2$ `Dt[phi] Dt[r] Dt[theta] Sin[theta]` |
| Here is the gradient of the function $r^2 \cos(\theta) \sin(\phi)$, in spherical coordinates. | `In[3]:= Grad[ r^2 Cos[theta], Spherical ]`<br>`Out[3]= {2 r Cos[theta], -(r Sin[theta]), 0}` |

## ■ A.3.2  Laplace Transforms

Laplace transforms are a common type of integral transforms.  They are particularly important in "operational methods" for solving partial differential equations.

You can define Laplace transforms in *Mathematica* by giving almost directly the formulae for Laplace transforms that you would find in a standard mathematical handbook.  Each formula is implemented as a transformation rule for a pattern involving the object `Laplace`.

```
Laplace::usage = "Laplace[expr,t,s] gives the Laplace transform of expr."

(* constants *)
Laplace[c_,t_,s_] := c/s /; FreeQ[c,t]

(* linearity *)
Laplace[a_+b_,t_,s_] := Laplace[a,t,s] + Laplace[b,t,s]

(* pick off constants *)
Laplace[c_ a_,t_,s_] := c Laplace[a,t,s] /; FreeQ[c,t]

(* powers *)
Laplace[t_^n_.,t_,s_] := n!/s^(n+1) /;
                        (FreeQ[n,t] && n > 0)

(* products involving powers *)
Laplace[a_ t_^n_.,t_,s_] :=
     (-1)^n D[Laplace[a,t,s], {s, n}] /; (FreeQ[n,t] && n > 0)

(* negative powers *)
Laplace[a_/t_,t_,s_] :=
          Block[ { v = Unique["s"] },
               Integrate[Laplace[a,t,v],{v,s,Infinity}]
          ]

(* exponentials *)
Laplace[a_. Exp[b_. + c_. t_],t_,s_] :=
               Laplace[a Exp[b],t,s-c] /;
                         FreeQ[{b, c},t]
```

Laplace transforms.

Read in the file of Laplace transforms.          *In[1]:=* `<<Laplace.m`

Here is the Laplace transform of $t^2 e^{-2t}$.

$In[2]:=$ `Laplace[t^2 Exp[-2t], t, s]`

$Out[2]=$ $\dfrac{2}{(2 + s)^3}$

If you want *Mathematica* to find Laplace transforms of Bessel functions, you will have to give some more rules.

$In[3]:=$ `Laplace[BesselJ[0, t], t, s]`

$Out[3]=$ `Laplace[BesselJ[0, t], t, s]`

## ■ A.3.3  Modular Arithmetic

In doing mathematics, you often need to introduce objects that have special properties. This section gives an example of a package that deals with integers modulo $n$. The package works with *Mathematica* objects of the form `mod[a, n]`. It specifies the behavior of these objects under arithmetic operations such as addition and multiplication.

Notice the specification of transformation rules associated with the object `mod` for common operations such as addition. These rules essentially "overload" the standard addition function, to include special cases for sums involving the object `mod`.

```
Format[mod[a_,n_]]  := SequenceForm[a," mod ",n]

mod[0,n_]  := 0

mod[a_Integer,n_Integer]  := mod[Mod[a,n],n] /; a>=n
mod[a_Integer,n_Integer]  := mod[Mod[a,n],n] /; a<0

mod[b_Rational,n_Integer]  :=
      mod[Mod[Numerator[b]*PowerMod[Denominator[b],-1,n],n],n]

mod /: mod[a_Integer,n_Integer] + b_Integer :=
      mod[Mod[a+b,n],n]
mod /: mod[a_Integer,n_Integer] + b_Rational :=
      mod[Mod[a + Numerator[b]*PowerMod[Denominator[b],-1,n],n],n]
mod /: mod[a_Integer,n_Integer] + mod[b_Integer,n_Integer] :=
      mod[Mod[a+b,n],n]
mod /: mod[a_Integer,m_Integer] + mod[b_Integer,n_Integer] :=
      Block[{g=GCD[m,n]}, mod[a,g]+mod[b,g] ]

mod /: mod[a_Integer,n_Integer] * b_Integer :=
      mod[Mod[a*b,n],n]
mod /: mod[a_Integer,n_Integer] * b_Rational :=
      mod[Mod[a*Numerator[b]*PowerMod[Denominator[b],-1,n],n],n]
mod /: mod[a_Integer,n_Integer] * mod[b_Integer,n_Integer] :=
```

```
        mod[Mod[a*b,n],n]
mod /: mod[a_Integer,m_Integer] * mod[b_Integer,n_Integer] :=
        Block[{g=GCD[m,n]}, mod[a,g]*mod[b,g] ]

mod /: mod[a_Integer,n_Integer] ^ q_Integer :=
        mod[PowerMod[a,q,n],n]
```

Modular arithmetic.

| | |
|---|---|
| Read in the package for doing modular arithmetic. | `In[1]:= <<ModularArithmetic.m` |
| The package sets up a special print form for mod objects. | `In[2]:= mod[2, 7]`<br>`Out[2]= 2 mod 7` |
| You can use standard arithmetic operators on mod objects; the definitions in the package specify that appropriate modular arithmetic operations get done. | `In[3]:= %^19 + 6`<br>`Out[3]= 1 mod 7` |

# ■ A.4  Simplification and Transformation Rules

## ■ A.4.1  Simplification Rules for Combinatorial Functions

*Mathematica* has a number of "simplification rules" for combinatorial functions built in. You can, however, add further rules. Notice that you have to call `Unprotect` before making definitions for built-in objects.

```
Unprotect[Factorial, Binomial]

Factorial/: (k_)! k1_ := (k1)! /; k1 - k == 1
Factorial/: (n_)!/(m_)! := Product[i, {i, m+1, n}] /; n - m > 0 && IntegerQ[n-m]
Factorial/: (n_)!/(m_)! := 1/Product[i, {i, n+1, m}] /; m - n > 0 && IntegerQ[m-n]

Binomial/: Binomial[n_, k_]/Binomial[n_, k1_] := (n-k+1)/k /; k1 == k-1
Binomial/: Binomial[n_, k1_]/Binomial[n_, k_] := k/(n-k+1) /; k1 == k-1
```

Simplification rules for combinatorial functions.

*Mathematica* does not automatically simplify this expression.

$In[1]:=$ **(n + 2)! / n!**

$Out[1]=$ $\dfrac{(2 + n)!}{n!}$

This reads in the package of combinatorial simplification rules.

$In[2]:=$ **<<CombinatorialSimplification.m**

Now *Mathematica* does simplify the expression.

$In[3]:=$ **(n + 2)! / n!**

$Out[3]=$ **(1 + n) (2 + n)**

## ■ A.4.2  Trigonometric Simplification Rules

If you make assignments that implement simplification rules, then these rules will be used whenever they apply. Often, however, you want to set up rules that can be used in a more controlled fashion.

This section shows part of a package for reducing trigonometric expressions, using a sequence of transformation rules. The goal is to write expressions that involve trigonometric functions of multiple angles in terms of powers of trigonometric functions.

The package defines some lists of transformation rules, then applies these rules using the `/.` and `//.` operators.

```
TrigReduceRel = {
    Cos[(n_Integer?Positive) x_] :> 2^(n-1) Cos[x]^n +
        Sum[ Binomial[n-i-1, i-1] (-1)^i n/i 2^(n-2i-1) Cos[x]^(n-2i),
            {i, 1, n/2} ],

    Sin[(m_Integer?OddQ) x_] :> Block[{p = -(m^2-1)/6, s = Sin[x]},
        Do[s += p Sin[x]^k;
            p = p * -(m^2 - k^2)/(k+2)/(k+1),
            {k, 3, m, 2}];
        m s]                                        /; m > 0,

    Sin[(n_Integer?EvenQ) x_] :>
        Sum[ Binomial[n, i] (-1)^((i-1)/2) Sin[x]^i Cos[x]^(n-i),
            {i, 1, n, 2} ]                          /; n > 0,

    Sin[x_ + y_] :> Sin[x] Cos[y] + Sin[y] Cos[x],
    Sin[x_ - y_] :> Sin[x] Cos[y] - Sin[y] Cos[x],
    Cos[x_ + y_] :> Cos[x] Cos[y] - Sin[x] Sin[y],
    Cos[x_ - y_] :> Cos[x] Cos[y] + Sin[x] Sin[y],
}

TrigCanonicalRel = {
    (* Sin is an odd function *)
    Sin[(n_?Negative) x_.]      :> -Sin[-n x],
    Sin[(n_?Negative) x_ + y_] :> -Sin[-n x - y] /; Order[x, y] == 1,

    (* Cos is an even function *)
    Cos[(n_?Negative) x_.]      :>  Cos[-n x] /; n < 0,
    Cos[(n_?Negative) x_ + y_] :>  Cos[-n x - y] /; Order[x, y] == 1,

    a_. Sin[x_]^2 + a_. Cos[x_]^2 :> a,
    n_Integer a_. Sin[x_]^2 + m_Integer a_. Cos[x_]^2 :> a (m + (n-m)Sin[x]^2)
}

TrigReduce[e_] :=
        e /. TrigCanonicalRel //. TrigReduceRel /. TrigCanonicalRel
```

Trigonometric simplification rules.

Read in the trigonometric simplification package.

```
In[1]:= <<Trigonometry.m
Out[1]= Trigonometry`
```

*Mathematica* makes no automatic transformations on this expression.

```
In[2]:= Sin[4x]
Out[2]= Sin[4 x]
```

`TrigReduce` converts the trigonometric function of a multiple angle into powers of trigonometric functions of single angles.

*In[3]:=* **TrigReduce[%]**

*Out[3]=* $4 \cos[x]^3 \sin[x] - 4 \cos[x] \sin[x]^3$

Here is a slightly more complicated case.

*In[4]:=* **TrigReduce[Sin[2x + y]]**

*Out[4]=* $2 \cos[x] \cos[y] \sin[x] + (-1 + 2 \cos[x]^2) \sin[y]$

# ■ A.5  Setting up Mathematical Databases

## ■ A.5.1  Units Conversions

By giving a sequence of definitions for symbolic objects, you can effectively set up a "database" of information in *Mathematica*. Here is part of a database of units, together with a function **Convert** that converts between different units. Notice that **Convert** prints a message if the units are not compatible.

```
Convert::usage =
"Convert[old,new] coverts old to a form involving the combination of units new."
Convert[old_, new_] :=
        Block[{t},
                t = t //. $ToSI ;
                t = N[t] ;
                If[!NumberQ[t], Message[Convert::incomp, old, new]; Return[old],
                        Return[t new]
                ]
        ]

Convert::incomp = "Incompatible units in `1` and `2`."

$ToSI =
        {
        Inch -> 2.54*10^-2 Meter,
        Foot -> 30.48*10^-2 Meter,
        Mile -> 1.609344*10^3 Meter,
        Minute -> 60 Second,
        Hour -> 60 Minute,
        Day -> 24 Hour,
        Year -> 365 Day
}
```

Part of a package that does units conversions.

Read in the units conversion package.

```
In[1]:= <<Units.m
```

This converts 6 miles per day into meters per second.

```
In[2]:= Convert[6 Mile/Day, Meter/Second]
```

$$Out[2]= \frac{0.11176 \text{ Meter}}{\text{Second}}$$

If you try to convert between incompatible units, the package prints a message.

```
In[3]:= Convert[6 Year, Inch]

Convert::incomp: Incompatible units in 6 Year and Inch.

Out[3]= 6 Year
```

## ■ A.5.2 Properties of Polyhedra

This section gives part of a database on properties of polyhedra. It is a common thing to use symbols like `Tetrahedron` to represent mathematical objects, and then symbolically to define properties such as `Area[Tetrahedron]`. Notice the use of `^=` to associate definitions with objects like `Tetrahedron`, rather than properties like `Area`.

```
(* Dcdecahedron *)
Vertices[Dodecahedron]  ^= 20
Edges[Dodecahedron]  ^= 30
Faces[Dodecahedron]  ^= 12
Area[Dodecahedron]  ^= Sqrt[25+10 Sqrt[5]]/4
Inscribed[Dodecahedron]  ^= Sqrt[250+110 Sqrt[5]]/20
Circumscribed[Dodecahedron]  ^= (Sqrt[15]+Sqrt[3])/4
Volume[Dodecahedron]  ^= (15 + 7 Sqrt[5])/4
Dual[Dodecahedron]  ^= Icosahedron
```

Properties of polyhedra.

# ■ A.6  Graphics Programming

## ■ A.6.1  Pictures of Polyhedra

As well as storing various numerical properties of polyhedra, you can also use *Mathematica* definitions to specify the geometrical properties of polyhedra, in a form that can be converted to pictures using *Mathematica* graphics functions.

```
Icosahedron::usage =
        "Icosahedron[(pos:{0,0,0}, (scale:1))] gives a graphics
        object representing an icosahedron with specified center
        position and scale."

MakePolyhedron[coords_, pos:{_?NumberQ, _?NumberQ, _?NumberQ}, scale_?NumberQ] :=
                               Map[Polygon, Map[# + pos &, scale coords, {2}] ]
MakePolyhedron[coords_, pos_] := MakePolyhedron[coords, pos, 1.]
MakePolyhedron[coords_] := MakePolyhedron[coords, {0.,0.,0.}, 1.]

Icosahedron[opts___] := MakePolyhedron[`IcosahedronCoords, opts]

Stellate::usage =
        "Stellate[polyhedron, (stellation ratio:2)] generates a stellated
        polyhedron from a polygon list. Negative stellation ratios give
        concave figures."

StellateFace[face_List, k_] :=
        Block[ { apex,
                 n = Length[face] } ,
               apex = N [ k Apply[Plus, face] / n ] ;
               Table[ Polygon[ {apex, face[[i]], face[[ Mod[i, n] + 1 ]] }
                             ],
                    {i, n} ]
        ]

Stellate[poly_, k_:2?NumberQ] :=
        Flatten [ poly /. Polygon[x_] :> StellateFace[x, k]  ]
```

Geometrical structure of polyhedra.

Read in the file of polyhedra.

```
In[1]:= <<Polyhedra.m
Out[1]= Polyhedra`
```

This generates a graphical object that represents an icosahedron.

```
In[2]:= Icosahedron[ ] // Short
Out[2]//Short= {Polygon[<<1>>], <<18>>, Polygon[{<<3>>}]}
```

This makes a picture of the icosahedron.         *In[3]:=* `Show[Graphics3D[Icosahedron[ ]]]`

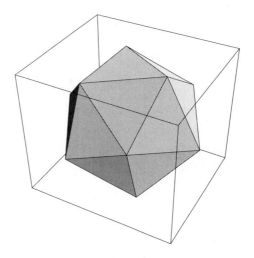

`Stellate` takes the symbolic representation         *In[4]:=* `Show[Graphics3D[Stellate[Icosahedron[ ]]]]`
of the icosahedron, and produces a
representation of a stellated icosahedron.

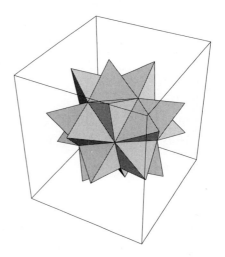

## ■ A.6.2  Plotting Data with Error Bars

The built-in *Mathematica* function `ListPlot` allows you to plot data points, but
gives you no way to include errors bars for each point.

This package defines the function `DataPlot`, which is an analog of `ListPlot` for
data with error bars.

```
DataPlot::usage =
        "DataPlot[list] plots a list of data with error bars. The
        data can be given either in the form {{y1, dy1}, {y2, dy2}, ...}
        or {{x1, y1, dy1}, ...}."

DataPlot[l2:{{_, _}..}] :=
        Block[ {i}, DataPlot[ Table[Prepend[l2[[i]], i], {i, Length[l2]}] ] ]

DataPlot[l3:{{_, _, _}..}] :=
        Show[ Graphics[ { PointSize[0.015], Thickness[0.002],
                Block[ {i, x, y, dy} ,
                Table[
                        {x, y, dy} = l3[[i]] ;
                        { Line[ {{x, y-dy}, {x, y+dy}} ],
                        Point[ {x, y} ] } ,
                        {i, Length[l3]}
                ] ] } ], Axes -> Automatic ]
```

Plotting data with error bars.

Notice the use of pattern objects such as {_,_}.. to recognize sequences of lists of two elements.

The basic way that DataPlot works is to construct a graphics object which is then displayed using Show.

Read in the package.                    *In[1]:=* **<<DataPlot.m**

This makes a list of 10 pairs of random     *In[2]:=* **data =**
numbers, with the second number in the             **Table[{Random[Real, 10], Random[Real, 1]}, {10}]  ;**
pair on average a factor of ten smaller than
the first.

Here is the list data, with the first number    *In[3]:=* **DataPlot[%]**
in each pair interpreted as $y$ position, and
the second number as $y$ error.

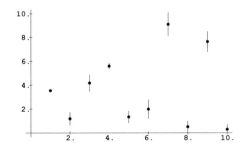

### ■ A.6.3  Three-Dimensional Parametric Plots

Section 1.8.6 discussed the built-in *Mathematica* function `ParametricPlot`, which
generates two-dimensional parametric plots. Here is a package for producing various
kinds of three-dimensional parametric plots.

```
ParametricPlot3D::usage =
    "ParametricPlot3D[{x,y,z}, {u,u0,u1,(du)}, {v,v0,v1,(dv)}, (options..)]
      plots a 3D parametric surface. Options are passed to Show[]"

SpaceCurve::usage =
    "SpaceCurve[{x,y,z}, {u,u0,u1,(du)}, (options..)]
      plots a 3D parametric curve. Options are passed to Show[]"

MakePolygons[vl_List] :=
    Block[{l = vl,
           l1 = Map[RotateLeft, vl],
           mesh},
        mesh = {l, l1, RotateLeft[l1], RotateLeft[l]};
        mesh = Map[Drop[#, -1]&, mesh, {1}];
        mesh = Map[Drop[#, -1]&, mesh, {2}];
        Polygon /@ Transpose[ Map[Flatten[#, 1]&, mesh] ]
    ]

plotpoints = PlotPoints /. Options[Plot3D]; (* default *)

Attributes[ParametricPlot3D] = {HoldFirst}

ParametricPlot3D[ fun:{_, _, _},
                  ul:{_, u0_, u1_, du_},
                  vl:{_, v0_, v1_, dv_},
                  opts___] :=
    Show[Graphics3D[MakePolygons[Table[N[fun], ul, vl]]], opts] /;
            NumberQ[N[u0]] && NumberQ[N[u1]] && NumberQ[N[du]] &&
                NumberQ[N[v0]] && NumberQ[N[v1]] && NumberQ[N[dv]]

ParametricPlot3D[fun_, {u_, u0_, u1_}, {v_, v0_, v1_}, opts___] :=
        ParametricPlot3D[ fun,
                    {u, u0, u1, (u1-u0)/(plotpoints-1)},
                    {v, v0, v1, (v1-v0)/(plotpoints-1)},
                    opts ]

Attributes[SpaceCurve] = {HoldFirst}

SpaceCurve[ fun:{_, _, _}, ul:{_, u0_, u1_, du_}, opts___] :=
        Show[ Graphics3D[Line[Table[N[fun], ul]]], opts ] /;
                    NumberQ[N[u0]] && NumberQ[N[u1]] && NumberQ[N[du]]
```

```
SpaceCurve[fun_, {u_, u0_, u1_}, opts___] :=
      SpaceCurve[ fun, {u, u0, u1, (u1-u0)/(plotpoints-1)}, opts ]
```

Three-dimensional parametric plots.

The function `ParametricPlot3D` plots surfaces generated by varying two parameters. The basic way that it works is to make an array of function values, then extract quadruples from the array, and render them as squares.

Read in the package.

```
In[1]:= <<ParametricPlot3D.m
```

Here is a sphere, generated from a parametric representation. The `BoxRatios` option is passed straight through to `Show`.

```
In[2]:= ParametricPlot3D[
            {Sin[u] Cos[v], Sin[u] Sin[v], Cos[u]},
            {u, 0, Pi, Pi/15}, {v, 0, 2Pi, Pi/15},
        BoxRatios->{1,1,1}]
```

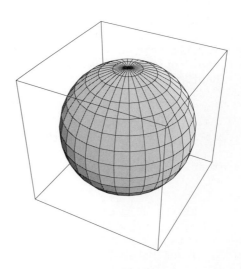

The function `PointParametricPlot3D` is
also defined in the package. It draws points
on the surface, but does not fill in
polygons.

```
In[3]:= PointParametricPlot3D[
          {Sin[u] Cos[v], Sin[u] Sin[v], Cos[u]},
          {u, 0, Pi, Pi/15}, {v, 0, 2Pi, Pi/15},
       BoxRatios->{1,1,1}]
```

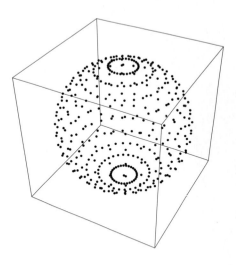

Here is an example of a curve in space,
specified by a single parameter.

```
In[4]:= SpaceCurve[{u Sin[u], u Cos[u], u},
          {u, 0, 15, 0.15}, BoxRatios->{1,1,1}]
```

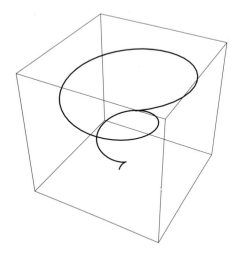

# Appendix B:
## *Mathematica Reference Guide*

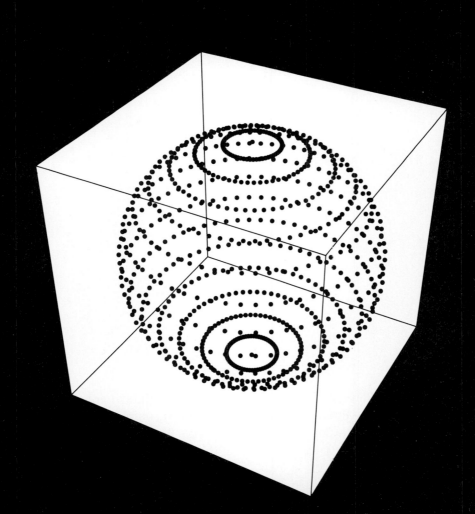

This Appendix gives a definitive summary of the complete *Mathematica* system. Most of what it contains you will never need to know for any particular application of *Mathematica*.

You should realize that this Appendix describes *all* the features of *Mathematica*, independent of their importance in typical usage.

Other parts of this book are organized along pedagogical lines, emphasizing important points, and giving details only when they are needed.

This Appendix gives all the details of every feature. As a result, you will often find obscure details discussed alongside very common and important functions. Just remember that this Appendix is intended for *reference purposes*, not for sequential reading. Do not be put off by the complexity of some of what you see; you will almost certainly never have to use it. But if you do end up having to use it, you will probably be happy that it is there.

By experimenting with *Mathematica*, you may find features that go beyond what is described in this Appendix. You really should not use any such features: there is no guarantee that features which are not documented will continue to be supported in future versions of *Mathematica*.

**About the illustration overleaf:**

This is a parametric plot of a sphere, made up from a sequence of points at equally-spaced parameter values. The command used was PointParametricPlot3D[*list*, *urange*, *vrange*], where *list* is {Sin[u] Cos[v], Sin[u] Sin[v], Cos[u]}, *urange* is {u, 0, Pi, Pi/15}, and *vrange* is {v, 0, 2Pi, Pi/30}. The option setting BoxRatios->{1,1,1} was used.

# ■ B.1  Basic Objects

## ■ B.1.1  Expressions

*Expressions* are the main type of data in *Mathematica*.

Expressions can be written in the form $h[e_1, e_2, ...]$. The object $h$ is known generically as the *head* of the expression.  The $e_i$ are termed the *elements* of the expression. Both the head and the elements may themselves be expressions.

The *parts* of an expression can be referred to by numerical indices.  The head has index 0; element $e_i$ has index $i$. $expr[[i]]$ gives the part of *expr* with index $i$. Negative indices count from the end.

$expr[[i_1, i_2, ...]]$ gives the piece of *expr* found by successively extracting parts of subexpressions with indices $i_1$, $i_2$, .... If you think of expressions as trees, the indices specify which branch to take at each node as you descend from the root.

The pieces of an expression that are specified by giving a sequence of exactly $n$ indices are defined to be at *level* $n$ in the expression. You can use levels to determine the domain of application of functions like `Map`. Level 0 corresponds to the whole expression.

The *depth* of an expression is defined to be the maximum number of indices needed to specify any part of it. A negative level number $-n$ refers to all parts of an expression that have depth $n$.

## ■ B.1.2  Symbols

*Symbols* are the basic named objects in *Mathematica*.

The name of a symbol can be any sequence of letters and digits, not starting with a digit. Symbol names can also contain the character $. Upper and lower case letters are always distinguished in *Mathematica*.

| | |
|---|---|
| *aaaaa* | user-defined symbol |
| *Aaaaa* | system-defined symbol |
| *$Aaaa* | global or internal system-defined symbol |

Symbol naming conventions.

It is a convention that the names of system-defined symbols usually consist of one or more complete English words. The first letter of each word is capitalized, and the words are run together.

On computer systems that use ASCII, *Mathematica* supports the ASCII international character set. Characters with decimal codes between 160 and 255 are treated as alphabetic, and can thus appear in symbol names.

## ■ B.1.3 Contexts

Every *Mathematica* symbol is associated with a particular *context*. The full specification of a *Mathematica* symbol is *context`name*. Context names can consist of any sequence of letters, digits, $ and `, but cannot start with either ` or a digit. All context names must end with `.

Built-in *Mathematica* symbols are in the context `System`. The default context for user-defined symbols is `Global`. Packages conventionally define symbols in a context whose name corresponds to the name of the package.

At any point in a *Mathematica* session, there is a *current context* `$Context`, together with a list of contexts `$ContextPath`. These allow symbols to be specified without explicitly giving their contexts. Functions like `Begin` and `End` change the current context.

| | |
|---:|:---|
| *name* | search `$Context`, then `$ContextPath`; create in `$Context` if necessary |
| `` `name `` | search `$Context` only; create there if necessary |
| *context`name* | search *context* only; create there if necessary |
| `` `context`name `` | search `$Context`*context* only; create there if necessary |

Contexts used for various specifications of symbols.

It is conventional for packages to prepend their context to `$ContextPath`.

Context is included in the printed form of a symbol only if it would be needed to specify the symbol *at the time of display*.

## ■ B.1.4 Aliases

*Aliases* may be defined for symbols.

*alias* `::=` *symbol* specifies that when *alias* is entered, it is immediately converted to the symbol specification *symbol*.

Aliases that can be used in normal *Mathematica* input must have the same form as symbol names. Aliases apply independent of context. Aliases can be translated to symbols with any context specification.

Aliases may be defined for arbitrary strings, and will be used by ?.

## ■ B.1.5  Special Objects

There are a number of types of special objects, which form the indivisible elements of expressions in *Mathematica*.

These objects have heads which are symbols that can be thought of as "tagging" their types. The objects contain "raw data", which can  usually be accessed only by functions specific to the particular type of object. You can extract the head of a special object using `Head`, but you cannot explicitly extract any of its other parts.

| | |
|---:|:---|
| `Symbol` | symbol |
| `String` | character string "*cccc*" |
| `Integer` | integer *nnnn* |
| `Real` | real (floating point) number *nnn.nnn* |
| `Rational` | rational number *nnn/nnn* |
| `Complex` | complex number *nnn* + *nnn* I |
| `RawMedium` | raw descriptor for an input-output medium |

Special objects.

Most special objects are input and output in special forms.

As an optimization for some special kinds of computations, the raw data in *Mathematica* special objects can be given explicitly using `Raw[`*head*`, "`*hexstring*`"]`. The data is specified as a string of  hexadecimal digits, corresponding to an array of bytes. When no special output form exists, `InputForm` prints special objects using `Raw`. *The behaviour of* `Raw` *differs from one implementation of Mathematica to another; its general use is strongly discouraged.*

## ■ B.1.6  Numbers

| | |
|---|---|
| Integer | integer |
| Real | real (floating point) number |
| Rational | rational number |
| Complex | complex number |

Basic types of numbers.

All numbers in *Mathematica* can contain any number of digits. Floating point numbers can have any exponent up to some maximum absolute value which depends on the implementation.

Numbers with sufficiently few digits are usually implemented as "machine numbers". On most computer systems, this is true for integers less than $2^{31} \simeq 2 \times 10^9$ and floating point numbers with fewer than 16 digits. Operations on machine numbers are usually much more efficient than operations on arbitrary-precision numbers.

Floating point numbers input with a small number of digits are treated with the precision of machine numbers.

Numbers can be entered in any base from 2 to 36, using the notation *base*^^*digits*. *base* is given in decimal. For bases larger than 10, additional digits are chosen from the letters a–z or A–Z. Upper and lower case letters are equivalent for these purposes. Floating point numbers can be specified by including . in the *digits* sequence.

## ■ B.1.7  Character Strings

Character strings are input in the form "*cccc*".

Newlines (line feeds and returns) and tabs within character strings are converted to spaces on input.

| | |
|---|---|
| \n | newline (line feed) |
| \t | tab |
| \*nnn* | character with octal code *nnn* |
| `` or `*n*` | a marker used by **StringForm** |

Special codes used in strings.

Note that octal codes for characters depend on the character set (e.g. ASCII or EBCDIC) used in a particular implementation.

# ■ B.2  Input Syntax

## ■ B.2.1  Bracketed Objects

| | |
|---|---|
| *(expr)* | parenthesization: grouping of input |
| $h[e_1, e_2, ...]$ | standard expression |
| $e[[i_1, i_2, ...]]$ | $Part[e, i_1, i_2, ...]$ |
| $\{e_1, e_2, ...\}$ | $List[e_1, e_2, ...]$ |
| (* *any text* *) | comment |

Bracketed objects.

$h[\ ]$ is an expression with zero elements. $\{\}$ is $List[\ ]$.

Expressions like $f[e_1, , e_2]$, $\{e_1, , e_2\}$ and so on, are interpreted with the symbol Null inserted between each pair of adjacent commas.

Comments can be nested, and may continue for any number of lines.

## ■ B.2.2  Special Input Forms

Everything you type into *Mathematica* is interpreted as an expression. Many objects that are fundamental to *Mathematica*, or in common usage, can however be input in special forms. Often you will only ever see the special forms of these objects. They are nevertheless all expressions. The table in this section gives the correspondence of special forms with standard *Mathematica* expressions.

Some special input forms, such as $a + b$ can be thought of as "operators". Other input forms, such as $a::b$ are not so naturally considered as operators. All of them, however, are ultimately just short forms for standard *Mathematica* expressions.

| input form | full form | grouping |
|---|---|---|
| *digits*. *digits* | (approximate number) | |
| $n$^^*digits* | (base $n$ integer) | |
| $n$^^*digits*. *digits* | (base $n$ approximate number) | |
| *expr*::*string* | `MessageName`[*expr*, `"`*string*`"`] | |
| forms containing `#` | (see below) | |
| forms containing `%` | (see below) | |
| forms containing `_` | (see below) | |
| $expr_1$?$expr_2$ | `PatternTest`[$expr_1$, $expr_2$] | |
| $expr_1$[$expr_2$, ...] | $expr_1$[$expr_2$, ...] | (e[e])[e] |
| $expr_1$[[$expr_2$, ...]] | `Part`[$expr_1$, $expr_2$, ...] | (e[[e]])[[e]] |
| *expr*++ | `Increment`[*expr*] | |
| *expr*-- | `Decrement`[*expr*] | |
| ++*expr* | `PreIncrement`[*expr*] | |
| --*expr* | `PreDecrement`[*expr*] | |
| $expr_1$ @ $expr_2$ | $expr_1$[$expr_2$] | e @ (e @ e) |
| $expr_1$ ~ $expr_2$ ~ $expr3$ | $expr_2$[$expr_1$, $expr3$] | (e ~ e ~ e) ~ e ~ e |
| $expr_1$ /@ $expr_2$ | `Map`[$expr_1$, $expr_2$] | e /@ (e /@ e) |
| $expr_1$ //@ $expr_2$ | `MapAll`[$expr_1$, $expr_2$] | e //@ (e //@ e) |
| $expr_1$ @@ $expr_2$ | `Apply`[$expr_1$, $expr_2$] | e @@ (e @@ e) |
| *expr*! | `Factorial`[*expr*] | |
| *expr*!! | `Factorial2`[*expr*] | |
| *expr*′ | `Derivative`[1][*expr*] | |
| $expr_1$ ** $expr_2$ ** $expr_3$ | `NonCommutativeMultiply`[$expr_1$, $expr_2$, $expr_3$] | |
| | | e ** e ** e |
| $expr_1$ . $expr_2$ . $expr_3$ | `Dot`[$expr_1$, $expr_2$, $expr_3$] | e . e . e |
| $expr_1$^$expr_2$ | `Power`[$expr_1$, $expr_2$] | e^(e^e) |
| -*expr* | `Times`[-1, *expr*] | |
| +*expr* | *expr* | |
| $expr_1$/$expr_2$ | $expr_1$ ($expr_2$)^-1 | (e / e) / e |
| $expr_1$  $expr_2$  $expr3$ | `Times`[$expr_1$, $expr_2$, $expr3$] | e e e |
| $expr_1$ * $expr_2$ * $expr3$ | `Times`[$expr_1$, $expr_2$, $expr3$] | e * e * e |
| $expr_1$ + $expr_2$ + $expr3$ | `Plus`[$expr_1$, $expr_2$, $expr3$] | e + e + e |
| $expr_1$ - $expr_2$ | `Subtract`[$expr_1$, $expr_2$] | (e - e) - e |

Special input forms, part one.

| input form | full form | grouping |
|---|---|---|
| $expr_1$ == $expr_2$ | Equal[$expr_1$,$expr_2$] | $e$ == $e$ == $e$ |
| $expr_1$ != $expr_2$ | Unequal[$expr_1$,$expr_2$] | $e$ != $e$ != $e$ |
| $expr_1$ > $expr_2$ | Greater[$expr_1$,$expr_2$] | $e$ > $e$ > $e$ |
| $expr_1$ >= $expr_2$ | GreaterEqual[$expr_1$,$expr_2$] | $e$ >= $e$ >= $e$ |
| $expr_1$ < $expr_2$ | Less[$expr_1$,$expr_2$] | $e$ < $e$ < $e$ |
| $expr_1$ <= $expr_2$ | LessEqual[$expr_1$,$expr_2$] | $e$ <= $e$ <= $e$ |
| !$expr$ | Not[$expr$] | !(!$e$) |
| $expr_1$ && $expr_2$ && $expr_3$ | And[$expr_1$,$expr_2$,$expr3$] | $e$ && $e$ && $e$ |
| $expr_1$ \|\| $expr_2$ \|\| $expr_3$ | Or[$expr_1$,$expr_2$,$expr3$] | $e$ \|\| $e$ \|\| $e$ |
| $expr$.. | Repeated[$expr$] | |
| $expr$... | RepeatedNull[$expr$] | |
| $symb$:$expr$ | Pattern[$symb$,$expr$] | |
| $expr_1$ /; $expr_2$ | Condition[$expr_1$,$expr_2$] | ($e$/;$e$)/;$e$ |
| $expr_1$ -> $expr_2$ | Rule[$expr_1$,$expr_2$] | $e$->($e$->$e$) |
| $expr_1$ :> $expr_2$ | RuleDelayed[$expr_1$,$expr_2$] | $e$->($e$->$e$) |
| $expr_1$ /. $expr_2$ | ReplaceAll[$expr_1$,$expr_2$] | ($e$/.$e$)/.$e$ |
| $expr_1$ //. $expr_2$ | ReplaceRepeated[$expr_1$,$expr_2$] | ($e$//.$e$)//.$e$ |
| $expr_1$ += $expr_2$ | AddTo[$expr_1$,$expr_2$] | |
| $expr_1$ -= $expr_2$ | SubtractFrom[$expr_1$,$expr_2$] | |
| $expr_1$ *= $expr_2$ | TimesBy[$expr_1$,$expr_2$] | |
| $expr_1$ /= $expr_2$ | DivideBy[$expr_1$,$expr_2$] | |
| $expr$ & | Function[$expr$] | |
| $expr_1$ // $expr_2$ | $expr_2$[$expr_1$] | ($e$//$e$)//$e$ |
| $expr_1$ = $expr_2$ | Set[$expr_1$,$expr_2$] | $e$ = ($e$ = $e$) |
| $expr_1$ := $expr_2$ | SetDelayed[$expr_1$,$expr_2$] | |
| $expr_1$ ^= $expr_2$ | UpSet[$expr_1$,$expr_2$ | |
| $expr_1$ ^:= $expr_2$ | UpSetDelayed[$expr_1$,$expr_2$ | |
| $symb$/: $expr_1$ = $expr_2$ | TagSet[$symb$,$expr_1$,$expr_2$] | |
| $symb$/: $expr_1$ := $expr_2$ | TagSetDelayed[$symb$,$expr_1$,$expr_2$] | |
| $expr$ =. | UnSet[$expr$] | |
| $symb$/: $expr$=. | TagUnSet[$symb$,$expr$] | |
| $expr$ ::= $symb$ | Alias[$expr$, $symb$] | |
| $expr$ ::=. | UnAlias[$expr$] | |

Special input forms, part two.

B.2 Input Syntax

| input form | filename |
| expr >> filename |
| expr >>> filename |
| expr ; expr3 |
| expr ; |

| full form | grouping |
| --- | --- |
| Put[expr,"filename"] | |
| PutAppend[expr,"filename"] | |
| CompoundExpression[expr_1,expr_2,expr3] | |
| CompoundExpression[expr_1,expr_2,Null] | |

Special input forms, part three.

| input form | full form |
| --- | --- |
| # | Slot[1] |
| #n | Slot[n] |
| ## | SlotSequence[1] |
| ##n | SlotSequence[n] |
| % | Out[ ] |
| %% | Out[-2] |
| %%...% (n times) | Out[-n] |
| %n | Out[n] |
| _ | Blank[ ] |
| _expr | Blank[expr] |
| __ | BlankSequence[ ] |
| __expr | BlankSequence[expr] |
| ___ | BlankNullSequence[ ] |
| ___expr | BlankNullSequence[expr] |
| _. | Optional[Blank[ ]] |
| symb_ | Pattern[symb,Blank[ ]] |
| symb_expr | Pattern[symb,Blank[expr]] |
| symb__ | Pattern[symb,BlankSequence[ ]] |
| symb__expr | Pattern[symb,BlankSequence[expr]] |
| symb___ | Pattern[symb,BlankNullSequence[ ]] |
| symb___expr | Pattern[symb,BlankNullSequence[expr]] |
| symb_. | Optional[Pattern[symb,Blank[ ]]] |

Additional special input forms.

| | |
|---|---|
| *expr* and *expr$_i$* | any expression |
| *symb* | any symbol |
| *n* | a non-negative integer |
| *string* | "*cccc*" or a sequence of letters and digits |
| *filename* | like *string*, but can also include any of the chara ., /, ~, _ and $ |
| *digits* | a sequence of digits (including letters when *base* is above 10) |

Objects used in the tables of special input forms.

## Precedence and the Ordering of Input Forms

The tables of input forms are arranged in decreasing order of *precedence*. Input forms in the same box have the same precedence. Precedence determines how *Mathematica* groups terms in input expressions.

When you type 2 + 5 * 6, *Mathematica* must decide whether this means (2 + 5) * 6 or 2 + (5 * 6). Following the standard mathematical convention, *Mathematica* chooses the second form. This choice follows from the fact that *Mathematica* assigns * a "higher precedence" than +. The operator * effectively binds its operands more tightly than + does.

The general rule is that if $\otimes$ has higher precedence than $\oplus$, then $a \oplus b \otimes c$ is interpreted as $a \oplus (b \otimes c)$, and $a \otimes b \oplus c$ is interpreted as $(a \otimes b) \oplus c$.

You can always control the grouping of terms in input expressions by explicitly inserting parentheses. The precedences of different operators in *Mathematica* have been chosen so that you have to type as few parentheses as possible in typical applications. In some cases, you will still have to put in parentheses to make clear what you mean. For example, you have to distinguish a = (b; c = d) from a = b; c = d, which means (a = b); (c = d).

## Grouping of Input Forms

The third columns in the tables show how multiple occurrences of a single input form, or of several input forms with the same precedence, are grouped. For example, a/b/c is grouped as (a/b)/c ("left associative"), while a^b^c is grouped as a^(b^c) ("right associative"). No grouping is needed in an expression like a + b + c, since

`Plus` can take any number of arguments.

Where the third column of the table is left blank, the input forms cannot be grouped: you always have to insert explicit parentheses.

## Spaces and Multiplication

Spaces in *Mathematica* denote multiplication, just as they do in standard mathematical notation. In addition, complete expressions that are adjacent, not necessarily separated by spaces, are also multiplied together.

```
x y z ⟶ x*y*z

2x ⟶ 2*x

2(x+1) ⟶ 2*(x+1)

c(x+1) ⟶ c*(x+1)

(x+1)(y+2) ⟶ (x+1)*(y+2)

x! y ⟶ x!*y

x!y ⟶ x!*y
```

Alternative forms for multiplication.

An expression like `x!y` could potentially mean either `(x!)*y` or `x*(!y)`. The first interpretation is chosen because `Factorial` has higher precedence than `Not`.

Spaces within single input forms are ignored. Thus, for example, `a + b` is equivalent to `a+b`. You will often want to insert spaces around lower precedence operators to improve readability.

You can give a "coefficient" for a symbol by preceding it with any sequence of digits. When you use numbers in bases larger than 10, the digits can include letters. (In bases other than 10, there must be a space between the end of the coefficient, and the beginning of the symbol name.)

```
x^2y, like x^2 y, means (x^2) y

x/2y, like x/2 y, means (x/2) y

xy is a single symbol, not x*y
```

Some cases to be careful about.

## Spaces to Avoid

You should avoid inserting any spaces between the different characters in composite operators such as /., =. and >=. Although in some cases such spaces are allowed, they are liable to lead to confusion.

Another case where spaces must be avoided is between the characters of the pattern object x_. If you type x _, *Mathematica* will interpret this as x*_, rather than the single named pattern object x_.

Similarly, you should not insert any spaces inside pattern objects like *x*:*value*.

## Relational Operators

Relational operators can be mixed. An expression like a > b >= c is converted to Inequality[a, Greater, b, GreaterEqual, c], which effectively evaluates as (a > b) && (b >= c). (The reason for the intermediate Inequality form is that it prevents objects from being evaluated twice when something like a > b >= c is processed.)

## ■ B.2.3  Input Control

*Mathematica* expressions can continue for several lines. Newlines (line feeds or returns) are equivalent to spaces.

With many front ends, *Mathematica* tests to see whether your input is finished every time you get to the end of a line. This means that you can open a bracket on one line, then type several lines of input. *Mathematica* will assume that you have not finished giving your input until you type a matching close bracket.

If the presence of unmatched brackets, or some other input structure, does not already indicate it, you can always show that your input continues for several lines by typing \ at the end of the line.

## ■ B.2.4  Formatting Conventions

Good formatting conventions are essential in making *Mathematica* code easy to read. Here are a few suggestions.

- Insert spaces around operators like + that have comparatively low precedence.
- Leave spaces after commas and semicolons.
- Break lines so as to keep logically-connected units on the same line.

- Use a separate line for different transformation rules, or different steps in a program.

- Try to use temporary variables to avoid deep nesting of functions.

- Leave spaces in expressions like `f[ g[h[x]] ]` to emphasize outer brackets.

- Indent blocks of code in programs.

- Insert comments when you need to label arguments of functions, such as `f[e, (*variable=*)x]`.

| | |
|---|---|
| $f$ @ $x$ | $f[x]$ |
| $x$ // $f$ | $f[x]$ |
| $x$~ $f$~ $y$ | $f[x, y]$ |

Alternative input forms for functions.

## ■ B.2.5  Special Input

| | |
|---|---|
| ?*symbol* | get information |
| ??*symbol* | get more information |
| ?$s_1$ $s_2$ ... | get information on several objects |
| !*command* | execute an external command |
| !!*file* | display the contents of an external file |

Special input lines.

In most implementations of *Mathematica*, you can give a line of special input anywhere in your input. The only constraint is that the special input must start at the beginning of a line.

Some implementations of *Mathematica* may not allow you to execute external commands using !*command*.

| | | |
|---|---|---|
| * | any sequence of letters and digits | |
| @ | any sequence of lower-case letters and digits | |
| ** | any sequence of letters, digits and $ | |

Metacharacters recognized by ?.

You can ask for information from *Mathematica* without specifying the name of an object exactly. You can include special "metacharacters", which can stand for different sequences of ordinary characters. Functions like `Names` and `StringMatchQ` allow the same metacharacters.

# ■ B.3  Some General Notations and Conventions

## ■ B.3.1  Function Names

The names of built-in functions follow some general guidelines.

- The name consists of complete English words, or standard mathematical abbreviations.

- The first letter of each word is capitalized.

- Functions whose names end with `Q` usually "ask a question", and return either `True` or `False`.

- Mathematical functions that are named after people usually have names in *Mathematica* of the form *PersonSymbol*.

## ■ B.3.2  Function Arguments

The main expression or object on which a built-in function acts is usually given as the first argument to the function. Subsidiary parameters appear as subsequent arguments.

The following are exceptions:

- In functions like `Map` and `Apply`, the function to apply comes before the expression it is to be applied to.

- In `Block` and `Function`, local variables and parameter names come before bodies.

- In functions like `Write` and `Display`, the name of the file is given before the objects to be written to it.

For mathematical functions, arguments that are written as subscripts in standard mathematical notation are given before those that are written as superscripts.

## ■ B.3.3  Options

Some built-in functions can take *options*. Each option has a name, represented as a symbol. Options are set by giving rules of the form *name->value*. Such rules must appear after all the other arguments in a function. Rules for different options can be given in any order. If you do not explicitly give a rule for a particular option, a default setting for that option is used.

| | |
|---:|:---|
| Options[$f$] | show the default rules for all options associated with $f$ |
| Options[$expr$] | give the options set in a particular expression |
| SetOptions[$f$, *name->value*, ...] | set default rules for options associated with $f$ |

Operations on options.

## ■ B.3.4  Part Numbering

| | |
|---:|:---|
| $n$ | element $n$ (starting at 1) |
| $-n$ | element $n$ from the end |
| 0 | head |
| \{$n_1$, $n_2$, ...\} | a list of parts $n_i$ |

Numbering of parts.

## ■ B.3.5  Sequence Specifications

| | |
|---:|:---|
| $n$ | elements 1 through $n$ |
| $-n$ | last $n$ elements |
| \{$n$\} | element $n$ only |
| \{$m$, $n$\} | elements $m$ through $n$ (inclusive). |

Specifications for sequences of parts.

## ■ B.3.6  Level Specifications

| | |
|---:|:---|
| $n$ | levels 1 through $n$ |
| Infinity | all levels |
| \{$n$\} | level $n$ only |
| \{$n_1$, $n_2$\} | levels $n_1$ through $n_2$ |

Level specifications.

The level in an expression corresponding to a non-negative integer $n$ is defined to consist of parts specified by $n$ non-negative indices. A negative level number $-n$ represents all parts of an expression that have depth $n$. The depth of an expression, `Depth[`*expr*`]`, is the maximum number of indices needed to specify any part, plus one. Levels *do not* include heads of expressions. Level 0 is the whole expression. Level -1 contains all symbols and other objects that have no subparts.

Ranges of levels specified by {$n_1$, $n_2$} contain all parts that are neither above level $n_1$, nor below level $n_2$ in the tree. The $n_i$ need not have the same sign. Thus, for example, {2, -2} specifies subexpressions which occur anywhere below the top level, but above the leaves, of the expression tree.

Level specifications are used by the functions `Apply`, `Count`, `Level`, `Map` and `Scan`.

Functions with level specifications visit different subexpressions in an order that corresponds to depth-first traversal of the expression tree, with leaves visited before roots. The subexpressions visited have part specifications which occur in an order which is lexicographic, except that longer sequences appear before shorter ones.

## ■ B.3.7   Iterators

| | |
|---|---|
| {*imax*} | iterate *imax* times |
| {*i*, *imax*} | *i* goes from *1* to *imax* in steps of *1* |
| {*i*, *imin*, *imax*} | *i* goes from *imin* to *imax* in steps of *1* |
| {*i*, *imin*, *imax*, *di*} | *i* goes from *imin* to *imax* in steps of *di* |
| {*i*, *imin*, *imax*}, {*j*, *jmin*, *jmax*}, ... | *i* goes from *imin* to *imax*, and for each value of *i*, *j* goes from *jmin* to *jmax*, etc. |

Iterator notation.

Iterator notation is used in such functions as `Sum`, `Table`, `Do` and `Range`.

The iteration parameters *imin*, *imax* and *di* do not need to be integers. The variable *i* is given a sequence of values starting at *imin*, and increasing in steps of *di*, stopping when the next value of *i* would be greater than *imax*. The iteration parameters can be arbitrary symbolic expressions, so long as (*imax*-*imin*)/*di* is a number.

When several iteration variables are used, the limits for the later ones can depend on the values of earlier ones.

The variable $i$ can be any symbolic expression; it need not be a single symbol. However, the expression given for $i$ must have no value assigned to it at the time when the iteration function is evaluated.

The procedure for evaluating iteration functions is described on page 569.

## ■ B.3.8  Mathematical Functions

The mathematical functions such as `Log[x]` and `BesselJ[n, x]` which are built into *Mathematica* have a number of features in common.

- They carry the attribute `Listable`, so that they are automatically "threaded" over any lists that appear as arguments.

- They give exact results in terms of integers, rational numbers and algebraic expressions in special cases.

- Except for functions whose arguments are always integers, mathematical functions in *Mathematica* can be evaluated to any numerical precision, with any complex numbers as arguments. If a function is undefined for a particular set of arguments, it is returned in symbolic form in this case.

- When possible, symbolic derivatives and integrals of built-in mathematical functions are evaluated in terms of other built-in functions.

## ■ B.3.9  Mathematical Constants

Mathematical constants such as `E` and `Pi` that are built into *Mathematica* have the following properties:

- They do not have values as such.

- They have numerical values that can be found to any precision.

- They carry the attribute `Constant`, and so are treated as constants in derivatives.

## ■ B.3.10  Protection

*Mathematica* allows you to make assignments that override the standard operation and meaning of built-in *Mathematica* objects.

To make it difficult to make such assignments by mistake, most built-in *Mathematica* objects have the attribute `Protected`. If you want to make an assignment for a built-in object, you must first remove this attribute. You can do this by calling the function `Unprotect`.

There are a few fundamental *Mathematica* objects to which you absolutely cannot assign your own values. These objects carry the attribute `Locked`, as well as `Protected`. The `Locked` attribute prevents you from changing any of the attributes, and thus from removing the `Protected` attribute.

# ■ B.4  Evaluation

## ■ B.4.1  The Standard Evaluation Sequence

The following is the sequence of steps that *Mathematica* follows in evaluating an expression like $h[e_1, e_2, \ldots]$. Every time the expression changes, *Mathematica* effectively starts the evaluation sequence over again.

- If the expression is a special object (e.g. `Integer`, `String`, etc.), leave it unchanged.

- Evaluate the head $h$ of the expression.

- Evaluate each element $e_i$ of the expression in turn. If $h$ is a symbol with attributes `HoldFirst`, `HoldRest` or `HoldAll`, then skip evaluation of certain elements.

- If $h$ has attribute `Flat`, then flatten out all nested expressions with head $h$.

- If $h$ has attribute `Orderless`, then sort the $e_i$ into order.

- If $h$ has attribute `Listable`, then thread through any $e_i$ that are lists.

- Use any applicable transformation rules that you have defined for objects of the form $f[\ h[e_1, \ldots], \ldots\ ]$. (Also use transformation rules in which $h$ appears in the head of an expression.)

- Use any built-in transformation rules for objects of the form $f[\ h[e_1, \ldots], \ldots]\ ]$.

- Use any applicable transformation rules that you have defined for $h[e_1, e_2, \ldots]$.

- Use any built-in transformation rules for $h[e_1, e_2, \ldots]$.

## ■ B.4.2  Non-standard Argument Evaluation

There are a number of built-in *Mathematica* functions that evaluate their arguments in special ways. The control structure `While` is an example. The symbol `While` has the attribute `HoldAll`. As a result, the arguments of `While` are not evaluated as part of the standard evaluation process. Instead, the internal code for `While` evaluates the arguments in a special way. In the case of `While`, the code evaluates the arguments repeatedly, so as to implement a loop.

| Control structures | arguments evaluated in a sequence determined by control flow (e.g. `CompoundExpression`, `Repeat`) |
| --- | --- |
| Conditionals | arguments evaluated only when they correspond to branches that are taken (e.g. `If`, `Which`) |
| Logical operations | arguments evaluated only when they are needed in determining the logical result (e.g. `And`, `Or`) |
| Iteration functions | first argument evaluated for each step in the iteration (e.g. `Do`, `Sum`, `Plot`) |
| Assignments | first argument only partially evaluated (e.g. `Set`, `AddTo`) |
| Pure functions | function body not evaluated (e.g. `Function`) |
| Holding functions | argument maintained in unevaluated form (e.g. `Hold`, `Literal`) |

Built-in functions that evaluate their arguments in special ways.

## Logical Operations

In an expression of the form $e_1$&&$e_2$&&$e_3$ the $e_i$ are evaluated in order. As soon as any $e_i$ is found to be `False`, evaluation is stopped, and the result `False` is returned. This means that you can use the $e_i$ to represent different "branches" in a program, with a particular branch being evaluated only if certain conditions are met.

The `Or` function works much like `And`; it returns `True` as soon as it finds any argument that is `True`. `Xor`, on the other hand, always evaluates *all* its arguments.

## Iteration Functions

An iteration function such as `Do[f, {i, imin, imax}]` is evaluated as follows.

- The iteration specification is evaluated. If it is not found to be of the form {*i*, *imin*, *imax*}, the evaluation stops.
- If the iteration variable *i* already has a value, a message is printed, and the evaluation stops.
- *imin* and *imax* are used to determine the sequence of values to be assigned to the iteration variable *i*.

- The iteration variable is successively set to each value, and $f$ is evaluated in each case.
- The values assigned to $i$ are cleared.

If there are several iteration variables, the same procedure is followed for each variable in turn.

Unless otherwise specified, $f$ is not evaluated until a specific value has been assigned to $i$, and is then evaluated for each value of $i$ chosen. You can use `Release[f]` to make $f$ be evaluated immediately, rather than only after a specific value has been assigned to $i$.

## Assignments

The left-hand sides of assignments are only partially evaluated.

- If the left-hand side is a symbol, no evaluation is performed.

- If the left-hand side is a function, the arguments of the function are evaluated, but the function itself is not evaluated.
  The right-hand side is evaluated for immediate, but not for delayed, assignments.

Any subexpression of the form `Literal[`*expr*`]` that appears on the left-hand side of an assignment is not evaluated, but is replaced by the unevaluated form of *expr* before the assignment is done.

## ■ B.4.3 Overriding Non-Standard Argument Evaluation

| |
|---|
| $F[expr_1, \ldots, \texttt{Release}[expr_n], \ldots]$ <br><br> evaluates the argument $expr_n$, whether or not the attributes of $F$ specify that it should be held |

Overriding holding of arguments.

By using `Release`, you can get any argument of a function evaluated immediately, even if the argument would usually be evaluated later under the control of the function.

## ■ B.4.4 Recursion Limits

*Mathematica* usually goes on evaluating an expression according to the procedure described above until the expression no longer changes.

There are, however, some expressions for which this procedure will never terminate. For example, if you make the assignment x=x+1, then ask for the value of x, the standard evaluation procedure will lead to an infinite loop.

*Mathematica* has various mechanisms which protect it from this kind of situation.

First, you can always interrupt the operation of *Mathematica*, as discussed in Section 1.3.6.

In addition, *Mathematica* has a built-in "recursion limit", which stops evaluation after a fixed number of "levels". If *Mathematica* reaches the recursion limit, it returns the expression it is trying to evaluate, wrapped in a `Hold` function to prevent further evaluation.

| | |
|---|---|
| $RecursionLimit | the current setting of the recursion limit |
| $RecursionLimit=$n$ | set the recursion limit to $n$ levels |
| $RecursionLimit=Infinity | allow unrestricted recursion |

Functions for manipulating the global recursion limit.

The exact counting of "recursion levels" depends on many details of the *Mathematica* definitions you are using. In a typical case, one recursion level is used every time a function that depends on another function is evaluated.

# ■ B.5  Patterns and Transformation Rules

## ■ B.5.1  Patterns

*Patterns* stand for classes of expressions. They contain *pattern objects* which represent sets of possible expressions.

| | |
|---:|:---|
| _ | any expression |
| $x\_$ | any expression, given the name $x$ |
| $x:pattern$ | a pattern, given the name $x$ |
| $pattern\ ?\ test$ | a pattern that yields **True** when *test* is applied to its value |
| $\_h$ | any expression with head $h$ |
| $x\_h$ | any expression with head $h$, given the name $x$ |
| __ | any sequence of one or more expressions |
| ___ | any sequence of zero or more expressions |
| $x\_\_$ and $x\_\_\_$ | sequences of expressions, given the name $x$ |
| $\_\_h$ and $\_\_\_h$ | sequences of expressions, each with head $h$ |
| $x\_\_h$ and $x\_\_\_h$ | sequences of expressions with head $h$, given the name $x$ |
| $x\_:v$ | an expression with default value $v$ |
| $x\_h:v$ | an expression with head $h$ and default value $v$ |
| $x\_.$ | an expression with a globally-defined default value |
| Optional$[x\_h]$ | an expression that must have head $h$, and has a globally-defined default value |
| $pattern..$ | a pattern repeated one or more times |
| $pattern...$ | a pattern repeated zero or more times |

Pattern objects.

When several pattern objects with the same name occur in a single pattern, all the objects must stand for the same expression. Thus f[x_, x_] can stand for f[2, 2] but not f[2, 3].

In a pattern object such as _h, the head *h* can be any expression, but cannot itself be a pattern.

A pattern object such as x__ stands for a *sequence* of expressions. So, for example, f[x__] can stand for f[a, b, c], with x being the *sequence* (a, b, c). If you use x, say in the result of a transformation rule, the sequence will be spliced into the function in which x appears. g[u, x, u] would thus become g[u, a, b, c, u].

When the pattern objects x_:v and x_. appear as arguments of functions, they represent arguments which may be omitted. When the argument corresponding to x:v is omitted, x is taken to have value v. When the argument corresponding to x_. is omitted, x has a *default value* that is associated with the function in which it appears. You can specify this default value by making assignments for Default[*f*] and so on.

| | |
|---|---|
| Default[*f*] | default value for x_. when it appears as any argument of the function *f* |
| Default[*f*, *n*] | default value for x_. when it appears as the *n*th argument (negative *n* count from the end) |
| Default[*f*, *n*, *tot*] | default value for the $n^{\text{th}}$ argument when there are a total of *tot* arguments |

Default values.

A pattern like f[x__, y__, z__] can match an expression like f[a, b, c, d, e] with several different choices of x, y and z. The choices with x and y of minimum length are tried first. In general, when there are multiple __ or ___ in a single function, the case that is tried first takes all the __ and ___ to stand for sequences of minimum length, except the last one, which stands for "the rest" of the arguments.

When x_:v or x_. are present, the case that is tried first is the one in which none of them correspond to omitted arguments. Cases in which later arguments are dropped are tried next.

| | |
|---|---|
| Orderless | *f*[*x*, *y*] and *f*[*y*, *x*] are equivalent |
| Flat | *f*[*f*[*x*], *y*] and *f*[*x*, *y*] are equivalent |
| OneIdentity | *f*[*x*] and *x* are equivalent |

Attributes used in matching patterns.

Pattern objects like x_ can represent any sequence of arguments in a function

$f$ with attribute `Flat`. The value of $x$ in this case is $f$ applied to the sequence of arguments. If $f$ has the attribute `OneIdentity`, then $e$ is used instead of $f[e]$ when $x$ corresponds to a sequence of just one argument.

## ■ B.5.2 Assignments

| | |
|---|---|
| $lhs$ = $rhs$ | immediate assignment: $rhs$ is evaluated at the time of assignment |
| $lhs$ := $rhs$ | delayed assignment: $rhs$ is evaluated when the value of $lhs$ is requested |

The two basic types of assignment in *Mathematica*.

Assignments in *Mathematica* specify transformation rules for expressions. Every assignment that you make must be associated with a particular *Mathematica* symbol.

| | |
|---|---|
| $f[args]$ = $rhs$ | assignment is associated with $f$ |
| $t/:$ $f[args]$ = $rhs$ | assignment is associated with $t$ |
| $f[g[args]]$ ^= $rhs$ | assignment is associated with $g$ |

Assignments associated with different symbols.

In the case of an assignment like $f[args]$ = $rhs$, *Mathematica* looks at $f$, then the head of $f$, then the head of that, and so on, until it finds a symbol with which to associate the assignment.

When you make an assignment like $lhs$ ^= $rhs$, *Mathematica* will set up transformation rules associated with each distinct symbol that occurs either as an argument of $lhs$, or as the head of an argument of $lhs$.

The transformation rules associated with a particular symbol $s$ are always stored in a definite order, and are tested in that order when they are used. Each time you make an assignment, the corresponding transformation rule is inserted at the end of the list of transformation rules associated with $s$, except in the following cases:

- The left-hand side of the transformation rule is identical to a transformation rule that has already been stored, and any /; conditions on the right-hand side are also identical. In this case, the new transformation rule is inserted in place of the old one.

- Transformation rules that are already in the list have left-hand sides which are patterns that match the left-hand side of the transformation rule being inserted. In this case, the new transformation rule is inserted immediately before the first transformation rule that matches it. (Neither new nor old transformation rules can have /; conditions attached in this case.)

## ■ B.5.3  Types of Values

There are several different sets of transformation rules that can be associated with a particular symbol.

| | |
|---:|:---|
| $f$ | the value of $f$ itself |
| `f[args]` etc. | values of expressions associated with $f$ |
| `Attributes[f]` | attributes of $f$ |
| `Default[f]` | default values for arguments of $f$ |
| `Format[f]` etc. | print forms associated with $f$ |
| `Messages[f]` | messages associated with $f$ |
| `N[f]` etc. | numerical values associated with $f$ |
| `Options[f]` | defaults for options associated with $f$ |

Types of values associated with symbols.

## ■ B.5.4  Clearing and Removing Objects

| | |
|---:|:---|
| *expr* `=.` | clear a value defined for *expr* |
| $f$ `/:` *expr* `=.` | clear a value associated with $f$ defined for *expr* |
| `Clear[`$s_1$`, `$s_2$`, ...]` | clear all values for the symbols $s_i$, except for attributes, messages and defaults |
| `ClearAll[`$s_1$`, `$s_2$`, ...]` | clear all values for the $s_i$, including attributes, messages and defaults |
| `Remove[`$s_1$`, `$s_2$`, ...]` | clear all values, and then remove the names of the $s_i$ |

Ways to clear and remove objects.

`Clear`, `ClearAll` and `Remove` can all take strings as arguments, to specify action on all symbols whose names match the strings given according to `StringMatchQ`.

`Clear`, `ClearAll` and `Remove` do nothing to symbols with the attribute `Protected`.

## ■ B.5.5  Transformation Rules

| | | |
|---|---|---|
| *lhs* `->` *rhs* | immediate rule: *rhs* is evaluated when the rule is first given |
| *lhs* `:>` *rhs* | delayed rule: *rhs* is evaluated when the rule is used |

The two basic types of transformation rules in *Mathematica*.

# ■ B.6 *Mathematica* Sessions

## ■ B.6.1 Global Variables

| | |
|---:|:---|
| In[$n$] | the $n^{\text{th}}$ input line |
| Environment["$var$"] | the value of an operating system environment variable, or Failed if the variable is not found |
| Out[$n$] or %$n$ | the $n^{\text{th}}$ output line |
| $CommandLine | a list of the elements of the original operating system command line with which *Mathematica* was called |
| $Context | the current context |
| $ContextPath | the current context path |
| $Epilog | an expression to be executed when you exit *Mathematica* |
| $IgnoreEOF | whether to exit an interactive *Mathematica* session when an end-of-file character is received |
| $Line | the current line number |
| $Path | the current path to search for files |
| $Pre | a function applied to each input expression before evaluation |
| $Post | a function applied after evaluation |
| $PrePrint | a function applied after Out[$n$] is assigned, but before the result is printed |
| $RecursionLimit | the current recursion limit for evaluation |
| $System | the type of computer system on which *Mathematica* is running |
| $Version | the version of *Mathematica* being used |

General global variables.

Input and output media can be either files or pipes.

| | |
|---|---|
| $Display | list of default media to use for graphics output |
| $DisplayFunction | default function to use for graphics output |
| $Echo | media to echo each line of input to |
| $Messages | media to send messages to |
| $Output | media to send standard output to |
| $Urgent | media to send urgent messages to |
| $$Media | list of all active output media |

Global variables for output.

## ■ B.6.2  The Main Loop

- Read in input.

- Make translations specified by aliases.

- Apply $Pre function, if defined.

- Assign In[*n*].

- Evaluate expression.

- Apply $Post function, if defined.

- Assign Out[*n*].

- Apply $PrePrint function, if defined.

- Print expression, if it is not Null.

- Increment $Line.

An important point is that when the value of Out[*n*] (and thus %) is assigned, certain formatting functions are stripped off.  In addition to the format types OutputForm, InputForm, CForm, etc., the following formatting functions are removed: Short, TreeForm, MatrixForm, TableForm.  As a result, even if you type Short[*expr*], the value assigned to Out[*n*] will still be *expr*.

If your input consists of a compound expression ending with ;, then Null will be returned, and no output will be printed. The value of Out[*n*] will nevertheless be assigned to be the last element in the compound expression.

## ■ B.6.3  Interrupts

Most versions of *Mathematica* provide some mechanism for you to interrupt calculations that are running.

| | |
|---|---|
| `abort` | abort this particular calculation |
| `continue` | continue the calculation |
| `exit` | exit *Mathematica* completely |
| `show` | show a trace of functions that *Mathematica* uses |

Some typical options when you interrupt a calculation.

When you quit a calculation, the result you get will usually be the special symbol `$Interrupted`.

## ■ B.6.4  Initialization

| | |
|---|---|
| `init.m` | file to read when *Mathematica* starts |

Conventional *Mathematica* initialization file.

The details of initialization and termination in *Mathematica* depend on various aspects of its external interface, as discussed in the next section.

*Mathematica* searches for the file `init.m` in the sequence of directories you have specified in the list `$Path`.

On many systems, you will need to read in a file which specifies what graphics output device you intend to use. Typically the name of the file you need will be the name of the device you intend to use.

## ■ B.6.5  Termination

| | |
|---|---|
| `Exit[ ]` or `Quit[ ]` | terminate *Mathematica* |
| `$Epilog` | symbol to evaluate before *Mathematica* exits |
| `$IgnoreEOF` | whether to exit an interactive *Mathematica* session when an end-of-file character is received |
| `end.m` | file to read when *Mathematica* terminates |

*Mathematica* termination.

There are several ways to end a *Mathematica* session. If you are using *Mathematica* interactively, typing `Exit[ ]` or `Quit[ ]` on an input line will always terminate *Mathematica*.

If you are taking input for *Mathematica* from a file, *Mathematica* will exit when it reaches the end of the file. If you are using *Mathematica* interactively, it will still exit if it receives an end-of-file character (typically CONTROL-D). You can stop *Mathematica* from doing this by setting `$IgnoreEOF=False`.

# ■ B.7   External Interface

## ■ B.7.1   Introduction

While the computational aspects of *Mathematica* are essentially identical on all kinds of computers that run *Mathematica*, the external interface to *Mathematica* inevitably varies somewhat from one computer system to another.

*Mathematica* is usually divided into two parts: the *kernel* that actually does computations, and a *front end* that deals with interaction with the user. The kernel is set up to be as similar as possible on every different kind of computer; the front end varies from one computer to another, taking advantage of particular features of each computer.

The kernel and front end of *Mathematica* communicate by exchanging packets of standard printable ASCII. (The front end can also usually send interrupt signals to the kernel.) The kernel generates all graphics in POSTSCRIPT form.

Under multi-tasking operating systems (such as UNIX), the front end is usually a separate process, which communicates with the kernel through a bidirectional pipe.

Sometimes the front end may be a generic program, such as a shell window or an EMACS editor; in other cases, the front end may be a special program built specially for use with *Mathematica*. The same goes for POSTSCRIPT interpreters: on some systems *Mathematica* may use built-in POSTSCRIPT interpreters; on others, a special POSTSCRIPT interpreter program may be needed.

The front end and kernel need not both be on the same computer; they can be running on separate computers, connected by a network or other communications link.

This Section primarily concerns the external interface to the kernel of *Mathematica*. It does not discuss in any detail issues associated with the front end.

Even in discussing the external interface to the kernel, there are many details that depend on the operating system you are using. What is said in this Section mostly applies to UNIX-like operating systems. It should nevertheless be valid, at least in general terms, for any operating system that supports analogs of pipes and shell files.

## ■ B.7.2   The *Mathematica* Executable

The file you execute to run *Mathematica* is usually called `math`. This file is in fact a shell script, which calls the actual *Mathematica* binary with an appropriate set of command line arguments. If you use *Mathematica* with a front end, this shell script may also start the front end.

The `math` shell script is usually created at the time when *Mathematica* is installed on your system. The shell script contains various directory names which are determined during installation. If you reorganize your directories, you may need to redo the installation.

Set up the processes and pipes needed to run a *Mathematica* front end, if this is being used

Set the UNIX **PATH** environment variable to include the *Mathematica* utilities directory

Set up the record file to keep the input you give to *Mathematica* (optional)

Set up appropriate interrupt handling

Call the actual *Mathematica* binary, with command line arguments to specify directories etc.

Save the record file (optional)

Typical operations carried out in the `math` shell script.

The actual *Mathematica* binary is usually called `mathexe`. Any command line arguments that you give to `math` will be passed through to `mathexe`.

| | |
|---|---|
| -noprompt | do not issue input prompts or output labels |
| -remote | use remote-mode packet communication |
| -run "*command*" | execute a *Mathematica* command during start-up |

Command line arguments for `mathexe`.

The *Mathematica* kernel can accept input and generate output in several forms. If you give the command line argument **-remote**, then the kernel will accept input only in special packets, and will give output only in the form of such packets. This packet-based protocol is appropriate for communication with sophisticated front ends.

If you do not give the command line argument **-remote**, then *Mathematica* will accept input terminated by newlines. The input can go on for several lines, but will be evaluated as soon as it forms a complete expression.

In this mode, *Mathematica* usually issues input prompts of the form `In[`$n$`]:=`, and output labels of the form `Out[`$n$`]=`. If you run *Mathematica* in a pipe, or from within another program, you may want to suppress this ancillary output. You can do this by giving the command line argument `-noprompt`.

On most computer systems, the file `mathexe` is not just the pure executable code and static data for the *Mathematica* kernel. It is in fact a "core image" obtained by dumping the state of a running *Mathematica* job after initialization is complete.

`mathexe` is usually created by starting the original *Mathematica* binary, and then calling `Dump` from within the *Mathematica* session. When it is distributed, the original *Mathematica* binary is usually called `mathraw`.

When `mathraw` starts up, it tries to read the file `sysinit.m`. If it cannot read this file, `mathraw` simply exits. `sysinit.m` contains *Mathematica* commands which initialize various elements of the *Mathematica* system. In a typical case, `sysinit.m` reads in data for rule-based operations such as integration. In addition, `sysinit.m` reads the file `info.m` which contains information about built-in *Mathematica* objects, together with the file `msg.m`, which gives the text of messages associated with built-in functions.

---

Run any commands given by `-run` command line arguments

Read the file `init.m`

---

Typical start-up operations carried out by `mathexe`.

## ■ B.7.3   Files

When you use a command like `<<`*name*, *Mathematica* uses the following procedure to try and resolve the name of the file you want:

- If the name starts with `!`, *Mathematica* treats the remainder of the name as an external command, and uses a pipe to this command.

- *Mathematica* scans the name for the characters `*`, `$`, `~`, `?`, `[`, `"`, `\`, `` ` `` and `'`. If it finds any of these characters, then it passes the complete name to your operating system or shell. Under UNIX, *Mathematica* asks the shell to `echo` the file name, so that whatever globbing, quote-stripping or variable expansion the shell usually does is done. So long as the resulting file is unique, *Mathematica* then uses its name.

- If the file you specify is to be used for output, then *Mathematica* performs no further transformations.

- If the file you specify is to be used for input, then *Mathematica* can search a list of directories to try and find the file. It will not do this if the name you gave contained any of the special characters listed above, or if it starts with a slash. Otherwise, *Mathematica* goes down the list `$Path`, taking each element as a string which specifies a directory name. *Mathematica* concatenates each directory name, followed by a slash, with the name you specified, and then looks for a file with the resulting name.

| | |
|---|---|
| ! *command* | a pipe to an external command |
| / *directory* / *name* | a file in an absolutely-specified directory |
| $DIR/*name* etc. | a file whose name is to be resolved using the shell |
| *name* | a file to be searched for in the list of directories `$Path` |

Forms of file names.

When *Mathematica* starts up, the initial value of `$Path` is usually set by a `-run` command line argument in the `math` shell script. `$Path` typically contains the current directory, the user's home directory, the main *Mathematica* directory and the directory or directories for *Mathematica* notebooks and packages.

Note that the `$Path` mechanism is used *only* for files being read into *Mathematica*. Names of files to be written out by *Mathematica* are always specified relative to the current directory.

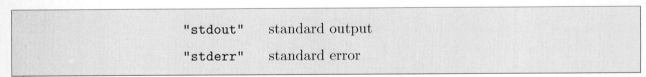

| | |
|---|---|
| `"stdout"` | standard output |
| `"stderr"` | standard error |

Special files recognized by *Mathematica*.

If *Mathematica* runs into a syntax error in an input file, it reports the error in the standard form *filename*: *linenumber*: `syntax error in` *inputstring*. By dissecting this form, you can make external programs, such as text editors, go to lines with syntax errors.

## ■ B.7.4  Pipes

You can use pipes in place of files in *Mathematica* input-output functions. *Mathematica* uses the rule that any "file name" beginning with a ! is in fact a pipe. The remainder of the name is used to specify the external command to which the pipe is attached. When the external command contains spaces or other special characters, you have to enclose the whole name in double quotes.

The text you give after ! is passed to your operating system or shell for execution. Under UNIX, external programs will be sought using whatever UNIX `PATH` you have specified. You should realize that this `PATH` has no connection with the `$Path` variable that you use within *Mathematica*. Nevertheless, the `math` shell script often resets your UNIX `PATH` so as to include directories of *Mathematica* utility programs.

## ■ B.7.5 External Programs

There are a number of different ways to run external programs from within *Mathematica*. The main difference between them is how input and output from the programs are connected to *Mathematica*. All these mechanisms work only under operating systems such as UNIX which support multitasking and pipes.

| | |
|---|---|
| `Run["`*command*`"]` | run an external command, with neither standard input nor standard output connected to *Mathematica* |
| *expr* `>> "!`*command*`"` | give the textual form of *expr* as the standard input to the command |
| `<< "!`*command*`"` | take the standard output of the command as *Mathematica* input |
| `RunThrough[`*expr*`, "`*command*`"]` | give *expr* as the standard input to the command, and take the standard output from the command as *Mathematica* input |

Functions for communicating with external programs.

## ■ B.7.6 External Functions

If you include the appropriate hooks in an external program, then you can call individual functions in the external program directly from *Mathematica*. In addition, you can have the external program call *Mathematica* back to perform calculations. All the necessary communications are done through a bidirectional pipe between *Mathematica* and the external program.

*Mathematica* sends "packets" containing requests for particular external function evaluations; the evaluations are performed by the external program, and the results are sent as a packet back to *Mathematica*. Routines for decoding and creating packets in the external program are typically distributed in source code form with *Mathematica*.

| | |
|---|---|
| MathInit() | initialize communications |
| MathInstall(*f*, "*fname*", "*ftype*", "*argnames*", "*argtypes*") | |
| | install the C function with pointer *f* so that it can be called from *Mathematica* with the name *fname* |
| MathStart() | put the external program in a state to be called by *Mathematica* |
| MathExec("*expr*") | evaluate *expr* as *Mathematica* input, and return the result as a string |

Typical C functions for setting up communication with *Mathematica*.

```
main()
{
int BitAnd();
double DoubleShift();

MathInit();

MathInstall(BitAnd, "BitAnd", "int", "x_Integer, y_Integer", "int, int");

MathInstall(DoubleShift, "DoubleShift", "double", "x, n_Integer", "double, int");

MathExec("BitAnd::usage = \"BitAnd[x, y] computes the bitwise AND of x and y.\"");

MathExec(
"DoubleShift::usage = \"DoubleShift[x] shifts the double representation of x by n bits.\"");

MathStart();
}

int BitAnd(x, y)
int x, y;
{
return( x&y );
}

double DoubleShift(x, n)
double x;
int n;
{
return( x >> n );
}
```

An external C program set up to be called from *Mathematica*.

The C types typically handled by `MathInstall` are `int`, `double` and `char *`.

## ■ B.7.7  Setting Up Textual Output

Output from *Mathematica* calculations is usually written to the special file named `"stdout"`. You can specify various properties of the output you want by setting different options for the file `"stdout"`.

| | |
|---|---|
| `ResetMedium[`*options*`]` | reset the specified options for the standard output from *Mathematica* |
| `ResetMedium[PageWidth->`*n*`]` | set up output for a text width of *n* characters |

Setting text output options.

| *option name* | *default value* | |
|---|---|---|
| `FormatType` | `OutputForm` | default format for printing expressions |
| `PageHeight` | `22` | number of lines per page |
| `PageWidth` | `78` | number of character widths per line |
| `TextRendering` | `Plain` | type of text output |
| `TotalHeight` | `Infinity` | maximum number of lines for a single expression |
| `TotalWidth` | `Infinity` | maximum number of character widths for a single expression |

Some options for text output.

Particularly when you first start *Mathematica*, you will often want to set `PageWidth` to correspond to the actual width of the text area available for *Mathematica* output. You can typically do this by running an external program that calls `stty` and so on, and using the result as the value of `PageWidth`.

| | |
|---|---|
| Format[In] := *nameIn* | specify alternative input prompts |
| Format[Out] := *nameOut* | specify alternative output labels |
| Format[Continuation[n_]] := *form* | |
| | specify continuation line marks |
| $PrePrint := *function* | specify a function to apply to every output expression |

Some characteristics of text output that you can specify.

Particularly if you run the kernel of *Mathematica* on a different computer than you run the front end, you may find it convenient to set up prompts and output labels that tell you what computer is being used.

| | |
|---|---|
| Continuation[*n*] | the object whose print form is given at the beginning of the $n^{\text{th}}$ line in multiline output (default: >) |
| Indent[*d*] | the object whose print form gives the indentation to be used on a line that begins with a depth $d$ subexpression (default: $d$ spaces) |
| LineBreak[*n*] | the object whose print form is given between the $n^{\text{th}}$ and $(n+1)^{\text{th}}$ line in multiline output (default: a blank line) |
| Skeleton[*n*] | the object whose print form is given in place of $n$ omitted elements in Short output (default: <<*n*>>) |
| StringBreak[*n*] | the object whose print form is given at the end of the $n^{\text{th}}$ part of a string that is broken onto several lines (default: \\) |
| StringSkeleton[*n*] | the object whose print form is given in place of $n$ omitted characters in Short output of a string (default: ..) |

Other objects whose print forms can be defined.

## ■ B.7.8  Setting Up Graphics

*Mathematica* generates all its graphics in PostScript.

The basic scheme is to send graphics output from *Mathematica* to a PostScript interpreter, usually through a pipe.

| | |
|---|---|
| `$DisplayFunction` | default function to apply to generate graphics output |
| `$Display` | default media to which to send graphics output |
| `Display[`*media*`, `*graphics*`]` | output *graphics* in POSTSCRIPT form to *media* |

Basic graphics output objects.

| | |
|---|---|
| `Identity` | no graphics output |
| `Function[ Display[$Display, #] ]` | |
| | graphics output to the media `$Display` |
| `Function[ Display["`*file*`", #] ]` | graphics output to a particular file |
| `Function[ Display["!`*command*`", #] ]` | |
| | graphics output through a pipe to an external command |
| `Function[ Run["`*begin*`"]; Display["!`*command*`", #]; Run["`*end*`"] ]` | |
| | graphics output through a pipe, running external initialization and termination programs |

Typical settings for `$DisplayFunction`.

### ■ B.7.9 POSTSCRIPT Output

| | |
|---:|:---|
| `%!` | standard POSTSCRIPT file beginning |
| `%%Creator: Mathematica` | standard POSTSCRIPT convention |
| `%%AspectRatio:` *r* | the "suggested" ratio of height to width for the final POSTSCRIPT image |
| `MathPictureStart` | initialization of *Mathematica* graphics state |
| *objects* `MathScale` | POSTSCRIPT computation for scaling of the final picture |
| `% Start of Graphics` | marker for the beginning of actual graphics |
| *graphics* | POSTSCRIPT for actual *Mathematica* graphics |
| `% End of Graphics` | marker for the end of actual graphics |
| `MathPictureEnd` | termination of *Mathematica* graphics |

Typical sequence of POSTSCRIPT generated by *Mathematica*.

The POSTSCRIPT output generated directly by the *Mathematica* kernel uses a number of special POSTSCRIPT procedures. Most *Mathematica* front ends automatically interpret these special procedures. However, if you want to send POSTSCRIPT from *Mathematica* to a generic POSTSCRIPT output device, you will have to include definition of the procedures, written in POSTSCRIPT. On most systems, the shell script `psfix` inserts the necessary definitions, and also adds POSTSCRIPT commands to set up output for $8\frac{1}{2} \times 11$ inch pages, and to specify standard fonts.

The treatment of text is the most complicated aspect of POSTSCRIPT output from *Mathematica*.

The basic problem is that different devices have different styles and sizes of fonts available. *Mathematica* functions like `FontForm` allow you to give strings which specify fonts for particular pieces of output. Typically these strings are generic font specifications, such as `Plain`, `Italic` or `Bold`. They have to be mapped into the particular fonts that are available on the output device you use. If your output goes through a *Mathematica* front end, the front end will usually take care of the necessary mappings. For output to generic POSTSCRIPT devices, the mapping must be done by an external program such as `psfix`. You may well have to modify `psfix` to deal with different sets of fonts on different output devices.

A second complication concerns the size of text. Although some POSTSCRIPT fonts can in principle be scaled arbitrarily, actual finite-resolution output devices typically use a discrete set of different-sized fonts. This means that the size of a particular piece of text can be determined only when the POSTSCRIPT for it is actually being rendered. As a result, the precise position of the text, and, in fact, the overall scaling of the whole picture, must be determined during POSTSCRIPT rendering, by executing the special POSTSCRIPT procedure `MathScale`.

The graphics output produced by *Mathematica* can be rendered on any device that supports a full version of standard POSTSCRIPT. The definitions for the special POSTSCRIPT procedures used in *Mathematica* output are sufficiently complicated that few subsets of POSTSCRIPT will be adequate.

## ■ B.7.10  Saving the State of *Mathematica*

On many computer systems, you can save the complete state of your *Mathematica* session, so you can start it up again exactly where you left off.

The basic mechanism for this is to save a "core image" file, and then to execute this core image when you want to start again.

| | |
|---|---|
| `Dump["file"]` | write out the core image of a *Mathematica* session |
| `Dump["file", start]` | insert the expression *start* in the core image, so the expression is evaluated when the image starts up |
| `Dump["file", start, "code"]` | take the file *code*, rather than `$CommandLine[[1]]`, to be the original *Mathematica* executable |

Saving the state of a *Mathematica* session.

A common way to use `Dump` is in creating copies of *Mathematica* that have certain data "pre-loaded". If you want these copies to start up like a standard *Mathematica* session, you can use `Dump["file", $Line=0; <<init.m]`.

You should realize that on most systems `Dump` creates a file that is more than two megabytes in size. If you want to save only some aspects of your *Mathematica* session, it is much more economical of storage space to save what you need in standard ASCII form using `Save`, rather than saving a complete core image using `Dump`.

If you have files open in *Mathematica* when you call `Dump`, these files will be closed. There would be no point in saving the file pointers in the core image, since there is no guarantee that the files will still exist, or be in the same place, when the core image is restarted.

## ■ B.7.11 *Mathematica* Files

| | |
|---|---|
| Notebooks | *Mathematica* notebooks |
| Packages | *Mathematica* packages |
| Utilities | utility programs and files for use with *Mathematica* |

Directories of files typically provided with *Mathematica*.

| | |
|---|---|
| math | shell script that runs *Mathematica* |
| mathremote | shell script that runs *Mathematica* in remote mode |
| mathexe | executable code for *Mathematica* |
| math.install | *Mathematica* installation script |
| init.m | *Mathematica* initialization file |
| end.m | *Mathematica* termination file |
| README | information file |

Files typically in the main *Mathematica* directory.

| | |
|---|---|
| mdefs.h | C language macro definitions for objects used in CForm output |
| mlink.c | C language code for setting up links between external functions and *Mathematica* |
| mlink.h | macro definitions associated with mlink.c |
| psfix | an annotated shell file for adapting *Mathematica* POSTSCRIPT output for rendering by a standard POSTSCRIPT interpreter |

Typical *Mathematica* utility files.

# ■ Listing of Built-in *Mathematica* Objects

## ■ Introduction

This section gives an alphabetical list of all the built-in *Mathematica* objects.

At the end of the section is a list of special input forms.

Much of the information in this section can be accessed directly from *Mathematica*. Assuming that your *Mathematica* implementation or initialization procedure has read in the file `info.m`, you can find information on a built-in object $F$ by typing `?F`. Typing `??F` gives you more information on $F$.

Note that all the built-in objects in this listing are in the context `System`.

## ■ Conventions in This Listing

| | |
|---|---|
| `text in this style` | literal *Mathematica* input that you type in as it is printed (e.g. function names) |
| *text in this style* | expressions that you fill in (e.g. function arguments) |
| $object_1$, $object_2$, ... | a sequence of any number of expressions |

Conventions used in the list of built-in objects.

■ **Abs**

> Abs[z] gives the absolute value of the real or complex number $z$.

For complex numbers $z$, Abs[z] gives the modulus $|z|$. ■ Abs[z] is left unevaluated if *expr* is not a number. ■ See pages 341 and 342. ■ See also: Re, Im, Arg, Mod.

■ **Accumulate**

> Accumulate[$f$, $g[e_1, e_2, ...]$] gives $g[e_1, f[e_1, e_2], f[f[e_1, e_2], e_3], ...]$.

Accumulate[Plus, {$e_1$, $e_2$, ...}] gives cumulative sums of elements in a list. ■ When you use Accumulate on a list of length $n$, you get a list of length $n$. ■ Accumulate is a generalized "prefix operation". ■ See page 182. ■ See also: Apply, Nest, NestList, Partition.

■ **Accuracy**

> Accuracy[x] gives the number of digits to the right of the decimal point in the number $x$.

If $x$ is not a number, Accuracy[x] gives the minimum value of Accuracy for all the numbers that appear in $x$. ■ Accuracy gives Infinity when applied to exact numbers, such as integers. ■ See page 331. ■ See also: Precision, N, Chop.

■ **AccuracyGoal**

> AccuracyGoal is an option for various numerical operations which specifies how many digits of accuracy should be sought in the final result.

AccuracyGoal is an option for such functions as NIntegrate and FindRoot. ■ Even though you may specify AccuracyGoal->$n$, the results you get may have much less than $n$ digit accuracy. ■ In most cases, you must set WorkingPrecision to be at least as large as AccuracyGoal. ■ See page 472. ■ See also: WorkingPrecision.

■ **AddTo**

> $x$ += $dx$ adds $dx$ to $x$ and returns the new value of $x$.

AddTo has the attribute HoldFirst. ■ $x$ += $dx$ is equivalent to $x = x + dx$. ■ See page 257. ■ See also: Increment, PreIncrement, Set, PrependTo.

■ **AiryAi**

> AiryAi[z] gives the Airy function Ai($z$).

Mathematical function (see Section B.3.8). ■ The Airy function Ai($z$) is a solution to the differential equation $\frac{d^2 y}{dx^2} - xy = 0$. ■ See page 363.

## ■ AlgebraicRules

**AlgebraicRules**[*eqns*, {$x_1$, $x_2$, ...}] generates a set of algebraic rules which replace variables earlier in the list of $x_i$ with ones later in the list, according to the equation or equations *eqns*.

You can use **AlgebraicRules** to set up algebraic transformations which you need to apply many times. ■ The argument *eqns* can be a single equation of the form *lhs*==*rhs*, or a list of equations {*lhs₁*==*rhs₁*, *lhs₂*==*rhs₂*, ...}. ■ **AlgebraicRules** generates an **AlgebraicRulesData** object, which contains a representation of the Gröbner basis for the equations *eqns*. In standard **OutputForm**, the output from **AlgebraicRules** is printed like a list of replacements. ■ You can use *expr*/.*arules* to apply a set of algebraic rules to a particular expression. ■ See page 410. ■ See also: **Eliminate**, **Replace**.

## ■ Alias

*in* ::= *trans* defines an alias, which causes *in* to be textually translated to the symbol *trans* on input. *in* can be either a string, or a symbol name, possibly including context marks.

**Alias**["*in*"] gives any aliases that have been defined for the string "*in*".

**Alias**[ ] gives all aliases that have been defined.

Example: m::=Statistics`Mean specifies that m should be textually translated to Statistics`Mean. ■ Alias translations are done only on complete symbol names. Defining an alias for m does not affect mm. ■ Aliases are translated as soon as input is read. They are independent of context, and of evaluation. ■ You can give an alias for any string. "++" ::= Increment defines an alias for ++. This will not be used in ordinary expressions, but will be retrieved if you type ?++. ■ See page 305. ■ See also: **UnAlias**.

## ■ All

**All** is a setting used for certain options.

PlotRange -> All specifies that all points are to be included in a plot. ■ See page 110.

## ■ AmbientLight

**AmbientLight** is an option to **Graphics3D** and related functions that gives the level of simulated ambient illumination in a three-dimensional picture.

AmbientLight -> GrayLevel[*intensity*] specifies a gray level;
AmbientLight -> RGBColor[*red*, *green*, *blue*] specifies color. ■ See page 129. ■ See also: **Lighting**, **LightSources**.

## ■ And

$e_1$ && $e_2$ && ... is the logical AND function. It evaluates its arguments in order, giving **False** immediately if any of them are **False**, and **True** if they are all **True**.

**And** evaluates its arguments in a non-standard way (see page 569). ■ **And** gives symbolic results when necessary, and applies various simplification rules to them. ■ When **And** gives a symbolic result, all its arguments are evaluated. ■ See page 73. ■ See also: **LogicalExpand**.

## Apart

Apart[*expr*] rewrites a rational expression as a sum of terms with minimal denominators.

Apart[*expr*, *var*] treats all variables other than *var* as constants.

Example: Apart[(x^2+1)/(x-1)] $\longrightarrow$ 1 + x + $\dfrac{2}{-1 + x}$. ▪ Apart gives the partial fraction decomposition of a rational expression. ▪ See page 386. ▪ See also: Together, Cancel, PolynomialQuotient.

## Append

Append[*expr*, *elem*] gives *expr* with *elem* appended.

Examples: Append[{a,b}, c] $\longrightarrow$ {a, b, c}; Append[f[a], b+c] $\longrightarrow$ f[a, b + c]. ▪ See page 102. ▪ See also: Prepend, Insert, AppendTo.

## AppendTo

AppendTo[*s*, *elem*] appends *elem* to the value of *s*, and resets *s* to the result.

AppendTo[*s*, *elem*] is equivalent to *s* = Append[*s*, *elem*]. ▪ AppendTo[*s*, *elem*] does not evaluate *s*. ▪ You can use AppendTo repeatedly to build up a list. ▪ See page 257. ▪ See also: PrependTo.

## Apply

Apply[*f*, *expr*] or *f* @@ *expr* replaces the head of *expr* by *f*.

Apply[*f*, *expr*, *levelspec*] replaces heads in parts of *expr* specified by *levelspec*.

Examples: Apply[f, {a, b, c}] $\longrightarrow$ f[a, b, c]; Apply[Plus, g[a, b]] $\longrightarrow$ a + b. ▪ Level specifications are described on page 564. ▪ The default value for *levelspec* in Apply is {0}. ▪ Examples: Apply[f, {{a,b},{c,d}}] $\longrightarrow$ f[{a, b}, {c, d}]; Apply[f, {{a,b},{c,d}}, 1] $\longrightarrow$ {f[a, b], f[c, d]}; Apply[f, {{a,b},{c,d}}, {1}] $\longrightarrow$ {f[a, b], f[c, d]}; Apply[f, {{a,b},{c,d}}, -2] $\longrightarrow$ {f[a, b], f[c, d]}. ▪ See page 169. ▪ See also: Map, Scan, Level.

## ArcCos

ArcCos[*z*] gives the arc cosine $\cos^{-1}(z)$ of *z*.

Mathematical function (see Section B.3.8). ▪ All results are given in radians. ▪ For real *z*, the results are always in the range $-\pi$ to $\pi$. ▪ See page 353.

## ArcCosh

ArcCosh[*z*] gives the hyperbolic arc cosine $\cosh^{-1}(z)$ of *z*.

See page 353. ▪ See also: ArcSech.

## ArcCot

ArcCot[*z*] gives the arc cotangent $\cot^{-1}(z)$ of the complex number *z*.

See page 353. ▪ See notes for ArcCos.

■ **ArcCoth**

ArcCoth[z] gives the hyperbolic arc cotangent $\coth^{-1}(z)$ of the complex number z.

See page 353.

■ **ArcCsc**

ArcCsc[z] gives the arc cosecant $\csc^{-1}(z)$ of the complex number z.

See notes for ArcCos. ▪ See page 353.

■ **ArcCsch**

ArcCsch[z] gives the hyperbolic arc cosecant $\operatorname{csch}^{-1}(z)$ of the complex number z.

See page 353.

■ **ArcSec**

ArcSec[z] gives the arc secant $\sec^{-1}(z)$ of the complex number z.

See notes for ArcCos. ▪ See page 353.

■ **ArcSech**

ArcSech[z] gives the hyperbolic arc secant $\operatorname{sech}^{-1}(z)$ of the complex number z.

See page 353.

■ **ArcSin**

ArcSin[z] gives the arc sine $\sin^{-1}(z)$ of the complex number z.

See notes for ArcCos. ▪ See page 353.

■ **ArcSinh**

ArcSinh[z] gives the hyperbolic arc sine $\sinh^{-1}(z)$ of the complex number z.

See page 353. ▪ See also: ArcCsch.

■ **ArcTan**

ArcTan[z] gives the arc tangent $\tan^{-1}(z)$ of the complex number z.

ArcTan[x, y] gives the arc tangent of $\frac{y}{x}$, taking into account which quadrant the point $(x, y)$ is in.

See notes for ArcCos. ▪ If x or y is complex, then ArcTan[x, y] gives $-i\,\log\left(\frac{x+i\,y}{\sqrt{x^2+y^2}}\right)$. When $x^2 + y^2 = 1$, ArcTan[x, y] gives the number $\phi$ such that $x = \cos\phi$ and $y = \sin\phi$. ▪ See page 353. ▪ See also: Arg.

■ **ArcTanh**

> `ArcTanh[z]` gives the hyperbolic arc tangent $\tanh^{-1}(z)$ of $z$.

> See page 353. ▪ See also: `ArcCoth`.

■ **Arg**

> `Arg[z]` gives the argument of $z$.

> Mathematical function (see Section B.3.8). ▪ `Arg[z]` gives the phase angle of $z$ in radians. ▪ The result from `Arg[z]` is always between $-\pi$ and $+\pi$. ▪ See page 342. ▪ See also: `ArcTan`.

■ **ArithmeticGeometricMean**

> `ArithmeticGeometricMean[a, b]` gives the arithmetic-geometric mean of $a$ and $b$.

> See page 374.

■ **Array**

> `Array[f, n]` generates a list of length $n$, with elements `f[i]`.

> `Array[f, {n1, n2, ...}]` generates a $n_1 \times n_2 \times ...$ array of nested lists, with elements $f[i_1, i_2, ...]$.

> `Array[f, dims, origin]` generates a list using the specified index origin (default **1**).

> `Array[f, dims, origin, h]` uses head $h$, rather than `List`, for each level of the array.

> Example: `Array[f, 3]` $\longrightarrow$ `{f[1], f[2], f[3]}`. ▪
> `Array[f, {2, 3}]` $\longrightarrow$ `{{f[1, 1], f[1, 2], f[1, 3]}, {f[2, 1], f[2, 2], f[2, 3]}}` generates a $2 \times 3$ matrix. ▪ `Array[#1^#2 &, {2, 2}]` $\longrightarrow$ `{{1, 1}, {2, 4}}`. ▪
> `Array[f, 3, 0]` $\longrightarrow$ `{f[0], f[1], f[2]}` generates an array with index origin 0. ▪
> `Array[f, 3, 1, Plus]` $\longrightarrow$ `f[1] + f[2] + f[3]`. ▪ Note that the dimensions given to `Array` are *not* in standard *Mathematica* iterator notation. ▪ See page 182. ▪ See also: `Table`.

■ **AspectRatio**

> `AspectRatio` is an option for `Show` and related functions which specifies the ratio of height to width for a plot.

> `AspectRatio` determines the scaling for the final image shape. ▪ `AspectRatio -> Automatic` determines the ratio of height to width from the actual coordinate values in the plot. ▪ The default value `AspectRatio -> 1/GoldenRatio` is used for two-dimensional plots. `AspectRatio -> 1` is used for three-dimensional plots. ▪ See page 109. ▪ See also: `BoxRatios`.

■ **AtomQ**

> `AtomQ[expr]` yields `True` if *expr* is an expression which cannot be divided into subexpressions, and yields `False` otherwise.

> You can use `AtomQ` in a recursive procedure to tell when you have got the bottom of the tree corresponding to an expression. ▪ `AtomQ` gives `True` for symbols, numbers, strings and other raw objects. ▪ `AtomQ` gives `True` on any object whose subparts cannot be accessed using functions like `Map`. ▪ See page 230. ▪ See also: `NumberQ`, `Head`, `LeafCount`.

# ■ Attributes

**Attributes**[*symbol*] gives the list of attributes for a symbol.

The attributes of a symbol can be set by assigning a value to **Attributes**[s]. If a single attribute is assigned, it need not be in a list. ■ **Attributes**[s] = {} clears all attributes of a symbol. ■ **Attributes**[{$s_1$, $s_2$, ...}] gives a list of the attributes for each of the $s_i$. ■ Attributes for functions must be set before any definitions that involve the functions are given. ■ The complete list of possible attributes for a symbol *f* is:

| | |
|---|---|
| Constant | all derivatives of *f* are zero |
| Flat | associative |
| HoldAll | all the arguments of *f* are not evaluated |
| HoldFirst | the first argument of *f* is not evaluated |
| HoldRest | all but the first argument of *f* is not evaluated |
| Listable | *f* is automatically "threaded" over lists |
| Locked | attributes of *f* cannot be changed |
| OneIdentity | *f*[a], *f*[*f*[a]], etc. are equivalent to *a* |
| Orderless | commutative |
| Protected | values of *f* cannot be changed |
| ReadProtected | values of *f* cannot be read |

■ See page 214. ■ See also: **SetAttributes**, **ClearAttributes**.

# ■ Automatic

**Automatic** represents an option value that is to be chosen automatically by a built-in function.

See page 110.

# ■ Axes

**Axes** is an option for **Show** that specifies how axes should be drawn in a plot.

Axes -> None specifies that no axes should be drawn. ■ Axes -> Automatic automatically selects the axis origin. ■ Axes -> {$x$, $y$} specifies the axis origin explicitly. ■ See page 109. ■ See also: **Framed**.

# ■ AxesLabel

**AxesLabel** is an option for graphics functions that specifies labels for axes.

AxesLabel -> None specifies that no labels should be given. ■ AxesLabel -> *label* specifies a label for the *y* of a two-dimensional plot, or the *z* axis of a three-dimensional plot. ■ AxesLabel -> {*xlabel*, *ylabel*} specifies labels for different axes. ■ Any expression can be specified as a label. It will be given in **OutputForm**. Arbitrary strings of text can be enclosed in ". ■ See page 109. ■ See also: **PlotLabel**.

# ■ BaseForm

**BaseForm**[*expr*, *n*] prints with the numbers in *expr* given in base *n*.

The maximum allowed base is 36. For bases larger than 10, additional digits are chosen from the letters a–z. ■ You can enter a number in an arbitrary base using *base*^^*digits*. ■ When a number in an arbitrary base is given in scientific notation, the exponent is still given in base 10. ■ See page 329. ■ See also: **NumberForm**.

■ Begin

> Begin["*context*`"] resets the current context.

Begin resets the value of $Context. ▪ The interpretation of symbol names depends on context. Begin thus affects the parsing of input expressions. ▪ See pages 310 and 313. ▪ See also: End, EndAdd, $ContextPath.

■ BeginPackage

> BeginPackage["*context*`"] makes *context*` and System` the only active contexts.

> BeginPackage["*context*`", {"*need₁*`", "*need₂*`", ...}] includes the *need*ᵢ in the list of active contexts.

BeginPackage is typically used at the beginning of a *Mathematica* package. ▪ BeginPackage resets the values of both $Context and $ContextPath. ▪ The interpretation of symbol names depends on context. BeginPackage thus affects the parsing of input expressions. ▪ See page 310. ▪ See also: EndPackage.

■ BernoulliB

> BernoulliB[*n*] gives the Bernoulli number $B_n$.

> BernoulliB[*n*, x] gives the Bernoulli polynomial $B_n(x)$.

Mathematical function (see Section B.3.8). ▪ The Bernoulli polynomials satisfy the generating function relation $\frac{te^{xt}}{e^t-1} = \sum_{n=0}^{\infty} B_n(x)\frac{t^n}{n!}$. ▪ The Bernoulli numbers are given by $B_n = B_n(0)$. ▪ See page 350. ▪ See also: NBernoulliB.

■ BesselI

> BesselI[*n*, z] gives the modified Bessel function of the first kind $I_n(z)$.

Mathematical function (see Section B.3.8). ▪ $I_n(z)$ satisfies the differential equation $z^2\frac{d^2y}{dz^2} + z\frac{dy}{dz} - (z^2 + n^2)y = 0$. ▪ See page 363.

■ BesselJ

> BesselJ[*n*, z] gives the Bessel function of the first kind $J_n(z)$.

Mathematical function (see Section B.3.8). ▪ $J_n(z)$ satisfies the differential equation $z^2\frac{d^2y}{dz^2} + z\frac{dy}{dz} + (z^2 - n^2)y = 0$. ▪ See page 363.

■ BesselK

> BesselK[*n*, z] gives the modified Bessel function of the second kind $K_n(z)$.

Mathematical function (see Section B.3.8). ▪ $K_n(z)$ satisfies the differential equation $z^2\frac{d^2y}{dz^2} + z\frac{dy}{dz} - (z^2 + n^2)y = 0$. ▪ See page 363.

■ BesselY

> BesselY[*n*, z] gives the Bessel function of the second kind $Y_n(z)$.

Mathematical function (see Section B.3.8). ▪ $Y_n(z)$ satisfies the differential equation $z^2\frac{d^2y}{dz^2} + z\frac{dy}{dz} + (z^2 - n^2)y = 0$. ▪ See page 363.

■ **Beta**

Beta[$x$, $y$] gives the Euler beta function $B(x, y)$.

Beta[$a$, $x$, $y$] gives the incomplete Beta function $B_a(x, y)$.

Mathematical function (see Section B.3.8). ▪ $B(x, y) = \frac{\Gamma(x)\Gamma(y)}{\Gamma(x+y)} = \int_0^1 t^{x-1}(1-t)^{y-1}dt.$ ▪ $B_a(x, y) = \int_0^a t^{x-1}(1-t)^{y-1}dt.$ ▪ See page 363.

■ **Binomial**

Binomial[$n$, $m$] gives the binomial coefficient $\binom{n}{m}$.

Integer mathematical function (see Section B.3.8). ▪ Binomial is evaluated whenever $n$ and $m$ differ by an integer. ▪ Example: Binomial[x+2, x] $\longrightarrow \dfrac{(1 + x)\ (2 + x)}{2}$. ▪ See page 350. ▪ See also: Multinomial, Pochhammer.

■ **Blank**

_ or Blank[ ] is a pattern object that can stand for any *Mathematica* expression.

_$h$ or Blank[$h$] can stand for any expression with head $h$.

The head $h$ in _$h$ cannot itself contain pattern objects. ▪ See page 224. ▪ See also: Pattern, Optional.

■ **BlankNullSequence**

___ (three _ characters) or BlankNullSequence[ ] is a pattern object that can stand for any sequence of zero or more *Mathematica* expressions.

___$h$ or BlankNullSequence[$h$] can stand for any sequence of expressions, all of which have head $h$.

Blank sequences work slightly differently depending on whether or not the head of the expression in which they appear is a symbol with the attribute Flat. ▪ Consider matching the pattern $f[a_1, a_2, \ldots, \_\_\_, c_1, \ldots]$ against the expression $f[a_1, a_2, \ldots, b_1, \ldots, c_1, \ldots]$. If $f$ is a symbol with attribute Flat, then the ___ will be taken to stand for the expression $f[b_1, \ldots]$. If $f$ is not a symbol with attribute Flat, then ___ will be taken to stand for the sequence of expressions $b_1, \ldots$. With a named pattern, such as $x\_\_\_$, $x$ can be used only as an element in an expression. The sequence of expressions $b_1, \ldots$ is "spliced in" to replace $x$, thereby usually increasing the length of the expression. ▪ See page 557. ▪ See also: Pattern.

■ **BlankSequence**

___ (two _ characters) or BlankSequence[ ] is a pattern object that can stand for any sequence of one or more *Mathematica* expressions.

___$h$ or BlankSequence[$h$] can stand for any sequence of expressions, all of which have head $h$.

See notes for BlankNullSequence. ▪ See page 557.

■ Block

Block[{$x_1$, $x_2$, ...}, *expr*] specifies that *expr* is to be evaluated with the symbols $x_i$ taken as local variables.

Block[{$x_1$ = $v_1$, ...}, *expr*] defines initial values for local variables.

The initial values specified for local variables are found before the variables are "localized". As a result, the initial values of different local variables are therefore effectively assigned in parallel. ■ A local variable x is represented by the same *symbol* as a global x. The two are considered identical in pattern matching or == comparisons. Any values of the global x are, however, removed when the local x is created, and are restored when the local x is destroyed. ■ Block has attribute HoldAll. ■ See page 252. ■ See also: CompoundExpression.

■ Boxed

Boxed is an option for **Graphics3D** which specifies whether to draw the edges of the bounding box in a three-dimensional picture.

Boxed -> True draws the box; Boxed -> False does not. ■ See page 123.

■ BoxRatios

BoxRatios is an option for **Graphics3D** and **SurfaceGraphics** which gives the ratios of side lengths for the bounding box of the three-dimensional picture.

BoxRatios -> {$s_x$, $s_y$, $s_z$} gives the side-length ratios. ■ See page 123.

■ Break

Break[ ] exits the nearest enclosing **For** or **While**.

Break is effective only if it is generated as the value of a segment in a compound expression, or as the body of a control structure. ■ The value Null is returned from the enclosing control structure. ■ Break does not work inside Do. ■ See page 260. ■ See also: Continue, Return.

■ Byte

Byte represents a single byte of data in **Read**.

See page 301.

■ ByteCount

ByteCount[*expr*] gives the number of bytes used internally by *Mathematica* to store *expr*.

ByteCount does not take account of any sharing of subexpressions. The results it gives assume that every part of the expression is stored separately. ByteCount will therefore often given an overestimate of the amount of memory currently needed to store a particular expression. When you manipulate the expression, however, subexpressions will often stop being shared, and the amount of memory needed will be close to the value returned by ByteCount. ■ See page 318. ■ See also: LeafCount, MemoryInUse, MaxMemoryUsed.

■ CallProcess

> CallProcess["*command*", *f*, {*x₁*, *x₂*, ...}] calls the function *f* in an external process, with arguments $x_i$.

> CallProcess exchanges data with an external process using pipes. The external process must have been started using StartProcess. ▪ The arguments $x_i$ are passed in textual form to the external process. ▪ See page 304. ▪ See also: RunThrough, Put.

■ Cancel

> Cancel[*expr*] cancels out common factors in the numerator and denominator of *expr*.

> Example: Cancel[(x^2-1)/(x-1)] ⟶ 1 + x. ▪ Cancel is Listable. ▪ Cancel cancels out the greatest common divisor of the numerator and denominator. ▪ See page 386. ▪ See also: Apart, GCD.

■ Cases

> Cases[{*e₁*, *e₂*, ...}, *pattern*] gives a list of the $e_i$ which match the pattern.

> Cases[{*e₁*, ...}, *rhs*, *pattern*] gives a list of the values of *rhs* corresponding to the $e_i$ which match the pattern.

> Examples: Cases[{5, k[3], 2, k[1], k[2]}, k[_]] ⟶ {k[3], k[1], k[2]}. ▪ Cases[{5, k[3], k[5]}, k[x_], 4 x + 1] ⟶ {13, 21}. ▪ The first argument to Cases need not have head List. ▪ See page 235. ▪ See also: Select, Position.

■ Catalan

> Catalan is Catalan's constant, with numerical value $\simeq 0.915966$.

> Catalan's constant is given by the sum $\sum_{k=0}^{\infty}(-1)^k(2k+1)^{-2}$. ▪ See page 359.

■ Catch

> Catch[*expr*] returns the argument of the first Throw generated in the evaluation of *expr*.

> Throw and Catch can be used to implement non-local returns and jumps in procedural programs. ▪ See page 260.

■ Ceiling

> Ceiling[x] gives the smallest integer greater than *x*.

> Mathematical function (see Section B.3.8). ▪ Examples: Ceiling[2.4] ⟶ 3; Ceiling[2.6] ⟶ 3; Ceiling[-2.4] ⟶ -2; Ceiling[-2.6] ⟶ -2. ▪ See page 341. ▪ See also: Floor, Round, Chop.

## CellArray

CellArray[{{$a_{11}$, $a_{12}$, ...}, ...}] is a two-dimensional graphics primitive which generates an array of rectangular gray cells.

The full form is CellArray[*array*, {{*xmin*, *ymin*}, {*xmax*, *ymax*}}, {*zmin*, *zmax*}]. The default value of {*zmin*, *zmax*} is {0, 1}. The displayed cells fill the rectangle {{*xmin*, *ymin*}, {*xmax*, *ymax*}}.

The array of cell values must be rectangular. ▪ The cell values must be numbers between *zmin* and *zmax*. ▪ Notice the order of $x$ and $y$ limits. Scaled coordinates can be used. ▪ See page 142. ▪ See also: GrayLevel.

## CForm

CForm[*expr*] prints as a C language version of *expr*.

Standard arithmetic functions and certain control structures are translated. ▪ No declarations are generated. ▪ See page 157. ▪ See also: FortranForm.

## Character

Character represents a single character in Read.

See page 301.

## Characters

Characters[*expr*] gives a list of the characters in the printed form of *expr*.

Each character is given as a length one string. ▪ Example: Characters[3412] $\longrightarrow$ {3, 4, 1, 2}. ▪ The InputForm of *expr* is used. ▪ See page 279.

## ChebyshevT

ChebyshevT[*n*, *x*] gives the Chebyshev polynomial of the first kind $T_n(x)$.

Mathematical function (see Section B.3.8). ▪ Explicit polynomials are given for integer $n$. ▪ $T_n(\cos\theta) = \cos(n\theta)$. ▪ See page 360.

## ChebyshevU

ChebyshevU[*n*, *x*] gives the Chebyshev polynomial of the second kind $U_n(x)$.

Mathematical function (see Section B.3.8). ▪ Explicit polynomials are given for integer $n$. ▪ $U_n(x) = \frac{\sin(n+1)\theta}{\sin\theta}$. ▪ See page 360.

## Check

Check[*expr*, *failexpr*] evaluates *expr*, and returns the result, unless messages were generated, in which case it evaluates and returns *failexpr*.

Check[*expr*, *failexpr*, $s_1$::$t_1$, $s_2$::$t_2$, ...] checks only for the specified messages.

Check has attribute HoldAll. ▪ Check tests for messages, whether or not actual output of the messages has been suppressed using Off. ▪ See page 261. ▪ See also: Message, Indeterminate, TimeConstrained.

■ **Chop**

> Chop[*expr*] replaces approximate real numbers in *expr* that are close to zero by the exact integer 0.
>
> Chop[*expr*, *delta*] replaces numbers smaller in absolute magnitude than *delta* by 0. ■ Chop uses a default tolerance of $10^{-10}$. ■ Chop works on both Real and Complex numbers. ■ See page 332. ■ See also: Rationalize, Round.

■ **Clear**

> Clear[*symbol₁*, *symbol₂*, ...] clears values defined for the *symbolᵢ*.
>
> Clear["*form₁*", "*form₂*", ...] clears values for all symbols whose names textually match any of the *formᵢ*.
>
> Clear does not clear attributes, messages, or defaults associated with symbols. ■ Clear["*form*"] allows metacharacters such as *, as specified in the notes on StringMatchQ. ■ Clear["*context*`*"] clears all symbols in a particular context. ■ Clear is HoldAll. ■ Clear does not affect symbols with the attribute Protected. ■ See pages 87, 188 and 575. ■ See also: Remove.

■ **ClearAll**

> ClearAll[*symb₁*, *symb₂*, ...] clears all values, attributes, messages and defaults associated with symbols.
>
> ClearAll["*form₁*", "*form₂*", ...] clears all symbols whose names textually match any of the *formᵢ*.
>
> See notes for Clear. ■ See page 575. ■ See also: Remove.

■ **ClearAttributes**

> ClearAttributes[*s*, *attr*] removes *attr* from the list of attributes of the symbol *s*.
>
> ClearAttributes modifies Attributes[*s*]. ■ ClearAttributes[*s*, {*attr₁*, *attr₂*, ...}] removes several attributes at a time. ■ ClearAttributes[{*s₁*, *s₂*, ...}, *attrs*] removes attributes from several symbols at a time. ■ ClearAttributes has the attribute HoldFirst. ■ See also: SetAttributes, Unprotect. ■ See page 214.

■ **ClipFill**

> ClipFill is an option for SurfaceGraphics that specifies how clipped parts of the surface are to be drawn.
>
> ClipFill specifies what
> is to be shown in places where the surface would extend beyond the bounding box. ■ The possible settings are:
>
> | | |
> |---|---|
> | Automatic | show clipped areas like the rest of the surface |
> | None | make holes in the surface where it would be clipped |
> | GrayLevel[*i*] | show clipped areas with a particular gray level |
> | RGBColor[*r*, *g*, *b*] | show clipped areas with a particular color |
> | {*top*, *bottom*} | use different specifications for top and bottom clipped areas |
>
> ■ See page 131.

■ Close

Close["*file*"] closes a file.

Close can be used to close any kind of file or pipe. It deletes the record of the object from the list $$Media.
■ See page 292. ■ See also: OpenAppend, ResetMedium.

■ Coefficient

Coefficient[*expr*, *form*] gives the coefficient of *form* in the polynomial *expr*.

Coefficient[*expr*, *form*, *n*] gives the coefficient of *form*∧*n* in *expr*.

Coefficient picks only terms that contain the particular form specified. $x^2$ is not considered part of $x^3$. ■
*form* can be a product of powers. ■ Coefficient[*expr*, *form*, 0] picks out terms that are not proportional
to *form*. ■ See page 383. ■ See also: Exponent.

■ CoefficientList

CoefficientList[*poly*, *var*] gives a list of coefficients of powers of *var* in *poly*, starting
with power 0.

CoefficientList[*poly*, {*var₁*, *var₂*, ...}] gives a matrix of coefficients of the *var_i*.

Example: CoefficientList[x∧2 + 2 x y - y, {x, y}] ⟶ {{0, -1}, {0, 2}, {1, 0}}. ■ The
dimensions of the matrix returned by CoefficientList are determined by the values of the
Exponent[*poly*, *var_i*]. ■ Terms that do not contain positive integer powers of a particular variable are
included in the first element of the list for that variable. ■ CoefficientList always returns a rectangular
matrix. Combinations of powers that do not appear in *poly* give zeroes in the matrix. ■ See page 383. ■ See
also: Series, Collect, FactorList.

■ Collect

Collect[*expr*, *x*] collects together terms involving the same power of *x*.

Collect[*expr*, {*x₁*, *x₂*, ...}] collects together terms that involve the same powers of *x₁*,
*x₂*, . . . .

Collect[*expr*, *x*] effectively writes *expr* as a polynomial in *x*. ■ Examples:
Collect[x + n x + m, x] ⟶ m + x (1 + n); Collect[Expand[(1+x+y)∧3], x] ⟶
$1 + x^3 + 3 y + 3 y^2 + y^3 + x^2 (3 + 3 y) + x (3 + 6 y + 3 y^2)$. ■ The "variables" $x_i$ can themselves
be products. ■ See page 381. ■ See also: Series, CoefficientList, Together.

## ◼ ColumnForm

> ColumnForm[{$e_1$, $e_2$, ...}]] prints as a column with $e_1$ above $e_2$ etc.
>
> ColumnForm[*list*, *horiz*] specifies the horizontal alignment of each element.
>
> ColumnForm[*list*, *horiz*, *vert*] also specifies the vertical alignment of the whole column.

Possible horizontal alignments are:

| | |
|---|---|
| Center | centered |
| Left | left justified (default case) |
| Right | right justified |

◾ Possible vertical alignments are:

| | |
|---|---|
| Above | the bottom element of the column is aligned with the baseline |
| Below | the top element is aligned with the baseline (default case) |
| Center | the column is centered on the baseline |

◾ The first argument of ColumnForm can have any head, not necessarily List. ◾ See page 276. ◾ See also: TableForm, MatrixForm, Subscripted, SequenceForm.

## ◼ Complement

> Complement[*eall*, $e_1$, $e_2$, ...] gives the elements in *eall* which are not in any of the $e_i$.

The list returned by Complement is sorted into standard order. ◾ Example: Complement[{a,b,c,d,e}, {a,c}, {d}] $\longrightarrow$ {b, e}. ◾ See page 103. ◾ See also: Intersection, Union.

## ◼ Complex

> Complex is the head used for complex numbers.

You can enter a complex number in the form $x$ + I $y$. ◾ _Complex can be used to stand for a complex number in a pattern. ◾ You have to use Re and Im to extract parts of Complex numbers. ◾ Only the real part is printed in complex numbers of the form $x$ + 0. I. ◾ See page 325. ◾ See also: Real, Re, Im.

## ◼ ComplexInfinity

> ComplexInfinity represents a quantity with infinite magnitude, but undetermined complex phase.

ComplexInfinity is converted to DirectedInfinity[ ]. ◾ In OutputForm, DirectedInfinity[ ] is printed as ComplexInfinity. ◾ See page 338. ◾ See also: Infinity, Indeterminate.

## ◼ Compose

> Compose[$a$, $b$, $c$, $d$] gives $a[b[c[d]]]$.

Compose implements functional composition. ◾ $a$ @ $b$ @ $c$ gives $a[b[c]]$. ◾ $a$ // $b$ // $c$ gives $c[b[a]]$. ◾ See page 248. ◾ See also: HeadCompose, Nest, Function.

■ CompoundExpression

$expr_1$; $expr_2$; ... evaluates the $expr_i$ in turn, giving the last one as the result.

CompoundExpression evaluates its arguments in a sequence corresponding to the control flow. ▪ The returned value can be the result of Return[*expr*]. ▪ The evaluation of the $expr_i$ can be affected by Return, Throw and Goto. ▪ $expr_1$; $expr_2$; returns value Null. If it is given as input, the resulting output will not be printed. Out[*n*] will nevertheless be assigned to be the value of $expr_2$. ▪ See page 556. ▪ See also: Block.

■ Condition

*expr* /; *test* gives *expr* if *test* is True.

You can use /; to control the applicability of rules.

Example: f[x_] := fp[x] /; x > 1 defines a function in the case when $x > 1$. ▪ *lhs* := *rhs* /; *test* defines *lhs* to be transformed to *rhs* so long as *test* is True. ▪ *lhs* :> *rhs* /; *test* is a rule that represents replacement of *lhs* by *rhs*, so long as *test* is True. ▪ *lhs* = *rhs* /; *test* and *lhs* -> *rhs* /; *test* are not usually useful, since the Condition in these cases is evaluated at the time when the transformation rule is given, not at the time when it is used. ▪ Condition returns the value Null when the test is not True. ▪ Condition does not evaluate its first argument when the test does not yield True. ▪ See page 229. ▪ See also: If, Switch, Which, PatternTest.

■ Conjugate

Conjugate[*z*] gives the complex conjugate $z^*$ of the complex number *z*.

Mathematical function (see Section B.3.8). ▪ See page 342.

■ Constant

Constant is an attribute which indicates zero derivative of a symbol with respect to all parameters.

Constant is used by Dt. ▪ Functions $f$[...] are taken to have zero total derivative if $f$ has attribute Constant. ▪ Mathematical constants such as Pi have attribute Constant. ▪ See pages 214 and 413.

■ Constants

Constants is an option for Dt which gives a list of objects to be taken as constants.

If $f$ appears in the list of Constants, then both Dt[$f$] and Dt[$f$[...]] are taken to be zero. ▪ See page 413. ▪ See also: D.

■ Context

Context[ ] gives the current context.

Context[*symbol*] gives the context in which a symbol appears.

The current context is the value of $Context. ▪ Context[*s*] searches for a symbol first in $Context, then in each element of $ContextPath. ▪ See page 309. ▪ See also: Begin, $ContextPath, Remove.

# ■ Continuation

Continuation[*n*] is output at the beginning of the $n^{\text{th}}$ line in a multiline printed expression.

Redefining Format[Continuation[n_]] changes the way continuation lines are printed.  ■ See page 588. ■ See also: StringBreak, LineBreak, Indent.

# ■ Continue

Continue[ ] exits to the nearest enclosing For or While in a procedural program.

Continue is effective only if it is generated as the value of a segment in a ; compound expression, or as the body of a control structure.  ■ Continue does not work inside Do.  ■ See page 260.  ■ See also: Break.

# ■ ContourGraphics

ContourGraphics[*array*] is a representation of a contour plot.

ContourGraphics can be displayed using Show.  ■ The following options can be given:

| | | |
|---|---|---|
| AspectRatio | 1 | ratio of height to width |
| Axes | Automatic | whether to include axes |
| AxesLabel | None | axes labels |
| ContourLevels | 10 | number of contour levels |
| ContourSpacing | Automatic | spacing in $z$ between contour levels |
| DisplayFunction | $DisplayFunction | function for generating output |
| Framed | True | whether to draw a frame |
| PlotColor | True | whether to plot in color |
| PlotLabel | None | a label for the plot |
| PlotRange | Automatic | range of $z$ values to include |
| Ticks | Automatic | tick marks |

■ *array* must be a rectangular array of real numbers, representing $z$ values. ■ ContourGraphics[*array*, {{*xmin*, *xmax*}, {*ymin*, *ymax*}}] can be used to specify $x$ and $y$ coordinates for axes.  ■ ContourGraphics is generated by ContourPlot and ListContourPlot.  ■ See page 134. ■ See also: ListContourPlot, DensityGraphics.

# ■ ContourLevels

ContourLevels is an option for ContourGraphics giving the number of contour levels to use.

See page 135.

# ■ ContourPlot

ContourPlot[*f*, {*x*, *xmin*, *xmax*}, {*y*, *ymin*, *ymax*}] generates a contour plot of *f* as a function of $x$ and $y$.

ContourPlot evaluates its arguments in a non-standard way (see page 569).  ■ The same options can be specified as for ContourGraphics, with the following addition:

| | | |
|---|---|---|
| PlotPoints | 15 | the number of points in each direction at which to sample the function |

■ ContourPlot returns a ContourGraphics object.  ■ See page 134. ■ See also: DensityPlot.

## ContourSpacing

ContourSpacing is an option for ContourGraphics that specifies the spacing between contour levels.

ContourSpacing -> Automatic causes a number of equally-spaced contour levels specified by ContourLevels to be used. ■ Giving a specific value for ContourSpacing overrides a value for ContourLevels. ■ See page 135.

## Cos

Cos[*z*] gives the cosine of *z*.

Mathematical function (see Section B.3.8). ■ The argument of Cos is assumed to be in radians. (Multiply by Degree to convert from degrees.) ■ See page 353. ■ See also: ArcCos, Sec.

## Cosh

Cosh[*z*] gives the hyperbolic cosine of *z*.

Mathematical function (see Section B.3.8). ■ $\cosh(z) = \frac{1}{2}(e^z + e^{-z})$. ■ See page 353. ■ See also: ArcCosh, Sech.

## Cot

Cot[*z*] gives the cotangent of *z*.

Mathematical function (see Section B.3.8). ■ The argument of Cot is assumed to be in radians. (Multiply by Degree to convert from degrees.) ■ $\cot(z) = \frac{1}{\tan(z)}$. ■ See page 353. ■ See also: ArcCot.

## Coth

Coth[*z*] gives the hyperbolic cotangent of *z*.

Mathematical function (see Section B.3.8). ■ See page 353. ■ See also: ArcCoth.

## Count

Count[*list, pattern*] gives the number of elements in *list* that match *pattern*.

Count[*expr, pattern, levelspec*] gives the total number of subexpressions matching *pattern* that appear at the levels in *expr* specified by *levelspec*.

Level specifications are described on page 564. ■ See page 235. ■ See also: FreeQ, MemberQ, Cases, Select, Position.

## Csc

Csc[*z*] gives the cosecant of *z*.

Mathematical function (see Section B.3.8). ■ The argument of Csc is assumed to be in radians. (Multiply by Degree to convert from degrees.) ■ $\csc(z) = \frac{1}{\sin(z)}$. ■ See page 353. ■ See also: ArcCsc.

## Csch

Csch[*z*] gives the hyperbolic cosecant of *z*.

Mathematical function (see Section B.3.8). ■ $\operatorname{csch}(z) = \frac{1}{\sinh(z)}$. ■ See page 353. ■ See also: ArcCsch.

■ Cubics

> **Cubics** is an option for **Roots**, **Solve** and related functions which specifies whether explicit solutions should be generated for irreducible cubic equations.
>
> **Cubics->False** causes irreducible cubics to be left unsolved in their original symbolic form. Numerical solutions can be found by applying **N**. ▪ Setting **Cubics->True** causes explicit solutions to be generated. These solutions are usually very complicated. ▪ See also: **Quartics**, **NRoots**.

■ Cyclotomic

> **Cyclotomic[**$n$, $x$**]** gives the cyclotomic polynomial of order $n$ in $x$.
>
> The cyclotomic polynomial $C_n(x)$ of order $n$ is defined to be $\prod_k (x - e^{2\pi i k/n})$, where the product runs over integers $k$ less than $n$ that are relatively prime to $n$. ▪ See page 388. ▪ See also: **Factor**.

■ D

> **D[**$f$, $x$**]** gives the partial derivative $\frac{\partial}{\partial x} f$.
>
> **D[**$f$, **{**$x$, $n$**}]** gives the multiple derivative $\frac{\partial^n}{\partial x^n} f$.
>
> **D[**$f$, $x_1$, $x_2$, ...**]** gives $\frac{\partial}{\partial x_1} \frac{\partial}{\partial x_2} ... f$.
>
> All quantities that do not explicitly depend on the $x_i$ are taken to have zero partial derivative. ▪ **D[**$f$, $x_1$, ..., **NonConstants -> {**$v_1$, ...**}]** specifies that the $v_i$ implicitly depend on the $x_i$, so that they do not have zero partial derivative. ▪ The derivatives of built-in mathematical functions are evaluated when possible in terms of other built-in mathematical functions. ▪ **D** uses the chain rule to simplify derivatives of unknown functions. ▪ See page 412. ▪ See also: **Dt**, **Derivative**.

■ Dashing

> **Dashing[{**$d_1$, $d_2$, ...**}]** is a two-dimensional graphics primitive which specifies that lines which follow are to be drawn dashed, with successive segments of lengths $d_1$, $d_2$, ... (repeated cyclically). The $d_i$ is given as a fraction of the total width of the graph.
>
> See page 142. ▪ See also: **Thickness**, **GrayLevel**, **RGBColor**.

## ■ Debug

Debug[*expr*] evaluates *expr*, allowing you to stop at function calls and in control structures.

Debug[*expr*, {$f_1$, $f_2$, ...}] stops only in evaluation of the functions $f_i$.

The following actions are possible in Debug:

| | |
|---|---|
| inspect (i) | inspect current state |
| step (s) | step through the execution of the current expression |
| next (n) | continue to the next expression (default action) |
| continue (c) | continue to the end of the current control structure |
| finish (f) | continue to the end of the whole computation |
| abort (a) | abort the computation |

▪ When you inspect the current state, you can look at the values of any objects. However, you cannot perform any operation which assigns values. ▪ Quit[ ] or Exit[ ] exits the inspector. ▪ See page 264. ▪ See also: On, $IgnoreEOF.

## ■ Decompose

Decompose[*poly*, *x*] decomposes a polynomial, if possible, into a composition of simpler polynomials.

Decompose gives a list of the polynomials $P_i$ which can be composed as $P_1(P_2(...(x)...))$ to give the original polynomial. ▪ The set of polynomials $P_i$ is not necessarily unique. ▪ Decomposition is an operation which is independent of polynomial factorization. ▪ See page 388. ▪ See also: FactorList, Solve.

## ■ Decrement

*x*-- decreases the value of *x* by 1, returning the old value of *x*.

Decrement has attribute HoldFirst. ▪ See page 257. ▪ See also: PreDecrement, SubtractFrom, Set.

## ■ Default

Default[*f*], if defined, gives the default value for arguments of the function *f* obtained with a _. pattern object.

Default[*f*, *i*] gives the default value to use when _. appears as the $i^{\text{th}}$ argument of *f*.

Default[*f*, *i*, *n*] gives the default value for the $i^{\text{th}}$ argument out of a total of *n* arguments.

_. represents an optional argument to a function, with a default value specified by Default. ▪ The necessary values for Default[*f*] must always be defined before _. is used as an argument of *f*. ▪ Values defined for Default[*f*] are stored with the Options values of *f*. ▪ See page 573. ▪ See also: Options.

## ■ Definition

Definition[$s_1$, $s_2$, ...] prints the definitions given for the symbols $s_i$.

Definition has attribute HoldAll. ▪ Definition[$s_1$, ...] prints all values and attributes defined for the symbols $s_i$. ▪ ?*s* uses Definition. ▪ See page 289. ▪ See also: FullDefinition, Information.

## ■ Degree

**Degree** represents the number of degrees in one radian. It has a numerical value of $\frac{\pi}{180}$.

You can use **Degree** to convert from degrees to radians.  ■ Example: 30 **Degree** represents 30°.  ■ See page 359.

## ■ Denominator

**Denominator**[*expr*] gives the denominator of *expr*.

**Denominator** picks out terms which have superficially negative exponents. **Numerator** picks out all remaining terms.  ■ An exponent is "superficially negative" if it has a negative number as a factor.  ■ The standard representation of rational expressions as products of powers means that you cannot simply use **Part** to extract denominators.  ■ **Denominator** can be used on rational numbers.  ■ See page 60.  ■ See also: **ExpandDenominator**.

## ■ DensityGraphics

**DensityGraphics**[*array*] is a representation of a density plot.

**DensityGraphics** can be displayed using **Show**.  ■ The following options can be given:

| AspectRatio | 1 | ratio of height to width |
|---|---|---|
| Axes | Automatic | whether to include axes |
| AxesLabel | None | axes labels |
| DisplayFunction | $DisplayFunction | function for generating output |
| Framed | True | whether to draw a frame |
| Mesh | True | whether to draw a mesh |
| PlotColor | True | whether to plot in color |
| PlotLabel | None | a label for the plot |
| PlotRange | Automatic | range of $z$ values to include |
| Ticks | Automatic | tick marks |

■ *array* must be a rectangular array of real numbers, representing $z$ values.  ■ **DensityGraphics**[*array*, {{*xmin*, *xmax*}, {*ymin*, *ymax*}}] can be used to specify $x$ and $y$ coordinates for axes.  ■ **DensityGraphics** is generated by **DensityPlot** and **ListDensityPlot**.  ■ See page 136.  ■ See also: **ListDensityPlot**, **ContourGraphics**.

## ■ DensityPlot

**DensityPlot**[*f*, {*x*, *xmin*, *xmax*}, {*y*, *ymin*, *ymax*}] makes a density plot of *f* as a function of *x* and *y*.

**DensityPlot** evaluates its arguments in a non-standard way (see page 569).  ■ The same options can be specified as for **DensityGraphics**, with the following addition:

| PlotPoints | 15 | the number of points in each direction at which to sample the function |
|---|---|---|

■ **DensityPlot** returns a **DensityGraphics** object.  ■ See page 136.  ■ See also: **ContourPlot**.

## ■ Depth

Depth[*expr*] gives the maximum number of indices needed to specify any part of *expr*, plus one.

Raw objects have depth 1. ■ The computation of Depth does not include heads of expressions. ■ See page 175. ■ See also: TensorRank, Level, LeafCount, Length, Nest.

## ■ Derivative

*f′* represents the derivative of a function *f* of one argument.

Derivative[$n_1$, $n_2$, ...][*f*] is the general form, representing a function obtained from *f* by differentiating $n_1$ times with respect to the first argument, $n_2$ times with respect to the second argument, and so on.

*f′* is equivalent to Derivative[1][*f*]. ■ *f′′* evaluates to Derivative[2][*f*]. ■ You can think of Derivative as a *functional operator* which acts on functions to give derivative functions. ■ Derivative is generated when you apply D to functions whose derivatives *Mathematica* does not know. ■ *Mathematica* attempts to convert Derivative[*n*][*f*] and so on to pure functions. Whenever Derivative[*n*][*f*] is generated, *Mathematica* rewrites it as D[f[#]&, {#, *n*}]. If *Mathematica* finds an explicit value for this derivative, it returns this value. Otherwise, it returns the original Derivative form. ■ Example: Cos′ $\longrightarrow$ -Sin[#1] &. ■ See page 416. ■ See also: D, Dt.

## ■ Det

Det[*m*] gives the determinant of the square matrix *m*.

See page 446. ■ See also: Minors, RowReduce, NullSpace.

## ■ DiagonalMatrix

DiagonalMatrix[*list*] gives a matrix with the elements of *list* on the leading diagonal, and 0 elsewhere.

See page 437. ■ See also: IdentityMatrix.

## ■ Dimensions

Dimensions[*expr*] gives a list of the dimensions of *expr*.

Dimensions[*expr*, *n*] gives a list of the dimensions of *expr* down to level *n*.

*expr* must be a *full array*, with all the pieces of *expr* at a particular level having the same length. (The elements of *expr* can then be thought of as filling up a hyper-rectangular region.) ■ Each successive level in *expr* sampled by Dimensions must have the same head. ■ Example: Dimensions[{{a,b,c},{d,e,f}}] $\longrightarrow$ {2, 3}. ■ See page 440. ■ See also: TensorRank, VectorQ, MatrixQ.

### ■ DirectedInfinity

DirectedInfinity[ ] represents an infinite numerical quantity whose direction in the complex plane is unknown.

DirectedInfinity[*z*] represents an infinite numerical quantity that is a positive real multiple of the complex number *z*.

You can think of DirectedInfinity[*z*] as representing a point in the complex plane reached by starting at the origin and going an infinite distance in the direction of the point *z*. ■ The following conversions are made:

| | |
|---|---|
| Infinity | DirectedInfinity[1] |
| -Infinity | DirectedInfinity[-1] |
| ComplexInfinity | DirectedInfinity[ ] |

■ Certain arithmetic operations are performed on DirectedInfinity quantities. ■ In OutputForm, DirectedInfinity[*z*] is printed in terms of Infinity, and DirectedInfinity[ ] is printed as ComplexInfinity. ■ See page 338. ■ See also: Indeterminate.

### ■ Display

Display[*channel*, *graphics*] writes graphics to the specified output channel.

The output channel can be a single file or pipe, or a list of them. ■ Display writes graphics in POSTSCRIPT form. ■ The *graphics* in Display can be Graphics, Graphics3D, SurfaceGraphics, ContourGraphics or DensityGraphics. ■ The POSTSCRIPT produced by Display does not include initialization or termination commands, nor does it include text font definitions. ■ $DisplayFunction is usually given in terms of Display. ■ If any of the specified files or pipes in *channel* are not open, Display uses OpenWrite to open them, then closes these particular files or pipes when it has finished. ■ See page 292. ■ See also: Write, Show.

### ■ DisplayFunction

DisplayFunction is an option for graphics functions that specifies the function to apply to the graphics primitives that are generated in order to display them.

The default setting for DisplayFunction is $DisplayFunction. ■ A typical setting is DisplayFunction->Display[*channel*, #]&. ■ Setting DisplayFunction->Identity will cause graphics primitives to be returned, but no display to be generated. ■ See page 109.

### ■ Distribute

Distribute[*f*[*x_1*, *x_2*, ...]] distributes *f* over Plus appearing in any of the $x_i$.

Distribute[*expr*, *g*] distributes over *g*.

Distribute[*expr*, *g*, *f*] performs the distribution only if the head of *expr* is *f*.

Distribute effectively implements the distributive law for operators *f* and *g*. ■ Distribute explicitly constructs the complete result of a distribution; Expand, on the other hand, builds up results iteratively, simplifying at each stage. ■ Example:
Distribute[f[a+b,c+d]] ⟶ f[a, c] + f[a, d] + f[b, c] + f[b, d]. ■
Distribute[f[a+b,g[x,y],c], g] ⟶ g[f[a + b, x, c], f[a + b, y, c]]. ■
Distribute[*expr*, *g*, *f*, *gp*, *fp*] gives *gp* and *fp* in place of *g* and *f* respectively in the result of the distribution. ■ See page 250. ■ See also: Expand, Thread.

### ■ Divide

$x/y$ or Divide[$x$, $y$] is equivalent to $x$ $y$^-1.

$x/y$ is converted to $x$ $y$^-1 on input.  ▪ See page 25.

### ■ DivideBy

$x$ /= $c$ divides $x$ by $c$ returns the new value of $x$.

DivideBy has the attribute HoldFirst.  ▪ $x$ /= $c$ is equivalent to $x$ = $x/c$.  ▪ See page 257.  ▪ See also: TimesBy, SubtractFrom, Set.

### ■ Divisors

Divisors[$n$] gives a list of the integers that divide $n$.

Example: Divisors[12] $\longrightarrow$ {1, 2, 3, 4, 6, 12}.  ▪ See page 346.  ▪ See also: FactorInteger.

### ■ DivisorSigma

DivisorSigma[$k$, $n$] gives the divisor function $\sigma_k(n)$.

Integer mathematical function (see Section B.3.8).  ▪ $\sigma_k(n)$ is the sum of the $k$th powers of the divisors of $n$.  ▪ See page 347.  ▪ See also: EulerPhi.

### ■ Do

Do[*expr*, {*imax*}] evaluates *expr* *imax* times.

Do[*expr*, {*i*, *imax*}] evaluates *expr* with the variable *i* successively taking on the values 1 through *imax* (in steps of 1).

Do[*expr*, {*i*, *imin*, *imax*}] starts with *i* = *imin*. Do[*expr*, {*i*, *imin*, *imax*, *di*}] uses steps *di*.

Do[*expr*, {*i*, *imin*, *imax*}, {*j*, *jmin*, *jmax*}, ...] evaluates *expr* looping over different values of *j*, etc. for each *i*.

Do uses the standard *Mathematica* iteration specification.  ▪ Do evaluates its arguments in a non-standard way (see page 569).  ▪ The result of Do is Null.  ▪ See page 254.  ▪ See also: For, While, Table, Nest.

■ **Dot**

$a.b.c$ or $\texttt{Dot}[a,\ b,\ c]$ gives products of vectors, matrices and tensors.

$a.b$ gives an explicit result when $a$ and $b$ are lists with appropriate dimensions. It contracts the last direction in $a$ with the first direction in $b$. ■ Various applications of Dot:

| | |
|---|---|
| $\{a_1,\ a_2\}\ .\ \{b_1,\ b_2\}$ | scalar product of vectors |
| $\{a_1,\ a_2\}\ .\ \{\{m_{11},\ m_{12}\},\ \{m_{21},\ m_{22}\}\}$ | product of a vector with a matrix |
| $\{\{m_{11},\ m_{12}\},\ \{m_{21},\ m_{22}\}\}\ .\ \{a_1,\ a_2\}$ | product of a matrix with a vector |
| $\{\{m_{11},\ m_{12}\},\ \{m_{21},\ m_{22}\}\}\ .\ \{\{n_{11},\ n_{12}\},\ \{n_{21},\ n_{22}\}\}$ | product of two matrices |

■ Example: $\{a, b\}\ .\ \{c, d\} \longrightarrow a\ c\ +\ b\ d$. ■
$\{\{a, b\}, \{c, d\}\}\ .\ \{x, y\} \longrightarrow \{a\ x\ +\ b\ y,\ c\ x\ +\ d\ y\}$. ■ The result of applying Dot to two tensors $T_{i_1 i_2 \ldots i_n}$ and $U_{j_1 j_2 \ldots j_m}$ is the tensor $\sum_k T_{i_1 i_2 \ldots i_{n-1} k}\ U_{k j_2 \ldots j_m}$. Dot effectively contracts the last index of the first tensor with the first index of the second tensor. Applying Dot to a rank $n$ tensor and a rank $m$ tensor gives a rank $n + m - 1$ tensor. ■ When its arguments are not lists, Dot remains unevaluated. It has the attribute **Flat**. ■ See pages 94 and 442. ■ See also: **Inner, Outer, NonCommutativeMultiply**.

■ **Drop**

$\texttt{Drop}[list,\ n]$ gives *list* with its first $n$ elements dropped.

$\texttt{Drop}[list,\ -n]$ gives *list* with its last $n$ elements dropped.

$\texttt{Drop}[list,\ \{m,\ n\}]$ gives *list* with elements $m$ through $n$ dropped.

Drop uses the standard *sequence specification*. ■ Example: $\texttt{Drop}[\{a,b,c,d,e\}, 2] \longrightarrow \{c, d, e\}$. ■
$\texttt{Drop}[\{a,b,c,d,e\}, -3] \longrightarrow \{a, b\}$. ■ Drop can be used on any function, not necessarily List. ■ See page 99. ■ See also: **Rest, Take, Cases**.

■ **Dt**

$\texttt{Dt}[f,\ x]$ gives the total derivative $\frac{d}{dx}\ f$.

$\texttt{Dt}[f]$ gives the total differential $df$.

$\texttt{Dt}[f,\ \{x,\ n\}]$ gives the multiple derivative $\frac{d^n}{dx^n}\ f$.

$\texttt{Dt}[f,\ x_1,\ x_2,\ \ldots]$ gives $\frac{d}{dx_1}\frac{d}{dx_2}\ldots\ f$.

$\texttt{Dt}[f,\ x_1,\ \ldots,\ \texttt{Constants} \rightarrow \{c_1,\ \ldots\}]$ specifies that the $c_i$ are constants, which have zero total derivative. ■ Symbols with attribute **Constant** are taken to be constants, with zero total derivative. ■ If an object is specified to be a constant, then all functions with that object as a head are also taken to be constants. ■ All quantities not explicitly specified as constants are assumed to depend on the $x_i$. ■ Example: $\texttt{Dt}[x\ y] \longrightarrow y\ \texttt{Dt}[x]\ +\ x\ \texttt{Dt}[y]$. ■ $\texttt{Dt}[x\ y,\ \texttt{Constants} \rightarrow \{x\}] \longrightarrow x\ \texttt{Dt}[y]$. ■ You can specify total derivatives by assigning values to $\texttt{Dt}[f]$ etc. ■ See page 413. ■ See also: **D, Derivative**.

■ **Dump**

> `Dump["`*filename*`"]` writes a complete image of the current state of your *Mathematica* session to a file.
>
> `Dump["`*filename*`",` *startup*`]` includes the command *startup*, to be run when the image is executed.
>
> `Dump["`*filename*`",` *startup*`,` `"`*code*`"]` uses the executable binary in the file `"`*code*`"`. The default for `"`*code*`"` is `$CommandLine[[1]]`.
>
> Dump is only available on certain computer systems.  ▪ The files produced by Dump may be very large.  ▪ Dump closes any files that are open. (Files could have been changed when the image is restarted.)  ▪ See page 591.  ▪ See also: Save.

■ **E**

> E is the exponential constant $e$ (base of natural logarithms), with numerical value $\simeq 2.71828$.
>
> Mathematical constant (see Section B.3.9).  ▪ See page 359.  ▪ See also: Exp.

■ **EdgeForm**

> `EdgeForm[`*p*`]` is a three-dimensional graphics primitive which specifies that edges between polygons are to be drawn using the graphics primitive *p*.
>
> EdgeForm[ ] draws no edges between polygons.  ▪ The primitives RGBColor, GrayLevel and Thickness can be used in EdgeForm.  ▪ See page 149.  ▪ See also: Line.

■ **Eigensystem**

> `Eigensystem[`*m*`]` gives a list {*values, vectors*} of the eigenvalues and eigenvectors of the square matrix *m*.
>
> Eigensystem finds numerical eigenvalues and eigenvectors if *m* contains approximate real numbers.  ▪ The elements of *m* can be complex.  ▪ All the eigenvectors given are independent. If the number of eigenvectors is equal to the number of eigenvalues, then corresponding eigenvalues and eigenvalues are given in corresponding positions in their respective lists.  ▪ The eigenvalues and eigenvectors satisfy the matrix equation m.Transpose[*vectors*] == Transpose[*vectors*].DiagonalMatrix[*values*].  ▪ See page 452.  ▪ See also: NullSpace.

■ **Eigenvalues**

> `Eigenvalues[`*m*`]` gives a list of the eigenvalues of the square matrix *m*.
>
> Eigenvalues finds numerical eigenvalues if *m* contains approximate real numbers.  ▪ Repeated eigenvalues appear with their appropriate multiplicity.  ▪ An $n \times n$ matrix gives a list of exactly $n$ eigenvalues, not necessarily distinct.  ▪ See page 452.  ▪ See also: Det.

■ **Eigenvectors**

Eigenvectors[*m*] gives a list of the eigenvectors of the square matrix *m*.

Eigenvectors finds numerical eigenvectors if *m* contains approximate real numbers. ▪ Eigenvectors corresponding to degenerate eigenvalues are chosen to be linearly independent. ▪ Eigenvectors are not normalized. ▪ Only independent eigenvectors are given. ▪ The number of eigenvectors for an $n \times n$ matrix may be less than $n$. ▪ Eigenvectors[*m*, ZeroTest -> *test*] applies *test* to determine whether expressions should be assumed to be zero. ▪ See page 452. ▪ See also: NullSpace.

■ **Eliminate**

Eliminate[*eqns*, *vars*] eliminates variables between a set of simultaneous equations.

Equations are given in the form *lhs* == *rhs*. ▪ Simultaneous equations can be combined either in a list or with &&. ▪ A single variable or a list of variables can be specified. ▪ Example: Eliminate[{x == 2 + y, y == z}, y] ⟶ z == -2 + x. ▪ Variables can be any expressions. ▪ Eliminate works primarily with linear and polynomial equations. ▪ Additional options to Eliminate can be specified, as in MainSolve. ▪ See page 404. ▪ See also: Reduce, SolveAlways, Solve, MainSolve, AlgebraicRules.

■ **EllipticE**

EllipticE[*phi*, *m*] gives the elliptic integral of the second kind $E(\phi|m)$.

EllipticE[*m*] gives the complete elliptic integral $E(m)$.

Mathematical function (see Section B.3.8). ▪ $E(\phi|m) = \int_0^\phi (1 - m \sin^2(\theta))^{\frac{1}{2}} d\theta$. ▪ $E(m) = E(\frac{\pi}{2}|m)$. ▪ See page 375 for a discussion of argument conventions for elliptic integrals. ▪ See page 374.

■ **EllipticExp**

EllipticExp[*u*, {*a*, *b*}] gives the generalized exponential associated with the elliptic curve $y^2 = x^3 + ax^2 + bx$.

EllipticExp is the inverse function for EllipticLog. ▪ EllipticExp is the basis for all elliptic functions in *Mathematica*. ▪ See page 374.

■ **EllipticF**

EllipticF[*phi*, *m*] gives the elliptic integral of the first kind $F(\phi|m)$.

Mathematical function (see Section B.3.8). ▪ $F(\phi|m) = \int_0^\phi (1 - m \sin^2(\theta))^{-\frac{1}{2}} d\theta$. ▪ The complete elliptic integral associated with EllipticF is EllipticK. ▪ See page 375 for a discussion of argument conventions for elliptic integrals. ▪ See page 374.

■ **EllipticK**

EllipticK[*k*] gives the complete elliptic integral of the first kind $K(m)$.

Mathematical function (see Section B.3.8). ▪ EllipticK is given terms of the incomplete elliptic integral of the first kind by $K(m) = F(\frac{\pi}{2}|m)$. ▪ See page 375 for a discussion of argument conventions for elliptic integrals. ▪ See page 374.

■ **EllipticLog**

EllipticLog[{x, y}, {a, b}] gives the generalized logarithm associated with the elliptic curve $y^2 = x^3 + ax^2 + bx$.

EllipticLog[{x, y}, {a, b}] is defined as the value of the integral $\int_{\infty}^{x}(t^3 + at^2 + bt)^{-\frac{1}{2}}\,dt$, where the sign of the square root is specified by giving the value of $y$ such that $y = \sqrt{x^3 + ax^2 + bx}$. ■ EllipticLog is the basis for all elliptic integrals in *Mathematica*. ■ See page 374. ■ See also: EllipticExp.

■ **EllipticPi**

EllipticPi[n, m] gives the complete elliptic integral of the third kind $\Pi(n|m)$.

EllipticPi[n, phi, m] gives the incomplete elliptic integral $\Pi(n; \phi|m)$.

Mathematical function (see Section B.3.8). ■ $\Pi(n; \phi|m) = \int_0^{\phi}(1 - n\sin^2(\theta))^{-1}[1 - \sin^2(\alpha)\sin^2(\theta)]^{-\frac{1}{2}}\,d\theta$. ■ $\Pi(n|m) = \Pi(n; \frac{\pi}{2}|m)$. ■ See page 374.

■ **EllipticTheta**

EllipticTheta[a, u, q] gives the elliptic theta functions $\theta_a(u|q)$ $(a = 1, ..., 4)$.

Mathematical function (see Section B.3.8). ■ $\theta_1(u, q) = 2q^{\frac{1}{4}}\sum_{n=0}^{\infty}(-1)^n q^{n(n+1)}\sin((2n+1)u)$, $\theta_2(u, q) = 2q^{\frac{1}{4}}\sum_{n=0}^{\infty}q^{n(n+1)}\cos((2n+1)u)$, $\theta_3(u, q) = 1 + 2\sum_{n=1}^{\infty}q^{n^2}\cos(2nu)$, $\theta_4(u, q) = 1 + 2\sum_{n=1}^{\infty}(-1)^n q^{n^2}\cos(2nu)$. ■ See page 374.

■ **End**

End[ ] returns the present context, and reverts to the previous one.

Every call to End must be balanced by an earlier call to Begin. ■ End[ ] resets the value of $Context. ■ End[ ] returns the present context name as a string of the form "*context*`". ■ End[ ] does not modify $ContextPath. ■ See pages 310 and 313.

■ **EndAdd**

EndAdd[ ] returns the present context, and reverts to the previous one, prepending the present context to $ContextPath.

EndAdd[ ] resets $Context and $ContextPath. ■ See notes for End. ■ See page 313.

■ **EndOfFile**

EndOfFile is a symbol returned by Read when it reaches the end of a file.

Subsequent calls to Read will also give EndOfFile. ■ See page 303.

■ **EndPackage**

> **EndPackage[ ]** restores **$Context** and **$ContextPath** to their values before the preceding **BeginPackage**, and prepends the current context to the list **$ContextPath**.

> Every call to **EndPackage** must be balanced by an earlier call to **BeginPackage**. ■ **EndPackage** is typically used at the end of a *Mathematica* package. ■ **EndPackage** returns the name of context it ends. ■ **EndPackage** resets the values of both **$Context** and **$ContextPath**. ■ See page 310.

■ **EndProcess**

> **EndProcess["***command***"]** terminates an external process in which functions could be called from *Mathematica*.

> See page 304. ■ See also: **StartProcess**, **CallProcess**.

■ **EngineeringForm**

> **EngineeringForm[***expr***]** prints with all real numbers in *expr* given in engineering notation.

> In "engineering notation" the exponent is always arranged to be a multiple of 3. ■ See page 328. ■ See also: **EngineeringForm**, **NumberForm**.

■ **Environment**

> **Environment["***var***"]** gives the value of an operating system environment variable.

> The values of environment values are returned by **Environment** as strings. ■ **Environment** returns **Null** if it cannot find a value for the operating system variable you requested. ■ The behavior of **Environment** depends on the computer system you are using. ■ See page 577. ■ See also: **Run**, **$CommandLine**, **$System**.

■ **Equal**

> *lhs* **==** *rhs* returns **True** if *lhs* and *rhs* are identical.

> *lhs* **==** *rhs* is used to represent a symbolic equation, to be manipulated using functions like **Solve**. ■ *lhs* **==** *rhs* returns **True** if *lhs* and *rhs* are identical expressions. ■ *lhs* **==** *rhs* returns **False** if *lhs* and *rhs* are determined to be unequal by comparisons between numbers or other raw data, such as strings. ■ Real numbers are considered equal if their difference is less than the precision of either of them. ■ 2 **==** 2. gives **True**. ■ $e_1$ **==** $e_2$ **==** $e_3$ gives **True** if all the $e_i$ are equal. ■ **Equal[***e***]** gives **True**. ■ See page 72. ■ See also: **SameQ**, **Unequal**, **Order**.

■ **Erf**

> **Erf[***z***]** gives the error function $\mathrm{erf}(z)$.

> **Erf[***z₀***, ***z₁***]** gives the generalized error function $\mathrm{erf}(z_1) - \mathrm{erf}(z_0)$.

> Mathematical function (see Section B.3.8). ■ **Erf[***z***]** is the integral of the Gaussian distribution, given by $\mathrm{erf}(z) = \frac{2}{\sqrt{\pi}} \int_0^z e^{-t^2}\,dt$. ■ **Erf[***z₀***, ***z₁***]** is given by $\frac{2}{\sqrt{\pi}} \int_{z_0}^{z_1} e^{-t^2}\,dt$. ■ The complementary error function $\mathrm{erfc}(z)$ is **Erf[***z***, Infinity]**. ■ See page 363. ■ See also: **ExpIntegralE**, **ExpIntegralEi**.

## EulerE

EulerE[$n$] gives the Euler number $E_n$.

EulerE[$n$, $x$] gives the Euler polynomial $E_n(x)$.

Mathematical function (see Section B.3.8). ▪ The Euler polynomials satisfy the generating function relation $\frac{2e^{xt}}{e^t+1} = \sum_{n=0}^{\infty} E_n(x)\frac{t^n}{n!}$. ▪ The Euler numbers are given by $E_n = 2^n E_n(\frac{1}{2})$. ▪ See page 350.

## EulerGamma

EulerGamma is Euler's constant $\gamma$, with numerical value $\simeq 0.577216$.

Mathematical constant (see Section B.3.9). ▪ See page 359. ▪ See also: PolyGamma.

## EulerPhi

EulerPhi[$n$] gives the Euler totient function $\phi(n)$.

Integer mathematical function (see Section B.3.8). ▪ $\phi(n)$ gives the number of positive integers less than $n$ which are relatively prime to $n$. ▪ See page 347. ▪ See also: FactorInteger, Divisors, MoebiusMu.

## ◼ EvenQ

EvenQ[$expr$] gives True if $expr$ is an even integer, and False otherwise.

EvenQ[$expr$] returns False unless $expr$ is manifestly an even integer (i.e. has head Integer, and is even). ▪ You can use EvenQ[$x$] = True to override the normal operation of EvenQ, and effectively define $x$ to be an even integer. ▪ See pages 230 and 326. ▪ See also: IntegerQ, OddQ, TrueQ.

## Exit

Exit[ ] terminates a *Mathematica* session, or an inspection session initiated within Debug.

Exit is a synonym for Quit. ▪ See page 579. ▪ See also: $IgnoreEOF.

## Exp

Exp[$z$] is the exponential function.

Mathematical function (see Section B.3.8). ▪ Exp[$z$] is converted to E^$z$. ▪ See page 353. ▪ See also: Power, E.

## Expand

Expand[$expr$] expands out products and positive powers in $expr$.

Expand works only on positive integer powers. ▪ Expand applies only to the top level in $expr$. ▪ See page 381. ▪ See also: Distribute, Apart, Series, Factor, LogicalExpand.

## ExpandAll

ExpandAll[$expr$] expands out all products and powers in any part of $expr$.

ExpandAll[$expr$] effectively maps Expand and ExpandDenominator onto every part of $expr$. ▪ See page 385.

■ **ExpandDenominator**

ExpandDenominator[*expr*] expands out products and powers that appear as denominators in *expr*.

ExpandDenominator works only on negative integer powers. ■ ExpandDenominator applies only to the top level in *expr*. ■ See page 385. ■ See also: Together.

■ **ExpandNumerator**

ExpandNumerator[*expr*] expands out products and powers that appear in the numerator of *expr*.

ExpandNumerator works on terms that have positive integer exponents. ■ ExpandNumerator applies only to the top level in *expr*. ■ See page 385.

■ **ExpIntegralE**

ExpIntegralE[*n*, *z*] gives the exponential integral function $E_n(z)$.

Mathematical function (see Section B.3.8). ■ $E_n = \int_1^{\infty} \frac{e^{-zt}}{t^n} dt$. ■ See page 363. ■ See also: Erf, LogIntegral.

■ **ExpIntegralEi**

ExpIntegralEi[*z*] gives the exponential integral function $\mathrm{Ei}(z)$.

Mathematical function (see Section B.3.8). ■ $\mathrm{Ei}(z) = -\int_{-z}^{\infty} \frac{e^{-t}}{t} dt$, where the principal value of the integral is taken. ■ See page 363. ■ See also: Erf, LogIntegral.

■ **Exponent**

Exponent[*expr*, *form*] gives the maximum power with which *form* appears in *expr*.

Exponent[*expr*, *form*, *h*] applies *h* to the set of exponents with which *form* appears in *expr*.

*expr* is assumed to be a single term, or a sum of terms. Exponent applies only to the top level in *expr*. ■ Example: Exponent[x^2 + a x^3, x] ⟶ 3. ■ The default taken for *h* is Max. ■ Example: Exponent[x^2 + a x^3, x, List] ⟶ {2, 0, 3}. ■ *form* can be a product of terms. ■ See page 383. ■ See also: Coefficient, Cases.

■ **Expression**

Expression is a symbol that represents an ordinary *Mathematica* expression.

Expression is used in such functions as Read and CallProcess. ■ See page 301. ■ See also: ToExpression.

■ **ExtendedGCD**

ExtendedGCD[*n*, *m*] gives the extended greatest common divisor of the integers *n* and *m*.

Integer mathematical function (see Section B.3.8). ■ ExtendedGCD[*n*, *m*] returns the list {*g*, *r*, *s*}, where *g* is GCD[*n*, *m*], and *r* and *s* satisfy the relation $g = nr + ms$. ■ See page 347. ■ See also: GCD.

■ **FaceForm**

FaceForm[*pf*, *pb*] is a three-dimensional graphics primitive which specifies that the front faces of polygons are to be drawn with the graphics primitive *pf*, and the back faces with *pb*.

The graphics specifications *pf* and *pb* must be either GrayLevel[*i*] or RGBColor[*r*, *g*, *b*]. ▪ Specifications given outside of FaceForm will apply both to the front and back faces of polygons. ▪ The front face of a polygon is defined to be the one that has an outward normal when the corners are taken in the order you specify them. ▪ See page 149. ▪ See also: EdgeForm.

■ **Factor**

Factor[*poly*] factors a polynomial over the integers.

Factor[*poly*, Modulus->*p*] factors a polynomial modulo a prime *p*.

Factor applies only to the top level in an expression. You may have to use Map, or apply Factor again, to reach other levels. ▪ Factor[*poly*, Variables->{$x_1$, $x_2$, ...}] allows you to specify an ordering on the variables in *poly*. The time needed to do the factorization may depend on the ordering you specify. ▪ Factor works only with exact Integer or Rational coefficients, not with Real numbers. ▪ The exponents of variables need not be positive integers. Factor can deal with exponents that are linear combinations of symbolic expressions. ▪ See page 381. ▪ See also: FactorTerms, Solve, Expand, Simplify, FactorInteger.

■ **FactorComplete**

FactorComplete is an option for FactorInteger which specifies whether complete factorization is to be performed.

FactorComplete->False causes at most one factor to be extracted. ▪ See page 346.

■ **Factorial**

*n*! gives the factorial of *n*.

Mathematical function (see Section **??**). ▪ For non-integer *n*, the numerical value of *n*! is given by Gamma[1 + *n*]. ▪ See page 350. ▪ See also: Gamma, Binomial.

■ **Factorial2**

*n*!! gives the double factorial of *n*.

Mathematical function (see Section **??**). ▪ $n!! = n(n-2)(n-4) \times \dots$. *n*!! is a product of even numbers for *n* even, and odd numbers for *n* odd. ▪ See page 350. ▪ See also: Gamma.

■ **FactorInteger**

FactorInteger[*n*] gives a list of the prime factors of the integer *n*, together with their exponents.

Example: FactorInteger[2434500] ⟶ {{2, 2}, {3, 2}, {5, 3}, {541, 1}}. ▪ For negative integers, {-1, 1} is included in the list of factors. ▪ FactorInteger[*n*, *pmax*] factors only over primes up to size *pmax*. Any unfactored part of *n* is left as an element of the returned list. ▪ FactorInteger[*n*, FactorComplete->False] finds only the first factor of *n*. ▪ See page 346. ▪ See also: Prime, PrimeQ, Divisors.

## FactorList

FactorList [*poly*] gives a list of the factors of a polynomial, together with their exponents.

The first element of the list is always the overall numerical factor. It is {1, 1} if there is no overall numerical factor. ∎ Example: FactorList[3 (1+x)∧2 (1-x)] ⟶ {{-3, 1}, {-1 + x, 1}, {1 + x, 2}}. ∎ FactorList[*poly*, Modulus->*p*] factors modulo a prime *p*. ∎ See page 388. ∎ See also: CoefficientList.

## FactorSquareFree

FactorSquareFree [*poly*] pulls out any squared factors in a polynomial.

FactorSquareFree[*poly*, Modulus->*p*] pulls out squared factors modulo a prime *p*. ∎ See page 388.

## FactorSquareFreeList

FactorSquareFreeList [*poly*] gives a list of square-free factors of a polynomial, together with their exponents.

See page 388.

## FactorTerms

FactorTerms [*poly*] pulls out common factors that appear in each term of a polynomial.

Example: FactorTerms[3 - 3x∧2] ⟶ 3 (1 - $x^2$). ∎ FactorTerms[3 y - 3 x∧2 y] ⟶ 3 (y - $x^2$ y). ∎ See notes for Factor. ∎ See page 381.

## FactorTermsList

FactorTermsList [*poly*] gives a list containing factors common to all terms of a polynomial, together with the polynomial with these factors removed.

The first element of the list is always the overall numerical factor. ∎ See notes for FactorList. ∎ See page 388.

## False

False is the symbol for the Boolean value false.

See page 71. ∎ See also: TrueQ, True.

■ **FindMinimum**

FindMinimum[f, {x, $x_0$}] searches for a local minimum in $f$, starting from the point $x=x_0$.

FindMinimum returns a list of the form {$f_{min}$, {x->$x_{min}$}}, where $f_{min}$ is the minimum value of $f$ found, and $x_{min}$ is the value of $x$ for which it is found. ■ FindMinimum[f, {x, {$x_0$, $x_1$}}] searches for a local minimum in $f$ using $x_0$ and $x_1$ as the first two values of $x$. This form must be used if symbolic derivatives of $f$ cannot be found. ■ FindMinimum[f, {x, xstart, xmin, xmax}] searches for a local minimum, stopping the search if $x$ ever gets outside the range *xmin* to *xmax*. ■ FindMinimum[f, {x, $x_0$}, {y, $y_0$}, ...] searches for a local minimum in a function of several variables. ■ FindMinimum works by following the path of steepest descent from each point that it reaches. The minima it finds are local, but not necessarily global, ones. ■ The following options can be given:

| | | |
|---|---|---|
| AccuracyGoal | 6 | the accuracy sought in the value of the function at the minimum |
| Gradient | Automatic | the list of gradient functions {D[f, x], D[f, y], ...} |
| MaxIterations | 30 | maximum number of iterations used |
| WorkingPrecision | Precision[1.] | the number of digits used in internal computations |

■ See page 481. ■ See also: D, Fit.

■ **FindRoot**

FindRoot[*lhs*==*rhs*, {x, $x_0$}] searches for a numerical solution to the equation *lhs*==*rhs*, starting with $x=x_0$.

FindRoot[*lhs*==*rhs*, {x, {$x_0$, $x_1$}}] searches for a solution using $x_0$ and $x_1$ as the first two values of $x$. This form must be used if symbolic derivatives of the equation cannot be found. ■ FindRoot[*lhs*==*rhs*, {x, xstart, xmin, xmax}] searches for a solution, stopping the search if $x$ ever gets outside the range *xmin* to *xmax*. ■ FindRoot[{$eqn_1$, $eqn_2$, ...}, {x, $x_0$}, {y, $y_0$}, ...] searches for a numerical solution to the simultaneous equations $eqn_i$. ■ FindRoot returns a list of replacements for $x$, $y$, ..., in the same form as obtained from Solve. ■ If you specify only one starting value of $x$, FindRoot searches for a solution using Newton's method. If you specify two starting values, FindRoot uses a variant of the secant method. ■ The following options can be given:

| | | |
|---|---|---|
| AccuracyGoal | 6 | the accuracy sought in the value of the function at the minimum |
| MaxIterations | 15 | maximum number of iterations used |
| WorkingPrecision | Precision[1.] | the number of digits used in internal computations |

■ If FindRoot does not succeed in finding a solution to the accuracy you specify within MaxIterations steps, it returns the most recent approximation to a solution that it found. You can then apply FindRoot again, with this approximation as a starting point. ■ See page 478. ■ See also: NRoots, Solve.

■ **First**

First[*expr*] gives the first element in *expr*.

First[*expr*] is equivalent to *expr*[[1]]. ■ See page 99. ■ See also: Part, Last, Rest.

## ■ Fit

Fit[*data*, *funs*, *vars*] finds a least-squares fit to a list of data as a linear combination of the functions *funs* of variables *vars*.

The data can have the form $\{\{x_1,\ y_1,\ ...,\ f_1\},\ \{x_2,\ y_2,\ ...,\ f_2\},\ ...\}$, where the number of coordinates $x$, $y$, ... is equal to the number of variables in the list *vars*.

The data can also be of the form $\{f_1,\ f_2,\ ...\}$, with a single coordinate assumed to take values 1, 2, ....

The argument *funs* can be any list of functions that depend only on the objects *vars*.

Fit[$\{f_1,\ f_2,\ ...\}$, $\{1,\ x,\ x\wedge 2\}$, x] gives a quadratic fit to a sequence of values $f_i$. The result is of the form $a_0\ +\ a_1\ x\ +\ a_2\ x\wedge 2$, where the $a_i$ are real numbers. The successive values of x needed to obtain the $f_i$ are assumed to be 1, 2, .... ■ Fit[$\{\{x_1,\ f_1\},\ \{x_2,\ f_2\},\ ...\}$, $\{1,\ x,\ x\wedge 2\}$, x] does a quadratic fit, assuming a sequence of x values $x_i$. ■ Fit[$\{\{x_1,\ y_1,\ f_1\},\ ...\}$, $\{1,\ x,\ y\}$, $\{x,\ y\}$] finds a fit of the form $a_0\ +\ a_1\ x\ +\ a_2\ y$. ■ Fit[*data*, $\{\{fn_1,\ fn_2,\ ...\},\ \{fd_1,\ ...\}\}$, *vars*] fits the data to rational function of the form $(an_1\ fn_1\ +\ an_2\ fn_2\ +\ ...)\ /\ (ad_1\ fd_1\ +\ ...)$. ■ Fit always finds the linear combination of the functions in the list *forms* that minimizes the sum of the squares of deviations from the values $f_i$. ■ Exact numbers given as input to Fit are converted to approximate numbers with machine precision. ■ See page 461. ■ See also: Solve, PseudoInverse, FindMinimum.

## ■ FixedPoint

FixedPoint[*f*, *expr*] starts with *expr*, then generates a sequence of expressions by repeatedly applying *f*, until the result no longer changes.

FixedPoint[*f*, *expr*, *n*] stops after at most *n* steps.

See page 254. ■ See also: Nest, ReplaceRepeated.

## ■ Flat

Flat is an attribute that can be assigned to a symbol *f* to indicate that all expressions involving nested functions *f* should be flattened out. This property is accounted for in pattern matching.

Flat corresponds to the mathematical property of associativity. ■ For a symbol *f* with attribute Flat, f[f[a, b], f[c]] is automatically reduced to f[a, b, c]. ■ Functions like Plus, Times and Dot are Flat. ■ For a Flat function *f*, the variables x and y in the pattern f[x_, y_] can correspond to any sequence of arguments. ■ The Flat attribute must be assigned before defining any values for an Flat function. ■ See page 214. ■ See also: Orderless, OneIdentity.

## ■ Flatten

Flatten[*list*] flattens out nested lists.

Flatten[*list*, *n*] flattens to level *n*.

Example: Flatten[{a,{b,c},{d}}] ⟶ {a, b, c, d}. ■ Flatten "unravels" lists, effectively just deleting inner braces. ■ Flatten[*list*, *n*] effectively flattens the top level in *list* *n* times. ■ Flatten[*f*[e, ...]] flattens out subexpressions with head *f*. ■ Flatten[*expr*, *n*, *h*] flattens only subexpressions with head *h*. ■ See page 104. ■ See also: Partition.

■ **Floor**

> Floor[*x*] gives the greatest integer less than or equal to *x*.
>
> Mathematical function (see Section B.3.8). ▪ Examples: Floor[2.4] ⟶ 2; Floor[2.6] ⟶ 2; Floor[-2.4] ⟶ -3; Floor[-2.6] ⟶ -3. ▪ See page 341. ▪ See also: Ceiling, Round, Chop.

■ **FontForm**

> FontForm[*expr*, "*fontname*", *size*] requests that *expr* be printed in the specified font and relative size.
>
> FontForm is used primarily for text included in graphics. ▪ The font name in FontForm is used in the POSTSCRIPT form of *expr*. Most POSTSCRIPT rendering systems translate the specifications into ones appropriate for the particular output device being used. ▪ The font size is specified in points. ▪ Typical font names are "Plain", "Bold" and "Italic". ▪ See page 281. ▪ See also: Text, PlotLabel.

■ **For**

> For[*start*, *test*, *incr*, *body*] executes *start*, then repeatedly evaluates *body* and *incr* until *test* fails to give True.
>
> For evaluates its arguments in a non-standard way. ▪ For[*start*, *test*, *incr*] does the loop with a null body. ▪ The sequence of evaluation is *test*, *body*, *incr*. The For exits as soon as *test* fails. ▪ If Break[ ] is generated in the evaluation of *body*, the For loop exits. ▪ Continue[ ] exits the evaluation of *body*, and continues the loop by evaluating *incr*. ▪ Unless Return[ ] or Throw[ ] are generated, the final value returned by For is Null. ▪ Example: For[tot=0; i=0, i < 3, i++, tot += f[i]]. Note that the roles of ; and , are *reversed* relative to the C programming language. ▪ See page 254. ▪ See also: Do, While.

■ **Format**

> Format[*expr*] prints as the formatted form of *expr*.
>
> Assigning values to Format[*expr*] defines print forms for expressions.
>
> Format[*expr*, *type*] gives a format of the specified type.
>
> Standard format types are:
>
> | | |
> |---|---|
> | CForm | C language input form |
> | FortranForm | FORTRAN input form |
> | InputForm | one-dimensional form suitable for input to *Mathematica* |
> | OutputForm | two-dimensional mathematical form |
> | TeXForm | TEX input form |
> | TextForm | textual form |
>
> ▪ You can add your own format types. ▪ Example: Format[*s*] := *form* defines a special print form for a symbol *s*. ▪ Format[*f*[...]] := *form* defines a print form for a function *f*. ▪ Definitions for Format are stored in the PrintValue of a symbol. ▪ See page 273. ▪ See also: ToString, Short.

■ **FormatType**

> FormatType is an option for OpenWrite and ResetMedium which specifies the default format type used when printing expressions.
>
> Standard values for FormatType are given in the notes for Format. ▪ See page 295. ▪ See also: TextRendering.

■ **FortranForm**

FortranForm[*expr*] prints as a FORTRAN language version of *expr*.

Standard arithmetic functions and certain control structures are translated. ■ Output lines are assumed to have 80 columns. ■ No declarations are generated. ■ See page 157. ■ See also: CForm.

■ **Fourier**

Fourier[*list*] finds the Fourier transform of a list of complex numbers.

The Fourier transform $b_s$ of a list $a_r$ of length $n$ is defined to be $\frac{1}{\sqrt{n}} \sum_{r=1}^{n} a_r e^{2\pi i (r-1)(s-1)/n}$. ■ Note that the zero frequency term appears at position 1 in the resulting list. ■ The list of data need not have a length equal to a power of two. ■ See page 465. ■ See also: InverseFourier, Fit.

■ **Framed**

Framed is an option for graphics functions that specifies whether a frame should be drawn around a plot.

Framed -> True draws a rectangular frame around the outside of the plot. ■ See page 109. ■ See also: Boxed.

■ **FreeQ**

FreeQ[*expr*, *form*] yields True if no subexpression in *expr* matches *form*, and yields False otherwise.

*form* can be a pattern. ■ Example: FreeQ[f[x∧2] + y∧2, x∧_] ⟶ False. ■ See page 230. ■ See also: MemberQ, Count.

■ **FromASCII**

FromASCII[*i*] gives a string consisting of the character which has the integer *i* as its ASCII code.

The value of *i* must be between 0 and 255, inclusive. ■ FromASCII uses character codes in the native character set on your computer. These codes may not necessarily be true ASCII. ■ See page 279. ■ See also: ToASCII.

■ **FullDefinition**

FullDefinition[$s_1$, $s_2$, ...] prints the definitions given for the symbols $s_i$, and all symbols on which these depend.

FullDefinition has attribute HoldAll. ■ FullDefinition[$s_1$, ...] recursively prints all definitions for the symbols $s_i$, and for the symbols that appear in these definitions. ■ FullDefinition does not look at rules or attributes of symbols that have the attribute Protected. ■ See page 289. ■ See also: Definition, Save, Information.

■ **FullForm**

> FullForm[*expr*] prints as the full form of *expr*, with no special syntax.

> Example: FullForm[a + b^2] ⟶ Plus[a, Power[b, 2]]. ▪ See page 270. ▪ See also: InputForm, TreeForm.

■ **Function**

> Function[*body*] or *body*& is a pure function. The formal parameters are # (or #1), #2, etc.

> Function[*x*,  *body*] is a pure function with a single formal parameter *x*.

> Function[{*x₁*,  *x₂*,  ...},  *body*] is a pure function with a list of formal parameters.

> Example: (# + 1)&[x] ⟶ 1 + x. ▪ Map[(# + 1)&, {x, y, z}] ⟶ {1 + x, 1 + y, 1 + z}. ▪ When Function[*body*] or *body*& is applied to a set of arguments, # (or #1) is replaced by the first argument, #2 by the second, and so on. ▪ If there are more arguments supplied than #*i* in the function, the remaining arguments are ignored. ▪ Function has attribute HoldAll. The function body is evaluated only after the formal parameters have been replaced by arguments. ▪ The named formal parameters $x_i$ in Function[{*x₁*,  ...},  *body*] are treated as local. ▪ ## stands for the sequence of all arguments supplied. ▪ ##*n* stands for arguments from number *n* on. ▪ f[##, ##2]& [x, y, z] ⟶ f[x, y, z, y, z]. ▪ Function is analogous to $\lambda$ in LISP or formal logic. ▪ Formal parameters inside nested Function objects are not modified when the outer objects are applied. ▪ See page 179. ▪ See also: Apply.

■ **Gamma**

> Gamma[*z*] is the Euler gamma function $\Gamma(z)$.

> Gamma[*a*,  *z*] is the incomplete gamma function $\Gamma(a, z)$.

> Gamma[*a*,  *z₀*,  *z₁*] is the generalized incomplete gamma function $\Gamma(a, z_0) - \Gamma(a, z_1)$.

> Mathematical function (see Section B.3.8). ▪ The gamma function satisfies $\Gamma(z) = \int_0^\infty t^{z-1} e^{-t} dt$. ▪ The incomplete gamma function satisfies $\Gamma(a, z) = \int_z^\infty t^{a-1} e^{-t} dt$. ▪ See page 363. ▪ See also: Factorial, PolyGamma.

■ **GCD**

> GCD[*expr₁*,  *expr₂*,  ...] gives the greatest common divisor of the expressions $expr_i$.

> The $expr_i$ may be either integers or polynomials.

> GCD[*expr₁*,  ...,  Modulus->*n*] evaluates the GCD modulo the integer *n*.

> Integer mathematical function (see Section B.3.8). ▪ GCD[*expr₁*, ...] gives the factors common to all the $expr_i$. ▪ See pages 345 and 388. ▪ See also: Rational, LCM, ExtendedGCD, Cancel.

■ **GegenbauerC**

> GegenbauerC[*n*,  *m*,  *x*] gives the Gegenbauer polynomial $C_n^m(x)$.

> Mathematical function (see Section B.3.8). ▪ Explicit polynomials are given for integer *n* and *m*. ▪ The Gegenbauer polynomials are orthogonal with weight function $(1 - x^2)^{m-1/2}$, corresponding to integration over a unit hypersphere. ▪ See page 360. ▪ See also: LegendreP, ChebyshevT.

# ■ General

**General** is a symbol to which general system messages are attached.

When you refer to a message with name $s$::$tag$ in On or Off, the text of the message is obtained from General::$tag$ if no specific message named $s$::$tag$ exists. ■ See page 284.

# ■ Get

**<<**$filename$ reads in a file, evaluating each expression in it, and returning the last one.

On systems with advanced graphical interfaces, there will usually be graphical tools for reading in files. ■ The .m extension in *Mathematica* file names must be included explicitly. ■ Get is for reading in files that contain *Mathematica* input only. ■ The list of directories $Path is searched for a file with the specified name. ■ <<"$filename$" is equivalent to <<$filename$. The " can be omitted if the filename contains only the following non-alphanumeric characters: ., / and ~. ■ Syntax errors in files are reported in the standard form: $filename$: $line$: syntax error in $expr$. Get continues attempting to read a file even after a syntax error has been detected. ■ See page 286. ■ See also: Read, StartProcess, RunThrough, Put, Splice.

# ■ GoldenRatio

**GoldenRatio** is the golden ratio $\phi = (1 + \sqrt{5})/2$, with numerical value $\simeq 1.61803$.

Mathematical constant (see Section B.3.9). ■ See page 359.

# ■ Goto

**Goto[**$tag$**]** scans the current compound expression for Label[$tag$], and transfers control to that point.

See page 260.

# ■ Graphics

Graphics[*primitives*, *options*] represents a two-dimensional graphical image.

Graphics is displayed using Show.  ■ The following primitives can be used:

| | |
|---|---|
| Point[{*x*, *y*}] | point |
| Line[{{*x₁*, *y₁*}, ...}] | line |
| Rectangle[{*xmin*, *ymin*}, {*xmax*, *ymax*}] | filled rectangle |
| Polygon[{{*x₁*, *y₁*}, ...}] | filled polygon |
| CellArray[*array*] | array of gray levels |
| Text[*expr*, {*x*, *y*}] | text |
| GrayLevel[*i*] | intensity specification |
| RGBColor[*r*, *g*, *b*] | color specification |
| PointSize[*s*] | point size specification |
| Thickness[*t*] | line thickness specification |
| Dashing[{*d₁*, ...}] | line dashing specification |

■ The following options can be given:

| | | |
|---|---|---|
| AspectRatio | 1/GoldenRatio | ratio of height to width |
| Axes | None | whether to include axes |
| AxesLabel | None | axes labels |
| DisplayFunction | $DisplayFunction | function for generating output |
| Framed | False | whether to draw a frame |
| PlotColor | True | whether to plot in color |
| PlotLabel | None | a label for the plot |
| PlotRange | Automatic | range of $z$ values to include |
| Ticks | Automatic | tick marks |

■ Nested lists of graphics primitives can be given. The scope of specifications such as GrayLevel is the list that contains them.  ■ The standard print form for Graphics[...] is -Graphics-. InputForm prints the explicit list of primitives.  ■ See page 140.  ■ See also: Plot.

■ **Graphics3D**

Graphics3D[*primitives, options*] represents a three-dimensional graphical image.

Graphics3D is displayed using Show. ▪ The following primitives can be used:

| | |
|---|---|
| Point[{$x$, $y$, $z$}] | point |
| Line[{{$x_1$, $y_1$, $z_1$}, ...}] | line |
| Polygon[{{$x_1$, $y_1$, $z_1$}, ...}] | polygon |
| GrayLevel[$i$] | gray level specification |
| RGBColor[$r$, $g$, $b$] | color specification |
| PointSize[$s$] | point size specification |
| Thickness[$t$] | line thickness specification |
| FaceForm[*spec*] | polygon face specification |
| EdgeForm[*spec*] | polygon edge specification |

▪ The following options can be given:

| | | |
|---|---|---|
| AmbientLight | GrayLevel[0.] | ambient illumination level |
| AspectRatio | 1 | ratio of height to width |
| BoxRatios | Automatic | bounding 3D box ratios |
| Boxed | True | whether to draw the bounding box |
| DisplayFunction | $DisplayFunction | function for generating output |
| Framed | False | whether to draw a frame |
| LightSources | (see below) | positions and colors of light sources |
| Lighting | True | whether to use simulated illumination |
| Plot3Matrix | Automatic | perspective transformation matrix |
| PlotColor | True | whether to plot in color |
| PlotLabel | None | a label for the plot |
| PlotRange | Automatic | range of values to include |
| RenderAll | True | whether to render all polygons |
| Shading | True | whether to shade polygons |
| ViewPoint | {1.3, -2.4, 2.} | viewing position |

▪ Nested lists of graphics primitives can be given. The scope of specifications such as GrayLevel is the list that contains them. ▪ The standard print form for Graphics3D[...] is -Graphics3D-. InputForm prints the explicit list of primitives. ▪ The default light sources used are
{{{1,0,1}, RGBColor[1,0,0]}, {{1,1,1}, RGBColor[0,1,0]}, {{0,1,1}, RGBColor[0,0,1]}} ▪ See page 148. ▪ See also: Plot3D, SurfaceGraphics.

■ **Greater**

$x > y$ yields True if $x$ is determined to be greater than $y$.

$x_1 > x_2 > x_3$ yields True if the $x_i$ form a strictly decreasing sequence.

Greater gives True or False when its arguments are real numbers. ▪ Greater does some simplification when its arguments are not numbers. ▪ See page 72. ▪ See also: Less, Positive.

■ **GreaterEqual**

$x$ >= $y$ yields **True** if $x$ is determined to be greater than or equal to $y$.

$x_1$ >= $x_2$ >= $x_3$ yields **True** if the $x_i$ form a non-increasing sequence.

GreaterEqual gives **True** or **False** when its arguments are real numbers. ■ GreaterEqual does some simplification when its arguments are not numbers. ■ See page 72.

■ **GrayLevel**

GrayLevel[*level*] is a graphics primitive which specifies that graphical objects which follow are to be displayed, if possible, with the gray level intensity specified.

The gray level must be a number between 0 and 1. ■ 0 represents black; 1 represents white. ■ On display devices with no native gray-level capability, dither patterns are typically used, as generated by the POSTSCRIPT interpreter. ■ See pages 129, 142 and 149. ■ See also: RGBColor, ContourGraphics.

■ **Head**

Head[*expr*] gives the head of *expr*.

Examples: Head[f[x]] $\longrightarrow$ f; Head[a + b] $\longrightarrow$ Plus; Head[4] $\longrightarrow$ Integer; Head[x] $\longrightarrow$ Symbol. ■ See page 166.

■ **HeadCompose**

HeadCompose[$a$, $b$, $c$, $d$] gives $a[b][c][d]$.

See page 248. ■ See also: Compose.

■ **HermiteH**

Hermite[$n$, $x$] gives the Hermite polynomial $H_n(x)$.

Mathematical function (see Section B.3.8). ■ Explicit polynomials are given for integer $n$. ■ The Hermite polynomials satisfy the differential equation $\frac{d^2y}{dx^2} - 2x\frac{dy}{dx} + 2ny = 0$. ■ They are orthogonal polynomials with weight function $e^{-x^2}$. ■ See page 360.

■ **HiddenSurface**

HiddenSurface is an option for **SurfaceGraphics** which specifies whether hidden surfaces are to be eliminated.

HiddenSurface -> True eliminates hidden surfaces. ■ See page 127. ■ See also: Shading.

■ **Hold**

Hold[*expr*] maintains *expr* in an unevaluated form.

Hold has attribute HoldAll, and performs no operation on its argument. ■ Example: Hold[1+1] $\longrightarrow$ Hold[1 + 1]. ■ Hold is removed by Release. ■ See page 220. ■ See also: Literal, HoldForm.

## HoldAll

**HoldAll** is an attribute which specifies that all arguments to a function are to be maintained in an unevaluated form.

You can use **Release** to evaluate the arguments of a **HoldAll** function in a controlled way. ■ See page 214.

## HoldFirst

**HoldFirst** is an attribute which specifies that the first argument to a function is to be maintained in an unevaluated form.

See page 214.

## HoldForm

**HoldForm**[*expr*] prints as the expression *expr*, with *expr* maintained in an unevaluated form.

**HoldForm** allows you to see the output form of an expression without evaluating the expression. ■ **HoldForm** has attribute **HoldFirst**. ■ See page 274. ■ See also: **ToString**, **WriteString**.

## HoldRest

**HoldRest** is an attribute which specifies that all but the first argument to a function are to be maintained in an unevaluated form.

See page 214.

## Hypergeometric0F1

**Hypergeometric0F1**[*a*, *z*] is the hypergeometric function $_0F_1(;a;z)$.

Mathematical function (see Section B.3.8). ■ The $_0F_1$ function has the series expansion $_0F_1(;a;z) = \sum_{k=0}^{\infty} \frac{z^k}{(a)_k k!}$. ■ See page 363.

## Hypergeometric1F1

**Hypergeometric1F1**[*a*, *b*, *z*] is the Kummer confluent hypergeometric function $_1F_1(a;b;z)$.

Mathematical function (see Section B.3.8). ■ The $_1F_1$ function has the series expansion $_1F_1(a;b;z) = \sum_{k=0}^{\infty} \frac{(a)_k}{(c)_k} \frac{z^k}{k!}$. ■ See page 363.

## Hypergeometric2F1

**Hypergeometric2F1**[*a*, *b*, *c*, *z*] is the hypergeometric function $_2F_1(a,b;c;z)$.

Mathematical function (see Section B.3.8). ■ The $_2F_1$ function has the series expansion $_2F_1(a,b;c;z) = \sum_{k=0}^{\infty} \frac{(a)_k(b)_k}{(c)_k} \frac{z^k}{k!}$. ■ See page 363.

## HypergeometricU

HypergeometricU[*a*,  *b*,  *z*] is the confluent hypergeometric function $U(a, b, z)$.

Mathematical function (see Section B.3.8).  ▪ The function $U(a, b, z)$ has the integral representation $U(a,b,z) = \frac{1}{\Gamma(a)} \int_0^\infty e^{-zt} t^{a-1} (1+t)^{b-a-1} \, dt$.  ▪ See page 363.

## I

I represents the imaginary unit $\sqrt{-1}$.

Numbers containing I are converted to the type Complex.  ▪ See page 359.  ▪ See also: Re, Im.

## Identity

Identity[*expr*] gives *expr* (the identity operation).

See page 246.  ▪ See also: Compose, Through.

## IdentityMatrix

IdentityMatrix[*n*] gives the $n \times n$ identity matrix.

See page 437.  ▪ See also: DiagonalMatrix, Table.

## If

If[*condition*,  *t*,  *f*] gives *t* if *condition* is True, and *f* if it is False.

If[*condition*,  *t*,  *f*,  *u*] gives *u* if *condition* is neither True nor False.

If evaluates only the argument determined by the value of the condition.  ▪ If[*condition*,  *t*,  *f*] is left unevaluated if *condition* is neither True nor False.  ▪ If[*condition*,  *t*] gives Null if *condition* is False.  ▪ See page 258.  ▪ See also: Switch, Which, Condition.

## Im

Im[*z*] gives the imaginary part of the complex number *z*.

Im[*expr*] is left unevaluated if *expr* is not a number.  ▪ See page 342.  ▪ See also: Re, Abs, Arg.

## Implies

Implies[*p*,  *q*] represents the logical implication $p \Rightarrow q$.

Implies[*p*,  *q*] is equivalent to !*p* || *q*.  ▪ See page 73.  ▪ See also: LogicalExpand, If.

## In

In[*n*] is a global object that is assigned to have a delayed value of the $n^{\text{th}}$ input line.

Typing In[*n*] causes the $n^{\text{th}}$ input line to be reevaluated.  ▪ In[ ] gives the last input line.  ▪ In[-k] gives the input *k* lines back.  ▪ See page 577.  ▪ See also: Out, $Line.

■ **Increment**

*x*++ increases the value of *x* by 1, returning the old value of *x*.

Increment has attribute HoldFirst.  ■ See page 257.  ■ See also: PreIncrement, AddTo, Set.

■ **Indent**

Indent[*d*] is printed as the indentation for a depth *d* subexpression.

You can redefine Indent[*d*] to change the indentation in the printed forms of expressions.  ■ See page 588.  ■ See also: LineBreak, Continuation, StringBreak.

■ **Indeterminate**

Indeterminate is a symbol that represents a numerical quantity whose magnitude cannot be determined.

Computations like 0/0 generate Indeterminate.  ■ A message is produced whenever an operation first yields Indeterminate as a result.  ■ See page 338.  ■ See also: DirectedInfinity, Check.

■ **Infinity**

Infinity is a symbol that represents a positive infinite quantity.

Infinity is converted to DirectedInfinity[1].  ■ Certain arithmetic operations work with Infinity.  ■ Example: 1/Infinity $\longrightarrow$ 0.  ■ See pages 338 and 359.  ■ See also: ComplexInfinity, Indeterminate.

■ **Infix**

Infix[*f*[*e₁*, *e₂*, ...]] prints with *f*[*e₁*, *e₂*, ...] given in default infix form: $e_1 \sim f \sim e_2 \sim f \sim e_3$ ....

Infix[*expr*, *h*] prints with arguments separated by *h*: $e_1 \ h \ e_2 \ h \ e_3$ ....

Infix[*expr*, *h*, *precedence*, *grouping*] can be used to specify how the output form should be parenthesized.  ■ Precedence levels are specified by integers. In OutputForm, some precedence levels are:

| | |
|---|---|
| *x* . *y* . *z* | 210 |
| *x y z* | 150 |
| *x* + *y* + *z* | 140 |
| *x* == *y* | 130 |
| *x* = *y* | 60 |

■ Possible grouping (associativity) specifications are:

| | |
|---|---|
| NonAssociative | not associative – always parenthesized |
| None | always associative – never parenthesized |
| Left | left associative (e.g. $(a/b)/c$) |
| Right | right associative (e.g. $a\wedge(b\wedge c)$) |

■ See page 278.  ■ See also: Postfix, Prefix, PrecedenceForm.

■ **Information**

Information[*symbol*] prints as information about a symbol.

Information[*symbol*] prints the same information as the input escape ?*symbol* would give.   ■ **Information** has attribute **HoldAll**.   ■ See also: **Definition**, **Names**, **ValueQ**.

■ **Inner**

Inner[*f*, *list₁*, *list₂*, *g*] is a generalization of **Dot** in which *f* plays the role of multiplication and *g* of addition.

Example: `Inner[f,{a,b},{x,y},g]` ⟶ `g[f[a, x], f[b, y]]`.  ■
`Inner[f,{{a,b},{c,d}},{x,y},g]` ⟶ `{g[f[a, x], f[b, y]], g[f[c, x], f[d, y]]}`.  ■ Like **Dot**, **Inner** effectively contracts the last index of the first tensor with the first index of the second tensor. Applying **Inner** to a rank $r$ tensor and a rank $s$ tensor gives a rank $r + s - 1$ tensor.  ■ Inner[*f*, *list₁*, *list₂*] uses **Plus** for *g*.  ■ Inner[*f*, *list₁*, *list₂*, *g*, *n*] contracts index *n* of the first tensor with the first index of the second tensor.  ■ The heads of *list₁* and *list₂* must be the same, but need not necessarily be **List**.  ■ See page 457.  ■ See also: **Outer**, **Thread**.

■ **Input**

Input[ ] interactively reads in one *Mathematica* expression.

Input["*prompt*"] requests input, using the specified string as a prompt.

**Input** returns the expression it read.  ■ The operation of **Input** may vary from one computer system to another. When a *Mathematica* front end is used, **Input** may work through a dialog box.  ■ When no front end is used, **Input** reads from standard input.  ■ If the standard input is a file, then **Input** returns **EndOfFile** if you try to read past the end of the file.  ■ On most systems, Input[ ] uses ? as a prompt.  ■ When **Input** is evaluated, *Mathematica* stops until the input has been read.  ■ See page 300.  ■ See also: **InputString**, **Read**, **Get**.

■ **InputForm**

InputForm[*expr*] prints as a version of *expr* suitable for input to *Mathematica*.

Example: `InputForm[x^2 + 1/a]` ⟶ `a^(-1) + x^2`.  ■ **InputForm** always produces one-dimensional output, suitable to be typed as lines of *Mathematica* input.  ■ **Put** (`>>`) produces **InputForm** by default.  ■ See page 268.  ■ See also: **OutputForm**, **FullForm**.

■ **InputString**

InputString[ ] interactively reads in a character string.

InputString["*prompt*"] requests input, using the specified string as a prompt.

See notes for **Input**.  ■ See page 300.

■ **Insert**

Insert[*list*, *elem*, *n*] inserts *elem* at position *n* in *list*. If *n* is negative, the position is counted from the end.

Example: `Insert[{a, b, c}, x, 2]` ⟶ `{a, x, b, c}`.  ■ *list* can have any head, not necessarily **List**.  ■ See page 102.  ■ See also: **Prepend**, **Append**.

## ■ Integer

**Integer** is the head used for integers.

_Integer can be used to stand for an integer in a pattern. ▪ Integers can be of any length. ▪ You can enter an integer in base $b$ using $b \wedge \wedge digits$. The base must be less than 36. The letters are used in sequence to standard for digits 10 through 35. ▪ See page 325. ▪ See also: **BaseForm**.

## ■ IntegerQ

**IntegerQ**[*expr*] gives **True** if *expr* is an integer, and **False** otherwise.

**IntegerQ**[*expr*] returns **False** unless *expr* is manifestly an integer (i.e. has head **Integer**). ▪ You can use **IntegerQ**[$x$] = **True** to override the normal operation of **IntegerQ**, and effectively define $x$ to be an integer. ▪ See pages 230 and 326. ▪ See also: **EvenQ**, **OddQ**, **NumberQ**, **TrueQ**.

## ■ Integrate

**Integrate**[*f*, *x*] gives the indefinite integral $\int f \, dx$.

**Integrate**[*f*, {*x*, *xmin*, *xmax*}] gives the definite integral $\int_{xmin}^{xmax} f \, dx$.

**Integrate**[*f*, {*x*, *xmin*, *xmax*}, {*y*, *ymin*, *ymax*}] gives the multiple integral $\int_{xmin}^{xmax} dx \int_{ymin}^{ymax} dy \, f$.

Multiple integrals use a variant of the standard iterator notation. The first variable given corresponds to the outermost integral, and is done last. ▪ **Integrate** can evaluate integrals of rational functions. It can also evaluate integrals that involve exponential, logarithmic, trigonometric and inverse trigonometric functions, so long as the result comes out in terms of the same set of functions. ▪ **Integrate** carries out some simplifications on integrals it can explicitly do. ▪ You can get a numerical result by applying **N** to a definite integral. ▪ You can assign values to patterns involving **Integrate** to give results for new classes of integrals. ▪ The integration variable can be any expression. However, **Integrate** uses only its literal form. The object $d(x^n)$, for example, is not converted to $nx^{n-1}dx$. ▪ See page 419. ▪ See also: **NIntegrate**.

## ■ Intersection

**Intersection**[*list₁*, *list₂*, ...] gives a sorted list of the elements common to all the *listᵢ*.

If the *listᵢ* are considered as sets, **Intersection** gives their intersection. ▪ The *listᵢ* must have the same head, but it need not be **List**. ▪ See page 103. ▪ See also: **Union**, **Complement**.

## ■ Inverse

**Inverse**[*m*] gives the inverse of a square matrix *m*.

**Inverse** works on both symbolic and numerical matrices. ▪ For matrices with approximate real or complex numbers, the inverse is generated to the same precision as the input. A warning is given for ill-conditioned matrices. ▪ See page 443. ▪ See also: **PseudoInverse**, **LinearSolve**, **NullSpace**.

## ■ InverseFourier

**InverseFourier**[*list*] finds the inverse Fourier transform of a list of complex numbers.

The inverse Fourier transform $a_r$ of a list $b_s$ of length $n$ is defined to be $\frac{1}{\sqrt{n}} \sum_{s=1}^{n} b_s e^{-2\pi i(r-1)(s-1)/n}$. ▪ Note that the zero frequency term must appear at position 1 in the input list. ▪ The list of data need not have a length equal to a power of two. ▪ See page 465. ▪ See also: **Fourier**.

■ **InverseJacobiSN**

> InverseJacobiSN[v, m], InverseJacobiCN[v, m], etc. give the inverse Jacobi elliptic functions $\operatorname{sn}^{-1}(v|m)$ etc.
>
> There are a total of twelve functions, with the names of the form InverseJacobi$PQ$, where $P$ and $Q$ can be any distinct pair of the letters S, C, D and N.
>
> Mathematical functions (see Section B.3.8). ▪ $\operatorname{sn}^{-1}(v|m)$ gives the value of $u$ for which $v = \operatorname{sn}(u|m)$. ▪ The inverse Jacobi elliptic functions are related to elliptic integrals. ▪ See page 374.

■ **InverseSeries**

> InverseSeries[s] takes the series $s$ generated by Series, and gives a series for the inverse of the function represented by $s$.
>
> InverseSeries performs "reversion" of series. ▪ Given a series $s(x)$, InverseSeries gives a series $s^{-1}(x)$ such that $s(s^{-1}(x)) = x$. ▪ InverseSeries can only be used when the first term in the series $s(x)$ is of order $x$. ▪ See page 432.

■ **JacobiAmplitude**

> JacobiAmplitude[u, m] gives the amplitude for Jacobi elliptic functions $\operatorname{am}(u|m)$.
>
> JacobiAmplitude is the inverse of the elliptic integral of the first kind. If $u = F(\phi|m)$, then $\phi = \operatorname{am}(u|m)$. ▪ See page 374.

■ **JacobiP**

> JacobiP[n, a, b, x] gives the Jacobi polynomial $P_n^{(a,b)}(x)$.
>
> Mathematical function (see Section B.3.8). ▪ Explicit polynomials are given when possible. ▪ The Jacobi polynomials are orthogonal with weight function $(1-x)^a(1+x)^b$. ▪ See page 360.

■ **JacobiSN**

> JacobiSN[u, m], JacobiCN[u, m], etc. give the Jacobi elliptic functions $\operatorname{sn}(u|m)$ etc.
>
> There are a total of twelve functions, with the names of the form Jacobi$PQ$, where $P$ and $Q$ can be any distinct pair of the letters S, C, D and N.
>
> Mathematical functions (see Section B.3.8). ▪ $\operatorname{sn}(u) = \sin(\phi)$, $\operatorname{cn}(u) = \cos(\phi)$ and $\operatorname{dn}(u) = \sqrt{1 - m\sin^2(\phi)}$, where $\phi = \operatorname{am}(u|m)$. ▪ Other Jacobi elliptic functions can be found from the relation $\operatorname{pq}(u) = \operatorname{pr}(u)/\operatorname{qr}(u)$, where for these purposes $\operatorname{pp}(u) = 1$. ▪ See page 374. ▪ See also: InverseJacobiSN.

■ **JacobiSymbol**

> JacobiSymbol[n, m] gives the Jacobi symbol $\left(\frac{n}{m}\right)$.
>
> Integer mathematical function (see Section B.3.8). ▪ For prime $m$, the Jacobi symbol reduces to the Legendre symbol. The Legendre symbol is equal to $\pm 1$ depending on whether $n$ is a quadratic residue modulo $m$. ▪ See page 347.

■ Join

> Join[*list₁*, *list₂*, ...] concatenates lists together. Join can be used on any set of expressions that have the same head.

> See page 102. ▪ See also: Union, StringJoin.

■ Label

> Label[*tag*] represents a point in a procedure to which control can be transferred using Goto.

> Label must appear as an element of a CompoundExpression. ▪ Label has attribute HoldFirst. ▪ See page 260.

■ LaguerreL

> LaguerreL[*n*, *a*, *x*] gives the Laguerre polynomial $L_n^a(x)$.

> Mathematical function (see Section B.3.8). ▪ Explicit polynomials are given when possible. ▪ The Laguerre polynomials are orthogonal with weight function $x^a e^{-x}$. ▪ They satisfy the differential equation $x\frac{d^2 y}{dx^2} + (a + 1 - x)\frac{dy}{dx} + ny = 0$. ▪ See page 360.

■ Last

> Last[*expr*] gives the last element in *expr*.

> Last[*expr*] is equivalent to *expr*[[-1]]. ▪ See page 99. ▪ See also: Part, First.

■ LatticeReduce

> LatticeReduce[{*v₁*, *v₂*, ...}] gives a reduced basis for the set of integer vectors *vᵢ*.

> LatticeReduce uses the Lenstra-Lenstra-Lovasz lattice reduction algorithm. ▪ See page 347. ▪ See also: RowReduce.

■ LCM

> LCM[*expr₁*, *expr₂*, ...] gives the least common multiple of the expressions *exprᵢ*.

> The *exprᵢ* may be either integers or polynomials.

> LCM[*expr₁*, ..., Modulus->*n*] evaluates the LCM modulo the integer *n*.

> Integer mathematical function (see Section B.3.8). ▪ See page 345. ▪ See also: GCD.

■ LeafCount

> LeafCount[*expr*] gives the total number of indivisible subexpressions in *expr*.

> LeafCount gives a measure of the total "size" of an expression. ▪ LeafCount counts the number of subexpressions in *expr* which correspond to "leaves" on the expression tree. ▪ Example: LeafCount[1 + a + b^2] ⟶ 6. ▪ See page 318. ▪ See also: ByteCount, Length, Depth, AtomQ.

### ■ LegendreP

LegendreP[*n*, *x*] gives the Legendre polynomial $P_n(x)$.

LegendreP[*n*, *m*, *x*] gives the associated Legendre polynomial $P_n^m(x)$.

Mathematical function (see Section B.3.8). ▪ Explicit polynomials are given for integer $n$ and $m$. ▪ The Legendre polynomials satisfy the differential equation $(1 - x^2)\frac{d^2y}{dx^2} - 2x\frac{dy}{dx} + n(n+1)y = 0$. ▪ The Legendre polynomials are orthogonal with unit weight function. ▪ The associated Legendre polynomials are defined by $P_n^m(x) = (-1)^m(1 - x^2)^{m/2}\frac{d^m}{dx^m}P_n(x)$. ▪ For arbitrary complex values of $n$, $m$ and $z$, LegendreP[*n*, *z*] and LegendreP[*n*, *m*, *z*] give Legendre functions of the first kind. ▪ See pages 360 and 363. ▪ See also: SphericalHarmonicY.

### ■ LegendreQ

LegendreQ[*n*, *z*] gives the Legendre function of the second kind $Q_n(z)$.

LegendreQ[*n*, *m*, *z*] gives the associated Legendre function of the second kind $Q_n^m(z)$.

Mathematical function (see Section B.3.8). ▪ For integer $n$ and $m$, explicit formulae are generated. ▪ The Legendre functions satisfy the differential equation $(1 - z^2)\frac{d^2y}{dz^2} - 2z\frac{dy}{dz} + [(n(n+1) - \frac{m^2}{1-z^2}]y = 0$. ▪ See page 363.

### ■ LegendreType

LegendreType is an option for LegendreP and LegendreQ which specifies choices of branch cuts for Legendre functions in the complex plane.

The possible settings for LegendreType are Real and Complex. ▪ With LegendreType->Complex, there is a branch cut from $-\infty$ to $+1$. With LegendreType->Real, there are branch cuts from $-\infty\,to-1$ and $+1$ to $+\infty$. ▪ See page 371.

### ■ Length

Length[*expr*] gives the number of elements in *expr*.

See pages 98 and 171. ▪ See also: LeafCount, ByteCount, Depth.

### ■ LerchPhi

LerchPhi[*z*, *s*, *a*] gives the Lerch transcendent $\Phi(z, s, a)$.

Mathematical function (see Section B.3.8). ▪ $\Phi(z, s, a) = \sum_{k=0}^{\infty}\frac{z^k}{(a+k)^s}$, where any term with $k + a = 0$ is excluded. ▪ LerchPhi[*z*, *s*, *a*, DoublyInfinite->True] gives the sum $\sum_{k=-\infty}^{\infty}\frac{z^k}{(a+k)^s}$. ▪ LerchPhi is a generalization of Zeta and PolyLog. ▪ See page 364.

### ■ Less

*x* < *y* yields True if *x* is determined to be less than *y*.

*x₁* < *x₂* < *x₃* yields True if the $x_i$ form a strictly increasing sequence.

Less gives True or False when its arguments are real numbers. ▪ Less does some simplification when its arguments are not numbers. ▪ See page 72. ▪ See also: Greater, Positive.

# ■ LessEqual

$x$ <= $y$ yields **True** if $x$ is determined to be less than or equal to $y$.

$x_1$ <= $x_2$ <= $x_3$ yields **True** if the $x_i$ form a non-decreasing sequence.

LessEqual gives **True** or **False** when its arguments are real numbers.  ■ LessEqual does some simplification when its arguments are not numbers.  ■ See page 72.

# ■ Level

Level[*expr*, *levelspec*] gives a list of all subexpressions of *expr* on levels specified by *levelspec*.

Level[*expr*, *levelspec*, *f*] applies *f* to the list of subexpressions.

Level uses the standard level specification described on page 564.  ■ Level[*expr*, -1] gives a list of all "atomic" objects in *expr*.  ■ See page 175.  ■ See also: Apply, Map, Scan.

# ■ Lighting

Lighting is an option to Graphics3D and related functions that specifies whether to use simulated illumination in three-dimensional pictures.

Lighting -> True uses simulated illumination. The ambient light level is specified by the option AmbientLight. The option LightSources gives the positions and intensities of point light sources.  ■ Lighting -> False uses no simulated illumination. In SurfaceGraphics, polygons are then shaded according to their height.  ■ See pages 128 and 153.  ■ See also: Shading.

# ■ LightSources

LightSources is an option to Graphics3D and related functions that specifies the properties of point light sources for simulated illumination.

The basic form is LightSources -> {$s_1$, $s_2$, ...}, where the $s_i$ are the specifications for each light source. Each $s_i$ has the form {*direction*, *color*}. The direction is specified as {$x$, $y$, $z$}, where the components are with respect to the final viewing plane. The $x$ and $y$ axes are in the plane; $z$ is orthogonal to the plane; positive $z$ is in front. Only the relative magnitude of the components is relevant; the overall normalization of the vector is ignored. The color can be specified by GrayLevel[*graylevel*] or RGBColor[*red*, *green*, *blue*].  ■ Simulated illumination determines the shading of polygons in three-dimensional pictures.  ■ The shading of a particular polygon is computed as a sum of contributions from point light sources, plus a contribution from ambient light.  ■ If GrayLevel or RGBColor has been specified for a particular polygon, the value will be used to give the reflectivity of the polygon. If no such specifications have been made, the polygon is taken to be a perfect (diffuse) reflector.  ■ Polygons are assumed to be diffuse reflectors, and to follow Lambert's law. The intensity of reflected light is taken to be proportional to the cosine of the angle between the normal to the polygon and the direction to a particular light source.  ■ See page 129.  ■ See also: AmbientLight, ViewPoint.

# ■ Limit

Limit[*expr*, $x$->$x_0$] finds the limiting value of *expr* when $x$ approaches $x_0$.

Limit can handle power law and logarithmic limiting behavior.  ■ Limit prints a message if it encounters an essential singularity.  ■ See page 435.  ■ See also: Series.

■ **Line**

Line[{$pt_1$, $pt_2$, ...}] is a graphics primitive which represents a line joining a sequence of points.

Line can be used in both Graphics and Graphics3D (two- and three-dimensional graphics). ■ The positions of points can be specified either in absolute coordinates, as {$x$, $y$} or {$x$, $y$, $z$}, or in scaled coordinates as Scaled[{$x$, $y$}] or Scaled[{$x$, $y$, $z$}]. ■ The line consists of a sequence of straight segments joining the specified points. ■ In two and three dimensions, the line thickness can be specified using the graphics primitive Thickness. ■ Line shading or coloring can be specified using GrayLevel or RGBColor. ■ In two dimensions, dashed lines can be specified using Dashing. ■ In three dimensions, the properties of lines that appear at intersections between polygons can be specified using EdgeForm. ■ See pages 142 and 149. ■ See also: Polygon.

■ **LinearSolve**

LinearSolve[$m$, $b$] gives the vector $x$ which solves the matrix equation $m.x == b$.

LinearSolve works on both numerical and symbolic matrices. ■ The matrix $m$ can be square or rectangular. ■ LinearSolve[$m$, ZeroTest -> $test$] evaluates $test$[ $m$[[$i$, $j$]] ] to determine whether matrix elements are zero. The default setting is ZeroTest -> (# == 0)&. ■ See page 448. ■ See also: Inverse, PseudoInverse, Solve, NullSpace.

■ **LineBreak**

LineBreak[$n$] is output between the $n^{\text{th}}$ and $(n+1)^{\text{th}}$ lines in a multiline printed expression.

Redefining Format[LineBreak[n_]] changes the way spaces are printed between lines. ■ Setting Format[LineBreak[_]] = "" specifies that a zero-size object is to be used between lines, and causes successive lines to be printed with no intervening blank lines. ■ Additional blank lines can be inserted by setting Format[LineBreak[_]] to be an object that is several lines high. ■ See page 588. ■ See also: Continuation, StringBreak, Indent.

■ **List**

{$e_1$, $e_2$, ...} is a list of elements.

Lists are very general objects that represent collections of expressions. ■ Functions with attribute Listable are automatically "threaded" over lists, so that they act separately on each list element. Most built-in mathematical functions are Listable. ■ {$a$, $b$, $c$} represents a vector. ■ {{$a$, $b$}, {$c$, $d$}} represents a matrix. ■ Nested lists can be used to represent tensors. ■ See page 90.

■ **Listable**

Listable is an attribute that can be assigned to a symbol $f$ to indicate that the function $f$ should automatically be threaded over lists that appear as its arguments.

Listable functions are effectively applied separately to each element in a list. ■ Most built-in mathematical functions are Listable. ■ Example: Log is Listable. Log[{a,b,c}] ⟶ {Log[a], Log[b], Log[c]}. ■ All the arguments which are lists in a Listable function must be of the same length. ■ Arguments that are not lists are copied as many times as there are elements in the lists. ■ Example: Plus is Listable. {a, b, c} + x ⟶ {a + x, b + x, c + x}. ■ See page 214. ■ See also: Thread, Map.

■ ListContourPlot

> ListContourPlot[*array*] generates a contour plot from an array of height values.

> ListContourPlot returns a ContourGraphics object. ■ The array of height values must be square. ■ See notes for ContourGraphics. ■ See page 137.

■ ListDensityPlot

> ListDensityGraphics[*array*] generates a density plot from an array of height values.

> ListDensityPlot returns a DensityGraphics object. ■ See notes for DensityGraphics. ■ See page 137.

■ ListPlot

> ListPlot[{$y_1$, $y_2$, ...}] plots a list of values. The $x$ coordinates for each point are taken to be 1, 2, ....

> ListPlot[{{$x_1$, $y_1$}, {$x_2$, $y_2$}, ...}] plots a list of values with specified $x$ and $y$ coordinates.

> ListPlot returns a Graphics object. ■ Setting PlotJoined -> True gives a line joining the points. ■ The following options can be given:

| | | |
|---|---|---|
| AspectRatio | 1/GoldenRatio | ratio of height to width |
| Axes | Automatic | whether to include axes |
| AxesLabel | None | axes labels |
| DisplayFunction | $DisplayFunction | function for generating output |
| Framed | False | whether to draw a frame |
| PlotColor | True | whether to plot in color |
| PlotJoined | False | whether to join the points |
| PlotLabel | None | a label for the plot |
| PlotRange | Automatic | range of $z$ values to include |
| PlotStyle | Automatic | graphics primitives to specify the style for points or lines |
| Ticks | Automatic | tick marks |

> ■ You can specify properties of points or lines in the plot by setting the option PlotStyle to lists of such graphics primitives as PointSize, Thickness, GrayLevel and RGBColor. ■ See page 137. ■ See also: Plot.

■ ListPlot3D

ListPlot3D[*array*] generates a three-dimensional plot of a surface representing an array of height values.

ListPlot3D[*array, shades*] generates a plot with each element of the surface shaded according to the specification in *shades*.

ListPlot3D returns a SurfaceGraphics object, which can be displayed using Show. ■ The following options can be given:

| AmbientLight | GrayLevel[0.] | ambient illumination level |
| AspectRatio | 1 | ratio of height to width |
| BoxRatios | {1, 1, 0.4} | bounding 3D box ratios |
| Boxed | True | whether to draw the bounding box |
| ClipFill | Automatic | how to draw clipped parts of the surface |
| DisplayFunction | $DisplayFunction | function for generating output |
| Framed | False | whether to draw a frame |
| LightSources | (see below) | positions and colors of light sources |
| Lighting | False | whether to use simulated illumination |
| Mesh | True | whether to draw a mesh on the surface |
| Plot3Matrix | Automatic | perspective transformation matrix |
| PlotColor | True | whether to plot in color |
| PlotLabel | None | a label for the plot |
| PlotRange | Automatic | range of values to include |
| Shading | True | whether to shade polygons |
| ViewPoint | {1.3, -2.4, 2.} | viewing position |

■ *array* should be a rectangular array of real numbers, representing $z$ values. There will be holes in the surface corresponding to any array elements that are not real numbers. ■ If *array* has dimensions $m \times n$, then *shades* must have dimensions $(m-1) \times (n-1)$. ■ The elements of *shades* must be either GrayLevel[*i*] or RGBColor[*r, g, b*]. ■ The default light sources used are the same as for Graphics3D. ■ See page 137. ■ See also: Plot3D.

■ Literal

Literal[*expr*] represents *expr* on the left-hand side of an assignment, maintaining *expr* in an unevaluated form.

Literal has attribute HoldFirst. ■ Certain parts of the left-hand sides of assignments are usually evaluated. You can use Literal to stop any part from being evaluated. ■ Example: f[Literal[Integrate[y_, x_]]] := *value* can be used to make an assignment for expressions of the form f[Integrate[y_, x_]]. Without Literal, the Integrate function would be evaluated at the time of assignment. ■ See pages 221 and 570. ■ See also: Hold.

■ Locked

Locked is an attribute which, once assigned, prevents modification of any attributes of a symbol.

See page 214. ■ See also: Protected, ReadProtected.

## ■ Log

Log[*z*] gives the natural logarithm of *z* (logarithm to base *e*).

Log[*b*, *z*] gives the logarithm to base *b*.

Log gives exact rational number results when possible.  ▪ See page 353. ▪ See also: Exp, Power.

## ■ LogicalExpand

LogicalExpand[*expr*] expands out expressions containing logical connectives such as && and ||.

LogicalExpand applies distributive laws for logical operations.  ▪ Example:
LogicalExpand[p && !(q || r)] ⟶ p && !q && !r. ▪ See page 73. ▪ See also: Expand.

## ■ LogIntegral

LogIntegral[*z*] is the logarithmic integral function li(*z*).

Mathematical function (see Section B.3.8).  ▪ The logarithmic integral function is defined by $\mathrm{li}(z) = \int_0^z \frac{dt}{\log t}$, where the principal value of the integral is taken.  ▪ See page 364. ▪ See also: ExpIntegralE.

## ■ MainSolve

MainSolve[*eqns*] is the underlying function for transforming systems of equations. Solve and Eliminate call it.

The equations must be of the form *lhs* == *rhs*. They can be combined using && and ||.

MainSolve returns False if no solutions to the equations exist, and True if all values of variables are solutions.

MainSolve rearranges the equations using certain directives.

MainSolve[*eqns*, *vars*, *elim*, *rest*] attempts to rearrange the equations *eqns* so as to solve for the variables *vars*, and eliminate the variables *elim*. The list *rest* can be included to specify the elimination order for any remaining variables.

MainSolve is essentially an internal routine. The functions Solve and Eliminate should be used for most practical purposes.  ▪ MainSolve works by creating a Gröbner basis from the equations.  ▪ The following options can be given:

| | |
|---|---|
| Mode -> Generic | rational numbers and denominators depending on parameters can be introduced |
| Mode -> Integer | solutions must be over the integers; rational numbers cannot be introduced |
| Mode -> Modular | equality is required only modulo an integer |
| Mode -> Rational | rational numbers can be introduced (default) |
| Method -> 1 | do one pass of elimination of variables only |
| Method -> 2 | generate a disjunction of two equations to account for cases in which an expression can be zero |
| Method -> 3 | solve the final equations for their roots |

▪ See also: Solve, Eliminate, Reduce, SolveAlways.

### ■ Map

Map[*f*, *expr*] or *f* /@ *expr* applies *f* to each element on the first level in *expr*.

Map[*f*, *expr*, *levelspec*] applies *f* to parts of *expr* specified by *levelspec*.

Examples: Map[f, {a, b, c}] ⟶ {f[a], f[b], f[c]}; Map[f, a + b + c] ⟶ f[a] + f[b] + f[c]. ■
Level specifications are described on page 564. ■ The default value for *levelspec* in Map is {1}. ■ Examples:
Map[f, {{a,b},{c,d}}] ⟶ {f[{a, b}], f[{c, d}]};
Map[f, {{a,b},{c,d}}, 2] ⟶ {f[{f[a], f[b]}], f[{f[c], f[d]}]};
Map[f, {{a,b},{c,d}}, -1] ⟶ {f[{f[a], f[b]}], f[{f[c], f[d]}]}. ■ See page 169. ■ See also:
Apply, Scan, Level, Operate.

### ■ MapAll

MapAll[*f*, *expr*] or *f* //@ *expr* applies *f* to every subexpression in *expr*.

Example: MapAll[f, {{a,b},{c,d}}] ⟶ f[{f[{f[a], f[b]}], f[{f[c], f[d]}]}]. ■ MapAll[*f*, *expr*]
is equivalent to Map[*f*, *expr*, {0, Infinity}]. ■ See page 169. ■ See also: ExpandAll, ReplaceAll.

### ■ MapAt

MapAt[*f*, *expr*, *poslist*] applies *f* to parts of *expr* at positions specified in *poslist*. *poslist*
must be a list of part specification. Each part specification must be a single integer or a list
of integers.

Example: MapAt[f, {a, b, c, d}, {{1}, {4}}] ⟶ {f[a], b, c, f[d]}. ■
MapAt[*f*, *expr*, {$i_1$, $i_2$, ...}] applies *f* to parts *expr*[[$i_1$]], *expr*[[$i_2$]], .... ■
MapAt[*f*, *expr*, {{i, j, ...}}] applies *f* to the part *expr*[[i, j, ...]]. ■
MapAt[*f*, *expr*, {{$i_1$, $j_1$, ...}, {$i_2$, $j_2$, ...}, ...}] applies *f* to parts *expr*[[$i_1$, $j_1$, ...]],
*expr*[[$i_2$, $j_2$, ...]], .... ■ The list of positions used by *MapAt* is in the same form as is returned by the
function Position. ■ See page 177.

### ■ MatchQ

MatchQ[*expr*, *form*] returns True if the pattern *form* matches *expr*, and returns False
otherwise.

See page 230. ■ See also: StringMatchQ.

### ■ MatrixForm

MatrixForm[*list*] prints with the elements of *list* arranged in a regular array.

MatrixForm[*list*, *d*] puts elements down to level *d* in *list* into an array.

MatrixForm prints with every element in the array effectively enclosed in a square cell of the same size. ■
MatrixForm prints a single level list in a column. It prints a two-level list in standard matrix form. More
deeply nested lists are printed with successive dimensions alternating between rows and columns. ■ See page
272. ■ See also: ColumnForm, TableForm.

■ **MatrixQ**

> **MatrixQ**[*expr*] gives **True** if *expr* is a list of lists that can represent a matrix, and gives **False** otherwise.

> **MatrixQ**[*expr*] gives **True** only if *expr* is a list, and each of its elements are lists of equal length, containing no elements that are themselves lists. ▪ See pages 230 and 440. ▪ See also: **VectorQ**, **TensorRank**.

■ **Max**

> **Max**[$x_1$, $x_2$, ...] yields the numerically largest of the $x_i$.

> **Max**[{$x_1$, $x_2$, ...}, {$y_1$, ...}, ...] yields the largest element of any of the lists.

> **Max** yields a definite result if all its arguments are real numbers. ▪ In other cases, **Max** carries out some simplifications. ▪ **Max**[ ] gives **-Infinity**. ▪ See page 341. ▪ See also: **Min**, **Order**.

■ **MaxBend**

> **MaxBend** is an option for **Plot** which measures the maximum bend angle between successive line segments on a curve.

> **Plot** uses an adaptive algorithm to try and include enough sample points that there are no bends larger than **MaxBend** between successive segments of the plot. ▪ **Plot** will not, however, subdivide by a factor of more than **PlotDivision**. ▪ Smaller settings for **MaxBend** will lead to smoother curves, based on more sample points. ▪ See page 109.

■ **MaxMemoryUsed**

> **MaxMemoryUsed**[ ] gives the maximum number of bytes used to store data in this *Mathematica* session.

> On most computer systems, **MaxMemoryUsed**[ ] will give results close to those obtained from external process status requests. ▪ See page 318. ▪ See also: **MemoryInUse**, **ByteCount**.

■ **Medium**

> **Medium**["*name*", *options*, *rawptr*] represents an output medium (file or pipe) in the list **$$Media**.

> **Medium** specifications are created by **OpenWrite** etc. and removed by **Close**. ▪ *options* gives the current settings of options for the medium, as specified by **OpenWrite** etc. or **ResetMedium**. ▪ See also: **$$Media**, **OpenWrite**.

■ **MemberQ**

> **MemberQ**[*list*, *form*] returns **True** if an element of *list* matches *form*, and **False** otherwise.

> *form* can be a pattern. ▪ Example: **MemberQ**[x^_, {x^2, y^2}] $\longrightarrow$ **False**. ▪ The first argument of **MemberQ** can have any head, not necessarily **List**. ▪ See page 230. ▪ See also: **FreeQ**, **Count**, **Cases**.

## ■ MemoryConstrained

MemoryConstrained[*expr*, *b*] evaluates *expr*, stopping if more than *b* bytes of memory are requested.

MemoryConstrained generates an interrupt to stop the evaluation of *expr* if the amount of additional memory requested during the evaluation of *expr* exceeds *b* bytes. ■ MemoryConstrained returns $Interrupted if the evaluation is interrupted. ■ MemoryConstrained has attribute HoldFirst. ■ See page 321. ■ See also: TimeConstrained, MaxMemoryUsed, $RecursionLimit.

## ■ MemoryInUse

MemoryInUse[ ] gives the number of bytes currently being used to store data in this *Mathematica* session.

See page 318. ■ See also: MaxMemoryUsed, ByteCount.

## ■ Mesh

Mesh is an option for SurfaceGraphics and DensityGraphics that specifies whether an explicit $x$–$y$ mesh should be drawn.

See page 127. ■ See also: Framed, Boxed.

## ■ Message

Message[*symbol*::*tag*] prints the message *symbol*::*tag* unless it has been switched off.

Message[*mname*, $e_1$, $e_2$, ...] prints a message, inserting the values of the $e_i$ as needed.

Message generates output on the channel $Messages. ■ You can switch off a message using Off[*symbol*::*tag*]. You can switch on a message using On[*symbol*::*tag*]. ■ Between any two successive input lines, *Mathematica* prints a message with a particular name at most three times. On the last occurrence, it prints the message General::stop. ■ Message[*mname*, $e_1$, $e_2$, ...] as StringForm[*mess*, $e_1$, $e_2$, ...] where *mess* is the value of the message *mname*. Entries of the form `i` in the string *mess* are replaced by the corresponding $e_i$. ■ See page 285. ■ See also: Print, Write, On, Off, Check.

## ■ MessageName

*symbol*::*tag* is a name for a message.

You can specify messages by defining values for *symbol*::*tag*. ■ *symbol*::*tag* is converted to MessageName[*symbol*, "*tag*"]. *tag* can contain any characters that can appear in symbol names. *symbol*::"*tag*" can also be used. ■ Assignments for *s*::*tag* are stored in the Messages value of the symbol *s*. ■ The following messages for functions are often defined:

| | |
|---|---|
| *f*::usage | how to use the function |
| *f*::example | examples of the function |
| *f*::notes | notes on the function |

■ ?*f* prints out the message *f*::usage. ■ When ?*form* finds more than one function, only the names of each function are printed. ■ You can switch on and off messages using On[*s*::*tag*] and Off[*s*::*tag*]. ■ See page 285.

## Messages

**Messages**[*symbol*] gives all the messages assigned to a particular symbol.

Messages that have been switched off using Off are enclosed in Off. ▪ See page 285.

## Min

**Min**[$x_1$, $x_2$, ...] yields the numerically smallest of the $x_i$.

**Min**[{$x_1$, $x_2$, ...}, {$y_1$, ...}, ...] yields the smallest element of any of the lists.

Min yields a definite result if all its arguments are real numbers. ▪ In other cases, Min carries out some simplifications. ▪ Min[ ] gives Infinity. ▪ See page 341. ▪ See also: Max, Order.

## Minors

**Minors**[*m*, *k*] gives a matrix consisting of the determinants of all $k \times k$ submatrices of *m*.

The results for different submatrices are given in lexicographic order. ▪ See page 446. ▪ See also: Det.

## Minus

**-*x*** is the arithmetic negation of *x*.

-*x* is converted to Times[-1, *x*] on input. ▪ See page 25. ▪ See also: Subtract.

## Mod

**Mod**[*m*, *n*] gives the remainder on division of *m* by *n*.

Numerical results from Mod are always non-negative. ▪ Mod[*x*, *y*] can have Rational and Real as well as Integer arguments. ▪ Mod[*poly*, *n*] reduces each coefficient in a polynomial modulo *n*. ▪ See page 345. ▪ See also: Quotient, PolynomialRemainder.

## Modular

**Modular** is a setting for the option Mode in Solve and related functions, which specifies that equations need be satisfied only modulo an integer.

An explicit equation Modulus==*p* can be given to specify a particular modulus to use. If no such equation is given, Solve attempts to solve for possible moduli. ▪ See page 408.

## Modulus

**Modulus->*n*** is an option that can be given in certain algebraic functions to specify that integers should be treated modulo *n*.

Equations for **Modulus** can be given in Solve and related functions.

Modulus appears as an option in Factor, GCD, LCM. ▪ Arithmetic is usually done over the full field **Z** of integers; setting the option Modulus specifies that arithmetic should instead be done in the finite ring $\mathbf{Z}_n$. ▪ Some functions require that Modulus be set to a prime, or a power of a prime. ▪ See pages 391 and 408.

■ **MoebiusMu**

MoebiusMu[*n*] gives the Möbius function $\mu(n)$.

Integer mathematical function (see Section B.3.8). ■ $\mu(n)$ is 1 if $n$ is a product of an even number of distinct primes, $-1$ if it is a product of an odd number of primes, and 0 if it has a multiple prime factor. ■ See page 347. ■ See also: FactorInteger.

■ **Multinomial**

Multinomial[$n_1$, $n_2$, ...] gives the multinomial coefficient $\frac{(n_1+n_2+...)!}{n_1!n_2!...}$.

Integer mathematical function (see Section B.3.8). ■ The multinomial coefficient Multinomial[$n_1$, $n_2$, ...], denoted $(N; n_1, n_2, ..., n_m)$, gives the number of ways of partitioning $N$ distinct objects into $m$ sets, each of size $n_i$ (with $N = \sum_{i=1}^{m} n_i$). ■ See page 350. ■ See also: Binomial.

■ **N**

N[*expr*] gives the numerical value of *expr*.

N[*expr*, *n*] does computations to *n*-digit precision.

N[*expr*, *n*] performs computations to *n*-digit precision. Often, this will give a result to *n*-digit accuracy. Sometimes, however, precision will be lost during the computation. ■ N converts all numbers to Real form. ■ You can define numerical values of functions using *f*/: N[*f*[*args*]] := *value* and *f*/: N[*f*[*args*], *n*] := *value*. ■ See pages 26 and 30. ■ See also: Chop.

■ **NameQ**

NameQ["*string*"] yields True if there are any symbols whose names match the form given, and yields False otherwise.

You can test for classes of symbol names, using metacharacters such as *, as described in the notes on StringMatchQ. ■ See page 312.

■ **Names**

Names["*string*"] gives a list of the names of symbols which match the string.

Names["*string*"] gives the same list of names as ?*string*. ■ In the string, you can use the metacharacters *, ** and @, as described in the notes on StringMatchQ. ■ Notice that the symbols in the list returned by Names are always evaluated. ■ See page 306. ■ See also: Information, Unique, ValueQ.

■ **NBernoulliB**

NBernoulliB[*n*] gives the numerical value of the Bernoulli number $B_n$.

NBernoulliB[*n*, *d*] gives $B_n$ to *d*-digit precision.

NBernoulliB[*n*] gives the same results as N[BernoulliB[*n*]], but is considerably faster. ■ See notes for BernoulliB. ■ See page 351.

■ Needs

> Needs["*context*`"] loads a file if the specified context is not already in $ContextPath.

Needs[*string*] reads in a file with name *str*.m, where *str* is *string* with any trailing ` removed. ■ If there are ` within the string *str*, Needs constructs several different file names to try and read in. Needs replaces ` in order by /, _ and .. ■ See page 311. ■ See also: Get.

■ Negative

> Negative[*x*] gives True if *x* is a negative number.

Negative[*x*] gives False if *x* is manifestly a non-negative number. Otherwise, it remains unevaluated. ■ A definition like Negative[*x*] = True effectively specifies that *x* is a negative number. ■ Definitions for Sign are tested in determining whether linear combinations of expressions are negative. ■ See page 242. ■ See also: NonNegative, Positive, Sign.

■ Nest

> Nest[*f*, *expr*, *n*] gives an expression with *f* applied *n* times to *expr*.

Example: Nest[f, x, 3] $\longrightarrow$ f[f[f[x]]]. ■ See pages 169, 248 and 254. ■ See also: Function, FixedPoint, Do.

■ NestList

> NestList[*f*, *expr*, *n*] gives a list of the results of applying *f* to *expr* 0 through *n* times.

Example: NestList[f, x, 3] $\longrightarrow$ {x, f[x], f[f[x]], f[f[f[x]]]}. ■ NestList[*f*, *expr*, *n*] gives a list of length *n* + 1. ■ See page 182. ■ See also: Accumulate.

■ NIntegrate

> NIntegrate[*f*, {*x*, *xmin*, *xmax*}] gives a numerical approximation to the integral $\int_{xmin}^{xmax} f \, dx$.

Multidimensional integrals can be specified, as in Integrate. ■ NIntegrate tests for singularities at the end points of the integration range. ■ NIntegrate[*f*, {*x*, $x_0$, $x_1$, ..., $x_k$}] tests for singularities at each of the intermediate points $x_i$. If there are no singularities, the result is equivalent to an integral from $x_0$ to $x_k$. You can use complex numbers $x_i$ to specify an integration contour in the complex plane. ■ The following options can be given in NIntegrate:

| | | |
|---|---|---|
| AccuracyGoal | 6 | digits of absolute accuracy sought |
| MaxRecursion | 6 | maximum number of recursive subdivisions |
| MinRecursion | 1 | minimum number of recursive subdivisions |
| Points | Automatic | initial number of sample points |
| SingularityDepth | 3 | number of recursive subdivisions before changing variables |
| WorkingPrecision | Precision[1.] | the number of digits used in internal computations |

■ NIntegrate uses an adaptive algorithm, which recursively subdivides the integration region as needed. Points specifies the number of initial points to choose in each dimension. MinRecursion specifies the minimum number of recursive subdivisions to try. MaxRecursion gives the maximum number. ■ You should realize that with sufficiently pathological functions, the algorithms used by NIntegrate can give wrong answers. In most cases, you can test the answer by looking at its sensitivity to changes in the setting of options for NIntegrate. ■ N[Integrate[...]] calls NIntegrate. ■ See page 470.

## NonCommutativeMultiply

$a$ ** $b$ ** $c$ is a general associative, but non-commutative, form of multiplication.

NonCommutativeMultiply has attribute Flat. ▪ Instances of NonCommutativeMultiply are automatically flattened, but no other simplification is performed. ▪ You can use NonCommutativeMultiply as a generalization of ordinary multiplication for special mathematical objects. ▪ See page 555. ▪ See also: Dot, Times.

## NonConstants

NonConstants is an option for D which gives a list of objects to be taken to depend implicitly on the differentiation variables.

If $c$ does not appear in the list of NonConstants, then D[$c$, $x$] is taken to be 0 unless $c$ and $x$ are identical expressions. ▪ See page 412. ▪ See also: Dt.

## None

None is a setting used for certain options.

## NonNegative

NonNegative[$x$] gives True if $x$ is a non-negative number.

NonNegative[$x$] gives False if $x$ is manifestly a negative number. Otherwise, it remains unevaluated. ▪ A definition like NonNegative[$x$] = True effectively specifies that $x$ is a non-negative number. ▪ Definitions for Sign are tested in determining whether linear combinations of expressions are non-negative. ▪ See page 242. ▪ See also: Negative, Positive, Sign.

## Normal

Normal[$expr$] converts $expr$ to a normal expression, from a variety of special forms.

Normal[$expr$] converts a power series to a normal expression by truncating higher-order terms. ▪ When additional "data types" are introduced, Normal should be defined to convert them, when possible, to normal expressions. ▪ See page 434.

## Not

!$expr$ is the logical NOT function. It gives False if $expr$ is True, and True if it is False.

Not gives symbolic results when necessary, and applies various simplification rules to them. ▪ You cannot use the notation !$expr$ for Not[$expr$] if it appears at the very beginning of a line. In this case, !$expr$ is interpreted as a shell escape. ▪ See page 73. ▪ See also: LogicalExpand.

## NProduct

NProduct[$f$, {$i$, $imin$, $imax$}] gives a numerical approximation to the product $\prod_{i=imin}^{imax} f$.

NProduct[$f$, {$i$, $imin$, $imax$, $di$}] uses a step $di$ in the product.

See notes for NSum. Only the Wynn epsilon method can be used in NProduct. ▪ See page 474.

■ **NRoots**

NRoots[*lhs==rhs*, *var*] gives a list of numerical approximations to the roots of a polynomial equation.

NRoots[*eqn*, *var*, *n*] gives results to *n* digit precision. ▪ See pages 397 and 476. ▪ See also: Roots, Solve, ToRules.

■ **NSum**

NSum[*f*, {*i*, *imin*, *imax*}] gives a numerical approximation to the sum $\sum_{i=imin}^{imax} f$.
NSum[*f*, {*i*, *imin*, *imax*, *di*}] uses a step *di* in the sum.

NSum can be used for sums with both finite and infinite limits. ▪ The following options can be given:

| AccuracyGoal | 6 | number of digits of final accuracy to try and get |
| ExtraTerms | 11 | maximum number of terms to use in extrapolation |
| Method | Automatic | method to use: Integrate or Fit |
| Terms | 15 | number of terms to use before extrapolation |
| WorkingPrecision | Precision[1.] | the number of digits used in internal computations |

▪ NSum uses either the Euler-Maclaurin (Integrate) or Wynn epsilon (Fit) method. ▪ You should realize that with sufficiently pathological summands, the algorithms used by NSum can give wrong answers. In most cases, you can test the answer by looking at its sensitivity to changes in the setting of options for NSum. ▪ N[Sum[...]] calls NSum. ▪ See page 474.

■ **Null**

Null is a symbol used to indicate the absence of an expression or a result. When it appears as an output expression, no output is printed.

$e_1$; $e_2$; ...; $e_k$; returns Null, and prints no output. ▪ Expressions like $f[e_1,,e2]$ are interpreted to have Null between each pair of adjacent commas. ▪ See page 578.

■ **NullSpace**

NullSpace[*m*] gives a list of vectors that forms a basis for the null space of the matrix *m*.

NullSpace works on both numerical and symbolic matrices. ▪ NullSpace[*m*, ZeroTest -> *test*] evaluates *test*[ *m*[[*i*, *j*]] ] to determine whether matrix elements are zero. The default setting is ZeroTest -> (# == 0)&. ▪ See page 448. ▪ See also: RowReduce, LinearSolve.

■ **Number**

Number represents an exact integer or an approximate real number in Read.

An integer is returned if no explicit decimal point is present. ▪ Approximate real numbers can be given in C or FORTRAN forms, such as 2.4E5 or -3.4e-4. ▪ See pages 156 and 301. ▪ See also: Real.

■ **NumberForm**

NumberForm[*expr*, *n*] prints with approximate real numbers in *expr* given to *n* digit precision.

NumberForm can print the digits in a number in blocks, with breaks in between. ■ The following options can be given:

| | | |
|---|---|---|
| DigitBlock | Infinity | number of digits between breaks |
| ExponentStep | 1 | size of steps in the exponents generated |
| NumberPoint | "." | decimal point string |
| NumberSeparator | "," | character to insert at breaks between blocks |

■ The setting of the option DigitBlock affects the printing not only of approximate real numbers, but also of integers. ■ See page 328. ■ See also: ScientificForm, EngineeringForm.

■ **NumberQ**

NumberQ[*expr*] gives True if *expr* is a number, and False otherwise.

NumberQ[*expr*] returns False unless *expr* is manifestly a number (i.e. has head Complex, Integer, Rational or Real). ■ You can use NumberQ[x] = True to override the normal operation of NumberQ, and effectively define $x$ to be an integer. ■ See pages 230 and 326. ■ See also: IntegerQ, TrueQ.

■ **Numerator**

Numerator[*expr*] gives the numerator of *expr*.

Numerator picks out terms which do not have superficially negative exponents. Denominator picks out the remaining terms. ■ An exponent is "superficially negative" if it has a negative number as a factor. ■ The standard representation of rational expressions as products of powers means that you cannot simply use Part to extract numerators. ■ Numerator can be used on rational numbers. ■ See page 60. ■ See also: ExpandNumerator.

■ **O**

O[*x*]^*n* represents a term of order $x^n$.

O[*x*]^*n* is generated to represent omitted higher-order terms in power series.

O[*x*, $x_0$]^*n* represents a term of order $(x - x_0)^n$.

Normal can be used to truncate power series, and remove O terms. ■ See page 430. ■ See also: Series, SeriesData.

■ **OddQ**

OddQ[*expr*] gives True if *expr* is an odd integer, and False otherwise.

OddQ[*expr*] returns False unless *expr* is manifestly an odd integer (i.e. has head Integer, and is odd). ■ You can use OddQ[x] = True to override the normal operation of OddQ, and effectively define $x$ to be an odd integer. ■ See pages 230 and 326. ■ See also: IntegerQ, EvenQ, TrueQ.

■ Off

> Off[*symbol*::*tag*] switches off a message, so that it is no longer printed.

> Off[*s*] switches off tracing messages associated with the symbol *s*.

> Off[$m_1$, $m_2$, ...] switches off several messages.

> Off[ ] switches off all tracing messages.

The *value* of *symbol*::*tag* is not affected by Off. ▪ Off[*s*] is equivalent to Off[*s*::trace]. ▪ Off[ ] is equivalent to Off[*s*::trace] for all symbols. ▪ Switching off the printing of a message does not affect its detection by Check. ▪ See pages 264 and 285. ▪ See also: Message, Check.

■ On

> On[*symbol*::*tag*] switches on a message, so that it can be printed.

> On[*s*] switches on tracing for the symbol *s*.

> On[$m_1$, $m_2$, ...] switches on several messages.

> On[ ] switches on tracing for all symbols.

When tracing is switched on, each evaluation of a symbol, on its own, or as a function, is printed, together with the result. ▪ Note that the tracing information is printed when a function *returns*. As a result, traces of recursive functions appear in the opposite order from their calls. ▪ On[*s*] is equivalent to On[*s*::trace]. ▪ On[ ] is equivalent to On[*s*::trace] for all symbols. ▪ See pages 264 and 285.

■ OneIdentity

> OneIdentity is an attribute that can be assigned to a symbol *f* to indicate that *f*[*x*], *f*[*f*[*x*]], etc. are all equivalent to *x* for the purpose of pattern matching.

Functions like Plus and Times have the attribute OneIdentity. ▪ The fact that Times has attribute OneIdentity allows a pattern like n_. x_ to match x. ▪ See page 214. ▪ See also: Flat, Nest.

■ OpenAppend

> OpenAppend["*file*"] opens a file to append output to it.

The following options can be given:

| | | |
|---|---|---|
| FormatType | InputForm | default format for printing expressions |
| GraphicsFont | "DefaultFont" | default font for text in graphics output |
| PageHeight | 22 | number of lines per page |
| PageWidth | 78 | number of character widths per line |
| TextRendering | Plain | type of text output |
| TotalHeight | Infinity | maximum number of lines for a single expression |
| TotalWidth | Infinity | maximum number of character widths for a single expression |

■ Files are specified by their names. Only one file with a particular name can be open at once.  ■ On computer systems that support pipes, OpenAppend["!*command*"] runs the external program specified by *command*, and opens a pipe to send input to it.  ■ If OpenAppend succeeds in opening a particular file or pipe, it returns the name of the file or pipe. Otherwise, it generates a message, and returns Null.  ■ OpenAppend resolves file names according to the procedure described in Section B.7.3.  ■ The list $$Media gives names of all the files and pipes active at a particular time.  ■ ResetMedium can be used to change the properties of a file or pipe, after it is already open.  ■ Functions like Put and Write automatically open the files or pipes they need, if they are not already open.  ■ See page 292.  ■ See also: Close, Put.

■ OpenRead

> OpenRead["*file*"] opens a file to read data from.

OpenRead prepares to read from a file, starting at the beginning of the file.  ■ On systems that support pipes, OpenRead["!*command*"] runs the external program specified by *command*, and opens a pipe to get input from it.  ■ The function ReadList automatically opens files or pipes that it needs.  ■ See page 302.  ■ See also: Close, Read, ReadList.

■ OpenTemporary

> OpenTemporary[ ] opens a temporary file to which output can be written, and returns the name of the file.

OpenTemporary is often used in conjunction with Put and Get as a way of preparing data that is exchanged between *Mathematica* and external programs.  ■ OpenTemporary always creates a new file, that does not already exist.  ■ On UNIX systems, OpenTemporary typically creates a file in the /tmp directory.  ■ See page 298.  ■ See also: Close, Run.

■ OpenWrite

> OpenWrite["*file*"] opens a file to write output to it.

OpenWrite deletes any existing contents in a file, and prepares to write output starting at the beginning of the file.  ■ For output to pipes, OpenWrite and OpenAppend are equivalent.  ■ See notes for OpenAppend.  ■ See page 292.

# ■ Operate

Operate[$p$, $f$[$x$, $y$]] gives $p$[$f$][$x$, $y$].

Operate[$p$, *expr*, $n$] applies $p$ at level $n$ in the head of *expr*.

Examples: Operate[p, f[x,y]] $\longrightarrow$ p[f][x, y]; Operate[p, f[x][y][z], 1] $\longrightarrow$ p[f[x][y]][z]; Operate[p, f[x][y][z], 2] $\longrightarrow$ p[f[x]][y][z]. ▪ Operate[$p$, $f$[x]] effectively applies the functional operator $p$ to the function $f$. ▪ Operate plays essentially the same role for heads of expressions as Map plays for elements. Note, however, that the level specification for Operate works differently than for Map. ▪ See page 247. ▪ See also: HeadCompose, Through.

# ■ Optional

$p$:$v$ is a pattern object which represents an expression of the form $p$, which, if omitted, should be replaced by $v$.

Optional is used to specify "optional arguments" in functions represented by patterns. The pattern object $p$ gives the form the argument should have, if it is present. The expression $v$ gives the "default value" to use if the argument is absent. ▪ Example: the pattern f[x_, y_:1] is matched by f[a], with x taking the value a, and y taking the value 1. It can also be matched by f[a, b], with y taking the value b. ▪ The form s_:v is equivalent to Optional[s_, v]. This form is also equivalent to s:_:v. There is no syntactic ambiguity since s must be a symbol in this case. ▪ The special form s. is equivalent to Optional[s_] and can be used to represent function arguments which, if omitted, should be replaced by default values globally specified for the functions in which they occur. ▪ Values for Default[f, ...] specify default values to be used when _. appears as an argument of f. Any assignments for Default[f, ...] must be made *before* _. first appears as an argument of f. ▪ Optional[s_h] represents a function which can be omitted, but which, if present, must have head $h$. There is no simpler syntactic form for this case. ▪ Functions with built-in default values include Plus, Times and Power. ▪ See page 557.

# ■ Options

Options[*symbol*] gives the list of default options assigned to a symbol.

Options[$f$[$x$, $y$, ..., *name$_1$* -> *value$_1$*, ...]] gives the options explicitly specified in a particular expression.

Many built-in functions allow you to give additional arguments that specify options with rules of the form *name* -> *value*. ▪ Options[$f$] gives the list of rules to be used for the options associated with a function $f$ if no explicit rules are given when the function is called. ▪ Options always returns a list of transformation rules for option names. ▪ You can assign a value to Options[*symbol*] to redefine all the default option settings for a function. ▪ SetOptions[*symbol*, *name* -> *value*] can be used to specify individual default options. ▪ See pages 113 and 564.

# ■ Or

$e_1$ || $e_2$ || ... is the logical OR function. It evaluates its arguments in order, giving **True** immediately if any of them are **True**, and **False** if they are all **False**.

And evaluates its arguments in a non-standard way (see page 569). ▪ Or gives symbolic results when necessary, and applies various simplification rules to them. ▪ When Or gives a symbolic result, all its arguments are simplified. ▪ See page 73. ▪ See also: Xor, LogicalExpand.

## ■ Order

Order[$expr_1$, $expr_2$] gives 1 if $expr_1$ is before $expr_2$ in canonical order, and -1 if $expr_1$ is after $expr_2$ in canonical order. It gives 0 if $expr_1$ is identical to $expr_2$.

Canonical order has several properties. Smaller numbers of a particular type come first. Symbols are ordered lexicographically according to their textual names. Strings are ordered lexicographically. Shorter expressions come first. ■ Examples: Order[a, b] $\longrightarrow$ 1; Order[b, a] $\longrightarrow$ -1. ■ See also: Equal, SameQ, Sort.

## ■ OrderedQ

OrderedQ[$h[e_1$, $e_2$, ...]] gives True if the $e_i$ are in canonical order, and False otherwise.

See notes for Order. ■ OrderedQ[{e, e}] gives True. ■ See pages 106 and 230. ■ See also: Signature, Sort.

## ■ Orderless

Orderless is an attribute that can be assigned to a symbol $f$ to indicate that the elements $e_i$ in expressions of the form $f[e_1$, $e_2$, ...] should automatically be sorted into canonical order. This property is accounted for in pattern matching.

The Orderless attribute for a function corresponds to the mathematical property of commutativity. ■ For an object that represents a matrix or a tensor, the Orderless attribute represents symmetry among indices. ■ Functions like Plus and Times are Orderless. ■ In matching patterns with Orderless functions, all possible orders of arguments are tried. ■ The Orderless attribute must be assigned before defining any values for an Orderless function. ■ See page 214. ■ See also: Sort, Flat, OneIdentity.

## ■ Out

%$n$ or Out[$n$] is a global object that is assigned to be the value produced on the $n^{\text{th}}$ output line.

% gives the last result generated.

%% gives the result before last. %%...% ($k$ times) gives the $k^{\text{th}}$ previous result.

Out[ ] is equivalent to %. ■ Out[-$k$] is equivalent to %%...% ($k$ times). ■ See page 577. ■ See also: In, $Line.

## ■ Outer

Outer[$f$, $list_1$, $list_2$, ...] gives the generalized outer product of the $list_i$.

Example: Outer[f,{a,b},{x,y}] $\longrightarrow$ {{f[a, x], f[a, y]}, {f[b, x], f[b, y]}}. ■ Outer[Times, $list_1$, $list_2$, ...] gives an outer product. ■ The result of applying Outer to two tensors $T_{i_1 i_2 ... i_r}$ and $U_{j_1 j_2 ... j_s}$ is the tensor $V_{i_1 i_2 ... i_r j_1 j_2 ... j_s}$ with elements f[$T_{i_1 i_2 ... i_r}$, $U_{j_1 j_2 ... j_s}$]. Applying Outer to two tensors of ranks $r$ and $s$ gives a tensor of rank $r + s$. ■ The heads of all the $list_i$ must be the same, but need not necessarily be List. ■ The $list_i$ need not necessarily be cuboidal arrays. ■ See page 457. ■ See also: Inner, Distribute.

## ■ OutputForm

OutputForm[*expr*] prints as the standard *Mathematica* output form for *expr*.

OutputForm imitates standard two-dimensional mathematical notation. ■ The OutputForm of many kinds of expressions is quite different from their internal representation. ■ In some versions of *Mathematica* with advanced graphical interfaces, you will be able to select parts of OutputForm expressions graphically. ■ See page 268. ■ See also: InputForm, TeXForm, Short, FullForm.

## ■ PageHeight

PageHeight is an option for OpenWrite etc. and ResetMedium which specifies how many lines of text should be printed between page breaks.

With TextRendering -> Plain, PageHeight gives the actual numbers of lines generated. ■ With TextRendering -> PostScript, PageHeight gives the number of m spaces (number of times the width of an m character). ■ PageHeight -> Infinity specifies that there should be no page breaks. ■ See page 295. ■ See also: TotalHeight.

## ■ PageWidth

PageWidth is an option for OpenWrite etc., ResetMedium and Splice which specifies how wide each line of printed text should be.

With TextRendering -> Plain, PageWidth gives the actual number of characters allowed on each line. ■ With TextRendering -> PostScript, PageWidth gives the number of m spaces (number of times the width of an m character) allowed. ■ PageWidth -> Infinity specifies that individual lines can be arbitrarily long. ■ See page 295. ■ See also: TotalWidth.

## ■ ParametricPlot

ParametricPlot[{$f_x$, $f_y$}, {$t$, *tmin*, *tmax*}] produces a parametric plot with $x$ and $y$ coordinates $f_x$ and $f_y$ generated as a function of $t$.

ParametricPlot[{{$f_x$, $f_y$}, {$g_x$, $g_y$}, ...}, {$t$, *tmin*, *tmax*}] plots several parametric curves.

ParametricPlot evaluates its arguments in a non-standard way (see page 569). ■ The options that can be given for ParametricPlot are the same as for Plot. ■ ParametricPlot returns a Graphics object. ■ See page 117.

# ■ Part

*expr*[[*i*]] gives the $i^{\text{th}}$ part of *expr*.

*expr*[[-*i*]] counts from the end.

*expr*[[0]] gives the head of *expr*.

*expr*[[*i*, *j*, ...]] is equivalent to *expr*[[*i*]] [[*j*]] ....

*expr*[[ {*i₁*, *i₂*, ...} ]] gives a list of the parts $i_1$, $i_2$, ... of *expr*.

You can make an assignment like *t*[[*i*]] = *value* to modify part of an expression. ■ When *expr* is a list, *expr*[[ {*i₁*, *i₂*, ...} ]] gives a list of parts. In general, the head of *f* is applied to the list of parts. ■ You can get a nested listing of parts from *expr*[[*list₁*, *list₂*, ...]]. Each part has one index from each list. ■ Notice that lists are used differently in Part than in MapAt and Position. ■ *expr*[[ Range[*i*, *j*] ]] can be used to extract sequences of parts. ■ See page 178. ■ See also: First, Head, Last, MapAt, Take.

# ■ Partition

Partition[*list*, *n*] partitions *list* into non-overlapping sublists of length *n*.

Partition[*list*, *n*, *di*] generates sublists with offset *di*.

Example: Partition[{a,b,c,d,e,f}, 2] ⟶ {{a, b}, {c, d}, {e, f}}. ■ All the sublists generated by Partition[*list*, *n*, *di*] are of length *n*. As a result, some elements at the end of *list* may not appear in any sublist. ■ The element e in Partition[{a,b,c,d,e}, 2] ⟶ {{a, b}, {c, d}} is dropped. ■ Partition[{a,b,c,d,e}, 3, 1] ⟶ {{a, b, c}, {b, c, d}, {c, d, e}} generates sublists with offset 1. ■ The object *list* need not have head List. ■ Partition[f[a,b,c,d], 2] ⟶ f[f[a, b], f[c, d]]. ■ See page 105. ■ See also: Flatten.

# ■ PartitionsP

PartitionsP[*n*] gives the number $p(n)$ of unrestricted partitions of the integer *n*.

Integer mathematical function (see Section B.3.8). ■ See page 350.

# ■ PartitionsQ

PartitionsQ[*n*] gives the number $q(n)$ of partitions of the integer *n* into distinct parts.

Integer mathematical function (see Section B.3.8). ■ See page 350.

# ■ Pattern

*s*:*obj* represents the pattern object *obj*, assigned the name *s*.

The name *s* must be a symbol. ■ The object *obj* can be any pattern object. ■ When a transformation rule is used, any occurrence of *s* on the right-hand side is replaced by whatever expression it matched on the left-hand side. ■ The operator : has a comparatively low precedence. The expression x:(_+_) is thus interpreted as x:(_+_), not (x:_)+_. ■ The form *s*_ is equivalent to *s*:_. Similarly, *s*_*h* is equivalent to *s*:_*h*, *s*__ to *s*:__, and so on. ■ See page 557.

■ **PatternTest**

> *p?test* is a pattern object that stands for any expression which matches *p*, and on which the application of *test* gives **True**.

Any result for *test*[*pval*] other than **True** is taken to signify failure. ■ Example: _?NumberQ represents a number of any type. The _ matches any expression, and ?NumberQ restricts to any expression which gives **True** on application of the number test NumberQ. ■ The operator ? has a high precedence. Thus _^_?t is _^(_?t) not (_^_)?t. ■ See page 557. ■ See also: Condition.

■ **Permutations**

> **Permutations**[*list*] generates a list of all possible permutations of the elements in *list*.

Example:
Permutations[{a,b,c}] ⟶ {{a, b, c}, {a, c, b}, {b, a, c}, {b, c, a}, {c, a, b}, {c, b, a}}.
■ There are *n*! permutations of a list of *n* elements. ■ Each element of the original list is treated as distinct. ■ The object *list* need not have head List. ■ See page 106. ■ See also: Sort, Signature, Reverse, RotateLeft.

■ **Pi**

> **Pi** is $\pi$, with numerical value $\simeq 3.14159$.

Mathematical constant (see Section B.3.9). ■ See page 359. ■ See also: Degree.

■ **Plain**

> **Plain** is a setting that can be given for the option TextRendering to specify output on a character-oriented display device.

See page 295. ■ See also: PostScript, PageWidth, PageHeight.

■ Plot

   Plot[$f$, {$x$, $xmin$, $xmax$}] generates a plot of $f$ as a function of $x$ from $xmin$ to $xmax$.

   Plot[{$f_1$, $f_2$, ...}, {$x$, $xmin$, $xmax$}] plots several functions $f_i$.

   Plot evaluates its arguments in a non-standard way (see page 569).  ■ The following options can be given:

| | | |
|---|---|---|
| AspectRatio | 1/GoldenRatio | ratio of height to width |
| Axes | Automatic | whether to include axes |
| AxesLabel | None | axes labels |
| DisplayFunction | $DisplayFunction | function for generating output |
| Framed | False | whether to draw a frame |
| MaxBend | 10. | maximum bend between segments |
| PlotColor | True | whether to plot in color |
| PlotDivision | 20. | maximum subdivision factor in sampling |
| PlotLabel | None | a label for the plot |
| PlotPoints | 25 | initial number of sample points |
| PlotRange | Automatic | range of $z$ values to include |
| PlotStyle | Automatic | graphics primitives to specify the style for each curve |
| Ticks | Automatic | tick marks |

   ■ Plot initially evaluates $f$ at a number of equally-spaced sample points specified by PlotPoints. Then it uses an adaptive algorithm to choose additional sample points, attempting to produce a curve in which the bend between successive segments is less than MaxBend. It subdivides a given interval by a factor of at most PlotDivision.  ■ You should realize that with the finite number of sample points used, it is possible for Plot to miss features in your function. To check your results, you should increase the setting for PlotPoints.  ■ Plot returns a Graphics object.  ■ See page 107.  ■ See also: ListPlot, Graphics.

# ■ Plot3D

Plot3D[*f*, {*x*, *xmin*, *xmax*}, {*y*, *ymin*, *ymax*}] generates a three-dimensional plot of *f* as a function of *x* and *y*.

Plot3D[{*f*, *s*}, {*x*, *xmin*, *xmax*}, {*y*, *ymin*, *ymax*}] generates a three-dimensional plot in which the height of the surface is specified by *f*, and the shading is specified by *s*.

Plot3D evaluates its arguments in a non-standard way (see page 569).  ■ The following options can be given:

| | | |
|---|---|---|
| AmbientLight | GrayLevel[0.] | ambient illumination level |
| AspectRatio | 1 | ratio of height to width |
| BoxRatios | {1, 1, 0.4} | bounding 3D box ratios |
| Boxed | True | whether to draw the bounding box |
| ClipFill | Automatic | how to draw clipped parts of the surface |
| DisplayFunction | $DisplayFunction | function for generating output |
| Framed | False | whether to draw a frame |
| LightSources | (see below) | positions and colors of light sources |
| Lighting | False | whether to use simulated illumination |
| Mesh | True | whether to draw a mesh on the surface |
| Plot3Matrix | Automatic | perspective transformation matrix |
| PlotColor | True | whether to plot in color |
| PlotLabel | None | a label for the plot |
| PlotPoints | 15 | the number of sample points in each direction |
| PlotRange | Automatic | range of values to include |
| Shading | True | whether to shade polygons |
| ViewPoint | {1.3, -2.4, 2.} | viewing position |

■ Plot3D returns a SurfaceGraphics object.  ■ The function *f* should give a real number for all values of *x* and *y* at which it is evaluated. There will be holes in the final surface at any values of *x* and *y* for which *f* does not yield a real number value.  ■ If Lighting->False and no shading function *s* is specified, the surface is shaded with gray levels according to height.  ■ The shading function *s* must yield values of the form GrayLevel[*i*] or RGBColor[*r*, *g*, *b*].  ■ The default light sources used are as for Graphics3D.  ■ See page 120.  ■ See also: ListPlot3D, ContourPlot, DensityPlot, Graphics3D.

# ■ Plot3Matrix

Plot3Matrix is an option to Graphics3D and related functions that can be used to specify the explicit homogeneous perspective transformation matrix.

Plot3Matrix can be set to a $4 \times 4$ matrix which is applied to vectors $(x, y, z, 1)$ for each point. The *x* and *y* components of the results give the screen positions of the points.  ■ Plot3Matrix -> Automatic specifies that the matrix should be computed automatically from the settings of ViewPoint and other options.

■ PlotColor

> PlotColor is an option for graphics functions that specifies whether color output should be produced.

> PlotColor -> True generates color POSTSCRIPT. ▪ Colors are specified by RGBColor graphics primitives, or by giving colors for simulated illumination. ▪ POSTSCRIPT interpreters should average colors to give gray scales on monochrome display devices. ▪ When PlotColor -> False, no color primitives appear in the POSTSCRIPT output. ▪ See page 109. ▪ See also: AmbientLight, LightSources.

■ PlotDivision

> PlotDivision is an option for Plot which specifies the maximum amount of subdivision to be used in attempting to generate a smooth curve.

> Plot initials uses PlotPoints equally-spaced sample points. In attempting to generate curves with no bends larger than MaxBend, Plot subdivides by at most a factor of PlotDivision. ▪ The finest resolution in plot is of order 1/(PlotPoints PlotDivision). ▪ See page 109. ▪ See also: MaxBend.

■ PlotJoined

> PlotJoined is an option for ListPlot that specifies whether the points plotted should be joined by a line.

■ PlotLabel

> PlotLabel is an option for graphics functions that specifies an overall label for a plot.

> PlotLabel -> None specifies that no label should be given. ▪ PlotLabel -> *label* specifies a label to give. ▪ Any expression can be used as a label. It will be given in OutputForm. Arbitrary strings of text can be enclosed in ". ▪ See page 109. ▪ See also: AxesLabel.

■ PlotPoints

> PlotPoints is an option for plotting functions that specifies how many sample points to use.

> The sample points are equally spaced. ▪ In Plot, an adaptive procedure is used to choose more sample points. ▪ PlotPoints -> $\{n_x, n_y\}$ specifies different numbers of sample points in the $x$ and $y$ directions. ▪ See pages 109 and 113. ▪ See also: PlotDivision.

# ■ PlotRange

**PlotRange** is an option for graphics functions that specifies what points to include in a plot.

The following settings can be used for two-dimensional graphics:

| | |
|---|---|
| All | all points are included |
| Automatic | outlying points must be dropped |
| {*min*, *max*} | explicit $y$ limits; Automatic is used for $x$ |
| {{*xmin*, *xmax*}, {*ymin*, *ymax*}} | explicit limits for $x$ and $y$ |
| {$s_x$, $s_y$} | specifications for each coordinate |

■ For three-dimensional graphics, a setting of {*min*, *max*} applies to the $z$ coordinate. ■ With the Automatic setting, the distribution of coordinate values is found, and any points sufficiently far out in the distribution are dropped. Such points are often produced as a result of singularities in functions being plotted. ■ See pages 109 and 112.

# ■ PlotStyle

**PlotStyle** is an option for **Plot** and **ListPlot** that specifies the style of lines or points to be plotted.

PlotStyle -> *prim* specifies that all lines or points are to be generated with the specified graphics primitive, or list of graphics primitives. ■ PlotStyle -> {*style*$_1$, *style*$_2$, ...} specifies that successive lines generated should use graphics primitives *style*$_1$, .... Each *style*$_i$ must always be a *list* of graphics primitives, perhaps of length one. The list of *style*$_i$ is used cyclically. ■ Graphics primitives such as RGBColor, Dashing, GrayLevel, Thickness and PointSize can be used. ■ See pages 109 and 147. ■ See also: Graphics.

# ■ Plus

$x$ + $y$ + $z$ represents a sum of terms.

Plus has attributes Flat, Orderless and OneIdentity. ■ The default value for arguments of Plus, as used in x_. patterns, is 0. ■ Plus[ ] is taken to be 0. ■ Plus[x] is x. ■ See page 25. ■ See also: Minus, Subtract, AddTo, Increment.

# ■ Pochhammer

**Pochhammer**[$a$, $n$] gives the Pochhammer symbol $(a)_n$.

Mathematical function (see Section B.3.8). ■ $(a)_n = \frac{\Gamma(a+n)}{\Gamma(a)}$. ■ See page 364. ■ See also: Beta, Binomial, Gamma, Factorial.

# ■ Point

**Point**[*coords*] is a graphics primitive that represents a point.

The coordinates can be given either in the absolute form {$x$, $y$} or {$x$, $y$, $z$} or in scaled form Scaled[{$x$, $y$}] or Scaled[{$x$, $y$, $z$}]. ■ Points are rendered if possible as circular regions. Their radius can be specified using the graphics primitive PointSize. ■ Shading and coloring of points can be specified using GrayLevel or RGBColor. ■ See pages 142 and 149. ■ See also: Text.

## ■ PointSize

PointSize[$r$] is a graphics primitive which specifies that points which follow are to be shown if possible as circular regions with radius $r$. The radius $r$ is given as a fraction of the total width of the graph.

See pages 142 and 149. ■ See also: Thickness.

## ■ PolyGamma

PolyGamma[$z$] gives the digamma function $\psi(z)$.

PolyGamma[$n$, $z$] gives $n^{\text{th}}$ derivative of the digamma function $\psi^{(n)}(z)$.

PolyGamma[$z$] is the logarithmic derivative of the gamma function, given by $\psi(z) = \frac{\Gamma'(z)}{\Gamma(z)}$. ■
PolyGamma[$n$, $z$] is given by $\psi^{(n)}(z) = \frac{d^n}{dz^n}\psi(z)$. ■ The digamma function is $\psi(z) = \psi^{(0)}(z)$: $\psi^{(n)}(z)$ is the $(n+1)^{\text{th}}$ logarithmic derivative of the gamma function. ■ See page 364. ■ See also: Gamma, EulerGamma.

## ■ Polygon

Polygon[{$pt_1$, $pt_2$, ...}] is a graphics primitive that represents a filled polygon.

Polygon can be used in both Graphics and Graphics3D (two- and three-dimensional graphics). ■ The positions of points can be specified either in absolute coordinates as {$x$, $y$} or {$x$, $y$, $z$}, or in scaled coordinates as Scaled[{$x$, $y$}] or Scaled[{$x$, $y$, $z$}]. ■ The boundary of the polygon is formed by joining the last point you specify to the first one. ■ In two dimensions, self-intersecting polygons are allowed. ■ In three dimensions, the two-dimensional convex hull of the points is formed. For a planar polygon that does not intersect itself, the polygon drawn will be exactly as you specified it. ■ You can use the graphics primitives GrayLevel or RGBColor to specify how polygons should be filled. ■ In three dimensions, the shading can be produced from simulated illumination. ■ In three-dimensional graphics, polygons are considered to have both a front and a back face. The sense of a polygon is defined in terms of its first three vertices. When taken in order, these vertices go in a *counter-clockwise* direction when viewed from the *front*. (The frontward normal is thus obtained from a *right hand* rule.) ■ You can use FaceForm to specify gray level or color for the the front and back faces of polygons. ■ In three-dimensional graphics, intersections between polygons are shown as lines, with forms specified by the graphics primitive EdgeForm. ■ See pages 142 and 149. ■ See also: CellArray, Rectangle.

## ■ PolyLog

PolyLog[$n$, $z$] gives the polylogarithm function $\text{Li}_n(z)$.

Mathematical function (see Section B.3.8). ■ $\text{Li}_n(z) = \sum_{k=1}^{\infty} \frac{z^k}{k^n}$. ■ See page 364. ■ See also: Zeta, PolyGamma, LerchPhi.

## ■ PolynomialQ

PolynomialQ[$expr$, $var$] yields True if $expr$ is a polynomial in $var$, and yields False otherwise.

PolynomialQ[$expr$, {$var_1$, ...}] tests whether $expr$ is a polynomial in the $var_i$.

The $var_i$ need not be symbols; PolynomialQ[f[a] + f[a]^2, f[a]] $\longrightarrow$ True. ■ See pages 230 and 383. ■ See also: Collect, Series.

■ **PolynomialQuotient**

PolynomialQuotient[$p$, $q$, $x$] gives the quotient of the polynomials $p$ and $q$ in $x$, with any remainder dropped.

See page 388. ▪ See also: `Apart`, `Cancel`, `Quotient`.

■ **PolynomialRemainder**

PolynomialRemainder[$p$, $q$, $x$] gives the remainder from division of the polynomials $p$ and $q$ in $x$.

The degree of the result in $x$ is guaranteed to be smaller than the degree of $q$. ▪ See page 388. ▪ See also: `Apart`, `Cancel`, `Mod`.

■ **Position**

Position[$expr$, $pattern$] gives a list of the positions at which objects matching $pattern$ appear in $expr$.

Example: `Position[{1+x^2, 5, x^4}, x^_]` $\longrightarrow$ `{{1, 2}, {3}}`. ▪ Position[$expr$, $pattern$] tests all the subparts of $expr$ in turn to try and find ones that match $pattern$. ▪ `Position` returns a list of positions in a form suitable for use in `MapAt`. ▪ See pages 177 and 235. ▪ See also: `Cases`, `Count`.

■ **Positive**

Positive[$x$] gives `True` if $x$ is a positive number.

Positive[$x$] gives `False` if $x$ is manifestly a negative number, or zero. Otherwise, it remains unevaluated. ▪ A definition like `Positive[x] = True` effectively specifies that $x$ is a positive number. ▪ Definitions for `Sign` are tested in determining whether linear combinations of expressions are positive. ▪ See page 242. ▪ See also: `Negative`, `NonNegative`, `Sign`.

■ **Postfix**

Postfix[$f$[$expr$]] prints with $f$[$expr$] given in default postfix form: $expr$ // $f$.

Postfix[$f$[$expr$], $h$] prints as $expr h$.

Postfix[$expr$, $h$, $precedence$, $grouping$] can be used to specify how the output form should be parenthesized. ▪ See the notes for `Infix` about precedence and grouping. ▪ See page 278. ▪ See also: `Infix`, `Prefix`.

■ **PostScript**

PostScript is a setting that can be given for the option `TextRendering` to specify output in POSTSCRIPT form.

See page 295. ▪ See also: `Plain`.

■ **Power**

$x$∧$y$ gives $x$ to the power $y$.

Mathematical function (see Section B.3.8).   ■ Exact integer results are given when possible for roots of the form $n^{\frac{1}{m}}$.   ■ For approximate complex numbers $x$ and $y$, **Power** gives the principal value of $e^{y \log(x)}$.   ■ For powers $x^{p/q}$ with exact rational exponents, real number results are given when possible.   ■ Examples: (-2.)∧(1/3) ⟶ -1.25992; (-2.)∧(1./3) ⟶ 0.629961 + 1.09112 I.   ■ See page 25.

■ **PowerMod**

**PowerMod**[$a$, $b$, $n$] gives $a^b$ mod $n$.

For negative $b$, **PowerMod**[$a$, $b$, $n$] gives modular inverses.

Integer mathematical function (see Section B.3.8).   ■ For positive $b$, **PowerMod**[$a$, $b$, $n$] gives the same answers as **Mod**[$a$∧$b$, $n$] but is much more efficient.   ■ For negative $b$, **PowerMod**[$a$, $b$, $n$] gives the integer $k$ such that $a \equiv k^b$ mod $n$. If no such integer exists, **PowerMod** returns unevaluated.   ■ See page 347.

■ **PrecedenceForm**

**PrecedenceForm**[*expr*, *prec*] prints with *expr* parenthesized as it would be if it contained an operator with precedence *prec*.

*prec* must be an integer. See notes for **Infix**.   ■ Example: a + PrecedenceForm[b c, 10] ⟶ a + (b c).   ■ See page 278.

■ **Precision**

**Precision**[$x$] gives the number of digits of precision in the number $x$.

If $x$ is not a number, **Precision**[$x$] gives the minimum value of **Precision** for all the numbers that appear in $x$.   ■ **Precision** gives **Infinity** when applied to exact numbers, such as integers.   ■ See page 331.   ■ See also: **Accuracy**, **N**, **Chop**.

■ **PreDecrement**

--$x$ decreases the value of $x$ by 1, returning the new value of $x$.

**PreDecrement** has attribute **HoldFirst**.   ■ --$x$ is equivalent to $x$=$x$-1.   ■ See page 257.   ■ See also: **Decrement**, **SubtractFrom**, **Set**.

■ **Prefix**

**Prefix**[$f$[*expr*]] prints with $f$[*expr*] given in default prefix form: $f$ @ *expr*.

**Prefix**[$f$[*expr*], $h$] prints as $h$*expr*.

**Prefix**[*expr*, $h$, *precedence*, *grouping*] can be used to specify how the output form should be parenthesized.   ■ See the notes for **Infix** about precedence and grouping.   ■ See page 278.   ■ See also: **Infix**, **Postfix**.

■ **PreIncrement**

++$x$ increases the value of $x$ by 1, returning the new value of $x$.

**PreIncrement** has attribute **HoldFirst**.   ■ ++$x$ is equivalent to $x$=$x$+1.   ■ See page 257.   ■ See also: **Increment**, **AddTo**, **Set**.

■ **Prepend**

> Prepend[*expr*, *elem*] gives *expr* with *elem* prepended.

Examples: Prepend[{a,b}, x] ⟶ {x, a, b}; Prepend[f[a], x+y] ⟶ f[x + y, a]. ■ See page 102. ■
See also: Append, Insert.

■ **PrependTo**

> PrependTo[*s*, *elem*] prepends *elem* to the value of *s*, and resets *s* to the result.

PrependTo[*s*, *elem*] is equivalent to s = Prepend[s, *elem*]. ■ PrependTo[*s*, *elem*] does not evaluate *s*. ■
You can use PrependTo repeatedly to build up a list. ■ See page 257. ■ See also: AppendTo.

■ **Prime**

> Prime[*n*] gives the $n^{\text{th}}$ prime number.

Prime[1] is 2. ■ On most computer systems, Prime[*n*] for *n* up to $10^8$ can be obtained quite quickly. ■ See
page 346. ■ See also: FactorInteger.

■ **PrimeQ**

> PrimeQ[*expr*] yields **True** if *expr* is a prime number, and yields **False** otherwise.

PrimeQ[1] gives False. ■ PrimeQ[-*n*], where *n* is prime, gives True. ■ See pages 230 and 346. ■ See also:
FactorInteger.

■ **Print**

> Print[*expr₁*, *expr₂*, ...] prints the *exprᵢ*, followed by a newline (line feed).

Print sends its output to the channel $Output. ■ Print uses OutputForm as the default format type. ■
Print concatenates the output from each *exprᵢ* together, effectively using SequenceForm. ■ You can arrange
to have expressions on several lines by using ColumnForm. ■ See page 282. ■ See also: Message, Put, Write.

■ **PrintForm**

> PrintForm[*expr*] prints as the internal printform representation of *expr*.

The printform consists of a nested collection of the primitives:

| | |
|---|---|
| String | raw character string |
| HorizontalForm | horizontal array of print objects |
| VerticalForm | vertical array of print objects |

■ See page 270. ■ See also: FullForm, TreeForm.

## ■ Product

Product[*f*, {*i*, *imax*}] evaluates the product $\prod_{i=1}^{imax} f$.

Product[*f*, {*i*, *imin*, *imax*}] starts with *i* = *imin*. Product[*f*, {*i*, *imin*, *imax*, *di*}] uses steps *di*.

Product[*f*, {*i*, *imin*, *imax*}, {*j*, *jmin*, *jmax*}, ...] evaluates the multiple product $\prod_{i=imin}^{imax} \prod_{j=jmin}^{jmax} \cdots f$.

Product evaluates its arguments in a non-standard way (see page 569). ■ Product uses the standard *Mathematica* iteration specification. ■ The iteration variable *i* is treated as local. ■ In multiple products, the range of the outermost variable is given first. ■ See page 69. ■ See also: Do, Sum, Table.

## ■ Protect

Protect[*s₁*, *s₂*, ...] sets the attribute Protected for the symbols $s_i$.

Protect["*form₁*", "*form₂*", ...] protects all symbols whose names textually match any of the $form_i$.

Protect["*form*"] allows metacharacters such as *, as specified in the notes on StringMatchQ. ■ Protect["*context*`*"] protects all symbols in a particular context. ■ See pages 196 and 566. ■ See also: Unprotect.

## ■ Protected

Protected is an attribute which prevents any values associated with a symbol from being modified.

Many built-in *Mathematica* functions have the attribute Protected. ■ See page 214. ■ See also: Locked, ReadProtected.

## ■ PseudoInverse

PseudoInverse[*m*] finds the pseudoinverse of a rectangular numerical matrix.

PseudoInverse[*m*, Tolerance -> *t*] specifies that singular values smaller than *t* times the maximum singular value are to be removed. ■ The default setting Tolerance -> Automatic takes *t* to be 10 times the numerical precision of the input. ■ For square matrices **M**, the pseudoinverse $\mathbf{M}^{(-1)}$ is equivalent to the standard inverse. ■ See page 454. ■ See also: Inverse, SingularValues, Fit.

## ■ Put

*expr* >> *filename* writes *expr* to a file.

Put[*expr₁*, *expr₂*, ..., "*filename*"] writes a sequence of expressions $expr_i$ to a file.

On systems with advanced graphical interfaces, there will usually be graphical tools for saving expressions in files. ■ Put uses the format type InputForm by default. ■ Put starts writing output at the beginning of the file. It deletes whatever was previously in the file. ■ Put inserts a newline (line feed) at the end of its output. ■ *expr* >> *filename* is equivalent to *expr* >> "*filename*". The double quotes can be omitted if the filename contains only the following non-alphanumeric characters: ., / and ~. ■ It is conventional to use names that end with .m for files containing *Mathematica* input. ■ See page 286. ■ See also: Save, Definition, Dump, Get.

■ **PutAppend**

> *expr* >>> *filename* appends *expr* to a file.
>
> Put[*expr₁*, *expr₂*, ..., "*filename*"] appends a sequence of expressions $expr_i$ to a file.
>
> PutAppend works the same as Put, except that it adds output to the end of file, rather than replacing the complete contents of the file. ▪ See page 286. ▪ See also: Write.

■ **Quartics**

> Quartics is an option for Roots, Solve and related functions which specifies whether explicit solutions should be generated for irreducible quartic equations.
>
> Quartics->False causes irreducible fourth degree equations to be left unsolved in their original symbolic form. Numerical solutions can be found by applying N. ▪ Setting Quartics->True causes explicit solutions to be generated. These solutions are usually very complicated. ▪ See also: Cubics, NRoots.

■ **Quit**

> Quit[ ] terminates a *Mathematica* session, or an inspection session initiated within Debug.
>
> All definitions that you have not explicitly saved in files are lost when the *Mathematica* session terminates. ▪ Before terminating a session, *Mathematica* executes any delayed value that has been assigned to the global variable $Epilog. Conventionally, this attempts to read in a file end.m of commands to be executed before termination. ▪ On most computer systems, Quit[*n*] terminates *Mathematica*, passing the integer *n* as an exit code to the operating system. ▪ Exit is a synonym for Quit. ▪ See page 579. ▪ See also: $IgnoreEOF.

■ **Quotient**

> Quotient[*n*, *m*] gives the integer quotient of *n* and *m*.
>
> Integer mathematical function (see Section B.3.8). ▪ Quotient[*n*, *m*] is equivalent to Floor[*n*/*m*]. ▪ See page 345. ▪ See also: Mod, PolynomialQuotient.

■ **Random**

> Random[ ] gives a uniformly-distributed pseudorandom Real in the range 0 to 1.
>
> Random[*type*, *range*] gives a pseudorandom number of the specified type, lying in the specified range. Possible types are: Integer, Real and Complex. The default range is 0 to 1. You can give the range {*min*, *max*} explicitly; a range specification of *max* is equivalent to {0, *max*}.
>
> Random[Integer] gives 0 or 1 with probability $\frac{1}{2}$. ▪ Random[Complex, {*zmin*, *zmax*}] gives a pseudorandom complex number in the rectangle defined by *zmin* and *zmax*. ▪ Random[Real, *range*, *n*] generates a pseudorandom real number with a precision of *n* digits. ▪ Random gives a different sequence of pseudorandom numbers whenever you run *Mathematica*. You can start Random with a particular seed using SeedRandom. ▪ See page 343.

# ■ Range

**Range**[*imax*] generates the list {1, 2, ..., *imax*}.

**Range**[*imin*, *imax*] generates the list {*imin*, ..., *imax*}. **Range**[*imin*, *imax*, *di*] uses step *di*.

Example: `Range[4]` ⟶ {1, 2, 3, 4}. ▪ The arguments to `Range` need not be integers. ▪ `Range` starts from *imin*, and successively adds increments of *di* until the result is greater than *imax*. ▪ `Range[0, 1, .3]` ⟶ {0, 0.3, 0.6, 0.9}. ▪ `Range[x, x+2]` ⟶ {x, 1 + x, 2 + x}. ▪ `Range` uses the standard *Mathematica* iteration specification, as applied to a single variable. ▪ See page 36. ▪ See also: `Table`.

# ■ Rational

**Rational** is the head used for rational numbers.

You can enter a rational number in the form *n*/*m*. ▪ The pattern object `_Rational` can be used to stand for a rational number. It cannot stand for a single integer. ▪ You have to use `Numerator` and `Denominator` to extract parts of `Rational` numbers. ▪ See page 325. ▪ See also: `Integer`, `Numerator`, `Denominator`.

# ■ Rationalize

**Rationalize**[*x*] takes `Real` numbers in *x* that are close to rationals, and converts them to exact `Rational` numbers.

**Rationalize**[*x*, *dx*] performs the conversion whenever the error made is smaller in magnitude than *dx*.

Example: `Rationalize[3.78]` ⟶ $\frac{189}{50}$ . ▪ `Rationalize[N[Pi]]` ⟶ 3.14159 does not give a rational number, since there is none "sufficiently close" to `N[Pi]`. ▪ A rational number $p/q$ is considered "sufficiently close" to a `Real` $x$ if $|p/q - x| < c/q^2$, where $c$ is chosen to be $10^{-4}$. See page 328. ▪ See also: `Chop`, `Round`.

# ■ Raw

**Raw**[*h*, "*hexstring*"] constructs a raw data object with head *h*, and with contents corresponding the binary bit pattern represented by the string *hexstring*, interpreted as a hexadecimal number.

`Raw` should be used only under very special circumstances. ▪ It is possible to crash *Mathematica* by creating a fundamental *Mathematica* data object with `Raw`, and specifying illegal internal data for it. If you create an object with head `Real`, but with internal data incompatible with *Mathematica* `Real` numbers, you may end up crashing your whole *Mathematica* session. ▪ `Raw` encodes data so that two hexadecimal digits represent one byte. Identical *hexstring* may lead to different internal data on different computer systems. ▪ You cannot necessarily transport raw arrays of bytes from one type of computer to another without encountering byte swap incompatibilities. ▪ See page 551. ▪ See also: `Run`.

# ■ Re

**Re**[*z*] gives the real part of the complex number *z*.

**Re**[*expr*] is left unevaluated if *expr* is not a number. ▪ See page 342. ▪ See also: `Im`, `Abs`, `Arg`.

## ■ Read

Read["*file*"] reads one expression from a file, and returns the expression.

Read["*file*", *type*] reads one object of the specified type.

Read["*file*", {*type₁*, *type₂*, ...}] reads a sequence of objects of the specified types.

Possible types to read are:

| | |
|---|---|
| Byte | a single byte, returned as an integer code |
| Character | a single character, returned as a one-character string |
| Number | an integer or an approximate number, given in "E" format |
| String | a string |
| Real | an approximate number, given in "E" format |
| Expression | a complete *Mathematica* expression |

■ Objects of type Real can be given in the scientific notation format used by languages such as C and FORTRAN. A form like 2.e5 or 2E5 can be used to represent the number $2 \times 10^5$. Objects read as type Real are always returned as approximate numbers. Objects read as type Number are returned as integers if they contain no explicit decimal points. ■ Objects of type String must be terminated by newlines (line feeds or returns). ■ You can specify any nested list of types for Read to look for. Each successive object read will be placed in the next position in the list structure. A depth-first traversal of the list structure is used. ■ Example: Read["*file*", {Number, Number}] reads a pair of numbers from a file, and gives the result as a two-element list. ■ Read["*file*", {{Number, Number}, {Number, Number}}] reads a $2 \times 2$ matrix, going through each column, then each row. ■ You can use Read to get objects to insert into any expression structure, not necessarily a list. Example: Read["*file*", Hold[Expression]] gets an expression and places it inside Hold. ■ If the file you specify is not already open, Read opens the file, and starts reading at the beginning. You can open a file for reading using OpenRead. ■ There is always a "current point" maintained for any file. When you read an object from a file, the current point is left after the input you read. Successive calls to Read can therefore be used to read successive objects in a file. ■ You can reset the current point to the beginning of a file by closing the file, and then reopening it. ■ Read returns EndOfFile for each object you try to read after you have reached the end of the file. ■ Read returns Null if it cannot read an object of the type you requested. ■ You can use Read["!*command*"] to read through a pipe from an external program. ■ See page 302. ■ See also: Input, Get.

## ■ ReadList

ReadList["*file*"] reads all the remaining expressions in a file, and returns a list of them.

ReadList["*file*", *type*] reads objects of the specified type from a file, until the end of the file is reached. The list of objects read is returned.

ReadList["*file*", {*type₁*, *type₂*, ...}] reads objects with a sequence of types, until the end of the file is reached.

If *file* is not already open for reading, ReadList opens it, then closes it when it is finished. If the file is already open, ReadList does not close it at the end. ■ ReadList prints a message if any of the objects remaining in the file are not of the specified types. ■ ReadList["*file*", {*type₁*, ...}] looks for the sequence of *typeᵢ* in order. If the end of file is reached while part way through the sequence of *typeᵢ*, EndOfFile is returned in place of the elements in the sequence that have not yet been read. ■ See notes for Read. ■ See pages 156 and 300.

### ■ ReadProtected

**ReadProtected** is an attribute which prevents any values associated with a symbol from being printed.

Individual values can nevertheless be used during evaluation. However, functions like **Definition** and **Information** which show the complete set of values, cannot be used. ■ See page 214. ■ See also: **Locked**, **Protected**.

### ■ Real

**Real** is the head used for real (floating-point) numbers.

_**Real** can be used to stand for a real number in a pattern. ■ You can enter a floating point number of any length. ■ You can enter a number in scientific notation by explicitly giving the form *mantissa* 10^*exponent*. ■ You can enter a floating point number in base *b* using *b*^^*digits*. The base must be less than 36. The letters are used in sequence to standard for digits 10 through 35. ■ **Real** is also used to indicate an approximate real number in **Read**. ■ See page 325. ■ See also: **BaseForm**, **Number**.

### ■ Rectangle

**Rectangle[{*xmin*, *ymin*}, {*xmax*, *ymax*}]** is a two-dimensional graphics primitive that represents a filled rectangle, oriented parallel to the axes.

**Rectangle[{Scaled[{*xmin*, *ymin*}], Scaled[{*xmax*, *ymax*}]}]** can also be used. ■ **Rectangle** is equivalent to a suitable **Polygon** with four corners. ■ You can use the graphics primitives **GrayLevel** and **RGBColor** to specify how rectangles should be filled. ■ See page 142. ■ See also: **Polygon**, **CellArray**.

### ■ Reduce

**Reduce[*eqns*, *vars*]** simplifies the equations *eqns*, attempting to solve for the variables *vars*. The equations generated by **Reduce** are equivalent to *eqns*, and contain all the possible solutions.

**Reduce[*eqns*, *vars*, *elims*]** simplifies the equations, trying to eliminate the variables *elims*.

The equations given to **Reduce** are in the form *lhs* == *rhs*. Simultaneous equations can either be given in a list, or combined with **&&**. ■ Example: **Reduce[a x + b == 0, x]** $\longrightarrow$ a != 0 && x == $-(\frac{b}{a})$ || a == 0 && b == 0. ■ **Reduce** generates equations (==) and nonequalities (!=), combined with && and ||. ■ **Reduce** primarily deals with polynomial equations. ■ You can give options to **Reduce**, as described in the notes on **MainSolve**. ■ See page 401. ■ See also: **Solve**, **Eliminate**, **LogicalExpand**, **ToRules**.

### ■ Release

**Release[*expr*]** causes *expr* to be evaluated, removing any "holding".

**Release** can be used to override the "holding" of function arguments. ■ When *Release*[*expr*] appears as the argument of the function, that argument is immediately replaced by the evaluated form of *expr*, whether or not the attributes associated with the function specified that the argument should be held. ■ When **Release** is applied to an expression that is not a held function argument. it returns the expression with subexpressions of the form **Hold[*e*]** replaced by the evaluated form of *e*. ■ See page 220. ■ See also: **Hold**, **HoldAll**.

■ **Remove**

Remove[*symbol$_1$*, ...] removes symbols completely, so that their names are no longer recognized by *Mathematica*.

Remove["*form$_1$*", "*form$_2$*", ...] removes all symbols whose names textually match any of the *form$_i$*.

You can use Remove to get rid of symbols that you do not need, and which interfere with context paths that you are using. ■ Remove uses ClearAll to remove all values and attributes associated with symbols, before removing their names. ■ Remove["*form*"] allows metacharacters such as *, as specified in the notes on StringMatchQ. ■ Remove["*context*`*"] removes all symbols in a particular context. ■ Remove does not affect symbols with the attribute Protected. ■ Once you have removed a symbol, you will never be able to refer to it again, unless you recreate it. ■ If you have an expression that contains a symbol which you remove, the removed symbol will be printed as Removed["*name*"], where its name is given in a string. ■ See pages 312, 315 and 575. ■ See also: Clear.

■ **RenderAll**

RenderAll is an option to Graphics3D which specifies whether or not POSTSCRIPT should be generated for *all* polygons.

When RenderAll->False, POSTSCRIPT will be generated only for those polygons or parts of polygons which are visible in the final picture. ■ If RenderAll->True, POSTSCRIPT is generated for *all* polygons. The POSTSCRIPT for polygons that are further back is given before the POSTSCRIPT for those in front. If the POSTSCRIPT is displayed incrementally, you can see the object being drawn from the back. ■ Setting RenderAll->False will usually lead to a smaller amount of POSTSCRIPT code, but may take longer to run. ■ See page 155.

■ **Repeated**

*p*.. is a pattern object which represents a sequence of one or more expressions, each matching *p*.

*p*.. can appear as an argument of any function. It represents any sequence of arguments. ■ All the objects in the sequence represented by *p*.. must match *p*, but the objects need not be identical. ■ The expression *p* may, but need not, itself be a pattern object. ■ See page 556. ■ See also: BlankSequence.

■ **RepeatedNull**

*p*... is a pattern object which represents a sequence of zero or more expressions, each matching *p*.

See notes for Repeated. ■ See page 556.

## ■ Replace

`Replace[`*expr,  rules*`]` applies a rule or list of rules in an attempt to transform the complete expression *expr*.

Example: `Replace[x∧2, x∧2 -> a]` ⟶ a. ■ `Replace[x + 1, x -> a]` ⟶ 1 + x. ■ The rules must be of the form *lhs* `->` *rhs* or *lhs* `:>` *rhs*. ■ A list of rules can be given. The rules are tried in order. The result of the first one that applies is returned. If none of the rules apply, the original *expr* is returned. ■ If the rules are given in nested lists, `Replace` is effectively mapped onto the inner lists. Thus `Replace[`*expr*`, {{`$r_{11}$`, `$r_{12}$`}, {`$r_{21}$`, ...}, ...}]` is equivalent to `{Replace[`*expr*`, {`$r_{11}$`, `$r_{12}$`}], Replace[`*expr*`, {`$r_{21}$`, ...}], ...}`. ■ Delayed rules defined with `:>` can contain `/;` conditions. ■ `Replace[`*expr, rules*`]` applies rules only to the complete expression *expr*. You can use `Map` and `MapAt` to apply rules to specific parts of an expression, or you can use `ReplaceAll` to apply rules to all parts of an expression. ■ See page 207. ■ See also: `Rule`, `Set`, `AlgebraicRules`.

## ■ ReplaceAll

*expr* `/.` *rules* applies a rule or list of rules in an attempt to transform each subpart of an expression *expr*.

Example: `x + 2 /. x -> a` ⟶ 2 + a. ■ `ReplaceAll[`*expr, rules*`]` is equivalent to `MapAll[Replace[#, `*rules*`]&, `*expr*`]`. ■ `ReplaceAll` looks at each part of *expr*, tries all the *rules* on it, and then goes on to the next part of *expr*. The first rule that applies to a particular part is used; no further rules are tried on that part, or on any of its subparts. ■ `ReplaceAll` applies a particular rule only once to an expression. ■ Example: `x /. x -> x + 1` ⟶ 1 + x. ■ See the notes on `Replace` for a description of how rules are applied to each part of *expr*. ■ *expr* `/.` *rules* returns *expr* if none of the rules apply. ■ See page 199. ■ See also: `Rule`, `Set`.

## ■ ReplaceRepeated

*expr* `//.` *rules* repeatedly performs replacements until *expr* no longer changes.

*expr* `//.` *rules* effectively applies `/.` repeatedly, until the results it gets no longer change. ■ It performs one complete pass over the expression using `/.`, then carries out the next pass. ■ You should be very careful to avoid infinite loops when you use the `//.` operator. `x //. x -> x + 1` will, for example, lead to an infinite loop. ■ See page 208. ■ See also: `Rule`, `Set`, `FixedPoint`.

## ■ ResetMedium

`ResetMedium["`*file*`", `*options*`]` resets the options associated with a file that is already open.

`ResetMedium[`*options*`]` resets the options for the standard output.

See the notes on `OpenAppend` for the possible options. ■ `ResetMedium[PageWidth -> `*n*`]` resets the standard output to have a width of *n*. ■ `ResetMedium` can be used with pipes as well as files. ■ See pages 292 and 587. ■ See also: `Close`.

## ■ Rest

`Rest[`*expr*`]` gives *expr* with the first element removed.

Example: `Rest[{a, b, c}]` ⟶ {b, c}. ■ `Rest[`*expr*`]` is equivalent to `Drop[`*expr*`, 1]`. ■ See page 99. ■ See also: `Drop`, `First`, `Part`, `Take`.

## ■ Resultant

Resultant[$poly_1$, $poly_2$, $var$] computes the resultant of the polynomials $poly_1$ and $poly_2$ with respect to the variable $var$.

Resultant[$poly_1$, $poly_2$, $var$, Modulus->$p$] computes the resultant modulo the prime $p$.

The resultant of two polynomials $a$ and $b$, both with leading coefficient one, is the product of all the differences $a_i - b_j$ between roots of the polynomials. The resultant is always a number or a polynomial. ■ See page 388. ■ See also: GCD, Eliminate.

## ■ Return

Return[$expr$] returns the value $expr$ from a function.

Return[ ] returns the value Null.

Return[$expr$] exits control structures within the definition of a function, and gives the value $expr$ for the whole function. ■ Return is effective only if it is generated as the value of a segment in a compound expression, or as the body of a control structure. Return also works in Scan. ■ See page 260. ■ See also: Break, Throw.

## ■ Reverse

Reverse[$expr$] reverses the order of the elements in $expr$.

Example: Reverse[{a, b, c}] ⟶ {c, b, a}. ■ See page 103. ■ See also: Permutations, RotateLeft, RotateRight.

## ■ RGBColor

RGBColor[$red$, $green$, $blue$] is a graphics primitive which specifies that graphical objects which follow are to be displayed, if possible, in the color given.

Red, green and blue color intensities outside the range 0 to 1 will be clipped. ■ On monochrome displays, a gray level based on the average of the color intensities is used. ■ See pages 129, 142 and 149. ■ See also: GrayLevel, PlotColor.

## ■ Roots

Roots[$lhs$==$rhs$, $var$] yields a disjunction of equations which represent the roots of a polynomial equation.

Roots uses Factor and Decompose in trying to find roots. ■ You can find numerical values of the roots by applying N. ■ Roots can take the following options:

| | | |
|---|---|---|
| Cubics | True | whether to generate explicit solutions for cubics |
| EquatedTo | Null | expression to which the variable solved for should be equated |
| Modulus | Infinity | integer modulus |
| Multiplicity | 1 | multiplicity in final list of solutions |
| Quartics | True | whether to generate explicit solutions for quartics |
| Using | True | subsidiary equations to be solved |

■ Roots is generated when Solve and related functions cannot produce explicit solutions. Options are often given in such cases. ■ Roots gives several identical equations when roots with multiplicity greater than one occur. ■ See page 393. ■ See also: NRoots, Solve, FindRoot, ToRules.

## RotateLeft

RotateLeft[*expr*, *n*] cycles the elements in *expr* *n* positions to the left.

RotateLeft[*expr*] cycles one position to the left.

Example: RotateLeft[{a, b, c}, 1] ⟶ {b, c, a}. ▪ RotateLeft[*expr*, -*n*] rotates *n* positions to the right. ▪ See page 103. ▪ See also: Reverse.

## RotateRight

RotateRight[*expr*, *n*] cycles the elements in *expr* *n* positions to the right.

RotateRight[*expr*] cycles one position to the right.

Example: RotateRight[{a, b, c}, 1] ⟶ {c, a, b}. ▪ RotateRight[*expr*, -*n*] rotates *n* positions to the left. ▪ See page 103. ▪ See also: Reverse.

## Round

Round[*x*] gives the integer closest to *x*.

Mathematical function (see Section B.3.8). ▪ Examples: Round[2.4] ⟶ 2; Round[2.6] ⟶ 3; Round[-2.4] ⟶ -2; Round[-2.6] ⟶ -3. ▪ Round rounds numbers of the form *x*.5 towards 0. ▪ See page 341. ▪ See also: Floor, Ceiling, Chop.

## RowReduce

RowReduce[*m*] gives the row-reduced form of the matrix *m*.

RowReduce adds multiples of rows together, producing zero elements when possible. The final matrix is in reduced row echelon form. ▪ RowReduce works on both numerical and symbolic matrices. ▪ RowReduce[*m*, ZeroTest -> *test*] evaluates *test*[ *m*[[*i*, *j*]] ] to determine whether matrix elements are zero. The default setting is ZeroTest -> (# == 0)&. ▪ See page 448. ▪ See also: NullSpace, LatticeReduce.

## Rule

*lhs* -> *rhs* represents a rule that transforms *lhs* to *rhs*.

*lhs* -> *rhs* evaluates *rhs* immediately. ▪ You can apply rules using Replace. ▪ The assignment *lhs* = *rhs* specifies that the rule *lhs* -> *rhs* should be used whenever it applies. ▪ When you enter a rule like *lhs* -> *rhs* or Rule[*lhs*, *rhs*], *Mathematica* inserts a "compiled" form of the rule as a third, hidden, element. ▪ See page 576. ▪ See also: Replace, Set, AlgebraicRules.

## RuleDelayed

*lhs* :> *rhs* represents a rule that transforms *lhs* to *rhs*, evaluating *rhs* only when the rule is used.

RuleDelayed has the attribute HoldRest. ▪ You can apply rules using Replace. ▪ The assignment *lhs* := *rhs* specifies that the rule *lhs* :> *rhs* should be used whenever it applies. ▪ You can use Condition to specify when a particular rule applies. ▪ When you enter a rule like *lhs* :> *rhs* or RuleDelayed[*lhs*, *rhs*], *Mathematica* inserts a "compiled" form of the rule as a third, hidden, element. ▪ See page 576. ▪ See also: Replace, SetDelayed.

## ■ Run

Run[*expr₁*, *expr₂*, ...] generates the printed form of the expressions *exprᵢ*, separated by spaces, and runs it as an external, operating system, command.

Run is not available on all computer systems. ■ Run prints the *exprᵢ* in InputForm format. ■ Run returns an integer which corresponds, when possible, to the exit code for the command returned by the operating system. ■ The command executed by Run cannot usually require interactive input. On most computer systems, it can, however, generate textual output. ■ You can enter the input line !*command* to execute an external command. ■ See page 297. ■ See also: Put, Splice.

## ■ RunThrough

RunThrough["*command*", *expr*] executes an external command, giving the printed form of *expr* as input, and taking the output, reading it as *Mathematica* input, and returning the result.

RunThrough is not available on all computer systems. ■ RunThrough writes the InputForm of *expr* on the standard input for *command*, then reads its standard output, and feeds it into *Mathematica*. ■ RunThrough starts *command*, then gives input to *command*, then terminates the input. ■ See page 298. ■ See also: StartProcess, Put, Get, Splice.

## ■ SameQ

SameQ[*expr₁*, *expr₂*, ...] yields True if all the *exprᵢ* are identical, and yields False otherwise.

SameQ requires exact correspondence between expressions, except that it considers Real numbers equal if their difference is less than the precision of either of them. ■ SameQ[2, 2.] gives False. ■ See page 259. ■ See also: Equal, Order.

## ■ Save

Save["*filename*", *symb₁*, *symb₂*, ...] appends the definitions of the symbols *symbᵢ* to a file.

Save uses FullDefinition to include subsidiary definitions. ■ Save writes out definitions in InputForm. ■ See page 289. ■ See also: PutAppend, Get, Dump.

## ■ Scaled

Scaled[{*x*, *y*, ...}] gives coordinates for a graphical object, scaled to run from 0 to 1 across the whole plot in each direction.

Scaled can be used to specify scaled coordinates in any two or three-dimensional graphics primitive. ■ See page 146. ■ See also: PlotRange.

■ **Scan**

>   Scan[*f*, *expr*] evaluates *f* applied to each element of *expr* in turn.

>   Scan[*f*, *expr*, *levelspec*] applies *f* to parts of *expr* specified by *levelspec*.

>   Scan[*f*, *expr*] discards the results of applying *f* to the subexpressions in *expr*. Unlike Map, Scan does not build up a new expression to return.  ▪ You can use Return to exit from Scan. Return[*ret*] causes the final value of Scan to be *ret*. If no explicit return values are specified, the final result from Scan is Null.  ▪ Scan is useful in carrying out an operation on parts of expressions where the operation has a "side effect", such as making an assignment.  ▪ Level specifications are described on page 565.  ▪ The default value for *levelspec* in Scan is {1}.  ▪ See page 183.  ▪ See also: Apply, Map, Level.

■ **ScientificForm**

>   ScientificForm[*expr*] prints with all real numbers in *expr* given in scientific notation.

>   See page 328.  ▪ See also: EngineeringForm, NumberForm.

■ **Sec**

>   Sec[*z*] gives the secant of *z*.

>   Mathematical function (see Section B.3.8).  ▪ The argument of Sec is assumed to be in radians. (Multiply by Degree to convert from degrees.)  ▪ $\sec(z) = \frac{1}{\cos(z)}$.  ▪ See page 353.  ▪ See also: ArcSec.

■ **Sech**

>   Sech[*z*] gives the hyperbolic secant of *z*.

>   Mathematical function (see Section B.3.8).  ▪ $\operatorname{sech}(z) = \frac{1}{\cosh(z)}$.  ▪ See page 353.  ▪ See also: ArcSech.

■ **SeedRandom**

>   SeedRandom[*n*] resets the pseudorandom number generator, using the integer *n* as a seed.

>   SeedRandom[ ] resets the generator, using as a seed an external quantity such as the exact time of day.

>   You can use SeedRandom[*n*] to make sure you get the same sequence of pseudorandom numbers on different occasions.  ▪ You can also use SeedRandom["*string*"], although the seed set in this way may be different on different computer systems.  ▪ See page 343.  ▪ See also: Random.

■ **Select**

>   Select[*list*, *crit*] picks out elements $e_i$ of *list* for which *crit*[$e_i$] is True.

>   Example: Select[{1,4,2,7,6}, EvenQ] ⟶ {4, 2, 6}.  ▪ The object *list* can have any head, not necessarily List.  ▪ See pages 172 and 235.  ▪ See also: Cases, Take, Drop.

■ **SequenceForm**

>   SequenceForm[*expr₁*, *expr₂*, ...] prints as the textual concatenation of the printed forms of the *exprᵢ*.

>   Expressions printed by SequenceForm have their baselines aligned.  ▪ See page 276.  ▪ See also: ColumnForm, TableForm.

■ Series

Series[$f$, {$x$, $x_0$, $n$}] generates a power series expansion for $f$ about the point $x = x_0$ to order $(x - x_0)^n$.

Series[$f$, {$x$, $x_0$, $n_x$}, {$y$, $y_0$, $n_y$}] successively finds series expansions with respect to $y$, then $x$.

Series can construct standard Taylor series, as well as certain expansions involving negative powers, fractional powers and logarithms. ■ Series detects certain essential singularities. ■ Series can expand about the point $x = \infty$. ■ Series[$f$, {$x$, 0, $n$}] constructs Taylor series for any function $f$ according to the formula $f(0) + f'(0)x + f''(0)x^2/2 + ... f^{(n)}x^n/n!$. ■ Series effectively evaluates partial derivatives using D. It assumes that different variables are independent. ■ The result of Series is a SeriesData object, which you can manipulate with other functions. ■ See page 427. ■ See also: InverseSeries, Limit, Normal.

■ SeriesData

SeriesData[$x$, $x_0$, {$a_0$, $a_1$, ...}, $nmin$, $nmax$, $den$] represents a power series in the variable $x$ about the point $x_0$. The $a_i$ are the coefficients in the power series. The powers of $(x-x_0)$ that appear are $nmin/den$, $(nmin+1)/den$, ..., $nmax/den$.

SeriesData objects are generated by Series. ■ SeriesData objects are printed as sums of the coefficients $a_i$, multiplied by powers of $x - x_0$. A SeriesData object representing a power series is printed with O[x]^p added, to represent omitted higher-order terms. ■ When you apply certain mathematical operations to SeriesData objects, new SeriesData objects truncated to the appropriate order are produced. ■ The operations you can perform on SeriesData objects include arithmetic ones, mathematical functions with built-in derivatives, and integration and differentiation. ■ Normal[$expr$] converts a SeriesData object into a normal expression, truncating omitted higher-order terms. ■ If the variable in a SeriesData object is itself a SeriesData object, then the composition of the SeriesData objects is computed. Substituting one series into another series with the same expansion parameter therefore automatically leads to composition of the series. Composition is only possible if the first term of the inner series involves a positive power of the variable. ■ InverseSeries can be applied to SeriesData objects to give series for inverse functions. ■ See page 430.

■ Set

$lhs$ = $rhs$ evaluates $rhs$ and assigns the result to be the value of $lhs$. $lhs$ is then replaced by $rhs$ whenever it appears.

{$l_1$, $l_2$, ...} = {$r_1$, $r_2$, ...} evaluates the $r_i$, and assigns the results to be the values of the corresponding $l_i$.

$lhs$ can be any expression, including a pattern. ■ f[x_] = x^2 is a typical assignment for a pattern. Notice the presence of _ on the left-hand side, but not the right-hand side. ■ An assignment of the form f[$args$] = $rhs$ sets up a transformation rule associated with the symbol $f$. ■ Different rules associated with a particular symbol are usually placed in the order that you give them. If a new rule that you give is *more general* than existing rules, it is, however, placed after them. One rule is considered more general than another if its left-hand side is a pattern that matches the left-hand side of the other. When the rules are used, they are tested in order. ■ New assignments with identical $lhs$ overwrite old ones. ■ You can see all the assignments associated with a symbol $f$ using ?f or Definition[f]. ■ If you make assignments for functions that have attributes like Flat and Orderless, you must make sure to set these attributes before you make assignments for the functions. ■ Set has attribute HoldFirst. ■ If $lhs$ is of the form f[$args$], then $args$ are evaluated. In addition, the flattening and sorting associated with attributes Flat and Orderless on $f$ are done. ■ There are some special functions for which an assignment to s[f[$args$]] is automatically associated with $f$ rather than s. These functions are: N, Format, Options, Default. ■ See page 574. ■ See also: TagSet, Unset, Clear, Literal.

■ SetAttributes

> SetAttributes[s, *attr*] adds *attr* to the list of attributes of the symbol *s*.

SetAttributes modifies Attributes[s]. ■ SetAttributes[s, {*attr₁*, *attr₂*, ...}] sets several attributes at a time. ■ SetAttributes[{*s₁*, *s₂*, ...}, *attrs*] sets attributes of several symbols at a time. ■ SetAttributes has the attribute HoldFirst. ■ See also: ClearAttributes, Protect. ■ See page 214.

■ SetDelayed

> *lhs* := *rhs* assigns *rhs* to be the delayed value of *lhs*. *rhs* is maintained in an unevaluated form. When *lhs* appears, it is replaced by *rhs*, evaluated afresh each time.

See notes for Set. ■ SetDelayed has attribute HoldAll, rather than HoldFirst. ■ You can make assignments of the form *lhs* := *rhs* /; *test*, where *test* gives conditions for the applicability of each transformation rule. You can make several assignments with the same *lhs* but different forms of *test*. ■ See page 574. ■ See also: TagSetDelayed, Unset, Clear.

■ SetOptions

> SetOptions[s, *name₁*->*value₁*, *name₂*->*value₂*, ...] sets the specified default options for a symbol *s*.

SetOptions is equivalent to an assignment which redefines certain elements of the list Options[s] of default options. ■ SetOptions can be used on Protected symbols. ■ SetOptions returns the new form of Options[s]. ■ See pages 113 and 564.

■ Shading

> Shading is an option for SurfaceGraphics that specifies whether the surfaces should be shaded.

With Shading -> False, the surface will be white all over. So long as Mesh -> True, however, mesh lines will still be drawn. ■ When Shading -> True, the actual shading used can either be determined by the height, or, when Lighting -> True, from simulated illumination. ■ See page 127. ■ See also: HiddenSurface, ClipFill.

■ Share

> Share[*expr*] changes the way *expr* is stored internally, to try and minimize the amount of memory used.

> Share[ ] tries to minimize the memory used to store all expressions.

Share works by sharing the storage of common subexpressions between different parts of an expression, or different expressions. ■ Using Share will never affect the results you get from *Mathematica*. It may, however, reduce the amount of memory used, and in many cases also the amount of time taken. ■ See page 318. ■ See also: MemoryInUse, ByteCount.

■ Short

> Short[*expr*] prints as a short form of *expr*, less than about one line long.

> Short[*expr*, *n*] prints as a form of *expr* about *n* lines long.

Short[*expr*] gives a "skeleton form" of *expr*, with omitted sequences of *k* elements indicated by <<*k*>>. ■ See page 269. ■ See also: Skeleton, StringSkeleton, Format.

■ Show

> Show[*graphics*, *options*] displays two- and three-dimensional graphics, possibly with options changed.
>
> Show[$g_1$, $g_2$, ...] shows several plots combined.

Show can be used with Graphics, Graphics3D, SurfaceGraphics, ContourGraphics and DensityGraphics. ▪ Options explicitly specified in Show override those included in the graphics expression. ▪ Only plots based on Graphics and Graphics3D can be combined. When plots are combined, their lists of non-default options are concatenated. ▪ Show is effectively the analog of Print for graphics. The option DisplayFunction determines the actual output mechanism used. ▪ Functions like Plot automatically apply Show to the graphics expressions they generate. ▪ See pages 113 and 140. ▪ See also: Plot, etc., and Display.

■ Sign

> Sign[*x*] gives -1, 0 or 1 depending on whether the real number *x* is negative, zero, or positive.

Sign tries simple transformations in trying to determine the sign of symbolic expressions. ▪ You can define values for Sign[*expr*] which are used when *expr*, and linear combinations involving it, appear in Sign, as well as functions like Positive and Negative. ▪ See page 341. ▪ See also: Abs, Positive, Negative, NonNegative.

■ Signature

> Signature[*list*] gives the signature of the permutation needed to place the elements of *list* in canonical order. by *list*.

Examples: Signature[{a,b,c}] $\longrightarrow$ 1; Signature[{a,c,b}] $\longrightarrow$ -1. ▪ The signature of the permutation is $(-1)^n$, where $n$ is the number of transpositions of pairs of elements that must be composed to build up the permutation. ▪ If any two elements of *list* are the same, Signature[*list*] gives 0. ▪ See pages 106 and 460. ▪ See also: Sort.

■ Simplify

> Simplify[*expr*] performs a sequence of algebraic transformations on *expr*, and returns the simplest form it finds.

Simplify[*expr*] returns the form of *expr* that it finds which has the smallest LeafCount. ▪ Simplify tries expanding and factoring parts of expressions, keeping track of which transformations make the parts simplest. ▪ See page 56. ▪ See also: Factor, Expand.

■ Sin

> Sin[*z*] gives the sine of *z*.

Mathematical function (see Section B.3.8). ▪ The argument of Sin is assumed to be in radians. (Multiply by Degree to convert from degrees.) ▪ See page 353. ▪ See also: ArcSin, Csc.

■ **SingularValues**

SingularValues[$m$] gives the singular value decomposition for a numerical matrix $m$. The result is a list {$u$, $w$, $v$}, where $w$ is the list of nonzero singular values, and $m$ can be written as Transpose[$u$].DiagonalMatrix[$w$].$v$.

SingularValues[$m$, Tolerance -> $t$] specifies that singular values smaller than $t$ times the maximum singular value are to be removed. ■ The default setting Tolerance -> Automatic takes $t$ to be 10 times the numerical precision of the input. ■ $u$ and $v$ can be considered as lists of orthonormal vectors. ■ See page 454. ■ See also: PseudoInverse.

■ **Sinh**

Sinh[$z$] gives the hyperbolic sine of $z$.

Mathematical function (see Section B.3.8). ■ See page 353. ■ See also: ArcSinh, Csch.

■ **Skeleton**

Skeleton[$n$] represents a sequence of $n$ omitted elements in an expression printed with Short.

The standard print form for Skeleton is <<$n$>>.

You can reset the print form of Skeleton. ■ See page 588. ■ See also: Short, StringSkeleton, TotalWidth.

■ **Slot**

# represents the first argument supplied to a pure function.

#$n$ represents the $n^{\text{th}}$ argument.

# is used to represent arguments or formal parameters in pure functions of the form *body*& or Function[*body*]. ■ # is equivalent to Slot[ ] or Slot[1]. ■ #$n$ is equivalent to Slot[$n$]. $n$ must be a positive integer. ■ See page 180.

■ **SlotSequence**

## represents the sequence of arguments supplied to a pure function.

##$n$ represents the sequence of arguments supplied to a pure function, starting with the $n^{\text{th}}$ argument.

## is used to represent sequences of arguments in pure functions of the form *body*& or Function[*body*]. ■ ## is equivalent to SlotSequence[ ] or SlotSequence[1]. ■ ##$n$ is equivalent to SlotSequence[$n$]. $n$ must be a positive integer. ■ A sequence of arguments supplied to a pure function is "spliced" into the body of the function wherever ## and so on appear. ■ See page 181.

■ Solve

Solve[*eqns*, *vars*] attempts to solve an equation or set of equations for the variables *vars*.

Solve[*eqns*, *vars*, *elims*] attempts to solve the equations for *vars*, elmininating the variables *elims*.

Equations are given in the form *lhs* == *rhs*. ▪ Simultaneous equations can be combined either in a list or with &&. ▪ A single variable or a list of variables can be specified. ▪ Solve[*eqns*] try to solve for all variables in *eqns*. ▪ Example: Solve[3 x + 9 == 0, x]. ▪ Solve gives explicit solutions as rules of the form *x* -> *sol*. ▪ When there are several variables, the solution is given as a list of rules: {*x* -> $s_x$, *y* -> $s_y$, ...}. ▪ When there are several solutions, Solve gives a list of them. ▪ When a particular root has multiplicity greater than one, Solve gives several copies of the corresponding solution. ▪ Solve deals primarily with linear and polynomial equations. ▪ Solve gives generic solutions only. It discards solutions that are valid only when the parameters satisfy special conditions. Reduce gives the complete set of solutions. ▪ Solve will not always be able to get explicit solutions to equations. It will give the explicit solutions it can, then give a symbolic representation of the remaining solutions, in terms of the function Roots. If there are sufficiently few symbolic parameters, you can then use N to get numerical approximations to the solutions. ▪ Solve gives {} if there are no possible solutions to the equations. ▪ Solve[*eqns*, ..., Mode->Modular] solves equations with equality required only modulo an integer. You can specify a particular modulus to use by including the equation Modulus==*p*. If you do not include such an equation, Solve will attempt to solve for the possible moduli. ▪ See page 400. ▪ See also: Reduce, Eliminate, Roots, NRoots, FindRoot, LinearSolve.

■ SolveAlways

SolveAlways[*eqns*, *vars*] gives the values of parameters that make the equations *eqns* valid for all values of the variables *vars*.

Equations are given in the form *lhs* == *rhs*. ▪ Simultaneous equations can be combined either in a list or with &&. ▪ A single variable or a list of variables can be specified. ▪ Example: SolveAlways[a x + b == 0, x] ⟶ {{b -> 0, a -> 0}}. ▪ SolveAlways works primarily with linear and polynomial equations. ▪ SolveAlways produces relations between parameters that appear in *eqns*, but are not in the list of variables *vars*. ▪ SolveAlways[*eqns*, *vars*] is equivalent to Solve[!Eliminate[!*eqns*, *vars*]]. ▪ See page 408. ▪ See also: Eliminate, Solve, Reduce, AlgebraicRules.

■ Sort

Sort[*list*] sorts the elements of *list* into canonical order.

Sort[*list*, *p*] sorts using the ordering function *p*.

Example: Sort[{b, c, a}] ⟶ {a, b, c}. ▪ Canonical order has several properties. Smaller numbers of a particular type come first. Symbols are ordered lexicographically according to their textual names. Strings are ordered lexicographically. Shorter expressions come first. ▪ Sort[*list*, *p*] applies the function *p* to pairs of elements in *list* to determine whether they are in order. The default function *p* is OrderedQ[{#1, #2}]&. ▪ Example: Sort[{4, 1, 3}, Greater] ⟶ {4, 3, 1}. ▪ Sort can be used on expressions with any head, not necessarily List. ▪ See page 103. ▪ See also: Order, OrderedQ, Orderless.

■ SphericalHarmonicY

SphericalHarmonicY[*l*, *m*, *theta*, *phi*] gives the spherical harmonic $Y_l^m(\theta, \phi)$.

Mathematical function (see Section B.3.8). ▪ The spherical harmonics are orthogonal with respect to integration over the surface of the unit sphere. ▪ See page 360. ▪ See also: LegendreP.

## ■ Splice

`Splice["`*file*`"]` splices *Mathematica* output into an external file. It takes text enclosed between `<*` and `*>` in the file, evaluates the text as *Mathematica* input, and replaces the text with the resulting *Mathematica* output.

`Splice["`*infile*`", "`*outfile*`"]` processes text from the file *infile*, and writes output into *outfile*. ■ `Splice["\#`*file*`"]` takes files with names of the form *name*`.mx` and writes output in files with names *name*`.x`. ■ Text in the input file not enclosed between `<*` and `*>` is copied without change to the output file. ■ The default format for *Mathematica* output is determined by the extension of the input file name:

| | |
|---|---|
| *name*`.mc` | `CForm` |
| *name*`.mf` | `FortranForm` |
| *name*`.mtex` | `TeXForm` |

■ The following options for `Splice` can be used:

| | | |
|---|---|---|
| `Delimiters` | `{"<*", "*>"}` | delimiters to search for |
| `FormatType` | `Automatic` | default format for *Mathematica* output |
| `PageWidth` | `78` | number of character widths per output line |

■ You can use pipes instead of files for input and output to `Splice`. ■ See page 158. ■ See also: `RunThrough`, `CallProcess`.

## ■ Sqrt

`Sqrt[`*z*`]` gives the square root of *z*.

Mathematical function (see Section B.3.8). ■ `Sqrt[`*z*`]` is converted to *z*`^(1/2)`. ■ See page 28. ■ See also: `Power`.

## ■ StartProcess

`StartProcess["`*command*`"]` starts up an external process in which functions can be called from *Mathematica*.

`StartProcess` returns a list of the functions that you can call in the external process. ■ `StartProcess` makes assignments in terms of `CallProcess` for functions that you can call in the external process. ■ See page 304. ■ See also: `EndProcess`.

## ■ StirlingS1

`StirlingS1[`*n*`,` *m*`]` gives the Stirling number of the first kind $S_n^{(m)}$.

Integer mathematical function (see Section B.3.8). ■ $(-1)^{n-m} S_n^{(m)}$ gives the number of permutations of $n$ elements which contain exactly $m$ cycles. ■ See page 350.

## ■ StirlingS2

`StirlingS2[`*n*`,` *m*`]` gives the Stirling number of the second kind $\mathcal{S}_n^{(m)}$.

Integer mathematical function (see Section B.3.8). ■ $\mathcal{S}_n^{(m)}$ gives the number of ways of partitioning a set of $n$ elements into $m$ non-empty subsets. ■ See page 350.

■ String

> String is the head of a string "*text*".

The following codes can be used for special characters in strings:

| | |
|---|---|
| \" | a " to be included in the string |
| \n | a newline (line feed) |
| \t | a tab |
| \\*nnn* | a character with octal code *nnn* |

▪ Note that the correspondence of octal codes with characters may depend on the computer system you are using. ▪ *x*_String can be used as a pattern that represents a string. ▪ String is used as a tag to indicate strings in Read. ▪ See page 278. ▪ See also: ToExpression.

■ StringBreak

> StringBreak[*n*] is output at the end of the $n^{\text{th}}$ line where a string is broken.

StringBreak is used when symbol names, strings and numbers are broken. ▪ You can think of StringBreak as being like a "hyphenation character". ▪ The default setting for Format[StringBreak[_]] is "\". ▪ You can specify what is printed when a string is broken by defining a new value for Format[StringBreak[n_]]. ▪ See page 588. ▪ See also: Continuation, LineBreak, Indent.

■ StringForm

> StringForm["*controlstring*", *expr*$_1$, ...] prints the text of the *controlstring*, with the printed forms of the *expr*$_i$ embedded.

`i` in the control string indicates a point at which to print *expr*$_i$. ▪ `` includes the next *expr*$_i$ not yet printed. ▪ \` prints a raw ` in the output string. ▪ You can use StringForm to set up "formatted output". ▪ The messages in the file msg.m are all used as control strings in StringForm. ▪ See page 283. ▪ See also: SequenceForm.

■ StringJoin

> StringJoin["*s₁*", "*s₂*", ...] concatenates the strings *s*$_i$.

Example: StringJoin["the", " ", "cat"] $\longrightarrow$ the cat. ▪ See page 280. ▪ See also: Join, Characters.

■ StringLength

> StringLength["*string*"] gives the number of characters in a string.

Example: StringLength["tiger"] $\longrightarrow$ 5. ▪ See page 280. ▪ See also: Length, Characters.

■ **StringMatchQ**

StringMatchQ["*string*", "*pattern*"] yields True if *string* matches the string *pattern*, and yields False otherwise.

The pattern string can contain literal characters, together with the following special characters:

| | |
|---|---|
| * | zero or more alphanumeric characters |
| ** | zero or more alphanumeric characters, or $ |
| @ | one or more lower-case letters |
| \* etc. | literal * etc. |

■ Example: StringMatchQ["apppbb", "a*b"] $\longrightarrow$ True. ■ See page 307. ■ See also: Equal, Names, MatchQ.

■ **StringSkeleton**

StringSkeleton[*n*] represents a sequence of *n* omitted characters in a string printed with Short.

The standard print form for StringSkeleton is an ellipsis.

You can reset the print form of StringSkeleton. ■ See page 588. ■ See also: Short, Skeleton, TotalWidth.

■ **Subscript**

Subscript[*expr*] prints *expr* as a subscript.

Subscript[*expr*] prints with the top of *expr* below the baseline. ■ Example: f[Subscript[x], y] $\longrightarrow$ f[$_x$, y]. ■ See page 277. ■ See also: Superscript, ColumnForm.

■ **Subscripted**

Subscripted[*f*[$arg_1$, $arg_2$, ...]] prints with the $arg_i$ given as subscripts of *f*.

Subscripted[*expr*, *sub*, *sup*] prints with the arguments specified by *sub* as subscripts, and the arguments specified by *sup* as superscripts. Arguments not included either in *sub* or *sup* are printed in standard functional form.

The specification *n* takes the first *n* arguments. -*n* takes the last *n* arguments. {*m*, *n*} takes arguments *m* through *n*.

Example: Subscripted[f[a,b]] $\longrightarrow$ f$_{a,b}$. ■ Subscripted takes standard sequence specifications, as used by Take and Drop. ■ Example: Subscripted[f[a,b,c], 1] $\longrightarrow$ f$_a$[b,c]. ■ Subscripted[*expr*, {}, *sup*] can be used to specify superscripts only. ■ Subscripted does not allow subscript and superscript specifications that overlap. ■ See page 275. ■ See also: ColumnForm.

■ **Subtract**

*x* - *y* is equivalent to *x* + (-1 * *y*).

See page 25. ■ See also: Minus, Decrement.

■ SubtractFrom

> $x$ -= $dx$ subtracts $dx$ from $x$ and returns the new value of $x$.

> SubtractFrom has the attribute HoldFirst. ▪ $x$ -= $dx$ is equivalent to $x = x - dx$. ▪ See page 257. ▪ See also: Decrement, PreDecrement, Set.

■ Sum

> Sum[$f$, {$i$, $imax$}] evaluates the sum $\sum_{i=1}^{imax} f$.

> Sum[$f$, {$i$, $imin$, $imax$}] starts with $i = imin$. Sum[$f$, {$i$, $imin$, $imax$, $di$}] uses steps $di$.

> Sum[$f$, {$i$, $imin$, $imax$}, {$j$, $jmin$, $jmax$}, ...] evaluates the multiple sum $\sum_{i=imin}^{imax} \sum_{j=jmin}^{jmax} \cdots f$.

> Sum evaluates its arguments in a non-standard way (see page 569). ▪ Sum uses the standard *Mathematica* iteration specification. ▪ The iteration variable $i$ is treated as local. ▪ In multiple sums, the range of the outermost variable is given first. ▪ See page 69. ▪ See also: Do, Product, Table.

■ Superscript

> Superscript[$expr$] prints $expr$ as a superscript.

> Superscript[$expr$] prints with the bottom of $expr$ one character height above the baseline. ▪ Example: f[Superscript[x], y] $\longrightarrow$ f[$^x$, y]. ▪ See page 277. ▪ See also: Subscript, Subscripted, ColumnForm.

■ SurfaceGraphics

> SurfaceGraphics[$array$] is a representation of a three-dimensional plot of a surface, with heights of each point on a grid specified by values in $array$.

> SurfaceGraphics[$array$, $shades$] represents a surface, whose parts are shaded according to the array $shades$.

> SurfaceGraphics can be displayed using Show. ▪ The same options can be given for SurfaceGraphics as for ListPlot3D. ▪ $array$ should be a rectangular array of real numbers, representing $z$ values. There will be holes in the surface corresponding to any array elements that are not real numbers. ▪ If $array$ has dimensions $m \times n$, then $shades$ must have dimensions $(m-1) \times (n-1)$. ▪ The elements of $shades$ must be either GrayLevel[$i$] or RGBColor[$r$, $g$, $b$]. ▪ SurfaceGraphics is generated by Plot3D and ListPlot3D. ▪ See page 120. ▪ See also: ListPlot3D, Plot3D, ContourGraphics, DensityGraphics.

■ Switch

> Switch[$expr$, $form_1$, $value_1$, $form_2$, $value_2$, ...] evaluates $expr$, then compares it with each of the $form_i$ in turn, evaluating and returning the $value_i$ corresponding to the first match found.

> Only the $value_i$ corresponding to the first $form_i$ that matches $expr$ is evaluated. Each $form_i$ is evaluated only when the match is tried. ▪ If the last $form_i$ is the pattern _, then the corresponding $value_i$ is always returned if this case is reached. ▪ If no $value_i$ is returned, the final value of the Switch is Null. ▪ You can use Break, Return and Throw in Switch. ▪ See page 258. ▪ See also: If, Condition, Which.

■ **Symbol**

Symbol is the head associated with a symbol.

Example: Head[x] ⟶ Symbol. ▪ *x*_Symbol can be used as a pattern than represents a symbol. ▪ See page 551.

■ **Table**

Table[*expr*, {*imax*}] generates a list of *imax* copies of *expr*.

Table[*expr*, {*i*, *imax*}] generates a list of the values of *expr* when *i* runs from 1 to *imax*.

Table[*expr*, {*i*, *imin*, *imax*}] starts with *i* = *imin*. Table[*expr*, {*i*, *imin*, *imax*, *di*}] uses steps *di*.

Table[*expr*, {*i*, *imin*, *imax*}, {*j*, *jmin*, *jmax*}, ...] gives a nested list. The list associated with *i* is outermost.

Table evaluates its arguments in a non-standard way (see page 569). ▪ Example: Table[f[i], {i, 4}] ⟶ {f[1], f[2], f[3], f[4]}. ▪ Table uses the standard *Mathematica* iteration specification. ▪ Example: Table[i-j, {i, 2}, {j, 2}] ⟶ {{0, -1}, {1, 0}}. ▪ You can use Table to build up vectors, matrices and tensors. ▪ See page 90. ▪ See also: Range, DiagonalMatrix, IdentityMatrix, Array, Do, Sum, Product.

■ **TableForm**

TableForm[*list*] prints with the elements of *list* arranged in tabular form.

TableForm[*list*, *d*] puts elements down to level *d* in *list* in tabular form.

TableForm prints the elements arranged in an array of rectangular cells. ▪ The height of each row and the width of each column are determined by the maximum size of an element in the row or column. ▪ Unlike MatrixForm, TableForm does not require all cells in the table to be the same size, or to be square. ▪ TableForm prints a single level list in a column. It prints a two-level list as a two-dimensional table. More deeply nested lists are printed with successive dimensions alternating between rows and columns. ▪ See page 272. ▪ See also: ColumnForm, MatrixForm.

■ **TagSet**

*f*/: *lhs* = *rhs* assigns *rhs* to be the value of *lhs*, and associates the assignment with the symbol *f*.

You can associate a particular transformation rule with any of the symbols that appear in it. ▪ A common case is *f*: *h*[*f*[*args*]] = *rhs*. ▪ You can see all the rules associated with a particular symbol by typing ?*symbol*. ▪ If *f* appears several times in *lhs*, then *f*/: *lhs* = *rhs* associates the assignment with each occurrence. ▪ See pages 208 and 574. ▪ See also: Set, UpSet.

■ **TagSetDelayed**

*f*/: *lhs* := *rhs* assigns *rhs* to be the delayed value of *lhs*, and associates the assignment with the symbol *f*.

See notes for TagSet and SetDelayed. ▪ See page 208.

■ **TagUnset**

$f/$: *lhs* =. removes any rules defined for *lhs*, associated with the symbol $f$.

Rules are removed only when their left-hand side is identical to *lhs*, and the tests in `Condition` given on the right-hand side are also identical. ■ See page 575. ■ See also: `Clear`, `Unset`.

■ **Take**

`Take[`*list*`, ` *n*`]` gives the first $n$ elements of *list*.

`Take[`*list*`, ` *-n*`]` gives the last $n$ elements of *list*.

`Take[`*list*`, {`*m*`, ` *n*`}]` elements $m$ through $n$ of *list*.

Take uses the standard *sequence specification*. ■ Example: `Take[{a,b,c,d,e}, 3]` ⟶ `{a, b, c}`. ■ `Take[{a,b,c,d,e}, -2]` ⟶ `{d, e}`. ■ `Take` can be used on an object with any head, not necessarily `List`. ■ See page 99. ■ See also: `Part`, `Drop`, `Cases`.

■ **Tan**

`Tan[`*z*`]` gives the tangent of $z$.

Mathematical function (see Section B.3.8). ■ The argument of `Tan` is assumed to be in radians. (Multiply by `Degree` to convert from degrees.) ■ See page 353. ■ See also: `ArcTan`, `Cot`.

■ **Tanh**

`Tanh[`*z*`]` gives the hyperbolic tangent of $z$.

Mathematical function (see Section B.3.8). ■ See page 353. ■ See also: `ArcTanh`, `Coth`.

■ **TensorRank**

`TensorRank[`*expr*`]` gives the depth to which *expr* is a full array, with all the parts at a particular level being lists of the same length.

`TensorRank[`*list*`]` is equivalent to `Length[Dimensions[`*list*`]]`. ■ Examples: `TensorRank[{a,b}]` ⟶ 1; `TensorRank[{a,{b}}]` ⟶ 1. ■ `TensorRank[`*expr*`, ` *h*`]` looks for head $h$ at each level. ■ See page 456. ■ See also: `Dimensions`, `Depth`, `VectorQ`, `MatrixQ`.

■ **TeXForm**

`TeXForm[`*expr*`]` prints as a TEX language version of *expr*.

TeXForm produces plain TEX. Its output should be suitable for both LATEX and AMSTEX. ■ `TeXForm` translates standard mathematical functions and operations. ■ Symbols with names like `alpha` and `ALPHA` that correspond to TEX symbols are translated into their corresponding TEX symbols. ■ Following standard mathematical conventions, single character symbol names are given in italic font, while multiple character names are given in roman font. ■ Print forms such as `ColumnForm`, `MatrixForm` and `Subscripted` are translated by `TeXForm`. ■ See page 157.

## ■ Text

Text[*expr*, *coords*] is a graphics primitive that represents text corresponding to the printed form of *expr*, centered at the point specified by *coords*.

The *text* is printed by default in OutputForm. ▪ Text can be used in both Graphics and Graphics3D. ▪ The coordinates can be specified either as {*x*, *y*, ...} or as Scaled[{*x*, *y*, ...}]. ▪ Text[*expr*, *coords*, *offset*] specifies an offset for the block of text relative to the coordinates given. Giving an offset {*sdx*, *sdy*} specifies that the point {*x*, *y*} should lie at relative coordinates {*sdx*, *sdy*} within the bounding rectangle that encloses the text. Each relative coordinate runs from −1 to 1 across the bounding rectangle. ▪ Here are sample offsets to use in two-dimensional graphics:

{0, 0}          text centered at {*x*, *y*}
{-1, 0}          left-hand end at {*x*, *y*}
{1, 0}          right-hand end at {*x*, *y*}
{0, 1}          centered above {*x*, *y*}
{0, -1}          centered below {*x*, *y*}

▪ See page 142. ▪ See also: PlotLabel, AxesLabel.

## ■ TextForm

TextForm[*expr*] prints as a textual form of *expr*.

TextForm prints standard expressions in OutputForm. ▪ TextForm prints strings in a way that corresponds to standard text. It break lines only at word boundaries, and does not put blank lines between lines of text. ▪ See page 283.

## ■ TextRendering

TextRendering is an option for OpenWrite etc. and ResetMedium which specifies how text is to be rendered in a particular output file.

Possible settings are:

Plain          plain character display
PostScript          POSTSCRIPT

▪ See page 295.

## ■ Thickness

Thickness[*x*] is a graphics primitive which specifies that lines which follow are to be drawn with a thickness *x*. The thickness *x* is given as a fraction of the total width of the graph.

Thickness can be used with both Graphics and Graphics3D. ▪ See pages 142 and 149. ▪ See also: PointSize, Dashing, GrayLevel, RGBColor.

## ■ Thread

Thread[*f*[*args*]] "threads" *f* over any lists that appear in *args*.

Thread[*f*[*args*], *n*] threads *f* over lists that appear in the first *n args*.

Thread[*f*[*args*], -*n*] threads over the last *n args*.

Thread[*f*[*args*], {*n*, *m*}] threads over arguments *n* through *m*.

Thread[*f*[*args*], *spec*, *h*] threads *f* over any objects with head *h* that appear.

Example: Thread[f[{a,b}, c, {d,e}]] $\longrightarrow$ {f[a, c, d], f[b, c, e]}. ■ Functions with attribute Listable are automatically threaded over lists. ■ All the elements in *args* whose head is *h* must be of the same length. ■ Arguments that do not have head *h* are copied as many times as there are elements in the arguments that do have head *h*. ■ Thread uses the standard *sequence specification*. ■ See page 250. ■ See also: Distribute, Map, Inner.

## ■ Through

Through[*p*[*f₁*, *f₂*][*x*]] gives *p*[*f₁*[*x*], *f₂*[*x*]].

Through[*expr*, *h*] performs the transformation wherever *h* occurs in the head of *expr*.

Example: Through[(f + g)[x, y]] $\longrightarrow$ f[x, y] + g[x, y]. ■ Through distributes operators that appear inside the heads of expressions. ■ See page 246. ■ See also: Operate.

## ■ Throw

Throw[*expr*] causes exit from nested control structures, returning the value *expr* to the nearest enclosing Catch.

You can use Throw and Catch to implement non-local returns. ■ See page 260. ■ See also: Return, Goto.

## ■ Ticks

Ticks is an option for graphics functions that specifies tick marks for axes.

Ticks -> None specifies that no tick marks should be given. ■ Ticks -> Automatic specifies that tick marks should be chosen automatically. They are usually placed at points whose coordinates have the minimum number of digits in their decimal representation. ■ Ticks -> {*xticks*, *yticks*} specifies tick marks for different axes. Each specification is None, Automatic, or an explicit list of tick mark positions. ■ Ticks can be used in both two- and three-dimensional graphics. ■ See page 109. ■ See also: Axes, AxesLabel.

## ■ TimeConstrained

TimeConstrained[*expr*, *t*] evaluates *expr*, stopping after *t* seconds.

TimeConstrained generates an interrupt to stop the evaluation of *expr* if the evaluation is not completed within the specified time. ■ TimeConstrained returns $Interrupted if the evaluation is interrupted. ■ TimeConstrained has attribute HoldFirst. ■ See page 321. ■ See also: MemoryConstrained, Timing, $RecursionLimit.

■ Times

> $x*y*z$ or $x\ y\ z$ represents a product of terms.

Times has attributes Flat, Orderless and OneIdentity. ■ The default value for arguments of Times, as used in $x_-$. patterns, is 1. ■ Times[ ] is taken to be 1. ■ Times[x] is $x$. ■ See page 25. ■ See also: Divide, NonCommutativeMultiply, Dot.

■ TimesBy

> $x$ *= $c$ multiplies $x$ by $c$ returns the new value of $x$.

TimesBy has the attribute HoldFirst. ■ $x$ *= $c$ is equivalent to $x = x*c$. ■ See page 257. ■ See also: DivideBy, AddTo, Set.

■ Timing

> Timing[*expr*] evaluates *expr*, and returns a list of time used, together with the result obtained.

Timing has attribute HoldAll. ■ Timing[*expr*;] will give {*timing*, Null}. ■ See page 317. ■ See also: TimeConstrained, ByteCount.

■ ToASCII

> ToASCII["*c*"] gives the ASCII integer code corresponding to the character *c*.

ToASCII gives character codes in the native character set used by your computer. These codes may not necessarily be true ASCII. ■ ToASCII works only on single-character strings. ■ See page 279. ■ See also: Characters, FromASCII.

■ ToExpression

> ToExpression["*string*"] gives the expression obtained by taking *string* as *Mathematica* input.

Example: ToExpression["1 + 1"] $\longrightarrow$ 2. ■ ToExpression remains unevaluated if a *Mathematica* syntax error occurs when *string* is parsed. ■ See page 281. ■ See also: ToString, Read.

■ Together

> Together[*expr*] puts terms in a sum over a common denominator, and cancels factors in the result.

Example: Together[1/x + 1/(1-x)] $\longrightarrow$ $-\left(\dfrac{1}{-x + x^2}\right)$. ■ Together makes a sum of terms into a single rational function. ■ The denominator of the result of Together is the lowest common multiple of the denominators of each of the terms in the sum. ■ Together is effectively the inverse of Apart. ■ See page 386. ■ See also: Collect, Cancel, Factor.

■ **ToRules**

ToRules[*eqns*] takes logical combinations of equations, in the form generated by Reduce or Roots, and converts them to lists of rules, of the form produced by Solve.

Example: {ToRules[x==1 || x==2]} $\longrightarrow$ {{x -> 1}, {x -> 2}}. ■ ToRules discards nonequalities (!=), and thus gives only "generic" solutions. ■ See pages 394 and 476.

■ **ToString**

ToString[*expr*] gives a string corresponding to the printed form of *expr*.

ToString uses InputForm by default. ■ See page 281. ■ See also: ToExpression, HoldForm, WriteString.

■ **TotalHeight**

TotalHeight is an option for OpenWrite etc. and ResetMedium which specifies the maximum number of lines of text that should be printed for each output expression. Short forms of expressions are given if the number of lines needed to print the whole expression is too large.

With TextRendering -> Plain, TotalHeight bounds the actual numbers of lines generated. ■ With TextRendering -> PostScript, TotalHeight bounds the number of em spaces (number of times the width of an m character). ■ TotalHeight -> Infinity allows expressions of any length to be printed. ■ See also: Short, Skeleton, PageHeight.

■ **TotalWidth**

TotalWidth is an option for OpenWrite etc. and ResetMedium which specifies the maximum total number of characters of text that should be printed for each output expression. Short forms of expressions are given if the number of characters needed to print the whole expression is too large.

With TextRendering -> Plain, TotalWidth bounds the actual numbers of characters generated. Line breaks are not counted. ■ With TextRendering -> PostScript, TotalWidth bounds the number of em spaces (number of times the width of an m character). ■ TotalWidth -> Infinity allows expressions of any length to be printed. ■ See also: Short, Skeleton, PageWidth.

■ **Transpose**

Transpose[*list*] transposes the first two levels in *list*.

Transpose[*list*, {$n_1$, $n_2$, ...}] transposes *list* so that the $n_k$<sup>th</sup> level in *list* is the $k$<sup>th</sup> level in the result.

Example: Transpose[{{a,b},{c,d}}] $\longrightarrow$ {{a, c}, {b, d}}. ■ Transpose gives the usual transpose of a matrix. ■ Acting on a tensor $T_{i_1 i_2 i_3 \ldots}$ Transpose gives the tensor $T_{i_2 i_1 i_3 \ldots}$. ■ Transpose[*list*, {$n_1$, $n_2$, ...}] gives the tensor $T_{i_{n_1} i_{n_2} \ldots}$. ■ The level specifications $n_k$ do not necessarily have to be distinct. ■ See page 446. ■ See also: Flatten.

■ **TreeForm**

TreeForm[*expr*] prints with different levels in *expr* shown with different indentations.

See pages 173 and 270. ■ See also: FullForm, MatrixForm.

■ True

    **True** is the symbol for the Boolean value true.

    See page 71. ■ See also: `True`, `TrueQ`.

■ TrueQ

    **TrueQ**[*expr*] yields **True** if *expr* is **True**, and yields **False** otherwise.

    Example: `TrueQ[x==y]` $\longrightarrow$ `False`. ■ You can use `TrueQ` to "assume" that a test fails when its outcome is not clear. ■ `TrueQ[`*expr*`]` is equivalent to `If[`*expr*`, True, False, False]`. ■ See page 259. ■ See also: `If`, `Condition`, `SameQ`.

■ UnAlias

    `"`*input*`" ::=.`   removes any alias defined for *input*.

    **UnAlias**[ ] removes all aliases that have been defined.

    See page 305. ■ See also: `Alias`, `Names`, `Remove`.

■ Unequal

    *lhs* `!=` *rhs* returns **False** if *lhs* and *rhs* are identical.

    *lhs* `!=` *rhs* returns **True** if *lhs* and *rhs* are determined to be unequal by comparisons between numbers or other raw data, such as strings. ■ **Real** numbers are considered unequal if their difference is larger than the precision of either of them. ■ $e_1$ `!=` $e_2$ `!=` $e_3$ `!=` ... gives **True** only if none of the $e_i$ are equal. `2 != 3 != 2` $\longrightarrow$ `False`. ■ *lhs* `!=` *rhs* represents a symbolic condition, that can be generated and manipulated by functions like `FullSolve` and `LogicalExpand`. ■ `Unequal[`*e*`]` gives **True**. ■ See page 72. ■ See also: `Equal`, `Order`.

■ Union

    **Union**[*list₁*, *list₂*, ...] gives a sorted list of all the distinct elements that appear in any of the *listᵢ*.

    **Union**[*list*] gives a sorted version of a list, in which all duplicated elements have been dropped.

    If the *listᵢ* are considered as sets, **Union** gives their union. ■ The *listᵢ* must have the same head, but it need not be **List**. ■ See page 103. ■ See also: `Join`, `Intersection`, `Complement`.

■ Unique

    **Unique**[ ] generates a new symbol, whose name is of the form $\$n$.

    **Unique**[`"`*name*`"`] generates a new symbol, with a name of the form *namen*.

    **Unique** uses the smallest positive integer *n* that gives a symbol that does not already exist. ■ See page 308. ■ See also: `ToExpression`, `Names`.

■ Unprotect

>    Unprotect[$s_1$, $s_2$, ...] removes the attribute Protected for the symbols $s_i$.
>
>    Unprotect["$form_1$", "$form_2$", ...] unprotects all symbols whose names textually match any of the $form_i$.
>
>    A typical sequence in adding your own rules for built-in functions is Unprotect[$f$]; *definition*; Protect[$f$]. ■ See notes for Protect. ■ See pages 196 and 566. ■ See also: Protect, Locked, SetOptions.

■ Unset

>    *lhs* =. removes any rules defined for *lhs*.
>
>    Rules are removed only when their left-hand side is identical to *lhs*. ■ See page 575. ■ See also: Clear, TagUnset.

■ Update

>    Update[*symbol*] specifies that hidden changes have been made which could affect values associated with a symbol.
>
>    Update[ ] specifies that the value of any symbol could be affected.
>
>    Update manipulates internal optimization features of *Mathematica*. It should not need to be called except under very special circumstances that very rarely occur in practice. ■ One special circumstance is that changes in the value of one symbol can affect the value of another symbol by changing the outcome of Condition tests. In such cases, you may need to use Update on the symbol you think may be affected. ■ Using Update will never give you incorrect results, although it will slow down the operation of the system. ■ See page 223.

■ UpSet

>    *lhs*^=*rhs* assigns *rhs* to be the value of *lhs*, and associates the assignment with symbols that occur at level one in *lhs*.
>
>    $f[g[x]]$=*value* makes an assignment associated with $f$. $f[g[x]]$^=*value* makes an assignment associated instead with $g$. ■ UpSet associates an assignment with *all* the distinct symbols that occur either directly as arguments of *lhs*, or as the heads of arguments of *lhs*. ■ See pages 210 and 574. ■ See also: TagSet.

■ UpSetDelayed

>    *lhs*^:=*rhs* assigns *rhs* to be the delayed value of *lhs*, and associates the assignment with symbols that occur at level one in *lhs*.
>
>    See notes for UpSet and SetDelayed. ■ See page 210.

■ ValueQ

>    ValueQ[*expr*] gives True if a value has been defined for *expr*, and gives False otherwise.
>
>    ValueQ has attribute HoldFirst. ■ ValueQ gives False only if *expr* would not change if it was to be entered as *Mathematica* input. ■ See page 230. ■ See also: Information.

# ■ Variables

Variables[*poly*] gives a list of all independent variables in a polynomial.

See page 383. ■ See also: Coefficient.

### VectorQ

VectorQ[*expr*] gives True if *expr* is a list, none of whose elements are themselves lists, and gives False otherwise.

See pages 230 and 440. ■ See also: MatrixQ, TensorRank.

### ViewPoint

ViewPoint is an option for Graphics3D and SurfaceGraphics which gives the point in space from which the objects plotted are to be viewed.

ViewPoint -> {x, y, z} gives the position of the viewpoint relative to the center of the three-dimensional box that contains the object being plotted. The coordinates are scaled so that the longest side of the box has length 1. ■ Common settings for ViewPoint are:

| | |
|---|---|
| {0, -2, 0} | directly in front |
| {0, -2, 2} | in front and up |
| {0, -2, -2} | in front and down |
| {-2, -2, 0} | left-hand corner |
| {2, -2, 0} | right-hand corner |
| {0, 0, 2} | directly above |

■ Choosing ViewPoint further away from the object reduces the distortion associated with perspective. ■ See page 123. ■ See also: Plot3Matrix.

### WeierstrassP

WeierstrassP[*u*, *g2*, *g3*] gives the Weierstrass elliptic function $\wp(u; g_2, g_3)$.

$\wp(u; g_2, g_3)$ gives the value of $x$ for which $u = \int_{\infty}^{x} (4t^3 - g_2 t - g_3)^{-\frac{1}{2}} \, dt$. ■ See page 374.

### WeierstrassPPrime

WeierstrassPPrime[*u*, *g2*, *g3*] gives the derivative Weierstrass elliptic function $\wp'(u; g_2, g_3)$.

$\wp'(u; g_2, g_3) = \frac{\partial}{\partial u} \wp(u; g_2, g_3)$. ■ See page 374.

# ■ Which

Which[*test₁*, *value₁*, *test₂*, *value₂*, ...] evaluates each of the *testᵢ* in turn, returning the value of the *valueᵢ* corresponding to the first one that yields True.

Example: Which[a==b, x, 1==1, y] ⟶ y. ■ Which has attribute HoldAll. ■ If none of the *testᵢ* give True, Which returns Null. ■ You can make Which return a "default value" by taking the last *valueᵢ* to be True. ■ See page 258. ■ See also: Switch.

## ■ While

While[*test*, *body*] evaluates *test*, then *body*, repetitively, until *test* first fails to give **True**.

While[*test*] does the loop with a null body. ■ If Break[ ] is generated in the evaluation of *body*, the While loop exits. ■ Continue[ ] exits the evaluation of *body*, and continues the loop. ■ Unless Return[ ] or Throw[ ] are generated, the final value returned by While is Null. ■ Example: i=0; While[i < 0, tot += f[i]; i++]. Note that the roles of ; and , are *reversed* relative to the C programming language. ■ See page 254. ■ See also: Do, For.

## ■ WorkingPrecision

WorkingPrecision is an option for various numerical operations which specifies how many digits of precision should be maintained in internal computations.

WorkingPrecision is an option for such functions as NIntegrate and FindRoot. ■ Setting WorkingPrecision->*n* causes all internal computations to be done to at most *n*-digit precision. ■ Even if internal computations are done to *n*-digit precision, the final results you get may have much lower precision. ■ See page 472. ■ See also: AccuracyGoal, Precision, Accuracy, N.

## ■ Write

Write[*channel*, *expr_1*, *expr_2*, ...] writes the expressions *expr_i* in sequence to the specified output channel.

The output channel can be a single file or pipe, or list of them, each specified by a string giving their name. ■ Write is the basic *Mathematica* output function. Print and Message are defined in terms of it. ■ If any of the specified files or pipes are not already open, Write calls OpenWrite to open them. ■ Write does not close files and pipes after it finishes writing to them. ■ By default, Write generates output in the form specified by the setting of the FormatType option for the output media used. ■ See page 292. ■ See also: Print, Display, Message, Read.

## ■ WriteString

WriteString[*channel*, *expr_1*, *expr_2*, ...] converts the *expr_i* to strings, and then writes them in sequence to the specified output channel.

WriteString uses the InputForm of the *expr_i*. ■ WriteString allows you to create files which are effectively just streams of bytes. ■ See notes for Write. ■ See page 292.

## ■ Xor

Xor[*e_1*, *e_2*, ...] is the logical XOR (exclusive OR) function.

It gives **True** if an odd number of the *e_i* are **True**, and the rest are **False**. It gives **False** if an even number are **True**, and the rest are **False**.

Xor gives symbolic results when necessary, and applies various simplification rules to them. ■ Unlike And and Or, Xor is not a control structure, and does not have attribute HoldAll. ■ See page 73. ■ See also: LogicalExpand.

■ ZeroTest

> **ZeroTest** is an option for **LinearSolve** and other linear algebra functions, which gives a function to be applied to combinations of matrix elements to determine whether or not they should be considered equal to zero.

> For matrices with symbolic entries, `ZeroTest->(Expand[#]==0 &)` is often appropriate.  ▪ See page 451.

■ Zeta

> **Zeta[s]** gives the Riemann zeta function $\zeta(s)$.

> **Zeta[s, a]** gives the generalized Riemann zeta function $\zeta(s, a)$.

> Mathematical function (see Section B.3.8).  ▪ $\zeta(s) = \sum_{k=1}^{\infty} k^{-s}$.  ▪ $\zeta(s, a) = \sum_{k=0}^{\infty} (k + a)^{-s}$, where any term with $k + a = 0$ is excluded.  ▪ See page 364.  ▪ See also: **PolyLog**, **LerchPhi**.

■ \$CommandLine

> **\$CommandLine** is a list of strings giving the elements of the original operating system command line with which *Mathematica* was invoked.

> See page 577.  ▪ See also: **Environment**.

■ \$Context

> **\$Context** is a global variable that gives the current context.

> Contexts are specified by strings of the form `"name`"`.  ▪ **\$Context** is modified by **Begin**, **End** and **EndAdd**.  ▪ **\$Context** is a rough analog for *Mathematica* symbols of the current working directory for files in many operating systems.  ▪ See pages 313, 550 and 577.  ▪ See also: **Context**.

■ \$ContextPath

> **\$ContextPath** is a global variable that gives a list of contexts to search in trying to find a symbol that has been entered.

> Each context is specified by a string of the form `"name`"`.  ▪ The elements of **\$ContextPath** are tested in order to try and find a context containing a particular symbol.  ▪ **\$ContextPath** is modified by **Begin**, **End** and **EndAdd**.  ▪ **\$ContextPath** is a rough analog for *Mathematica* symbols of the "search path" for files in many operating systems.  ▪ See pages 313, 550 and 577.

■ \$Display

> **\$Display** gives a list of files and pipes to be used with the default **\$DisplayFunction**.

> The initial setting of **\$Display** is {}.  ▪ See pages 294 and 578.

## $DisplayFunction

$DisplayFunction gives the default setting for the option DisplayFunction in graphics functions.

The initial setting of $DisplayFunction is Display[$Display, #]&. ▪ $DisplayFunction is typically set to a procedure which performs the following: (1) open an output channel; (2) send a POSTSCRIPT prolog to the output channel; (3) use Display to send POSTSCRIPT graphics; (4) send POSTSCRIPT epilog; (5) close the output channel and execute the external commands needed to produce actual display. ▪ See page 578. ▪ See also: Display, Put, Run.

## $Echo

$Echo gives a list of files and pipes to which all input is echoed.

You can use $Echo to keep a file of all your input commands. ▪ See pages 294 and 578.

## $Epilog

$Epilog is a symbol whose value, if any, is evaluated when a *Mathematica* session is terminated.

$Epilog is conventionally defined to read in a file named end.m. ▪ See page 577. ▪ See also: Exit, Quit.

## $IgnoreEOF

$IgnoreEOF specifies whether *Mathematica* should terminate when it receives an end-of-file character as input.

$IgnoreEOF defaults to False. ▪ $IgnoreEOF is assumed to be False if the input to *Mathematica* comes from a file, rather than an interactive device. ▪ See pages 577 and 580. ▪ See also: Exit, Quit.

## $Interrupted

$Interrupted is a special symbol that is returned as the result from a calculation that has been interrupted.

See page 579.

## $Line

$Line is a global variable that specifies the number of the current input line.

You can reset $Line. ▪ See page 577. ▪ See also: In, Out.

## $Messages

$Messages gives the list of files and pipes to which message output is sent.

Output from Message is always given on the $Messages channel. ▪ See pages 294 and 578.

## $Output

$Output gives the list of files and pipes to which standard output from *Mathematica* is sent.

Output from Print is always given on the $Output channel.  ▪ See pages 294 and 578. ▪ See also: ResetMedium.

## $Path

$Path gives a list of directories to search in attempting to find an external file.

$Path is used by Get.  ▪ The structure of directory and file names may differ from one computer system to another.  ▪ The directory names are specified by strings. The full file names tested are of the form *directory*/*name*, where the separator / is taken to be the appropriate one for the computer system used.  ▪ On most computer systems, the following special characters can be used in directory names:

.         the current directory

..       the directory one level up in the hierarchy

~       the user's home directory

▪ See pages 296, 577 and 584.

## ■ $Post

$Post is a global variable whose value, if set, is applied to every output expression.

See page 577. ▪ See also: $Pre, $PrePrint.

## $Pre

$Pre is a global variable whose value, if set, is applied to every input expression.

See page 577. ▪ See also: $Post.

## $PrePrint

$PrePrint is a global variable whose value, if set, is applied to every expression before it is printed.

$PrePrint is applied after Out[*n*] is assigned, but before the output result is printed.  ▪ See page 577. ▪ See also: $Post.

## ■ $RecursionLimit

$RecursionLimit gives the current limit on the number of levels of recursion that *Mathematica* can use.

$RecursionLimit=*n* sets the limit on the number of recursion levels that *Mathematica* can use to be *n*.  ▪ $RecursionLimit=Infinity removes any limit on the number of recursion levels.  ▪ Each time the evaluation of a function requires the nested evaluation of the same or another function, one recursion level is used up.  ▪ On most computers, each level of recursion uses a certain amount of stack space. $RecursionLimit allows you to control the amount of stack space that *Mathematica* can use from within *Mathematica*. On some computer systems, your whole *Mathematica* session may crash if you allow it to use more stack space than the computer system allows.  ▪ MemoryInUse and related functions do not count stack space.  ▪ See pages 223, 320, 571 and 577. ▪ See also: MemoryConstrained.

■ **$System**

> **$System** is a string specifying the type of computer system used.
>
> See page 577. ■ See also: **$Version**.

■ **$Urgent**

> **$Urgent** gives the list of files and pipes to which urgent output from *Mathematica* is sent.
>
> Urgent output includes reports of syntax errors in input, and results from ?*name* information requests. ■ See pages 294 and 578.

■ **$Version**

> **$Version** is a string that represents the version of *Mathematica* being used.
>
> See page 577. ■ See also: **$System**.

■ **$$Media**

> **$$Media** is a read-only list of active files and pipes.
>
> The list **$$Media** contains the actual media specifications for the various media that have been opened using **OpenWrite** etc. ■ You can find the options set for a particular medium using **Options**. ■ See pages 294 and 578. ■ See also: **ResetMedia**.

# ■ Special Forms

| | |
|---|---|
| !*expr* | Not[*expr*] |
| *n*! | Factorial[*n*] |
| !*command* | input escape |
| *n*!! | Factorial2[*n*] |
| !!*filename* | input escape |
| *x* != *y* | Unequal[*x*, *y*] |
| *f* @ *expr* | *f*[*expr*] |
| # | Slot[1] (in Function) |
| #*n* | Slot[*n*] |
| ## | SlotSequence[1] |
| ##*n* | SlotSequence[*n*] |
| $*aaa* | symbol name |
| % | Out[] |
| %%...% | Out[-*k*] |
| %*n* | Out[*n*] |
| *x* ∧ *y* | Power[*x*, *y*] |
| *base*∧∧*digits* | number |
| *lhs* ∧= *rhs* | UpSet[*lhs*, *rhs*] |
| *lhs* ∧:= *rhs* | UpSetDelayed[*lhs*, *rhs*] |
| *body*& | Function[*body*] |
| *expr*₁ && *expr*₂ | And[*expr*₁, *expr*₂] |
| *x* * *y* | Times[*x*, *y*] |
| *x* ** *y* | NonCommutativeMultiply[*x*, *y*] |
| (*expr*) | parentheses |
| -*x* | Minus[*x*] |
| *x* - *y* | Subtract[*x*, *y*] |
| *x*-- | Decrement[*x*] |
| --*x* | PreDecrement[*x*] |
| *x* -= *y* | SubtractFrom[*x*, *y*] |
| *lhs* -> *rhs* | Rule[*lhs*, *rhs*] |

| | |
|---|---|
| _ | Blank[] |
| _*h* | Blank[*h*] |
| *x*_ | Pattern[*x*, Blank[]] |
| __ | BlankSequence[] |
| ___ | BlankNullSequence[] |
| *x*. | Optional[*x*] |
| *x* = *y* | Set[*x*, *y*] |
| *x* == *y* | Equal[*x*, *y*] |
| *x* =. | Unset[*x*] |
| *x* + *y* | Plus[*x*, *y*] |
| *x* += *y* | AddTo[*x*, *y*] |
| *x*++ | Increment[*x*] |
| ++*x* | PreIncrement[*x*] |
| *text* \ | line continuation |
| "aaa \c bbb" | special character code |
| *expr*₁ \|\| *expr*₂ | Or[*expr*₁, *expr*₂] |
| *expr*₁~*f*~*expr*₂ | *f*[*expr*₁, *expr*₂] |
| *context*`*name* | context mark |
| *f*[*expr*] | *f*[*expr*] |
| *e*[[*i*, *j*]] | Part[*e*, {*i*, *j*}] |
| {*expr*₁, *expr*₂} | List[*expr*₁, *expr*₂] |
| *expr*₁; *expr*₂ | CompoundExpression[*expr*₁, *expr*₂] |
| *pattern*:*value* | Optional[*pattern*, *value*] |
| *x* := *y* | SetDelayed[*x*, *y*] |
| *s*::*tag* | MessageName[*s*, "*tag*"] |
| *lhs*::=*rhs* | Alias[*lhs*, *rhs*] |
| *lhs* :> *rhs* | RuleDelayed[*lhs*, *rhs*] |

| | |
|---|---|
| *f*' | Derivative[1][*f*] |
| "*text*" | string |
| *f*[*expr*₁,*expr*₂] | argument separator |
| *x* < *y* | Less[*x*, *y*] |
| *x* <= *y* | LessEqual[*x*, *y*] |
| <<*name* | Get["*name*"] |
| *a* . *b* | Dot[*a*, *b*] |
| *ddd*.*ddd* | number |
| *pattern*.. | Repeated[*pattern*] |
| *pattern*... | RepeatedNull[*pattern*] |
| *x* > *y* | Greater[*x*, *y*] |
| *x* >= *y* | GreaterEqual[*x*, *y*] |
| *expr* >> *name* | Put[*expr*, "*name*"] |
| *expr* >>> *name* | PutAppend[*expr*, "*name*"] |
| *x* / *y* | Divide[*x*, *y*] |
| *f* /@ *expr* | Map[*f*, *expr*] |
| *f* /@@ *expr* | Apply[*f*, *expr*] |
| *expr* /; *test* | Condition[*expr*, *test*] |
| *f*/: *x* = *y* | TagSet[*f*, *x*, *y*] |
| *expr* /. *rules* | ReplaceAll[*expr*, *rules*] |
| *expr* // *f* | *f*[*expr*] |
| *f* //@ *expr* | MapAll[*f*, *expr*] |
| *expr* //. *rules* | ReplaceRepeated[*expr*, *rules*] |
| *pattern* ? *test* | Test[*pattern*, *test*] |
| ?*name* | input escape |

# Index

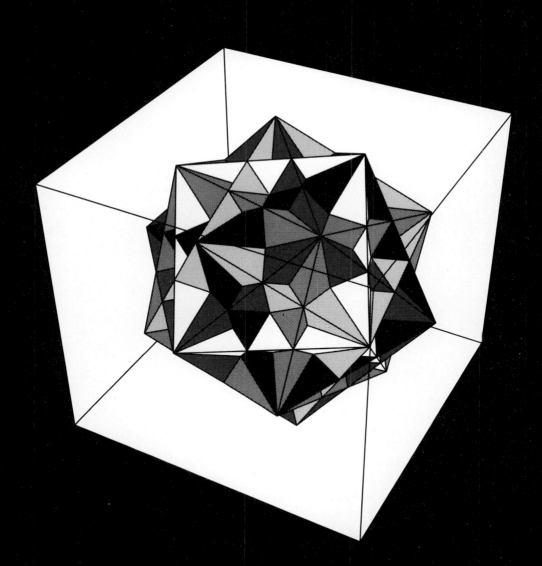

In this index, primary pages for each topic are given in boldface. When a topic continues for several pages, only the first one is listed.

The index includes many synonyms, some quite historical, for items discussed in the book. The particular words used in the index therefore do not always appear in the text.

Pages 743–749 list all the objects that are built into *Mathematica*. More details on them are given in the alphabetical listing that starts on page 593.

The special characters used by *Mathematica* are listed on page 706, and on pages 555–557.

**About the illustration overleaf:**

This picture shows five intersecting cubes, whose corners meet at the vertices of a dodecahedron. Each cube is shown in a different gray level. The picture was produced by first generating the faces of the cubes, and then rendering them by applying `Show` to the resulting `Graphics3D` object. The picture provides an illustration of some important features of the rotational symmetry group of the dodecahedron.

# ■ *Mathematica* Objects Grouped by Category

---

### ■ Mathematical Functions and Objects

| | | | |
|---|---|---|---|
| Abs | Csch | Hypergeometric1F1 | Pochhammer |
| AiryAi | Cyclotomic | Hypergeometric2F1 | PolyGamma |
| ArcCos | Degree | HypergeometricU | PolyLog |
| ArcCosh | DirectedInfinity | I | Power |
| ArcCot | Divide | Im | PowerMod |
| ArcCoth | Divisors | Indeterminate | Prime |
| ArcCsc | DivisorSigma | Infinity | Quotient |
| ArcCsch | Dot | Integer | Random |
| ArcSec | E | InverseJacobiSN | Rational |
| ArcSech | EllipticE | JacobiAmplitude | Rationalize |
| ArcSin | EllipticExp | JacobiP | Re |
| ArcSinh | EllipticF | JacobiSN | Real |
| ArcTan | EllipticK | JacobiSymbol | Round |
| ArcTanh | EllipticLog | LaguerreL | Sec |
| Arg | EllipticPi | LatticeReduce | Sech |
| BernoulliB | EllipticTheta | LCM | SeedRandom |
| BesselI | Erf | LegendreP | Sign |
| BesselJ | EulerE | LegendreQ | Signature |
| BesselK | EulerGamma | LegendreType | Sin |
| BesselY | EulerPhi | LerchPhi | Sinh |
| Beta | Exp | Log | SphericalHarmonicY |
| Binomial | ExpIntegralE | LogIntegral | Sqrt |
| Catalan | ExpIntegralEi | Max | StirlingS1 |
| Ceiling | ExtendedGCD | Min | StirlingS2 |
| ChebyshevT | Factorial | Minus | Subtract |
| ChebyshevU | Factorial2 | Mod | Tan |
| Complex | FactorInteger | MoebiusMu | Tanh |
| ComplexInfinity | Floor | Multinomial | Times |
| Conjugate | Gamma | NBernoulliB | WeierstrassP |
| Cos | GCD | NonCommutativeMultiply | WeierstrassPPrime |
| Cosh | GegenbauerC | PartitionsP | Zeta |
| Cot | GoldenRatio | PartitionsQ | |
| Coth | HermiteH | Pi | |
| Csc | Hypergeometric0F1 | Plus | |

### ■ Mathematical Operations and Options

| | | | |
|---|---|---|---|
| Accuracy | Eliminate | InverseSeries | Product |
| AccuracyGoal | Expand | LatticeReduce | PseudoInverse |
| AlgebraicRules | ExpandAll | Limit | Quartics |
| Apart | ExpandDenominator | LinearSolve | Rationalize |
| Cancel | ExpandNumerator | LogicalExpand | Reduce |
| Chop | Exponent | MainSolve | Resultant |
| Coefficient | Factor | Minors | Roots |
| CoefficientList | FactorComplete | Modular | RowReduce |
| Collect | FactorInteger | Modulus | Series |
| Constant | FactorList | N | SeriesData |
| Constants | FactorSquareFree | NIntegrate | Simplify |
| Cubics | FactorSquareFreeList | NonConstants | SingularValues |
| D | FactorTerms | Normal | Solve |
| Decompose | FactorTermsList | NProduct | SolveAlways |
| Denominator | FindMinimum | NRoots | Sum |
| Derivative | FindRoot | NSum | Together |
| Det | Fit | NullSpace | Transpose |
| DiagonalMatrix | Fourier | Numerator | Variables |
| Dot | IdentityMatrix | O | WorkingPrecision |
| Dt | Inner | Outer | ZeroTest |
| Eigensystem | Integrate | PolynomialQuotient | |
| Eigenvalues | Inverse | PolynomialRemainder | |
| Eigenvectors | InverseFourier | Precision | |

### ■ Predicates

| | | | |
|---|---|---|---|
| AtomQ | Implies | Negative | PolynomialQ |
| Equal | IntegerQ | NonNegative | Positive |
| EvenQ | Less | Not | PrimeQ |
| False | LessEqual | NumberQ | SameQ |
| FreeQ | MatchQ | OddQ | StringMatchQ |
| Greater | MatrixQ | Or | TrueQ |
| GreaterEqual | MemberQ | Order | Unequal |
| If | NameQ | OrderedQ | VectorQ |

### ■ Programming

| | | | |
|---|---|---|---|
| AddTo | Continue | Increment | Select |
| And | Debug | Label | SubtractFrom |
| AppendTo | Decrement | Nest | Switch |
| Array | DivideBy | NestList | Table |
| Block | Do | PreDecrement | Throw |
| Break | FixedPoint | PreIncrement | TimesBy |
| Catch | For | PrependTo | Which |
| Check | Function | Range | While |
| CompoundExpression | Goto | Return | Xor |
| Condition | If | Scan | |

## ■ Input-Output

| | | | |
|---|---|---|---|
| BaseForm | Infix | PageHeight | StringBreak |
| Byte | Information | PageWidth | StringForm |
| CForm | Input | Plain | StringSkeleton |
| Character | InputForm | Postfix | Subscript |
| Close | InputString | PostScript | Subscripted |
| ColumnForm | LineBreak | PrecedenceForm | Superscript |
| Continuation | MatrixForm | Prefix | TableForm |
| Definition | Medium | Print | TeXForm |
| Display | Message | PrintForm | TextForm |
| DisplayFunction | MessageName | Put | TextRendering |
| EndOfFile | Messages | PutAppend | TotalHeight |
| EngineeringForm | Number | Read | TotalWidth |
| Expression | NumberForm | ReadList | TreeForm |
| Format | Off | ResetMedium | Write |
| FormatType | On | Save | WriteString |
| FortranForm | OpenAppend | ScientificForm | $Echo |
| FullDefinition | OpenRead | SequenceForm | $Messages |
| Get | OpenTemporary | Short | $Output |
| HoldForm | OpenWrite | Skeleton | $$Media |
| Indent | OutputForm | Splice | |

## ■ Graphics Functions and Options

| | | | |
|---|---|---|---|
| AmbientLight | EdgeForm | ListPlot3D | PointSize |
| AspectRatio | FaceForm | MaxBend | Polygon |
| Axes | FontForm | Mesh | Rectangle |
| AxesLabel | Framed | ParametricPlot | RGBColor |
| Boxed | FullForm | Plot | Scaled |
| BoxRatios | Graphics | Plot3D | Shading |
| CellArray | Graphics3D | Plot3Matrix | Show |
| ClipFill | GrayLevel | PlotColor | SurfaceGraphics |
| ContourGraphics | HiddenSurface | PlotDivision | Text |
| ContourLevels | Lighting | PlotJoined | Thickness |
| ContourPlot | LightSources | PlotLabel | Ticks |
| ContourSpacing | Line | PlotPoints | ViewPoint |
| Dashing | ListContourPlot | PlotRange | $Display |
| DensityGraphics | ListDensityPlot | PlotStyle | $DisplayFunction |
| DensityPlot | ListPlot | Point | |

## ■ Structural Operations

| | | | |
|---|---|---|---|
| Accumulate | First | MapAt | Reverse |
| Append | Flat | Nest | RotateLeft |
| Apply | Flatten | NestList | RotateRight |
| Array | Head | Numerator | Select |
| Cases | HeadCompose | Operate | Sort |
| Complement | Inner | Part | Table |
| Compose | Insert | Partition | Take |
| Count | Intersection | Permutations | TensorRank |
| Denominator | Join | Position | Thread |
| Depth | Last | Prepend | Through |
| Dimensions | Length | Range | Transpose |
| Distribute | Level | Replace | Union |
| Drop | Listable | ReplaceAll | |
| Expand | Map | ReplaceRepeated | |
| Exponent | MapAll | Rest | |

## ■ Miscellaneous

| | | | |
|---|---|---|---|
| Alias | HoldFirst | Repeated | ToString |
| All | HoldRest | RepeatedNull | True |
| Attributes | Identity | Replace | UnAlias |
| Automatic | In | ReplaceAll | Unique |
| Begin | LeafCount | ReplaceRepeated | Unprotect |
| BeginPackage | List | Rule | Unset |
| Blank | Literal | RuleDelayed | Update |
| BlankNullSequence | Locked | Run | UpSet |
| BlankSequence | MaxMemoryUsed | RunThrough | UpSetDelayed |
| ByteCount | MemoryConstrained | Set | $CommandLine |
| CallProcess | MemoryInUse | SetAttributes | $Context |
| Characters | Names | SetDelayed | $ContextPath |
| Clear | Needs | SetOptions | $Epilog |
| ClearAll | None | Share | $IgnoreEOF |
| ClearAttributes | Null | Slot | $Interrupted |
| Context | OneIdentity | SlotSequence | $Line |
| Default | Optional | StartProcess | $Messages |
| Dump | Options | String | $Output |
| End | Orderless | StringJoin | $Path |
| EndAdd | Out | StringLength | $Post |
| EndPackage | Pattern | Symbol | $Pre |
| EndProcess | PatternTest | TagSet | $PrePrint |
| Environment | Protect | TagSetDelayed | $RecursionLimit |
| Exit | Protected | TagUnset | $System |
| FromASCII | Quit | TimeConstrained | $Urgent |
| Function | Raw | Timing | $Version |
| General | ReadProtected | ToASCII | |
| Hold | Release | ToExpression | |
| HoldAll | Remove | ToRules | |

# ■ Built-In *Mathematica* Objects

Abs
Accumulate
Accuracy
AccuracyGoal
AddTo
AiryAi
AlgebraicRules
Alias
All
AmbientLight
And
Apart
Append
AppendTo
Apply
ArcCos
ArcCosh
ArcCot
ArcCoth
ArcCsc
ArcCsch
ArcSec
ArcSech
ArcSin
ArcSinh
ArcTan
ArcTanh
Arg
ArithmeticGeometricMean
Array
AspectRatio
AtomQ
Attributes
Automatic
Axes
AxesLabel

BaseForm
Begin
BeginPackage
BernoulliB
BesselI
BesselJ
BesselK
BesselY
Beta
Binomial
Blank
BlankNullSequence

BlankSequence
Block
Boxed
BoxRatios
Break
Byte
ByteCount

CallProcess
Cancel
Cases
Catalan
Catch
Ceiling
CellArray
CForm
Character
Characters
ChebyshevT
ChebyshevU
Check
Chop
Clear
ClearAll
ClipFill
Close
Coefficient
CoefficientList
Collect
ColumnForm
Complement
Complex
ComplexInfinity
Compose
CompoundExpression
Condition
Conjugate
Constant
Constants
Construct
Context
Continuation
Continue
ContourGraphics
ContourLevels
ContourPlot
ContourSpacing
Cos
Cosh

Cot
Coth
Count
Csc
Csch
Cubics
Cyclotomic

D
Dashing
Debug
Decompose
Decrement
Default
Definition
Degree
Denominator
DensityGraphics
DensityPlot
Depth
Derivative
Det
DiagonalMatrix
Dimensions
DirectedInfinity
Display
DisplayFunction
Distribute
Divide
DivideBy
Divisors
DivisorSigma
Do
Dot
Drop
Dt
Dump

E
EdgeForm
Eigensystem
Eigenvalues
Eigenvectors
Eliminate
EllipticE
EllipticExp
EllipticF
EllipticK
EllipticLog

EllipticPi
EllipticTheta
End
EndAdd
EndOfFile
EndPackage
EndProcess
EngineeringForm
Environment
Equal
Erf
EulerE
EulerGamma
EulerPhi
EvenQ
Exit
Exp
Expand
ExpandAll
ExpandDenominator
ExpandNumerator
ExpIntegralE
ExpIntegralEi
Exponent
Expression
ExtendedGCD

FaceForm
Factor
FactorComplete
Factorial
Factorial2
FactorInteger
FactorList
FactorSquareFree
FactorSquareFreeList
FactorTerms
FactorTermsList
False
FindMinimum
FindRoot
First
Fit
FixedPoint
Flat
Flatten
Floor
FontForm
For

| | | | |
|---|---|---|---|
| PolynomialRemainder | Return | StringBreak | Unequal |
| Position | Reverse | StringForm | Union |
| Positive | RGBColor | StringJoin | Unique |
| Postfix | Roots | StringLength | Unprotect |
| PostScript | RotateLeft | StringMatchQ | Unset |
| Power | RotateRight | StringSkeleton | Update |
| PowerMod | Round | Subscript | UpSet |
| PrecedenceForm | RowReduce | Subscripted | UpSetDelayed |
| Precision | Rule | Subtract | |
| PreDecrement | RuleDelayed | SubtractFrom | Variables |
| Prefix | Run | Sum | VectorQ |
| PreIncrement | RunThrough | Superscript | ViewPoint |
| Prepend | | SurfaceGraphics | |
| PrependTo | SameQ | Switch | WeierstrassP |
| Prime | Save | Symbol | WeierstrassPPrime |
| PrimeQ | Scaled | | Which |
| Print | Scan | Table | While |
| PrintForm | ScientificForm | TableForm | WorkingPrecision |
| Product | Sec | TagSet | Write |
| Protect | Sech | TagSetDelayed | WriteString |
| Protected | SeedRandom | TagUnset | |
| PseudoInverse | Select | Take | Xor |
| Put | SequenceForm | Tan | |
| PutAppend | Series | Tanh | ZeroTest |
| | SeriesData | TensorRank | Zeta |
| Quartics | Set | TeXForm | |
| Quit | SetDelayed | Text | $CommandLine |
| Quotient | SetOptions | TextForm | $Context |
| | Shading | TextRendering | $ContextPath |
| Random | Share | Thickness | $Display |
| Range | Short | Thread | $DisplayFunction |
| Rational | Show | Through | $Echo |
| Rationalize | Sign | Throw | $Epilog |
| Raw | Signature | Ticks | $Interrupted |
| Re | Simplify | TimeConstrained | $Line |
| Read | Sin | Times | $Messages |
| ReadList | SingularValues | TimesBy | $Output |
| ReadProtected | Sinh | Timing | $Path |
| Real | Skeleton | ToASCII | $Pre |
| Rectangle | Slot | ToExpression | $PrePrint |
| Reduce | SlotSequence | Together | $Post |
| Release | Solve | ToRules | $RecursionLimit |
| Remove | SolveAlways | ToString | $System |
| Repeated | Sort | TotalHeight | $Urgent |
| RepeatedNull | SphericalHarmonicY | TotalWidth | $Version |
| Replace | Splice | Transpose | $$Media |
| ReplaceAll | Sqrt | TreeForm | |
| ReplaceRepeated | StartProcess | True | |
| ResetMedium | StirlingS1 | TrueQ | |
| Rest | StirlingS2 | | |
| Resultant | String | UnAlias | |